HOM

OPERATIONS MANAGEMENT SOFTWARE FOR WINDOWS®

Gaining Competitive Advantage from Operations

HOM

OPERATIONS MANAGEMENT SOFTWARE FOR WINDOWS®

Gaining Competitive Advantage from Operations

Michael A. Moses

Sridhar Seshardi

Michael Yakir

Stern School of Business • New York University

Boston   Burr Ridge, IL   Dubuque, IA   Madison, WI   New York   San Francisco
St. Louis   Bankok   Bogotá   Caracas   Lisbon   London   Madrid   Mexico City
Milan   New Delhi   Singapore   Sidney   Taipei   Toronto

Irwin/McGraw-Hill

A Division of The McGraw-Hill Companies

HOM OPERATIONS MANAGEMENT SOFTWARE FOR WINDOWS®:
Gaining Competitive Advantage from Operations
Copyright © 1999 by Michael A. Moses and Sridhar Seshadri. All rights reserved. Printed in the United States of America. Except as permitted under United States Copyright Act of 1976, no part of this publication may be reproduced or distributed in any form or by any means, or stored in a data base or retrieval system, without prior written permission of the publisher.

This book is printed on acid-free paper.

1 2 3 4 5 6 7 8 9 0 DOC/DOC 9 4 3 2 1 0 9

ISBN 0-07-366262-3

Vice president/Editor-in-chief: *Michael W. Junior*
Publisher: *Jeffery J. Shelstad*
Executive editor: *Richard T. Hercher, Jr.*
Editorial assistant: *Nicolle Schieffer*
Senior marketing manager: *Colleen J. Suljic*
Project manager: *Jim Labeots*
Production supervisor: *Scott M. Hamilton*
Designer: *Kiera Cunningham*
Senior supplement coordinator: *Cathy L. Tupper*
Compositor: *GAC Indianapolis*
Typeface: *10/12 Times Roman*
Printer: *R. R. Donnelley & Sons Company*

http://www.mhhe.com

We dedicate HOM

To

Our wives Liza, Shubha, and Julia

And

Our children Andrew & Daniel, and Padamavati & Sharada.

PREFACE

This project started over five years ago with our desire to give students a software package that was powerful enough to solve real business operations problems. We wanted to create a package that was flexible with regard to problem formulation, required minimum computer sophistication, and facilitated alternative scenario investigations. Our initial attempts were cumbersome but thanks to the development of both hardware and software over the time period and the continuous inputs of colleagues and students the current version of HOM, we feel, has finally satisfied our requirements.

We would first like to thank our graduate and undergraduate students here at the Leonard Stern School of Business at NYU for putting up with all of our initial attempts. They have "Beta" tested every release of every module with remarkable good spirit and understanding. Most of the "ease of use" changes emanated from their comments and concerns. Our project could not have continued to this final product without the support of the Stern School under the leadership of Dean George Daly and the continued encouragement of Deans Avijit Ghosh and Tom Pugel. This product has been facilitated by our publishers Irwin/McGraw Hill who supported the concept of a preview edition that was made available, free, to all interested faculty teaching operations management throughout the United States. In particular, we would like to thank our editor Dick Hercher for his tireless encouragement and enthusiastic support. Our editorial assistant Nicolle M. Schieffer also deserves our appreciation. She did much to give this document its current appearance and was always there to gather and distribute materials along the way to completion with good cheer and understanding.

No project can succeed without diligent critical review. We gratefully acknowledge the following faculty for reviewing and testing our ideas, programs, and manuscripts throughout the project: Joseph Biggs, Mohsen El Hafsi, Ananth Iyer, Bob Jacobs, Thomas Johnson, Duncan McDougall, Patrick McMullen, Steven Nahmias, William Peterson, Zinovy Radovilsky, Jeffrey Rinquest, Robert Schlesinger, Kannan Sethuraman, George Vairaktarakis, and Rachel Yang. In addition our faculty colleagues here at Stern were always available for advice and testing. In particular Matt Sobel (currently at Case Western Reserve University) and Mike Pinedo were particularly helpful.

Software development projects need excellent technical support. Under the management of Mabel Hsueh and Tom Oleszczuk our requests were always accommodated so that a "new" version of HOM could be made available to users every semester. Every organization has its jewels and for us that was Mathew Gee in our computer operations. His tireless optimism and professionalism insured that any thing we envisioned could be implemented.

We would also like to thank our administrative staff of Carmen Alvarado and Jennifer Bowe who typed so many versions of our text and cases that I am sure they can cite most of it by heart. Their continued cheerfulness and competence helped us meet many a deadline and overcome periods of self-doubt. We would finally like to thank Dinah Chang, Praveen Nayyar, and Don Weinstein for helping us create and use some of the cases.

TABLE OF CONTENTS

HOM Operations Management Software for Windows

Introduction   1

Mastercraftsmen of Newport: A HOM Tutorial Case   7

Project and Time Management Methods   54

    CASE: Toys City, Inc.   69

Process Analysis Methods   75

    CASE: Matthews Mug and Muffins (M^3)   110
    CASE: Tenafly Bagels   113
    CASE: The Violet Film Processing Agency   115

Waiting Line Management Methods   118

    CASE: Northeast Islands Air   144

Quality Management   149

Forecasting Methods   176

Independent Demand Inventory Management Methods   200

    CASE: The Nut Case   234

Dependent Demand Inventory Management Methods   236

Aggregate Planning   260

    CASE: TC Bank Corp.: Check Processing Unit   306

Integrative Cases:

    CASE: United Bank Branches:
        A Comprehensive Service Operations Case   308

    CASE: Ice Queen Snow Blowers Inc.:
        A Comprehensive Manufacturing Operations Case   330

HOM

OPERATIONS MANAGEMENT SOFTWARE FOR WINDOWS®

Gaining Competitive Advantage from Operations

INTRODUCTION

1. OVERVIEW

HOM is a software system designed to help mid level managers and owners of small businesses gain competitive advantage from operations. It is also useful for business school students, both undergraduate and graduate, who are trying to analyze cases and problems derived from situations these managers face on a regular basis. We developed this product based on the premise that an organization's operating system is its key source of competitive advantage. While large organizations can rely on internal staffs, well known consulting organizations (Anderson Consulting, A.T. Kearney, etc.) and complex and expensive software systems (SAP, BAAN, etc.) smaller independent organizations or operations within these firms require a different solution approach.

Our philosophy is based on two overlapping concepts. First, managers understand a problem environment and data availability in a language that is different from that required to develop and implement technical solutions to their problems. Second, the trade off between problem precision and rapid scenario evaluations should always come down on the side that facilitates the latter. Thus, our software stresses managerially oriented data inputs and problem formulation philosophy. We also facilitate alternative scenario analysis by having it built in whenever possible with simple, user initiated parameter selection windows.

The current version of HOM addresses five key competitive advantage drivers

- Process improvements by process analysis and waiting line management
- Response time improvement by time management and process analysis.
- Quality management using statistical process control and acceptance sampling.
- Supply chain management by inventory modeling and material requirement planning
- Capacity management by forecasting and aggregate planning.

HOM has been designed so that an unsophisticated user taking advantage of imbedded "How To Solve" help files and Tutorial Case- <u>Master Craftsmen of Newport</u> should be able to start analyzing real problems within a half-hour. This text and the unique "How To Solve" help files in the software can also be used as a stand alone vehicle for delivery of a basic course in operations management as long as key readings are given for every section. A list of such readings is available from the authors.

2. SOFTWARE OVERVIEW

An overview of the capabilities of the software is given below.

2.1 Competitive Advantage from Operations Using HOM

Competitive Advantage	Software Module
- Process Improvements	- Process Analysis - Waiting Line Analysis
- Supply Chain Management	- Independent Demand Inventory Systems - Material Requirements Planning (MRP) - Facility Location & Transportation (Fall 1999)
- Capacity Management	- Forecasting - Aggregate Planning - CPM-PERT-Crashing - Process Analysis
- Quality Management	- Statistical Process Control - Acceptance Sampling

2.2 Process Analysis

- Model Up to 15 Products
- Each Product has Unique Task Sequence, Priority, and Lot Size
- Model Several Types of Labor - General and Task Specific
- Each Task can
- Process Jobs One at a Time, Batch, Continuous Flow
- Require a Setup in Addition to Run Time
- Randomness Can Occur In Demand Arrival and Task Processing Time
- Job Selection -- FCFS, Set Up Saving
- Results - Production, Capacity Utilization for Each Resource and Delays Due to Labor and/or Material Unavailability, Product Flow Time Distribution

2.3 Waiting Line Management

- Arrival Pattern - Exponential, Erlang, General, Empirical
- Service Time Pattern - Exponential, Erlang, General, Empirical
- Queue Joining Discipline - Random, Shortest Line, Jockey, Cyclic
- Job Selection - FCFS and SPT
- Standard Waiting Line Outputs
- Wait Time Distribution

2.4 Project Management

- Critical Path Analysis
- PERT
  - Simulation Capability
- Crashing
  - Linear Programming Solution
- Output
  - Early/Late Start Gantt Chart Format
  - Completion Time Distribution
  - Criticality Index

2.5 Forecasting

- Techniques Available
  - Exponential Smoothing
  - Trend Regression
  - FIT Smoothing
  - Moving Average
  - Simple Average
  - Best of Above
  - Weighted Moving Average
  - Winter's Method
  - Multiple Regression
- Allows for User Determination or Program Optimization of Parameters
- Allows for De-seasonalization and De-trending of Data
- Automatic Plotting of Data, Results, and Deviations from Actual
- Robust Set of Statistical Measures
- Allows for MAD and Forecast Tailoring

2.6 Inventory

- Models Available
- EOQ -- Finite & Infinite Replenishment Rate, Quantity Discounts, Back Orders, Safety Stock
- Joint Optimization of Order Quantity and Safety Stock
- Periodic Review Model-- Safety Stock
- MRP
  - Low Level Coding
  - Different Batching Rules (FOQ, FPQ, LTL, LUC, LTC, Silver Meal)
  - Rescheduling/Expediting Options

2.7 Aggregate Planning

- Up to Three Products
- Up to 24 Time Periods
- Hire/Fire Costs
- Finite Setup Times and Relevant Costs Between Products
- Shift Employment Minimums and Maximums
- Lost Sales, Subcontracting, or Stockout Costing
- Develops Mixed Integer Optimal Solution
- Emulates Chase and Level Production and Workforce Strategies
- Variable Length of Time Periods Allowed

2.8 Quality Management

- Statistical Process Control
- Sampling by Variables ($\overline{X}$, R, s charts)
- Sampling by Attributes (p, np, c, u charts)
- Several Statistical Tests
- Acceptance Sampling
  - OC Curve
  - Determination of Sampling Plan

3. HOW TO USE HOM

HOM is a powerful software package that allows the user to analyze real-world operating problems. The software is designed to solve problems in the seven key Operations Management areas listed below.

- Project and Time Management
- Process Analysis and Design
- Waiting Line Design and Management
- Quality Management
- Forecasting Demand and Other Variables
- Inventory management and Material Requirements Planning
- Capacity Planning and Management

For detailed information on the capabilities of these modules, please consult their individual help files and technical manuals in the following chapters. The help files will be found in their respective sub-directories under C:\HOM. The technical manuals are WORD documents, and because of their size are placed on the CD-ROM.

The basic operating philosophy behind HOM is to have the user specify (1) broad problem-related input date (i.e., dependent and independent variables for forecasting demand) in a *spreadsheet* format and (ii) data needed for model specification (i.e., the number of periods to forecast in the forecasting model) called *parameters*, in a single dialog box. Data can be exported from and imported to HOM from commercial Windows based spreadsheet packages. Results can be exported to word processing software, commercial spreadsheet programs or saved for future reference. Each HOM module has a unique How to Solve help file, found by using the command line HELP option and then the Index. These help files sequentially move the user through all the steps that are required to solve a particular operations problem. We strongly recommend that the user follow the help steps until he or she has become familiar with a module. In addition to module-specific functions (which are explained in each of the How to Solve help files), there is a set of general capabilities that apply to all modules and are discussed in the How to Get Started help file.

If you are in WINDOWS 3.1, whenever you select HOM, you are always taken to the HOM-module selection window (i.e., the HOM group), which gives you the choice of starting one of the seven HOM analytical modules, the setup icon, or one of several help files. If you are in WINDOWS 95, 98, or NT you will see the HOM on the Start menu under Programs. The manual (the technical assumptions, examples and details that are the analytical underpinnings of each HOM module), and cases (the two comprehensive cases, Ice Queen and United Bank Branch, and the individual cases for each module) are WORD documents and are resident on the CD.

3.1 Menus and Toolbars

The initial window in all modules has the same visual topography: a command line; a tool bar; and an initial spreadsheet window for entering the broad problem input data. It also has the normal Windows dimensioning arrows in the upper right corner and the scroll bars on the bottom and right side for easy horizontal and vertical spreadsheet movements. As with any Windows-based product, HOM has a tool bar that gives direct access to the most-often-used functions. Again, we use a combination of Windows-specific and HOM-specific icons. The first eight icons are familiar to Windows users and invoke the functions of New, Open and Save files, Print and Preview print files, and information manipulation functions of Cut, Copy and Paste.

The next five icons are unique to HOM. These icons are shown below.

The first icon is in the format of a HOM Parameters Dialog box and allows the immediate jump to this dialog box from any stage in the problem-solving activity. However, if you have not input the basic data on the variables under analysis, the Parameters box will allow you to enter information, but not finally function (i.e., clicking on OK to exit to the next step will produce an error message that reminds you to input the base data, which can be done by clicking on Cancel and returning to and completing the base Data spreadsheet). The second icon unique to HOM is in the form of a graph, and it will automatically plot the data, if feasible, for the last specified variable. If no data exist, it will depict just the x and y axes. The third icon is in the form of a jogger and will automatically Run the last problem that was specified within the Parameters window. The fourth icon is in the form of a graph and text document and will display the Results of the last run. If you want to view a previously saved result, you must use the Results function on the command line and then use the Open option to retrieve any previously saved results. The fifth icon is in the form of a hand writing and is used to create a Log file for a data file or a result file. The log file is time stamped and useful for storing notes about what-if scenario analysis.

The last two icons in the HOM icon line allow the user to (1) get more general information about the current model, and (2) use a Bubble help for particular items. The Bubble Help is activated by clicking on the last icon, moving the cursor (notice the question mark comes with you), and clicking again on the item in question once the cursor has been moved to it. An explanation of the topic will then appear on the screen. Certain icons cannot be used during certain parts of a problem analysis. These will appear in light gray and you will be unable to invoke then at that time (e.g., the parameter's icon when a current result is on the screen.

4. INSTALLATION, FILE MANAGEMENT AND DOCUMENTATION

HOM will be installed in the directory C:\HOM. The seven HOM modules and cases are installed under the sub-directories of C:\HOM as shown below.
- Project and Time Management in C:\HOM\PROJMGMT.
- Process Analysis and Design in C:\HOM\PROCESS.
- Waiting Line Design and Management in C:\HOM\QUEUE.
- Quality Management in C:\HOM\QUALITY.
- Forecasting Demand and Other Variables in C:\HOM\FORECAST.
- Inventory Management and Material Requirements Planning (MRP) in C:\HOM\INVENTORY.
- Capacity Planning and Management in C:\HOM\AGGPLAN.
- Quality Management in C:\HOM\QUALITY.
- Cases in the CD.

Help files pertaining to the individual modules will be found in the respective sub-directories. There are eight technical manuals because Independent demand inventory management and MRP modules are described in separate manuals. These manuals are WORD documents located in the CD in a folder called "MANUALS." These can be opened, copied, or printed. The screen shots given in the manual will not appear as clear on the screen as they appear when they are printed. Please contact your Irwin/McGraw-Hill representative to order a copy of a color, indexed, and bound copy of the technical manuals.

Data files in HOM are given the extension DAT with the exceptions of MRP files which have the extension MRP and Quality Management Files (with extensions VAR, ATT and ACP). Result files are given the extension RES. These files unless explicitly specified by the user, will be saved in the respective sub-directories.

4.1 Manuals and Cases

Manuals are located on the CD under the folder called MANUALS. The names of the manuals are listed below.

Module	Manual
Project and Time Management	PROJECT.DOC
Process Analysis and Design	PROCESS.DOC.
Waiting Line Design and Management	QUEUE.DOC.
Quality Management	QUALITY.DOC.
Forecasting Demand and Other Variables	FORECAST.DOC.
Inventory Management and Material Requirements Planning (MRP)	INVENTRY.DOC and MRP.DOC.
Capacity Planning and Management	AGPLAN.DOC.

Several cases are located on the CD under the folder called CASES. The names of the cases are given below.

Project and Time Management -- Toys City in	TOYS.DOC.
Process Analysis and Design –	
Violet Film in	VIOLET.DOC
Mathew's Mug and Muffin in	MATHEW.DOC.
Tenafly Bagels in	TENAFLY.DOC.
Waiting Line Design and Management -- Northeast Island Airs in	NEISLAND.DOC.
Inventory Management -- Nut Case in	NUTCASE.DOC.
Capacity Planning and Management -- CB Check Processing in	TCBCHECK.DOC.
Integrated Cases	ICEQUEEN.DOC
	UNITED.DOC.

A comprehensive tutorial case (Mastercraftsmen of Newport) with data files and sample outputs can be found under the CD folder TUTORIAL. The data files for this tutorial case are found under each module sub-directory (for example, the data files pertaining to inventory, MAKETBLI.DAT & MAKETBLM.MRP, are located in C:\HOM\INVENTRY). In addition to the software and the Tutorial

Case, this package contains two integrated cases, Ice Queen Snow Blowers and United Bank Branches, that allow the user to apply many of the above models within a single organizational setting. Ice Queen presents a set of problems faced by a manufacturer of snow blowers, United Bank Branches presents a set of problems faced by a money center bank trying to gain efficiency by merging two branch locations. Cases involving only one task area (for example, Toy City Audit for Project and Time Management), as well as information-only databases for some classic Harvard Cases (for example, forecasting input data for the *Blanchard* case) are also included as listed above. Data files for all sample problems mentioned in the technical manuals are included in each module directory. Solutions to the cases are available upon request from the Authors (please email request to: mmoses@stern.nyu.edu or sseshadr@stern.nyu.edu).

Solutions to the problems in Stevenson Production/Operations Management 6/e and Chase, Aquilano and Jacobs Production and Operations Management 8/e are also available and can be downloaded, after registration, from the world wide web: http://www.stern.nyu.edu/HOM.

We recommend that you approach the use of any HOM module by first reading its help file and then working through that part of the Tutorial Case that pertains to the module.

MASTERCRAFTSMEN OF NEWPORT CASE[1]

A HOM Example[+]

Christopher Townsend, the co-founder of the Newport Cabinetmaking School, was thinking about his furniture making business in the summer of 1750. He had just returned from the Quaker summer meeting held in Salem, MA that year and had seen some of the latest production techniques used by the larger Quaker furniture making shops of that city. His son, John was almost finished with his seven-year apprenticeship and was demonstrating skill equal to his own in every facet of the furniture making craft.

PROJECT MANAGEMENT

Christopher currently built tables by completing every task himself (serial processing). He would select and trim the wood for the legs and top, which would take a total of one day, then cut and carve the legs (4 days), then cut and carve the top (3 days), then assemble the parts (2 days) then stain and finish (1 ½ days) and pack the table for delivery (½ day). Christopher usually worked 24 days a month.

In Salem, he learned that some tasks could be allocated to other workers and could be done at the same time as other tasks (parallel processing). Since John's skills were so advanced, Christopher was wondering by how much he could shorten the delivery time for a table (throughput time). At a minimum, he wanted to know what the effect would be if John would cut and carve the legs at the same time as he was making the top? (It also takes John four days to cut and carve a set of legs).

Christopher also knew that his brother, Job's sons were also gaining skill as cabinetmakers and that he could hire them to help with the work. At a cost of 2 pounds per day he could cut up to 2 days off the time to make legs. At 3 pounds per day he could cut 1 day off the time to make the top, at 4 pounds per day he could reduce the assembly time by 1 day and at 1.5 pounds per half day he could reduce the stain and finish time by ½ day. Christopher is wondering if he employed Job's sons how much it would cost for each day's reduction in the time it would take John and himself to produce a table.

Christopher knows that adding extra workers might add some uncertainty to certain of his completion time estimates. The new range of possibilities are given below:

		Times	
Task	Pessimistic	Expected	Optimistic
Buywood	2	1	1
Makeleg	5	4	3
Maketop	4	3	2
Assemble	5	2	1
Stain	3	1.5	1
Pack	0.5	0.5	0.5

Christopher would like to be 90% confident in any completion time estimate he gives his customers. What should his completion time quote be (service guarantee)? Christopher is very confident in his own abilities and knows he can always complete tasks in the expected time. Which tasks would you recommend he work on, and why?

---

[1] By Michael Moses, Operations Management Department, Stern School of Business. This case is for the use of students in a core course in Operations Management and is intended to have an actual relationship to the persons and organization described. (11/98)

[+] Sample HOM input data spreadsheets, parameters windows, and output graphs and tables are given at the end of each section.

The HOM module project management can be used to solve these questions. The required input file is given below.

<u>HOM Data</u>
MAKETBLJ.DAT - Project Management

Activity	Duration	Min.Durn	Cost/Time	Opt.Time	Likely T	Pess.Tim	Pred. 1	Pred. 2
Buywood	1	1		1	1	2		
Makeleg	4	2	2	3	4	5	Buywood	
Maketop	3	2	3	2	3	4	Buywood	
Assemble	2	1	4	1	2	5	Makeleg	Maketop
Stain	1.5	1	3	1	1.5	3	Assemble	
Pack	0.5	0.5		0.5	0.5	0.5	Stain	

Results

The data spreadsheet is the first input screen of the project management module. The project activities, their predecessors, and their duration times can be entered directly into this spreadsheet in their indicated rows. It is best not to leave any blank rows. Data entry for project crashing and PERT can also be entered at this time or postponed until they are needed. To solve the first questions requires the use of CPM. This is specified by clicking on the parameters icon, and then on the CPM button in the drop down parameters window and then setting the ACTIVITY range from 1-6. Click next on OK and then click on the RUN icon. The results report produces a Gant chart, a list of the activities on the critical path (Buy, Makeleg, Assemble, Stain, Pack) and its time (9 days). This is a 3 days improvement over Christopher's doing everything on his own. (Buy, Makeleg, Maketop, Assemble, Stain, Pack = 12 days)

To reduce the time it takes to make a table to less than nine days requires the enabling of the crashing option in the parameters window. Changing the value in the completion time box forces the computer to try and reach that time in the most efficient manner. In our example, it costs $2 to reach a completion time of 8 days, a total of $5.5 to reach 7 days ($3.5 extra) and a total of $10 to reach 6 days ($4.5 extra). For each of these scenarios a new Gant chart, critical path activities and time is developed. (Try to understand why these results occurred). The computer tells you that the project cannot be reduced to 5 days.

An alternative to doing this incrementally is to use the cost/time tradeoff option within crashing. This option computes the maximum feasible time reduction and then divides the time difference between it and the original into 10 equal time units and computes the cost of each of these. A run of this type can take 15 minutes of computer time for a big project. For MAKETBLJ it will usually take less than 1 minute.

To determine a service guarantee for Christopher requires the enabling of the PERT analysis option in the parameters dialogue box. The analytical result for these problem are developed by enabling PERT. The results of the run depict a completion time histogram and its digital analog. They indicate that a 10-day guarantee would have about a 90 percent likelihood of being correct. The simulation alternative, enabled by clicking on its indicator box, lists the percentage of the time that each activity was on the critical path in 1000 simulations of the problem (criticality index). Clearly, those with a percentage on or near 100 would be where Christopher should do the work since he knows his ability with certainty. The output shows that the maketop task is on the critical path only 1.8 percent of the time. Christopher should, thus, do any task other than this one since all the others are almost always on the critical path.

HOM SAMPLE INPUTS AND OUTPUTS

Name of Module: PROJMGMT
Data File: MAKETBLJ.DAT

Input Data Spreadsheet

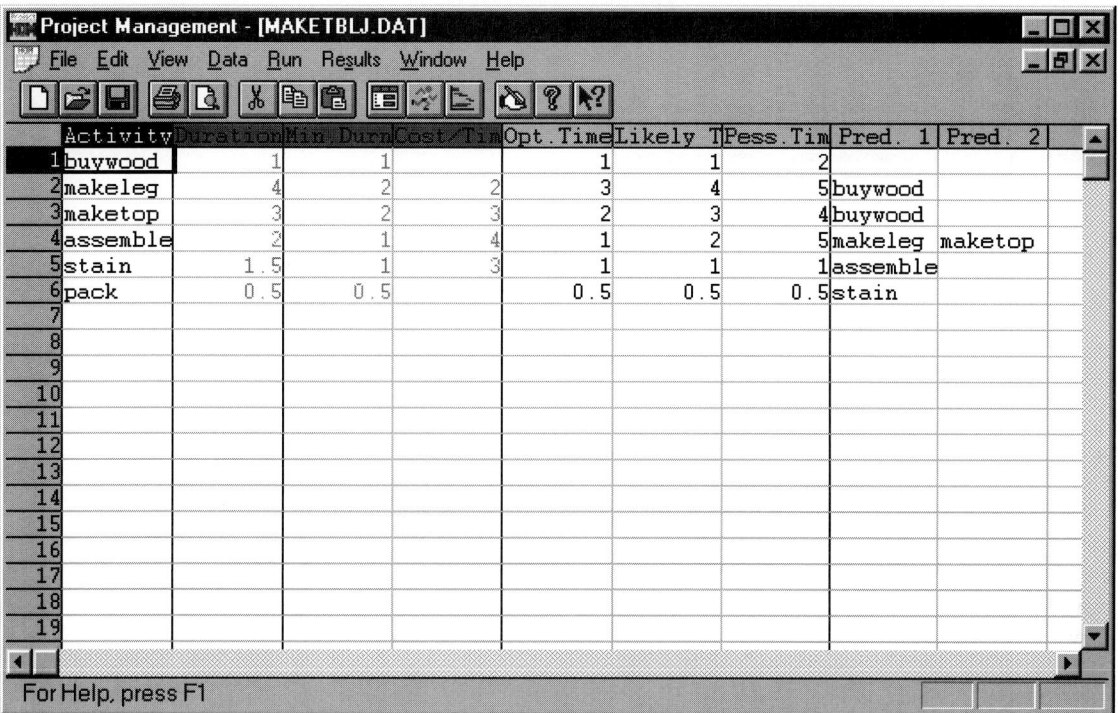

Parameters Window

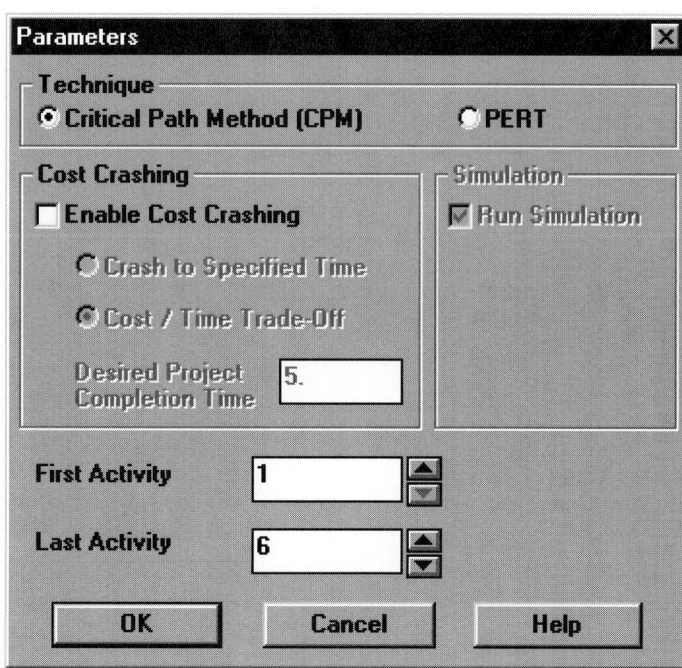

Output Graph

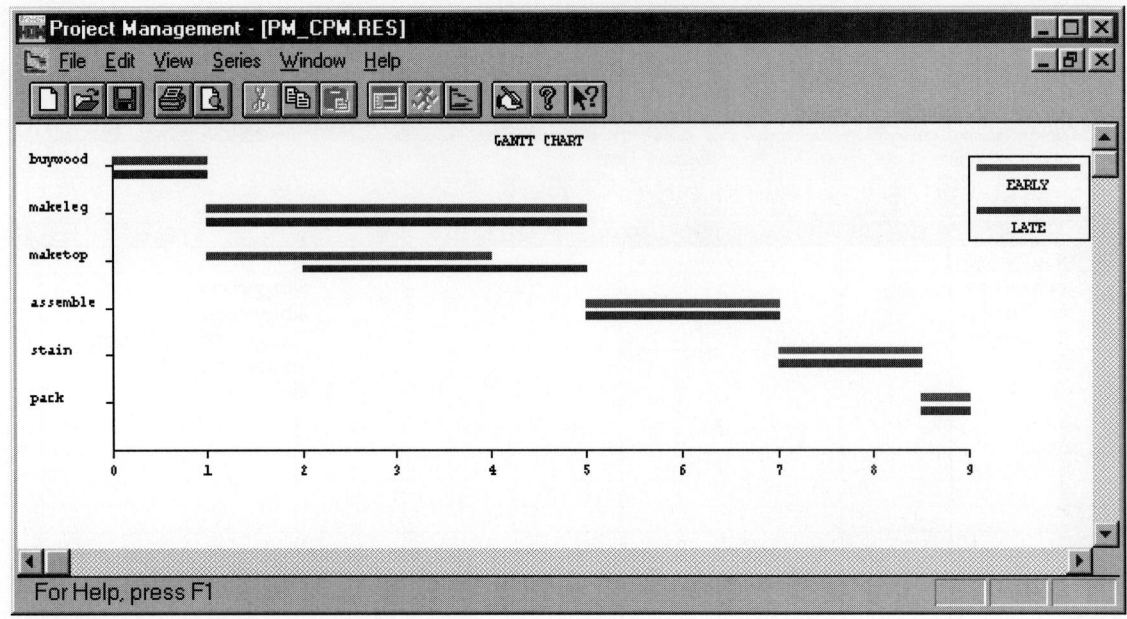

Output Table

Critical Path Method Calculations Results.

Activity Name	Early Start	Early Finish	Late Start	Late Finish	Slack	Description
buywood	0	1	0	1	0	
makeleg	1	5	1	5	0	
maketop	1	4	2	5	1	
assemble	5	7	5	7	0	
stain	7	8.5	7	8.5	0	
pack	8.5	9	8.5	9	0	

Expected Completion Time   :   9

Critical Path:
buywood   makeleg assemble   stain   pack

Output of Simulation

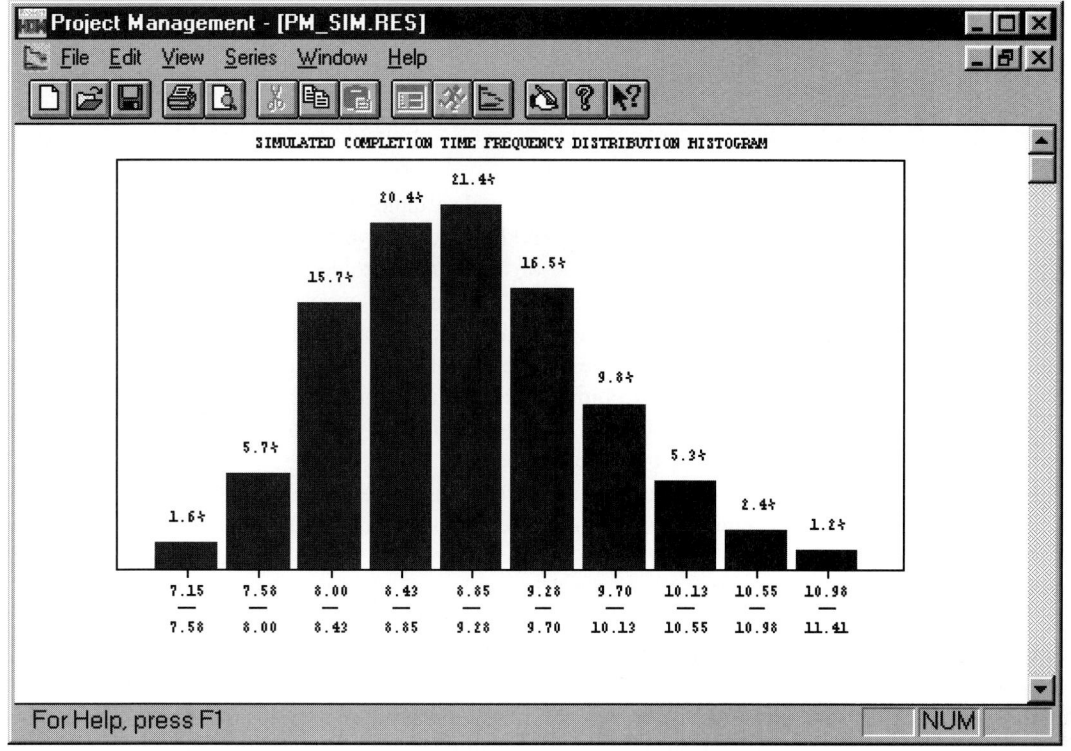

PERT Simulation (Criticality) Calculations Results.

Activity Criticality

Name	Indices	Description
==========	==========	==================
buywood	1	
makeleg	0.982	
maketop	0.018	
assemble	1	
stain	1	
pack	1	

Project completion time:
- Minimum : 7.14945
- Maximum : 11.4058
- Mean : 9.02302
- Standard Deviation : 0.766755

Completion frequency distribution (1000 runs performed):

Interval Start	Interval End	Frequency (%)	(Counts)
==========	==========	==========	==========
7.149	7.575	1.6	16
7.575	8.001	5.7	57
8.001	8.426	15.7	157
8.426	8.852	20.4	204
8.852	9.278	21.4	214
9.278	9.703	16.5	165
9.703	10.13	9.8	98
10.13	10.55	5.3	53
10.55	10.98	2.4	24
10.98	11.41	1.2	12

PROCESS ANALYSIS

Christopher's full attention for the entire duration of the task (set up and run time) was required for each of the tasks, except staining. Parts of the stain and finish process, however, could be done as a batch process. The stain and finish process could be broken into three sub-tasks. Mixing and heating the volatile substance that made up the stain took ½ day. Applying the stain to each piece took ½ day and an additional ½ day was required for drying before packing could commence. In the amount of time indicated, a batch of stain could be made that was sufficient for up to 3 tables.

Christopher's initial questions was, if he only makes tables by himself and orders are received evenly over each demand period how many tables could he make in a year?

Using process analysis allows the solution of this simple problem. The Maketable Process File (MAKETBLP) is illustrated at the end of this section. Your first opportunity to enter data is via the spreadsheet that appears after the process analysis module has been selected. We first enter the names of the three products (data, product, new) that have been established for each part of our analysis Tableself, Tablejohn, Tablenph . The data item on the command line is also used to enter the labor types that have been set up for all three potential possibilities. The data item is also used to specify the work centers that have been established for each step in the production process.

Double clicking on a product yields its unique right-hand side of the spreadsheet (columns D→N). Double clicking on each work center yields data as to the number of identical machines at that work center, and the number of units that they can run before the machine needs to be set up again. The type of this machine must also be specified at this time. For Christopher all his processes, except mix, are one at a time. A "one at a time" machine runs one unit until completion. It can not start processing the next job until the current job in the machine has finished. The Mix Process, however, is a "batch process" that has one machine. It can create enough stain for up to three tables in the same time it would take to make the stain for one table. Thus the units that can be run before setup is again required is three.

Information on the SCV and set up saving algorithm are more advanced topics and are discussed later and in the help files and manual.

Double clicking on each labor type gives the user the opportunity to specify data as to the number of individuals available in each labor type as well as SCV information. In our case there is one Christopher, one John and two nephews.

Double clicking on Tableself reveals the demand and process information if we assume that Christopher is making tables by himself. We have entered the processing times as indicated in the case for each operation. The only process to have a set up time was the batch operation of mixing. All batch process, in our system, only have set up times and no run times. It is our convention. Thus, if a batch process has both set up and run times they are combined and placed in the set up column. All other processes can have both. Since Christopher is the only worker we have filled his name in for all tasks. Labor times for our case are the same as machine run times. This may not always be the case, and smaller or larger numbers can be specified. Batch process entries must again be made only in the set up column. SCV is again left at zero at this stage.

Demand information is also entered at the top of this part of the spreadsheet. Order size is assumed to be one table and the assumed demand per demand period (month) is two. The Process Analysis module will not derive capacity for you since so many factors can affect it. It does however, derive the feasibility of your assumption for demand. Thus, in our case if Christopher can make two tables per month at capacity the model will show that output and the fact that he is working at 100% of that capacity. A percent greater than 100 indicates the need for overtime, more workers or less demand. A percent less than 100 indicates slack and the need for fewer workers or the ability to handle more demand. To determine those results the model needs to be run. But before you can do that you must finish the problem specification via the parameters window illustrated at the end of this section.

The first part of the Parameters window indicates that the Run/Setup time units for our case are in days. The demand time unit is months and the length of a simulation is a month. Since Christopher works six days a week, we assume he works 24 days a month and set this number in the appropriate counter box. (The default would have been 20 - 5 days/week times 4 weeks/month). Since demand and simulation tie units are the same the next box is one. If we wanted to simulate a year we would have set the simulation time period to a year and this box would then be 12.

The next part of the Parameters window allows the user to assign labor to the next task based on two rules. One rule assigns labor to the work center with the most waiting work (longest queue). The other rule assigns labor to the work center that has the highest utilization rate. Experimentation will show which is "better" since different case situations can lead to a different rule being optimal. The work center traces allows the user to see, in the results output, the buildup and reduction of work at the two chosen workcenters. (Makelegs and mix in our case). The length of the simulation box gives the user the opportunity to indicate the number of simulation time units that they want to run. The number, for our case, would be twelve months to simulate a year's work. The first solution techniques available is a computer-generated estimate of theoretical utilization. We recommend for a first pass, that this be used since it is fast and tests the feasibility of your demand guesses, etc. The simulation alternative gives a more elaborate output, which is discussed and illustrated below.

The use of the setup saving algorithm rule is discussed in detail in the help files and the manual.

Results

The first graph of the result output shows the theoretical and simulated utilization at each workstation. When there is no uncertainty and demand yields a utilization of less than 100%, both these levels should be approximately equal. Next is a similar utilization chart for labor. As we can see Christopher is utilized almost at 100% at our assumed demand level of two tables per month. The difference between the theoretical and simulated times in this instance are caused by the timing of the orders over the planning period. The next set of data show the numerical values of these graphs. Since Christopher is doing each task himself no one process is utilized at 100 percent. When they are all added together, however, they approximate full capacity. The next set of data illustrates the number of jobs waiting at each workcenter. When the system runs at less than capacity without bottlenecks this should equal the maximum value of the unit of demand, in our case one. Unavoidable delays happen when a system has either too much demand or is seriously out of balance. The percent of time that this happens at each workcenter is given in the last column.

The next set of results data indicates the amount of time each job spent in the facility on average (flowtime), its standard deviation and the quantity produced over the length of the simulation. In our case since we are running just at capacity that time it 12 days and we produce 22 units over the year. The reason this is 22 and not 24 is that there are subtle beginning of process and ending of process delays caused by the timing of the arrivals of the first and last jobs. The longer the simulation the closer to actual this number becomes. The next set of data shows the distribution of the variability of flow time, which in our case does not exist since there is no uncertainty to speak of. Every job gets done in 12 days. These data will be very important however when some uncertainty is allowed to exist in the arrival process for orders.

The last set of data is the actual trace of the time when a unit arrives at the previously chosen workcenter and how many items are in the queue at that time. The data in our case indicates that the first order arrives for cutting of the legs at time 13.06 days and finishes at 17.06 days. (We have two orders per 24 days and thus, the model assumes that orders arrive at days 12 and 24 plus round off error rather than 0,12,24. This is why we produced only 22 tables in a year. The first 12 days of production are lost waiting for the initial order and the last order to arrive at the shop was on the 24th day of the 12th month and is not completed by the time the simulation ends on the next day.)

Up to this point we have considered the case when demand is known with certainty and arrives evenly spaced over the planing horizon. The likelihood of this happening in reality is extremely small. The process analysis module of HOM allows for risk to enter the analysis in three ways. Demand arrival pattern, machine set up and run times and labor setup and run times. For each of these factors a unique squared coefficient of variation (SCV = (standard deviation/mean)^2 can be entered.

Thus, for our example instead of assuming a demand for a table arrives every 12 days with certainty we assumed that the mean customer demand is once every 12 days with a standard deviation of 4 days (thus, the SCV = $(4/12)^2$ = .11). We enter this SCV in the demand data section of our spreadsheet for this product - TABLESELF.

Since Christopher can do all his manufacturing tasks with certainty there would be no SCV for his work times. (SCV= 0) However, as we have seen his nephews are a different matter and thus any task they do might have a labor SCV which is non zero, lets say a standard deviation that is one half of its mean or an SCV of .25. (SCV= $(½)^2$). We also assume that the only mechanical process times where risk occurs is in the mixing, applying the stain and drying. Humidity effects these three processes very dramatically and uniformly. Assume that these processes have a standard deviation three quarters of the mean. (SCV = $(¾)^2$ = .56) These latter three SCVs can be entered globally via the drop down window for each workcenter and labor type or uniquely in the spreadsheet associated with each product.

We model only demand arrival variation in HOM. Changes in the level of demand are modeled by using alternative scenarios and setting the different demand levels for the product uniquely in each scenario. To see the Results of demand arrival variation set the SCV to .11 for product TABLESELF and change the length of the simulation to 120 in the parameters window, click OK and then click again on the Run Icon. We lengthen the simulation by 10 times since our demand per time unit is low and we want to get lots of opportunities for positive and negative variations.

An initial result message may appear warring of utilization less than .2%. This is caused, in this case, by the Dry Operation, which, we assume, has no real physical constraint (the size of the house). We had entered 100 in the number of identical machines at that workcenter and thus, this operation has very low utilization. Click OK and the Results appear in a few seconds on the screen. The Results indicate that this level of variation plays havoc with our service guarantee. Instead of all orders taking 12 days we see the average flow time is 68 days with a standard deviation of 53 days. Over the ten years we now produce 222 tables instead of 237 and a guarantee of 100 days would be required to have 90% probability of success. Changing to the most utilized machine rule in the parameters window makes things even worse. Try it and see if you can figure out why this has happened. [Hint, - where in the process in the most utilized machine located] [Since Makeleg is the most utilized machine and is early in the process every time there is a need for labor at two locations at the same time Christopher will go and make legs. Thus, everything at the end of the process has to wait. The result is that the queue length for drying goes from 3 to 33. Thus, product does not get out the door in an expeditious manner. Mean flow time increases to 116 days and 90% service guarantee would be over 330 days. Also the unavoidable delay due to waiting for labor or material at Makeleg goes to zero but at mixing it increases to 14%.

Including the SCV for the mixing, applying, drying processes, but excluding the SCV for demand has a much less dramatic effect. Average flow time increases to over 22 days with a standard deviation of approximately 4 days and with the 90 percent service guarantee now occurring at about 25 days. These results are obtained by filling in the spreadsheet SCV locations for the mix (in the workcenters set up SCV), Apply and Dry (in the workcenter run time SCV) locations.

When Christopher thought of adding his son John to his workforce he assumed that he would put him to work exclusively making table legs. The first question we would like to answer is what effect that might have on Christopher's output and service guarantee. We can again use HOM process analysis to investigate this scenario. We first set up a new product called Tablejohn by adding the product and adding a labor type called John. We then copy the right-hand side of the TABLESELF (without SCV information) spreadsheet (D12 through N19) and paste it into the right-hand side of the Tablejohn spreadsheet by double-clicking on Product Tablejohn and placing the cursor on D12, clicking and then moving the cursor to the paste icon and clicking again. Now, we only have to change Christopher's name to John in the Makeleg operation and we can then commence with our new analysis. Since we are now using zero SCV we can revert to a simulation length of 24 periods. We then click on OK and then, after entering a demand assumption, we click on run. With two workers you would assume that they could do twice the work so we should be able to average about 4 tables a period. To check this we set our analysis to "theoretical" in the parameters window and then click on Run. The result is surprising John is only used for 66% of his capacity or 16 days (2/3 of 24 days) a month and can produce legs for 4 tables but 4 tables requires 32 additional days of work which requires Christopher to work 8 additional days or 133% of his capacity (32/24 = 1.33). In order to produce more we need to add work to John and reduce work for Christopher. Without doing this we can only produce just under 3 tables a month. If no jobs are reallocated they might be better off building tables independently. Try some allocations and see if you can make some improvements. The best we did was to have John do Legs, Mix, Stain, Dry, and Pack. The result was not appreciably better than if both, Christopher and John made tables independently. Is there any benefit to them working together? See what happens if you use the demand SCV of .11 when both John and Christopher are working together. We see immediately that the average flow time has been reduced dramatically from the case when John was working alone to about 50 days with a standard deviation of less than half that value and a 90% service guarantee of about 90 days. Thus, the effect of having John and Christopher work on tables together is not to enhance output but to reduce the effects of uncertainty in the demand arrival process.

HOM SAMPLE INPUTS AND OUTPUTS

Name of Module: PROCESS
Data File: MAKETBLP.DAT

Input Data Spreadsheet

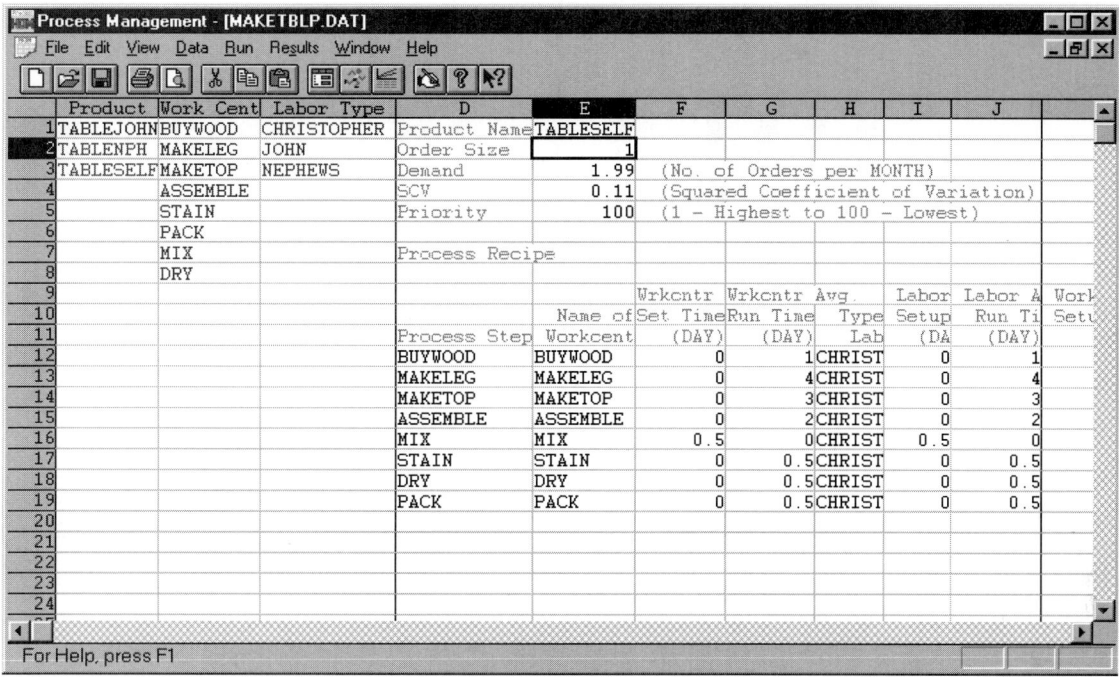

Parameters Window

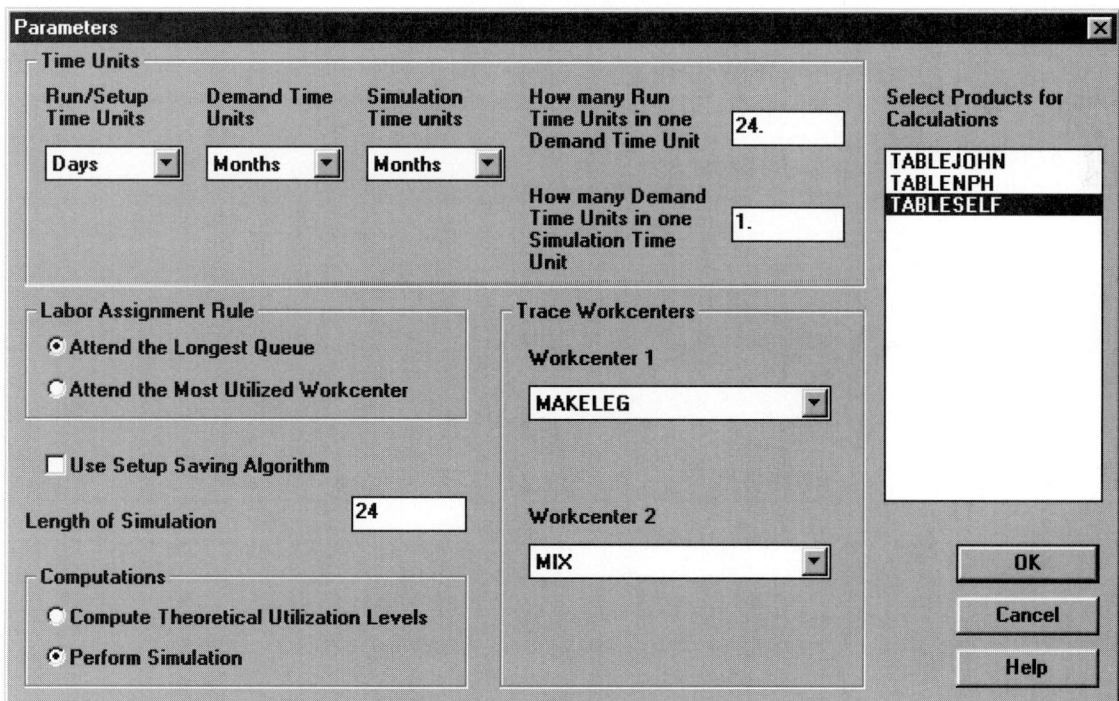

Output Graphs

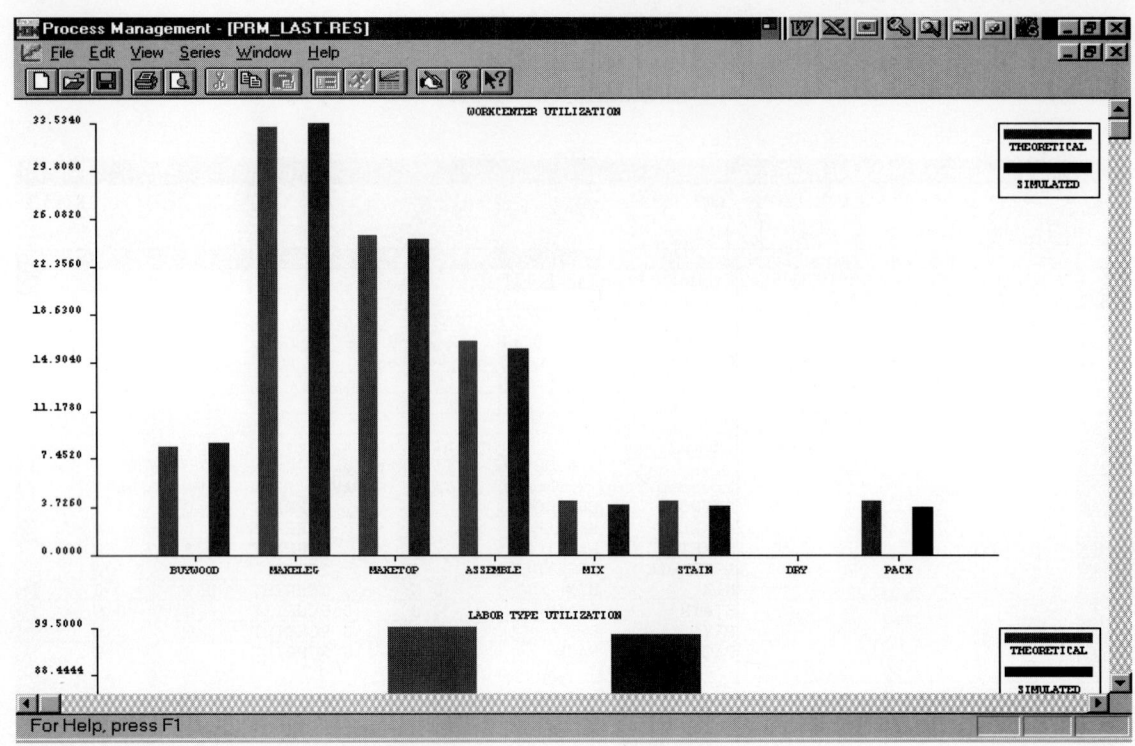

Output Tables

Process Analysis Calculations

Utilization (%)

Workcenter	Theoretic Util. (%)	Simulated Util. (%)
BUYWOOD	8.2917	8.1597
MAKELEG	33.167	32.639
MAKETOP	24.875	24.479
ASSEMBLE	16.583	16.175
MIX	4.1458	3.993
STAIN	4.1458	3.993
DRY	0.004146	0
PACK	4.1458	3.993

Labor Type	Theoretic Util. (%)	Simulated Util. (%)
CHRISTOPH	99.5	97.425

Simulation Results

Workcenter	Type of Processing	Average Jobs In Queue	Avg. Num. In Workcenter	Maximum Num. In Queue	Avoidable Delay (%)
BUYWOOD	One at Time	0	0.081597	1	0
MAKELEG	One at Time	0	0.32639	1	0
MAKETOP	One at Time	0	0.24479	1	0
ASSEMBLE	One at Time	0	0.15972	1	0
MIX	In Batches	0	0.039931	1	0
STAIN	One at Time	0	0.039931	1	0
DRY	One at Time	0	0.039931	1	0
PACK	One at Time	0	0.039931	1	0

** Avoidable delay is due to waiting for labor or material.

Product Name	Average Flow Time	Std. Dev. Flow Time	Quantity Produced/MONTH
TABLESELF	12	0.003258	46

Product Flow Time Distribution

TABLESELF

Left End Point (T1)	Right End Point (T2)	Fraction of Jobs w/Flow Time <= T2
12	12	1

Trace Workcenters

MAKELEG

Time	Number of Units
0	0
13.06	1

QUEUEING

By 1755, John and Christopher Townsend had become known throughout the religious freedom oriented colony of Rhode Island as its best furniture craftsmen. The popularity of their form of furniture, noted for its unique blocked shells and claw and ball feet, was such that the number of potential customers arriving at their family shop often could not be served without some waiting. The family's finely crafted furniture was, however, quite expensive (a desk could require a year's wages of a journeyman carpenter). Thus, not every potential customer visit turned into an order. In fact, it often took ten customer visits to generate a sale. Normally a customer required three visits at various times to finally consummate a purchase. Christopher had been keeping track of the amount of time he was spending on these customer visits and the results are tabulated in the Customer Service Time Distribution illustrated below.

Customer Service Time (In Hours)	Number of Customers
0-0.5	16
0.5-1.0	14
1.0-1.5	10
1.5-2.0	6

While Christopher was keeping track of service time, John was tabulating the time between customer arrivals (Interarrival Rate). These are listed below.

Time Between Arrivals	Number of Occurrences
0-2 Hours	29
2-4 Hours	9
4-6 Hours	3
6-8 Hours	4
8-10 Hours	2

There are times when Christopher is with a client, and another client arrives and needs attention. The operating rule for the shop is that, if at all possible, no customer should have to wait for more than ten minutes for service. Now with both John and Christopher available, this rarely happens. One night John and Christopher sat down to decide on what to do since their success was pulling in customers, but lengthening the throughput time since when they were with customers they were not working on other customers' orders. In particular, they are thinking of hiring one of Job's sons full-time to both take care of initial customer visits, and also to do some work in the shop. John and Christopher were curious about how much of Job's son's time would be occupied with customers and how much of his time would remain to work in the shop if customer visits remained at the level indicated previously. (Assume John and Christopher no longer visited with customers).

To solve this problem, we need to employ the Queue Module within HOM. We need to enter the interarrival time and service time distributions via the Data function on the command line. Doing this yields the following spreadsheet found under file MAKETBLQ. Notice that the midpoint of the arrival/service time intervals is to be used and that there are no blank lines within a data set.

MAKETBLQ.DAT

MidPt: arriva	Freq:arrival	MidPt:servic	Freq:service
1	10	0.25	16
3	6	0.75	8
5	3	1.25	6
7	4	1.75	2
9	2		

The next step is to specify the problem utilizing the Parameters window, which is reached by clicking on its unique icon. A completed parameters window is illustrated at the end of this section. We first specify the interarrival time distribution using the choices in the drop down window (our case empirical) and then specify the name of the empirical distribution we want to use in the lower drop-down window (our case arrival). We then indicate the number of rows to be included (in our case 1 through 5).

We similarly select the service time distribution and number of rows (in our case empirical, service and 1 through 4). We then specify the number of servers (Job's son, one), waiting room area (infinite), customer service rule (first come first served), length of simulation (at least 1,000), and then click OK. Remember, light gray areas can not be invoked due to previous selections. For example, one server forces all customers to join the end of the line.

After finishing the parameters window, click on OK and then click on the RUN icon to generate the desired Results. These results first show a graph that indicates that 68 percent of the time there is no one waiting, and that 94 percent of the time there are one or no customers waiting. The next set of data reviews the input data and gives the means and standard deviation of the arrival and service distributions. The main body of the results data indicates the server utilization and the mean and standard deviation of time in system and queue and number of customers in system and queue for the base case and four predetermined sensitivity analyses. For our example it shows that on average 33 percent of Job's son's time would be with customers and that the average wait in the queue is just under 10 minutes (.158 x 60). The last data shows that only 5.7 percent of the time are there two customers in the system and only .2 percent of the time are there 3 customers in the system. So with all three people working, and available to see customers, no one would ever have to wait.

There will be time when you do not have data on the complete arrival and service times distributions but you do know its type (exponential, Erlang, etc) and its mean and maybe its variance. How to use HOM under this environment is discussed in the Queueing help file.

HOM SAMPLE INPUTS AND OUTPUTS

Name of Module: QUEUE
Data File: MAKETBLQ.DAT

<u>Input Data Spreadsheet</u>

MidPt:arrival	Freq:arrival	MidPt:servic	Freq:service	MidPt:Dstr.3
1	29	0.25	16	1
3	9	0.75	14	2
5	3	1.25	10	3
7	4	1.75	6	
9	2			

Parameters Window

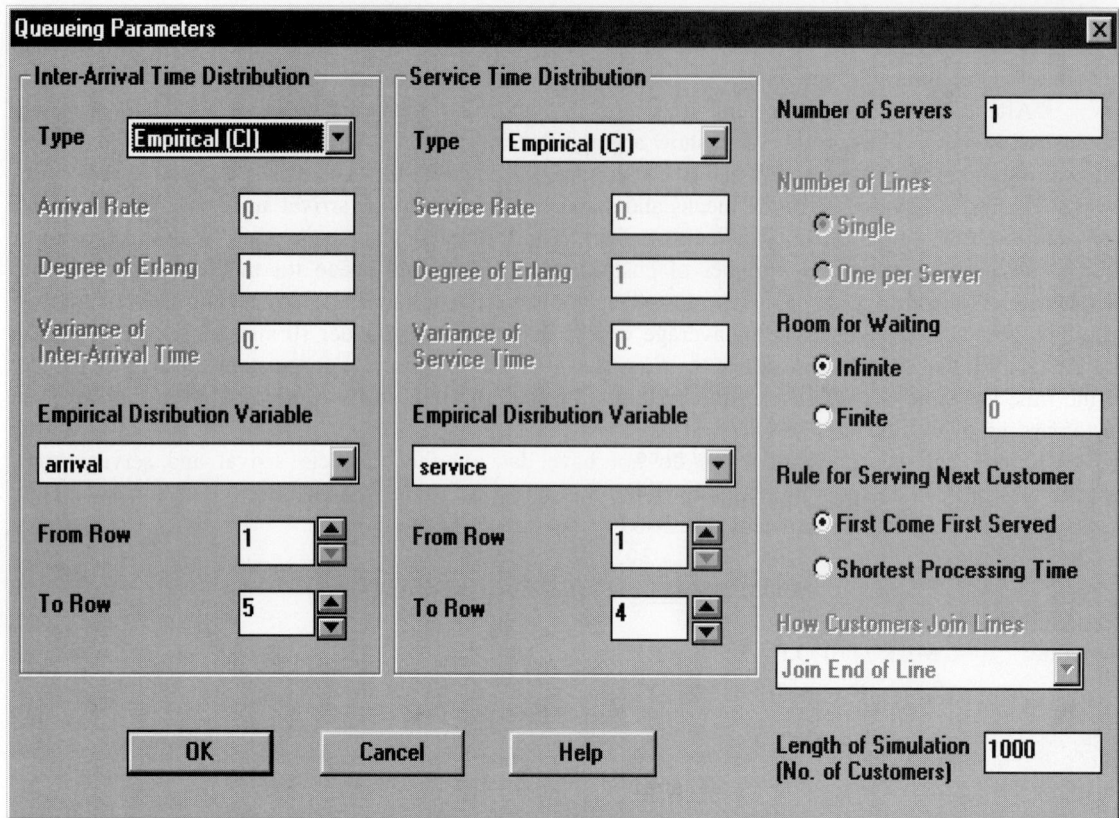

Output Graphs

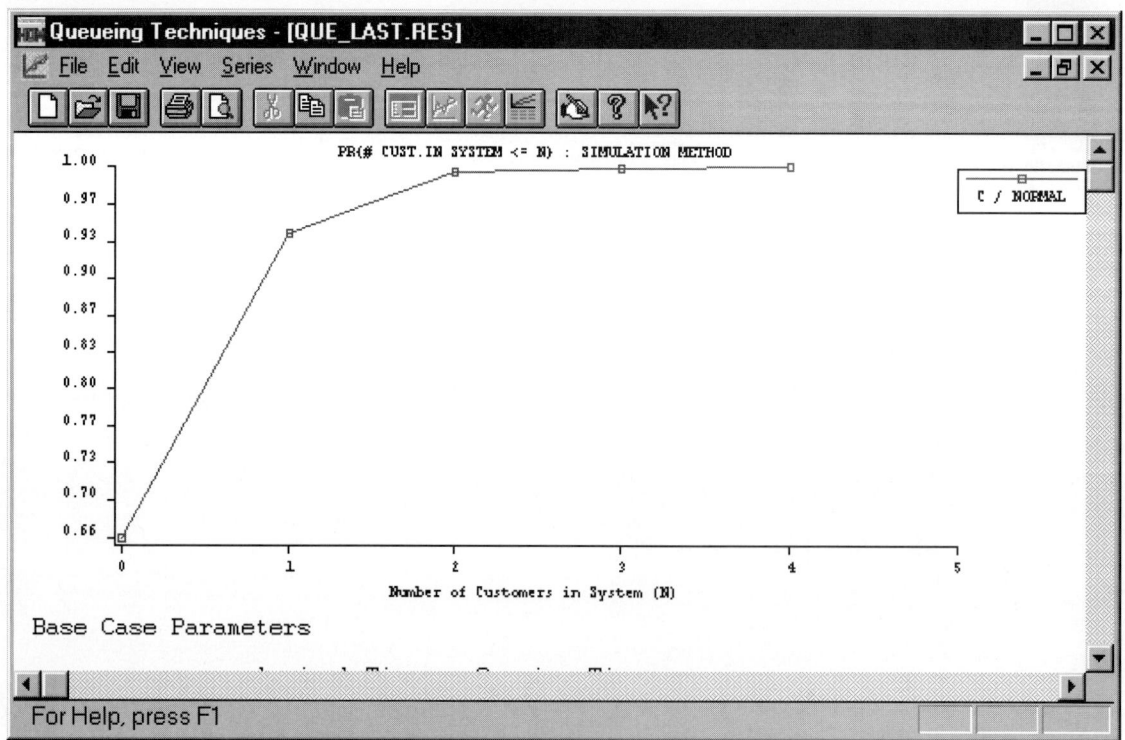

20

Output Tables

Base Case Parameters					
	Arrival Time	Service Time			
	===========	===========			
Distr. Type	C	CI			
Rate	0.401709	1.22667			
Degr. Erlang	N/	N/A			
Distr. Mean	2.48936	0.815217			
Variance	5.35627	0.267486			
Std. Dev.	2.31436	0.51719			
No. Servers	1				
No. Lines	1				
Wait. Space	Infinite				
Serving Rule	First Come First Served				
Cust. Behav.	Join End of Line				
Simul.Length	1000				

Results of Calculations

NOTE: The results are available only if the combination of the Number of Servers (C) and the Service Rate creates a stable system. For example, if C = 1, the results for C - 1 servers will not be available. Likewise, when Utilization exceeds 99%.

		Base Case	Sensitivity Analysis		
Number of Servers		1	1	1	0	2
Service Rate, (100%=1.2267)		Base Case	105% Base C	95% Base	Base Case	Base Case
Method (Model) Used		Simulation	Simulation	Simulation	Not Used	Simulation
		===========	===========	===========	===========	===========
Utilization		0.32748	0.311886	0.344716	N	0.16374
Avg. No. Customers in System		0.397595	0.362679	0.402201	N	0.355237
Std.Dev. of No.Cust in Syst.		0.608634	0.579434	0.607702	N	0.552254
Avg. No. Customers in Queue		0.0619669	0.0506834	0.0631681	N	0
Std.Dev. of No.Cust in Queue		0.255176	0.226601	0.248411	N	0
Average Time Spent in System		0.965967	0.904778	1.01581	N	0.815217
Std.Dev. of Time in System		0.615892	0.569612	0.624279	N	0.51719
Average Time Spent in Queue		0.15075	0.128381	0.157684	N	0
Std.Dev. of Time in Queue		0.33442	0.286077	0.305517	N	0
Fraction of Time Syst. Empty		0.664372	0.688004	0.660967	N	0.682734
Fraction of Customers Lost		0	0	0	N	0

Fraction of Time N Customers in the System

No. of Customers in System,N		-----------	-----------	-----------	-----------	-----------
	0	0.664372	0.688004	0.660967	N	0.682734
	1	0.277053	0.262929	0.27713	N	0.279295
	2	0.0552872	0.0474499	0.060638	N	0.0379707
	3	0.0031857	0.00161675	0.0012651	N	0
	4	0.00010276	0	0	N	0
	5	0	0	0	N	0

QUALITY CONTROL

By the early 1770's John Townsends' business was so successful that he was constantly ordering chair legs and parts from other local Newport craftsmen. He was becoming uneasy however since several of his old customers had commented that they could see a difference between the chairs they had ordered early on in his career and the chairs they were receiving now. John had been taking measurement on some key chair part dimensions and comparing them to the model he had given his suppliers. This data is given below. John was trying to decide if the differences were just normal variation or a sign of a more serious problem. What advice would you give him?

Height from Foot to Knee   Best Value = 10.5"

(inches)

Sample	Chair 1	Chair 2	Chair 3
1.00	10.69	10.67	10.29
2.00	10.37	10.50	10.45
3.00	10.36	10.76	10.57
4.00	10.59	10.49	10.37
5.00	10.39	10.51	10.51
6.00	10.44	10.79	10.36
7.00	10.24	10.46	10.47
8.00	10.48	10.33	10.56
9.00	10.62	10.53	10.23
10.00	10.29	10.54	10.78

Width at Knee   Best Value = 2.38"

Sample	Chair 1	Chair 2	Chair 3
1.00	2.36	2.37	2.31
2.00	2.29	2.29	2.31
3.00	2.26	2.27	2.28
4.00	2.33	2.35	2.39
5.00	2.36	2.27	2.25
6.00	2.39	2.29	2.28
7.00	2.39	2.31	2.37
8.00	2.38	2.34	2.27
9.00	2.36	2.31	2.30
10.00	2.40	2.33	2.31

This is an example in which every four days (for a total of ten) samples were drawn of three chairs and their dimensions recorded. As the height and width are measured in inches, we use HOM's sampling by variable module. Opening HOM's Quality Management module, we select the Sampling by Variable option and click on OK.

The first step is to open the Parameters Dialog box and select options before entering any data. The options are selected as shown below. We have chosen Actual Data as we will be entering each chair's dimension rather than aggregate data such as the mean height. We have also specified that the sample size is fixed as each sample consists of three chairs from a batch of chairs. We have set the sample size to be equal to three so that HOM will create three columns for us to enter the data. Finally, we have set the To Row to be 2. We will come back to this aspect after entering the spreadsheet data. Clicking on OK produces the data spreadsheet for this module. The data for both the height and width can be entered in the same sheet. The data file will be called MAKETBLQ.VAR. Notice that the extension is .VAR for Sampling by Variables.

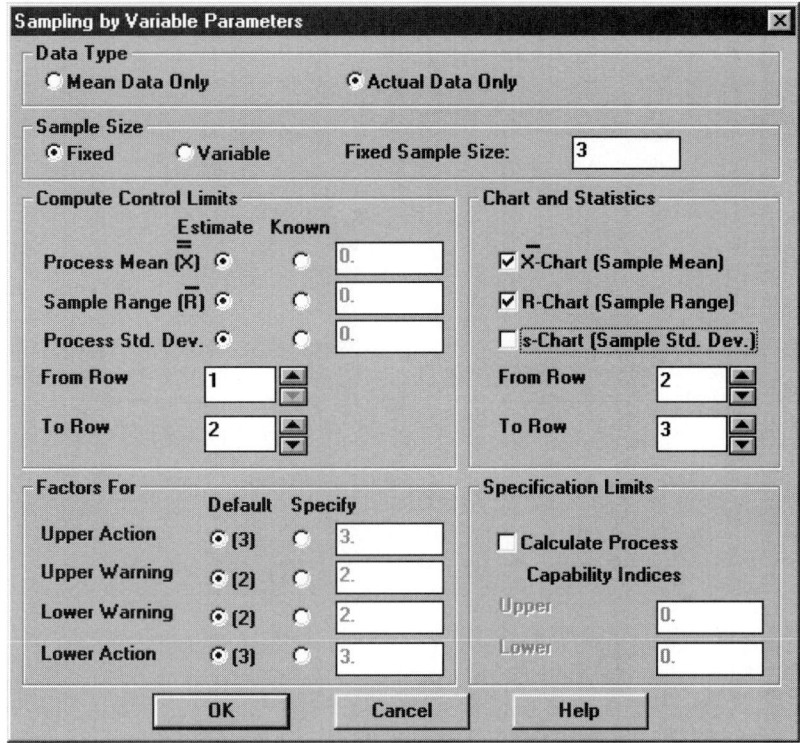

The data is entered as shown below. The variable identifier descriptions (Height ..., Chair 1, etc. can be entered in free form fashion as we have done here. What must be orderly is the number of each sample and its observations (that is, 1, 10.69, 10.67, and 10.29 for sample one).

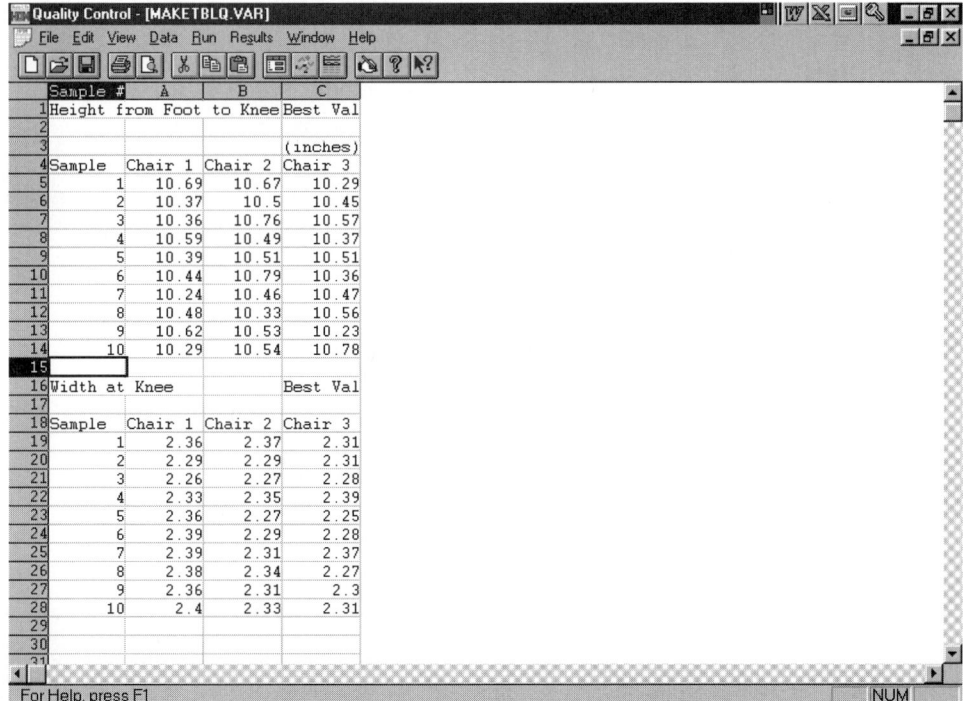

23

To determine whether the variations in height is random and get other useful information about this process, we modify the Parameters Dialog box as shown below. The From Row = 5 and the To Row = 14.

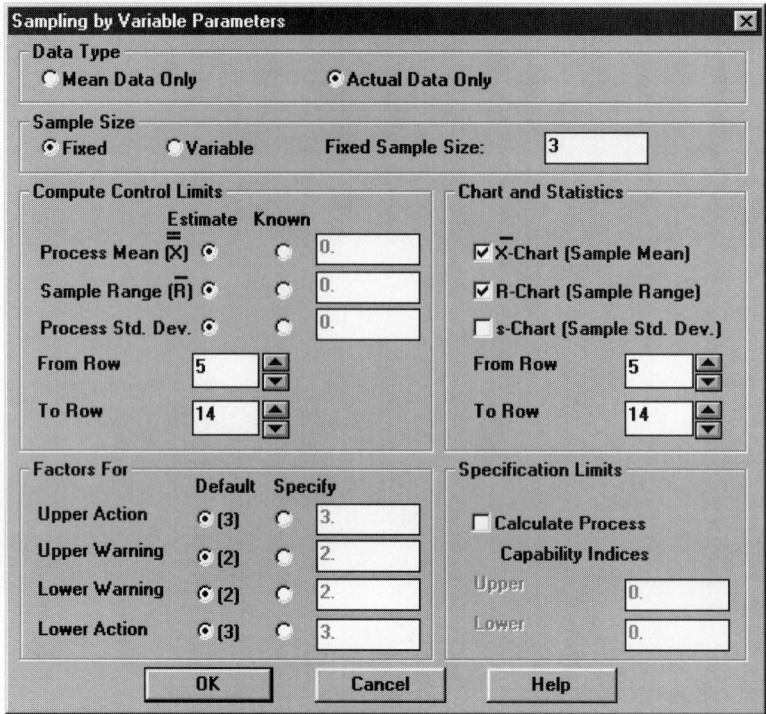

After clicking on OK and clicking on the Run icon, HOM's output is produced in the form of charts, tables and statistics. We see from the tables and the charts (tables not shown) that both the sample mean as well as the sample range are within control. This simply means that the variations are random and not due to any assignable cause. In managerial terms, if the variations are unacceptable then the process must be improved. Options such as using fixtures and templates could be considered to control the variation from chair to chair.

X-bar Chart or Control Chart for Sample Mean

This chart plots the mean of the height of the three chairs within each sample. The blue lines shown are called control limits. The pattern of sample means appears to be random, suggesting that the production process is within control. The control limits are rather wide indicating that the variability from chair to chair is large. The mean appears to be close to the desired value of 10.5".

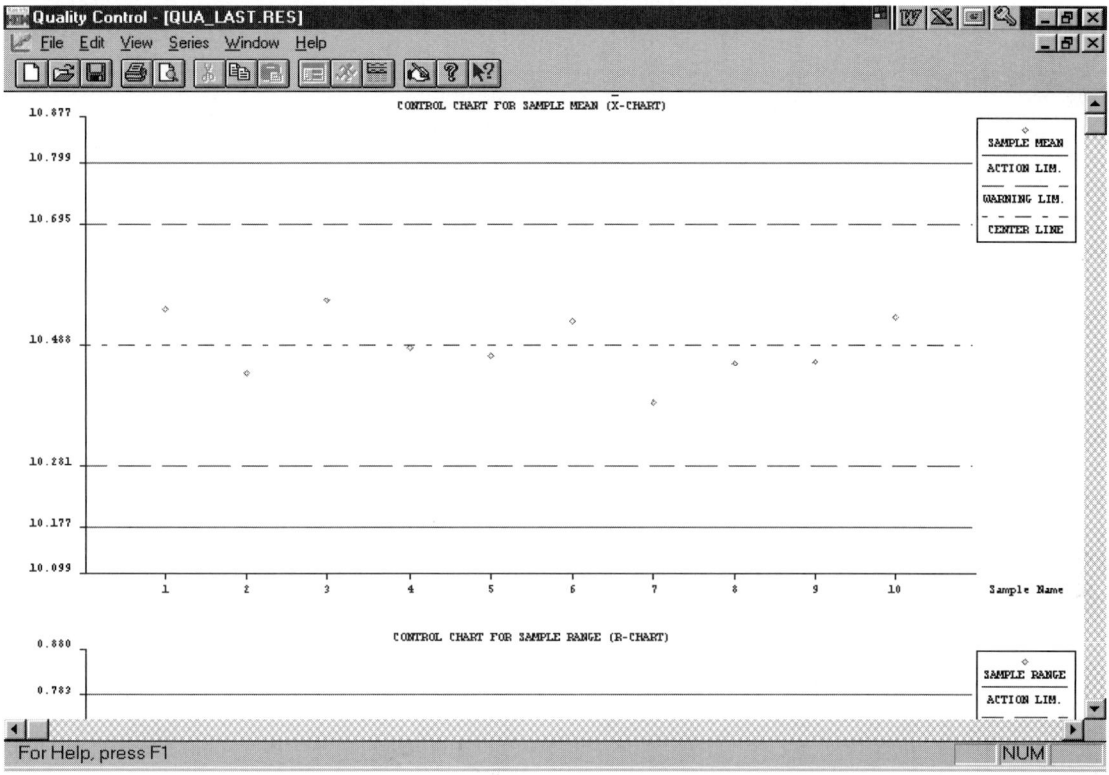

R Chart or the Plot of the Range of Height within each Sample

The range also appears to be within control, indicating that the changes in the range are random and thus can not be attributed to an assignable cause. However, the average range is large (0.304"). This causes some chairs to be 3 tenths of an inch higher (or lower) than another -- a difference a discerning customer can notice.

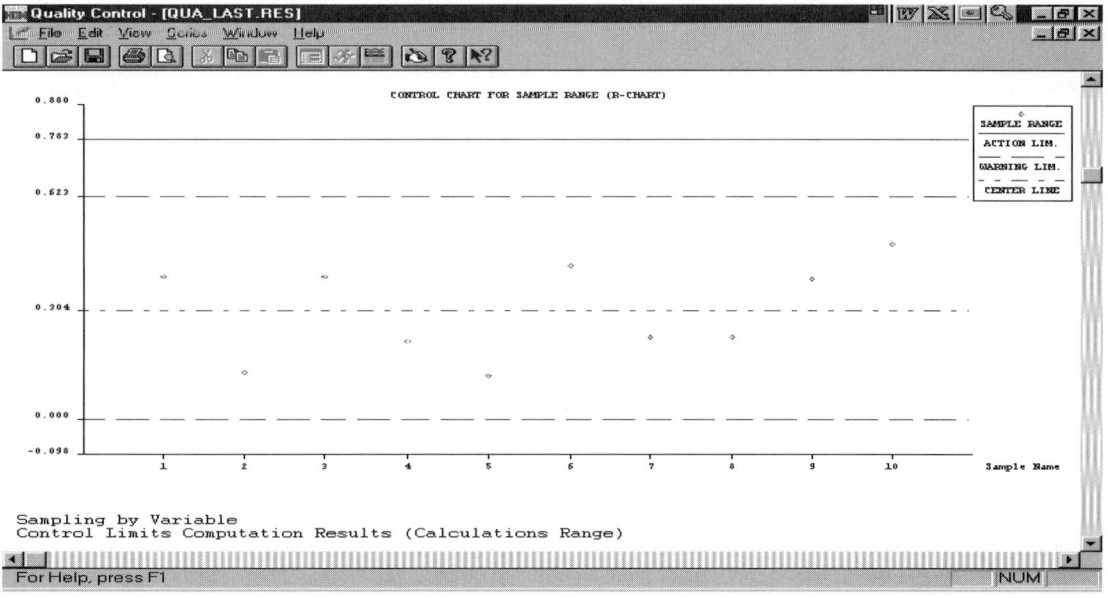

A similar analysis of the width of the knee indicates that the process used to produced the width is under control (outputs are not shown -- they can be obtained by setting the From Row = 19 and the To Row = 28). A more careful study reveals that the range of the width is not that large (average knee width = 2.324" and range = 0.072"). John should pay greater attention to the height while continuing monitoring the processes by collecting data on the two dimensions and plotting them as shown above. The processes are in control but not capable of meeting the quality expectations of John's customers (mean range of height, 0.30", is too high). As suggested earlier, he could consider experimenting with giving his suppliers a template which would reduce the variability.

FORECASTING

As the reputation of the quality of the Newport-created furniture continued to grow throughout the colonies, the need for raw materials increased. Fine wood was either cut locally (walnut, maple, chestnut) or imported from the Islands or Central America (Mahogany). This wood was imported as venture cargo and sold by the log to local dealers. These dealers would then pitsaw the wood into rough planks (often 40 feet long and 36 inches wide) of various depths (1"-4") and sell them to house carpenters, shipwrights and furniture makers such as the Townsends.

Isaac Stella, a longtime supplier of wood to Christopher Townsend (since the mid-1740's,) recently approached Christopher about a long-term commitment for wood. Stella would give Christopher a substantial discount on the coming year's wood purchase if Christopher would commit to a specific annual quantity purchase for the year. To obtain the discount, Christopher would have to guarantee a minimum purchase and commit to using no other suppliers. Christopher was considering the proposal and trying to decide how he would forecast next year's demand for mahogany. Over the past years he had kept data on a set of variables that he thought might be relevant. He had no idea how to forecast these variables into the future, so he was also wondering how else he might create the forecast and concomitant minimum annual purchase quantity for Stella.

To analyze this problem, we must use the forecasting module within HOM. After clicking on its icon we see a spreadsheet appear where the information on periods, dependent and independent variables can be input. We first would sequentially enter the years 1740-1755 into the period column. We would then use the data item on the command line to name a new variable for our dependent variable "board feet" and then enter its 15 data points corresponding to 1740-54. We then would add four additional variables for each of the independent variables and their data. The completed input table is stored in the file MAKETBLF.

MAKETBLF.DAT

Year	Board feet of Mahogany Used	Shop Revenue In Pounds	Percent of Furniture Made of Mahogany	Newport Population	Local Currency For 100 Pounds Sterling
1740	400	600	30	25,255	496
41	350	550	27	25,125	489
42	300	500	23	24,312	462
43	425	575	30	26,327	550
44	475	700	33	28,521	600
45	550	750	35	30,339	725
46	600	800	40	32,528	850
47	800	1000	50	33,239	1,075
48	1,000	1,200	55	34,300	1,300
49	900	1,100	52	33,927	1,248
50	800	1,000	50	32,213	1,188
51	875	1,075	54	33,628	1,218
52	925	1,300	59	34,112	1,249
53	1,075	1,700	67	38,329	1,405
54	1,200	2,000	75	40,128	1,561

To finish specifying the problem we need to use the Parameters window. Clicking on its icon moves it onto the screen. Our first choice is which forecast method to use. Clicking on the arrow reveals the available choices. If we want to use the independent variables, we click on multiple regression. We then choose the variable to forecast (board feet) and then choose which independent variable we would like to use by highlighting them in the independent variable box on the right hand side of the screen. We then specify the starting and ending periods of the forecast (1-15) and the number of periods we want to forecast. Remember, if we are using multiple regression we need a forecast for the independent variables to be able to obtain a forecast estimate. (Assume the following for our four independent variables in order of appearance: 2100; 78; 42171; 1650). These numbers must be entered into the data input spreadsheet in year 1755. This completes the problem specification. Therefore, click on OK and then Run. The Run icon reveals the forecast results. (Mad tailoring is left for more advanced discussions in the manual).

Choosing all four independent variables as forecast drivers does not yield meaningful results since for three of the variables their standard errors are greater than their means (SE less than 1/4 of the mean are much better). Experiment with different combinations or single variables and try to find one with a high R squared, Standard Errors less than 1/4 of the mean, and normally distributed error terms (plotted by activating the SERIES function on the results command line). To do another analysis, simply close the current file you are working on and reactivate the Parameters window. We found the best results by first using percent to forecast currency and then currency to forecast board feet. This also yields a better fit than using the "Best of the Above" time series model.

If, like Christopher, you are uncomfortable forecasting the independent variables, you must use a forecasting technique other than multiple regression. To specify which techniques we return to the Parameters window and click on the method of forecast arrow. Eight techniques are available. For this simple problem we will choose "Best of Above". We recommend you try some of the others. We assume no seasonality since this is annual data, and thus, we have completed our model specifications. Choices as to smoothing constants and initial values are not allowed when we let the computer pick the "Best of" the first five forecasting techniques. Choosing board feet as the variable to forecast, and the time periods as before, completes our specification. Click on OK and then Run and inspect the results.

We see the computer has chosen an exponential smoothing with trend with an alpha of almost one. The problem with this approach is that it misses the first year of any down turn almost completely (1741, 1749). Also, the deviations are quite large. However, the forecast using this method (1260 board feet) does not vary widely from those obtained using econometric forecasting. Forecasting is an art, and thus, model choice must be left up to you. Your comfort level with your ability to forecast the independent variable and the goodness of fit of actual to forecast values of the various models may help you make your choice.

HOM SAMPLE INPUTS AND OUTPUTS
Name of Module: FORECAST
Data File: MAKETBLF.DAT

Input Data Spreadsheet

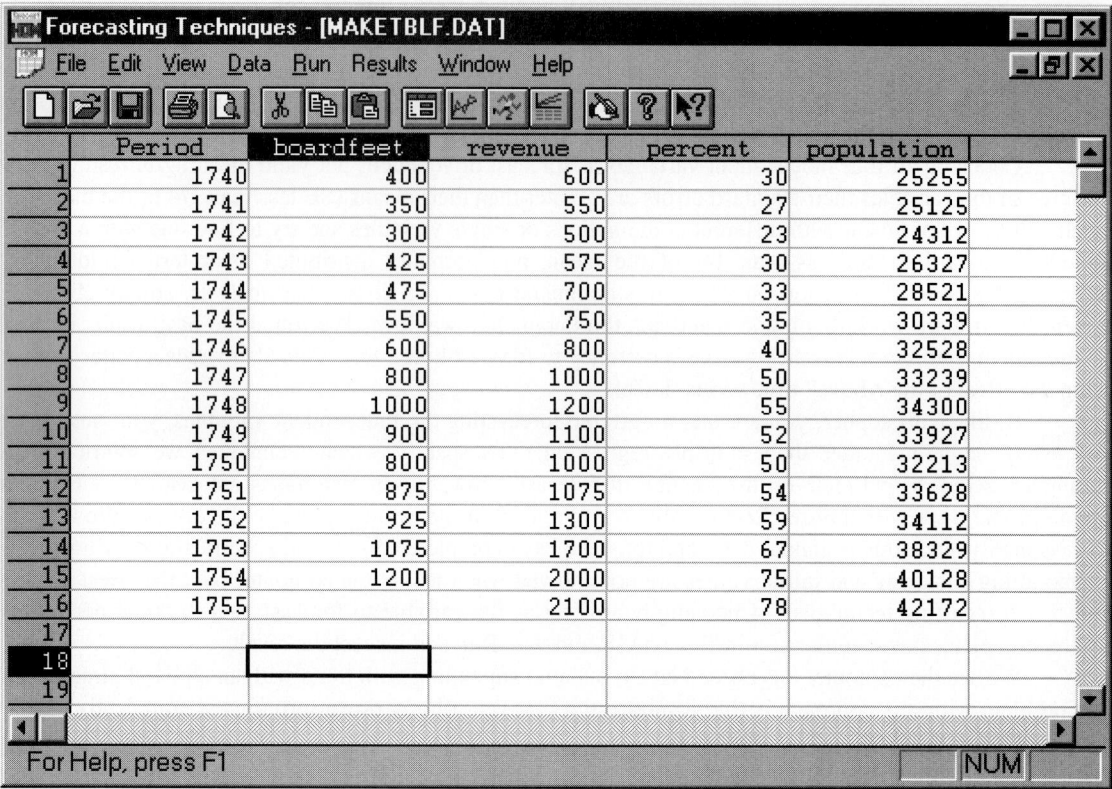

Parameters Window

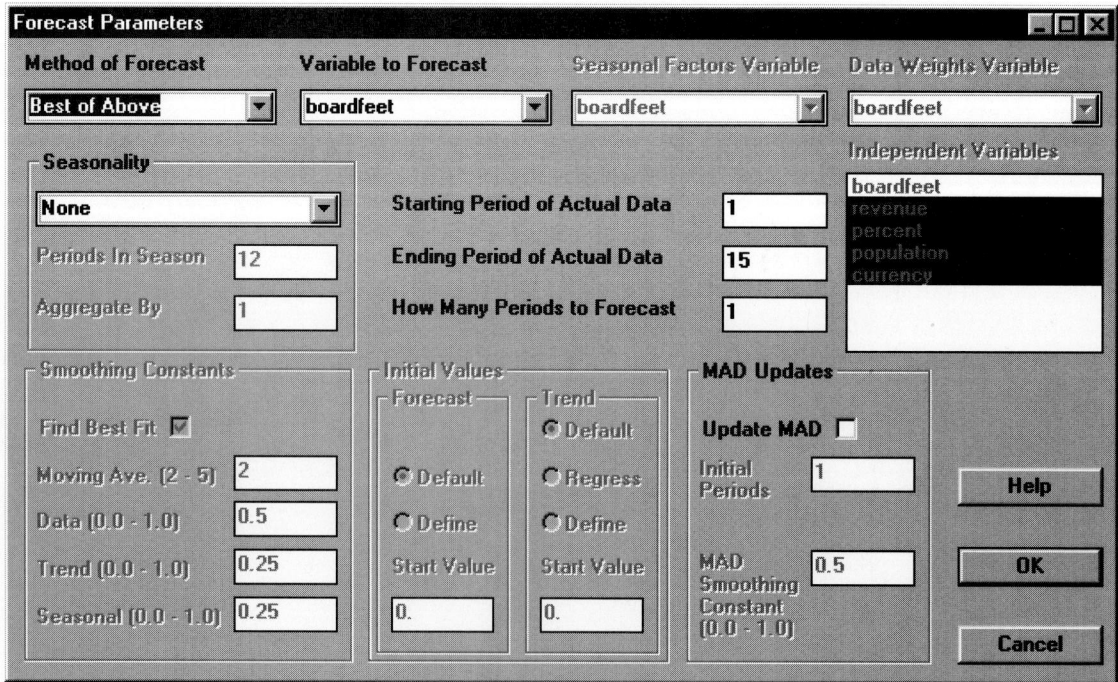

Output Graphs

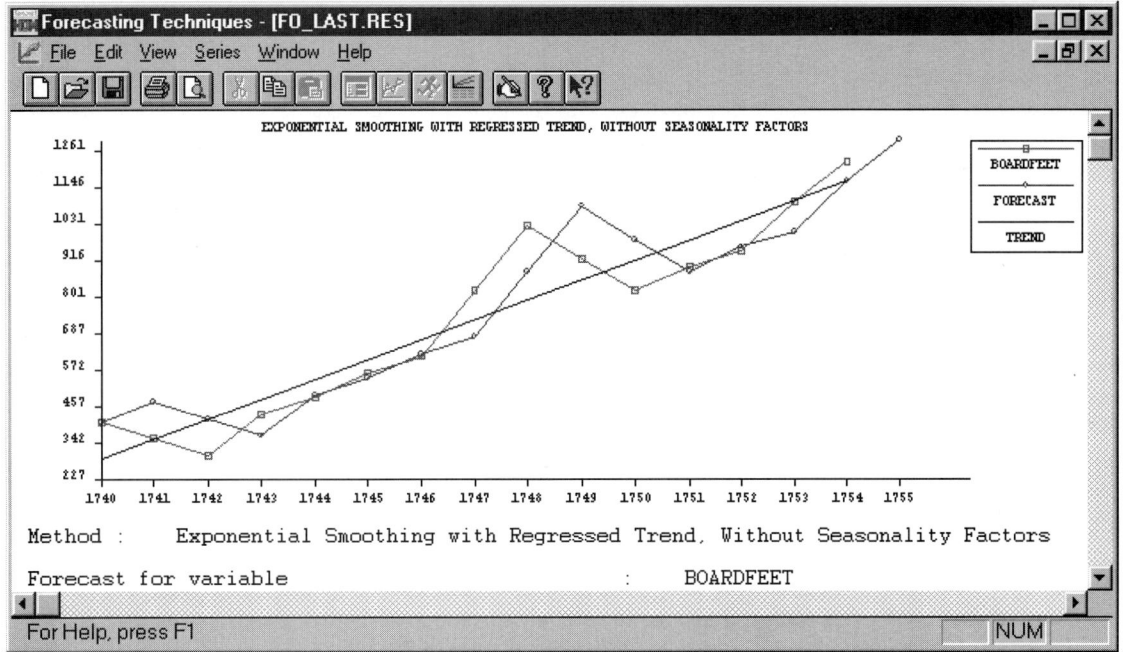

Output Tables

Method :	Exponential Smoothing with Regressed Trend, Without Seasonality Factors								
Forecast f	BOARDFEET								
Root Mean	97.0819								
Mean Absol	11.73%								
Trend Coef	60.5357								
Trend Y-In	227.381								
Best Fitti	0.999969								
Current Period	Actual Data	Data Without Trend	Forecast Without Trend	Forecast With Trend Added	Error (Deviation)	Absolute Deviation	Mean Absolute Deviatio	Running Sum of Errors	Tracking Signal
1740	400	400	400	400	0	0	0	0	0
1741	350	289.464	400	460.536	-110.536	110.536	55.2679	-110.536	-2
1742	300	178.929	289.468	410.539	-110.539	110.539	73.6916	-221.075	-3
1743	425	243.393	178.932	360.539	64.4609	64.4609	71.3839	-156.614	-2.19397
1744	475	232.857	243.391	485.534	-10.5337	10.5337	59.2139	-167.148	-2.82278
1745	550	247.321	232.857	535.536	14.464	14.464	51.7556	-152.684	-2.95009
1746	600	236.786	247.321	610.535	-10.5353	10.5353	45.867	-163.219	-3.55853
1747	800	376.25	236.786	660.536	139.464	139.464	57.5666	-23.755	-0.412652
1748	1000	515.714	376.246	860.531	139.469	139.469	66.6668	115.714	1.7357
1749	900	355.179	515.71	1060.53	-160.531	160.531	76.0533	-44.8179	-0.589296
1750	800	194.643	355.183	960.541	-160.541	160.541	83.7339	-205.359	-2.45251
1751	875	209.107	194.648	860.541	14.4594	14.4594	77.9611	-190.899	-2.44865
1752	925	198.571	209.107	935.535	-10.5353	10.5353	72.7745	-201.434	-2.76793
1753	1075	288.036	198.572	985.536	89.464	89.464	73.9666	-111.97	-1.5138
1754	1200	352.5	288.033	1135.53	64.467	64.467	73.3333	-47.5034	-0.647775
1755	0		352.498	1260.53	-1260.53	1260.53	147.533	-1308.04	-8.86605

INVENTORY

In the past, Christopher purchased wood on a monthly basis. Knowing the orders he had received during the previous month, he would take half a day off from work to visit the numerous enterprises selling lumber to select the planks that he needed. This selection process was very important because the success of the eventual piece of furniture had a lot to do with the characteristics (grain, density, etc.) of the wood used. To ensure continued output at the shop, Christopher hired a laborer for a full day to fill in for him while he was out wood shopping (2 pounds per day). The full day is required due to the difference in their skill levels. The lumber merchant required one-week lead time to trim the wood to Christopher's specification and make the delivery. There was a two pound delivery charge for each order. Mahogany cost 12 shillings a board foot (there are 20 shillings in a pound). For orders of more than 400 board feet there was a discount of 6 percent for the entire order. For orders of more than 800 board feet the discount was 7.5 percent for the entire order. Since the mahogany was imported, the King of England required a tax of 5 percent paid at the time the wood was removed from the merchant's premises. Money could be borrowed at 6 percent and Christopher felt he could earn 10 percent on every additional pound invested in the business. Christopher's shop was small so he stored his wood outside. This caused him to encounter a pilferage rate of 1 percent and a deterioration loss to termites, carpenter bees and assorted animals of 6 percent a year. In order to cure the wood, Christopher felt he needed to store any recently purchased wood for one month before he would consider using it in his furniture.

Assume that Christopher's annual demand for mahogany is what you forecast it to be in the last section and that it is used at a relatively uniform rate over the year. Should Christopher change his once-a-month wood shopping policy? Should he take the quantity discounts offered? If he gives up on curing the new wood for a month would that change the amount he should order?

To analyze these questions, we must use the independent demand section of the HOM Inventory module. After selecting independent demand and clicking on OK, the data input section spreadsheet is revealed. For these types of problems, it is best to specify the problem in the Parameters window first and then fill in the data. We do this because "specify the model" turns the words of the required data entries in the spreadsheet blue, facilitating data entry. Since we want to order based on our wood supply rather than a specific day of the month, we choose the continuous review model. Our demand has initially been assumed to be deterministic without the ability to back-order. We assume the chosen wood will arrive in one cart-full rather than a few pieces at a time and, thus, choose the infinite replenishment rate. We will also, at some time, want to allow for quantity discounts with 3 ranges (list, 6% off, and 7.5% off). This completes the current model specification and, thus, we click on OK and fill in the resulting blue sections of the data spreadsheet. The actual data used is given in the file MAKETBLI. Demand is assumed to be 1,260, cost per unit is .63 pounds (12/20 x 1.05), an annual holding cost rate of .17(.10+.01+.06), order costs of 4 pounds(2+2), and a lead time of 5 weeks (5/52=.096 of a year).

The output of the results for this case first indicates a tradeoff curve between order quantity and inventory cost. This indicates that a broad range of order quantities (290-324 board feet) have about the same cost. The next set of data shows the optimal order quantity (306.9 board feet of Mahogany), the number of orders per year (4.1), the level when our order should be made (120.96 board feet), and all relevant costs. These data show that Christopher should give up his once a month wood purchasing expeditions for an approach that is based on his stock of wood. This would cut his expeditions to about 4 per year.

To determine if we should accept the proposed quantity discounts, close this file and then revisit the Parameters window. Once there, enable the Quantity Discount mode by clicking on its box and indicating that we will use three ranges. Leaving the other settings as before, return to the data spreadsheet and fill in the required range data that is now highlighted in blue. These are the base case and the 6 and 7.5 percent price reductions with their concomitant minimum purchases (400, 800 board feet). Now, re-run the analysis to reveal which of the three alternatives is preferred. In our case, the 6% discount yields the best result with an order cycle of almost every four months.

We now assume that the demand of 1260 Board Feet of Mahogany is the mean of a distribution with a standard deviation of 1/10 the mean. Will this effect our inventory policy? To analyze this type of problem we must return to the parameter window and switch to stochastic demand. This will require additional decisions to be made (words turn black from grey). First is whether to use fill rate or lead time service levels. Fill rate implies that we have enough in stock to fill the given percent of demand during every inventory cycle (90% implies we will carry enough inventory to fill 90% of the orders in every cycle). Lead time implies that we will have enough in stock to fill all orders in the given percent of inventory cycles (90% implies we have enough inventory to fill all of the orders in 9 out of every 10 inventory cycles). We also get to choose how we want the data reported (safety stock; cost; service level).

In our case we use fill rate service and cost reporting. After clicking on OK the data spreadsheet reappears with the need for new blue highlighted data areas to be filled. We specify 126 for the standard deviation of demand (10%) and zero for the standard deviation of the lead time since it is not uncertain. We specify our service level of 99% and then click on run.

The result output again shows a trade off curve between inventory costs and order quantity. The two columns show results for an EOQ policy and an optimal Q policy. The EOQ results simply utilize the EOQ order quantity and adjust the safety stock to yield the desired service level. (In our case the EOQ is 306 and the safety stock is 40) You will also notice that the inventory cost has been augmented from the certain demand case to include the cost of holding the safety stock. The column headed by Best Q reveals the order quantity Q that minimizes the costs of ordering, and holding the base inventory as well as the safety stock. The Best Q results will always have lower costs, higher order quantity and lower safety stock then the EOQ results.

In the certain demand example we noticed that changing the lead time had no effect on the inventory decision. If John, however, abandons the curing of the wood in this environment what is the result? This scenario would reduce the lead time to 1 week (.02 of a year). If we close the current file and make the appropriate change to the data spreadsheet and rerun the analysis we get a different result. The cost and quantities change, why? [Hint: Remember that the variability of demand only effects us during the lead time if we are using the continuous review model. Thus, if the lead time is shorter the same degree of uncertainties occurs but over a shorter period of time and we thus need less safety stock to protect against it.] In our case it reduces to ten units from forty and our costs reduce to 827 from 831.

To investigate the modeling of other alternative situations when demand or lead time is uncertain, we refer the user to the Help files or the manual.

HOM SAMPLE INPUTS AND OUTPUTS
Name of Module: INVENTORY (INDEPENDENT DEMAND)
Data File: MAKETBLI.DAT

Input Data Spreadsheet

Continuous Review, Stochastic, Infinite Replenishment Rate			
Backorders not allowed, No Qty. Discounts, Calculate Costs			
BASIC MODEL DATA			
Annual Demand		1260.00	Units / Year
Cost per Unit [and]		0.63	$ / Unit
Annual Holding Cost Rate		0.17	Fraction of Cost
Annual Holding Cost per		0.107	$ / Unit / Year
Ordering Cost		4	$ / Order (Setup)
Annual Cost per Backorder			$ / Unit / Year
SUPPLEMENTAL DATA (YEARLY QUANTITIES)			
Usage Rate (Demand)		1260	Units / Year
Production Rate			Units / Year
Average Leadtime		0.096	in Years
Std.Dev. of Demand		126	Units / Year
Std.Dev. of Leadtime			in Years
Length of Review Period			in Years
Inventory on Hand			Units
Service Level		0.99	Fraction (0 - 1)
SENSITIVITY ANALYSIS	Alt.Order Quantity	Alt.Reorder Level	
Alternative Set 1			
Alternative Set 2			
Alternative Set 3			
QUANTITY DISCOUNT TABLE	Price	Min.Order Quantity	
Range 1	0.63	0	
Range 2	0.592	400	
Range 3	0.583	800	

Parameters Window

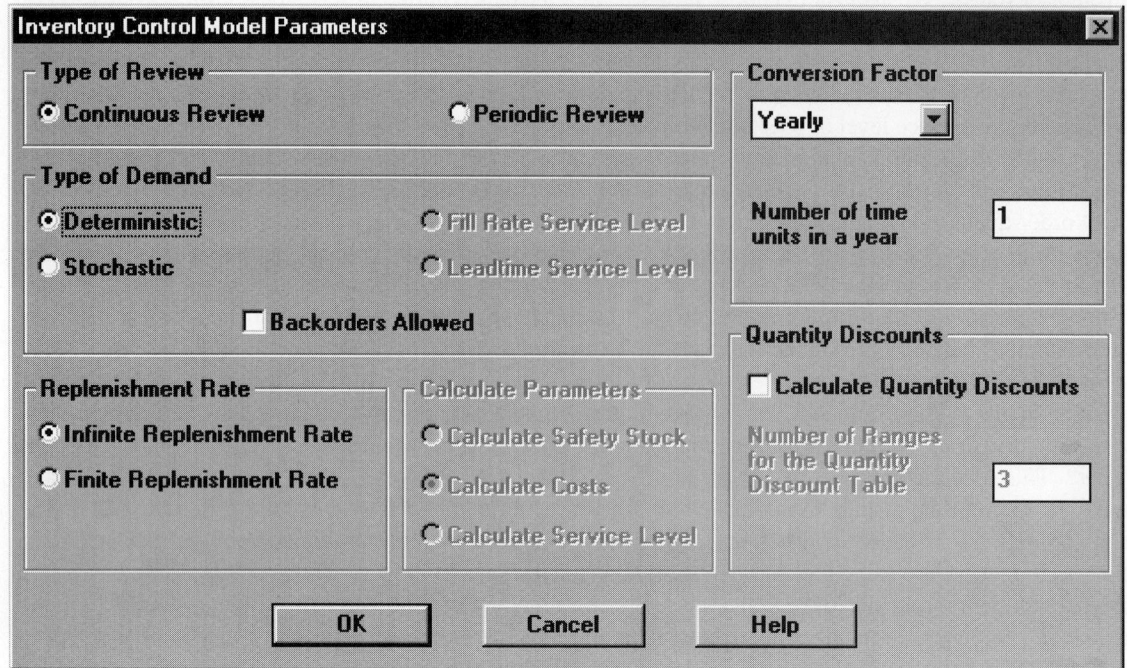

Output Graphs

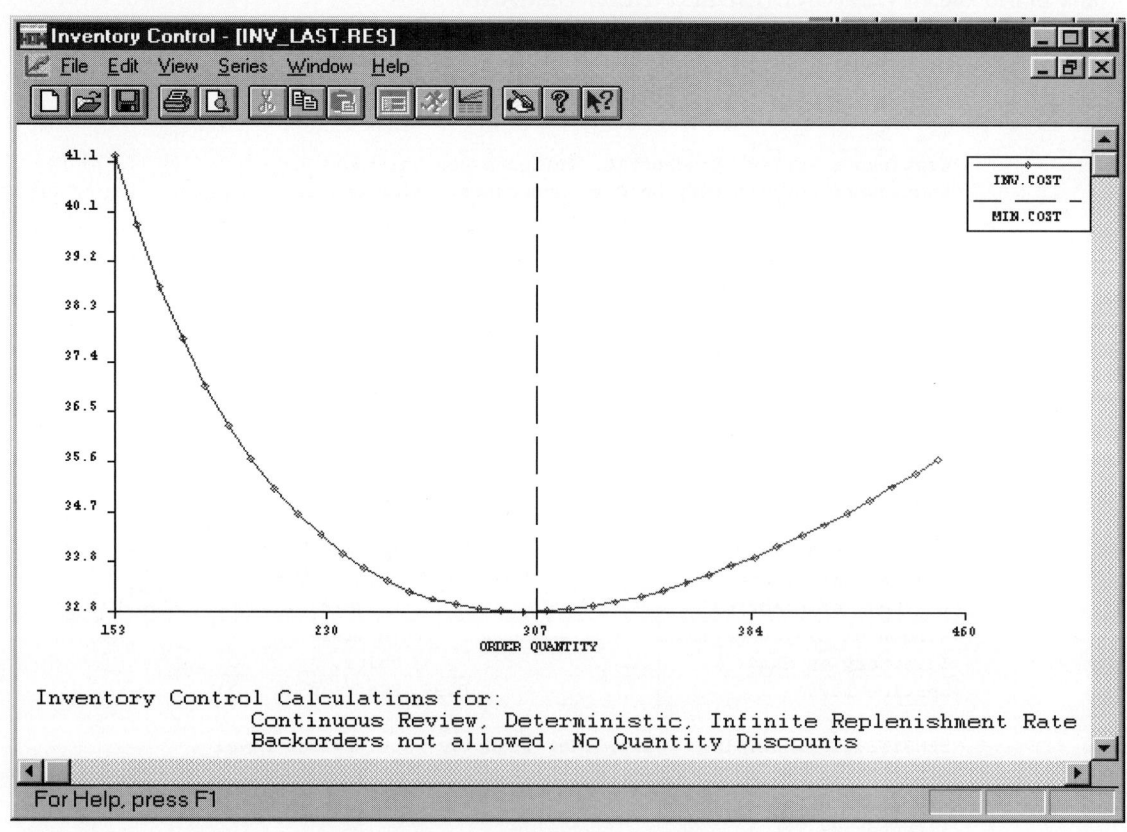

Output Tables

Inventory Control Calculations for:
Continuous Review, Deterministic, Infinite Replenishment Rate
Backorders not allowed, No Quantity Discounts

	EOQ (optimal)
Annual Demand	1260
Holding Cost (Unit/Year)	0.1071
Ordering Cost	4
Order Quantity	306.929
Number of Orders (Year)	4.10518
Average Inventory	153.465
Maximum Inventory	306.929
Reorder Level	120.96
Length of Order Cycle	0.243595
Annual Holding Cost	16.4207
Annual Ordering Cost	16.4207
Annual Inventory Cost	32.8414
Annual Purchase Cost	793.8
Total Annual Cost	826.641

MATERIALS REQUIREMENTS PLANNING

In addition to chairs and tables John and Christopher also made desks for domestic consumption as well as export to New York and the Southern Colonies as well as the Caribbean Islands. These required brass handles and escutcheons, locks, and in some cases casters. Brass was extremely expensive in the colonies and could constitute five percent of the cost of a desk or chest. The Townsends did not make these items but bought them on an as needed basis from their uncle Solomon Townsend who owned a hardware store in Newport. Brass was not allowed to be manufactured in the colonies and thus Solomon had to order them from London. Due to the perils of the oversea voyage, Solomon did not always have the brasses that his nephews required when they needed them. If not in stock, Christopher and John would often have to wait a month or two for delivery. Thus they were thinking of developing a brass materials inventory to insure against this occurrence. Their customers were not happy to have their chests and desks delivered without brasses. Can you devise a material requirements planning (MRP) system for them given the demand and cost data depicted below. The data is given for the three major options available with a desk. Option A desks had brass handles (in pairs), escutcheons, locks and casters. Option B desks had only brass handles and escutcheons, whereas option C desks had brass handles, escutcheons and locks. The Product Structure (for only brass items) was as follows (the product structure is called the Bill of Materials).

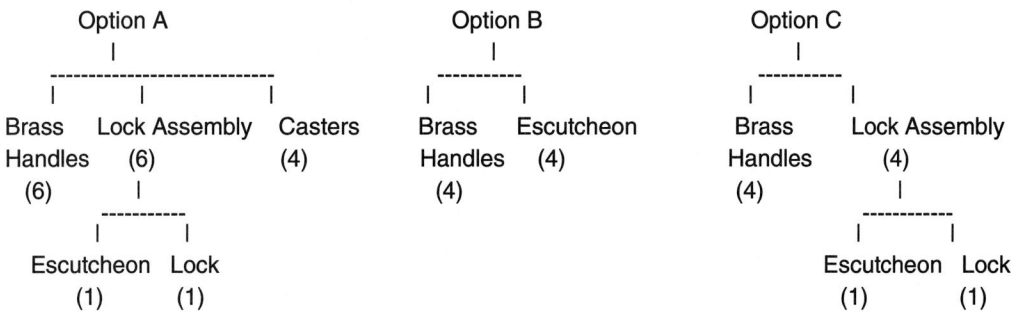

The numbers under each item indicate how many of the parts are necessary to make an assembly or sub-assembly. For example, six brass handles, six lock assemblies, and four casters are needed for an option A desk. Each lock assembly requires one escutcheon and one lock. The following leadtime and cost data are applicable. We shall assume that the time to make the desk or assemble the lock assembly are quite negligible (less than a week).

Part	Holding Cost/week	Leadtime for Procurement	Ordering Cost	Inventory On Hand
Brass Handle	£0.02	2 weeks	£1	5
Escutcheon	£0.05	2 weeks	£1	22
Lock	£0.025	4 weeks	£1	8
Caster	£0.05	6 weeks	£2	32

We are given that a shipment of handles (5 handles) and locks (3 locks) are expected in week 3. No other orders are outstanding. We shall also assume that the demand forecast for weeks 1 through 10 are as follows.

Option	Week									
	1	2	3	4	5	6	7	8	9	10
A	2	3	1	4	2	3	2	2	1	2
B	3	4	1	1	1	1	5	2	1	0
C	0	5	0	4	0	0	3	3	2	1

After clicking on the HOM inventory management identifier, choose "Dependent Demand (MRP)" in the dialog box and click on OK.

The first set of data that are entered correspond to the product structure. The structure has to be specified for each assembly as shown below (the HOM data file is called MAKETBLM.MRP -- please note that MRP files have the extension .MRP).

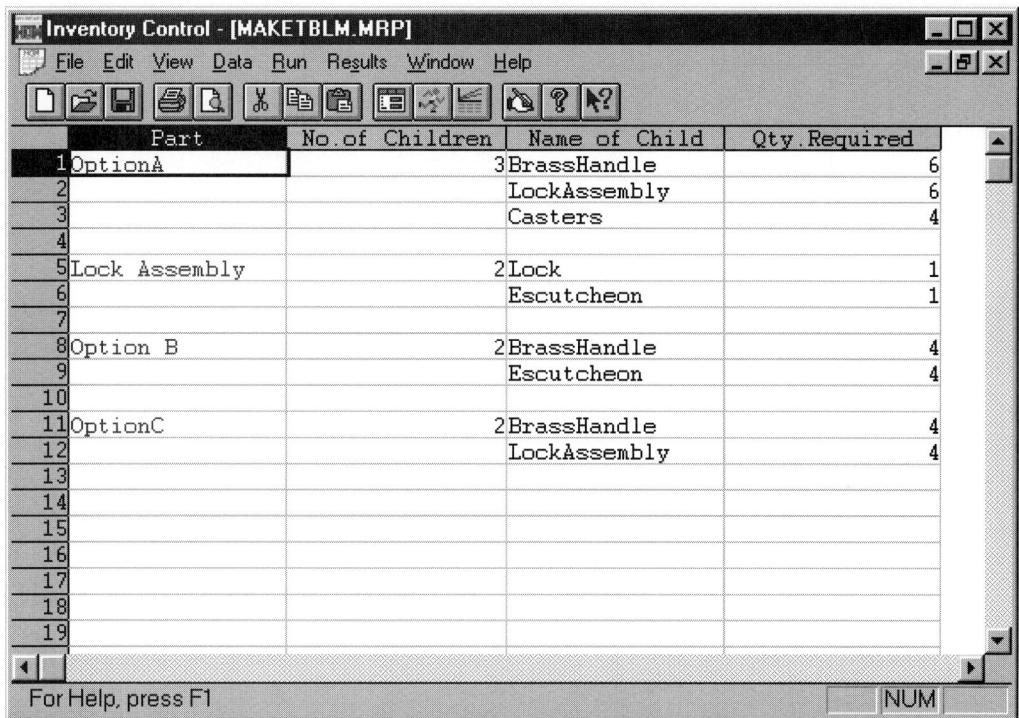

The rule for data entry is that every assembly should be listed but the order of listing them is unimportant (lock assembly comes before option C). Each assembly is listed only once (even though the lock assembly is used in two options it is defined only once). Right click any cell and the spreadsheet for entering the demand and cost data is revealed. The two spreadsheets are linked documents -- making changes in one will reflect changes in the other. The demand data for Option A is entered as shown below:

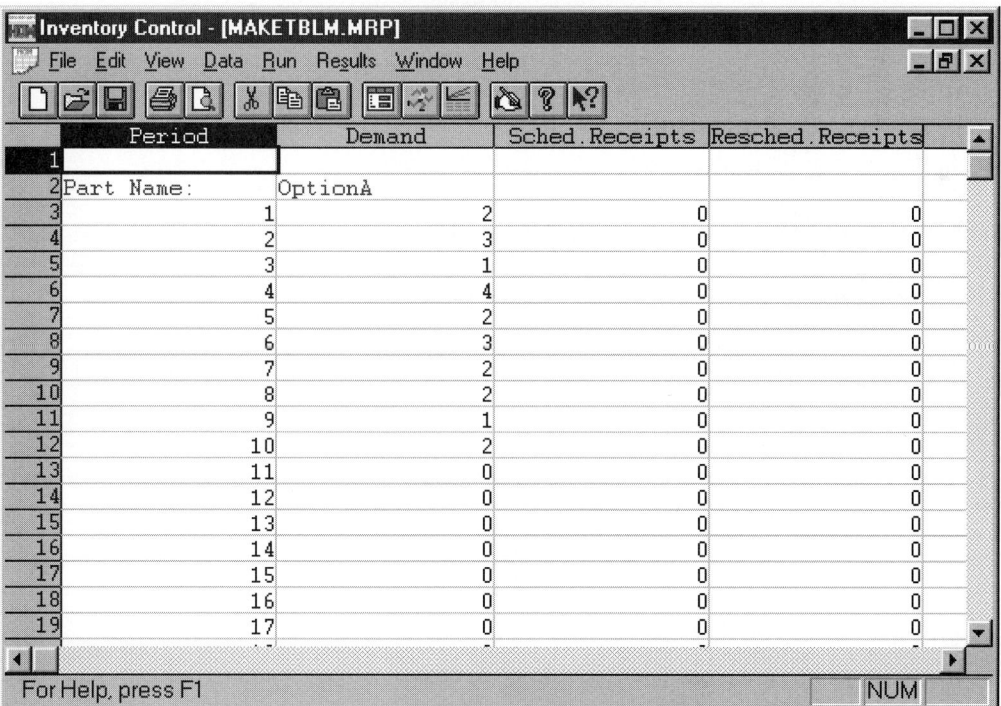

Demand data for Options B and C are entered in a similar fashion. The other parts (their names are highlighted in blue) are seen by scrolling down the spreadsheet. We are neglecting assembly time so there are no scheduled receipts for the three options. There will be receipts if and only if there are desks being assembled (that is in work-in-progress).

The scheduled receipts of the handles and locks are entered as shown below. Recall that a ship is due in 3 weeks from now carrying 5 handles and 3 locks.

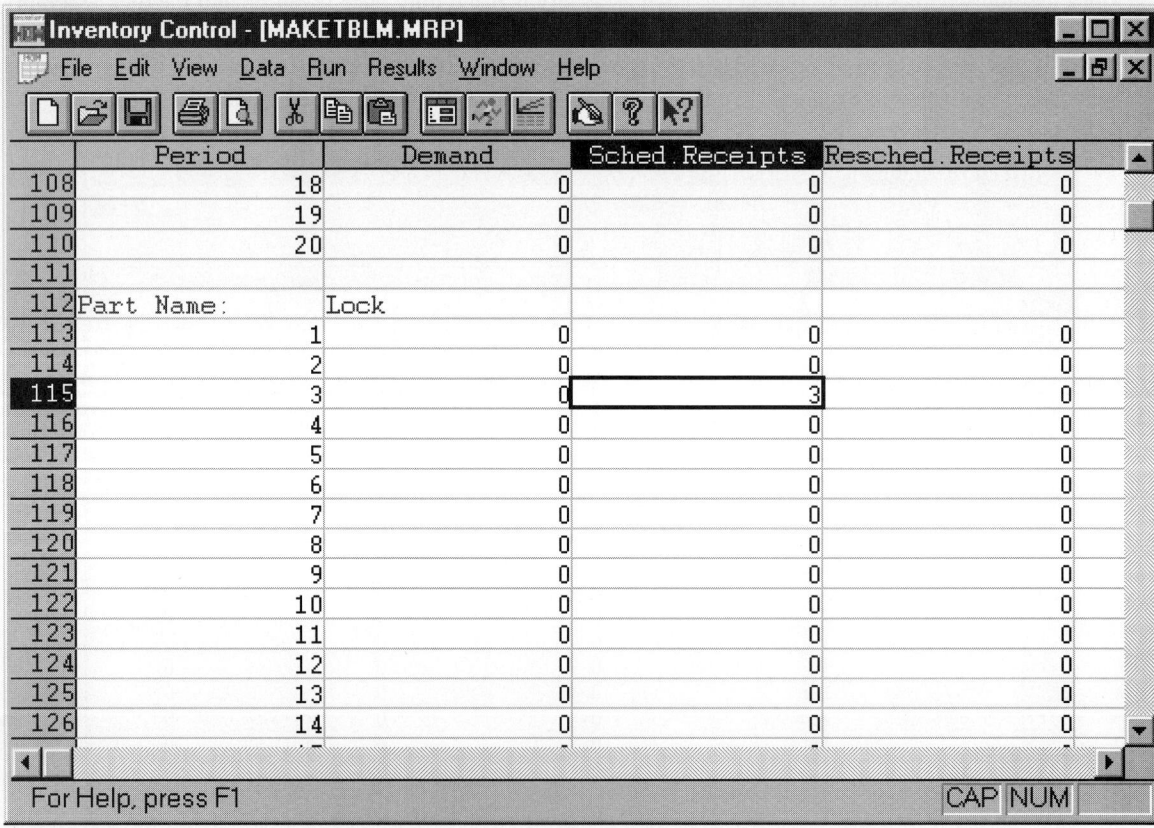

Now the order policy (batching rule), leadtime and cost data are added. This data is entered by clicking on the Parameters Dialog box as shown below for each assembly and part. For assembled parts, as assembly time is negligible, we have let HOM's default values stay unchanged except for the leadtime (which is set = 0) as shown below. (That is we have neglected assembled parts and concentrated on the problematic brass parts.)

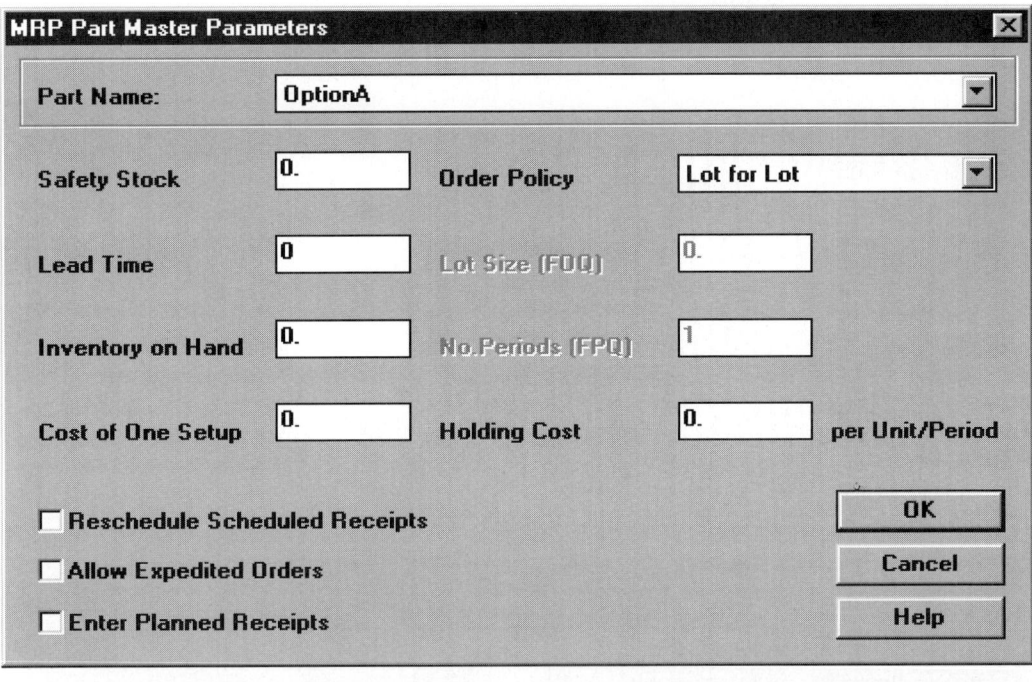

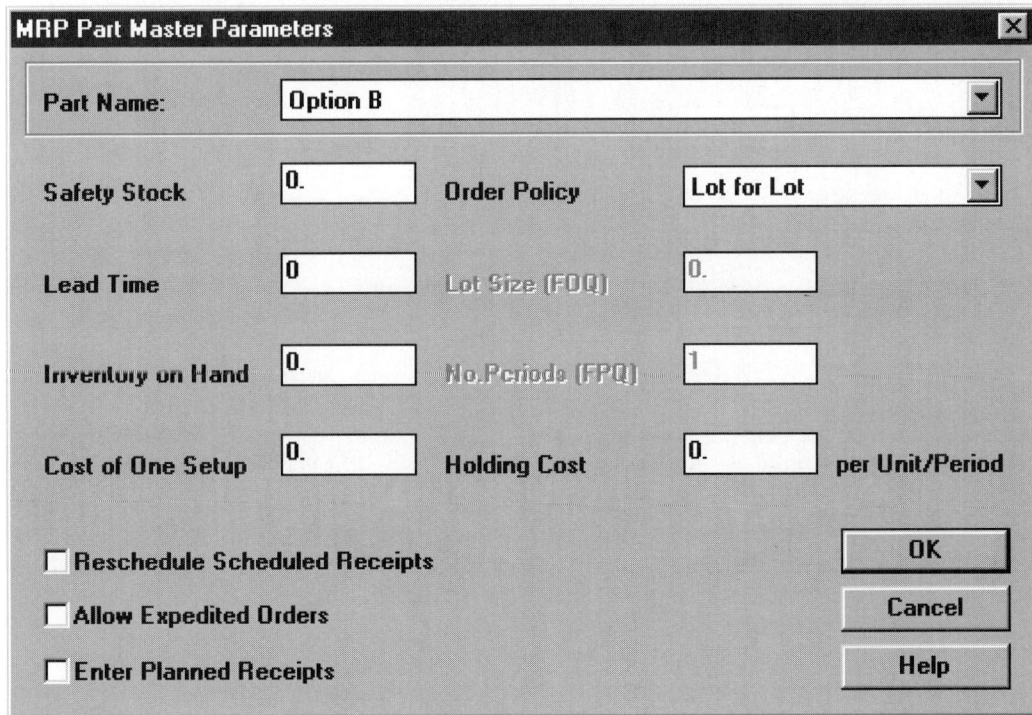

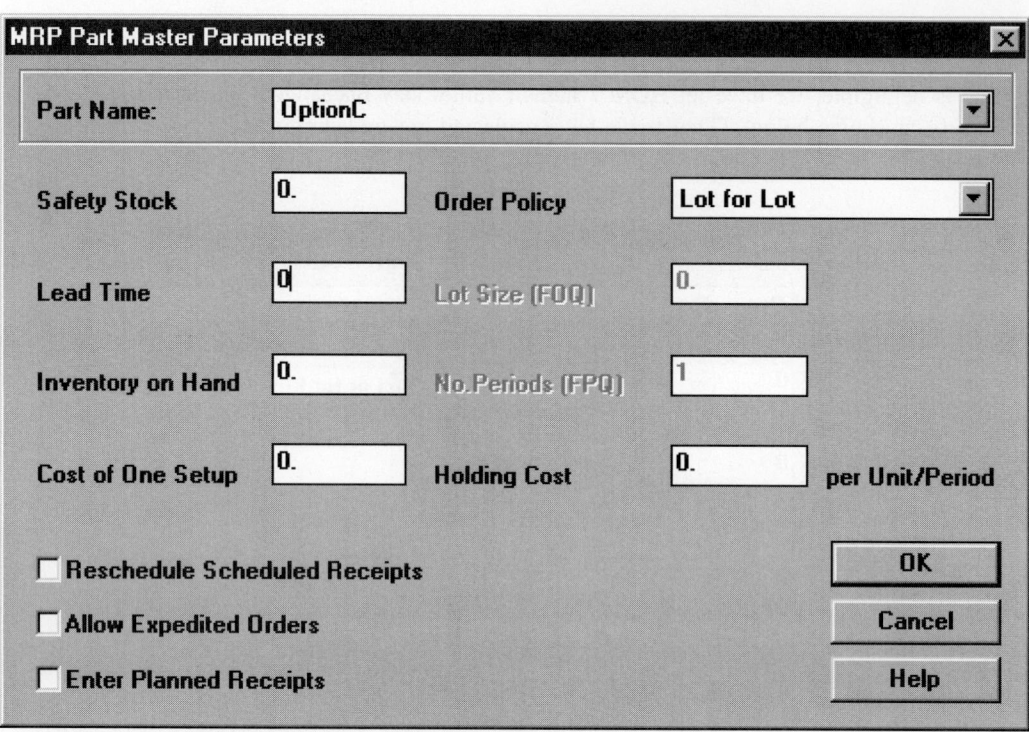
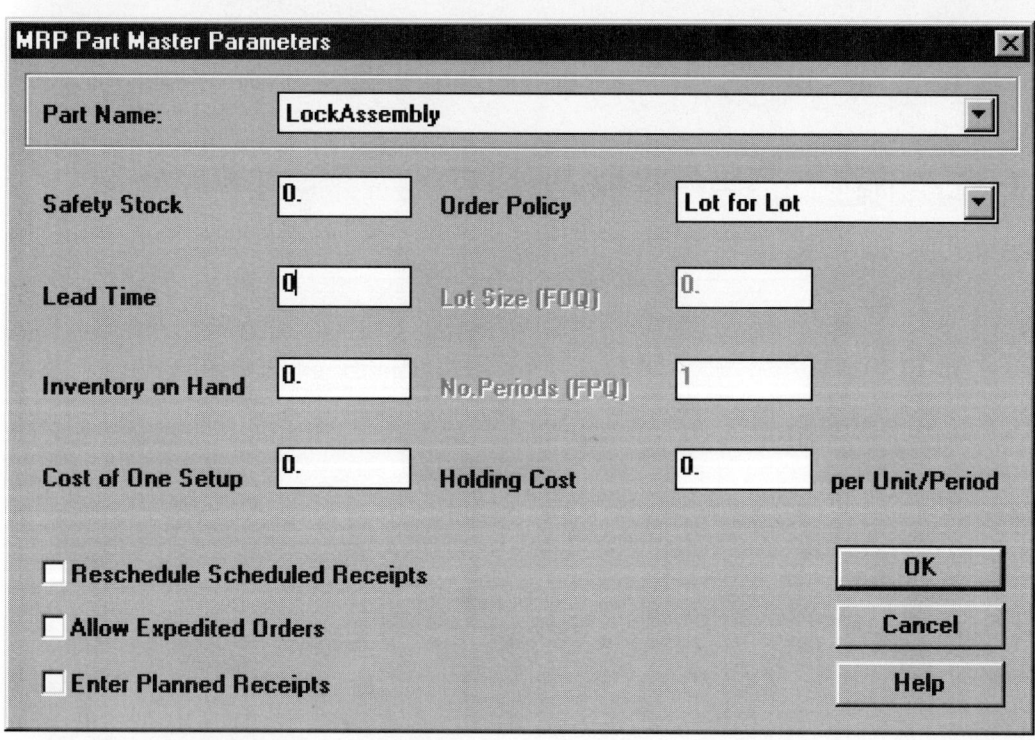

For the brass parts the data is entered as shown below:

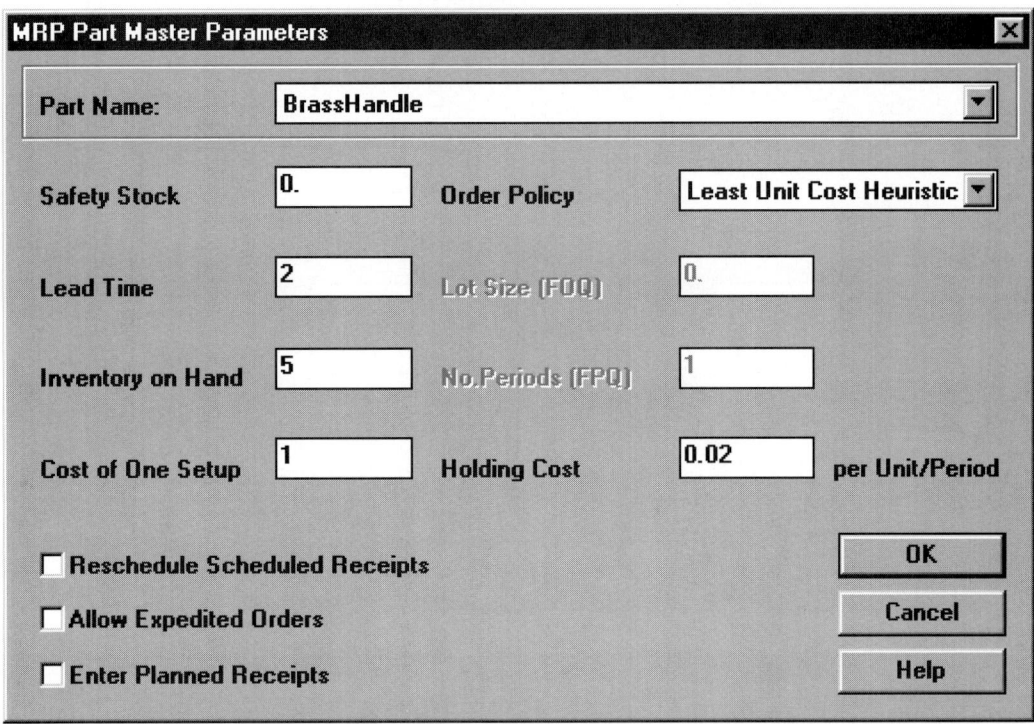

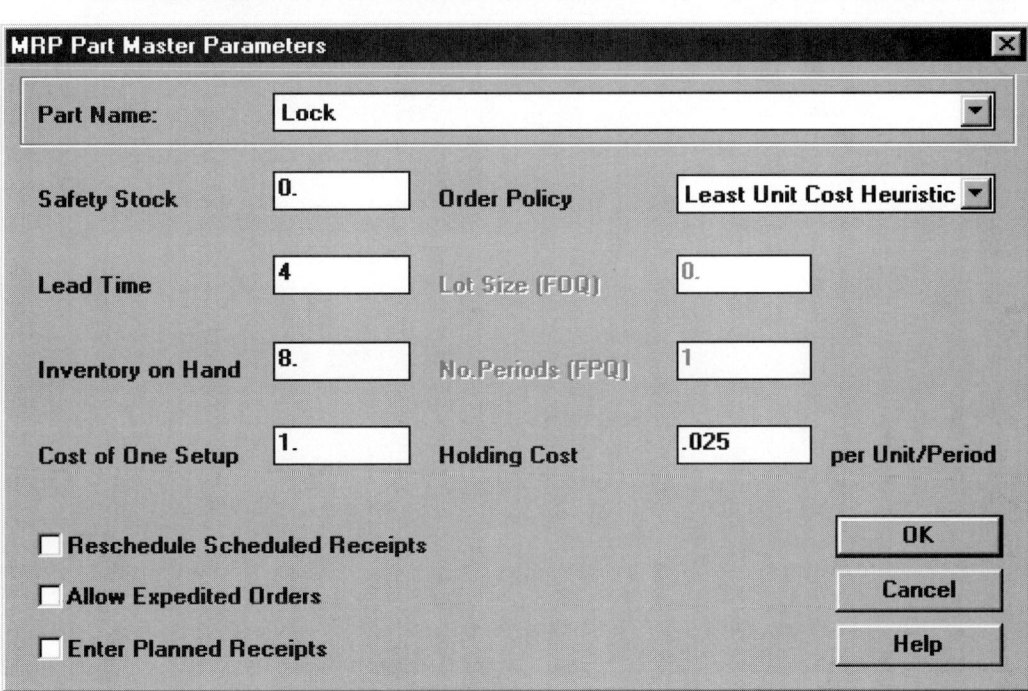

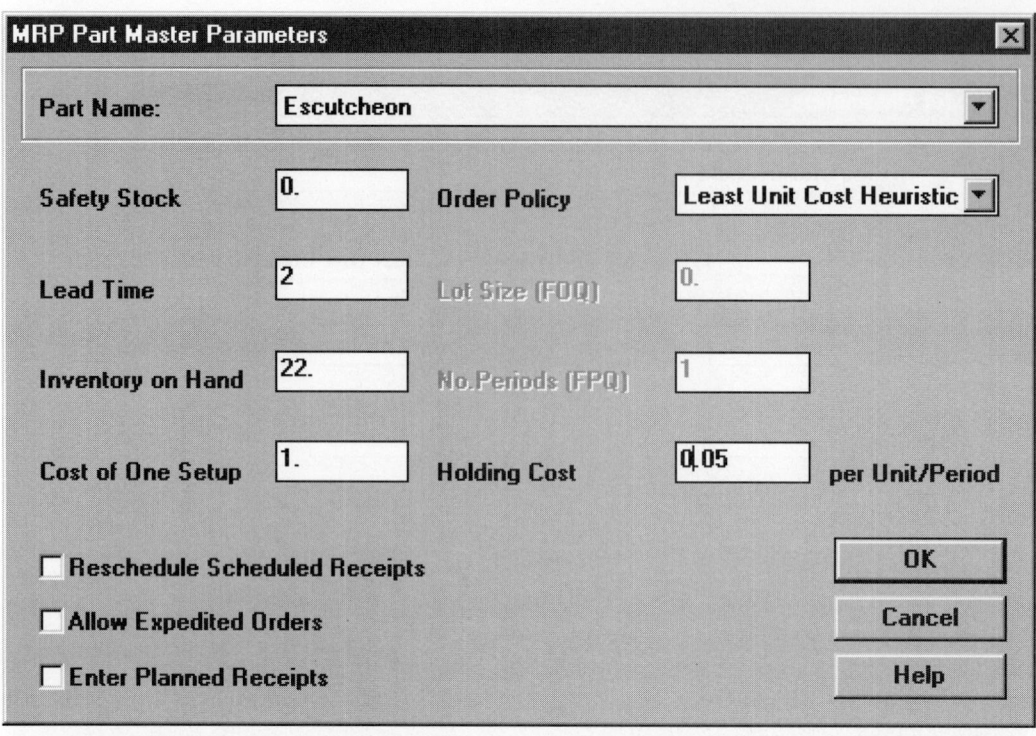

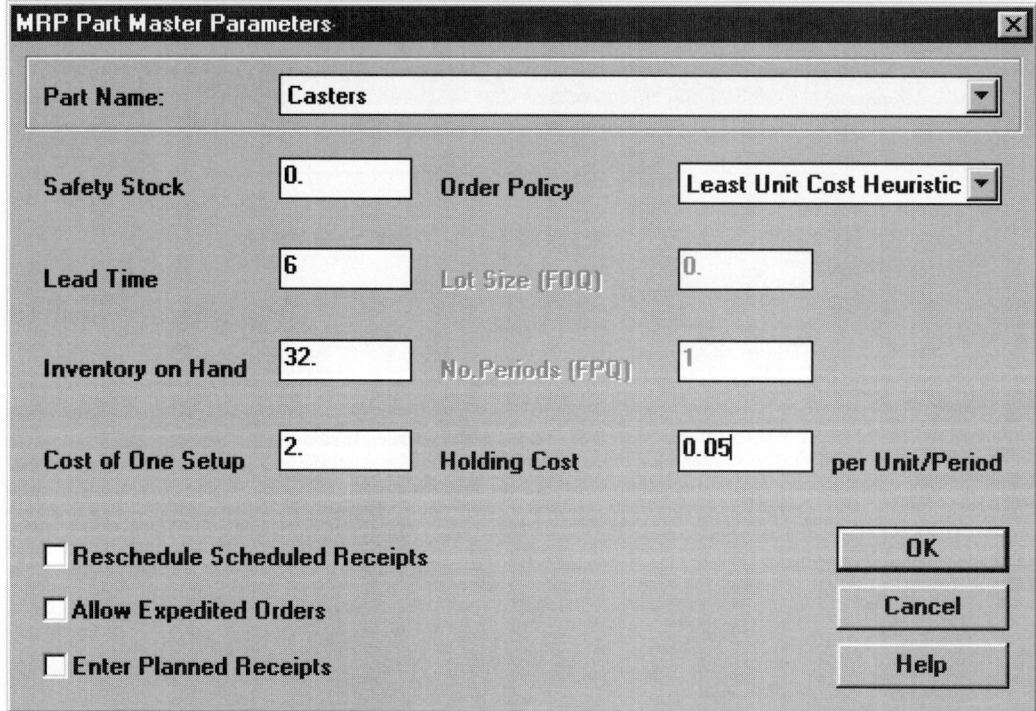

We have asked HOM to minimize the ordering plus holding cost using a rule known as the least unit cost heuristic. This rule attempts to heuristically minimize the sum of these two costs. The user could try other rules and study the impact on cost.

Finally, clicking on the right mouse button to reveal the Bill of Materials spreadsheet and opening its Parameters Dialog Box, we enter the data as shown below.

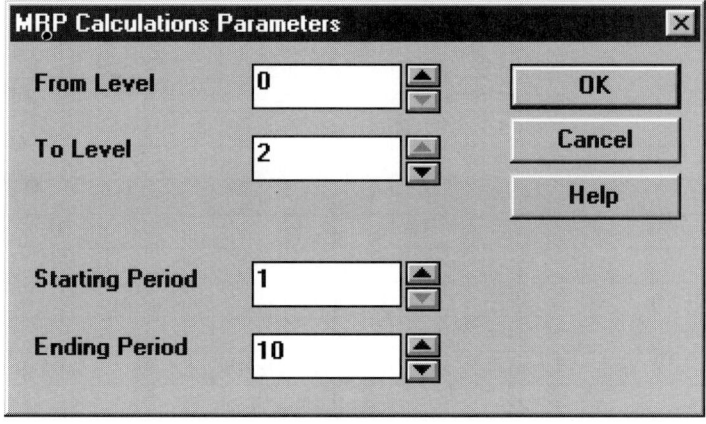

In this dialog box we have asked HOM to plan for all parts and assemblies (level zero corresponds to the topmost parts in the product structure and the largest level number to the bottommost part in the product structure). In this product structure there are only three levels. Level zero corresponds to the three options. Level 1 corresponds to Casters and Lock Assembly. Lock and Escutcheon are level 2 parts. We have also asked HOM to plan for the first ten periods. Click on RUN to produce the following reports (only data up to period 6 are shown). The most serious problem appears to be with Casters and Locks. The projected available balance is -28 in week 6 for Casters and -85 for locks in week 4 for locks. Clearly the long leadtime is contributing to the shortages. The user can experiment with a larger value of on hand inventory as well as carrying a safety stock for the brass products to see the effect on the materials plan. The best advice that you can give Christopher and John is to either carry a larger safety stock or plan eight weeks ahead or use a combination of the two solutions.

BILL OF MATERIAL						
==================================						
	Number of		Quantity			
Part Name	Children	Child Name	Required			
============	=========	============	============			
OptionA	3	BrassHandle	6			
		LockAssembly	6			
		Casters	4			
------------	---------	------------	------------			
LockAssembly	2	Lock	1			
		Escutcheon	1			
------------	---------	------------	------------			
Option B	2	BrassHandle	4			
		Escutcheon	4			
------------	---------	------------	------------			
OptionC	2	BrassHandle	4			
		LockAssembly	4			
MRP PARAMETERS						
==================================						
From Level	0					
To Level	2					
Start Period	1					
End Period	10					
MRP PART RECORDS						
==================================						
PART NAME	OptionA					
Low Level	0					
Ordering Policy	LTL					
Safety Stock	0					
Lead Time	0					
On Hand Inventory	0					
User Reschedules Receipts?	NO					
Expediting allowed	NO					
User Provides Planned Rcpts?	NO					
Setup plus Holding Cost	0					

Period		1	2	3	4	5	6
		---------	------------	---------	---------	---------	---------
Gross Requirements		2	3	1	4	2	3
Scheduled Receipts		0	0	0	0	0	0
Projected Available Balance		0	0	0	0	0	0
Planned Order Releases		2	3	1	4	2	3
Expedite Orders?		NO	NO	NO	NO	NO	NO
Rescheduled Scheduled Rcpts		0	0	0	0	0	0
Planned Order Receipts		2	3	1	4	2	3
Independent Demand		2	3	1	4	2	3
Dependent Demand		0	0	0	0	0	0

PART NAME	Option B						
Low Level	0						
Ordering Policy	LTL						
Safety Stock	0						
Lead Time	0						
On Hand Inventory	0						
User Reschedules Receipts?	NO						
Expediting allowed	NO						
User Provides Planned Rcpts?	NO						
Setup plus Holding Cost	0						
Period		1	2	3	4	5	6
		---------	------------	---------	---------	---------	---------
Gross Requirements		3	4	1	1	1	1
Scheduled Receipts		0	0	0	0	0	0
Projected Available Balance		0	0	0	0	0	0
Planned Order Releases		3	4	1	1	1	1
Expedite Orders?		NO	NO	NO	NO	NO	NO
Rescheduled Scheduled Rcpts		0	0	0	0	0	0
Planned Order Receipts		3	4	1	1	1	1
Independent Demand		3	4	1	1	1	1
Dependent Demand		0	0	0	0	0	0

PART NAME	OptionC						
Low Level	0						
Ordering Policy	LTL						
Safety Stock	0						
Lead Time	0						
On Hand Inventory	0						
User Reschedules Receipts?	NO						
Expediting allowed	NO						
User Provides Planned Rcpts?	NO						
Setup plus Holding Cost	0						
Period		1	2	3	4	5	6
		---------	------------	---------	---------	---------	---------
Gross Requirements		0	5	0	4	0	0
Scheduled Receipts		0	0	0	0	0	0
Projected Available Balance		0	0	0	0	0	0

Planned Order Releases		0	5	0	4	0	0
Expedite Orders?		NO	NO	NO	NO	NO	NO
Rescheduled Scheduled Rcpts		0	0	0	0	0	0
Planned Order Receipts		0	5	0	4	0	0
Independent Demand		0	5	0	4	0	0
Dependent Demand		0	0	0	0	0	0

PART NAME	Casters						
Low Level	1						
Ordering Policy	LUC						
Safety Stock	0						
Lead Time	6						
On Hand Inventory	32						
User Reschedules Receipts?	NO						
Expediting allowed	NO						
User Provides Planned Rcpts?	NO						
Setup plus Holding Cost	7						
Period		1	2	3	4	5	6
		---------	-------------	---------	---------	---------	---------
Gross Requirements		8	12	4	16	8	12
Scheduled Receipts		0	0	0	0	0	0
Projected Available Balance		24	12	8	-8	-16	-28
Planned Order Releases		44	0	12	0	0	0
Expedite Orders?		NO	NO	NO	NO	NO	NO
Rescheduled Scheduled Rcpts		0	0	0	0	0	0
Planned Order Receipts		0	0	0	0	0	0
Independent Demand		0	0	0	0	0	0
Dependent Demand		8	12	4	16	8	12

PART NAME	BrassHandle					
Low Level	1					
Ordering Policy	LUC					
Safety Stock	0					
Lead Time	2					
On Hand Inventory	5					
User Reschedules Receipts?	NO					
Expediting allowed	NO					
User Provides Planned rpt?	NO					
Setup plus Holding Cost	6.56					
Period		1	2	3	4	5	6
		---------	-------------	---------	---------	---------	---------
Gross Requirements		24	54	10	44	16	22
Scheduled Receipts		0	0	5	0	0	0
Projected Available Balance		-19	-73	0	16	0	44
Planned Order Releases		78	60	0	66	0	50
Expedite Orders?		NO	NO	NO	NO	NO	NO
Rescheduled Scheduled Rcpts		0	0	0	0	0	0
Planned Order Receipts		0	0	78	60	0	66
Independent Demand		0	0	0	0	0	0
Dependent Demand		24	54	10	44	16	22

PART NAME	LockAssembly					
Low Level	1					
Ordering Policy	LTL					
Safety Stock	0					
Lead Time	0					
On Hand Inventory	0					
User Reschedules Receipts?	NO					
Expediting allowed	NO					
User Provides Planned Rcpts?	NO					
Setup plus Holding Cost	0					
Period		1	2	3	4	5	6
		---------	-------------	---------	---------	---------	---------
Gross Requirements		12	38	6	40	12	18
Scheduled Receipts		0	0	0	0	0	0
Projected Available Balance		0	0	0	0	0	0
Planned Order Releases		12	38	6	40	12	18
Expedite Orders?		NO	NO	NO	NO	NO	NO
Rescheduled Scheduled Rcpts		0	0	0	0	0	0
Planned Order Receipts		12	38	6	40	12	18
Independent Demand		0	0	0	0	0	0
Dependent Demand		12	38	6	40	12	18

PART NAME	Lock
Low Level	2
Ordering Policy	LUC
Safety Stock	0
Lead Time	4

On Hand Inventory	8					
User Reschedules Receipts?	NO					
Expediting allowed	NO					
User Provides Planned Rcpts?	NO					
Setup plus Holding Cost	4.95					
Period	1	2	3	4	5	6
	---------	------------	---------	---------	---------	---------
Gross Requirements	12	38	6	40	12	18
Scheduled Receipts	0	0	3	0	0	0
Projected Available Balance	-4	-42	-45	-85	0	24
Planned Order Releases	97	42	0	38	0	16
Expedite Orders?	NO	NO	NO	NO	NO	NO
Rescheduled Scheduled Rcpts	0	0	0	0	0	0
Planned Order Receipts	0	0	0	0	97	42
Independent Demand	0	0	0	0	0	0
Dependent Demand	12	38	6	40	12	18

PART NAME	Escutcheon					
Low Level	2					
Ordering Policy	LUC					
Safety Stock	0					
Lead Time	2					
On Hand Inventory	22					
User Reschedules Receipts?	NO					
Expediting allowed	NO					
User Provides Planned Rcpts?	NO					
Setup plus Holding Cost	7.9					
Period	1	2	3	4	5	6
	---------	------------	---------	---------	---------	---------
Gross Requirements	24	54	10	44	16	22
Scheduled Receipts	0	0	0	0	0	0
Projected Available Balance	-2	-56	0	0	22	0
Planned Order Releases	66	44	38	0	44	32
Expedite Orders?	NO	NO	NO	NO	NO	NO
Rescheduled Scheduled Rcpts	0	0	0	0	0	0
Planned Order Receipts	0	0	66	44	38	0
Independent Demand	0	0	0	0	0	0
Dependent Demand	24	54	10	44	16	22

AGGREGATE PLANNING

After working with his father for several years, upon completion of his apprenticeship, John Townsend's skill and business sense had achieved a level of competency that he was able to open his own furniture making shop. This was not unusual for the Townsend family and by the late 1760's, there were at least 6 family shops in existence. All the shops were within a few blocks of each other within the Quaker community in the Eastons Point area of Newport, RI.

In late 1765, John completed a three-shell block front desk that would have sold for over 400 pounds (currently in the Diplomatic Reception Rooms at the State Department in Washington, DC). John had become the most successful member of the family, paying taxes of 2 pounds, one shillings in the 1772 census. John continued to create made-to-order pieces until the early 1800's. In addition to this line of extremely expensive furniture, John had established a pre-made line of high quality "Ready to Use" furniture to service the growing middle class community of farmers and merchants of Rhode Island. Since so much of the economy was based on agriculture and its by-products, the demand for these items peaked in December, January, and February. Once the harvests had been completed and all business transactions based on them were settled, a family knew how much money they had made and could decide on what it would be spent on over the slower winter months.

John employed his younger brother, Jonathan, and his cousin, Thomas, to create this "Ready to Use" line of three standard, but popular, furniture types. A Mahogany tea table with slipper feet costing 60 pounds, a pad-foot side chair costing 36 pounds, and a 4-foot square dining table with turned legs and pad-feet for 48 pounds. All these pieces were made by hand, but were not as sophisticated as John's finer examples. These pieces took 10, 6, and 8 days to make respectively. The length of the table legs allowed the use of a pole lathe, which required a half day to set up and take down. John's shop was not big enough to allow this piece of equipment to be setup when dining tables were not being made. It was, however, a major production improvement which had been added to the manufacturing process several years ago and allowed for the reduction in time to make a table from 10 days to the current 8. This device could not be used on the legs for the chair or tea table.

John felt that, if demand warranted it, he could train a local journeyman carpenter in a month so that he would be proficient enough to join the production process for this "Ready to Use" line of furniture. John's shop was small, however, and he felt it could only handle 4 workmen in addition to himself. John could only train two of these individuals at a time, and it cost him the individual's wage (2 pounds per day) for that time and a reduction of his own output with an implied cost of 20 pounds for the month. One such individual, Benjamin Baker, had worked in John's shop and then gone into business on his own. John had enough trust in his skills that he allowed him to make the chairs and dining tables in the "Ready to Use" line on a subcontracting basis. John was willing to pay Baker 24 pounds for a chair and 32 pounds for a dining room table. The most Baker could produce on this basis was 4 chairs and 2 tables in a month.

A normal work schedule for the shop was 10 hours a day, 24 days a month. Due to limited daylight hours and the lack of sufficient illumination from the 18th century candle, only one shift of operation was feasible. Overtime was feasible only during the longer summer days and an extra 4 hours could be achieved during the months of May, June, July and August. John felt an obligation to pay his workers time and a half for these incremental hours. John's policy was also to pay one month's severance pay to any worker that he dismissed without a cause.

It was now the first of March, and John was analyzing the results of last year's sales of the "Ready to Use" furniture line. It had been so successful that he had no current inventory and, thus, nothing to show or sell to a new customer. He was convinced that next year he wanted to have an ending inventory of 2 tea tables, 4 chairs and 1 dining room table. His shop was small, so inventory in general was a problem. He had just leased a small first floor front room from a clock maker just up the block by the name of W. Clagget. He occasionally made clock cases for him and had gotten a preferential rate that translated into 1 percent of the price of the piece per month. He could store 4 tea tables 32 chairs and 4 dining tables with sufficient display space. Interest rates had recently increased to 7 percent and John had just started investments in a molasses operation that he felt could return 15 percent per year.

John's forecast for the upcoming year is given below. He was trying to decide if and how he could produce this quantity of furniture given the constraints already discussed. John's time was not available for this project since he concentrated on special orders, meeting with customers, selecting the wood and administrating the business. Customers for the "Ready to Use" line are not willing to wait and would go to another maker if John did not have what they wanted in stock. Lost sales not only implied the loss of the

25 percent profit margin, but the loss of the future stream of profit from other furniture sales. John assumed this cost to be 50 pounds.

MAKETBLA.DAT

	Slipper Foot Tea Table	Pad Foot Side Chair	Pad Foot Dining Table
March	2	2	2
April	1	4	1
May	1	4	2
June	1	2	1
July	1	2	1
August	0	2	1
September	1	4	2
October	2	8	2
November	2	8	4
December	3	12	4
January	4	16	3
February	3	12	3

Given all this information, John was trying to decide if he should hire and train a new employee, forego some sales, subcontract work to Benjamin Baker, build inventory in front of demand or follow demand with changes in work force. To solve this type of complex problem requires the use of HOM Aggregate planning.

After clicking on the aggregate planning module identifier a data input spread sheet appears. The first task is to use the DATA item to introduce our 3 new products. Each named product adds demand and safety stock columns to the spreadsheet. We ignore the safety stock since we are assuming we know demand with certainty. After products have been named their demand values can be entered. We are assuming a 12 month planning horizon and thus we will only use the first 12 rows. If we had semi-monthly or 2 years worth of data we would use all 24 periods. Since we assume 24 day months and four hours of over time only during the summer months we adjust the preset entries as indicated in MAKE TBLA.DAT.

Below the demand data on the spreadsheet we have an opportunity to enter data on key cost and capabilities information by product. The inventory holding cost is the monthly cost of carrying the item. {(opportunity cost of capital + annual storage cost)(cost of item);ex((.15+.12)X(60))/12=1.35] Back orders are not allowed thus, their cost is very high. Lost sales cost is based on 25% of the price plus 50 pounds. The only product to have positive setup time is the dining table and we compute it by multiplying the number of people required to do the setup times the time each spends. In our case 1/2 day for 1 person or 5 hours. (set up time must always be converted to hours). Setup cost are extra charges over and above labor cost required to accomplish the setup. In our case it is the one pound John promised to pay his friend who taught him how to use a polelathe every time he set it up. Run time is in hours and it is the amount of time required for labor to complete the production of one unit of each of the products. In our case 100 hours for Tea Table (10 days x 10), 60 hours for chairs (six days x 10) etc. Subcontracting costs are by item and in our case are very large for tea tables since it is not allowed and 24 and 32 pounds for the other named products. The maximum subcontracting quantity per period is zero for tea tables and 4 and 2 for the other products. The next items are for starting and desired ending inventory and the entries come right from the case as does the maximum inventory level possible.

To specify the problem we now proceed to the parameter window. The planning horizon sub box allows us to specify up to 3 products for the analysis. The plan type we want to use (we suggest you start with optimal) the number of time periods to model (1 through 12 in our case) and the precision of the solution. (For small problems like this one using a quick computer (pentium 166+) we recommend optimal, for a big problem (3x24) or a slow computer (486) we recommend heuristic fast). In the work force sub box we specify the current work force (2); the maximum work force size (4), and the minimum work force required to run the shop at the stated run time values (2). In our case we do not have second shift entries since it is not feasible. The wages subbox gives us an opportunity to choose per hour or per period (1 month in our case) costs. We chose by hour. Our shift is 10 hours long and thus our 2 pounds per day yields .2 pounds per hour for regular shift and .35 (time and a half) for over time. We have no cost for under time and no shift premium since they are not allowed. Work force changes sub box allows us to cost the hiring and firing of an employee. (1 month (24x2=48) +20 pounds of John's lost .time=68; one month severance, 24x2=48). It also allows us to limit the numbers of people we can hire and fire in any period. (In our case it is two to hire and 4 to fire) After completing this box click on OK and then on the run icon to obtain results.

The first result is a graph depicting the amount of each product produced in each period. This graph can be confusing since all products are displayed at once. We often use the SERIES function on the results command line to show the demand, production and inventory level of each product one at a time by clicking on the appropriate enabling boxes and then printing it out. Closing this window brings you back to the spreadsheet and then clicking on the last results icon will return you to the original output.

Below the graph are per period results on production costs and work force costs. This is followed by results by period on units produced for each product including how much subcontracting and lost sales were incurred. The final output category deals with work force issues including number of workers per period, the amount of over time and under time in hours and the number of workers hired and fired. The latter can be seen by using the right arrow.

The optimal solutions for our case incurs a cost of 2227 pounds with some overtime, some subcontracting and the hiring of 2 additional workers in the second half of the planning horizon. To see how much better this solution is than the two classical approaches to this problem use the parameters window to set up two additional runs one for a chase strategy and the other for the level work force strategy.

We should point that while the workers are selected in integer values actual production is fractional in some time periods. This approximation occurs due to the complexity of the problem and our desire to insure relatively low running times (less than 15 minutes) for most problems. It should also be he pointed out that some amount of fractional production is feasible since it implies the starting of a piece in one period and its completion in another. Fractional production is also more pronounced when quantities of output are low (less than 10) as in our case. Rescaling of demand and cost by a factor of 100 would make the non-integer results less pronounced.

HOM SAMPLE INPUTS AND OUTPUTS
Name of Module: AGGPLAN
Data File: MAKETBLA.DAT

Input Data Spreadsheet

Period	Days in Peri	Max.Overti	D:teatble	D:chair	D:dinetbl	SS:teatble	SS:chair
Period 1	24	0	2	2	2		
Period 2	24	0	1	4	1		
Period 3	24	4	1	4	2		
Period 4	24	4	1	2	1		
Period 5	24	4	1	2	1		
Period 6	24	4	0	2	1		
Period 7	24	0	1	4	2		
Period 8	24	0	2	8	2		
Period 9	24	0	2	8	4		
Period 10	24	0	3	12	4		
Period 11	24	0	4	16	3		
Period 12	24	0	3	12	3		
Period 13	20	4					

(Periods 14-24 not shown)

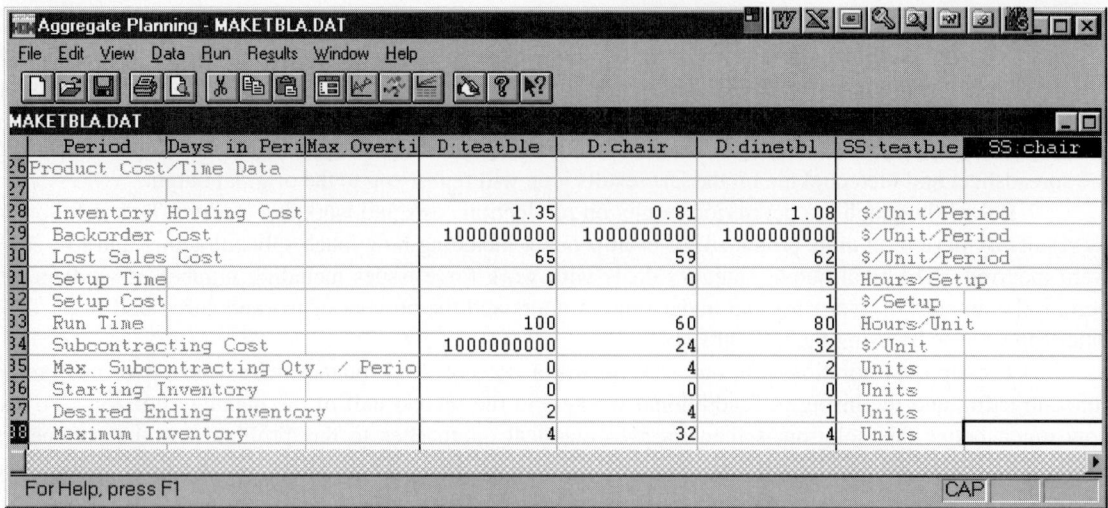

Parameters Window

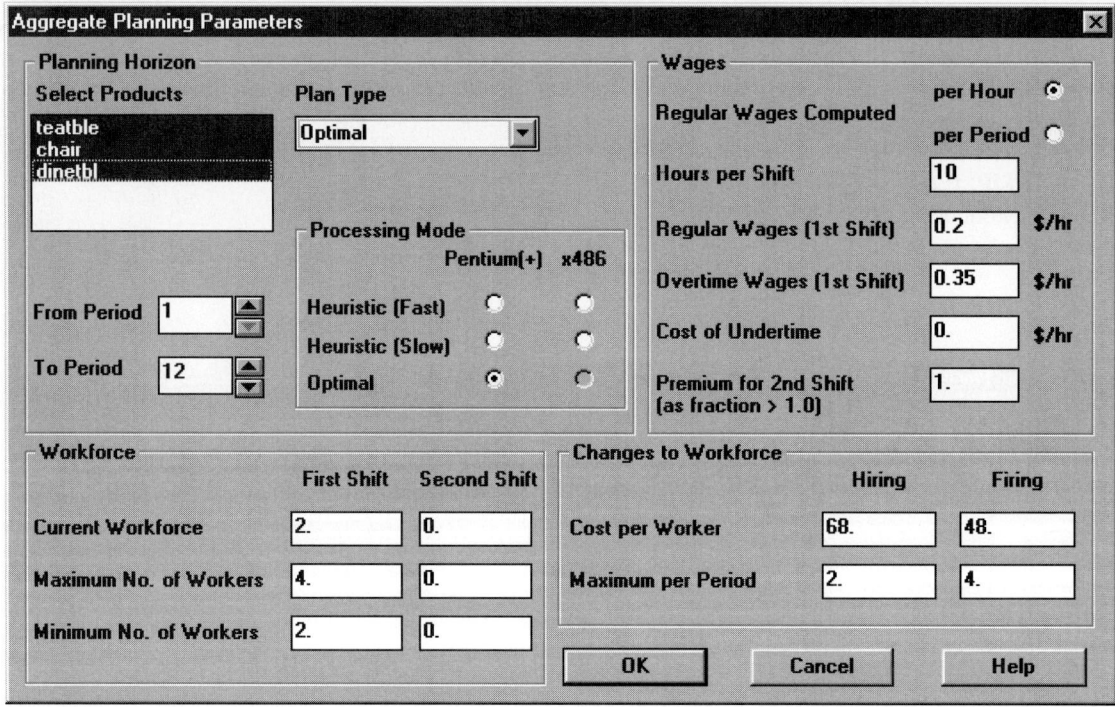

Output Graphs

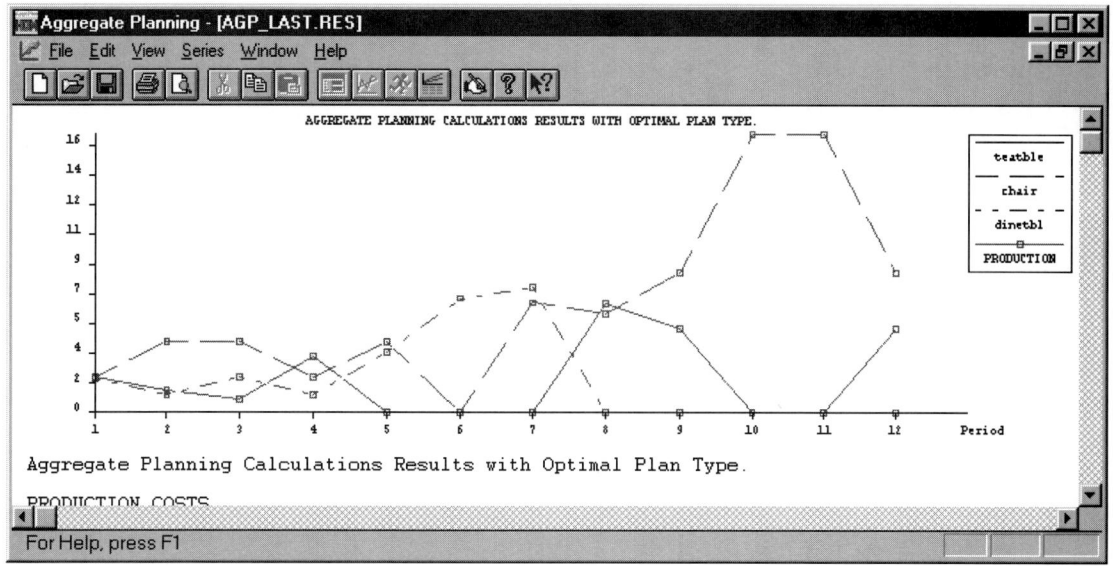

Output Tables

Aggregate Planning Calculations Results with Optimal Plan Type.

PRODUCTION COSTS

	Setup Cost	Subcontract	Inventory	Backlog	Lost Sales
Period 1	1	2	0	0	0
Period 2	1	0	0	0	0
Period 3	1	0	0.3375	0	0
Period 4	1	0	0	0	0
Period 5	1	0	2.9812	0	0
Period 6	1	0	5.9625	0	0
Period 7	1	0	10.294	0	0
Period 8	0	0	16.437	0	0
Period 9	0	0	18.057	0	0
Period 10	0	0	17.516	0	0
Period 11	0	57.002	12.386	0	0
Period 12	0	160	5.67	0	0
Total:	7	219.002	89.6412	0	0

WORKFORCE COSTS

	Wages	Overtime	Undertime	Hiring Cost	Firing Cost
Period 1	96	0	0	0	0
Period 2	96	0	0	0	0
Period 3	96	0	0	0	0
Period 4	96	16.044	0	0	0
Period 5	96	16.044	0	0	0
Period 6	96	16.044	0	0	0
Period 7	192	0	0	136	0
Period 8	192	0	0	0	0
Period 9	192	0	0	0	0
Period 10	192	0	0	0	0
Period 11	192	0	0	0	0
Period 12	192	0	0	0	0
Total:	1728	48.132	0	136	0

TOTAL COST: 2227.8

PRODUCTION (FOR EACH PRODUCT)

teatble

Period	Demand	Production	Sucontract	Opening Inventory	Opening Backlog	Lost Sales
Period 1	2	2	0	0	0	0
Period 2	1	1.25	0	0	0	0
Period 3	1	0.75	0	0.25	0	0
Period 4	1	3.2083	0	0	0	0
Period 5	1	0	0	2.2083	0	0
Period 6	0	0	0	1.2083	0	0
Period 7	1	0	0	1.2083	0	0
Period 8	2	6.1917	0	0.2083	0	0
Period 9	2	4.8	0	4.4	0	0
Period 10	3	0	0	7.2	0	0
Period 11	4	0	0	4.2	0	0
Period 12	3	4.8	0	0.2	0	0

chair

Period	Demand	Production	Sucontract	Opening Inventory	Opening Backlog	Lost Sales
Period 1	2	2	0	0	0	0
Period 2	4	4	0	0	0	0
Period 3	4	4	0	0	0	0
Period 4	2	2	0	0	0	0
Period 5	2	4.0278	0	0	0	0
Period 6	2	0	0	2.0278	0	0
Period 7	4	6.2917	0	0.027778	0	0
Period 8	8	5.6805	0	2.3195	0	0
Period 9	8	8	0	0	0	0
Period 10	12	16	0	0	0	0
Period 11	16	16	0	4	0	0
Period 12	12	8	4	4	0	0

dinetbl

Period	Demand	Production	Sucontract	Opening Inventory	Opening Backlog	Lost Sales
Period 1	2	1.9375	0.0625	0	0	0
Period 2	1	1	0	0	0	0
Period 3	2	2	0	0	0	0
Period 4	1	1	0	0	0	0
Period 5	1	3.4896	0	0	0	0
Period 6	1	6.5104	0	2.4896	0	0
Period 7	2	7.2187	0	8	0	0
Period 8	2	0	0	13.219	0	0
Period 9	4	0	0	11.219	0	0
Period 10	4	0	0	7.2187	0	0
Period 11	3	0	1.7813	3.2187	0	0
Period 12	3	0	2	2	0	0

WORKFORCE							
Period	No. Workers in 1st Shift	Overtime in 1st Shift	No. Workers in 2nd Shift	Overtime in 2nd Shift	Undertime	No. Workers to Hire	No. Workers to Fire
Period 1	2	0	0	0	0	0	0
Period 2	2	0	0	0	30	0	0
Period 3	2	0	0	0	0	0	0
Period 4	2	45.84	0	0	0	0	0
Period 5	2	45.84	0	0	0	0	0
Period 6	2	45.84	0	0	0	0	0
Period 7	4	0	0	0	0.002	2	0
Period 8	4	0	0	0	0	0	0
Period 9	4	0	0	0	0	0	0
Period 10	4	0	0	0	0	0	0
Period 11	4	0	0	0	0	0	0
Period 12	4	0	0	0	0	0	0

PROJECT AND TIME MANAGEMENT METHODS

The HOM Project Management calculation schema is given below.

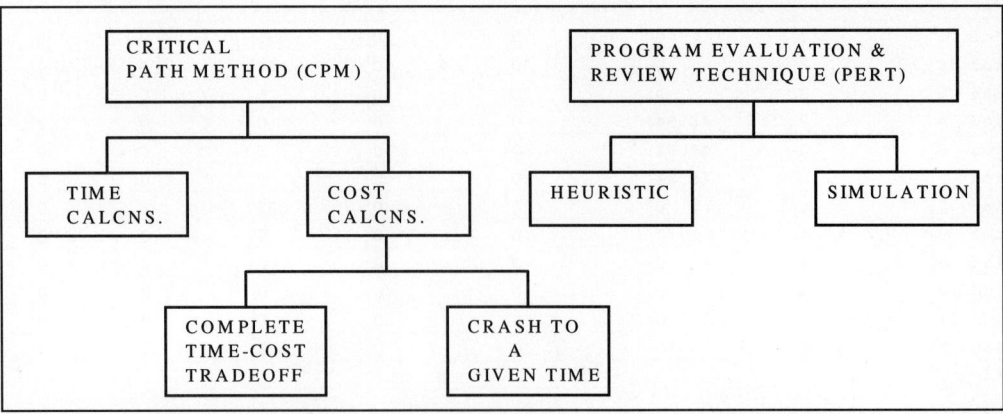

Five different methods for Project and Time Management are available in this application: (i) CPM Time Calculations - Determine Project Completion Time, Early Start, Late Start, Slack, and so on; (ii) CPM Cost Calculations - Generate Complete Time-Cost Trade-Off Curve; (iii) CPM Cost Calculations - Determine Activities to Crash to Attain a Given Project Completion Time; (iv) PERT - Heuristic Calculation of Expected Completion and Probability of Completion; and (v) PERT - Simulation.

Note: The model has to be selected before any data input is done. To select the model open the Parameters dialog box to make your choices.

1. CPM TIME CALCULATIONS

Inputs

Activity Name — Use a number, letter, or short abbreviation (less than 8 characters) in the ACTIVITY column. A more complete definition can be given for each activity, if desired, by moving the cursor to the extreme right of the spreadsheet to the activity DESCRIPTION column.

Activity Duration — After designating the task name in column one, the user should enter its duration in the next column, DURATION, in the same row.

Predecessors — Each task can have up to ten immediate predecessors. If a task has only one immediate predecessor, enter it in column PRED 1. If it has two, use columns PRED 1 and PRED 2, and so on. The name used to identify the predecessor must be identical to its short activity name. A task without predecessors (i.e., starting tasks) will have no predecessors listed in its appropriate row.

First Activity — Row number of the first activity to include in the project.

Last Activity — Row number of the last activity to include in the project. (All activities in between the 1st and the last are included in the project.)

Sample Data File

NETWORK.DAT [1]

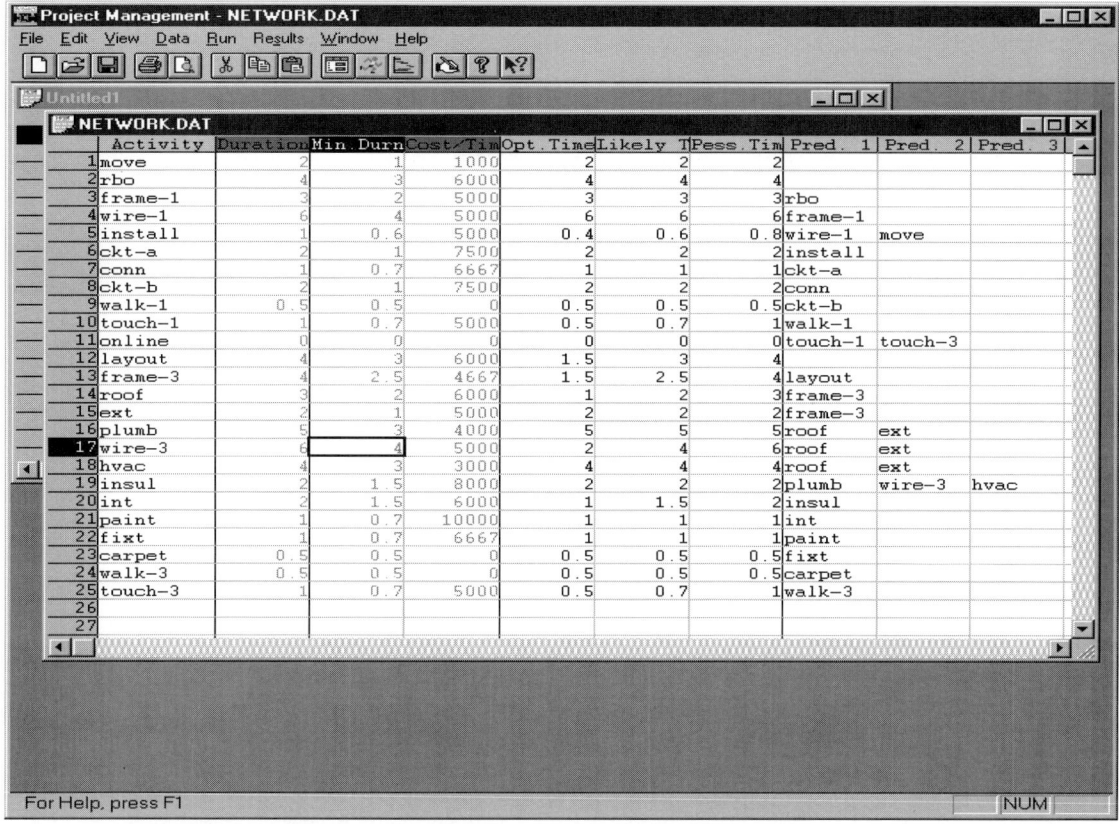

Sample Parameters Dialog Box

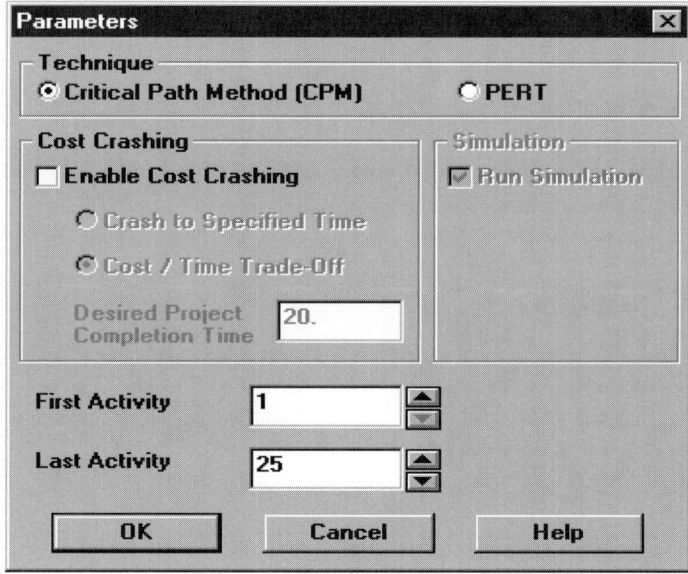

Note: Observe the choice of first and last activity -- all activities in rows 1 through 25 are included in the project.

---

[1] Data from the "United Bank Branches" case.

Output for Sample Data File NETWORK.DAT (CPM - Time Calculations)

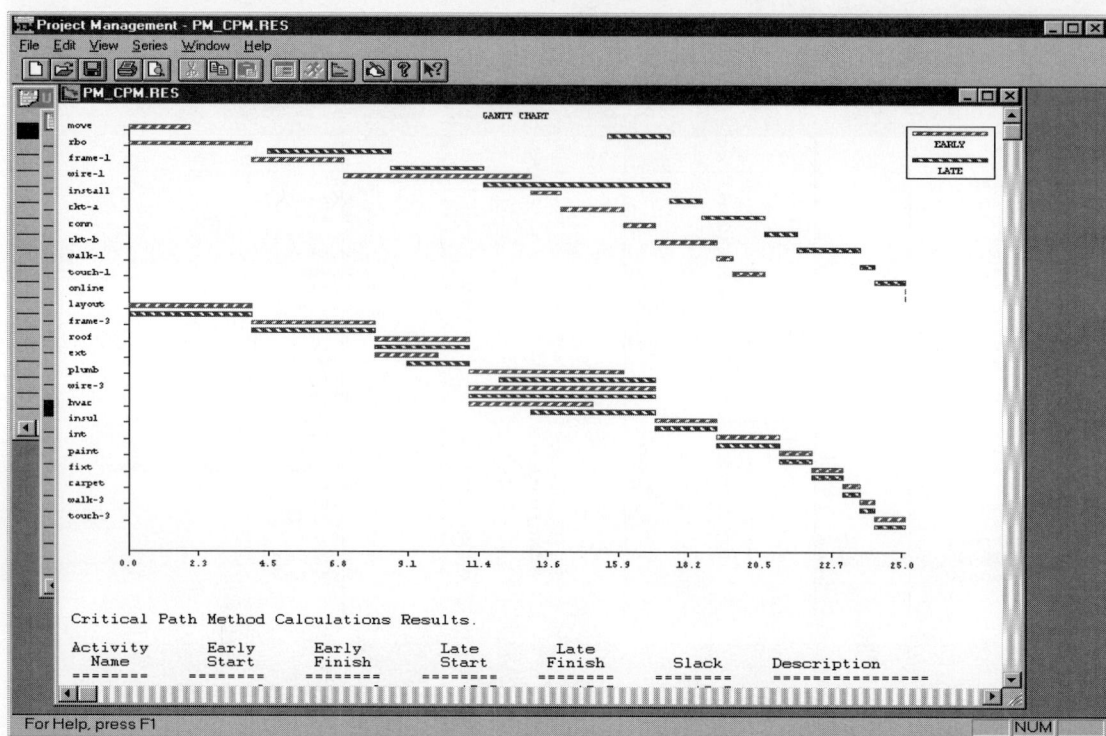

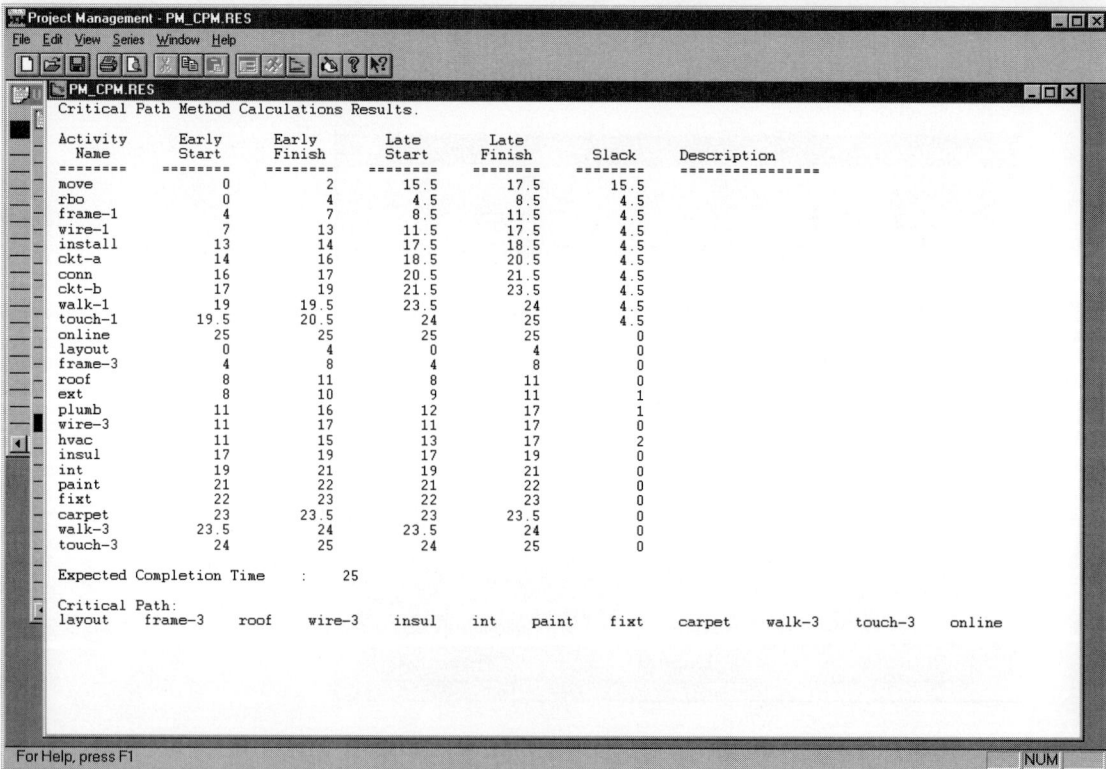

Note: When there are multiple critical paths, HOM lists all critical paths.

2. **CPM COST CALCULATIONS - GENERATE COMPLETE TIME-COST TRADE-OFF CURVE**

3. **CPM COST CALCULATIONS - DETERMINE ACTIVITIES TO INVEST IN TIME REDUCTION (CRASH) TO ATTAIN A GIVEN PROJECT DURATION**

Both these methods need two additional inputs when compared to CPM - Time Calculations:

Additional Inputs for Methods 2 and 3

Minimum Duration — This is the minimum duration to which the activity can be crashed. Please see picture below.

Cost/Time — The cost of reducing the duration of an activity (crashing) by a unit of time. Please see picture below.

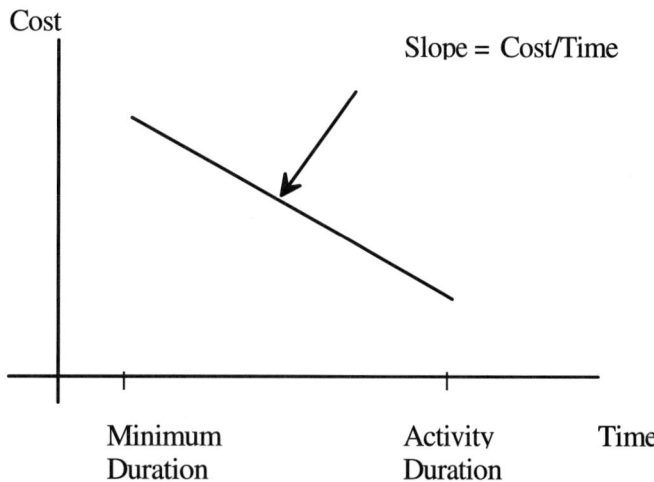

Additional Inputs for Methods 2 and 3 (continued)

The activity duration given in the third column of the input spreadsheet is usually referred to in the literature as the "Normal Duration."

For example, for the activity wire-1,
    Duration = 6,
    Minimum duration = 4,
    Cost/time = 5000.

This means activity wire-1 can be "normally" completed in 6 time units. However, its duration can be shortened by crashing it at a cost of 5000 per unit of time. The "minimum" duration to which it can be crashed is 4.

Linear Program: When the calculations start, the given data are first converted into a linear program. The conversion method is outlined in Eppen, Gould and Schmidt, (1993). Then the resulting LP is solved by a standard two-phase simplex method.

Infeasibility may occur in crashing if the project cannot be crashed to meet the target duration; that is, the desired completion time (in method 3) is too small. The program will notify you at that point and will ask you to input a different completion time.

Output for 2 (Complete Cost-Time Trade-Off): Choosing Cost/Time Trade-Off will produce the complete cost-time trade-off curve shown below. The optimal cost of crashing is calculated for ten values of the project duration - start from the minimum duration (obtained by first crashing all activities to their shortest durations) and increase in nine equal steps to the normal duration (i.e., the duration of the project with no activities crashed). The calculations could take a long time (3–5 minutes on a Pentium 100 MHZ machine) if the project is large.

Sample Parameters Dialog Box

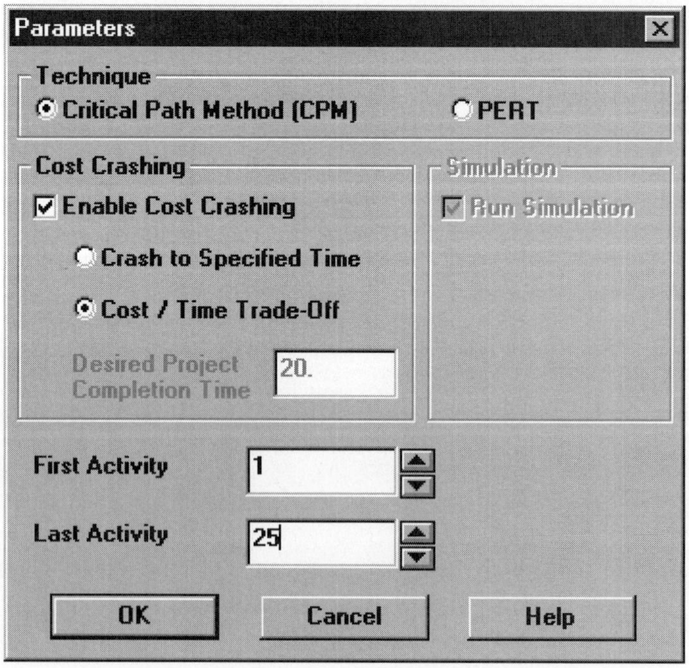

Output for Sample Data

NETWORK.DAT   (CPM - Complete Cost/Time Trade-Off)

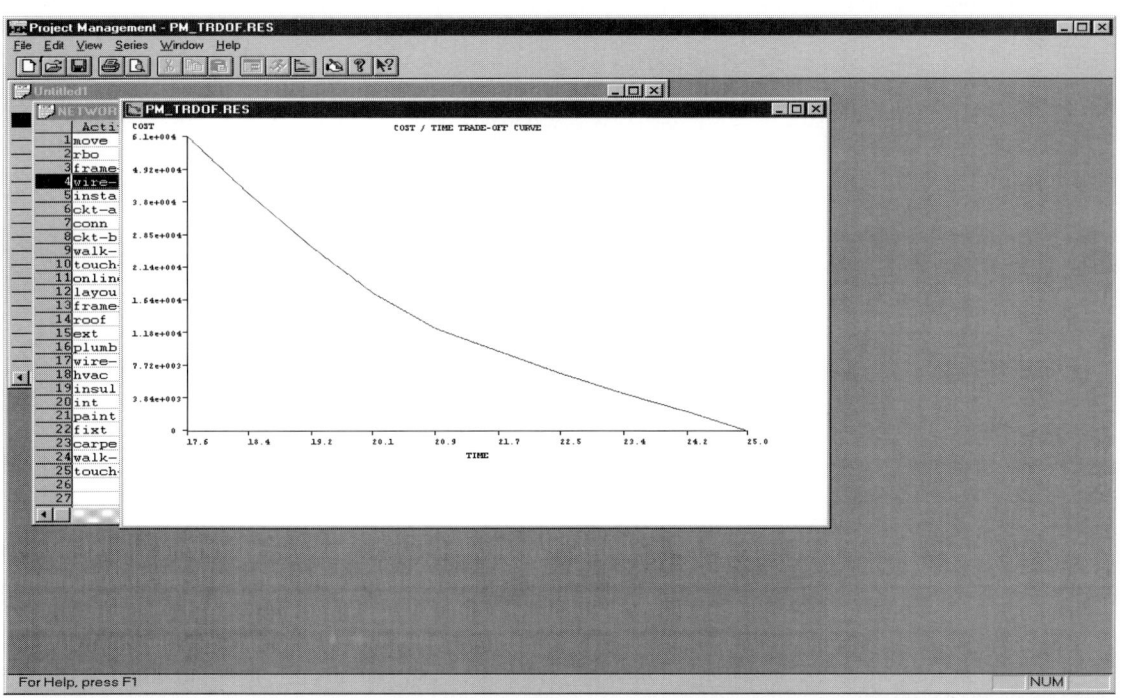

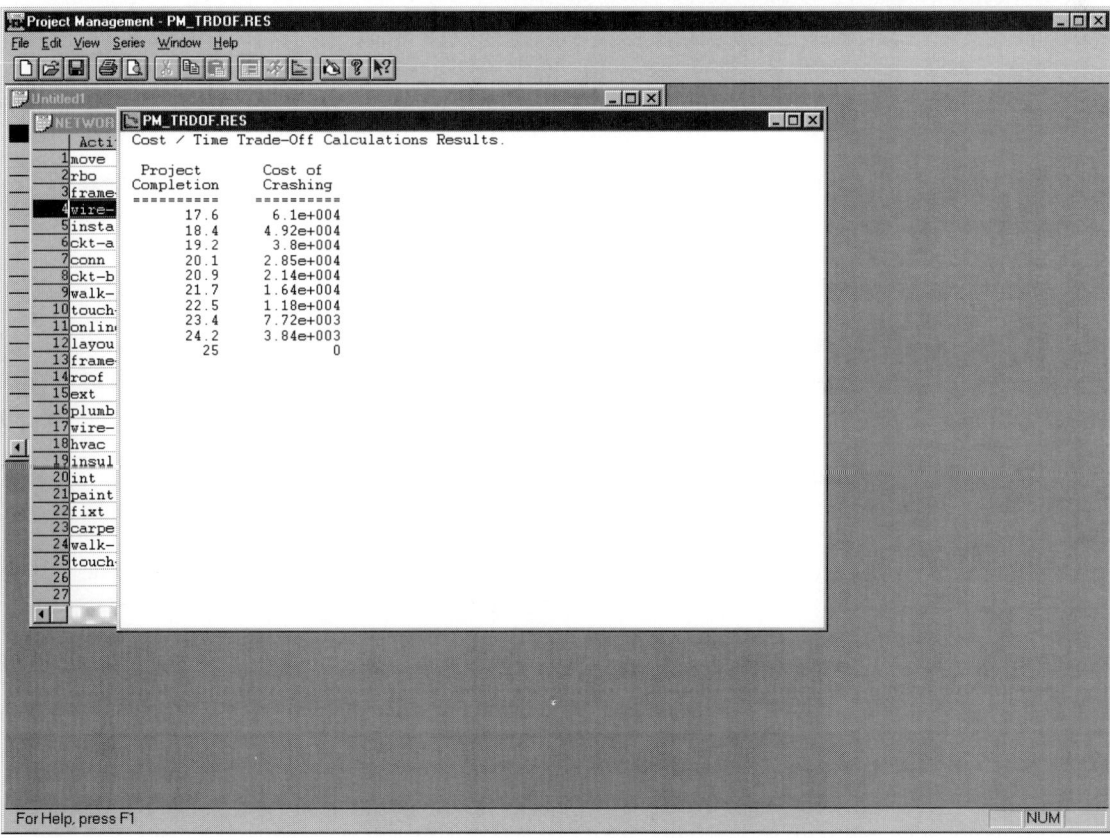

Output for 3 (Crash to Specified Time): Choosing Crash to a Specified Time will give the optimal cost of crashing to the desired completion time. If the project cannot be crashed to this duration, the program will prompt for another completion time.

Sample Parameters Dialog Box

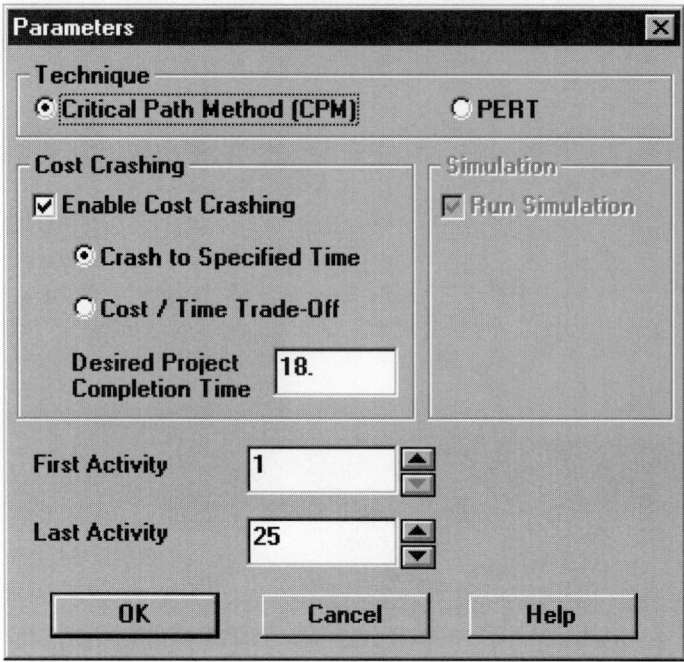

Output for Sample Data

NETWORK.DAT   (CPM - Crash to a Particular Duration)

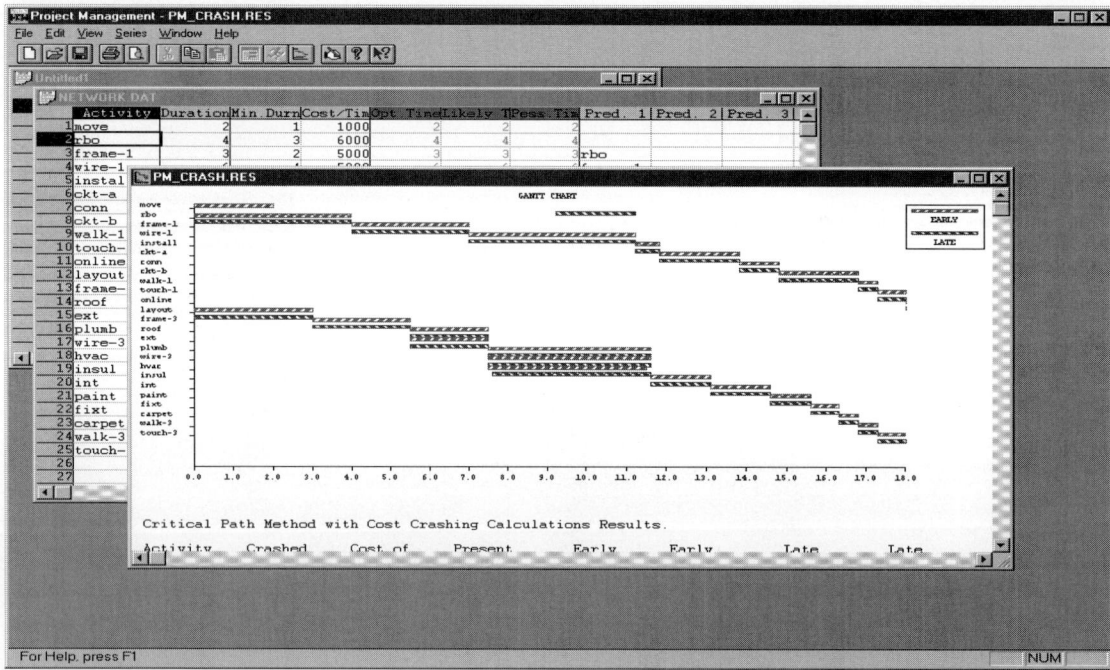

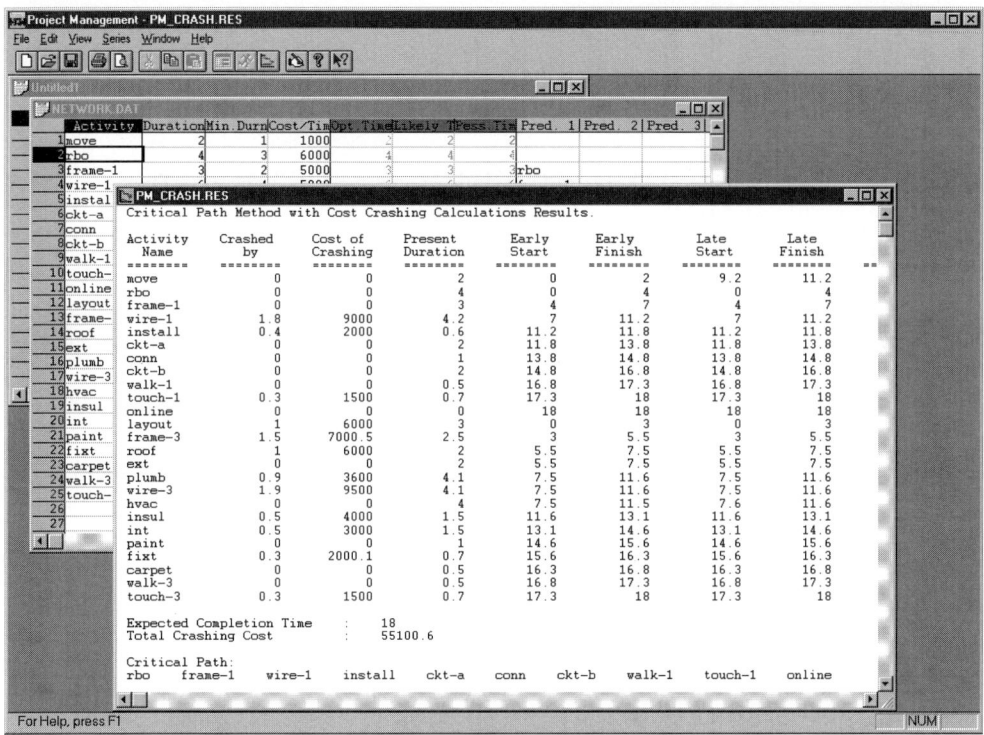

4. PERT - HEURISTIC &

5. PERT - SIMULATION

Inputs

Activity Name	Use a number, letter, or short abbreviation (less than 8 characters) in the ACTIVITY column. A more complete definition can be given for each activity, if desired, by moving the cursor to the extreme right of the spreadsheet to the activity DESCRIPTION column. (If you have already specified the names for a CPM - Time Calculation, you can use their rows to input the required data.)
Predecessors	Each task can have up to ten immediate predecessors. If a task has only one immediate predecessor, enter it in column PRED 1. If it has two, use columns PRED 1 and PRED 2, and so on. The name used to identify the predecessor must be identical to its short activity name. A task without predecessors (i.e., starting tasks) will have no predecessors listed in its appropriate row. (If you have already specified the network for a CPM - Time Calculation, you can use those rows to input the required data.)
First Activity	Row number of the first activity to include in the project.
Last Activity	Row number of the last activity to include in the project. (All activities in between the 1st and the last are included in the project.)
Optimistic, Likely, and Pessimistic Estimates of Activity Duration	Three time estimates are required for each activity. These must be placed in their appropriate columns.

The methods used and outputs are given below.

Method for 4 (PERT- Heuristic)

If an activity has three durations specified, then the average duration as well as the standard deviation of the activity's duration is computed using the following formulae:

Let a, m, and b stand for the optimistic, most likely, and pessimistic activity duration time. Then,

Mean Duration of Activity = $(a + 4m + b)/6$;
Standard Deviation of Activity Duration = $(b - a)/6$.

The critical path is determined using the CPM technique.

The mean project duration and the standard deviation of the project duration are approximated as follows:

Let t_i, s_i, $i = 1, 2, ..., M$, be the means and standard deviations of the M activities on the critical path. Then,

Mean Project Duration (approximate) $T = t_1 + t_2 + ... + t_M$

Standard Deviation of Project Duration (approximate), $S = \sqrt{s_1^2 + s_2^2 + ... + s_M^2}$.

Remarks:
(i) The latter formula assumes the independence of the M activities.
(ii) Moreover, the procedure assumes that an activity that is not on the critical path (determined by the CPM technique) never becomes critical.
(iii) Thus the heuristic estimate of the mean duration of the project is an optimistic estimate. To avoid this potential bias, the PERT - Simulation technique could be employed.

The project duration random variable is approximated by a normally distributed random variable with mean = T and standard deviation = S, that is, $N(T, S^2)$. The probability of the project completing within a given duration is calculated using the standard normal distribution.

The probability table for completing the project in a given time is calculated in addition to the critical path. The probability of completion is given for the range from expected completion time minus three standard deviations to expected completion time plus three standard deviations with a step size of 0.2 standard deviation. Thus, the table contains 31 entries.

Sample Data File

NETWORK.DAT

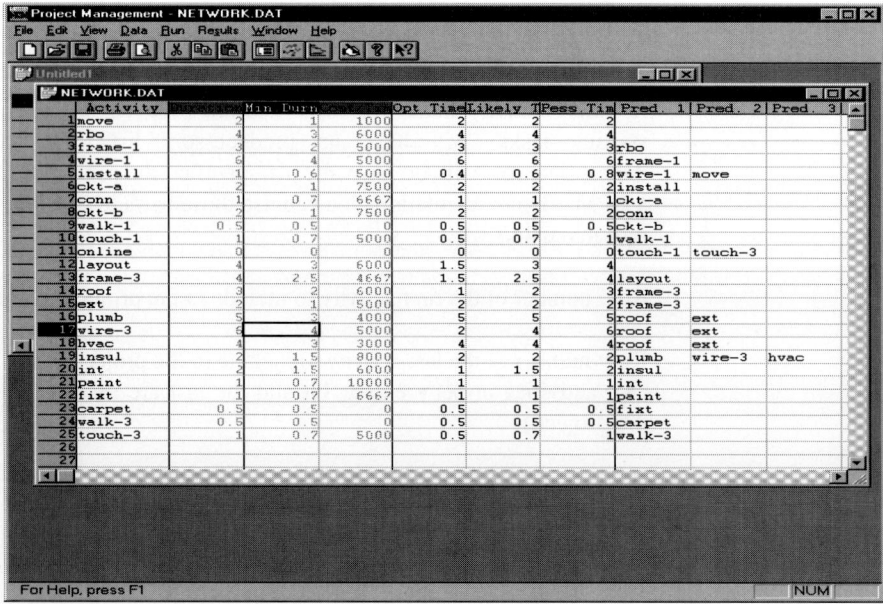

|< -- 3 Times Estimate -->|

Sample Parameters Dialog Box

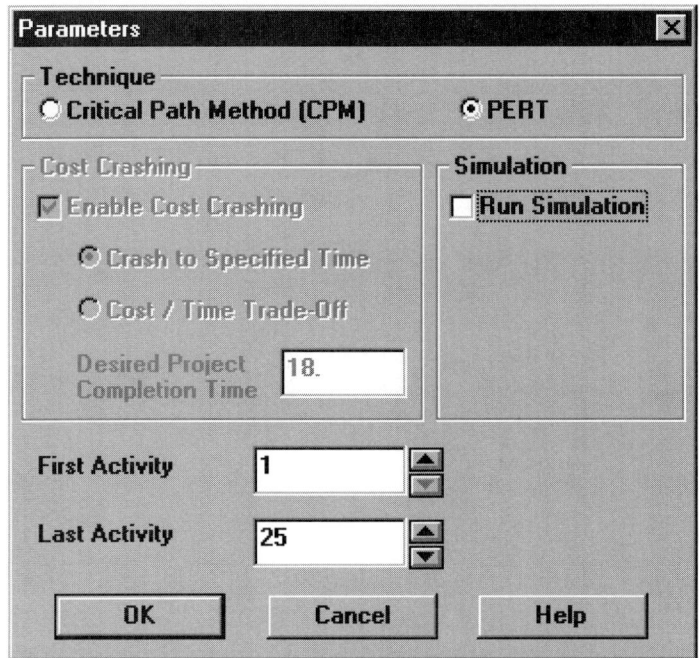

Outputs for Sample Data

NETWORK.DAT (PERT - Heuristic)

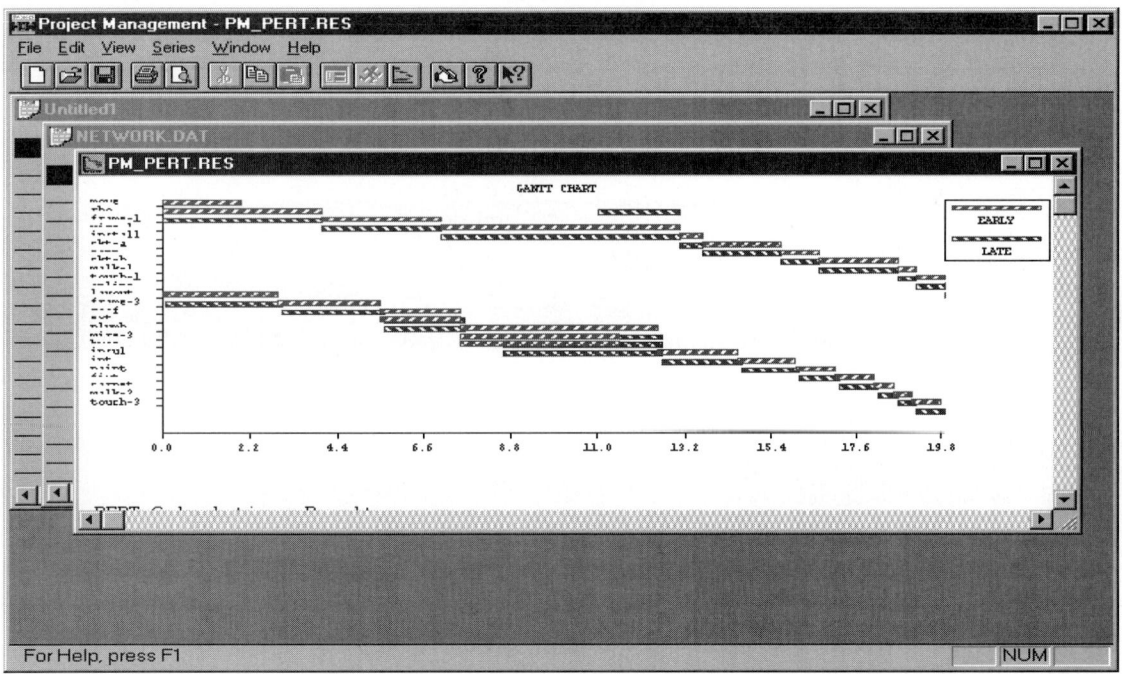

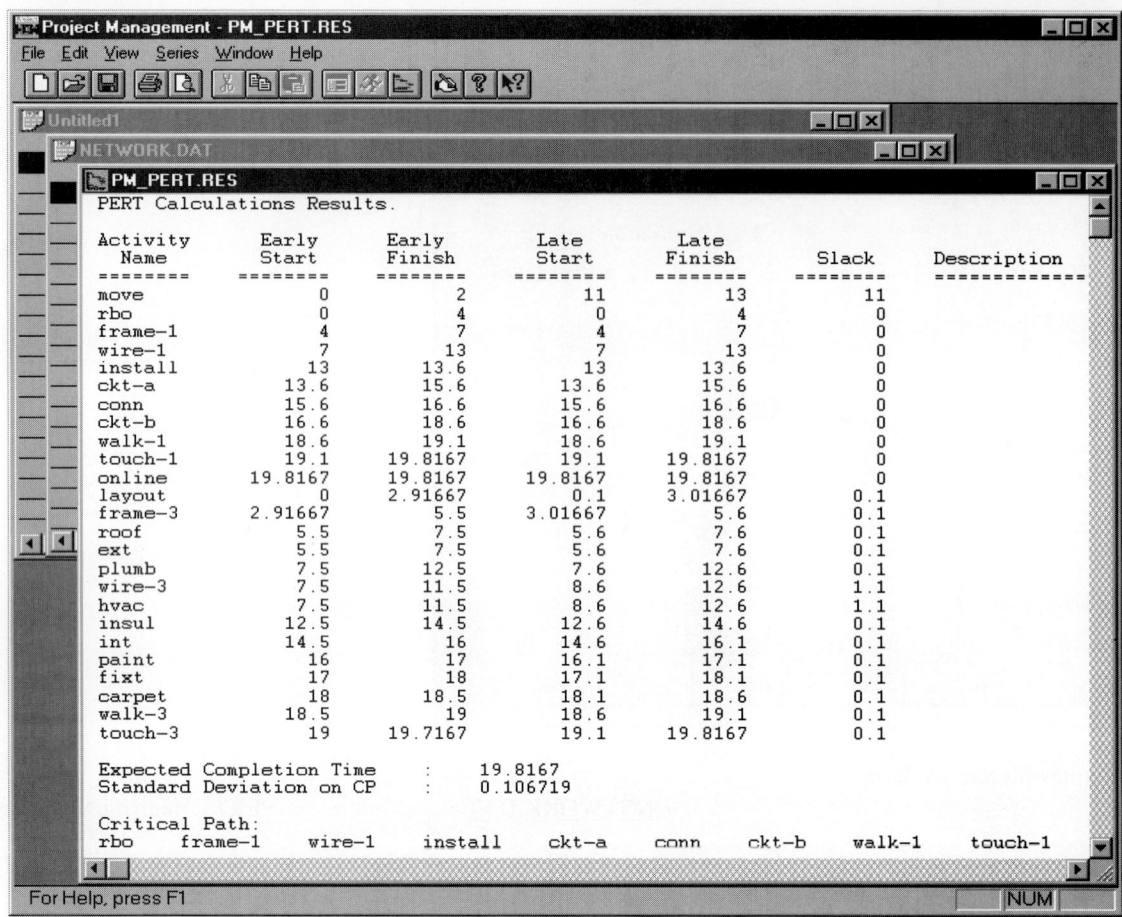

Outputs for Sample Data (continued)   NETWORK.DAT   (PERT - Heuristic)

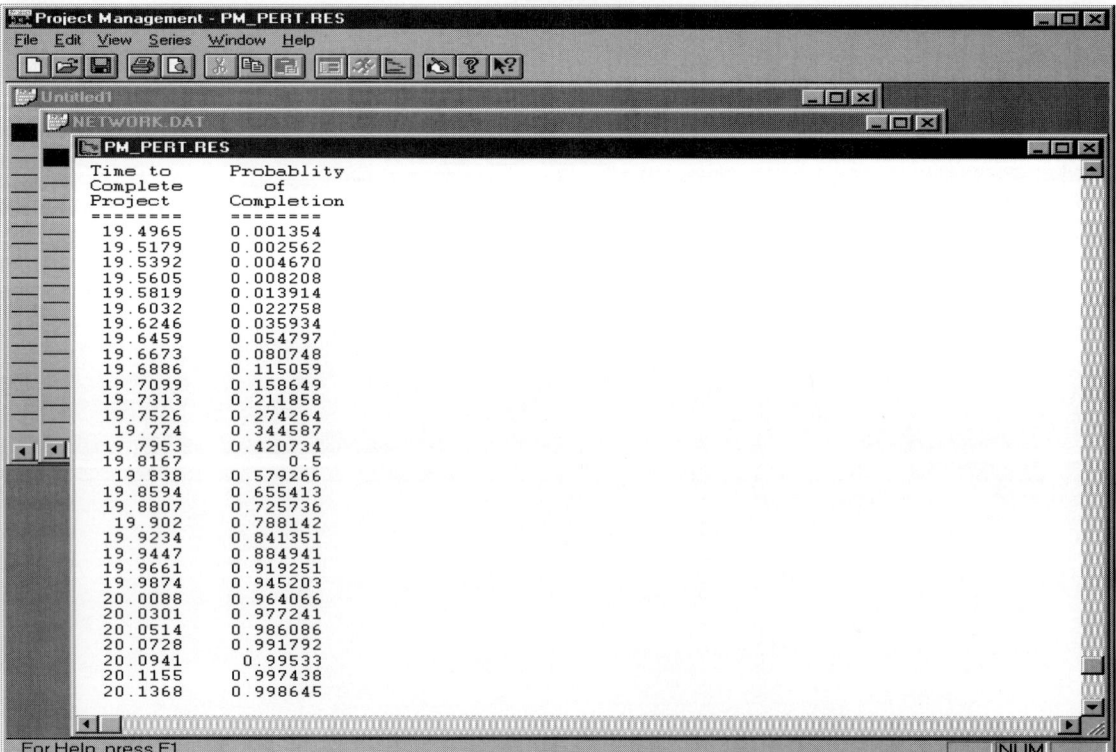

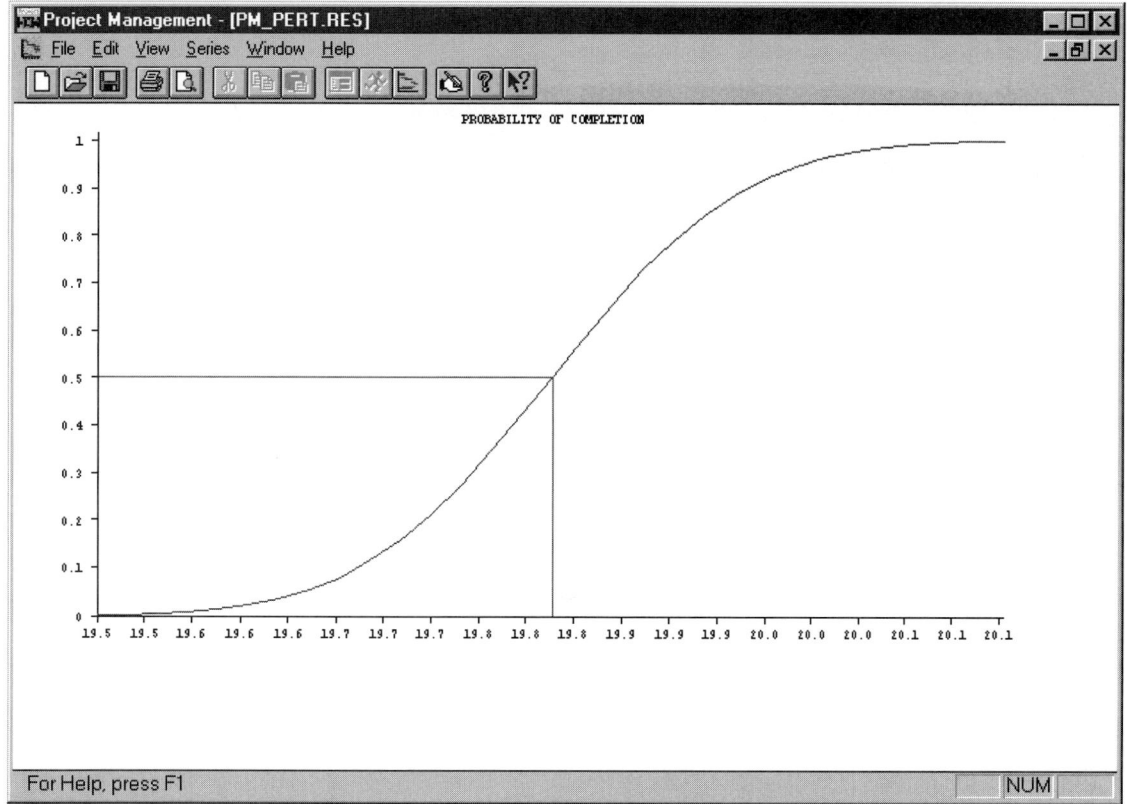

Method for 5 (PERT - Simulation)

Simulation is used to determine whether some of the noncritical activities become critical if their durations vary in a random manner. The simulation of the project is carried out 1,000 times. The CPM program is invoked 1,000 times and all CPM calculations are performed, such as finding the slacks, start and finish times, as well the project duration.

For each run the activity durations are each independently and randomly chosen from a suitable Beta distribution. The Beta distribution is chosen to fit the three time estimates for the activity duration.[2]

The frequency distribution of the project duration, as well as the mean and standard deviation of the project duration is found using the simulation statistics.

The criticality factor for each activity is determined by the formula:

>   Criticality Factor = (Number of Runs in which the Activity Was Ccritical)/1,000
>   The higher this factor, the more critical the activity. The value of the factor ranges between 0 and 1.

---

[2] The mean and variance based on the formulae given in Method 4 are used to determine the shape parameters of the Beta distribution, see Phillips et al (1976).

Sample Parameters Dialog Box

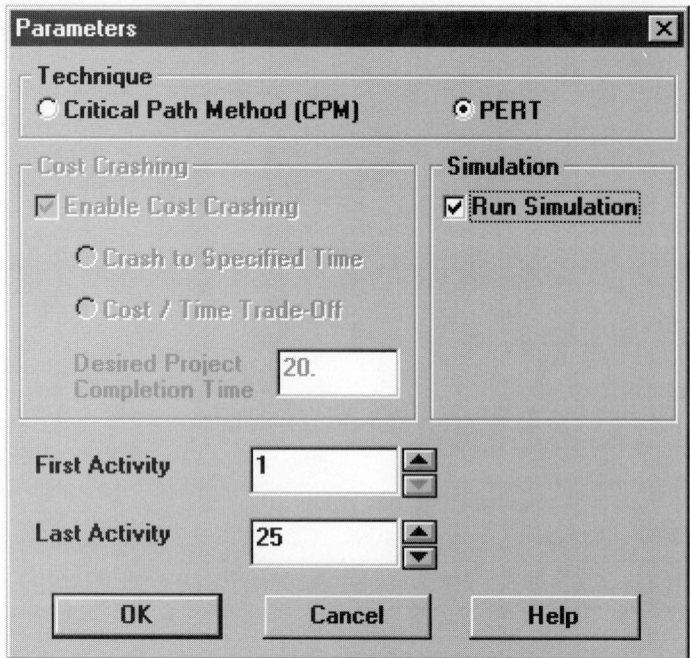

Outputs for Sample Data

NETWORK.DAT   (PERT - Simulation)

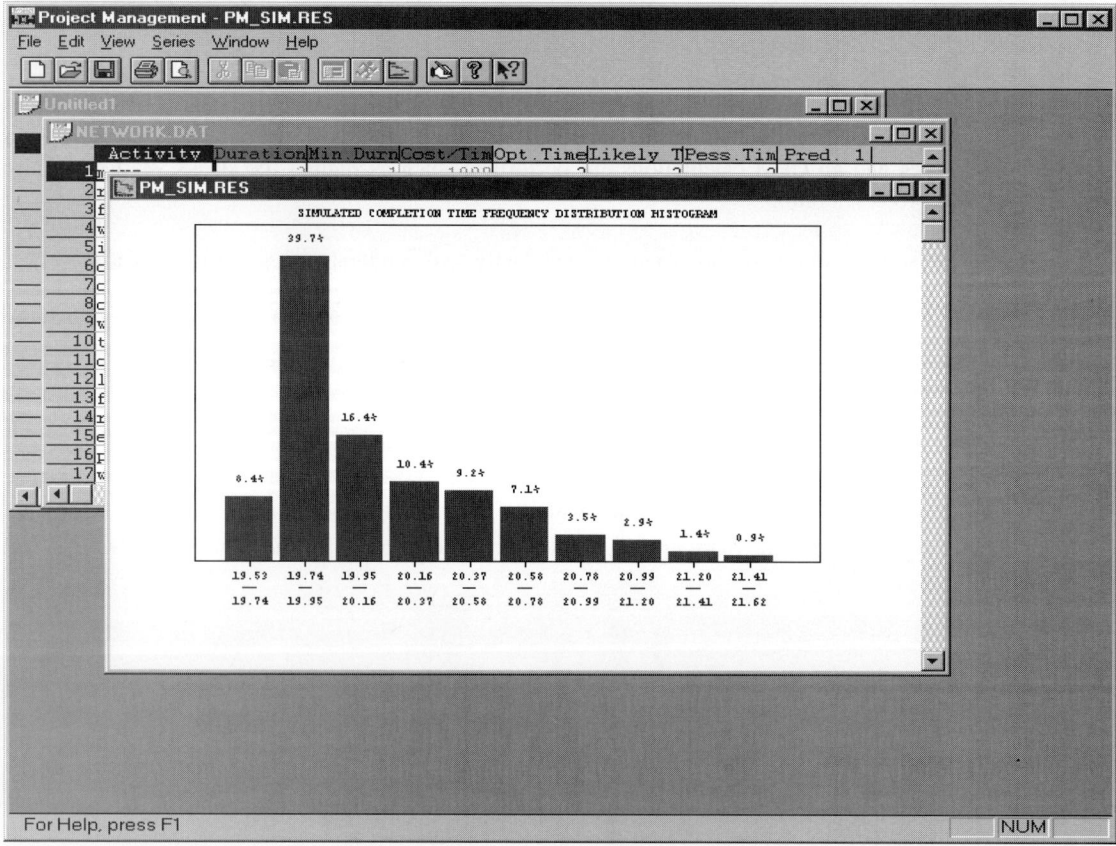

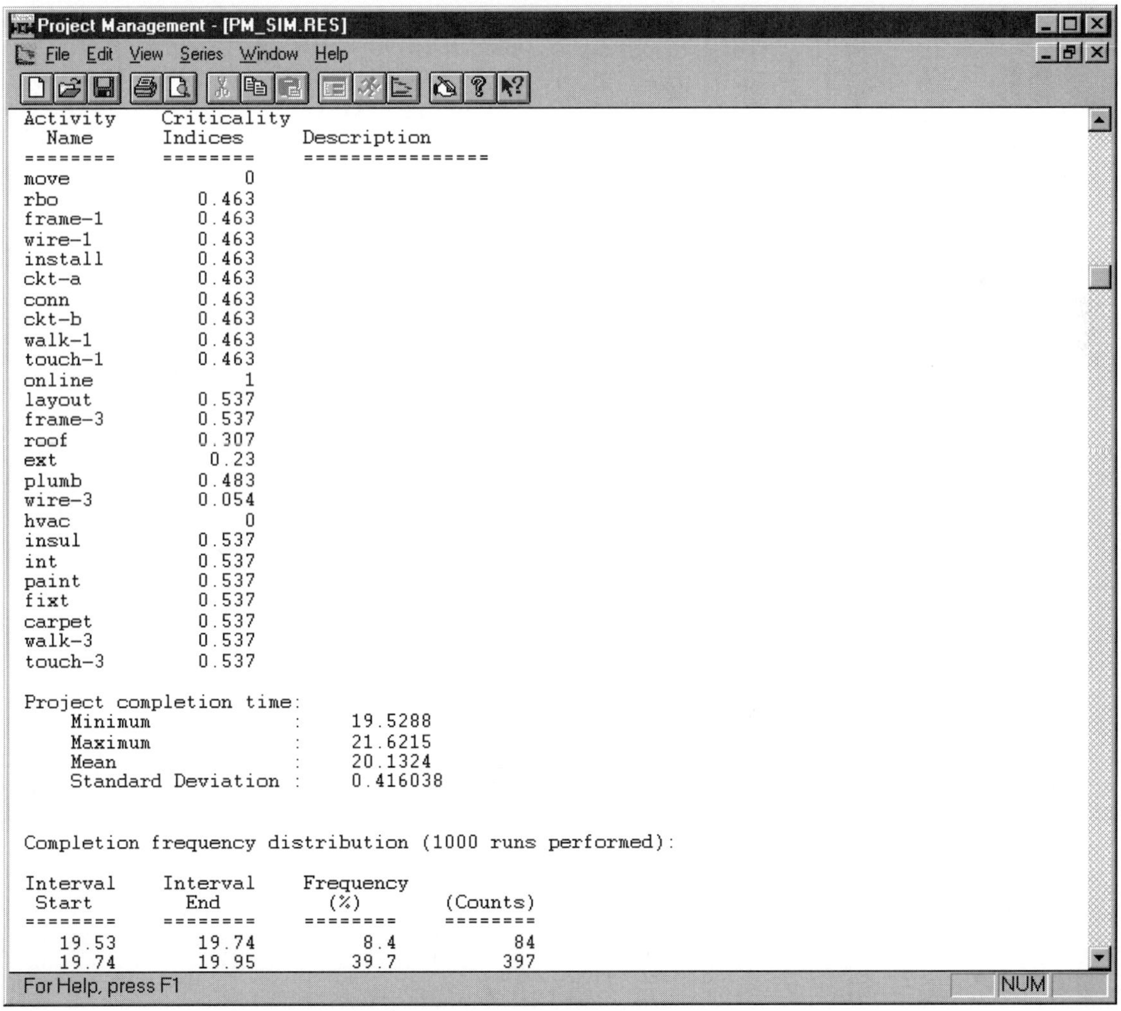

Outputs for Sample Data   (continued)

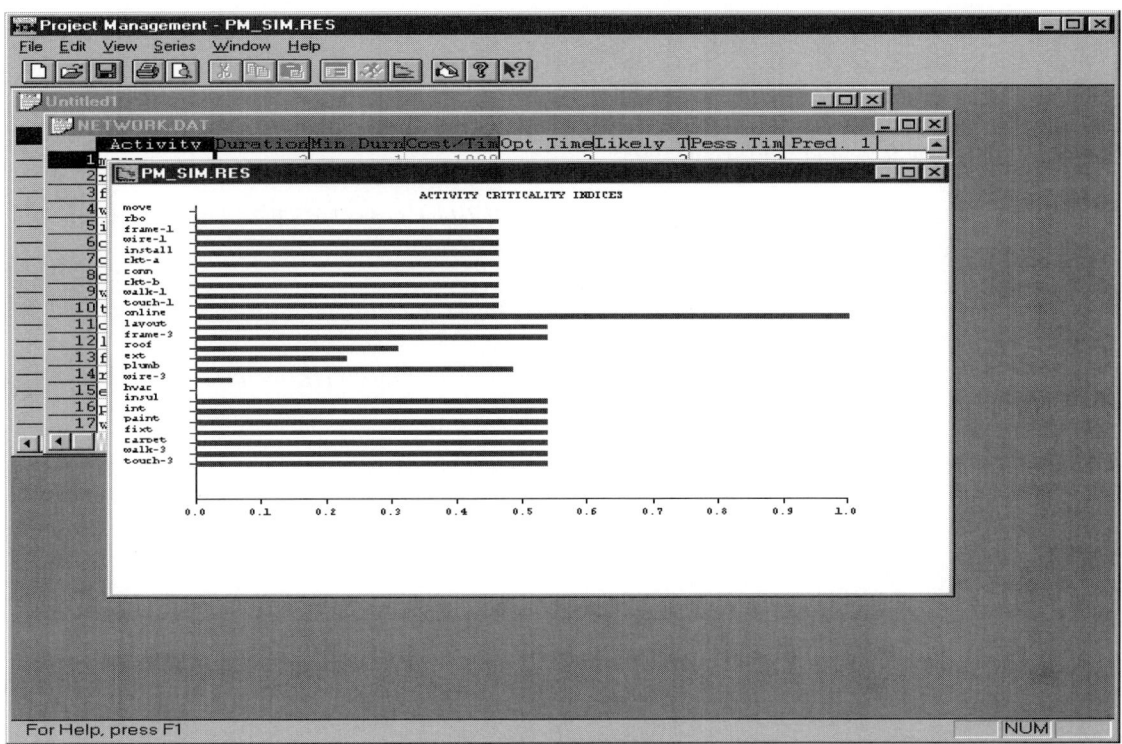

```
Activity      Criticality
  Name         Indices      Description
========     ==========     ================
move              0
rbo             0.463
frame-1         0.463
wire-1          0.463
install         0.463
ckt-a           0.463
conn            0.463
ckt-b           0.463
walk-1          0.463
touch-1         0.463
online            1
layout          0.537
frame-3         0.537
roof            0.307
ext             0.23
plumb           0.483
wire-3          0.054
hvac              0
insul           0.537
int             0.537
paint           0.537
fixt            0.537
carpet          0.537
walk-3          0.537
touch-3         0.537


Project completion time:
    Minimum              :    19.5288
    Maximum              :    21.6215
    Mean                 :    20.1324
    Standard Deviation   :     0.416038


Completion frequency distribution (1000 runs performed):

Interval     Interval     Frequency
  Start         End          (%)        (Counts)
========     ========     =========     ========
  19.53        19.74          8.4           84
  19.74        19.95         39.7          397
```

67

REFERENCES

Chase, R. B., and N. J. Aquilano *Production and Operations Management* 7th ed. Burr Ridge, IL: Richard D. Irwin, 1995.

Eppen, G. D.; F. J. Gould; and C. P. Schmidt *Introductory Management Science* Englewood Cliffs, New Jersey: Prentice Hall, 1993.

Law, Averill M., and W. David Kelton *Simulation Modeling & Analysis* 2nd ed. New York: McGraw-Hill, 1991.

Nahmias, S. *Production and Operations Analysis* 3rd ed. Burr Ridge, IL: Richard D. Irwin, 1997.

Phillips, D. T.; A. Ravindran; and J. J. Solberg *Operations Research Principles and Practices*, New York: John Wiley & Sons, 1976.

Stevenson, W. J. *Production/Operations Management* 5th ed. Burr Ridge, IL: Richard D. Irwin, 1996.

Toys City, Inc.[*]

Goodman & Goodman, a CPA firm, has audited Toys City, Inc., for the last three years. Toys City, Inc., is a regional retailer of children's toys and games. Each of the three previous audits resulted in unqualified opinions. Toys City's year end is December 31, and Goodman & Goodman has agreed to provide the audit report on March 1, 1998, ten days before the annual board of directors meeting. Bert, the manager from Goodman & Goodman in charge of the Toys City engagement, recalls that last year there was a 25 percent budget overrun. He attributes one-third of the overrun to unforeseen circumstances and the remaining two-thirds to poor planning. He estimates that poor planning resulted in approximately 130 hours and $3,400 in audit fees that were not billed to Toys City. In an effort to avoid another costly overrun, Bert wisely decided to devote more time to audit planning. By talking to various people, Bert learns that a project management technique known as Critical Path Method (CPM) could assist an auditor in sequencing all audit detail work (including work requested from client personnel), efficiently allocating personnel resources, highlighting potential audit bottlenecks, estimating completion time, determining the probability of meeting a completion deadline, and providing a framework for relevant feedback and control as the audit progresses. Thus, he decides to spend an additional 17 hours planning this year's audit, including computer setup and analysis time, using CPM.

Audit planning

During the slow month of August 1997, Bert and Craig, the senior-in-charge of the Toys City engagement, analyzed the audit plan for Toys City.

Basically the audit work could be divided into three phases: prior to year end, year end, and after year end. Exhibit 1 illustrates the work structure for Toys City's audit. Prior to year end the work is relatively simple and does not require much coordination. The work for the year end and after the year end, on the other hand, is mostly field work and requires much tighter control and coordination. This is the part of the audit that Bert feels the CPM method could help.

After a careful study, 22 audit areas are identified and budgeted hours for various levels of auditors are estimated (Exhibit 2). Billing rates for each auditor are indicated in parentheses below the various professional levels. Combining these rates with the budgeted hours leads to budgeted costs for the audit areas. The duration hours refer to the net time it takes to complete an audit area. Duration hours are less than total budgeted hours where audit areas permit simultaneous auditing by two or more audit personnel. Thus, to some extent, duration hours are variable depending upon the number of audit personnel available for an engagement and their assignment to various audit areas.

Each audit area is then analyzed as a separate work package in which detailed audit activities are specified in chronological order. For instance, the liabilities work package is composed of 10 tasks. First it takes 2 hours to obtain a schedule of liabilities. Then confirmations must be mailed out and processed, which take 12 hours and 39 hours respectively. After the confirmations are processed, the debit balances must be investigated, which takes 5 hours. While the confirmations are being mailed out, another staff auditor could first vouch selected liabilities and then test accruals and amortization, which takes 64 hours and 4 hours respectively. Also, after the schedule of liabilities had been obtained, a third staff auditor can spend 4 hours testing the pension plan. Once the pension plan, accruals, and amortization have been tested, the interest expense to debt can then be reconciled. This takes 8 hours. This is then followed by 5 hours of verification of the debt restriction compliance. Once the debit balances are investigated and debt restriction compliance verified, subsequent payments can then be reviewed, which takes 10 hours. Exhibit 3 summarizes the tasks for the liabilities work package and their duration.

---

[*] By Dinah W. Cheng and Mike Moses, Operations Management Area, Stern School of Business. This case is for the use of students in a core course in Operations Management and is intended to have no actual relationship to any real person or organization. (11/98)

The engagement network could be depicted at various levels. A relatively detailed schedule is used in assembling time estimates and controlling audit progress while a summary version is useful for an overview. The summary version depicts each work package (such as the liabilities work package) as a simple engagement activity with duration equal to the project completion for that work package.

Once the timing and duration of the various work packages have been worked out in detail, they are linked together in chronological order. The relationship among the various twenty two work packages is summarized in Exhibit 4. Using this information, a network diagram is drawn and all critical activities are identified. The minimum time to perform the entire engagement can also calculated.

One benefit that has come out of this audit planning is the cost reduction resulting from more efficient allocation of the audit staffs. For example, last year's inventory pricing required 192 hours of staff time, 30 hours of senior time, 8 hours of manager time, and 6 hours of partner time. Multiplying hours by the billing rates of the four professional levels shows that this personnel scheduling plan resulted in a total cost of $5,360. This year, Bert estimated the relative efficiency per dollar of cost for each professional level in each work package. For the inventory pricing area, it was found that it is more efficient to substitute 4 hours of manager time and 3 hours of senior time for 38 hours of staff time. The manager's and senior's general competence and familiarity with Toys City's inventory enabled them to apply overall tests of reasonableness to a major segment of inventory in lieu of staff performance of more time-consuming detail price vouching. Total cost for the inventory pricing work thereby was reduced to $4,850, resulting in saving $510.

Implementation

The actual audit began on January 4, 1998, as planned. Soon after the audit began, Bert received a request from John, one of the staff auditors who would be auditing the receivables. John was getting married and would like to take a week (40 audit hours) off for his honeymoon from January 16 to January 20. There was no other auditor available in the firm to replace him. To ensure that the audit would complete on schedule and on budget, John was advised to delay his honeymoon plan until the entire project was completed. After failing to convince Bert that his plan would not affect the progress of the project, John reluctantly postponed his honeymoon and the audit engagement proceeded without any interruption.

After the Toys City audit had progressed 106 duration hours, a need for acceleration arose when Bert was informed by the Toys City controller that merger negotiations had been initiated with a toy manufacturer. The controller urgently requested delivery of the audit report 1½ weeks (60 hours) earlier than originally agreed. Bert assured the Toys City controller that he would attempt to comply with the acceleration request.

Since it was an extremely busy period for Goodman & Goodman, no idle auditing personnel were available in the firm for assignment to the Toys City engagement. Thus work package durations (not budgeted hours) could be reduced only by application of personnel at overtime rates, increased use of more experienced professionals (i.e., seniors, managers, and partners), and similar cost-inflating alternatives. Since Bert's CPM knowledge is still rather elementary and it is important to be able to reduce the project completion time by 60 hours at the lowest cost, Bert decided to hire Gary Fay, an external consultant, to advise him on how to proceed. After talking to Bert and various people in personnel, Gary quickly came up with the estimated acceleration times and costs for various activities tabulated in Exhibit 5. Based on these costs, the schedule for the remaining auditing procedures was revised. Bert was happy with revised schedule as the additional cost was reasonable. The Toys City engagement was finally completed two days earlier than scheduled.

After the delivery of the audit report, Bert evaluated the auditing procedures. He realized that the completion time of several work packages in fact could fluctuate depending on the individual staff performing the audit as well as the actual amount of work load. This year they were lucky that the work load turned out to be much less (so that they actually completed early). For future planning, he felt that he needs more assurance about the completion time so that undesirable outcomes could be prevented.

Again he sought help from Gary Fay. Gary suggested that a procedure similar to CPM called PERT could be applied. First, from the large amounts of prior history on comparable audit activities, and by talking to auditors who are familiar with the condition of Toys City's books, the effectiveness of internal control, and the likely problem areas of the engagement, optimistic and pessimistic time estimates were obtained for the work packages whose completion time may fluctuate. The information is summarized in Exhibit 6. Based on this information and results from previous calculations, the probability that the entire engagement would complete within a certain time could then be calculated.

Questions:

1. Taking into consideration tasks that can be performed simultaneously, prepare a detailed CPM network for the liabilities work package. What is the earliest finish time for the package? What is the critical path?

2. Present a summary network for the entire audit plan with all the work prior to year end and each of the work packages presented as a single activity. Determine how long the entire audit will take.

3. If you were Bert, would you have accommodated John's vacation request? Why? What is the maximum time you would be comfortable giving John off if his only responsibility was the auditing of the receivables?

4. After examining the data in Exhibit 5, Bert notices that the normal time and normal cost are different from the ones shown in Exhibit 2. He suspects that there are some errors in the calculation. What do you think?

5. Recommend an accelerating plan that would reduce the auditing engagement by 60 hours at minimum additional costs. What is the additional cost? Is a 79-hour reduction feasible, and if so, at what cost? Would a corporate limit on per-hour reduction cost of $150 an hour ever become a problem if further reductions were required? Why?

6. Based on the information given in Exhibit 6, determine the probability that the entire audit would be completed within 311 duration hours. Is it likely that the engagement would be completed before the deadline? Is it likely that an activity that was not on the initial critical path would now be on the critical path? Which activity does this happen to? What percent of the time, and why?

Exhibit 1 Work structure of the Toys City engagement

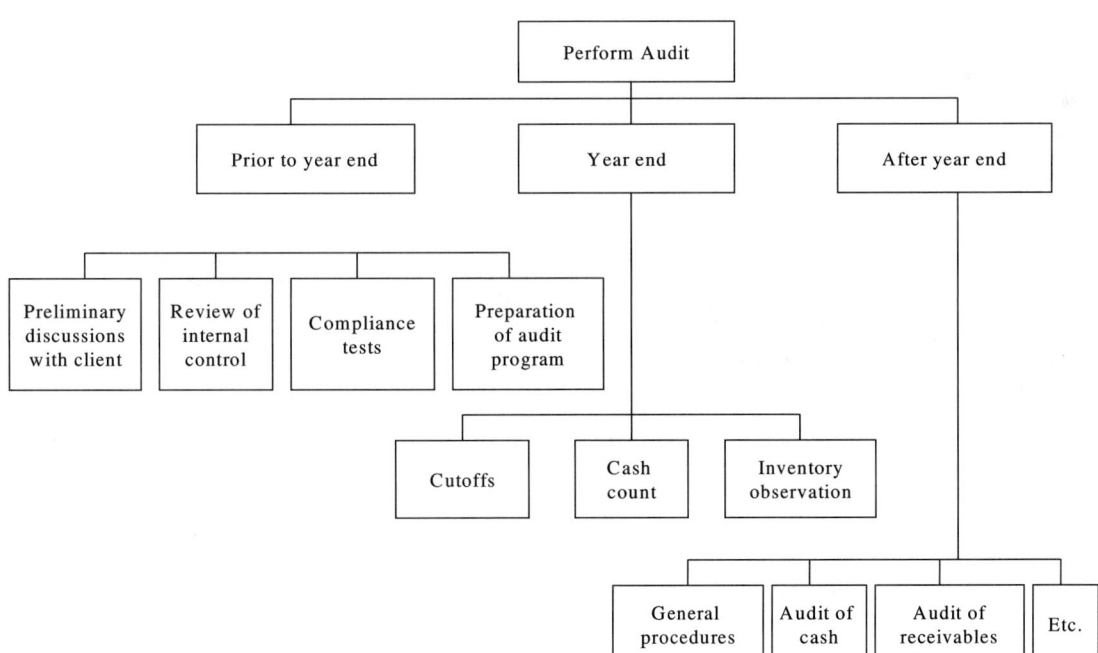

Exhibit 2 Audit plan

Audit areas	Time budget (in hours)				Total budgeted hours	Budgeted cost	Duration hours
	Staff ($20)	Senior ($30)	Manager ($40)	Partner ($50)			
Discussions with Toys City		1	2		3	110	2
Review of internal control		8	2		10	320	8
Compliance tests		5			5	150	5
Year-end procedures	20	3	1		24	530	13
Field work:							
Observation of inventory	16	12	8	2	38	1,100	25
General audit procedures	7			8	15	540	11
Audit of cash	31	7		3	41	980	19
Audit of receivables	10	8	2		20	520	10
Inventory pricing	154	33	12	6	205	4,850	145
Audit of other current assets	27	4			31	660	11
Audit of liabilities	102	28	15	8	153	3,880	93
Audit of fixed assets	29	9		4	42	1050	22
Audit of sales	10	5	1		16	390	6
Audit of COGS	42	7	4	2	55	1,310	25
Audit of other revenues and expenses	17	7	1		25	590	10
Audit of capital stock and R/E				1	1	50	1
Lawyer's letter			1		1	40	1
Management's letter			1		1	40	1
Subsequent review	12	8	6	4	30	920	18
Preparation of financial statements		12	3		15	480	15
Preparation of tax returns			12		12	480	12
Partner/manager review			4	4	8	360	6
Total hours	477	165	95	42	779	$ 20,390	479

Exhibit 3 Activities in the liabilities work package

Activity	Description	Duration (hours)
1.	Obtain schedule of liabilities	2
2.	Mail confirmations	12
3.	Process confirmations	39
4.	Investigate debit balances	5
5.	Test pension plan	4
6.	Vouch selected liabilities	64
7.	Test accruals and amortization	4
8.	Reconcile interest expense to debit	8
9.	Verify debt restriction compliance	5
10.	Review subsequent payments	10

Exhibit 4 Predecessors and successors relationship of the various work packages

Activity	Description	Immediate predecessors
1.	Discussions with Toys City	—
2.	Review internal control	1
3.	Compliance tests	2
4.	Year end procedures	3
5.	Observation of inventory	4
6.	General audit procedures	5
7.	Audit of cash	5
8.	Audit of receivables	7
9.	Inventory pricing	5
10.	Audit of other current assets	6
11.	Audit of liabilities	9
12.	Audit of fixed assets	10
13.	Audit of sales	8
14.	Audit of COGS	9
15.	Audit of other revenues and expenses	13, 14
16.	Audit of capital stock and R/E	15
17.	Lawyer's letter	11
18.	Management's letter	12, 16
19.	Subsequent review	12, 16
20.	Preparation of financial statements	17, 18, 19
21.	Preparation of tax returns	17, 18, 19
22.	Partner/manager review	20, 21

Exhibit 5 Time-cost trade-off of Toys City engagement

Activity	Description	Normal		Acceleration*	
		Time	Cost	Time	Cost
9.	Inventory pricing	92	$3,055	56	$4521
10.	Audit of other current assets	11	660	11	660
11.	Audit of liabilities	93	3,880	53	4,720
12.	Audit of fixed assets	22	1,050	22	1,050
13.	Audit of sales	6	390	6	390
14.	Audit of COGS	25	1,310	25	1,310
15.	Audit of other revenues and expenses	10	590	5	790
16.	Audit of capital stock and R/E	1	50	1	50
17.	Lawyer's letter	1	40	1	40
18.	Management's letter	1	40	1	40
19.	Subsequent review	18	920	3	1,670
20.	Preparation of financial statements	15	480	10	1080
21.	Preparation of tax returns	12	480	2	980
22.	Partner/manager review	6	360	6	360

*Acceleration time is the minimum time the activity can be completed. Acceleration cost is the total cost for the maximum reduction assuming that the cost is incurred in a linear fashion.

Exhibit 6 Alternate Completion Times for Some Activities in Toy City Engagement

Activity	Description	Optimistic	Most likely	Pessimistic
5.	Observation of inventory	20	25	40
9.	Inventory pricing	138	145	152
10.	Audit of other current assets	9	11	12
11.	Audit of liabilities	90	93	95
15.	Audit of other revenues and expenses	8	10	12
21.	Preparation of Tax Returns	10	12	25
22.	Partner/manager review	5	6	10

PROCESS ANALYSIS METHODS

1. INTRODUCTION

Some of the key information that any entrepreneur or manager wants to know about his or her business is how much can the business produce per unit of time and under what conditions; that is, how much can it produce of a single product or service or a mix of products and services, or how much can it produce given large or small or even a mixture of order sizes. Information on how long it takes to get orders through the manufacturing or service facility is also required to setup service guarantees regarding delivery and due dates; that is, film will be ready in an hour, loan will be approved in three days, and pizza will be delivered to the door in 30 minutes. Information on how much capital and labor are required in order to meet or exceed these guarantees is also necessary for making tactical as well as strategic decisions. HOM: Process Analysis is designed to help the entrepreneur or manager respond to these questions.

Since the types of problems in the real world that involve the analysis of processes vary dramatically from setting to setting, this HOM module has been designed to be very general and flexible. It facilitates the ability to model many different situations. Therefore, the Process Analysis module is also the most complex to populate with the correct information. We therefore recommend that the user follow the Help tutorial the first few times solving Process Analysis problems.

As with all HOM modules, the basic product data is entered through the data spreadsheet, while managerial choices that affect the Results are entered through the Parameters Dialog box. Due to the complexity of this module, a third data entry vehicle has been created. These are dialog boxes in which key workcenter and labor capabilities can be entered. To start the problem analysis, the resources must first be Named.

Before starting this task, however, we recommend that the user write down in a logical and sequential list the set of steps required to create the product or service to be analyzed (to bake cookies requires mixing ingredients, spooning cookies onto trays, baking, cooling, packing, paying).

Currently, HOM can be used to model make-to-order systems that create products or services in a linear sequence of steps. Hints for modeling some atypical situations are given in section 13.2.

2. NAMING PRODUCTS AND RESOURCES

On start-up, the basic problem data spreadsheet is presented. The three leftmost columns are where the directory of products, workcenters, and labor types are entered (and always indicated thereafter). These columns will be blank if no product or resource names have been specified. The remaining columns are for entering the demand and process-specific information for each product. These two parts of the spreadsheet are separated by a black line. For now we just want to restrict our attention to the first three columns: Products, Workcenters, and Labor Types.

2.1 Naming Products

Click on the DATA item on the HOM command line. A drop-down menu exhibits Product, Workcenter, Labor Type, Column, and Parameters. We recommend that you first name your products. Move the cursor to Product. This will produce the Add Product, Edit Product, Delete Product, and Rename Product features of the Product submenu. Only Add will be highlighted until the first product name has been entered.

Clicking on Add reveals a New Name dialog box with a computer-generated name (Product1) for the first product (or service). If this name is not acceptable, enter your preference and click on OK. You will now see your chosen product name displayed in the first row of the leftmost (first) column. (This column is labeled as Product.) Repeat this operation until you have named all your products (or services). HOM permits the modeling of up to 25 different products.

Each time you name a product, the right-hand side (i.e., the fourth column and beyond) of the spreadsheet will bear the name of the last product that you entered. Moving the cursor and double-clicking on any product name will produce the unique right-hand side associated with that product. The unique right-hand side contains the unique demand and process recipe data for that product. We strongly recommend that you wait to fill in the process recipe data until you have completed filling in all the resource names. We recommend that you use FILE --> Save to save the data entered so far.

2.2 Naming Workcenters

After product names come workcenter names. The workcenters are where value gets added to the products or services. Typical workcenters will be ovens in a bakery, drill presses in a machine shop, ATMs in a bank, Recovery Rooms in a hospital, and so on. Using DATA --> Workcenter reveals the choices: Add, Edit, Delete, and Rename Workcenter. Clicking on Add reveals an Add Workcenter dialog box with a computer-generated name (Workcenter1), which can be edited if it is not to your liking. This dialog box also contains information for this workcenter. The first few times you use Process Analysis we recommend that you refrain from completing the information at this point. Click on OK. The name of the workcenter now appears in the second column of the spreadsheet. Double-clicking on the name of the workcenter causes the Edit Workcenter dialog box to be displayed. Clicking on OK moves you back to the spreadsheet.

Enter all the names of the workcenters by following the steps described above. HOM allows the user to model up to 30 workcenters. We recommend that you use FILE --> Save to save the data entered so far.

2.3 Naming Labor Types

The last resource to be named is labor. This gives you the opportunity to specify up to 10 types (classes) of labor. A labor type (or, equivalently, labor class) could be used to denote a specific skill or experience category. For example, some workcenters might require labor with a particular skill (cook, machinist, repair person, cashier, or clerk). A bakery may require decorators, bakers, mechanics, and unskilled labor. Hospitals may need scrub nurses, floor nurses, nurse's aides, and so on. Repeated use of DATA --> Labor Type --> Add gives you the opportunity to enter all the types of labor that are required. The names appear after they are entered in the third column of the spreadsheet. Double-clicking on the name of a labor type produces the Edit Labor Type dialog box. This dialog box also contains information about the Labor Type. The first few times you use Process Analysis we recommend that you refrain from completing the information at this point. We recommend that you save the data using FILE --> Save and proceed to the next step.

3. ENTER PRODUCT DEMAND DATA

The first column of the problem data spreadsheet contains all the names of the products. Double-clicking a Product name reveals its unique right-hand side of the data spreadsheet. The demand data is entered in Column E, rows 2, 3, 4, and 5 of the spreadsheet. This data comprises four items: order size, demand, SCV (squared coefficient of variation), and priority. Detailed descriptions of these data items are given below.

3.1 Order Size (Enter Product Demand)

The order size is entered in Column E, row 2. The order size is the number of units demanded by a customer for that product. It is fixed for a given product and should be a positive integer. This particular choice of modeling the zero customer-to-customer variation in the number of units demanded is explained below.

HOM is not designed to be an exact Demand replicator since it can handle only 30 types of products. Thus, if the process were the baking of cookies as per customer orders, you should first decide the "units" of an order. Units of a single cookie, ½ dozen cookies, and 1 dozen cookies all are possible "units" for the analysis. If we assume that our "unit" is ½ dozen, then the possible products could be

Product	Order Size	Cookie Type	Description
A	1	Choc Chip	Orders of ½ dozen choc chip cookies
B	2	Choc Chip	Orders of 1 dozen choc chip cookies
C	3	Choc Chip	Orders of 1 and ½ doz. choc chip cookies
D	4	Choc Chip	Orders of 2 dozen choc chip cookies
E	1	Sugar	Orders of ½ dozen sugar cookies
F	2	Sugar	Orders of 1 dozen sugar cookies.

Notice that by specifying four different order sizes for the "same" product, namely choc chip cookies, we have created some degree of variation in the order size. This method allows the user to set different priorities for customers with different order sizes for choc chip cookies.

In other cases, order size could be used to emulate small, medium, and large orders, for example, 10, 100, and 1,000 circuit boards, with the single circuit board being the basic "unit." Alternate routing, rework, and scrap can also be modeled by creating multiple products, each with a different routing. The next item to be specified is the demand for the product.

3.2 Demand (Enter Product Demand)

The *average* demand is entered in Column E, row 3. Enter the expected number of orders per *time period*. The default value of the demand *time period* is a month; that is, if you enter a value of 20 in column E, row 3, HOM will assume that on the average there are 20 orders per month for this product.

If you do not like the choice of the time unit, "month," the demand time units can be changed in the Parameters dialog box. The choices available are: minutes, hours, days, weeks, months, or years. Also see section 7.

In our cookie-making example, the demand for product A could be 100 orders per month, that is, 100 orders for ½ dozen choc chip cookies per month. After entering the demand, proceed to the SCV (squared coefficient of variation) with regard to demand.

3.3 Squared Coefficient of Variation (SCV) with Regard to Demand (Enter Product Demand)

The next item describing the demand is the squared coefficient of variation, column E, row 4. This gives the user the opportunity to model uncertain demand arrival patterns. The squared coefficient of variation is the variance divided by the square of the mean. In this instance, it refers to the variance divided by the square of the mean time between two customer arrival epochs (i.e., the SCV of the inter-arrival time between orders; please see note below). The SCV must be nonnegative. The larger the value of the SCV, the greater the variability in the order arrival process. If the SCV is set to zero, then the associated interarrival times will be deterministic (no variability). If it is set to one, it will correspond to exponentially distributed times. Values greater than one will correspond to larger variability.

The default value for the SCV is zero. This implies that there is no variability and demand will be uniformly spread out over the demand time period. In our cookie-making example, assume that the demand for product A is 100 orders per month. Assume too (and it can be specified in the Parameters dialog box) that a month consists of 80 hours of operation. Then if the SCV for product A were zero, an order for ½ dozen choc chip cookies will arrive every 0.8 hour (i.e., 80/100 hour).

Notice that an SCV of 0.09 represents substantial variability in many instances. This value of SCV implies that the standard deviation of the time between arrivals is 30 percent (0.3) of the value of the mean. In our example, this would imply a standard deviation of 0.24 hour when the mean time between arrivals is 0.8 hour, that is, the range given by the mean +/- 3 standard deviations would be as large as [0.08, 1.52 hours]. An SCV of 0.01 can be used to emulate moderate variability.

Please see the section 10 on Modeling Variability for details about how HOM uses just the information about the mean and the variance (via the SCV) to fit a distribution. Also note that this method of approximating distributions is intended only to give the user a (rough-and-ready) feel for the effect of variability and is not guaranteed to be precise. Simulations that use analytical and empirical distributions to model single-stage queueing systems can be carried out using the HOM: Waiting Line Management module.

After entering the SCV, please proceed to specifying the priority of the product.

Note: Using a single product, we can only model variability in the arrival pattern (time between arrivals) but not in the volume of demand. Order size variation can be handled by using multiple products with different order sizes and carrying out sensitivity analysis with regard to the product mix as well as order size.

3.4 Priority of Product (Enter Product Demand)

The priority of a product is a device that allows the program to break ties when determining which product to schedule for processing next. The value for priority can range from 1 to 100 and should be an integer. The number one (1) represents the highest priority and the number 100 the lowest priority.

In our cookie example, we may decide that since orders for two dozen choc chip cookies (product D) are the most profitable, they should have precedence over the other products. So we may assign product D a priority of one (1). Orders for ½ dozen sugar cookies (product E) could be the least profitable, and thus assigned a priority of 10. The priorities of all other products could take values in between 1 and 10. The computer assumes that the ranking is ordinal and disregards the relative difference between the priority values.

The process recipe is still to be filled in, but we recommend doing this last. The next step should be entering the workcenter capabilities data.

4. ENTER WORKCENTER CAPABILITIES DATA

Double-clicking on any of the workcenters listed in the second column of the data spreadsheet will allow the editing of the workcenter capabilities. The Edit Workcenter dialog box will appear. If you notice at this stage that you have misspelled the workcenter name and this bothers you, then you have two choices: (1) either delete the name of the workcenter and create a new name or (2) use the DATA --> Workcenter --> Rename item from the command line to give the workcenter the correct name. The latter method is recommended once the process recipes have been entered. If the former method is employed, HOM will warn that the name of the workcenter will be deleted from the process recipes; however, the processing times entered in the recipes will stay intact (only the workcenter name will be blanked out).

The left-hand side of this dialog box is meant for entering the capabilities of the workcenter, whereas the right-hand side requests information for the type of processing done at the workcenter. The descriptions of the data items are given below.

4.1 Number of Identical Equipment

Enter how many identical machines there are at a workcenter. In a service operation or where no equipment is used, simply make this equal to the number of workers. There will often be just one machine, such as the oven in a bakery. But in some operations, such as ATMs in a bank, there could be several machines. If an operation has infinite capacity (for example, cooling hot cookies prior to packing), make this a large number, say, 100.

4.2 Maximum Units That Can Be Processed on a Machine without an Additional Setup

Enter the maximum number of units that can be processed at a time without additional setup. This number indicates either a physical capacity of the machine or a managerial decision on the maximum lot size allowed. We interpret a lot size to be the maximum number of units that can be processed before an additional setup is required. Note that orders cannot be combined for processing in this version of HOM. In addition, we use the term job to indicate a subset of a customer order that is available for processing at a workcenter. The maximum units information is used to schedule jobs at the workcenter.

Assume that we are discussing the oven in the bakery example. Assume that the oven can process three units (maximum) at a time. Recall that a unit is ½ dozen. Assume that a job waiting to be baked has the priority to be scheduled (i.e., it can be taken up for processing) next.

> If the order size of the job is less than 3 units (1 ½ dozen), and if the entire order is at the workcenter, then the job will be processed as a whole, that is, the full order will be baked at one time. An example would be product B that has an order size of 1 dozen. If the entire 1 dozen are available for baking (say, mixed and placed on trays), then the dozen cookies will be loaded.
>
> If the order size of the job exceeds 3 units, and if at least 3 units of this order are available for processing right now, then 3 units will be processed. In other words, the job will be broken up into smaller lots to accommodate the maximum units constraint. For example, product D, which has an order size of 2 dozen, will be processed as soon as 1½ dozen cookies are available without waiting for the remaining ½ dozen to arrive at the oven. Once the first 1½ dozen are baked, the oven would be setup again and the remaining ½ dozen of the order would be completed.
>
> Finally, note that in both cases described above, the scheduling rule will postpone the processing of a job if the lot size can be made as close to the maximum units (i.e., 3) as possible by waiting. The workcenter is programmed to wait for the rest of the order to arrive at the workcenter. This device is an automatic setup time–saving feature built into all the scheduling algorithms. Other setup time–saving features are described in section 4.6. In any case, this version of HOM does not permit the user to combine two or more orders to fill a machine to capacity.

In a process that allows for large order sizes, such as 1,000 circuit boards in one setup, you may want to test the effects on performance of stopping the machine and loading an order of a smaller size (say, 10 circuit boards) in between processing the large order. (This would be feasible only if the product with the smaller order size has higher priority.) This device *could* also be used to facilitate the flow of the product to the next processing step. By specifying a maximum unit of 100, an order of size 1,000 will get broken up into lots of size 100, processed in 100s and transferred to the next step for processing, without waiting for the entire 1,000 circuit boards to be completed. Remember too that if you have not specified Use Setup Saving Algorithm, you would have caused the process to incur additional setups each time you break up an order.

4.3 Default SCV of Setup Time

Enter the default value of the squared coefficient of the setup time for a machine in this workcenter. The ability to add this measure of uncertainty to the process makes the outcome more realistic.

> **Caution!** Once the default value of the setup time has been set, it can only be changed on the data spreadsheet. For example, if you have set the default SCV of setup time to be 0.3, this value is automatically entered when this workcenter is part of the process recipe of a product. However, after the process recipe has been created, changes in the default SCV of the setup time will *no longer* be automatically reflected in the process recipe. The SCV values will stay unchanged for the recipes created before the change. However, the new default value of the SCV will be used for any new recipes that you create.

> **Solution!** A possible solution *available for* replacing the default SCV globally would be to *delete* the workcenter. This will delete the *name* of the workcenter and not the setup or run times in the process recipe. Reenter the name of the workcenter and a new value of the default SCV. Enter the name of the workcenter once again in *all* process recipes that use this workcenter. The SCV values will be *replaced* by the default SCV. The flip side of this operation is that any SCV value that you have entered in the process recipe will be overwritten. A third alternative is to Edit the workcenter. Change its default SCV values. Copy the name of the workcenter using the Edit function. Then paste this name wherever you wish the new default values to take effect. Remember, the value of the SCV for any particular step in the process recipe for any particular product can always be modified on the data spreadsheet.

The squared coefficient of variation is the variance divided by the square of the mean. In this instance, it refers to the variance divided by the square of the average setup time. The SCV must be nonnegative. The larger the value of the SCV, the greater the variability in the setup time. If the SCV is set to zero, then the setup time will be deterministic (no variability). If it is set to one, it will correspond to exponentially distributed setup time.

The default value for the SCV is initially set equal to zero. This implies that there is no variability. Please see section 10 on Modeling Variability for details about how HOM uses just the information about the mean and the variance (via the SCV) to fit a distribution. Also note that this method of approximating distributions is intended only to give the user a (rough-and-ready) feel for the effect of variability and is not guaranteed to be precise. Simulations that use analytical and empirical distributions and model single-stage queueing systems can be carried out using the HOM: Waiting Line Management module.

4.4 Default SCV of Run Time

Enter the default value of the squared coefficient of the run time for a machine in this workcenter. The ability to add this measure of uncertainty to the process makes the outcome more realistic.

> **Caution!** Once the default value of the run time has been set, it can only be changed on the data spreadsheet. For example, if you have set the default SCV of run time to be 0.3, this value is automatically entered when this workcenter is part of the process recipe of a product. However, after the process recipe has been created, changes in the default SCV of the run time will *no longer* be automatically reflected in the process recipe. The SCV values will stay unchanged for the recipes created before the change. However, the new default value of the SCV will be used for any new recipes that you create.

Solution! A possible solution available for replacing the default SCV globally would be to *delete* the workcenter. This will delete the *name* of the workcenter and not the setup or run times in the process recipe. Reenter the name of the workcenter and a new value of the default SCV. Enter the name of the workcenter once again in *all* process recipes that use this workcenter. The SCV values will be *replaced* by the default SCV. The flip side of this operation is that any SCV value that you have entered in the process recipe will be overwritten. A third alternative is to Edit the workcenter. Change its default SCV values. Copy name of the workcenter using the Edit function. Then paste this name wherever you wish the new default values to take effect. Remember, the value of the SCV for any particular step in the process recipe for any particular product can always be modified on the data spreadsheet.

The squared coefficient of variation is the variance divided by the square of the mean. In this instance, it refers to the variance divided by the square of the average run time. The SCV must be nonnegative. The larger the value of the SCV, the greater the variability in the run time. If the SCV is set to zero, then the run time will be deterministic (no variability). If it is set to one, it will correspond to exponentially distributed run times.

The default value for the SCV is initially set equal to zero. This implies that there is no variability. Please see section 10 on Modeling Variability for details about how HOM uses just the information about the mean and the variance (via the SCV) to fit a distribution. Also note that this method of approximating distributions is intended only to give the user a (rough-and-ready) feel for the effect of variability and is not guaranteed to be precise. Simulations that use analytical and empirical distributions and model single-stage queueing systems can be carried out using the HOM: Waiting Line Management module.

4.5 Type of Processing

Three types of processes can be modeled using HOM. The user should select the type of process most appropriate for each workcenter from the list shown below. Please note that customer orders are not combined for processing in this version of HOM. For first-time users of HOM, we recommend you read all of section 4.5 before making your selection on which process type best resembles the situation you are modeling.

One Unit at a Time
In Batches
Continuous Flow

Also, remember that HOM is currently designed to model make-to-order systems that create products or services in a linear sequence of steps. Hints for modeling some atypical situations and machines are given in section 13.2.

4.5.1 One Unit at a Time (Type of Processing—Workcenter Dialog Box)

This is the model of a machine that has setup as well as run time. The setup is an internal setup, that is, the machine is idle while the setup is being done. Nothing else can be done on this machine during its setup and run time. This is typical of most machines available in industry. The machine setup is considered to be finished after the maximum of the machine setup time and the labor setup time has elapsed. For example, machine setup time is 6 min. and labor setup time is 10 min. If both these quantities are deterministic, then the setup is completed after max(6,10) = 10 min. If these quantities are the means of a random distribution, then two random variables having the means 6 and 10 (and appropriate SCVs) are first sampled, then the setup time is considered to be finished after a period of time equal to the maximum of these two quantities. The machine is considered to be free after the setup is completed and a duration equal to the machine run time has elapsed. Labor is considered to be free after the setup time for labor plus the run time (if any) for the labor has been completed. The job is completed after the setup has been finished and an additional duration equal to the maximum of the machine and labor run times has elapsed. This is not the only method of modeling the sequence of setup and run time activities, but has been chosen as a simple but reasonable representation of many actual sequences of activities. However, by appropriately specifying the process recipe, many other sequences can be modeled.

The jobs are processed in lot sizes equal to the minimum of the following quantities:
Order size or
Maximum units that can be processed on a machine without an additional setup

As described earlier, the scheduling rule will postpone the processing of a job if the lot size can be made as close to the maximum units as possible by waiting. The workcenter is programmed to wait for the rest of the order to arrive at the workcenter. This device is an automatic setup time–saving feature built into all the scheduling algorithms. Other setup time–saving features are described in section 4.6.

> **Caution!** The time to setup essentially becomes the maximum of the machine and labor setup times. The run time for the product becomes the maximum of the machine and labor run times. This could create a dramatic change in the utilization and flow times! For example, even if setup times were deterministic, if the labor setup time (say 10 min.) exceeds that of the machine (6 min.), then the machine will be idle longer than what the user might anticipate. This would in turn increase the machine utilization. This problem becomes heightened when the setup times are random variables. It is useful to remember that the expected value of the setup time in this case no longer equals the maximum of the two expected values, viz., expected value of the setup time and expected value of the run time.

> **Solution?** One solution would be to ensure that the labor setup time is smaller (and, if random, much smaller) than the machine setup time. Also see the examples given in section 14.

4.5.2 In Batches (Type of Processing—Workcenter Dialog Box)

This is the model of a machine that processes parts in a batch. The run time of such a machine does not depend on the quantity produced in a batch. In our previous example, it is possible to bake ½, 1, or 1½ dozen cookies in the oven at the same time. In HOM such a machine is modeled as having a setup time but no run time. Therefore the setup time entered in the process recipe for a product using this workcenter should be the sum of the setup and run time for the product. For example, if it takes 1 minute to setup the oven and 9 minutes to bake, and if the oven is modeled as a batch process, then enter 10 minutes for the setup time and zero for the run time. Also see the example given in section 6.

HOM will ignore (and warn) any run time entered in the process recipe for such workcenters. The machine is considered to be free after the maximum of the machine setup time and the labor setup time has elapsed. (Nothing else can be done using this machine while it is processing.) Labor is considered to be free after the setup time for labor. The job is completed as soon as the machine is free.

The jobs are processed in lot sizes equal to the minimum of the following quantities:

Order size or
Maximum units that can be processed on a machine without an additional setup

As described earlier, the scheduling rule will postpone the processing of a job if the lot size can be made as close to the maximum units as possible by waiting. The workcenter is programmed to wait for the rest of the order to arrive at the workcenter. This device is an automatic setup time–saving feature built into all the scheduling algorithms. Other setup time–saving features are described in section 4.6.

> **Caution!** The time to setup essentially becomes the maximum of the machine and labor setup times. The run time for the product becomes the maximum of the machine and labor run times. This could create a dramatic change in the utilization and flow times! For example, even if setup times were deterministic, if the labor setup time (say 10 min.) exceeds that of the machine (6 min.), then the machine will be idle longer than what the user might anticipate. This would in turn increase the machine utilization. This problem becomes heightened when the setup times are random variables. It is useful to remember that the expected value of the setup time in this case no longer equals the maximum of the two expected values, viz., expected value of the setup time and expected value of the run time.

Solution? One solution would be to ensure that the labor setup time is smaller (and, if random, much smaller) than the machine setup time. Also see the examples given in section 14.

4.5.3 Continuous Flow (Type of Processing—Workcenter Dialog Box)

The third type of machine processing is continuous flow. In this type of process environment, orders pass right behind one another without having to wait for the previous order to finish. In contrast to the one-unit-at-a-time and batch processes, jobs can be loaded one after the other, for example, to emulate a chain broiler. In our bakery example, a continuous flow oven would have openings at either end to allow for the entry of cookie trays as soon as the previous one clears the opening. The continuous flow process is modeled in HOM as one that has both a setup time and a run time. The setup time is the time during which the job is loaded onto the machine. The machine cannot be used for loading another job while a job is being loaded. The machine is considered to be free for *loading* another job after the maximum of the machine setup time and the labor setup time has elapsed. Labor is considered to be free after the setup time for labor. Once the setup has been completed, the job requires an additional duration equal to the run time to finish its processing. Please note that the run time (to be entered in the process recipe) for a continuous flow machine is equal to the time for the job to flow from one end of the machine to the other.

The capacity of such a process is determined by the loading time and physical size. The capacity is not determined by the run time. Throughput time, however, is affected by run time. The physical size is modeled in HOM as the input given in the "Maximum Units that can be Processed" edit box. The jobs are processed in lot sizes equal to the minimum of the following quantities:

> Order size or
> Maximum units that can be processed on a machine without an additional setup

As described earlier, the scheduling rule will postpone the processing of a job if the lot size can be made as close to the maximum units as possible by waiting. The workcenter is programmed to wait for the rest of the order to arrive at the workcenter. This device is an automatic setup time–saving feature built into all the scheduling algorithms. Other setup time–saving features are described in section 4.6.

> **Caution!** The time to setup essentially becomes the maximum of the machine and labor setup times. The run time for the product becomes the maximum of the machine and labor run times. This could create a dramatic change in the utilization and flow times! For example, even if setup times were deterministic, if the labor setup time (say 10 min.) exceeds that of the machine (6 min.), then the machine will be idle longer than what the user might anticipate. This would in turn increase the machine utilization. This problem becomes heightened when the setup times are random variables. It is useful to remember that the expected value of the setup time in this case no longer equals the maximum of the two expected values, viz., expected value of the setup time and expected value of the run time.
>
> **Solution?** One solution would be to ensure that the labor setup time is smaller (and, if random, much smaller) than the machine setup time. Also see the examples given in section 14.

4.6 Use the Setup-Saving Algorithm

The last entry in this (workcenter capabilities) dialog box is your decision on whether to use a setup saving algorithm. In order to use this feature, setup saving must first be activated in the Parameters dialog box. Then it must be individually selected for each workcenter in which the algorithm is to be used. An important restriction for using the setup saving algorithm in a workcenter is that the number of identical machines must be less than or equal to 20.

This algorithm when activated for a workcenter allows the workcenter operator to look down the queue of waiting jobs and select the order for processing that requires the same setup process as the order just processed at a machine. This would save the time required to reset the machine if a different order type or process step was run in between two similar jobs. When setup saving is activated, the priority of products is ignored. In case a similar setup cannot be performed, the scheduling rule reverts to the product priority–based scheduling rules described under Type of Processing.

In our cookie-making example, assume that choc chip cookies do not require a setup for mixing the ingredients if the previous order had been for a choc chip cookie, but need a five-minute setup to clean up after an order for sugar cookies has been processed. Assume also that the ingredients for choc chip cookies were mixed for the previous order and that the setup-saving algorithm had been involved. Then, five minutes will be saved if, from two waiting orders, one for sugar cookies and the other for choc chip cookies, the choc chip cookies order was taken up first for processing.

5. ENTER LABOR CLASSIFICATION DATA

Double-clicking any of the listed labor types will produce the Edit Labor Type dialog box. If you notice at this stage that you have misspelled the Labor Type name and this bothers you, then you have two choices: (1) either delete the name of the Labor Type and create a new name or (2) use the DATA --> Labor Type --> Rename item from the command line to give the correct name. The latter method is recommended once the process recipes have been entered. If the former method is employed, HOM will warn that the name of the workcenter will be deleted from the process recipes.

In this dialog box you get to enter the number of identical workers of this type that are currently available, as well as the default values for the SCVs of the labor setup and run times. Incorporating uncertainty in the labor setup and run times enhances the reality of HOM's modeling ability. The rules regarding the use and change of default SCVs are identical to the rules for a workcenter's default SCVs, and are explained under sections 4.3 and 4.4, Default SCV of Setup time and Default SCV of Run Time.

> **Note!** Please refer to section 4.5, Type of Processing, for the rules on scheduling labor, as well as the description of the Parameters dialog box given in Section 7, for the tie-breaking rule for deciding which workcenter to attend when there are multiple workcenters operated by the same type of labor. These rules become quite important when labor and (or) workcenter setup and (or) run times are stochastic (i.e., SCV > 0).

After completing the data entry for all labor types, proceed to Specify Process Recipe.

6. SPECIFY PROCESS RECIPE

To this point you have completed a list of all the resources that are available to your operating system (workcenters and labor), and the demand characteristics and priorities for all your products. All that remains to be done is to specify the process recipes that will allow you to use your resources in a unique step-by-step procedure to create your products or services. The current version of HOM allows you only to create products or services that are produced sequentially. Thus HOM cannot be used to model the simultaneous building of an engine and the body of a car, putting them in inventory, and drawing upon them later to build a car. The recipe must be stated in the logical order of processing, that is, Mix --> Bake --> Cool --> Pack --> Pay would be the logical sequence for baking cookies in our bakery example. In the same recipe, multiple visits to the same workcenter are allowed.

To start this step, double-click on the name of a product in the list of Product names. The right-hand side of the spreadsheet for that product will appear. If you have followed the steps thus far, you will see the demand information in column E, rows 2–5. The process recipe should be entered beginning from row 12, column D. Each row, beginning from row 12, corresponds to a step in the process. There can be up to 30 steps in your process recipe. Remember to save your work frequently.

Begin the data entry from column D, row 12. The data item is the name of the process step. Enter the first step of the process; in the bakery example, this might be mixing. Moving to the next column, that is, E, in the same row, enter the name of the workcenter that accomplishes this task. There could be several workcenters that could do the mixing, for example, hand mixing or automatic mixing, but you have to specify a unique workcenter that will accomplish this task. Either type in the name of the workcenter or use the cursor and the Edit function to copy the name of the workcenter from the second column and paste the name into the appropriate location. If you type in the name of a workcenter that is not in the list shown in the second column (under Workcenters), a dialog box will open asking, "Workcenter with the given name does not exist. Would you like to add it to the database?" If you answer yes, then the Add Workcenter dialog box will open up, and you can add the new workcenter to your list by following the instructions given in section 4. If you made a spelling mistake, answer no, and reenter the name of the workcenter.

In the next two columns enter the average run time and setup time for a machine in this workcenter for carrying out this process step. Repeat the procedure for the name of the labor type that will perform this step of the process recipe, and enter the average setup and run time for the labor as well. The manner in which HOM uses the setup and run time information to carry out the simulation is explained in section 4.5 on the Type of Processing. It has been assumed that the setup and run times will be given in minutes. This unit of time can be changed (only) globally by selecting the appropriate entry in the Parameters dialog box.

It is often the case that the labor time is less than the workcenter time. As an example, worker presence may be necessary to setup the oven, but once having set it up, the labor might not be necessary while the oven is baking.

Please note that a workcenter that performs a batch process has only a setup time. Any entry in the run time columns will be ignored (after warning the user). For example, the oven in our example can bake ½, 1, or 1½ dozen cookies in 10 minutes. The loading time for labor is 1 minute. Model this as a batch process, with the maximum number of units that can be processed without requiring an additional setup equal to three, workcenter setup time equal to 10, and labor setup time equal to one.

In a workcenter that performs a continuous flow operation, the setup time corresponds to the time for loading the job, whereas the run time corresponds to the time to flow from one end to the other. The run time for a job on a continuous flow machine therefore does *not* depend on the size of the job. For example, in the bakery example, a bread line requires a flow time of 48 minutes (from end to end), and 2 minutes are required to load a tray of dough (to be baked). The tray can hold up to 4 loaves. The unit for the product is a loaf of bread. Model this as a continuous flow process, with maximum units that can be processed without requiring an additional setup equal to 4, workcenter setup time and labor setup time equal to 2 min., and run time for the workcenter equal to 48 min. No labor run time is permitted for continuous flow processes.

The last four columns show the default values of the SCVs of setup and run times entered previously under workcenter and labor data. If you so desire, these values can be individually edited. Note that the SCV values cannot be changed globally in a simple manner. Please consult sections 4.3 and 4.4 on Default SCV of Setup Time and Default SCV of Run Time. The above procedure is followed for each step in the process recipe. Once all process recipes have been completed, move on to Specify Model.

> **Hint!** You cannot insert a row in the process recipe. Therefore, if you forget to include a step in the recipe, you must use the cut, copy, and paste spreadsheet operations to create an empty row for entering the forgotten step.

> **Hint!** You can copy and paste the entire process recipe for a product by selecting and copying just the process recipe portion of the data spreadsheet of, say, Product A, switching to Product B by double-clicking on its name in the Product column, and pasting the information in the appropriate location.

> **Hint!** Once you have become proficient with HOM: Process Analysis, you can skip the initial naming of workcenters and labor types and directly proceed to the Process Recipe step. Each time you enter a new name in the process recipe, you can answer yes (to whether to add the workcenter or labor to the database) and enter the workcenter or labor data.

7. SPECIFY MODEL

Model specification requires the user to make a set of decisions on operating procedures and units for measuring time. These alternatives are selected in the Parameters dialog box. The dialog box can be reached via DATA --> Parameters on the command line or by clicking on the Parameters dialog box icon. The items in the dialog box are as follows. Details are given after the table.

Item	Description
Time Units: Run/Setup Time Units	Choose the units in which setup and run times will be expressed. Minutes is the default value.
Time Units: Demand	Select the time units in which demand will be expressed, for example, 10 orders per day, 20 cars per month. The default value is months.
Time Units: Simulation	Decide the units of time in which the length of simulation will be expressed. The default unit is years.
Conversion factors	The next two boxes on the right side of the dialog box are for entering the relationship between the three time units.
Labor Assignment Rule	Specify the tie-breaking rule for deciding which workcenter to attend.
Use Setup Saving Algorithm	Force the scheduler to run together jobs requiring the same setup process.
Length of Simulation	Enter the length of simulation.
Computations	Specify whether you wish only the theoretical utilization to be computed and reported or whether the simulation is to be run and reported.
Trace Workcenters	Choose the workcenters whose queues will be traced during the simulation and plotted at the end of a successful run.
Select Products for Calculations	The last task in problem specification is to choose the set of products you want the process to produce.

7.1 Time Units   (Parameters Dialog Box)

Item	Description
Time Units: Run/Setup Time Units	Choose the units in which setup and run times will be expressed. Minutes is the default value. This choice will be the units for *all* the setup and run times entered in the process recipes. The unit of choice will be automatically reflected in the header (row 11, columns F, G, I, and J). The time units selected are assumed to be the same for all products.
Time Units: Demand	Select the time units in which demand will be expressed, For example, 10 orders per day, 20 cars per month. The default value is months. The choice will affect the unit of Demand you entered in Column E, row 3, and will be shown in column G of the same row. The time units selected are assumed to be the same for all products.
Time Units: Simulation	Decide the units of time in which the length of simulation will be expressed. The default unit is years. The time unit for the simulation should be greater than the time units for the Demand. The time units selected are assumed to be the same for all products.
Conversion factors	The next two boxes on the right side of the dialog box are for entering the relationship between the three time units. Without these conversion factors, the computer does not know how to make the basic calculations to simulate the operating process. In the first of these boxes, enter the number of run time units in a demand time unit. For example, if the run time unit is in minutes and the demand time unit is in months, then enter the number of minutes in a month. The precalculated default values assume that there are 8 hours in a day, 5 days in a week, 4 weeks in a month, 48 weeks (12 months) in a year. In the second box, enter the number of demand time units in a simulation time unit (e.g., enter 12 if the demand time unit is a month and the simulation time unit is a year). The time units selected are assumed to be the same for all products.

7.2 Labor Assignment Rule and Setup Saving Rule (Parameters Dialog Box)

Labor Assignment Rule — Specify the tie-breaking rule for deciding which workcenter to attend in case labor is free and there are two (or more) workcenters that require the use of the same type of labor. The choices are to attend to either the workcenter with the longest queue or the workcenter with the greater (theoretically computed) utilization.

Use Setup Saving Algorithm — Force the scheduler to run together jobs requiring the same setup process. In order to activate this mechanism, the user should additionally activate setup saving for the workcenters in which this algorithm will be applied. A description of the algorithm is given in section 4.6; Use the Setup-Saving Algorithm.

7.3 Length of Simulation and Type of Computations (Parameters Dialog Box)

Length of Simulation — Enter the length of simulation. If the unit of simulation was a week, and you wish to simulate 50 weeks demand, enter the number 50.

Computations — Specify whether you wish only the theoretical utilization to be computed and reported or whether the simulation is to be run and reported.

The theoretical utilization numbers could be used to make adjustments prior to running a long simulation. HOM will not carry out a simulation if the utilization of any resource (workcenter or labor) exceeds 100 percent. In that case, the theoretical utilization values will be useful in determining the cause for the overutilization.

7.4 Tracing Queues at Workcenters (Parameters Dialog Box)

Trace Workcenters — Choose the workcenters whose queues will be traced during the simulation and plotted at the end of a successful run.

This is a useful device for understanding the buildup and reduction of work at key workcenters. HOM has the capability of plotting up to 2,000 points on a graph. Thus, the trace will be for the last 2,000 points if the number of values exceeds 2,000. This is quite likely to happen during a long simulation.

7.5 Select Products for Calculations (Parameters Dialog Box)

Choose the set of products that you wish to produce. This option allows the user to carry out sensitivity analysis by running the simulation with a variety of product mixes.

The names of the products are selected by clicking on them using the mouse. Names in blue are the products currently selected. Names shown in white are the names of products that have not been selected.

8. RUN PROBLEM

In order to run a previously specified problem, you need only to click on the Run icon or the Run item on the command line. Simulation is a very CPU-intensive process. The run time could be several minutes to even hours on a Pentium machine. We recommend that you save the data before commencing the run.

We also recommend that the run time be gradually increased (after starting out with a small value for the length of simulation) until you are satisfied with the results. Long simulations also produce long trace files. If the available disk space is inadequate, the simulation will be terminated with a suitable error message.

9. RESULTS

After a successful run, the results will be displayed. If only the theoretical utilization is computed, the results will not include any simulated values. The results include

1. Two bar graphs, one each for workcenters and labor types, showing the theoretical versus simulated values of utilization (%).
2. A table of the theoretical versus the simulated values of resource (workcenter as well as labor) utilization (%).
3. For each workcenter, the average number of jobs in queue, the average number of units at the workcenter, the maximum number of units at the workcenter, and the unavoidable delay due to waiting for labor or material are shown.

    A job could be either a part or the whole of a customer order. Number of units at a workcenter is the number of units in all jobs at a workcenter (whether in queue or under process). In the bakery example, the unit was ½ dozen cookies. The number of units is then expressed as the total number of ½ dozen cookies either waiting to be processed or under process at a workcenter. The unavoidable delay is the delay due to unavailability of labor or the delay due to waiting for material to arrive. The latter is caused by the program's attempt to make the lot size as close as possible to the maximum number of units that can be processed at the workcenter without an additional setup; see Type of Processing.
4. For each product, the average and standard deviation of the flow time are given. The time unit for reporting the flow time is the unit chosen by the user for the setup and run time. The quantity produced of each product during the length of the simulation is also reported in number of units (i.e., number of ½ dozen cookies in our bakery example).

    Notice that orders can be split and processed in lots due to the fact that the maximum number of units that can be processed at a time at some workcenter may be smaller than the order size for the product. Therefore, the order might not be delivered in one complete whole (in the order size) at a time to the customer. The order may be delivered in one or more lots. In order to cope with this phenomenon, HOM computes flow time based on weighting the flow time by the quantity produced. For example, if the customer orders two dozen cookies, one dozen of which are delivered in 26 minutes and the rest in 36 minutes, then the weighted average flow time is 30 minutes.
5. The flow time distribution is reported for each product. The distribution is given as a table containing 10 class interval values and the fraction of units of the product that experienced a flow time less than or equal to the right endpoint of the class interval. This is a cumulative distribution of the flow time. If the user desires, these values can be copied using the EDIT --> Copy command and pasted for further analysis or plotting in a commercial spreadsheet program. See section 11 on exporting and importing.

10. MODELING VARIABILITY

SCV stands for the squared coefficient of variation, which is defined as the ratio of the variance to the square of the mean. The SCV must be nonnegative. The larger the value of the SCV, the greater the variability in processing (or interarrival) times. If the SCV is set to zero, then the associated processing times will be deterministic (no variability). If it is set to one, it will correspond to exponential processing times. Values greater than one will correspond to larger variability. The value of the SCV is used by the program to sample from an appropriate mixture of a constant (deterministic) and an exponential distribution.

11. EXPORT AND IMPORT OF DATA AS WELL AS RESULTS

HOM has the ability to export final and interim results to a spreadsheet or word processing program. To do this, you should have run and obtained results and must be in the Results window. Use the Edit function on the menu bar to copy the results, and then switch to the spreadsheet program and paste to export the results.

To import data into the HOM spreadsheet from your favorite spreadsheet program, simply copy the data from the spreadsheet, switch over to HOM, and paste it into the desired location.

Exporting/importing to a spreadsheet will also allow you to do more complex mathematical operations to your data, if you so desire, or create more elaborate graphs, and so forth.

12. SUMMARY OF PROCESSING SEQUENCE

1. Based on the input data, the program first creates an output showing the data input by the user.

2. The program calculates resource and labor utilization *assuming* that the lot size is equal to the minimum of the order size and the maximum size allowed by the resource. This value is simply an approximation, and simulated utilization values are later displayed. However, for practical purposes, the utilization computed in this fashion should be very close to the simulated utilization.

3. The program keeps track of the time during which resources are idling due to lack of materials (i.e., when a workcenter postpones the processing of a job, preferring to wait for more of the same order to arrive at the workcenter to better utilize the machine) or waiting for labor. The percentage of "unavoidable" idle time is reported. This time can be avoided by adding more labor or increasing the maximum size permitted (see section 4.2).

4. Customer orders arrive as per the random interarrival times specified by the user. They are given an order number (i.e., an ID). Each order has an order size equal to the value input for that type of product.

5. Each resource has a queue associated with it, and jobs wait in the queue until they are taken up for processing.

6. The program keeps track of customer orders as they flow through the shop. In particular, information on the number of units in the order that are still at previous processing steps is maintained. The program also keeps track of the time taken to flow through the shop.

7. When a resource falls idle, or when labor becomes available, or when an order either arrives or departs from a processing step, the program checks to see whether another job can be scheduled.

   7.1 The scheduling rules when a labor type becomes free:

   7.1.1 If the option of attending the longest queue has been chosen, then the workcenter queues are scanned in the order of decreasing number of waiting jobs— that is, highest priority is given to try and schedule the resource with the largest number of waiting jobs.

   7.1.2 If the option of attending the workcenter with the maximum utilization first has been chosen, then the workcenters are scanned in the descending order of machine utilization. The theoretical value of the utilization is used for this purpose.

   7.2 In order to schedule a job, a machine must be available, the correct type of labor must be available, and the job must be of sufficient size. Jobs are scanned in decreasing value of priority (priority is set at the level of products). Jobs further along the processing sequence are given higher priority (compared to jobs of the same product but lower down the processing sequence).

   7.2.1 If setup saving has not been activated for this workcenter, then a job is taken up for processing if it satisfies the priority rules, a machine of the right type is available, and the right type of labor is available, <u>and</u> (i) the number of units in the job is greater than or equal to the lot size for the resource <u>or</u> (ii) if the order size is less than the lot size, the entire order is available for processing.

7.2.2 Else, the workcenter operator looks down the queue of waiting jobs and selects the order for processing that requires the same setup process as the order just processed at a machine. This would save the time required to reset the machine if a different order type or process step was run in between two similar jobs. When setup saving is activated, the priority of products is ignored. In case a similar setup cannot be performed, the scheduling rule reverts to the product priority–based scheduling rules described above.

7.3 If a job does not satisfy any of the rules, then it waits in the queue and other jobs are scanned for scheduling.

7.4 The computation of processing times is as follows: (i) If the machine is either of the One Unit at a Time or Batch type of processing, then (a) the job finishes its processing after = maximum(machine's setup time, labor setup time) + maximum(machine run time, labor run time); (b) the machine is set free after = maximum(machine's setup time, labor setup time) + machine run time; (c) the labor becomes free after = labor setup time + labor run time. There is a slight inconsistency between (a) (b) and (c), but this usually does not create too much distortion from our experience in running the simulations. (ii) If the machine is of the continuous flow type, then (a) the job finishes its processing after = maximum(machine's setup time, labor setup time) + machine run time; (b) the machine is set free after = maximum(machine's setup time, labor setup time) + machine run time; the labor becomes free after = labor setup time. Note that the job has to flow through the machine for a fixed time = the run time of the machine. The machine is *busy* while the job is being loaded. The labor is *busy* when doing the loading.

8. Once a job has finished its processing it departs. It may depart from the system or go to the next step of processing, as the case might be. Jobs progress through the shop and leave as soon as all processing steps are complete. Customer orders do not wait to be completed to leave the system. For example, an order of size = 40 may be split into 2 lots according to the processing rules. Each lot will depart on its own. The flow time reported is a weighted average per unit—that is, it equals the flow time weighted by the number of units in the job.

9. Once a processing step has been completed, machine and labor are set free (Freemachine and Freelabor).

10. At the end of simulation, reports are generated by using the statistics generated during the simulation.

13. HINTS AND COMMON MISTAKES FOR THIS APPLICATION

13.1 Error Messages

If the input data was entered incorrectly, or the data integrity rules were not followed, the simulation will not be run. An appropriate error message will be given. Follow the directions in the message to correct the situation.

If the simulation aborts for some reason, please note down the error message that appears on the screen. Usually the cause for the program to abort execution is that some resource(s) or labor category(ies) are being heavily utilized or due to machine interference (due to the same labor type attending more than one workcenter). This (in extreme cases) causes the data to exceed the allowed maximum size (dimension) in the simulation program.

If the program stops execution (after clearing all data integrity checks), it will give a report on the utilization. If you see a resource or labor category over 100 percent utilization, add more resources, or change the product routing.

If the simulated values of utilization do not correspond to the theoretical values, or to your expectations, then the problem could be due either to machine interference (see example in section 14) or to the fact that the setup time for the machine is modeled as the maximum of the setup time for the labor and the setup time for the machine. Please see modeling hints given below.

13.2 Modeling Hints

Alternate Routes: A method for modeling alternate routes for the same product is to create two or more products with changes in the processing steps. For example, there are both manual and CNC drilling machines in the shop. There is only a single product with demand = 200/day. You have chosen to do a particular step (say #15) on the CNC drilling machine though it can be also done on the manual drill. The program aborts and shows that the CNC drilling machine's utilization is 150 percent whereas the manual drill has a utilization of 15 percent. You can correct this imbalance by creating two products: each, say, with demand = 100/day (total = original demand), but one of the products uses the CNC whereas the other uses the manual drill to do this step (#15).

Order Size: By specifying three different order sizes for the "same" product, we can create some degree of variation in the order size. This method allows the user to set different priorities for customers with different order sizes. In other cases, order size could be used to emulate small, medium, and large orders, for example, 10, 100, and 1,000 circuit boards, with the single circuit board being the basic "unit." The next item to be specified is the demand for the product. Alternate routing, rework, and scrap can also be modeled by creating multiple products, each with a different routing.

Priority Queues: The hint given above can be used to model a single or multistage priority queueing system. Please see discussions given below.

Setup Time: The time to setup essentially becomes the maximum of the machine and labor setup times. The run time for the product becomes the maximum of the machine and labor run times. This could create a dramatic change in the utilization and flow times! For example, even if setup times were deterministic, if the labor setup time (say 10 min.) exceeds that of the machine (6 min.), then the machine will be idle longer than what the user might anticipate. This would in turn increase the machine utilization. This problem becomes heightened when the setup times are random variables. It is useful to remember that the expected value of the setup time in this case no longer equals the maximum of the two expected values, viz., expected value of the setup time and expected value of the run time. One solution would be to ensure that the labor setup time is smaller (and, if random, much smaller) than the machine setup time. Also see the examples given in section 14.

Continuous Flow: Continuous flow processing can be mimicked by specifying a large number of "one at a time" machines. For an example, see the "cool" workcenter given in section 14.1.

Modeling Atypical Machines: Some machines exist that do not conform to the previous definitions (section 4) and that cannot be explicitly modeled in this version of HOM. One such machine is a batch machine that allows for interruption and replacement. Consider a pizza oven big enough for six pies. Clearly, once the oven reaches its cooking temperature, pies can be added at any time as long as there is a place to put them. Another such machine is one that makes its own inventory. A coffee brewer makes a batch of coffee (i.e., 8–12 cups) that is then poured to fill sequential orders until the reservoir (inventory) is consumed and another pot needs to be brewed.

Both of these machines can be "approximately" modeled in HOM by utilizing N one-at-a-time machines where N is the physical capacity of the current batch machine being modeled. An 8-cup automatic coffee pot takes 8 minutes to load and brew. The ½ minute to pour each cup would be approximated by 8 one-at-a-time machines each with a setup time of one minute and a run time of ½ minute. Similar assumptions would be made about setup labor. A six-pie pizza oven that takes 6 minutes to load and 18 minutes to bake could be approximated by 6 one-at-a-time machines with a setup time of 1 minute and run times of 18 minutes. The accuracy of these assumptions depends on the performance measure in use. They will give better results for utilization than for flow times. Modeling processes is an art form that is improved with experimentation and ingenuity.

13.3 Data Entry Hints

You cannot insert a row in the process recipe. Therefore, if you forget to include a step in the recipe, you must use the cut, copy, and paste spreadsheet operations to create an empty row for entering the forgotten step.

You can copy and paste the entire process recipe for a product by selecting and copying just the process recipe portion of the data spreadsheet of, say, Product A, switching to Product B by double-clicking on its name in the Product column, and pasting the information in the appropriate location.

Once you have become proficient with HOM: Process Analysis, you can skip the initial naming of workcenters and labor types and directly proceed to the Process Recipe step. Each time you enter a new name in the process recipe, you can answer Yes (to whether to add the workcenter or labor to the database) and enter the workcenter or labor data.

A possible solution *available for* replacing the default SCV globally would be to *delete* the workcenter. This will delete the *name* of the workcenter and not the setup or run times in the process recipe. Reenter the name of the workcenter and a new value of the default SCV. Enter the name of the workcenter once again in *all* process recipes that use this workcenter. The SCV values will be *replaced* by the default SCV. The flip side of this operation is that any SCV value that you have entered in the process recipe will be overwritten. A third alternative is to Edit the workcenter. Change its default SCV values. Copy the name of the workcenter using the Edit function. Then paste this name wherever you wish the new default values to take effect.

14. EXAMPLES

Note: The results will change from run to run because of the way random numbers are generated within HOM.

14.1 Cookie-Making Example

We model a *deterministic* process for making custom-baked cookies; that is, all SCVs are zero. We assume that

Number of products	:	1
Order size	:	1 dozen
Demand per day	:	44

Workcenters :

Name	Type	Number of Machines	Maximum Number of Dozen Cookies That Can Be Processed Without Additional Setup
MIXSPOON	One at a time	1	3
OVEN	Batch	1	1
COOL	One at a time	100	1
PACK	One at a time	1	1
PAY	Batch	1	100

Labor :

Name	Number of Workers
Baker	1
Helper	1
Dummy	100

Process Recipe :

Process Step	Name of Workcenter	Wrkcntr Avg. Setup Time/Lot (MIN)	Wrkcntr Avg. Run Time/Unit (MIN)	Type of Labor	Labor Avg. Setup Time (MIN)	Labor Avg. Run Time (MIN)
MIX&SPOON	MIXSPOON	6	2	Baker	6	2
BAKE	OVEN	10	0	Baker	1	0
COOL	COOL	0	5	Dummy	0	0
PACK	PACK	0	2	Helper	0	2
PAY	PAY	1	0	Helper	1	0

Some of the data entry screens are shown below during the data entry stage. The data file is COOKIE.DAT.

Screen 1: Add Product dialog box (has to be the first step).

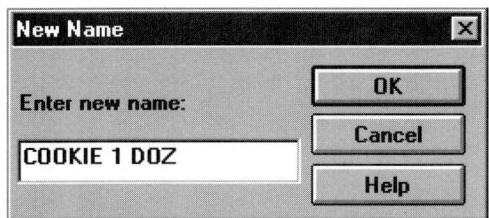

Screen 2: Entry of Workcenter data for MIXSPOON.

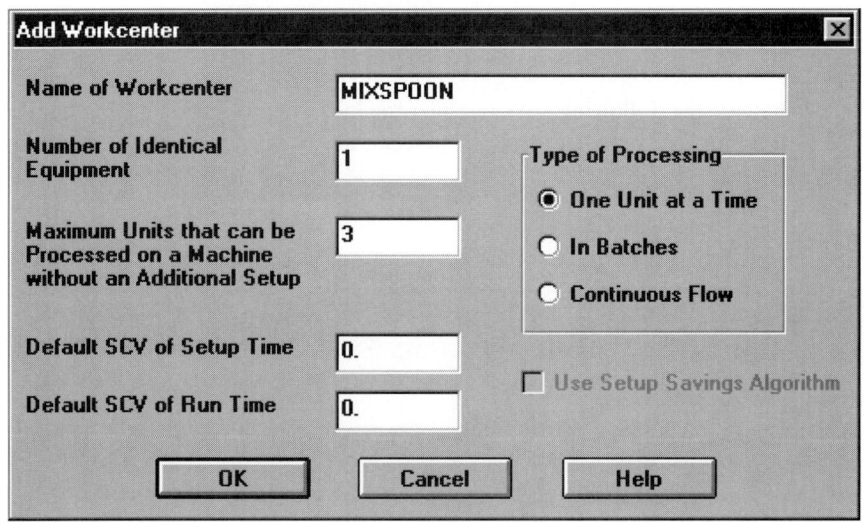

Screen 3: Entry of Labor Type Data for Baker.

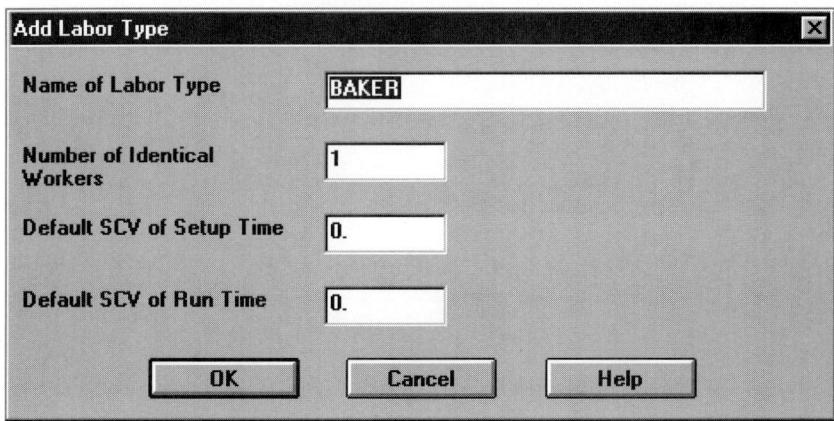

Screen 4: Parameters Dialog box

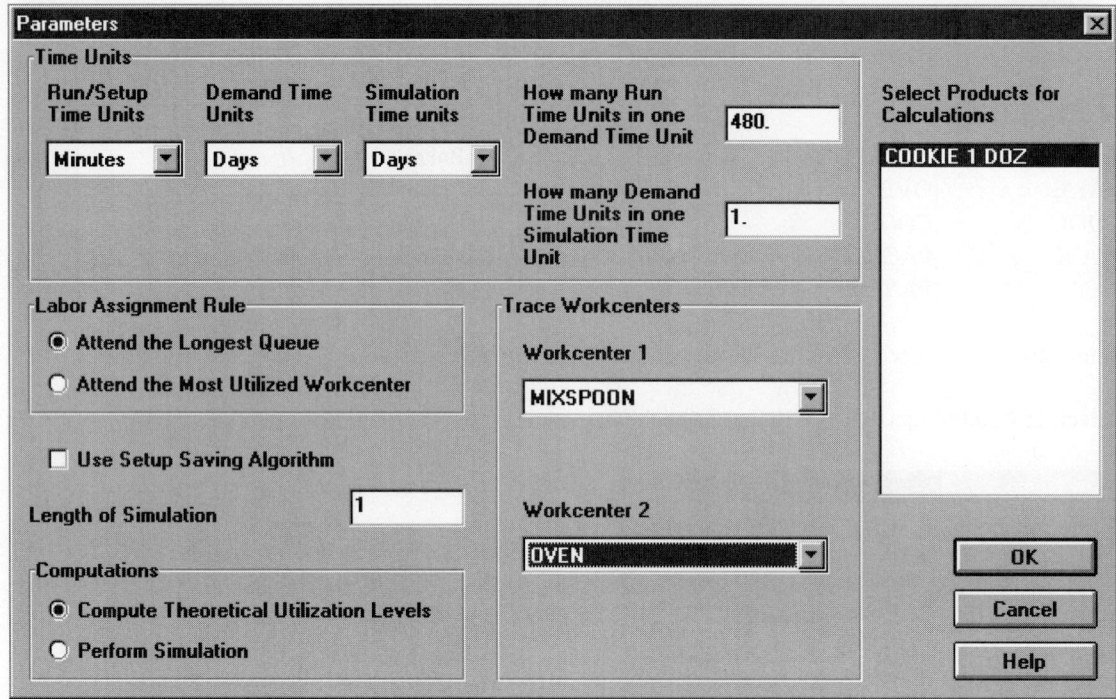

Notice the choice of time units as well as the conversion factors. We have asked HOM to trace the queues at two workcenters, MIXSPOON and OVEN.

On running HOM with these choices, the following text output (graphics suppressed using the Series command) was produced. The utilization levels are less than 100 percent, thus we can go to the second step of running the simulation.

Process Analysis Calculations

Theoretical Utilization (%)

Workcenter Name	Utilization
MIXSPOON	73.333
OVEN	91.667
COOL	0.45833
PACK	18.333
PAY	9.1667

Labor Type Name	Utilization
BAKER	82.5
DUMMY	0
HELPER	27.5

(The output was copied using the Edit --> Copy command and pasted into this file.)

The result of the simulation for one day is shown below. (The Perform Simulation radio button should be selected instead of Compute Theoretical Utilization Levels.)

Process Analysis Calculations

Utilization (%)

Workcenter Name	Theoretical Utilization	Simulated Utilization
MIXSPOON	73.333	71.667
OVEN	91.667	88.106
COOL	0.45833	0.43504
PACK	18.333	17.083
PAY	9.1667	8.5416

Labor Type Name	Theoretical Utilization	Simulated Utilization
BAKER	82.5	80.625
DUMMY	0	0
HELPER	27.5	25.625

Simulation Results

Workcenter Name	Average Jobs In Queue	Avg. Num. At Workcenter	Maximum Num. In Queue	Unavoidable Delay
MIXSPOON	0	0.71667	1	0
OVEN	0	0.87708	1	0
COOL	0	0.43106	1	0
PACK	0	0.17083	1	0
PAY	0	0.085417	1	0

** Unavoidable delay is due to waiting for labor or material.

Product Name	Average Flow Time	Std. Dev. of Flow Time	Quantity Produced
COOKIE 1 DOZ	26	0	41

Product Flow Time Distribution

COOKIE 1 DOZ

Left End Point (T1)	Right End Point (T2)	Fraction of Jobs w/Flow Time <= T2
26	26	1

The trace of queues has been cut along with the bar graphs showing the utilization.
The two traces are shown below:

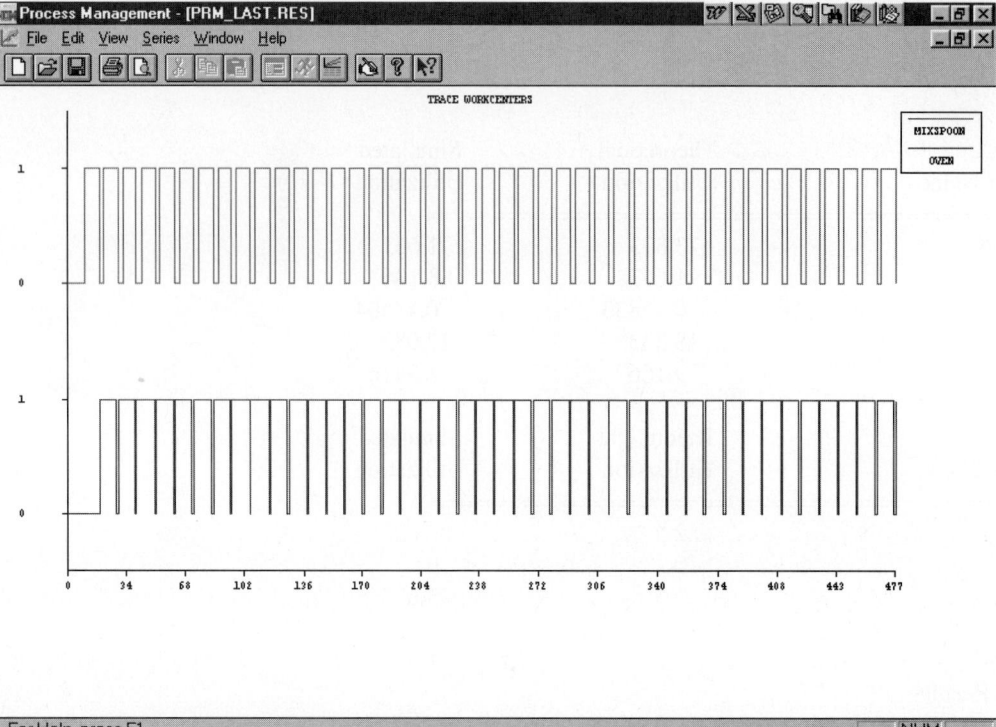

14.2 Cookie-Making Example—Variations

The following variations of this example can be created:

1. Instead of the orders arriving in a deterministic manner, the SCV of demand has been changed to 1 in the file COOKIE1.DAT. You will notice that the queue at the oven will be built up and that the system is unstable!

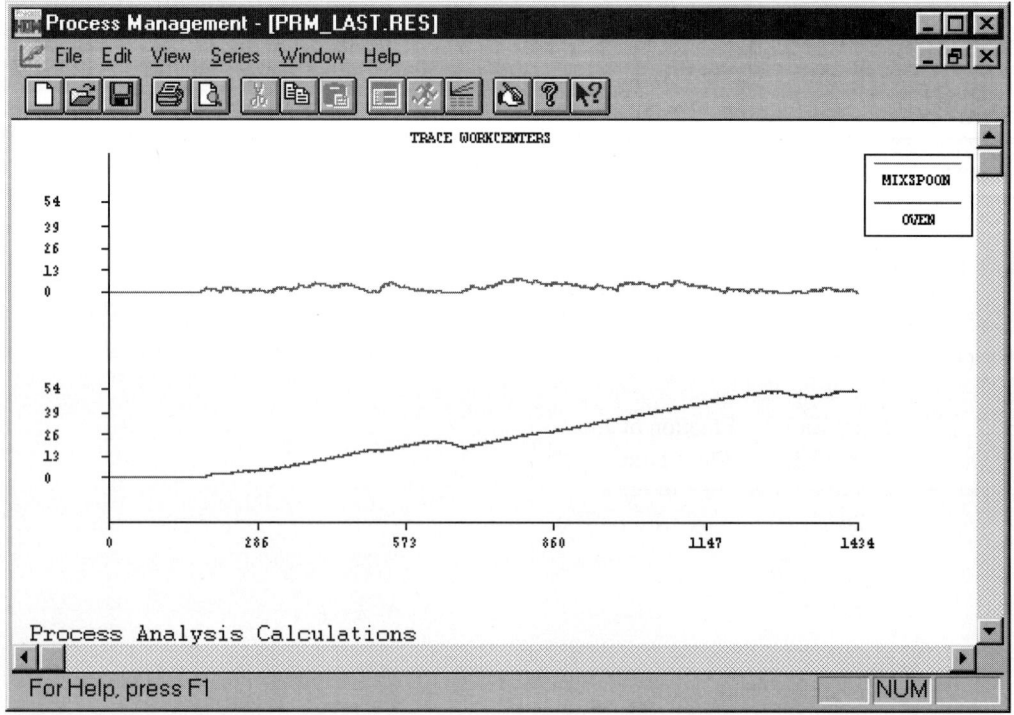

This is due to a phenomenon called *machine interference*. Notice that the unavoidable delay at the OVEN is in excess of 27 percent. The problem arises because the Baker is also heavily utilized, and therefore cannot be in two places (the MIXSPOON and the OVEN) at the same time. A simple solution would be to assign the Baker's work to the Helper so far as the loading of the oven is concerned. See COOKIE2.DAT for this solution. Now the system becomes stable. The traces are given below.

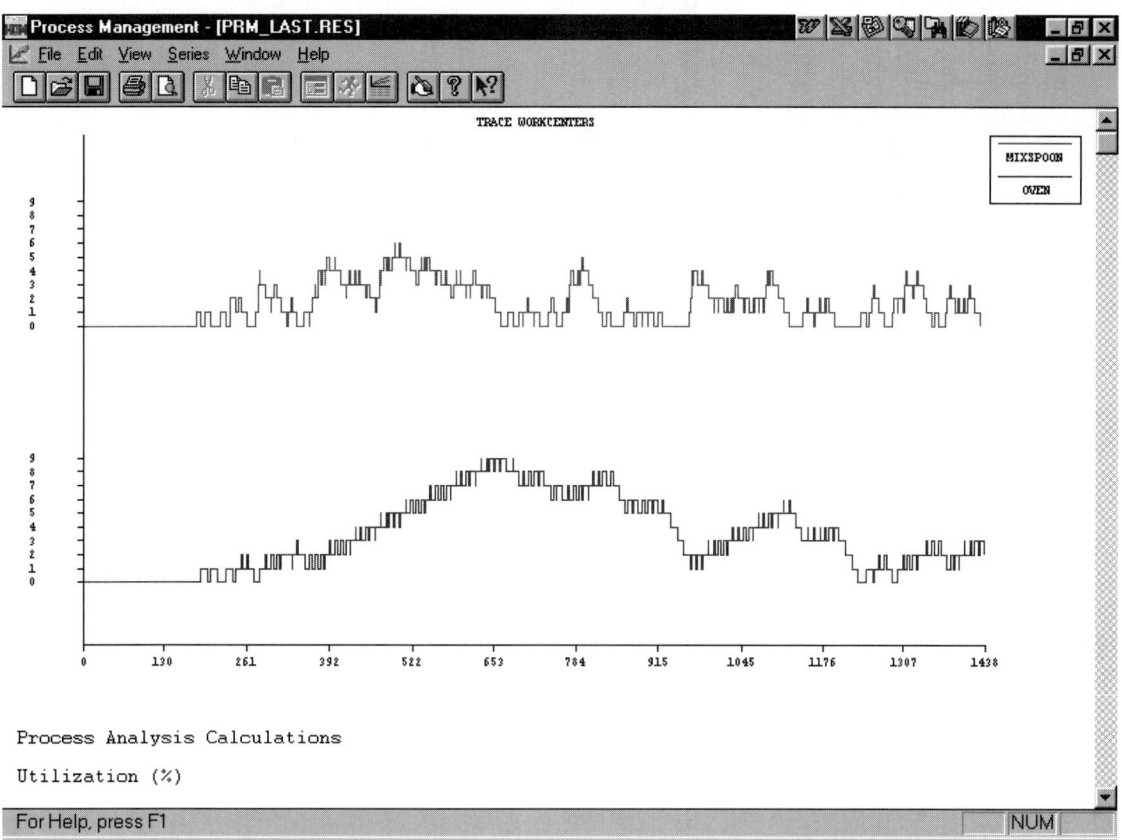

Another simple solution is to activate the setup saving-algorithm at MIXSPOON. This essentially eliminates the setup time at this workcenter. The algorithm has to be first activated in the Parameters dialog box and then for the MIXSPOON workcenter; the data file is COOKIE3.DAT. This action eliminates the setup time at MIX&SPOON and thus frees up the Baker to handle both operations without causing unnecessary idle time. (You will also notice that the simulated and the theoretical values of the utilization of MIXSPOON are very different from one another, 16.91 percent against 73.33 percent. This is due to setup savings.) The traces are shown below.

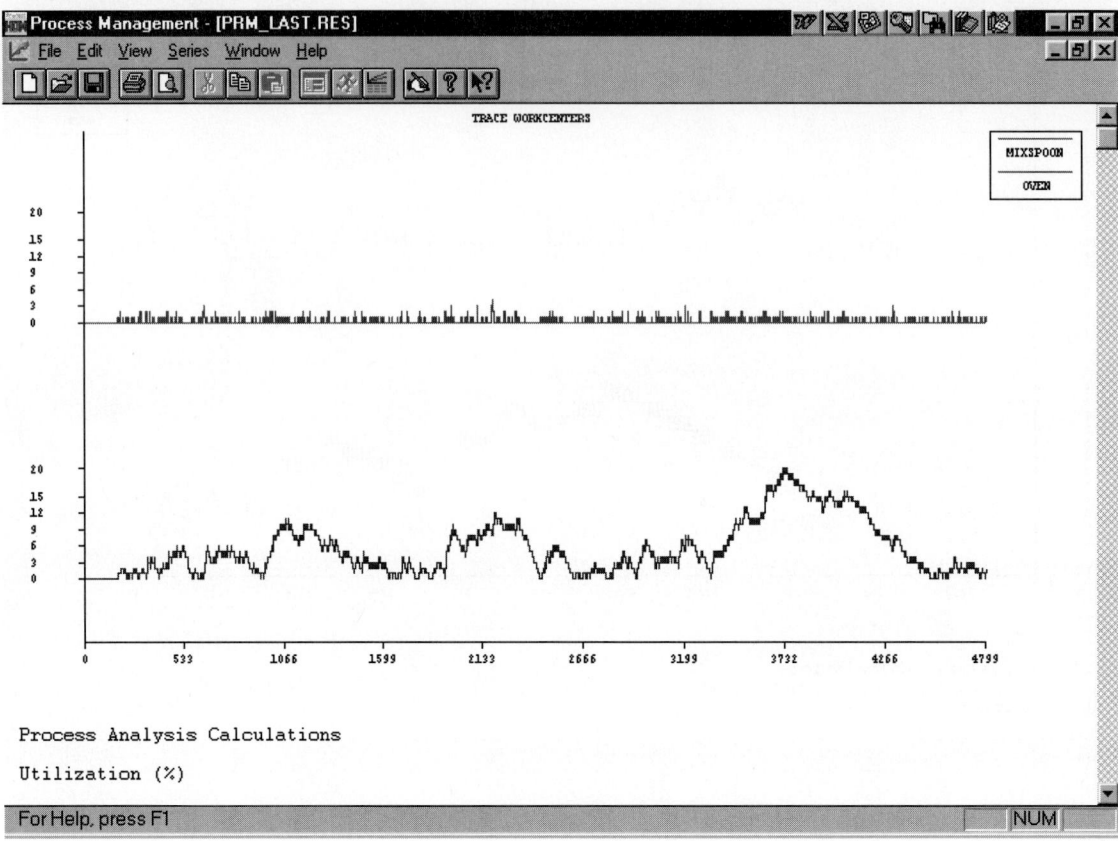

2. A second modeling variation has been created in COOKIE4.DAT. In this example, a second product has been introduced. This product models orders for two dozen cookies. The process recipe is identical to that used to make orders of a dozen cookies. The user could experiment the effect of product mix variation (by changing the demand values) as well as priority for the products (the priority for both types of orders has been set equal to 100 presently).

14.3 Circuit Board Manufacturing

The file CIRCUIT.DAT contains an example of circuit board manufacturing. There are three types of products, representing small, medium, and large orders. The process recipes are almost identical for the three products, except that the large product uses CNC machines. The priority for small orders is the highest (1). The priority has been set equal to 100 for the remaining types of orders. Demand as well as all processing times are deterministic (SCV = 0).

This model can be used to carry out complex what-if analyses, such as what happens if demand is no longer deterministic, what is the impact of setting different product priorities, what happens if the maximum lot size is reduced on some workcenters, what is the "best" number of workers, can small orders be given high priority while large orders are quoted with a delivery leadtime of 1 month, and so forth.

14.4 The M/M/1 Queue with Priority

The file MM1.DAT contains the data for an M/M/1 queue with two types of customers. The arrival rate of each class of customers is 0.4 customer per minute. The average machine run time is 1 min., while the setup time is zero. There is zero labor run time or setup time. (We could as well have modeled this as zero run and setup time for the machine, and average run time for labor equal to 1 minute. It is important to observe that the run time cannot be positive for both machine and labor—please see section 4.5 for the consequences of making the run time greater than zero for both types of resources.) The system models an M/M/1 queue because the SCV of demand as well as the machine run time have been set equal to one. Therefore, HOM will use an exponential distribution for generating the interarrival time as well as the run time; see section 10.

If both classes are given the same priority, the system behaves like an M/M/1 queue with arrival rate = 0.4 + 0.4 = 0.8 customer per minute. The performance measures for the two customer classes are given below (simulation length = 200 days). The two classes are called CUSTOMER and CUSTOMER1.

Process Analysis Calculations

Utilization (%)

Workcenter Name	Theoretical Util. (%)	Simulated Util. (%)
Q	80	79.823

Labor Type Name	Theoretical Util. (%)	Simulated Util. (%)
L	0	0

Simulation Results

Workcenter Name	Average Jobs In Queue	Avg. Num. At Workcenter	Maximum Num. In Queue	Unavoidable Delay (%)
Q	3.2272	4.025	34	0.13758

** Unavoidable delay is due to waiting for labor or material.

Product Name	Average Flow Time	Std. Dev. of Flow Time	Quantity Produced
CUSTOMER	5.0358	5.1680	38577
CUSTOMER1	4.9998	5.0319	38444

Product Flow Time Distribution
CUSTOMER

Left End Point (T1)	Right End Point (T2)	Fraction of Jobs w/Flow Time <= T2
0.00010967	4.3661	0.58444
4.3661	8.7322	0.82816
8.7322	13.098	0.92449
13.098	17.464	0.96508
17.464	21.83	0.98281
21.83	26.196	0.99204
26.196	30.562	0.99736
30.562	34.928	0.99917
34.928	39.294	0.99974
39.294	43.66	1

CUSTOMER1

Left End Point (T1)	Right End Point (T2)	Fraction of Jobs w/Flow Time <= T2
8.0109e-005	4.3988	0.5848
4.3988	8.7976	0.83176
8.7976	13.196	0.92803
13.196	17.595	0.96847
17.595	21.994	0.98517
21.994	26.393	0.99412
26.393	30.791	0.998
30.791	35.19	0.99948
35.19	39.589	0.9999
39.589	43.988	1

Notice that the performance measures are almost identical for both customer classes and coincide with those in an M/M/1 queue that has an utilization of 0.8 (i.e., 80 percent). Modify the model such that the class CUSTOMER has priority of 1 (i.e., higher priority with respect to CUSTOMER1). (The user has to modify the model.) The output is shown below (simulation length = 200 days).

Process Analysis Calculations

Utilization (%)

Workcenter Name	Theoretical Util. (%)	Simulated Util. (%)
Q	80	79.645

Labor Type Name	Theoretical Util. (%)	Simulated Util. (%)
L	0	0

Simulation Results

Workcenter Name	In Queue	Workcenter	In Queue	Delay (%)
Q	3.2094	4.0054	40	0.11956

** Unavoidable delay is due to waiting for labor or material.

Product Name	Average Flow Time	Std. Dev. of Flow Time	Quantity Produced
CUSTOMER	2.3178	1.9077	38224
CUSTOMER1	7.7027	9.6392	38427

Product Flow Time Distribution

CUSTOMER

Left End Point (T1)	Right End Point (T2)	Fraction of Jobs w/Flow Time <= T2
2.1219e-005	1.9376	0.52365
1.9376	3.8753	0.82741
3.8753	5.8129	0.94292
5.8129	7.7505	0.98148
7.7505	9.6881	0.99411
9.6881	11.626	0.99833
11.626	13.563	0.99948
13.563	15.501	0.99992
15.501	17.439	0.99995
17.439	19.376	1

CUSTOMER1

Left End Point (T1)	Right End Point (T2)	Fraction of Jobs w/Flow Time <= T2
0.00013828	7.8772	0.68038
7.8772	15.754	0.85809
15.754	23.631	0.92911
23.631	31.509	0.96526
31.509	39.386	0.98098
39.386	47.263	0.98964
47.263	55.14	0.99584
55.14	63.017	0.99852
63.017	70.894	0.99961
70.894	78.771	1

The class CUSTOMER now has smaller delay, whereas the class CUSTOMER1 has larger delay. The average delay of the two classes is the "same."

14.5 A Tandem Queue Example

The file TANDEM.DAT has the data for a five-stage queueing system. The data is shown below, along with the theoretical utilization levels for the five stages. The interarrival and service time distributions are exponential. There are 1, 2, 4, 1, and 1 servers at the five stages.

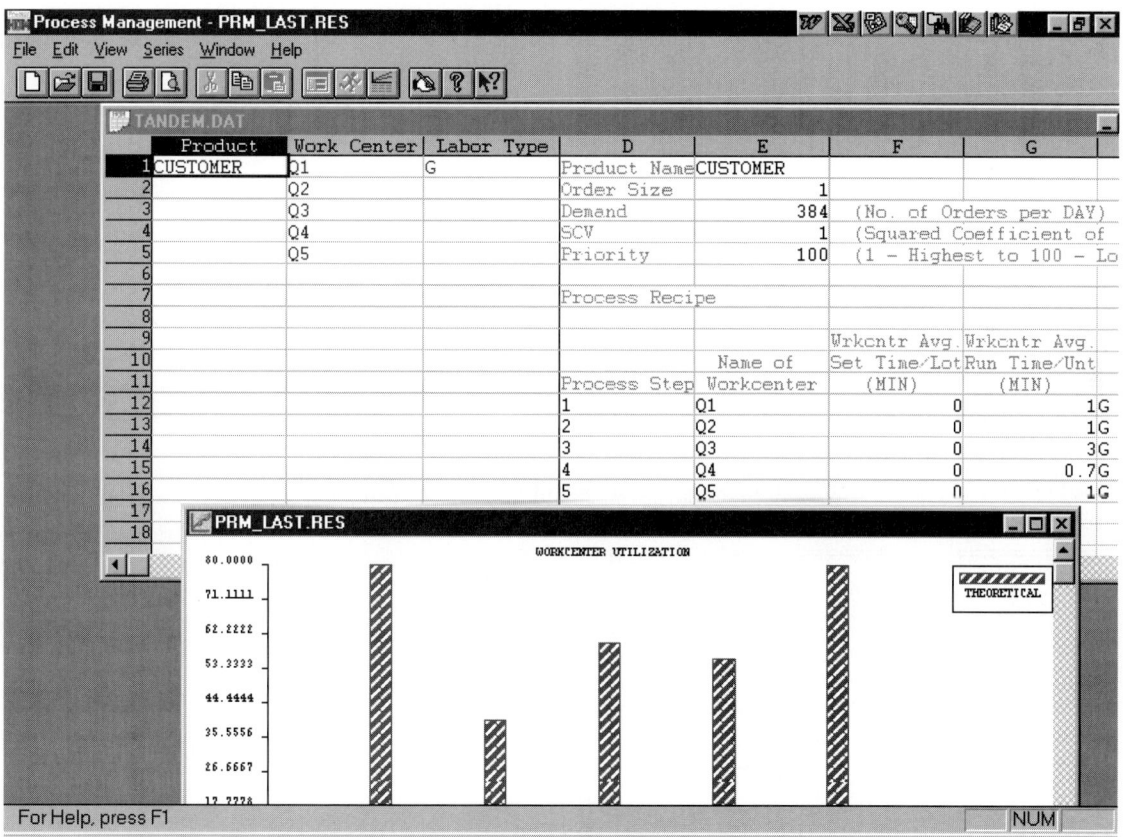

The output for this example is given below (for a simulation length of 200 days).

Process Analysis Calculations

Utilization (%)

Workcenter Name	Theoretical Util. (%)	Simulated Util. (%)
Q1	80	80.046
Q2	40	39.959
Q3	60	59.747
Q4	56	55.904
Q5	80	80.186

Labor Type Name	Theoretical Util. (%)	Simulated Util. (%)
G	0	0.019732

Simulation Results

Workcenter Name	Average Jobs In Queue	Avg. Num. At Workcenter	Maximum Num. In Queue	Unavoidable Delay (%)
Q1	3.2455	4.0438	38	0
Q2	0.15875	0.95849	11	0
Q3	0.42328	2.8147	21	0
Q4	0.72564	1.2846	19	0
Q5	3.2434	4.043	45	0

** Unavoidable delay is due to waiting for labor or material.

Product Name	Average Flow Time	Std. Dev. of Flow Time	Quantity Produced
CUSTOMER	16.416	8.3138	76913

Product Flow Time Distribution

CUSTOMER

Left End Point (T1)	Right End Point (T2)	Fraction of Jobs w/Flow Time <= T2
0	7.9376	0.11674
7.9376	15.875	0.53014
15.875	23.813	0.8187
23.813	31.75	0.94184
31.75	39.688	0.9859
39.688	47.626	0.99666
47.626	55.563	0.99898
55.563	63.501	0.99974
63.501	71.438	0.99996
71.438	79.376	1

For this system, it turns out that each stage behaves like an M/M/C queue, with the number of servers C = 1, 2, 4, 1, and 1. The expected number of customers at the five stages can be determined using the HOM: Waiting Line Management module, and are 4, 0.952, 2.831, 1.273, and 4, respectively. These numbers compare well with the simulated values.

14.6 An Example of Underwriting

There are four products, RUNS, RAPS, RAINS, and RERUNS, in this model. The products are produced in four processing steps. The data as given in the HOM file models the demand for the four products from *three* different regions. The demand from each region is identified using a number after the name of the four products, e.g., RUNS1, RUNS2, and RUNS3. Thus there are twelve products in the model. The process flow is nearly identical for all the products except that the underwriting is done by three different underwriters, one for each region. All products except RAPS851, RAPS852, and RAPS853 go through the same four steps of processing, namely, DISTRIBUTION, UNDERWRITE, RATE, and WRITE. Fifteen percent of the demand for RAPS goes to WRITE, after the RATE step. In contrast, 85 percent of the demand for RAPS leaves the system after RATE. This difference in route is modeled using three products, RAPS851, RAPS852, and RAPS853. The region 1 demand for the RAPS product has been allocated in the proportion 15:85 to the products RAPS151:RAPS851 (similarly RAPS152:RAPS852, RAPS153:RAPS853). The product RERUNS has the lowest priority. All the other products have the same priority.

The model as setup in HOM shows that UNDERWRITE3 is overloaded; see below for the theoretical utilization.

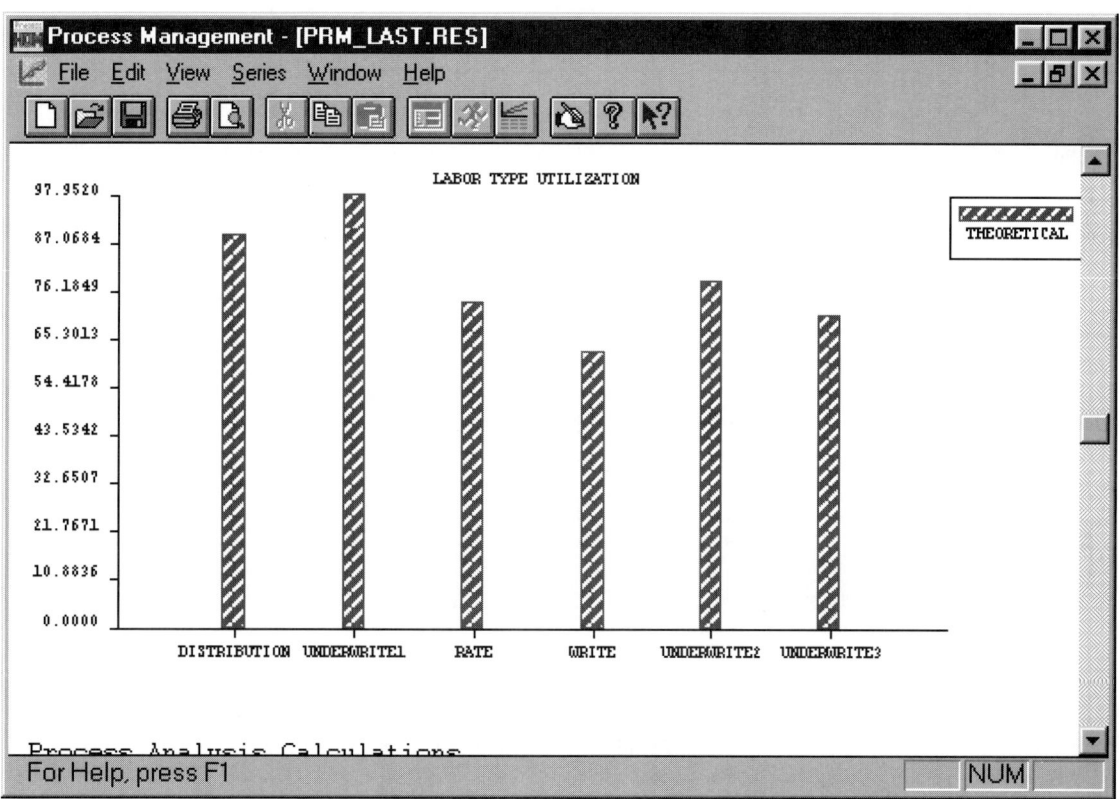

The simulation results for a year's operation are shown below.

Process Analysis Calculations

Utilization (%)

Workcenter Name	Theoretical Util. (%)	Simulated Util. (%)
DISTRIBUTION	0	0
UNDERWRITE1	0	0
RATE	0	0
WRITE	0	0
UNDERWRITE2	0	0
UNDERWRITE3	0	0

Labor Type Name	Theoretical Util. (%)	Simulated Util. (%)
DISTRIBUTION	89.596	87.937
UNDERWRITE1	97.952	95.180
RATE	74.183	72.183
WRITE	62.715	60.702
UNDERWRITE2	78.989	79.365
UNDERWRITE3	70.891	69.341

Simulation Results

Workcenter Name	Average Jobs In Queue	Avg. Num. At Workcenter	Maximum Num. In Queue	Unavoidable Delay (%)
DISTRIBUTION	6.0564	9.5728	60	0
UNDERWRITE1	22.938	23.886	67	0
RATE	0.77382	6.5484	26	0
WRITE	0.22841	3.2635	12	0
UNDERWRITE2	2.7122	3.5055	26	0
UNDERWRITE3	1.3248	2.0181	13	0

** Unavoidable delay is due to waiting for labor or material.

Product Name	Average Flow Time	Std. Dev. of Flow Time	Quantity Produced
RUNS1	371.08	114.03	322
RAPS151	378.27	112.11	173
RAPS851	291.72	109.48	1016
RAINS1	305.3	110.95	400
RERUNS1	2219.7	1599.1	1199
RUNS2	308.71	62.963	202
RAPS152	291.68	54.305	115
RAPS852	237.7	67.233	727
RAINS2	242.8	58.189	246
RERUNS2	489.94	280.19	1637
RUNS3	307.92	73.048	185
RAPS153	311.75	76.158	106
RAPS853	224.58	54.087	736
RAINS3	233.96	49.357	234
RERUNS3	439.35	271.5	1166

Product Flow Time Distribution

RUNS1

Left End Point (T1)	Right End Point (T2)	Fraction of Jobs w/Flow Time <= T2
192.95	253.45	0.068323
253.45	313.95	0.38509
313.95	374.45	0.61491
374.45	434.95	0.76398
434.95	495.45	0.87888
495.45	555.94	0.93789
555.94	616.44	0.95031
616.44	676.94	0.96584
676.94	737.44	0.98758
737.44	797.94	1

RAPS151

Left End Point (T1)	Right End Point (T2)	Fraction of Jobs w/Flow Time <= T2
217.44	275.1	0.14451
275.1	332.76	0.45665
332.76	390.43	0.6474
390.43	448.09	0.80925
448.09	505.75	0.86127
505.75	563.42	0.90751
563.42	621.08	0.95376
621.08	678.75	0.97688
678.75	736.41	0.98844
736.41	794.07	1

RAPS851

Left End Point (T1)	Right End Point (T2)	Fraction of Jobs w/Flow Time <= T2
119.52	182.86	0.056102
182.86	246.19	0.43504
246.19	309.52	0.68799
309.52	372.85	0.81004
372.85	436.19	0.89075
436.19	499.52	0.93898
499.52	562.85	0.96457
562.85	626.18	0.98327
626.18	689.52	0.99508
689.52	752.85	1

RAINS1

Left End Point (T1)	Right End Point (T2)	Fraction of Jobs w/Flow Time <= T2
143.99	205.18	0.155
205.18	266.38	0.4825
266.38	327.58	0.68
327.58	388.78	0.7975
388.78	449.98	0.8775
449.98	511.17	0.93
511.17	572.37	0.96
572.37	633.57	0.9925
633.57	694.77	0.9975
694.77	755.97	1

RERUNS1

Left End Point (T1)	Right End Point (T2)	Fraction of Jobs w/Flow Time <= T2
153.6	875.13	0.25688
875.13	1596.7	0.42118
1596.7	2318.2	0.59216
2318.2	3039.7	0.69475
3039.7	3761.2	0.81818
3761.2	4482.8	0.90325
4482.8	5204.3	0.94662
5204.3	5925.8	0.97748
5925.8	6647.3	0.98666
6647.3	7368.9	1

RUNS2

Left End Point (T1)	Right End Point (T2)	Fraction of Jobs w/Flow Time <= T2
162.14	199.57	0.034653
199.57	236.99	0.094059
236.99	274.42	0.30693
274.42	311.85	0.56436
311.85	349.27	0.78218
349.27	386.7	0.90594
386.7	424.13	0.94554
424.13	461.56	0.97525
461.56	498.98	0.9901
498.98	536.41	1

RAPS152

Left End Point (T1)	Right End Point (T2)	Fraction of Jobs w/Flow Time <= T2
188.77	227.64	0.069565
227.64	266.5	0.32174
266.5	305.37	0.72174
305.37	344.24	0.86957
344.24	383.11	0.95652
383.11	421.97	0.97391
421.97	460.84	0.98261
460.84	499.71	0.9913
499.71	538.57	0.9913
538.57	577.44	1

RAPS852

Left End Point (T1)	Right End Point (T2)	Fraction of Jobs w/Flow Time <= T2
97.56	158.31	0.030261
158.31	219.06	0.48968
219.06	279.8	0.81018
279.8	340.55	0.92847
340.55	401.3	0.96286
401.3	462.05	0.99175
462.05	522.8	0.99587
522.8	583.54	0.99725
583.54	644.29	0.99725
644.29	705.04	1

RAINS2

Left End Point (T1)	Right End Point (T2)	Fraction of Jobs w/Flow Time <= T2
143.3	186.14	0.10569
186.14	228.98	0.49593
228.98	271.82	0.75203
271.82	314.66	0.89837
314.66	357.5	0.95528
357.5	400.34	0.97561
400.34	443.18	0.99593
443.18	486.02	0.99593
486.02	528.86	0.99593
528.86	571.69	1

RERUNS2

Left End Point (T1)	Right End Point (T2)	Fraction of Jobs w/Flow Time <= T2
107.9	245.61	0.2022
245.61	383.32	0.43372
383.32	521.04	0.63042
521.04	658.75	0.78681
658.75	796.46	0.87355
796.46	934.18	0.90837
934.18	1071.9	0.94563
1071.9	1209.6	0.96885
1209.6	1347.3	0.99023
1347.3	1485	1

RUNS3

Left End Point (T1)	Right End Point (T2)	Fraction of Jobs w/Flow Time <= T2
184.56	239.66	0.091892
239.66	294.75	0.56757
294.75	349.85	0.78919
349.85	404.94	0.91351
404.94	460.04	0.95676
460.04	515.13	0.98378
515.13	570.23	0.99459
570.23	625.32	0.99459
625.32	680.42	0.99459
680.42	735.51	1

RAPS153

Left End Point (T1)	Right End Point (T2)	Fraction of Jobs w/Flow Time <= T2
195	237.41	0.11321
237.41	279.83	0.43396
279.83	322.24	0.66038
322.24	364.65	0.78302
364.65	407.07	0.90566
407.07	449.48	0.93396
449.48	491.89	0.9717
491.89	534.31	0.9717
534.31	576.72	0.99057
576.72	619.13	1

RAPS853

Left End Point (T1)	Right End Point (T2)	Fraction of Jobs w/Flow Time <= T2
85.759	138.12	0.0081522
138.12	190.48	0.26087
190.48	242.84	0.73641
242.84	295.2	0.90217
295.2	347.56	0.97011
347.56	399.92	0.98777
399.92	452.28	0.99592
452.28	504.64	0.99864
504.64	557.01	0.99864
557.01	609.37	1

RAINS3

Left End Point (T1)	Right End Point (T2)	Fraction of Jobs w/Flow Time <= T2
144.57	177.75	0.042735
177.75	210.92	0.39744
210.92	244.09	0.67949
244.09	277.26	0.84188
277.26	310.43	0.92308
310.43	343.61	0.96581
343.61	376.78	0.98291
376.78	409.95	0.99145
409.95	443.12	0.99573
443.12	476.29	1

RERUNS3

Left End Point (T1)	Right End Point (T2)	Fraction of Jobs w/Flow Time <= T2
133.68	306.66	0.39108
306.66	479.64	0.69039
479.64	652.62	0.83105
652.62	825.6	0.91424
825.6	998.58	0.95197
998.58	1171.6	0.97084
1171.6	1344.5	0.98971
1344.5	1517.5	0.99228
1517.5	1690.5	0.99485
1690.5	1863.5	1

The user could experiment with the different ways available for reducing the flow time. Some methods that can be used for this purpose are increasing the staffing, pooling the three underwriting teams into one underwriting center, and changing the priority for the products.

REFERENCES

Bohn, R.; K. Sommers and Greenberg *Kristen's Cookie Company (A)* Boston, MA: President and Fellows of Harvard College, 1986.

Donner Company. Boston, MA: President and Fellows of Harvard College, 1988.

Law, Averill M., and W. David Kelton *Simulation Modeling & Analysis.* 2nd ed. New York, NY: McGraw-Hill, 1991.

Loch, C.; D. Grant and M. Harrison *Manzana Insurance—Fruitvale Branch.* Stanford, CA: Board of Trustees of the Leland Stanford Junior University, 1989.

Ross, S. M. *A Course in Simulation.* New York, NY: Macmillan, 1990.

Matthew's Mug and Muffins (M³)©[1]

Matthew had spent most of the dinner hours during his senior year in high school listening to his parents, David and Sally Field, talk about the travails of the dorm room cookie business of his sister Kristen. He was planning to attend the same school in the fall and was looking forward to starting an entrepreneurial venture of his own. He did not want to compete with his sister's operation, and since he was a natural early riser and had always liked muffins and coffee for breakfast, he thought he would continue the family tradition and open up a dorm room mug of coffee and muffin shop. It would operate four hours a day for six days a week during the fall and spring semesters (15 weeks each).

Matthew knew that his dorm room would be equipped with a small oven capable of cooking up to four muffins at a time and a microwave oven capable of holding two muffins and two mugs of coffee, or any combination thereof. Muffin trays were readily available for either two or four muffins. After many years of experimentation, Matthew had decided that he would offer a plain muffin selection (corn, bran, etc.) or a filled muffin selection (fruit, caramel, honey, cinnamon, etc.). He had recently invented a hard biscotti type of non-filled muffin perfect for coffee dunking. Its only problem was that it required double baking. He would also offer coffee, changing the flavor on a daily basis. Matthew intended to bring his industrial strength mixer which could mix a dozen muffins of the same kind at one time, as well as his 12-cup coffee machine.

The muffin making process is as follows. The mixing bowl is washed and dried, and then flour, shortening and other ingredients are added. This takes four minutes (one minute to wash and dry, three minutes to measure and add ingredients) for up to a dozen muffins. If extra bowls are available, this process can be done while the mixer is occupied working on another batch since the bowl is detachable. The detaching/attaching of the fresh bowl and mixing the batch requires no setup and takes six minutes for between 1 and 12 muffins. Matthew's mixer is old, but reliable, and he has been unable to secure an additional bowl to the one he has. The mixed dough takes 60 seconds to spoon into the tray per muffin. The tray should be sprayed immediately before the dough is placed in the tray, and this takes 30 seconds, independent of the number of muffins being baked. All of these preliminary steps must be done by Matthew and require his presence during their entire operation.

The next step in the operation is to set up the oven for baking (loading and placing the tray in the oven and adjusting the temperature), which cannot be done while the oven is in operation (one minute). An additional 14 minutes of baking per tray whether it contains one to four muffins is then required. After baking the muffins, the tray is placed on a special rack (which holds up to a four-muffin tray) for cooling. Matthew has only one cooling rack. This cooling process takes five minutes. After cooling, any order of up to a dozen muffins can be bagged (one minute). Funds are then collected and recorded when the customer arrives, which takes another minute.

Matthew thinks that there is nothing worse than a cool muffin or cup of coffee, so he is planning to warm each order in the microwave for 30 seconds before it is sold. Paying and warming can be done simultaneously by his roommate, who is also responsible for loading the oven and bagging the order. While the muffins are baking and cooling, the roommate's talents are not needed and can be employed doing something else, like studying, showering, and so on. The microwave oven can also be used for baking (load and bake take only five minutes), but produce a somewhat inferior muffin with slightly soggy tops and a mealy consistency. Matthew has decided to run a first class operation using only the best ingredients and, thus, will only use the microwave for baking in an emergency, or for a non- "made to order" line of muffins.

After initially baking and cooling, the biscotti type of muffin must be sliced and then baked a second time. Slicing and laying the muffins on a flat oven tray (which are in plentiful supply) takes 30 seconds per muffin. Baking this tray takes five minutes for up to four sliced muffins. After the baking, another full five minutes of cooling on the special rack is required. Matthew can do the biscotti slicing while another order is baking in the oven. The biscotti-type muffin can not be baked in the microwave, even in an emergency. Matthew assumes that these muffins will cause a great deal of confusion in his manufacturing process and reduce capacity substantially. Therefore, he intends to charge a 20 percent premium for them over the plain muffins. Due to the extra ingredients, filled muffins will be sold at 25 percent above the retail price of the plain muffins.

---

[1] By Mike Moses, Operations Management, Stern School of Business, New York University. This case is for the use of students in a core course in Operations Management and is intended to have no actual relationship to any real person or organization. (11/98)

To brew up to 12 cups of coffee requires a setup time of two minutes and a brewing time of four minutes. Setup can not be done while the machine is brewing. Filling and covering a cup of coffee take 30 seconds. The roommate does this task, as well as the brewing task. Worker presence is required only for the brew setup and cup pouring.

Ingredients for a plain muffin cost $.50, a filled muffin $.70, and a mug of coffee $.40. Matthew is planning to charge a 100 percent markup for his plain muffin and coffee products. He is planning to sell coffee only to people who buy muffins. All orders are assumed to be for two of the same kind of muffin. On average, half of the customers are assumed to also want coffee. Orders will be accepted on Matthew's Web site, with an order pickup service <u>guarantee of 45 minutes</u> from the time of the placement of the order. Customers whose order fulfillment violates this guarantee receive a 50 percent refund. Processing new order data takes no time due to the strategic location of the roommate's computer monitor. It is right next to the kitchen area.

Demand is assumed to exist and be sufficient for full capacity operation. It was also assumed initially that it will be spread uniformly over the breakfast hours of operation. Customers will have available to them on the Web site a menu listing the coffee of the day, as well as the set of plain and filled muffins available. All muffin orders for Web customers will be made to order and available at, or before, the service guarantee. The web site designer can develop a reservation time slot system, reducing the possibility that too many customers will demand delivery at one specific time and exceed the capacity of Matthew's operation.

Matthew, on a late summer's afternoon at Mrs. Robinson's (a family friend) pool, is daydreaming about the following set of questions. Can you help him with the answers?

1. What is the minimum time from order to delivery for each class of muffin (throughput time)?

2. If only plain muffins are being produced, what is the cycle time of the operation?

3. What is the maximum number of orders for plain muffins that can be produced in a shift (4 hours -- approximate)? If the orders are for the typical product mix (50 percent plain, 25 percent filled, 25 percent biscotti), how much does the result change? Based on these results, would you change the service guarantee? How would you re-engineer the process so that you would not have to change the service guarantee?

4. If he gets more than enough orders in the typical mix, how much total gross profit (before labor costs) can the operation make in a school year?

5. Does the proposed process flow have his roommate working as much as he will? What changes would you make to even the workflow?

6. His parents called from a local flea market and said they saw a mixing bowl for his mixer. It was being sold as an antique, and thus, the price was $250. Should they buy it? Also available is another cooling stand for $50. Should they buy it?

7. How much could randomness in the timing of the arrivals of orders affect this guarantee and the profitability of his operation? Under these conditions, how much could he afford to spend on the development of the order reservation system?

8. A new industrial–strength mixer with six bowls costs $1,000. Its capacity setup and processing times are the same as for the old ones. Would it be a better investment? What would its setup and running times have to be to justify the investment (every five minute improvement in service time guarantees increases demand by 10 percent and chargeable price by 10 percent)?

9. In addition to the "made to order" business, Matthew is considering a "no order" walk up service. Customers would only be able to choose from a stock of product based on those generated by the "made to order" customers (i.e., a "made to order" customer asks for two corn muffins; Matthew makes four, two for the "made to order" customer and two for the "no order" walk up stock). What do you think of this idea? How much extra product does Matthew have the capacity to make? How much should he charge? How would it affect profitability? Would it affect his base business or his service guarantee for his prime customers? Again, assume the typical order mix for the prime customers.

10. Some free space has been offered to all students on the school's website. Matthew is trying to decide which muffin type he should advertise. What is your advice? (Remember to use your accounting skills).

11. In reality, due to the stickiness of the ingredients, the washing, adding ingredients and mixing processes take twice as long after filled muffins have been made than for plain muffins. (Honey is used as a sweetener for all filled muffins.) Conceptualize how the inclusion of this fact would affect your analysis.

Tenafly Bagels[1]

Since taking over the Tenafly Bagel Bakery two years ago in Northern New Jersey, demand has increased steadily, and its owners are considering their current position. Your parent, often a weekend retail customer, has offered your services during your spring recess from one of New York's leading Schools of Business. Since you are halfway through your Competitive Advantage From Operations Core Course, you are confident that you can be of assistance.

You decide to visit the bakery on your first Saturday at home, assuming that the weekend is the high point of weekly demand for bagels. You arrive at 4:30am on the invitation of the store owner. After exchanging very early morning pleasantries, you ask for a general description of the business, its key factors of success, and any particular current or continuing problems they are facing. Over freshly brewed Mocha-Java Decaf Colombian High Mountain Green Leaf Non-Pesticide Picked on Tuesday by 8am Coffee, the owner relates that his wholesale business has been growing at about 30% a year, and his retail business has been growing at 10% a year. There are times when he can not meet his wholesale customer service guarantee (one hour availability for order pick-ups from the time of order).

The indicated key factors of success for his wholesale business are this guarantee, mix flexibility, and quality at a competitive price. For the retail customer, mix availability and quality are the two key factors. When they took over the business, quality and pleasantness had decreased to such a level that a low price strategy was the only feasible way of getting customers into the store. Shortly after taking over, this strategy was abandoned in favor of the current more customer (especially wholesale) oriented approach. Building of the wholesale business and switching retail to a "buy the half-dozen" mentality has allowed the bakery to focus on the production process and minimized the inefficiency of responding to small orders. It also gave them the economies to reduce price on the wholesale level to be 25% below the market. Having completed your exotic morning brew, you were both ready for a tour of the facility.

From an ample inventory of flour, water, salt and assorted seeds and other ingredients, the bagel making process starts with mixing flour and water and salt in a commercial mixer which has the capacity to mix from one to six dozen bagels of the same kind in 10 minutes (the first two minutes of this time are taken to clean the bowl). After mixing, all the mixed dough is placed in a forming machine which can produce one dozen bagels every five minutes with no setup. The formed bagels are next placed in a vat of boiling water big enough to handle up to three dozen bagels at a time. The water must be at a rolling boil before the bagels are immersed. It takes ten minutes for the bagels, after loading, to float to the top where they must be skimmed off immediately with a large ladle net and placed on the rinsing table. The firm currently possesses only one vat capable of handling the boiling process. For high quality bagels, the water should be changed once an hour and requires 10 minutes to again reach a rolling boil. After boiling, the bagels must be rinsed and placed on wooden racks (rinse & rack) before baking. Rinse and rack takes two minutes per dozen. The physical space allows only one worker at a time to work at any production location.

The bagels are baked in a special oven (the oven is a continuous flow process). The full baking cycle requires 30 minutes. The oven has three rotating racks inside, each of which can handle four dozen bagels. The racks pass the easily opened door of the oven every 10 minutes. The racks pass the door slowly enough so that an experienced worker can load the oven in one minute without stopping the racks or the baking process. Inexperienced workers require the racks to be stopped for two minutes to load the four wooden boards each containing one dozen bagels. Before the bagels are loaded into the oven they receive the seeds and other additives (by the dozen) - garlic, onions, poppy seeds, etc. in a process that takes a worker one minute per dozen. Removing the bagels from the oven requires the same process as loading, except in reverse. The bagels are then cooled (infinite capacity) for 15 minutes before being packed in bags for commercial customers, or placed in bins for retail customers. Placing the still warm bagels in bags prematurely makes them soggy. They are then perceived to be of lesser quality by most customers.

Only the mixing, forming, seeding, oven loading, and rinse & rack operations require continuous presence of a worker while the machines are working. Boiling requires only one minute of worker content per dozen to load and one minute per dozen of worker content to unload. Cooking requires no worker effort and packing and paying each require only one minute per dozen. All labor is interchangeable, except that only the shift manager can accept payments.

---

[1] By Michael Moses, Operations Management Area, Stern School of Business. This case is for the use of students in a core course in Operations Management and is intended to have no actual relationship to any real person or organization. (11/98)

The current product mix does not include cinnamon raisin bagels. They require 2 1/2 more minutes of boiling, and five more minutes in mixing, due to the excessive clean up time of the squished raisins. The presence of the raisins also requires the water to be changed before any other bagel can proceed through the boiling process after the cinnamon raisin bagels.

Fifty percent of the wholesale orders are for six dozen bagels. The remainder are for four dozen. During the peak weekend period 3/4 of the orders are from wholesale customers. Retail customer orders are uniformly distributed across bagel types. The baking operations start at 6:00 AM, and the store retail hours are from 7:00 AM to 6:00 PM. At current volumes the bakery makes a profit of $2.40 per dozen bagels sold at the retail level, and $1.20 per dozen at the wholesale level.

After viewing the process in action, the owner asks you to respond to the following questions:

a) Draw a process flow diagram.

b) What is the cycle time and capacity of each step in the process, and, what is the steady state capacity of the entire operation per hour?

c) Does capacity depend on the type of bagels ordered (excluding cinnamon raisin)? Does it depend on the average order size?

d) Is the service guarantee reasonable?

e) What is the minimum labor content per dozen bagels and how many workers should be employed?

f) How much should the owner be willing to pay for an extra boiling vat?

g) What would be the effects on capacity and scheduling of adding cinnamon raisin bagels to your product mix? Assume that they will comprise 10% of wholesale and retail demand. Should they be required to yield a higher profit than the current product line? How much higher?

The Violet Film Processing Agency[1]

In the spring of 1998, two first year MBA students attending a major New York City business school decided to test some of the marketing and operations skills they had learned by analyzing whether or not they should ask their parents for sufficient funds to allow them to open a film processing store. They wanted to be in operation by the summer when neither one was intending to take classes. During the following year they decided that the demands of school would allow only one of them to work in the shop at a time, while the other studied or attended classes. They felt the shop needed to be open from 8:00 A.M. to 8:00 P.M., 6 days a week. After this first year the students hoped that the operation would not require their attention and that they could move on to more traditional jobs after graduation, and become absentee owners.

From a major supplier of photographic printing and developing equipment they learned a good bit about the film processing business. Current technology allows, for an investment of slightly less the $100,000, for the developing and printing of black-and-white and color 35mm film in sizes from 3½"x5" to 5"x7".

The normal flow of an order through the developing and printing process is as follows: A customer enters the store and gives the roll, or rolls, of film to a salesperson who discusses the price, size, finish and pick-up time that is desired and gives the customer a receipt for his or her order. This usually takes one minute. Each roll of black-and-white film is placed in the unloading bin, where it is taken out of its canister and prepared for developing. This takes one minute per roll. The film is next transferred to the black-and-white developer, which runs in a batch processing mode. The loading process (setup) takes five minutes for up to a batch of six rolls of film. An incremental 15 minutes of run time is required to complete the developing process of the batch (1–6 rolls). Once a batch is completed (loaded and developed), a new batch can begin. The developed film is then put on a rack (no time) from which it is removed when the printing machine operator decides that its turn for printing has arrived. There is sufficient rack space to hold hundreds of rolls of developed film. The transfer from rack to printer takes no time.

Color film canister unloading is automatically done by the separate color developing machine. The loading of this machine takes 2 minutes, independent of whether the rolls are 24 or 36 exposures. Up to two rolls can be loaded at a time on this machine and either 1 or 2 rolls can be loaded in the given time. This developing machine is a continuous process machine that can be reloaded as soon as the previous rolls have entered the system. The actual developing time (after loading) for the 1- or 2-roll batch is 15 minutes. A continuous process machine is one with which the operator can start loading the next batch as soon as the prior batch has started into the process rather than waiting until it has completed the process. The developed color film is then placed on the same rack as the black and white film. This transfer requires no time.

The person running the only film printing machine (which prints either black and white or color prints) selects film from the rack and adjusts the machine based on the type of film used (black and white, color, different manufacturers), makes minor adjustments based on the quality of the negatives, and selects the print size, number of copies, and length of roll. This whole process takes about 1 minute for any type of printing order. Processing time for this operation (one roll at a time) once the machine has been loaded is 5 minutes for rolls of 24 and 7 minutes for rolls of 36. Black and white or color film rolls can be set up while the machine is running and can be started through the process as soon as the last frame of the prior roll has completed the entire printing process. At the end of the printing process, the prints are spliced and automatically collated into single order stacks. The time for the machine to do this operation is included in the prior processing time.

After the collating step is completed, a worker must take the photos and place them in the order envelope, splice the negative roll so it fits into the envelope, stuff them in a cellophane protective sleeve, and place the completed order in the pick up box. This takes 1 minute for 24-shot rolls and 1½ minutes for 36-shot rolls. The final step in the process is obtaining payment when the customer arrives. This usually takes 1 minute for cash transactions and 2 minutes for credit card transactions.

The paper used in the printing process is wide and flexible enough to do either the 3½"x5" or 4"x6" size in either black and white or color without having to change the paper canister. However, to make 5"x7" enlargements requires the paper canister to be changed to a wider size. This operation requires

---

[1] By Michael Moses, Operations Management Area, Stern School of Business. This case is for the use of students in a core course in Operations Management and is intended to have no actual relationship to any real person or organization. (11/98)

the machine to be turned off, opened, canisters switched, and then restarted. This takes about 5 minutes, and usually involves the loss of about 3 feet of paper film at a cost of $1 a foot. The same process must be followed when the machine is switched back to the smaller paper size (same time and paper loss). It takes 1½ minutes to process two 5"x7" enlargements of the same negative and 1 minute to collate negatives and place prints in envelopes.

Photo processing has become a very competitive business in the New York City area. Total profit before labor and interest costs is $2 for a 24 shot roll of color, $3 for a 36 shot roll of color, $3 for a 24 shot roll of black and white, and $5 for a 36 shot roll of black and white. The first 5"x7" enlargement of a 5"x7" run loses $1, but every one thereafter yields $1 in profit. More profit is made on the black and white and enlargement processing, since most local photo processors do not have the most modern equipment. These shops must send those orders out to another vendor for processing.

An average day yields orders that conform to the following demand distribution:

Film Types

Size	Black and White	Color
3½"x5"	10%	10%
4"x6"	20%	40%
5"x7"	10%	10%

The number of 24- versus 36-shot rolls is normally split 50/50 within a class and the average order for 5"x7" enlargements is 2 each of 2 negatives, which takes a total of 3 minutes to print and 1 minute to pack.

The volume of customers on either Monday or Tuesday requiring film processing is 5 times the volume of customers any other day in the week.

Our erstwhile students decide that they need to answer many questions before a decision should be made about asking their folks for cash. They have made up the following list. How would you respond?

1. Construct a process flow diagram.
2. What is the capacity of the system and does it depend on the mix of orders? Why ? If so, what mix of orders yields maximum and minimum throughput?
3. What is the bottleneck operation?
4. Assuming no seasonality, what would weekly demand have to be, given the average order mix discussed in the case, for the operation to be profitable? At what wage rate? How many employees are required? (Assume that their parents are currently earning fifteen percent on their investments and bank debt costs ten percent.)
5. What level of service should be offered for each product (hours from drop off to pick up for black and white, color, enlargements, and so forth)?
6. How sensitive is the business plan to change in demand or the assumed order mix?
7. Would extra investment dollars be helpful and if so, where should they be expended? Assume the printer costs $75,000, color developer $15,000, black and white developer $5,000, and all other equipment $5,000. (Assume all original and incremental equipment have a life of three years and no salvage value.)
8. A new printer has come on the market. It costs $150,000 and has a five year life with zero salvage value. It has a ten percent improvement in cycle time compared to the existing machine, but it can do enlargements up to 12" x 18" without changing the film canister. The machine also has a small TV screen that allows the operator to better set the print parameters before processing a roll, yielding better quality prints for all kinds of film. The new machine has the same operating characteristics as the old machine. A new roll of film can not be entered into the printer until the prior roll has completed printing. Since the paper canister does not have to be changed, profit is now $1.50 for every enlargement including the first. Should this new printer be purchased?
9. Assume the capabilities and output qualities of the new machine (Question 8) increase general demand by 10 percent and produce an additional demand for twenty 10" x 12" enlargements per day. The profit for this size enlargement is $3 per enlargement and its cycle time is the same as a 5" x 7" enlargement. How would these facts affect your decision?

10. QUESTION TO PONDER BUT NOT COMPLETE: With the original equipment, does the sequence in which orders are released to the printer matter, and if so, what decision rule should they tell the operator to use in selecting the next job? (Some alternative rules: first come, first served; run what has just been run; run one size until it is exhausted; only run 5"x7" when there is no other work in the shop; run job with shortest processing time; run job with shortest setup time; run job with the closest due date, etc.)

WAITING LINE MANAGEMENT METHODS

1. GETTING STARTED

One of the factors that affects our assessment of the quality of a service organization is how long it takes us to be served. Whether waiting for our turn for a bank teller or ATM, airport airline reservation clerk, the longer the wait, the more unhappy we become. Thus, before making staffing decisions, a manager in charge of such an operation will want information on how long the customer, on the average, must wait for service, the number of people awaiting service, the utilization of the service staff, and so on. HOM — Waiting Line Management module allows the solution of problems of this type.

The determination of how long a customer or job must wait before being served depends on several factors, such as the distribution of the time between arrivals (inter-arrival time distribution), the distribution of the time required to serve a customer (service time distribution), the number of servers, the choice of whom to serve next, and how customers or jobs are organized in the waiting area. The choice of the inter-arrival and service distributions as well as other parameters of the waiting line will depend on the problem, the available data and the degree of detail required in the outputs. These issues are explained in the next section, Modeling Considerations.

2. MODELING CONSIDERATIONS

Distributions: The program automatically displays the HOM tool bar and a blank spreadsheet. The spreadsheet is used to enter any empirical data that you might have about the inter-arrival or service time distributions. Your choice in this matter will be determined by the information that is available on customer (or job) arrivals and service times. In particular, you may have empirical data on how long it takes to serve a customer. An example might be that you may have observed that bank ATM customers spend either 1-10, 11–30 or 31–60 seconds at the ATM and that 60 customers take 110 seconds, 30 customers take 11–30 seconds, and 10 customers take 31–60 seconds. Similarly, you may also have data on how long it takes between customer (or job) arrivals (i.e., empirical data about inter-arrival times). Customers of the bank may arrive, 0–1, 2–5, 6–9, or 10–20 minutes apart, and 50 customers arrive 0–1 minute apart, 30 arrive 2–5 minutes apart, 20 arrive 6–9 minutes apart, and 15 arrive 10–20 minutes apart. If you have the empirical distribution for either one or both the inter-arrival and service time distributions, enter the data as described in the next section on "Data Input of Empirical Distributions".

On the other hand, you might have information on the general shape of the distributions, that is exponential or erlang of degree greater than one, or even just the mean and variance of the distributions. HOM caters to such situations, and you should enter your information in the Parameters dialog box as described in section 5, "Model Specification".

Solutions: Typically, the more data available about the distributions, the greater the variety of modeling choices that become available and more complete the solution to the problems. For example, on entering only the mean and variance of the distributions, the model choices are restricted to the case when customers are served in the order they arrive and when there is an infinite waiting area for customers awaiting service. The results too are restricted to the average waiting time and the average number of customers waiting. At the other end of the spectrum, when empirical data are available or when the shapes of the distribution are known (or a combination thereof, i.e., empirical data about the inter-arrival time and the shape of the service time distribution), you could simulate service disciplines such as serving the customer with the shortest processing time and obtain results on the distribution of the number of customers in the system as well as the variance of the waiting time (along with its mean).

Solution Techniques: HOM, in keeping with the modern trends of analysis of waiting lines, uses a combination of analytical formulae, approximation techniques, and simulation to produce a wide range of outputs. The choice of the solution technique is dictated by the modeling choices made by the user. The actual techniques employed are enumerated under "Solution Techniques" and described in greater detail in section 8.

3. DATA INPUT OF EMPIRICAL DISTRIBUTIONS

In order to input empirical values, the data must be available for either one or both service time and inter-arrival time distributions. Several empirical distributions can be entered in the same spreadsheet.

The user chooses which distribution to use for the service time and inter-arrival time in the Parameters dialog box.

In order to add a distribution, select DATA item from the menu and then choose Add. A Variable Name dialog box opens up. The user has to name each distribution before being able to enter the data. The computer automatically gives default names for the distribution. You may edit the name given in the Edit box. After selecting a Variable Name, a pair of columns will be generated automatically in the spreadsheet. The first column of each pair is the midpoint of the range of values (i.e., the class interval for either the service time or inter-arrival time distribution). The service time ranges at our previously discussed bank example will be 1–10 seconds, 11–30 seconds, and 31–60 seconds, which would result in the midpoints 5.5, 20.5, and 45.5. The second column of the pair would be the number of observations that fell into each range (class interval). In the bank example, 1–10 had 60 observations, 11–30 had 30 and 31–60 had 10. When entering the data, ensure that you do not skip a row. Data entry can begin from any row.

Follow this procedure for either or both service time and inter-arrival time distributions. You may enter more than two distributions in order to carry out sensitivity analysis. The order of entry (service time or inter-arrival time) is not important. Also notice that the total number of observations need not be normalized (say, add up to 100). Finally, you could also enter fractional values for the number of observations. This would be appropriate if you are sampling or simulating using a distribution other than the exponential or the erlang. Examples of such usage would include, the beta, gamma, or uniform distributions. If the distribution is deterministic (degenerate), then HOM directly handles such cases; see the Parameters dialog box.

Once the data have been entered, ensure that the file is saved using the Save icon or the FILE Save item on the command line. HOM does not permit undo's, so save your data frequently or enter it into a commercial spreadsheet first and then copy it into the HOM spreadsheet. For use of this feature, see "Export and Import of Data as well as Results".

Example

Name the variable.

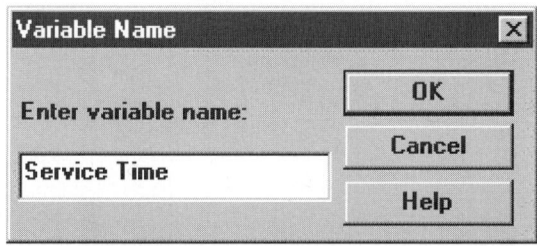

After entering the data, the spreadsheet will be as given below (see QEXAMPLE.DAT).

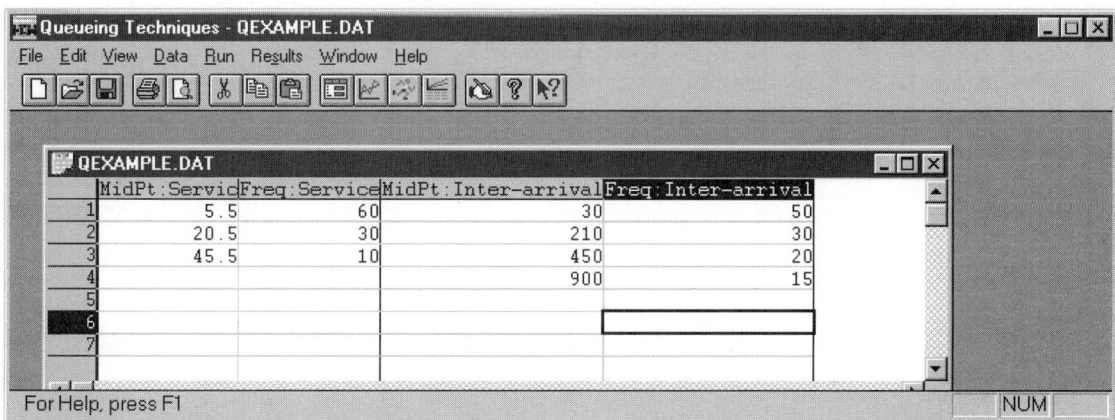

4. PLOT DATA

The DATA --> Plot item on the command line or the Plot icon allows the user to plot the previously entered data. However, before the user can plot a distribution, the user must designate the distribution to be either one of the inter-arrival or service time distribution. This choice must be made in the Parameters dialog box. After plotting one of the variables, say the arrivals, the Series function on the command line can be used to change to the variable designated to be the service time distribution. The Parameters dialog box can be reached via the Parameters icon or the DATA --> Parameters item on the command line. If the plot of the distribution appears to be distorted (zigzags across the plot area), please check and correct your selection of the From Row and To Row in the Parameters dialog box.

The plot of data has been added for two reasons. The first one is that this provides a visual check on the entered data. Second, a user interested in using the analytical formulation (i.e., the exponential or erlang distributions) to model distributional data could determine whether the histograms of the empirical data fit the shape of one of the analytical distributions. To aid in this determination, HOM will plot on the same graph the exponential or the erlang distribution that best approximates the mean and variance of the empirical distribution. The choice of fitting the mean and variance is dictated by the fact that several performance measures of waiting lines are closely connected to the first two moments of the inter-arrival and service time distributions. The chi-square test can be used to ensure that you are using the correct analytical distribution.

Example

The plots of the service and inter-arrival time distributions for the bank example are shown below.

<u>Service Time Distribution</u>

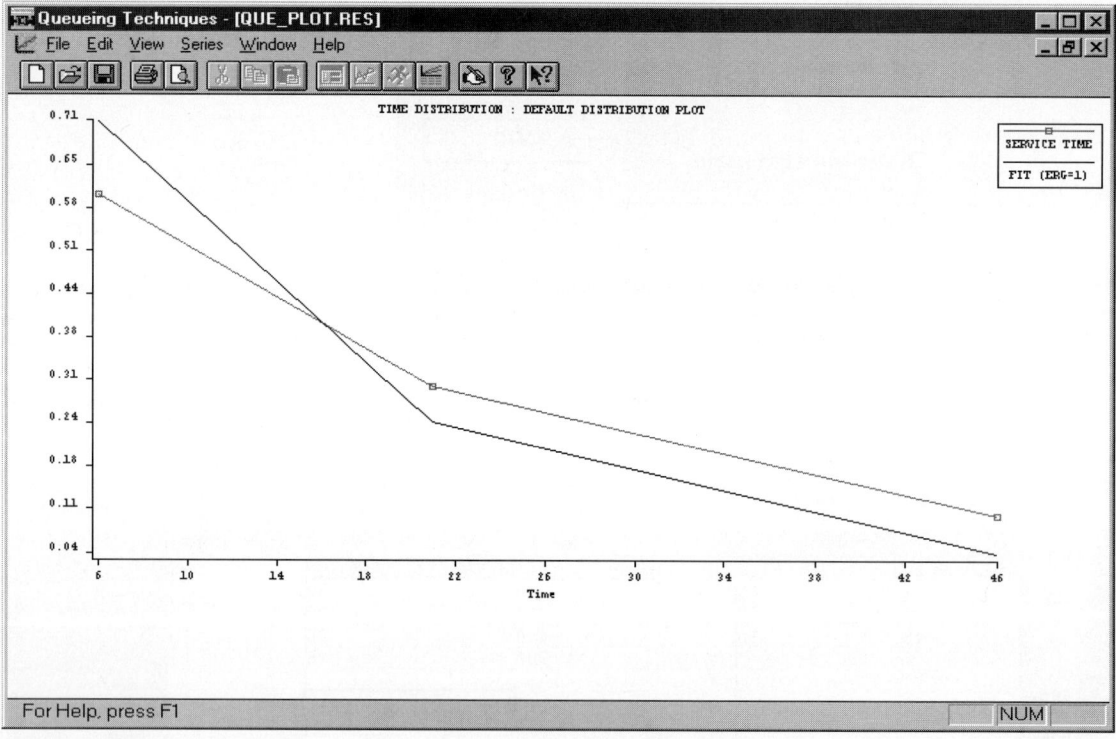

Inter-arrival Time Distribution

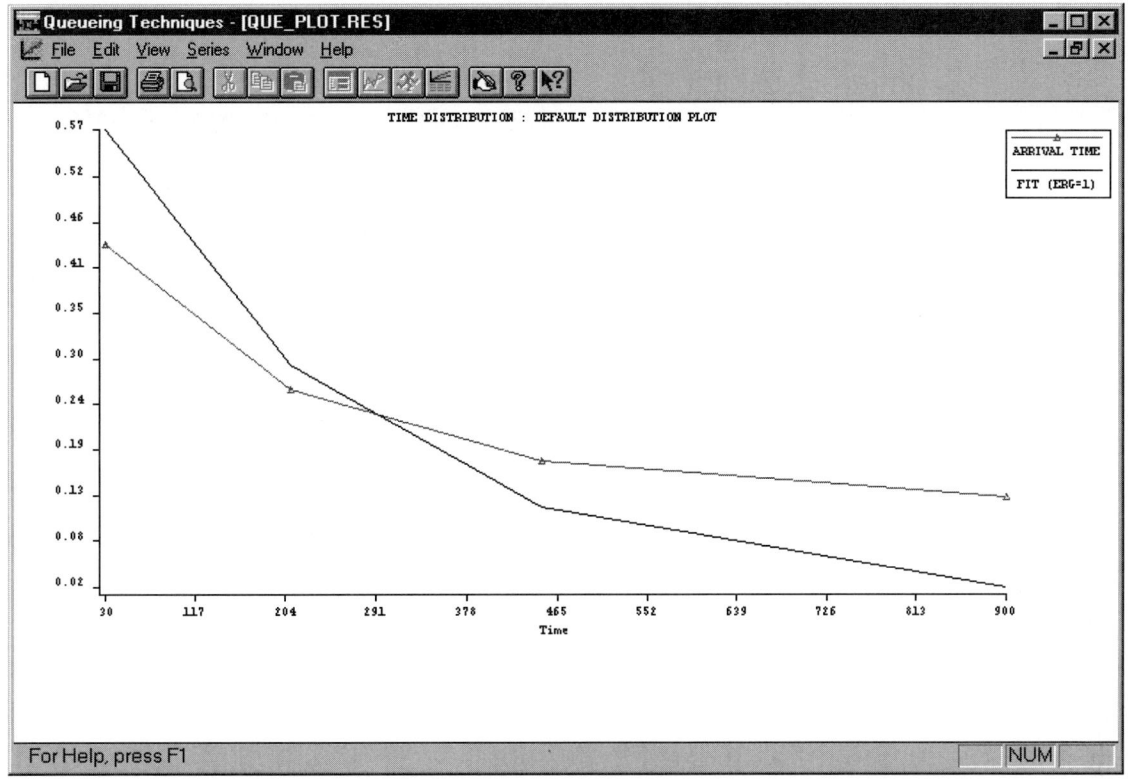

5. MODEL SPECIFICATION

The next stage in the problem solving for waiting time management is the specification of the model. This is true regardless of the type(s) of distributions you have chosen to use. To specify the model you need to reach the Parameters dialog box by using its icon or the DATA --> Parameters function on the command line. The dialog box that opens has three parts: namely, the inter-arrival time specification, the service time specification, and all the remaining information. The data items are described in brief in a summary table followed by a more detailed description.

It is useful to note that certain choices, such as the rules about which customer to serve next, or the size of the waiting area, or how customers behave while waiting in line or in joining lines, might seem at first glance to be better than others. However, this is not always true. We recommend that the user try many alternative rules and configurations of the waiting line to get a better feel for how changes in the specification of the problem affect the performance of the waiting line. When the problem has been completely specified, click on OK to close the dialog box. Use the Save icon or the FILE → Save item on the command line to save your data, and proceed to the next step.

> **Hint!** If you wish rough and ready results first, please reduce the length of simulation to 500–1000 customers.

> **Hint!** In order to force HOM to simulate am M/M/C queue, select the inter-arrival and/or the service time distribution to be erlang of degree one (1). This device also gives the user some feel for the usual length of simulation. For example, at low levels of utilization (or high loss rate of customers), a value of 1,000 or 5,000 customers should suffice. Whereas, at relatively high levels of utilization, a simulation length of 50,000 customers might be necessary.

Summary of Data Items in the Parameters Dialog Box

Item	Description
Inter-arrival Time Distribution	Select the type of distribution from the drop–down list. The available choices are: Exponential (M), Erlang (E), Deterministic (D), General (G), and Empirical (CI).
Service Time Distribution	Follow the procedure for specifying the Inter-Arrival Time Distribution.
Number of Servers	Enter the number of servers (max 30) in the edit box.
Number of Lines	You must choose whether the customers will wait in a single line (S-Line) that is in front of all servers (used at most retail banks) or whether they will wait by forming individual lines (as many as lines as there are servers) in front of each server (used at most supermarkets).
Room for Waiting	Select whether the waiting area is infinite or finite.
Rule for Serving Next Customer	Specify which customer to serve next.
How Customers Join Lines (when there are multiple lines)	Another modeling choice available to the user is how customers decide to join a line.
Length of Simulation (No. of Customers)	Choose the length of the simulation.

A more detailed description of each term is given below.

5.1 Inter-Arrival and Service Time Distributions (Parameters Dialog Box)

Inter-arrival Time Distribution	Select the type of distribution from the drop down list. The available choices are Exponential, Erlang, Deterministic, General, and Empirical.
If Exponential (M)	Enter the rate at which customers arrive. This quantity is denoted as λ in textbooks.
If Erlang (E)	Enter the rate at which customers arrive (λ) as well as the degree (max 10) of the erlang distribution.
If Deterministic (D)	Enter the rate at which customers arrive (λ).
If General (G)	Enter the rate at which customers arrive (λ) as well as the variance of the inter-arrival time.
If Empirical (CI)	Select the name of the distribution and its beginning and ending rows in the spreadsheet. Please take special care in this regard, because HOM automatically defaults the starting and ending rows based on the current position of the cursor.
Service Time Distribution	Follow the procedure for specifying the Inter-Arrival Time Distribution.

5.2 Number of Servers and Number of Lines (Parameters Dialog Box)

Number of Servers	Enter the number of servers (max 30) in the edit box.
Number of Lines	You must choose whether the customers will wait in a single line (S-Line) that is in front of all servers (used at most retail banks) or whether they will wait by forming individual lines (as many as lines as there are servers) in front of each server (used at most supermarkets). Make your choice by selecting the appropriate radio button.

5.3 Room for Waiting (Parameters Dialog Box)

Room for Waiting

Most waiting areas are larger than most probable queues (such as at an airline terminal). So the area would be considered to be infinite.

In some situations, found at car washes, gas stations, professional services, or in manufacturing operations, the waiting area is limited. This should be indicated along with the space available for waiting customers. Note that the waiting area when finite is for customers or jobs waiting to be served. For example, a waiting area of zero indicates that there is no room for any customer to wait.

Furthermore, customers that arrive and find the waiting area full are assumed to be lost to the system forever.

When there are multiple lines, the size of the waiting area is the size of each line. For example, there are 2 servers, and 2 lines. The waiting area is finite and has been specified as 10. This is interpreted as a waiting area for 10 customers to wait *in each line*.

5.4 Rule for Serving Next Customer? (Parameters Dialog Box)

Rule for Serving Next Customer

Which customer to serve next is often a vexing decision faced by managers of service organizations. HOM offers two different alternatives, the First Come First Served (FCFS) or the Shortest Processing Time (SPT) rule.

The use of the SPT rule presupposes that the manager can choose whom to serve next and has knowledge of the customers' service time even before the service has commenced.

HOM allows the FCFS rule to be chosen for all other parameter settings, however in order to apply the SPT rule neither the service time nor the inter-arrival distribution can be general. HOM uses simulation to evaluate the performance under the SPT rule. Also see the section on Solution Techniques.

5.5 How Customers Join Lines (Parameters Dialog Box)

How Customers Join Lines (when there are multiple lines)

Another modeling choice available to the user is how customers decide to join a line. Analytical solution methodologies do not (normally) allow for the variety of choices available in real life. HOM allows four different types of customer behavior: Random, Cyclic, Shortest Line, and Jockey. These choices are available only when there is a line in front of each server.

Random implies that the customer on entering the system, randomly chooses a line, joins that line, and continues to wait in it until served by the server.

Cyclic implies that if there are 5 lines (and 5 servers), the first customer joins the first line, the second customer the second line, ..., the sixth customer joins the first line, and so forth. They continue to wait in the line they joined until served.

When the behavior is Shortest Line, customers join the shortest line found on arrival and continue to wait in that line until served.

When Jockey is selected, customers join the shortest line on arrival. They switch one line to the left or right, if that line is shorter, at every simulation event, that is, an arrival or a service completion event.

5.6 Length of Simulation (Parameters Dialog Box)

Length of Simulation

You can choose the length of the simulation. The length is expressed in terms of number of customer arrivals simulated. We recommend the choice of 5,000 customers. The run time for the simulation will typically be 3–10 seconds for this value.

Example

The Parameters dialog box is shown below.

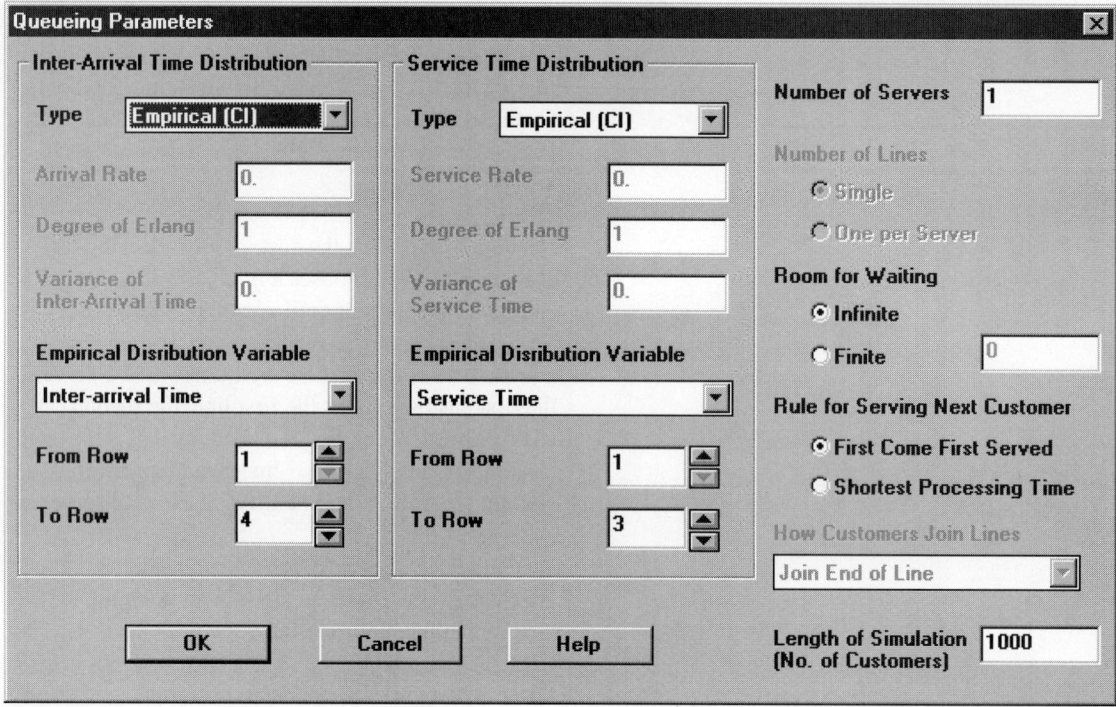

Please notice that both Inter-Arrival and Service Time distributions have been specified to be Empirical. The names of the distributions have been selected from the drop down list, and the From and To Row values have been selected. The number of servers has been set equal to one (1), with infinite Room for Waiting, the scheduling Rule for Serving Next Customer is First Come First Served; and the Length of Simulation has been chosen as 1,000.

6. RUN PROBLEM AND ANALYZE RESULTS

In order to run a previously specified problem, you need only to click upon the Run icon or the RUN item on the command line. If the simulation solution methodology is used, the run time could be as much as 30 seconds on a Pentium machine. We recommend that you save the data before commencing the run.

HOM automatically displays the results on the completion of a RUN. The first part of the Results file is a graph that shows the probability that there are "N" or fewer customers in the system. The range of "N" is determined by the probability of the outcome. When the probability that there are "N" customers is less than .001, no larger value of "N" is plotted. The text form of the probability that there are "N" customers in the system is given at the end of the Results file.

Paging down from the graph reveals a recapitulation of the summary data entered and the choices made during model specification. Paging down again reveals the main body of the Results file. To aid analysis,

HOM has been preprogrammed to automatically produce a sensitivity analysis on the service rate and the number of servers. A plus and minus five percent change in service rate is indicated in the two columns to the immediate right of the base case. The results of increasing and decreasing the number of servers by one is indicated by the next two columns to the right.

Performance measures for all the above scenarios including the server utilization, customer waiting time in the queue and in the system (waiting time in the queue plus service time), as well as the length of line, are given below each scenario's heading. The scenario heading contains information on the number of servers (C(Base), C+1, C-1), service rate normal, as entered in the Parameters window, 105% normal, five percent faster, 95% normal, 5 percent slower, and the solution methodology used (analytical (M/M/C), approximation, simulation, etc.). Standard deviations for most of the above measures are given so that measures such as confidence interval for the work flow completion times (the probability that a customer will have to wait less than "X" minutes) can be computed. The last measure, the percent of customers lost to the system, indicates the percent of customers that arrive, find the finite waiting area full, and, therefore, depart without getting served. These customers do not return and are lost to the system forever. These data and information on the cost of lost sales can be used to determine whether it is beneficial to add an incremental server to reduce the loss rate.

The command line for this sub-module contains the SERIES command. Clicking on it gives the user the opportunity to include (independently or simultaneously) the sensitivity analysis information (plus and minus five percent on service time, plus and minus one server) on the graph that shows the probability of "N" or fewer customers being in the system. Simply click on the box of the data that you want to be included and click again to have it excluded. The WINDOWS Tile function can also be used to exhibit multiple graphs on one screen.

Example 1

The results of a RUN using the parameters shown previously are given below. The text output was copied using EDIT --> Copy and pasted into Excel. Thereafter the text results were formatted and pasted into this document.

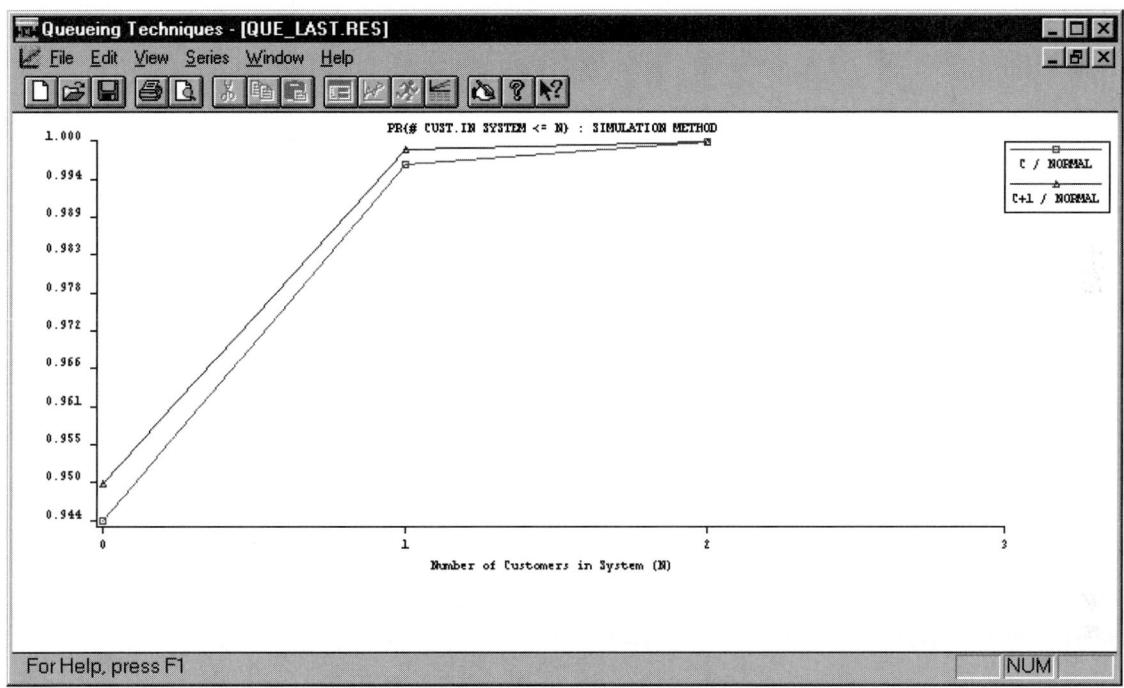

Base Case Parameters

	Arrival Time	Service Time
Distr. Type	CI	CI
Rate	N/A	N/A
Degr. Erlang	N/A	N/A
Distr. Mean	263.478	14
Variance	83344.4	155.25
Std. Dev.	288.694	12.4599

No. Servers	1
No. Lines	1
Wait. Space	Infinite
Serving Rule	First Come First Served
Cust. Behav.	Join End of Line
Simul.Length	1000

Results of Calculations

NOTE: The results are available only if the combination of the Number of Servers (C) and the Service Rate creates a stable system. For example, if C = 1, the results for C - 1 servers will not be available. Likewise, when Utilization exceeds 99%.

	Base Case	Sensitivity Analysis			
Number of Servers	C	C	C	C - 1	C + 1
Service Rate	Normal	105% Normal	95% Normal	Normal	Normal
Method (Model) Used	Simulation	Simulation	Simulation	Not Used	Simulation
Utilization	0.0531353	0.0506051	0.0559319	N/A	0.0265677
Avg. No. Customers in System	0.0594827	0.0538488	0.05781	N/A	0.0518596
Std.Dev. of No.Cust in Syst.	0.250497	0.236668	0.245311	N/A	0.227327
Avg. No. Customers in Queue	0.0033901	0.0025312	0.0028336	N/A	0
Std.Dev. of No.Cust in Queue	0.0583302	0.0502477	0.0535539	N/A	0
Average Time Spent in System	14.8555	13.9771	15.5105	N/A	14
Std.Dev. of Time in System	13.0277	12.2454	13.6234	N/A	12.4599
Average Time Spent in Queue	0.8555	0.64381	0.773684	N/A	0
Std.Dev. of Time in Queue	3.80399	3.02207	3.68433	N/A	0
Fraction of Time Syst. Empty	0.943907	0.948682	0.945024	N/A	0.949394
Fraction of Customers Lost	0	0	0	N/A	0

Fraction of Time N Customers in the System

No. of Customers in System, N					
0	0.943907	0.948682	0.945024	N/A	0.949394
1	0.0527144	0.0487863	0.052164	N/A	0.0493524
2	0.0033664	0.0025312	0.0027912	N/A	0.0012536
3	1.19E-05	0	2.12E-05	N/A	0

Example 2   M/M/C queue

The input file is called MMC.DAT. The model is of an M/M/2 queue. The solution method is analytical. The output is not given.

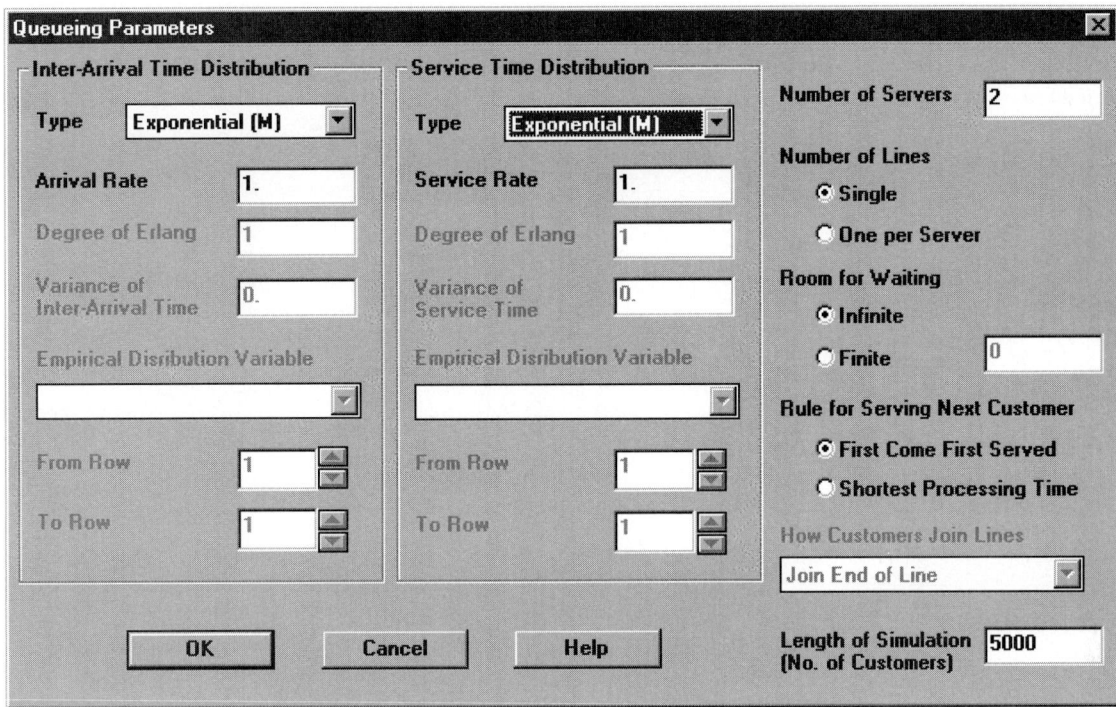

Example 3   M/G/C Queue

The input file is called MGC.DAT. The data are as given below. Output data not given.

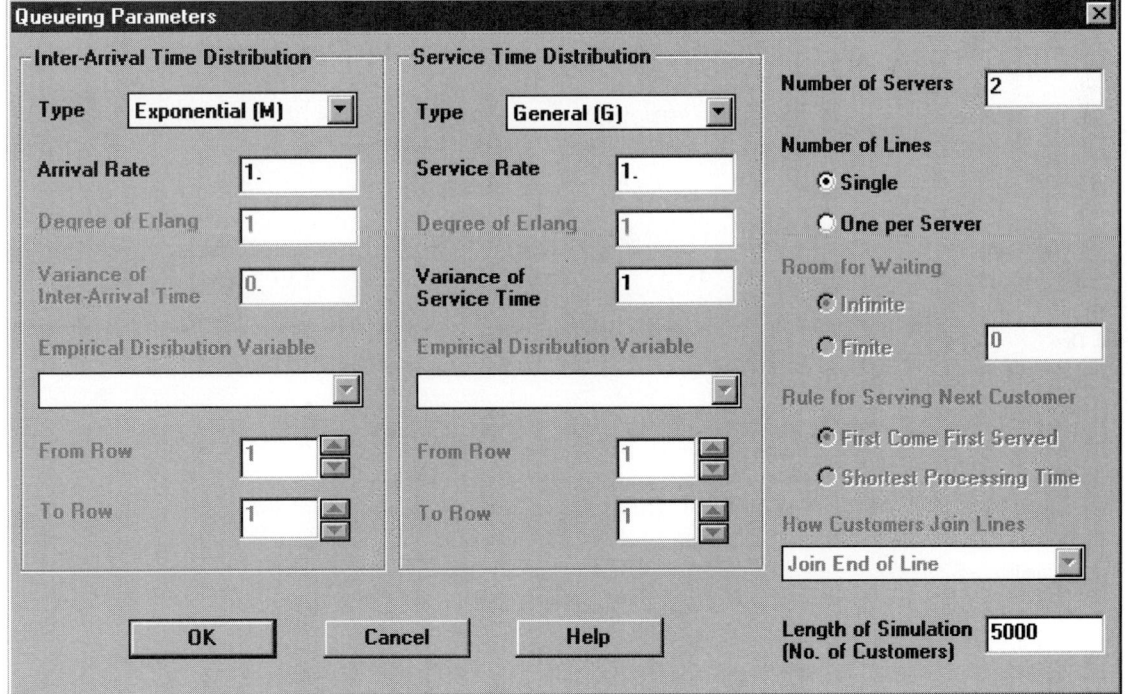

Example 4   M/M/C Queue — Force HOM to simulate

Retrieve the file MMC.DAT. In order to force HOM to simulate this queue, change the inter-arrival time distribution to erlang of degree one (which is the same distribution as the exponential). The change is shown below.

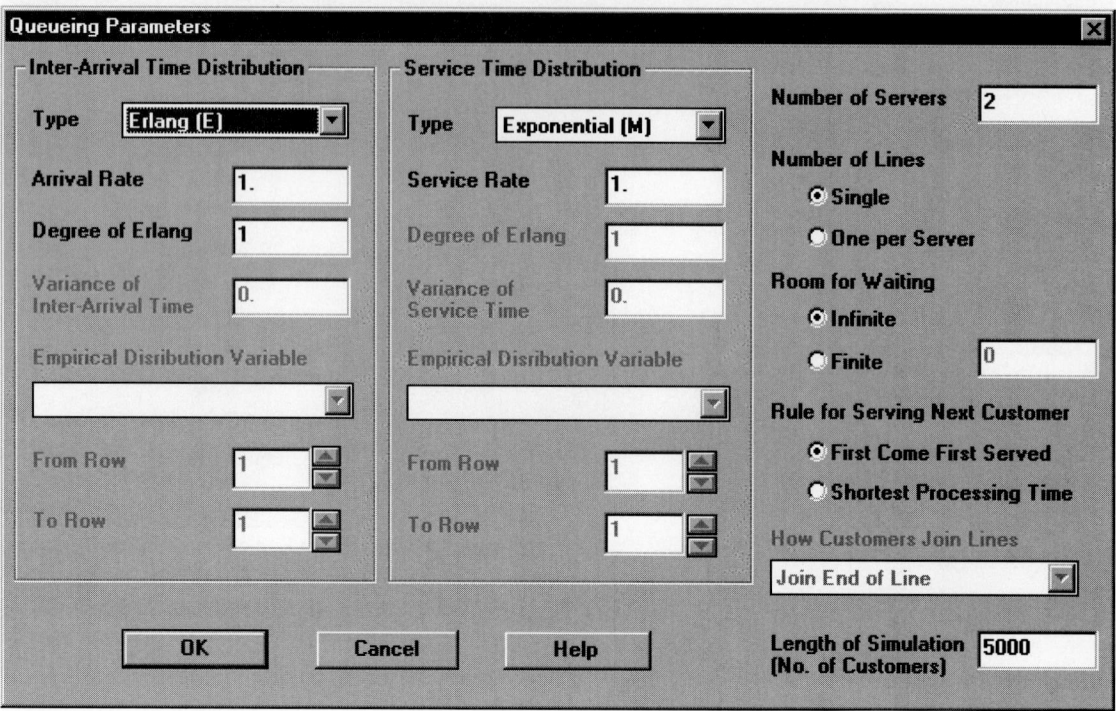

The outputs for the base case — one from calculations (i.e., example 2) and the other from simulation (this example) — are shown below side by side. To produce this output, two runs were made, the data copied after each run, pasted into Excel, formatted, and imported into this document.

	Base Case Parameters		Base Case Parameters	
	Arrival Time	Service Time	Arrival Time	Service Time
Distr. Type	M	M	E	M
Rate	1	1	1	1
Degr. Erlang	N/A	N/A	1	N/A
Distr. Mean	1	1	1	1
Variance	1	1	1	1
Std. Dev.	1	1	1	1
No. Servers	2		2	
No. Lines	1		1	
Wait. Space	Infinite		Infinite	
Serving Rule	First Come First Served		First Come First Served	
Cust. Behav.	Join End of Line		Join End of Line	
Simul.Length	5000		5000	

	Results of Calculations	Results of Calculations
	Base Case	Base Case
Number of Servers	C	C
Service Rate	Normal	Normal
Method (Model) Used	**M/M/C**	**Simulation**
	============	============
Utilization	0.5	0.5
Avg. No. Customers in System	1.33333	1.38838
Std.Dev. of No.Cust in Syst.	1.49071	1.52344
Avg. No. Customers in Queue	0.333333	0.367884
Std.Dev. of No.Cust in Queue	0.942809	0.960533
Average Time Spent in System	1.33333	1.36126
Std.Dev. of Time in System	1.24722	1.265
Average Time Spent in Queue	0.333333	0.361264
Std.Dev. of Time in Queue	0.745356	0.774746
Fraction of Time Syst. Empty	0.333333	0.328744
Fraction of Customers Lost	0	0

Fraction of Time N Customers in the System

No. of Cust. in System, N			
		------------	------------
	0	0.333333	0.328744
	1	0.333333	0.322013
	2	0.166667	0.167749
	3	0.0833333	0.0858557
	4	0.0416667	0.04536
	5	0.0208333	0.0265689
	6	0.0104167	0.0142016
	7	0.0052083	0.0047937
	8	0.0026042	0.0029585
	9	0.0013021	0.0010642
	10	0.000651	0.0006006
	11	0.0003255	9.12E-05
	12	0.0001628	0
	13	8.14E-05	
	14	4.07E-05	
	15	2.03E-05	
	16	1.02E-05	

Example 5   Deterministic Service Time

Please see the data file MDC.DAT for an example.

Example 6   **M/M/C Queue — with Multiple Lines and Alternate Customer Behavior**

Please see the file MCALT.DAT. The example is a two-server model with two lines (one per server). Customers join the shortest line on arrival.

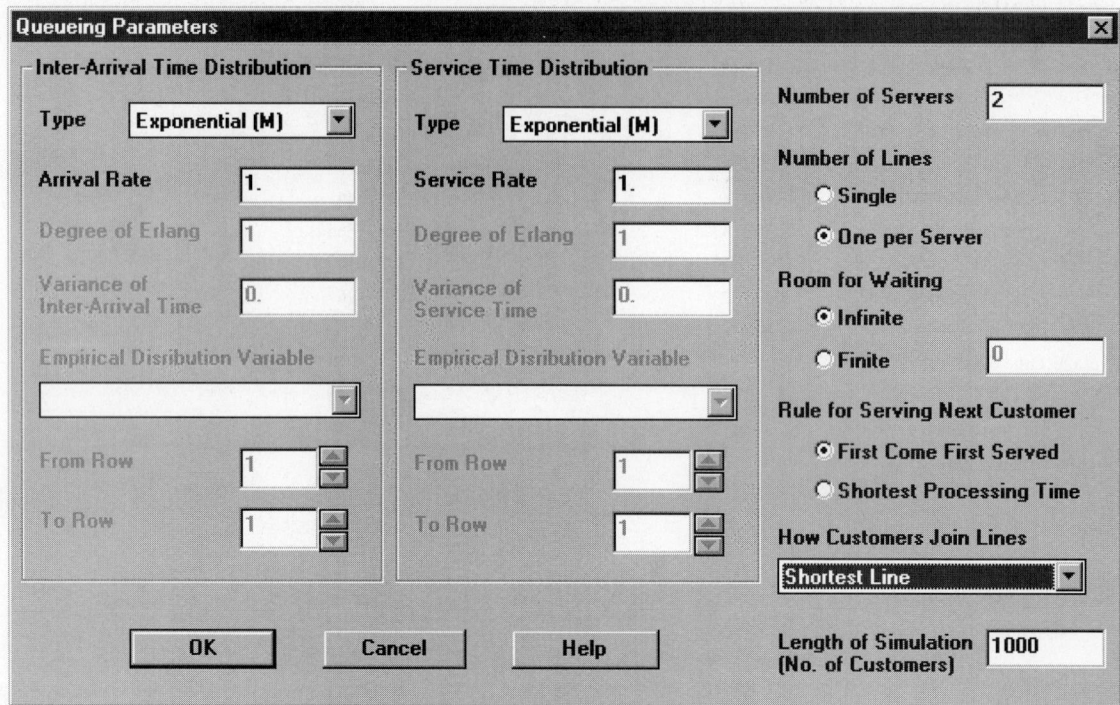

Given below are outputs from the base cases of five models, single line (FCFS), multiple line (random behavior), multiple lines (cyclic behavior), and multiple lines (join shortest queue), and multiple lines (jockeying behavior). The outputs were as before pasted into Excel and then imported after formatting.

	Base Case Parameters	
	Arrival Time	Service Time
	=========	==========
Distr. Type	M	M
Rate	1	1
Degr. Erlang	N/A	N/A
Distr. Mean	1	1
Variance	1	1
Std. Dev.	1	1
No. Servers	2	
No. Lines	1	
Wait. Space	Infinite	
Serving Rule	First Come First Served	
Cust. Behav.	Join End of Line	
Simul.Length	1000	

132

	Single Line	Random	Cyclic	Short. Line	Jockey
Number of Servers	C	C	C	C	C
Service Rate	Normal	Normal	Normal	Normal	Normal
Method (Model) Used	M/M/C	M/M/C/Rand	Simulation	Simulation	Simulation
=========	=========	=========	=========	=========	=========
Utilization	0.5	0.5	0.5	0.5	0.5
Avg. No. Customers in System	1.33333	2	1.37921	1.68255	1.67902
Std.Dev. of No.Cust in Syst.	1.49071	2	1.38039	1.67804	1.46261
Avg. No. Customers in Queue	0.333333	1	0.447271	0.682481	0.630676
Std.Dev. of No.Cust in Queue	0.942809	1.58114	0.911804	1.13422	0.893094
Average Time Spent in System	1.33333	2	1.46563	1.67473	1.62891
Std.Dev. of Time in System	1.24722	2	1.44959	1.48174	1.43201
Average Time Spent in Queue	0.333333	1	0.465635	0.674725	0.62891
Std.Dev. of Time in Queue	0.745356	1.73205	1.04943	1.09342	1.02502
Fraction of Time Syst. Empty	0.333333	0.25	0.303164	0.279789	0.241047
Fraction of Customers Lost	0	0	0	0	0

Fraction of Time N Customers in the System

No. of Cust. in System, N					
0	0.333333	0.25	0.303164	0.279789	0.241047
1	0.333333	0.25	0.322062	0.254037	0.276121
2	0.166667	0.1875	0.203544	0.217059	0.23487
3	0.0833333	0.125	0.0896203	0.121223	0.128451
4	0.0416667	0.078125	0.0476332	0.0701517	0.0697026
5	0.0208333	0.046875	0.0219029	0.0338121	0.0331979
6	0.0104167	0.0273438	0.0066157	0.0102698	0.0132626
7	5.21E-03	0.015625	0.0025419	0.005116	0.0033475
8	2.60E-03	0.0087891	0.0025696	0.0033027	0
9	1.30E-03	0.0048828	0.0003456	0.001075	0
10	6.51E-04	0.0026856	0	0.0010963	0
11	0.0003255	0.0014648	0	0.000928	0
		0.0007935	0	0.0014693	
		0.0004272	0	0.0006711	
		0.0002289	0	0	
		0.0001221	0		
		6.48E-05	0		
		3.43E-05	0		
		1.81E-05	0		
		9.54E-06			
		5.01E-06			

Example 7   **Finite Waiting Area in an M/Erlang$_2$/2 Queue**

An example of a two–server queue, with Erlang$_2$ service time distribution and exponential inter-arrival time with finite waiting area for six customers, is given below. The data are in MERL2.DAT. No outputs are shown.

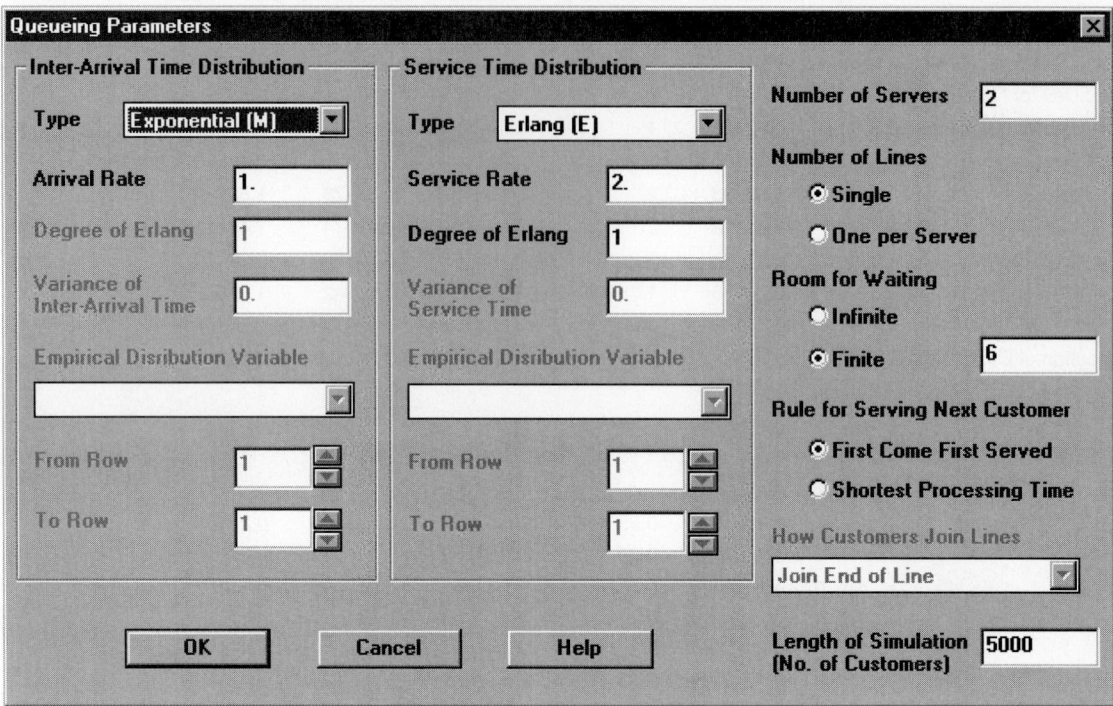

The plots of the service time and inter-arrival time distributions are shown below.

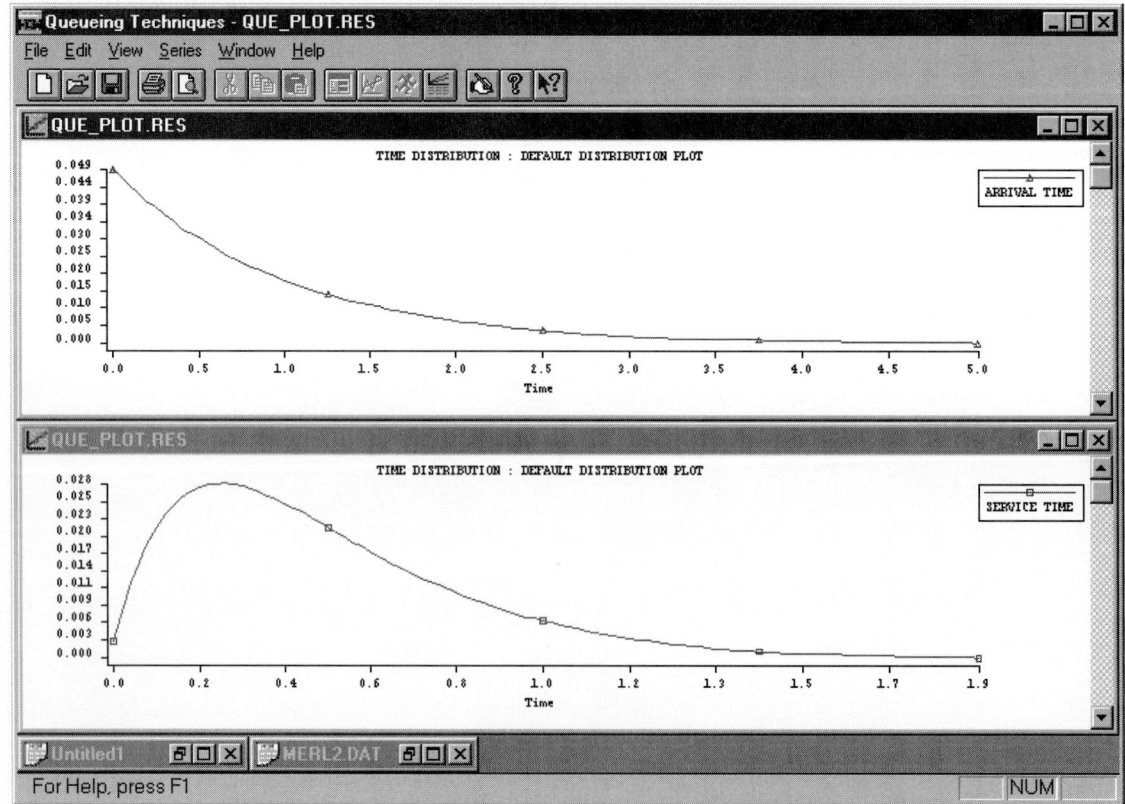

Example 8

The file MM1SPT.DAT contains the model of an M/M/1 queue in which the SPT discipline is used and there is waiting room for only two customers. The outputs for the SPT and FCFS discipline are compared below. The SPT example is shown on top, the FCFS example is given below. Notice the improvement in the number of lost customers due to the use of the SPT rule.

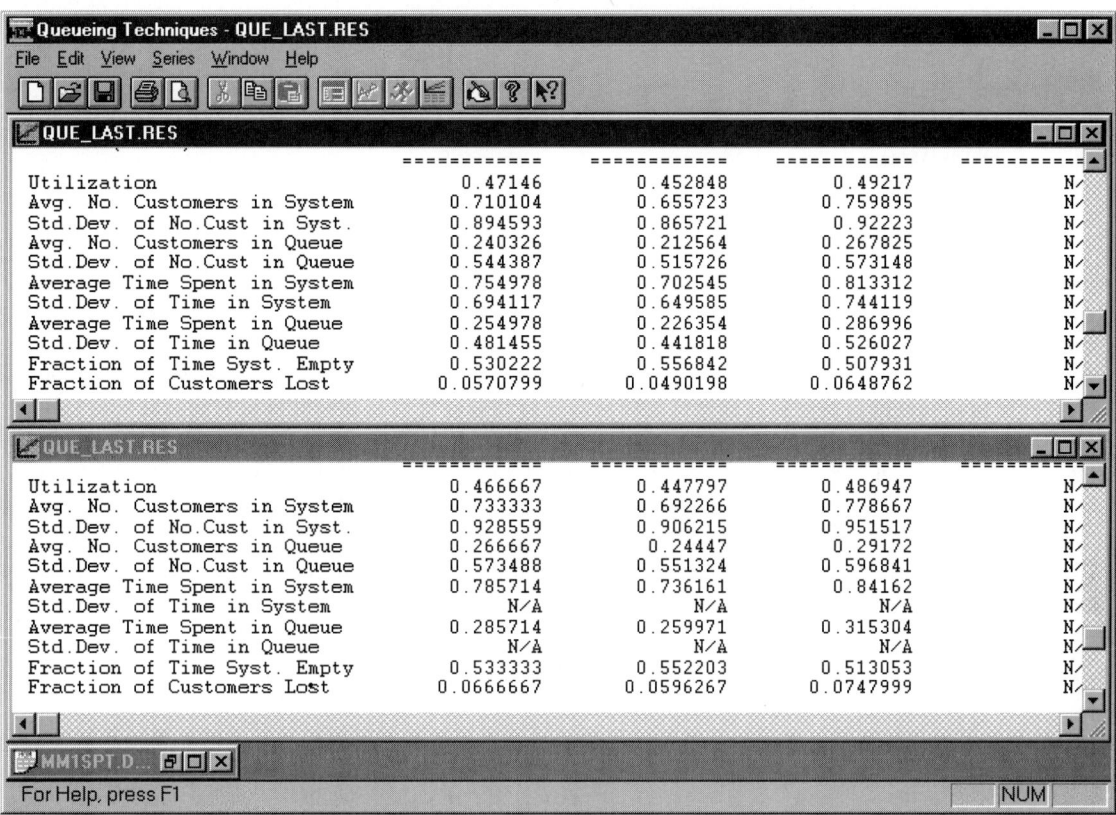

7. EXPORT AND IMPORT OF DATA AS WELL AS RESULTS

HOM has the ability to export final and interim results to a spreadsheet or word processing program. To do this you should have run and obtained results and must be in the Results window. Use the Edit function on the menu bar to copy the results, and then switch to the spreadsheet program and paste to export the results.

To import data into the HOM spreadsheet from your favorite spreadsheet program, simply copy the data from the spreadsheet, switch over to HOM, and paste it into the desired location.

Exporting/importing to a spreadsheet will also allow you to do more complex mathematical operations to your data, if you so desire, or create more elaborate graphs, and so on.

8. SOLUTION TECHNIQUES

The solution techniques used in HOM have been organized as per the Inter-Arrival Time Distribution. Select the inter-arrival time distribution from the list given below:

Exponential (M)

Deterministic (D)

Erlang (E)

General (G)

Empirical (CI)

Hint! In order to force HOM to simulate an M/M/C queue, select the inter-arrival and/or the service distribution to be erlang of degree one (1). This device also gives the user some feel for the usual length of simulation. For example, at low levels of utilization (or high loss rate of customers), a value of 1,000 or 5,000 customers should suffice. Whereas, at relatively high levels of utilization, a simulation length of 50,000 customers might be necessary.

Hint! HOM's Waiting Line Module can **not be used to simulate priority queues** to multiple types (classes) of customers. The Process Analysis Module should be used for that purpose. [A priority queue is one in which customers belonging to different classes (i.e., customers of different types) are assigned different priorities for obtaining service. A customer with a higher priority obtains service earlier in comparison to a customer with lower priority.]

8.1 Exponentially Distributed Inter-Arrival Time (Part 1)

Inter-Arrival Time Distribution	Exponential	Exponential	Exponential
Service Time Distribution	Exponential	Exponential	Exponential
Room for Waiting (buffer space) (max 200 if finite)	Finite or Infinite	Finite or Infinite	Finite or Infinite
Number of Servers (max 15)	1 to 15	1 to 15	1 to 15
Number Of Lines	Single or Multiple	Single or Multiple	Multiple
Rule for Serving Next Customer	FCFS	SPT	FCFS
How Customers Join Lines. (customer behavior)	Random if Multiple	Jockey not Allowed	Cyclic, Shortest Line Jockey
MODEL NAME (in output)	M/M/C or M/M/C/Rand	Simulation	Simulation
Solution Technique	Analytical if infinite waiting space, else Analytical + Simulation for the variance of the waiting time.	Simulation	Simulation

8.2 Exponentially Distributed Inter-Arrival Time (Part 2)

Inter-Arrival Time Distribution	Exponential	Exponential	Exponential
Service Time Distribution	General	General	General
Room for Waiting (buffer space) (max 200 if finite)	Infinite (finite not allowed)	Infinite (finite not allowed)	Infinite (finite not allowed)
NUMBER of SERVERS (max 15)	Single	2 to 15	2 to 15
Number of Lines	Single	Single	Multiple
Rule for Serving Next Customer	FCFS (SPT not allowed)	FCFS (SPT not allowed)	FCFS (SPT not allowed)
How Customers Join Lines. (customer behavior)	Not Applicable	Not Applicable	Random (Cyclic, Shortest Line, and Jockey not allowed)
Model Name (in output)	M/G/1	M/G/C	M/G/C/Rand
Solution Technique	Analytical And Approximation for probability there are "n" or fewer customers in the system	Approximation for all performance measures	Analytical And Approximation for Probability there are "n" or fewer customers in the system

8.3 Exponentially Distributed Inter-Arrival Time (Part 3)

Inter-Arrival Time Distribution	Exponential	Exponential
Service Time Distribution	Deterministic, Erlang, or Empirical	Deterministic, Erlang, or Empirical
Size of Waiting Area (buffer space) (max 200 if finite)	Infinite	All other combinations Except Multiple lines+SPT+Jockey
Number of Servers (max 15)	1 to 15	‖
Number of Lines	Single or Multiple	‖
Rule for Serving Next Customer	FCFS	‖
How Customers Join Lines. (customer behavior)	Random if Multiple	‖ V
Model Name (in output)	M/G/1/Sim or M/G/C/Sim when single line and multiple servers	Simulation
Solution Technique	Analytical using M/G/1 formulae or Approx. using M/G/C model and simulation for probability of "n" or fewer customers in the system	Simulation

8.4 Inter-Arrival Time Distribution General

Inter-Arrival Time Distribution	General
Service Time Distribution	All
Size of Waiting Area (buffer space)	Infinite (Finite not allowed)
Number of Servers	1 to 15
Number of Lines	Single (Multiple not allowed)
Rule for Serving Next Customer	FCFS (SPT not allowed)
How Customers Join Lines. (customer behavior)	Not applicable
Model Name (in output)	GI/G/1 if single server GI/G/C if multiple servers
Solution Technique	Approximation For all performance Measures. Variance of time in queue and Time in system not available

8.5 Inter-Arrival Time Distribution Deterministic, Erlang, or Empirical

Inter-Arrival Time Distribution	Deterministic, Erlang, or Empirical	Deterministic, Erlang, or Empirical
Service Time Distribution	General	All except General
Size of Waiting Area (buffer space)	Infinite (Finite not allowed)	All combinations Except
Number of Servers	1 to 15	Multiple lines+SPT+Jockey
		‖
		‖
Number of Lines	Single (Multiple not allowed)	‖
		‖
Rule for Serving Next Customer	FCFS (SPT not allowed)	‖
		‖
		‖
How Customers Join Lines. (customer behavior)	Not applicable	‖
		‖
		V
Model Name (in output)	GI/G/1 if single server GI/G/C if multiple servers	Simulation
Solution Technique	Approximation for all performance Measures. Variance of time in queue and time in system not available	Simulation

8.6 Formulae

The notation employed is as follows:

Exponential	M
Erlang of degree k	E_k
General	G
Deterministic	D
Empirical	CI (for class interval)
Arrival Rate	λ
Service Rate	μ
Number of Servers	C
Utilization	ρ
Prob. n customers in the system	P(n)

Customers in the System	Customers in the queue and being served
Customers in the Queue	Customers waiting in the queue

8.7.1 M/M/C — Single Line — FCFS — Infinite or Finite Waiting Area

The formulae for the average delay and the average number of customers in the queue for this case are omitted. These can be found in most textbooks; see, for example, Buzacott and Shanthikumar (1992) section 3.4. Denote the utilization of the system as $\rho = \lambda/(C\mu)$, where λ = the arrival rate, μ = the service rate, and C is the number of servers. Let P(n) denote the fraction of time there are n customers in the system. The probability that the waiting time in the queue exceeds x is given by

$$P(W > x) = e^{-(C\mu - \lambda)x} \left(\frac{C^C \rho^C}{C!(1-\rho)} \right) P(0), \quad x > 0.$$

8.7.2 M/M/C — Multiple Lines — Random Customer Behavior — Infinite or Finite Waiting Area

Each queue is modeled as an M/M/1 queue. The statistics are aggregated and given for the entire system. In particular, the probability distribution for the number of customers in the queue and system is obtained by convolving (adding up) the distributions for the M/M/1 queue.

8.7.3 M/G/1 — FCFS — Infinite Waiting Area

The formulae for the average number of customers in the queue and in the system, as well as the average waiting time in the queue and the system, are standard. These can be found in most textbooks; see, for example, Buzacott and Shanthikumar (1992) section 3.3.2. The approximation suggested in Buzacott and Shanthikumar (1992) for the probability distribution of the number of customers in the system is employed. The approximation procedure consists of following the steps given below. The procedure is employed in several places and is therefore presented for the general case.

Algorithm for Approximating P(n) in a single server queue

Step 1: Determine an exact or approximate value of the expected number of jobs in the system. Denote this value as N.

Step 2: Denote the utilization of the system as $\rho = \lambda/(C\mu)$, where λ = the arrival rate, μ = the service rate, and C is the number of servers.

Step 3: Let $\sigma = (N - \rho)/N$.

Step 4: $P(0) = 1 - \rho$, $P(n) = \rho(1- \sigma)\sigma^{n-1}$, for $n > 0$.

end

The approximation for $P(n)$ are based on the algorithm given above. These values tend to be indicative rather than precise measures of the values of $P(n)$. The variance of waiting times is not available for this model.

8.7.4 M/G/C — FCFS — Infinite Waiting Area

The approximations suggested in Buzacott and Shanthikumar (1992) section 3.4, are used to determine the average number of customers in the queue and in the system, as well as the average waiting time in the queue and the system. The key step in the approximation is given below.

Denote the utilization of the system as $\rho = \lambda/(C\mu)$, where λ = the arrival rate, μ = the service rate, and C is the number of servers. $P(n)$ is the fraction of time there are n customers in the system.

Let $E[W(M/M/1)]$ be the expected waiting time in the queue in an M/M/1 queue with $\rho = \lambda/(C\mu)$, λ = the arrival rate, $C\mu$ = the service rate, and the number of servers is one (1).

Let $E[W(M/M/C)]$ be the expected waiting time in the queue in an M/M/C queue with $\rho = \lambda/(C\mu)$, λ = the arrival rate, μ = the service rate, and the number of servers is C.

Let $E[W(M/G/1)]$ be the expected waiting time in the queue in an M/G/1 queue with $\rho = \lambda/(C\mu)$, λ = the arrival rate, $C\mu$ = the service rate, and the number of servers is one (1).

Let $E[W(M/G/C)]$ be the expected waiting time in the queue in an M/G/C queue with $\rho = \lambda/(C\mu)$, λ = the arrival rate, μ = the service rate, and the number of servers is C.

Then, the approximation consists of setting

$$E[W(M/G/C)] \approx (E[W(M/M/C)]/ E[W(M/M/1)]) \times E[W(M/G/1)].$$

The approximation for $P(n)$ are based on the algorithm given section 8.7.3. These values tend to be indicative rather than precise measures of the values of P(n). The variance of waiting times is not available for this model.

8.7.5 GI/G/1 — FCFS — Infinite Waiting Area

The approximations suggested in Table 3.1 of Buzacott and Shanthikumar (1992) are used to determine the average number of customers in the queue and in the system, as well as the average waiting time in the queue and the system. The algorithm given in section 8.7.3 is used to approximate the values of P(n).

These values tend to be indicative rather than precise measures. The variance of waiting times is not available for this model.

8.7.6 GI/G/C -- FCFS -- Infinite Waiting Area

The approximations suggested in Buzacott and Shanthikumar (1992) are used to determine the average number of customers in the queue and in the system, as well as the average waiting time in the GI/G/1 queue and the system. Thereafter, the procedures given in section 8.7.3 and 8.7.4 are used to approximate the performance measures for the GI/G/C queue.

These values tend to be indicative rather than precise measures. The variance of waiting times is not available for this model.

REFERENCES

Buzacott, J. A., and J. G. Shanthikumar. *Stochastic Models of Manufacturing Systems*. Englewood Cliffs, NJ: Prentice Hall, 1992.

Ross, S. M. *Stochastic Processes*. New York: John Wiley & Sons, 1983.

Wolff, R. W. *Stochastic Modeling and the Theory of Queues,* Englewood Cliffs, NJ: Prentice Hall, 1989.

Northeast Islands Air[1]

Northeast Islands Air (NIA) is a startup airline supplying four times a day service to the Major Northeast Islands of Martha's Vineyard, Nantucket, Prince Edward, etc. from New York, Philadelphia, Baltimore, Washington, D.C., and Atlanta. Newark airport's newly renovated north terminal is to be the principal hub of the system. As part of the design team, you have been asked to help select which of two check-in service area configurations that have been made available to NIA.

The Port Authority of New York and New Jersey can make available, at the chosen location, two basic customer check-in configurations. The first is the typical design (Chart I), found in most airports, with up to nine locations in a line with an automated baggage carrying system behind each location. Management and staff offices are behind the moving baggage beltway. There is enough depth in the front area of the terminal to support customer waiting systems of unlimited length in separate lines behind each location, or several "s" lines for different classes of ticket holding customers (first, tourist, frequent flyer, etc.).

The second configuration being offered has the capacity for ten service locations with a somewhat smaller, but sufficient, staff area. However, in this configuration, four locations would be at the back of the facility and six would be across the front with the baggage beltway running between them as illustrated in Chart II. There is sufficient space at both the front and back to allow for unlimited and unconstrained waiting line design.

In both configurations, the baggage beltway has been designed with a beneficial ergonomic height of two feet off the ground. The speed of the baggage beltway makes it quite unsafe to walk on or over it for either configuration.

The company has been in existence for two years at another location, and has been gathering data on service times and arrival patterns almost continuously. Due to the well trained staff, service times do not vary from day to day, or time of day, or length of line. However, there is more variability in service time between first class/ priority frequent flyer and normal tourist passengers. The service time distributions for the two classes of customers are given in Exhibit 1.

The time between passenger arrivals does not vary by customer class, but does vary significantly from day to day and at different times of the day. Fridays are always the busiest days at Newark Airport (independent of which of the three seasons is involved). Data for Peak (summer), Shoulder (late spring and early fall), and Off-peak (remainder) arrivals are given in Exhibits 2, 3, and 4. The maximum demand on the system is from 4-7 p.m. on Friday in any season. The arrival patterns for Peak season Friday afternoon (4-7 p.m.) are given in Exhibit 5. The 4-7 p.m. demand in the Off and Shoulder periods is light enough so that they need not be differentiated, and can be considered as one distribution (Exhibit 6).

The Airline does not want its first class/priority frequent flyer passengers, 25 percent of total customers, to wait more than four minutes on average, nor its other passengers to wait in line more than eight minutes on average. The Airline's most important customers (those who make more than 20 round trips per year to their second home on the Islands) have a preference for being serviced by particular customer service representatives, and desire to be able to queue up behind such individuals. These passengers either travel first class or are priority frequent flyers. Thus, some consideration is being given to serving them in individual rather than "s" lines. The Airline feels that it is necessary to maintain a utilization rate for service providers of at least 70%. The monthly rental for facility type one is $10,000, and for facility type two is $9,000. Service providers cost $2,500 per month including benefits.

Which configuration would you recommend? Why and how would you design the customer service system? What service guarantee could you give if you wanted to have at least 75% of each class of customer satisfied within the guaranteed time (try using Chebyshev's inequality[2])? What would your annual staffing plan be? HINT: Remember that if you intend to divide the arrival distributions between first class and tourist, you must think about how to adjust the interarrival times for each customer class to reflect the

---

[1] By Michael Moses, Operations Management Area, Stern School of Business. This case is for the use of students in a core course in Operations Management and is intended to have no actual relationship to any real person or organization. (11/98)

[2] Chebyshev's inequality states that given a random variable X, whose mean and standard deviation are μ and σ, and a constant $k > 0$, then the probability that X is greater than or equal to $\mu + k\sigma$ is less than or equal to $1/k^2$. Hint: Use $k = 2$.

reduced number of customers in each class. As an alternative you might want to think about how to adjust the arrival rates to reflect the same phenomenon.

CHART I - TYPE 1

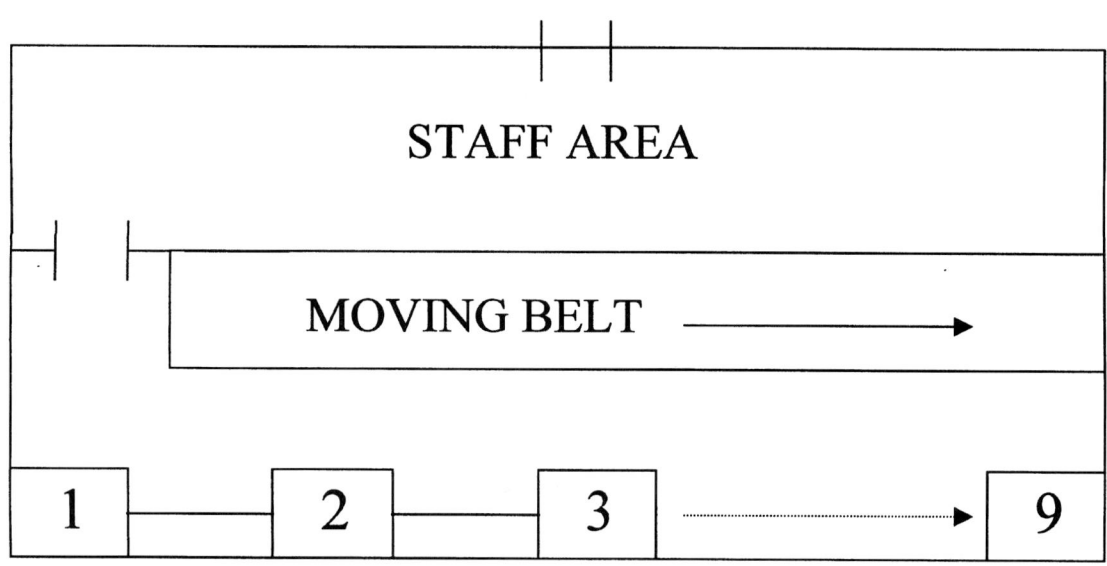

CHART II - TYPE II

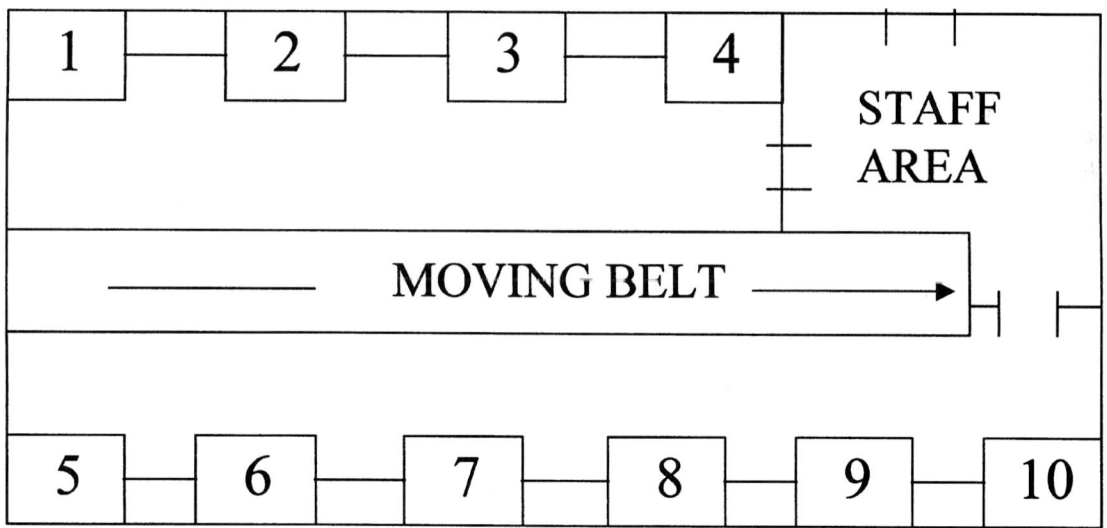

Exhibit 1

Service Time Distributions

Service Time Range (min.)	Total Number of First Class Customers Served	Total Number of Normal Customers Served	All Customers if 75% Normal, 25% First Class*
			.75N + .25F
.01-2	55	45	47.5
2-4	57	43	46.5
4-6	29	34	32.8
4-8	26	27	26.8
8-10	22	28	26.5
10-12	12	14	13.5
12-14	7	12	10.8
14-16	8	9	8.75
16-18	3	8	6.75
18-20	4	3	3.25
20-22	3	2	2.25
22-24	2	3	2.25
Total Observations	228	228	-----------

* Clearly assuming 100% Normal would be worst case or 100% first class would be best case.

Exhibit 2

Inter-Arrival Time Distribution for Peak Season

Time Interval (minutes)	Number of Customers
0-1	83
1-2	74
2-3	60
3-4	38
4-5	34
5-6	21
6-7	17
7-8	21
8-9	20
9-10	14
10-11	7
11-12	11
12-13	7
13-14	4
14-15	7
15-16	0
16-17	1
17-18	1
18-19	2

Exhibit 3

Inter-Arrival Time Distribution for Shoulder Season

Time Interval (minutes)	Number of Customers
0-2	77
2-4	66
4-6	49
6-8	43
8-10	34
10-12	27
12-14	30
14-16	14
16-18	19
18-20	16
20-22	14
22-24	6
24-26	8
26-28	6
28-30	3
30-32	4
32-34	4
34-36	3
36-38	5

Exhibit 4

Inter-Arrival Time and Distribution for Off-Season

Time Interval (minutes)	Number of Customers
0-2.5	62
2.5-5	55
5-7.5	46
7.5-10	52
10-12.5	28
12.5-15	36
15-17.5	16
17.5-20	21
20-22.5	21
22.5-25	11
25-27.5	20
27.5-30	17
30-32.5	6
32.5-35	11
35-37.5	5
37.5-40	3
40-42.5	5
42.5-45	3
45-47.5	3

Exhibit 5

Inter-Arrival Time Distribution for Friday's 4-7 PM Peak Season

Time Interval (minutes)	Number of Customers
0-.25	95
.25-.5	82
.5-.75	59
.75-1	50
1-1.25	32
1.25-1.5	26
1.5-1.75	17
1.75-2	16
2-2.25	9
2.25-2.5	5
2.5-2.75	10
2.75-3	3
3-3.25	3
3.25-3.5	1
3.5-3.75	2
3.75-4	0
4-4.25	2
4.25-4.5	1
4.5-4.75	1

Exhibit 6

Inter-Arrival Time Distribution for Friday's 4-7 PM Shoulder/Off-Season

Time Interval (minutes)	Number of Customers
0-.5	80
.5-1	71
1-1.5	61
1.5-2	52
2-2.5	36
2.5-3	28
3-3.5	24
3.5-4	26
4-4.5	6
4.5-5	8
5-5.5	11
5.5-6	8
6-6.5	5
6.5-7	4
7-7.5	2
7.5-8	3
8-8.5	2
8.5-9	2
9-9.5	3

QUALITY MANAGMENT

1. INTRODUCTION

The Quality Management module consists of three different submodules. The first two pertain to Statistical Process Control and the third to Acceptance Sampling. The three submodules are
- Statistical Process Control: Sampling by Variables (section 2)
- Statistical Process Control: Sampling by Attributes (section 3)
- Acceptance Sampling (section 4).

The Sampling by Variables submodule is used to determine parameters for and construct $\overline{X}$ (X bar or sample mean), R (range), and s (sample standard deviation) charts. These three charts can be used when the control is sought with regard to a dimension of the output that is measurable. For example, the weight of cereals in a box, the salt content of chips, or the percent of impurities in filtered water are important dimensions of the output of a process that are also measurable. The Sampling by Attributes submodule is used to construct p (fraction nonconforming), np (number nonconforming), c (number of nonconformities), and u (number of nonconformities per unit) charts. These charts are used either when each item in the output can be classified as good or bad, or when the number of defects in the output can be counted. The charts are used to plot certain statistics of samples drawn at periodic intervals. Control limits drawn on the chart help determine whether the process variations are random or not. If the only variations in the process are random in nature, then the process is said to be in control. Variations that are not random indicate that the process might have changed due to an assignable cause. The trade-off faced when designing these charts is stopping a process that is in control versus not stopping a process that has gone out of control.

Acceptance Sampling in HOM comprises drawing a sample from a lot and examining the sample to decide whether or not the lot should be rejected. There are many other sampling techniques that have been designed for a similar purpose, but these are not implemented in HOM. The interested reader should consult the references given at the end of this manual.

Sections 2, 3, and 4 contain instructions for using these submodules. Section 5 has several examples.

2. STATISTICAL PROCESS CONTROL: SAMPLING BY VARIABLES

Sampling by variables means that you are observing some process whose output is measurable as a number (10" or 101 degrees Fahrenheit). The objective is to determine the parameters of a chart that will help you determine whether the process is under statistical control. A process is said to be in statistical control if the variations observed in the output of the process are random in nature, that is, the variations cannot be attributed to a specific cause. The charts used for statistical process control are based on control limits (usually depicted as horizontal lines). The X-axis of the chart represents time and the Y-axis, the sample mean or the range of values in a sample or the sample standard deviation.

Samples are drawn at regular intervals and their parameters plotted on the chart. (There are separate charts for the mean, range, and standard deviation.) If the parameters of the sample (such as the mean and/or range) fall within the control limits and do not exhibit any nonrandom pattern, then there are grounds to believe that the process is under control.

Three types of charts can be produced using HOM: a chart for plotting the sample average ($\overline{X}$ chart), a chart for plotting the range of observed values in each sample (R chart), and a chart for plotting the sample standard deviation (s chart). The plot of such values allows you to predict with a certain degree of confidence whether or not the process is within statistical control.

The sampling of the output is carried out at predetermined intervals. HOM allows you to enter either each observation in a sample (e.g., 2, 3, 4, 5) or just the aggregate information, such as the sample average (e.g., (2 + 3 + 4 + 5)/4 = 3.5) and range (e.g., 5 – 2 = 3).of the observations in the sample

On starting the program for Sampling by Variables, you will see a HOM spreadsheet. Before you enter any data, open the Parameters dialog box to choose the parameters of the problem.

Caution: HOM does not have the capability to undo any command and cannot undertake algebraic manipulation of column or row data. These operations can be done by exporting and importing data as well as results to a spreadsheet program. Any word in the Help file that is highlighted leads to more context-sensitive help on the meaning of that word. Data files for sampling by variables have the extension, VAR.

2.1 Selecting the Charts and Parameters in Parameters Dialog Box

You will see several choices in the Parameters dialog box. These are described below. Having made your choices, click on OK to close the dialog box. Proceed to Entering Data.

2.1.1 *Data Type*

Your choice on this item determines the type of data that you will be entering. If you have data for each observation in a sample, then choose Actual Data Only. Otherwise, if the data are available in an aggregate form, that is, you have the average of the observations in each sample and the range (or sample standard deviation) for each sample, then choose Mean Data Only.

If you choose Actual Data Only, HOM will compute the average, range, and sample standard deviation for each sample. You cannot combine the two data types.

2.1.2 *Sample Size*

Fixed Sample Size. HOM by default assumes that the size of the sample (i.e., how many items are sampled each time) is fixed. If the sample size is fixed, then select the Fixed radio button, and enter the Fixed Sample Size in the adjoining edit box.

Variable Sample Size. HOM allows the sample size to vary from one sample to another. If this is the case, choose the radio button adjacent to Variable and enter the Maximum Sample Size in the edit box.

2.1.3 *Process Parameters and Control Limits*

Estimation of Process Parameters. The user can either let HOM estimate the process mean, sample, range, and process standard deviation or input known values for any of these three quantities. If any of these three values are known, then select the corresponding Known radio button and enter the appropriate value in the edit box.

Estimation of Parameters (Computing Control Limits). Each row in the HOM spreadsheet corresponds to a sample. The user specifies which of these samples, that is, the contiguous rows of data, will be used to estimate the process mean ($\overline{\overline{X}}$), the mean range ($\overline{R}$), and the process standard deviation. In other words, the user can specify that control limits should be determined using, for example, the 10 rows of data starting from row 5 through row 14 even though there are data in rows 1 through 50. (In this example, the From Row is 5 and the To Row is 14.) This permits the user to determine control limits using part of the data and plot the remaining data to verify whether the process is under control.

Enter the From Row and the To Row numbers. All the data between the two rows (From and To Row inclusive) will be used to determine the control limits. Please note that if the user has entered any of the three values (mean, range, and standard deviation) and also specified that these values are Known, then the known value(s) will be used to compute the control limits. For example, if the sample mean were known and entered as 4.3, then HOM will use this value for the centerline of the $\overline{X}$ chart.

> **Note**: The value entered for the To Row must be greater than the From Row. Otherwise HOM will not allow the user to close the Parameters dialog box.

2.1.4 *Chart and Statistics*

The user **must** select at least one of three charts to be plotted from:

- ❑ $\overline{X}$-Chart
- ❑ R-Chart
- ❑ s-Chart

The $\overline{X}$ chart is a plot of the sample means, the R chart is a plot of the range of values in each sample, and the s chart is a plot of the standard deviation of the sample. The user must select the rows of data (i.e., the sample mean/range/standard deviation) that will be plotted. These rows can be the same, inclusive, or different from the rows used to determine the control limits. The data are plotted starting from the value entered in the From Row edit box and ending with the value entered in To Row edit box.

2.1.5 Factors for Drawing the Control Limits (Optional Input)

The control limits are determined by multiplying the standard deviation of the quantity being plotted (sample mean, range, or standard deviation) by certain factors. Typically these factors are +/− 2 standard deviations for the Warning limits and +/− 3 standard deviation for the Action limits. The user can change any of these factors if so desired.

2.1.6 Process Capability Indices (Optional Input)

The process standard deviation and the process mean (or their estimates) can be used in combination with the upper and lower specification limits to compute process capability indices. The process capability index is a nonnegative number. A value of the capability index that is greater than one suggests that the process is capable of consistently producing items whose measurement lies within the lower and the upper specification limits. If the value is less than one, there is cause for concern that a significant part of the output from the process will not fall within the two specification limits. Please consult any of the references in Section 6 for details about the construction and use of these indices.

2.2 Entering Data

Enter the data depending on the choices you have made in the Parameters dialog box and after consulting the guidelines given below. After entering your data, save your data file and proceed to Obtaining Results.

Data Type: Mean Data and Fixed Sample Size. Each row contains the data from a sample. Enter the sample number (1, 2, 3,... or Mon, Tue, . . .) in the first column. Enter the sample mean and the sample range in the third and the fourth columns. Enter the sample standard deviation in fourth column only if you want the *s* chart to be plotted. Otherwise, this column can be left blank. All other columns must be filled in. Missing values of the sample mean ($\overline{X}$) and/or the sample range are not allowed. The second column shows the fixed sample size and cannot be edited.

Data Type: Mean Data and Variable Sample Size. Each row contains the data from a sample. Enter the sample number (1, 2, 3, . . . or Mon, Tue, . . .) in the first column. Enter the size of the sample in the second column (e.g., if the numbers of items sampled are 3, 4, 3, 5 in the first four samples; then enter 3, 4, 3, 5 in the second column). Enter the sample mean and the sample range in the next two columns. Enter the sample standard deviation in the fifth column only if you want the *s* chart to be plotted. Otherwise, this column can be left blank.

Enter the data in contiguous columns. Missing values of the sample mean ($\overline{X}$) and/or the sample range between two entries, such as 2, __, 2, will lead to an error message.

Data Type: Actual Data Only and Fixed Sample Size. Each row contains the data from a sample. Enter the sample number (1, 2, 3, . . . or Mon, Tue, . . .) in the first column. Enter the observations from each sample in the corresponding rows. The number of columns for entering the data equals the fixed sample size.

Data Type: Actual Data Only and Variable Sample Size. Each row contains the data from a sample. The size of each sample is determined implicitly based on the number of values that you enter. Enter the observations from each sample, row by row. Fill only as many *contiguous* columns as the size of the sample. (For example: you have specified the maximum size of a sample to be equal to 4. If sample 1 has two observations, then fill columns A and B of the first row. If sample 2 then has three observations, then fill columns A, B, and C of row 2.) The number of columns equals the maximum sample size.

> **Note:** Switching from one data type to another or from fixed sample size to variable sample size will cause you to lose your data. Save your data before making such a change. Data files for Sampling by Variables have the extension. VAR.

2.3 Obtaining Results

Once the data have been entered, click on the Run icon or RUN on the HOM command line to obtain the results. You will see the following outputs:

1. The charts that you have checked. The charts will contain a centerline as well as upper and lower warning and action limits. Please consult a standard textbook on statistical process control to interpret the charts.

2. Tables produced by HOM (corresponding to each type of chart selected by the user. Each table contains the data used to generate the chart. HOM also produces certain statistics that permit the user to interpret whether the pattern observed in the chart can be attributed to chance. The explanation of these statistics can be found in Section 5 of the manual. The output can be saved as a file, printed, or exported to a spreadsheet or word processing software for further analysis. Results files have the extension. RES. Please refer to the RESULTS command in the on-line Help.

3. Additional output that has been customized to some extent by clicking on the SERIES item on the HOM command line. For example, the user can request the plot of the sample mean as a histogram to verify whether the sample means follow a normal distribution.

3. STATISTICAL PROCESS CONTROL: SAMPLING BY ATTRIBUTES

Sampling by attributes means that you are observing some process whose output is such that either each item can be classified as good or bad, or the number of defects in each sample can be counted. The objective is to determine the parameters of a chart that will help you determine whether the process is under statistical control. A process is said to be in statistical control if the variations observed in the output of the process are random in nature, that is, the variations cannot be attributed to a specific cause. The charts used for statistical process control are based on control limits (usually depicted as horizontal lines). The X-axis of the chart represents time and the Y-axis, the fraction of defective items or the number of defects per sample.

Samples are drawn at regular intervals and the fraction of nonconforming items or the number of nonconformities in a sample are plotted on the chart. If the parameter of the sample (such as the fraction of nonconforming items or the number of nonconformities in a sample) falls within the control limits and does not exhibit any nonrandom pattern, then there are grounds to believe that the process is under control.

Four types of charts can be produced using HOM: (i) a chart for plotting the fraction of nonconforming items (p chart), (ii) a chart showing the number of nonconformities in a sample (np chart), and (iii) & (iv) charts of the number of nonconformities in a sample (c and u charts). The plot of such values allows you to predict with a certain degree of confidence whether or not the process is within statistical control.

On starting the program for Sampling by Attributes, you will see a HOM spreadsheet. Before you enter any data, open the Parameters dialog box to choose the parameters of the problem.

<u>Caution!</u> HOM does not have the capability to undo any command and cannot undertake algebraic manipulation of column or row data. These operations can be done by exporting and importing data as well as results to a spreadsheet program. Any word in the Help file that is highlighted leads to more context-sensitive help on the meaning of that word. Data files for sampling by attributes have the extension. ATT.

3.1 Selecting the Chart and its Parameters

You will see several choices in the Parameters dialog box. A brief description of these choices is given below. Having made your choices, click on OK to close the dialog box. Proceed to Entering Data.

3.1.1 Chart type

Four types of charts can be produced using HOM, namely the p chart, the np chart, the c chart, and the u chart. Only one type of chart can be drawn at a time.

The p chart is used when the sample size is fixed and when each item in the output can be classified only as good or bad. The p stands for the fraction of nonconforming items in a sample. The np chart is used when the sample size can be variable. The np stands for the number of nonconforming items in a sample.

The *c* chart is used when the sample size is fixed and the number of nonconformities (defects) in a sample can be counted. For example, the number of defects in a square yard of cloth can be counted and recorded on a *c* chart. The *c* stands for the number of nonconformities. The *u* chart is used to plot the number of nonconformities when the sample size is variable.

3.1.2 Sample Size

A fixed sample size means that each time the number of items sampled is the same. A variable sample size means that the number of items sampled can be different from sample to sample. The *p* (usually) and the *c* charts assume that the sample size is fixed. The *np* chart and the *u* chart are used when the sample size is variable.

Enter the value of the Fixed Sample Size or the Maximum Sample Size according to your choice of Fixed or Variable sample size.

3.1.3 Process Parameters and Control Limits

Estimation of Process Parameters. The user can either let HOM estimate the fraction of nonconforming items in a sample (*p* or *np* chart) or the average number of nonconformities (*c* or *u* chart), or input the known value for the process. If the value is known, then select the corresponding Known radio button and enter the appropriate value in the edit box.

Each row in the HOM spreadsheet corresponds to a sample. The user specifies which of these samples, that is, the contiguous rows of data, will be used to estimate the fraction of nonconforming items in a sample (*p* or *np* chart) or the average number of nonconformities (*c* or *u* chart). In other words, control limits can be determined, for example, using the 10 rows of data starting from row 5 through row 14 even though there are data in rows 1 through 50. (In this example, the From Row is 5 and the To Row is 14.) This permits the user to determine control limits using part of the data and plot the remaining data to verify whether the process is under control.

Enter the From Row and the To Row numbers. All the data between the two rows (From and To Row inclusive) will be used to determine the control limits. Please note that if the user has entered the value and also specified that the value is Known, then the known value will be used to compute the control limits. For example, if the fraction of nonconforming items were known and entered as 0.45, then HOM will use this value for the centerline of the $\bar{p}$ chart.

3.1.4 Chart and Statistics

The user must select the rows of data that will be plotted. These rows can be the same, inclusive, or different from the rows used to determine the control limits. Enter the From Row and the To Row of data that will be plotted.

3.1.5 Factors for Control Limits (Optional Input)

The control limits are determined by multiplying the standard deviation of the quantity being plotted (sample mean, range, or standard deviation) by certain factors. Typically these factors are +/– 2 standard deviations for the Warning limits and +/– 3 standard deviations for the Action limits. The user can change any of these factors if so desired.

3.2 Entering Data

Enter the data depending on the choices you have made in the Parameters dialog box and after consulting the guidelines given below. After entering your data, save your data file and proceed to Obtaining Results.

Data Type: p *or* np *Chart with Fixed Sample Size.* Enter the sample number (1, 2, 3, . . . or Mon, Tue, Wed, . . .) and the number of nonconforming items (for example, if there are two defective items and four defective items in the first two samples, then enter 2 and 4 in the third column of rows 1 and 2). The second column cannot be edited, it shows the fixed sample size.

Data Type: p *or* np *Chart with Variable Sample Size.* Enter the sample number, the sample size, and the number of nonconforming items in the sample. For example, say two samples are drawn, the first of 10 items and the second of 15 items. Let there be no nonconforming items in the first sample and one nonconforming item in the second sample. Then enter the values 10 and 15 in the second column of rows 1 and 2. Enter the values 0 and 1 in the third column of rows 1 and 2.

Data Type: c *Chart.* In each row enter the sample number and the number of nonconformities in the sample. The second column shows the fixed sample size and cannot be edited. For example, if the numbers of nonconformities are 1, 0, 2, 3 in the first four samples, enter these values in the third column of rows 1 to 4.

Data Type: u *Chart.* Enter the sample number, the sample size, and the number of nonconformities in the sample. For example, if the numbers of nonconformities are 1, 0, 2, 3 in the first four samples and the sample sizes are 1, 1, 2, 1 respectively, then enter values 1, 1, 2, and 1 in column two and the values 1, 0, 2, 3 in the third column of rows 1 to 4.

> **Note**: Please save your data often as HOM does not have an undo feature. Data files for Sampling by Attributes have the extension. ATT.

3.3 Obtaining Results

Once the data have been entered, click on the Run icon or RUN on the HOM command line to obtain the results. You will see as outputs
    1. The charts that you have checked. The charts will contain a centerline as well as upper and lower warning and action limits. Please consult a standard textbook on statistical process control to interpret the charts.
    2. Tables produced by HOM corresponding to each type of chart selected by the user. Each table contains the data used to generate the chart. HOM also produces certain statistics that permit the user to interpret whether the pattern observed in the chart can be attributed to chance. The explanation of these statistics can be found in Section 5 of the manual.

The output can be saved as a file, printed or exported to a spreadsheet or word processing software for further analysis. Please refer to the RESULTS command help in the on-line Help.

4. ACCEPTANCE SAMPLING

Acceptance sampling is a technique used to sample outputs or purchased material to determine whether or not to accept a lot. HOM has two options.
    In the first option, the user can specify a sampling plan and have HOM compute the probability of accepting the lot. A sampling plan consists of specifying two numbers, the Sample Size and the Acceptance Number. The Sample Size is the number of items sampled from the lot. The Acceptance Number is the cut-off value such that if the number of defective items in the sample is less than or equal to the Acceptance Number, then the lot is accepted; else it is rejected. There are several other types of sampling plans, but these are not implemented within HOM.
    In the second option, the user specifies the producer's and the consumer's risks. The user also specifies the Acceptable Quality Level and the Lot Tolerance % Defective. When designing the plan, the probability of rejecting a lot in which the defective proportion is less than or equal to the Acceptable Quality Level must be less than or equal to the Producer's Risk. Similarly, the probability of accepting a lot in which the defective proportion is greater than or equal to the Lot Tolerance % Defective should be less than or equal to the Consumer's Risk.
    Choose the option and specify the parameters in the Parameters dialog box. Data files for Acceptance Sampling have the extension. ACP.

4.1 Choosing Options and Specifying the Sampling Plan Parameters

In the Parameters dialog box, you will see several options. These are described below.

Calculated: The user chooses whether HOM should determine the Operating Characteristics (OC) Curve or a Sampling Plan. Given the sampling plan, the OC curve shows the probability of accepting a lot plotted versus the fraction of defective items in the lot. The Sampling Plan produces the sample size and the acceptance number given the Producer's Risk, the Consumer's Risk, the Acceptable Quality Level, and the Lot Tolerance % Defective.

OC Curve Parameters. Enter the Sample Size (n), the Acceptance Number (c), and the Defective Fraction (p). The Defective Fraction is used to print out the probability of acceptance for that value of the fraction defectives in the lot. However, the OC curve is drawn for a wide range of p.

Sampling Plan Parameters. Enter the Acceptable Quality Level (AQL), the Producer's Risk (Alpha), the Lot Tolerance % Defective (LTPD), and the Consumer's Risk.

Click on OK to close the Parameters dialog box. Proceed to Obtaining Results.

4.2 Obtaining Results

Once the data have been entered, click on the Run icon or RUN on the HOM command line to obtain the results. You will see the following outputs
Option Chosen Is OC Curve. HOM depicts the probability of accepting a lot as well as the average outgoing quality for different values of the fraction of defectives. The average outgoing quality is the fraction of defective items in a lot, given a sampling plan and the fraction of defectives in the lot. The assumption is that defective lots are 100 percent checked and defective items when found are replaced with good items. HOM also produces a table showing these values.

Option Chosen Is Sampling Plan. HOM produces the sampling plan with the smallest sample size that conforms to the user's requirements. HOM also shows the OC curve for this sampling plan and other outputs similar to those under the first option (OC curve).

Please consult the Results menu for help on customizing, saving, and printing the output.

5. EXAMPLES

5.1 Statistical Process Control: Sampling by Variables

Consider the following example in which samples are drawn from a process producing potato chips. Each hour a sample of three to four bags of chips is drawn. The chips are analyzed for salt content. The table below gives the salt content in the samples.

Time	Sample Size (# of bags)	Salt Content (grams)						
		Bag1	Bag2	Bag3	Bag4	Average	Range	Std Dev.
8 AM	3	0.091915	0.117895	0.071921		0.09391	0.045974	0.023052
9	3	0.148242	0.101775	0.055185		0.101734	0.093057	0.046528
10	3	0.141822	0.050377	0.07304		0.088413	0.091445	0.047621
11	3	0.11689	0.102611	0.064568		0.09469	0.052323	0.027046
12Noon	3	0.112367	0.075413	0.052377		0.080052	0.05999	0.030263
1 PM	3	0.148682	0.124649	0.09895		0.124094	0.049731	0.02487
2	3	0.123448	0.106555	0.096958		0.108987	0.02649	0.013411
3	3	0.104355	0.093819	0.117341		0.105172	0.023522	0.011782
4	3	0.138308	0.144186	0.076579		0.119691	0.067607	0.037452
5	3	0.136129	0.140473	0.107659		0.128087	0.032814	0.017824
6	4	0.089173	0.090657	0.062241	0.089941	0.083003	0.028416	0.013855
7	4	0.132546	0.05816	0.113316	0.094386	0.099602	0.074386	0.031718
8	4	0.135718	0.105984	0.090775	0.125823	0.114575	0.044942	0.020114
9	4	0.129322	0.095318	0.136883	0.144946	0.126617	0.049628	0.02182
10	4	0.103447	0.077689	0.107041	0.07201	0.090047	0.035031	0.017762
11	4	0.088027	0.132765	0.105822	0.099469	0.106521	0.044738	0.018982
12	4	0.098311	0.137633	0.115757	0.07505	0.106688	0.062583	0.026527

5.1.1 Using Mean Data Only

Let us consider only the data given from time 8 AM until time 5 PM. The sample size is fixed and equal to 3. Upon starting HOM: Quality Management, you will see the following screen:

Choose Sampling by Variables using the mouse and click on OK. You will see the following screen.

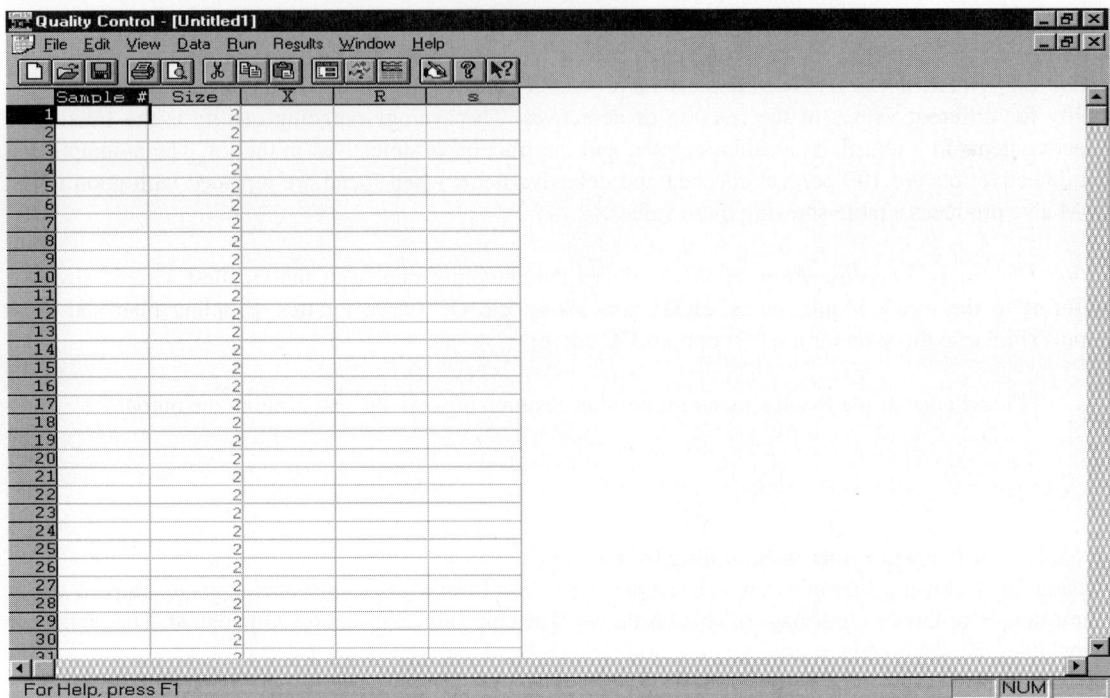

Before entering the data (you will notice that the sample size, for example, is not the one you want), open the Parameters dialog box. Make the following choices:

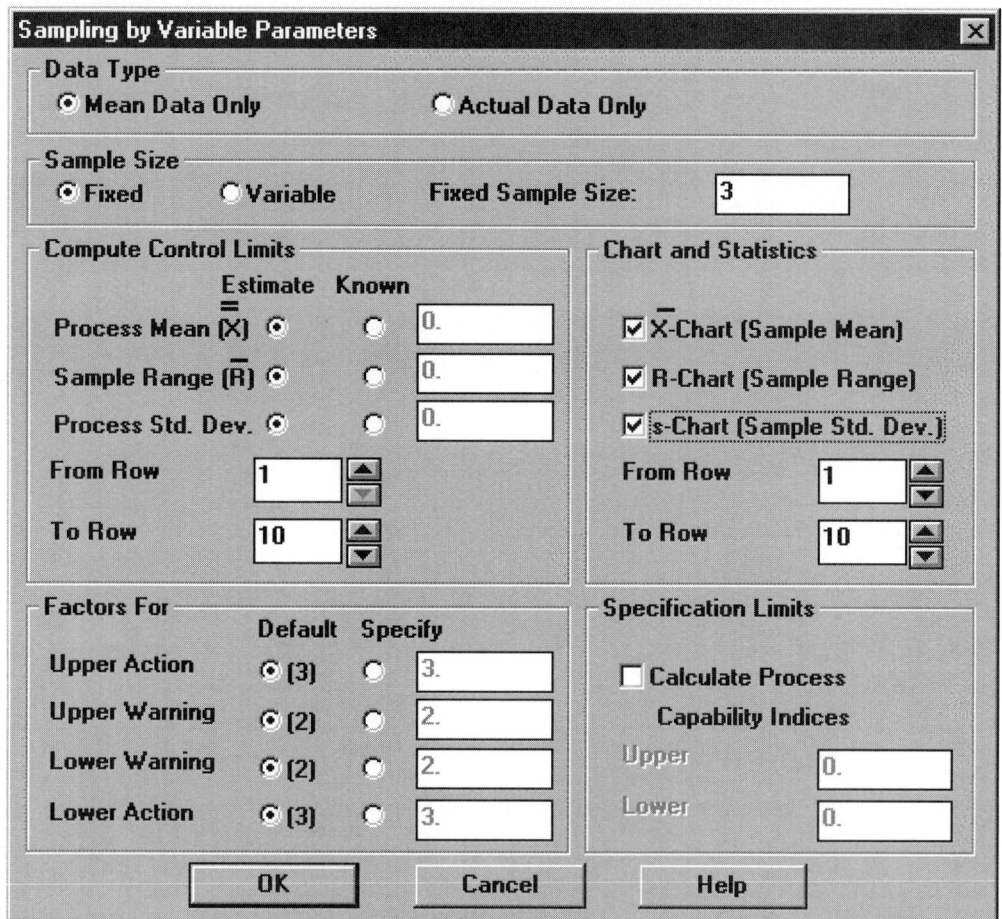

Notice that the To Row has been set equal to 10. This can be changed later. In this case we know there are 10 observations. Close the dialog box. Enter the following data in the spreadsheet.

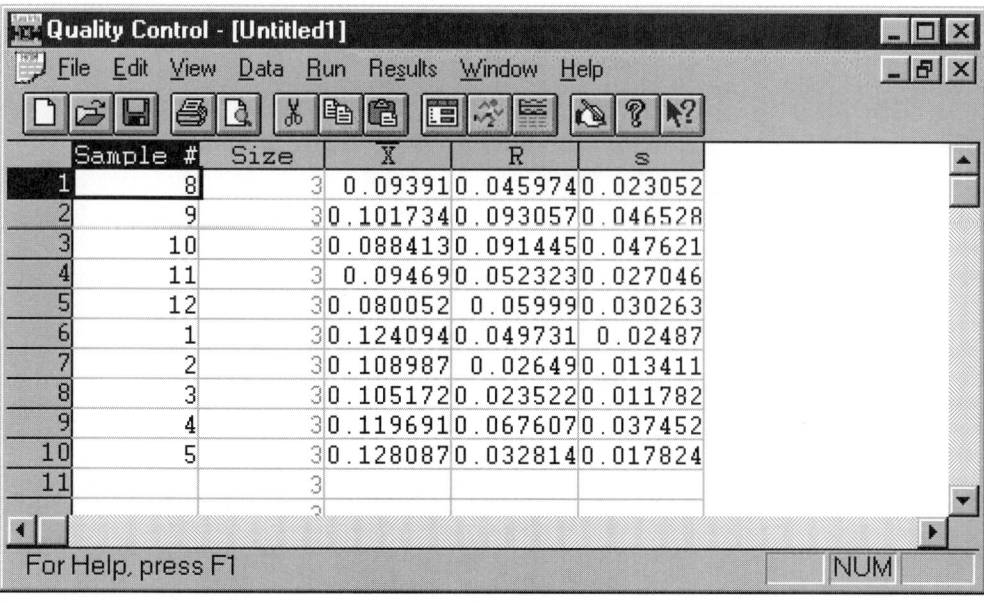

Save the data. These data have been saved under EXAMPLE1.VAR. Click on the Run or Run item to obtain the following output.

157

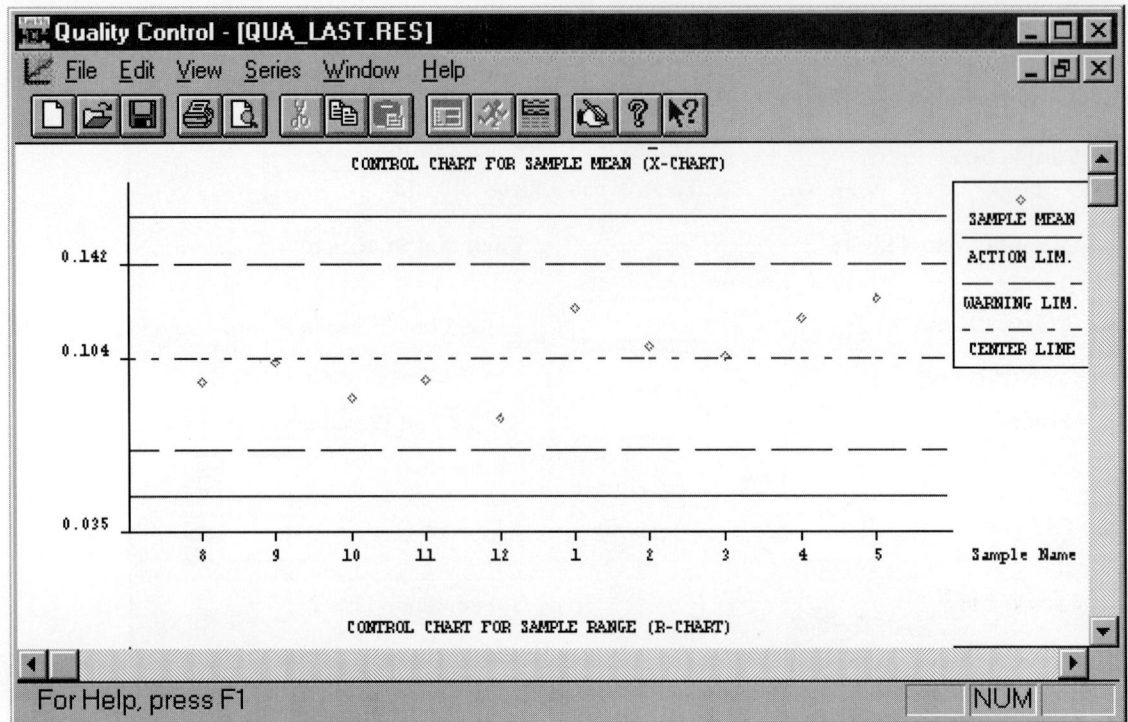

The text output is given below. It has been annotated to facilitate understanding (see notes in the output).

Sampling by Variable
Control Limits Computation Results (Calculations Range)

Estimated Process Mean :	0.104483		
Estimated Process Range :	0.0542953		
Estimated Process Std.Dev. :	0.0304448		
Between Group Std.Dev. :	0.015861		
F-statistic & Dgr.Freedom :	0.814248	9	20

Note: HOM gives the estimated values of the process parameters. The F-statistic compares the variance between the sample means and the process standard deviation. The ratio of the two (scaled for the size of the sample) should be close to one. Please see the technical notes given in Section 7.

Factors For the Charts

	X-Chart	R-Chart	s-Chart
Upper Action Factor :	1.02307	2.57425	2.5681
Upper Warning Factor :	0.682044	2.0495	2.0454
Lower Warning Factor :	0.682044	0	0
Lower Action Factor :	1.02307	0	0

Ratio of R-bar to Process Std. Dev. (d2) :   1.693
Ratio of Sample Std.Dev to Proc.Std.Dev (C4):   0.8862

Note: HOM produces the "standard" values used to construct the control charts. These values are drawn from standard tables stored within HOM. For example, when the Upper Action limit is three times the standard deviation of the sample mean, then the Upper Action Factor is denoted as A_2 as in textbooks. For a sample size of 3, this factor is 1.02307. Similarly, when the Upper and Lower Action Factors are three times the standard deviation of the range, they are designated as D_3 and D_4. In this example, for a sample size equal to 3, the corresponding values of D_3 and D_4 are 2.5681 and zero. The ratio of the mean range to the process standard deviation (d_2) and the ratio of the sample standard deviation to the process standard deviation ($C4$) are obtained from standard tables under the assumption that the true distribution of the quantity measured is the normal distribution.

Control Charts and Statistics (Chart Range)

Sample Mean (X) Control Chart

Sample No.	Sample Mean	LAL	LWL	Center	UWL	UAL
8	0.09391	0.0489353	0.0674512	0.104483	0.141515	0.160031
9	0.101734	0.0489353	0.0674512	0.104483	0.141515	0.160031
10	0.088413	0.0489353	0.0674512	0.104483	0.141515	0.160031
11	0.09469	0.0489353	0.0674512	0.104483	0.141515	0.160031
12	0.080052	0.0489353	0.0674512	0.104483	0.141515	0.160031
1	0.124094	0.0489353	0.0674512	0.104483	0.141515	0.160031
2	0.108987	0.0489353	0.0674512	0.104483	0.141515	0.160031
3	0.105172	0.0489353	0.0674512	0.104483	0.141515	0.160031
4	0.119691	0.0489353	0.0674512	0.104483	0.141515	0.160031
5	0.128087	0.0489353	0.0674512	0.104483	0.141515	0.160031

Run Test Results for X-chart

	Above/Below	Up/Down
Number of Runs :	2	7
Expected Number of Runs :	6	6.33333
Std.Dev. of Number of Runs :	1.5	1.20646
Z-statistic :	-2.66667	0.552579
Number of Sample Points :	10	10

Note: The run tests are of two types. The Above/Below run test looks at how the points fall above and below the median. The Up/Down run test looks at whether a point falls up or down relative to the previous point on the chart. These tests are described in Stevenson [1996] and a brief description is given in Section 7. The z statistic has (approximately) a normal distribution. If the value of z is significantly different from zero, then there is reason to believe that the process is not under control.

Sample Range (R) Control Chart

Sample No.	Sample Mean	LAL	LWL	Center	UWL	UAL
8	0.045974	0	0	0.0542953	0.111278	0.13977
9	0.093057	0	0	0.0542953	0.111278	0.13977
10	0.091445	0	0	0.0542953	0.111278	0.13977
11	0.052323	0	0	0.0542953	0.111278	0.13977
12	0.05999	0	0	0.0542953	0.111278	0.13977
1	0.049731	0	0	0.0542953	0.111278	0.13977
2	0.02649	0	0	0.0542953	0.111278	0.13977
3	0.023522	0	0	0.0542953	0.111278	0.13977
4	0.067607	0	0	0.0542953	0.111278	0.13977
5	0.032814	0	0	0.0542953	0.111278	0.13977

Run Test Results for R-chart

	Above/Below	Up/Down
Number of Runs :	7	6
Expected Number of Runs :	6	6.33333
Std.Dev. of Number of Runs :	1.5	1.20646
Z-statistic :	0.666667	-0.276289
Number of Sample Points :	10	10

Note: The run tests are similar to the ones described above.

Sample Standard Deviation (s) Control Chart

Sample No.	Sample Mean	LAL	LWL	Center	UWL	UAL
8	0.023052	0	0	0.0269802	0.0551853	0.0692879
9	0.046528	0	0	0.0269802	0.0551853	0.0692879
10	0.047621	0	0	0.0269802	0.0551853	0.0692879
11	0.027046	0	0	0.0269802	0.0551853	0.0692879
12	0.030263	0	0	0.0269802	0.0551853	0.0692879
1	0.02487	0	0	0.0269802	0.0551853	0.0692879
2	0.013411	0	0	0.0269802	0.0551853	0.0692879
3	0.011782	0	0	0.0269802	0.0551853	0.0692879
4	0.037452	0	0	0.0269802	0.0551853	0.0692879
5	0.017824	0	0	0.0269802	0.0551853	0.0692879

Run Test Results for s-chart

	Above/Below	Up/Down
Number of Runs :	3	6
Expected Number of Runs :	6	6.33333
Std.Dev. of Number of Runs :	1.5	1.20646
Z-statistic :	-2	-0.276289
Number of Sample Points :	10	10

<Frequency distribution table cut to save space>

Note: The value of F-statistic is expected to be 1.0. If it is significantly greater than that, it would suggest additional variation, i.e., variation produced other than by chance.

Note: The z-statistic of Run test could be used to determine whether the runs could have been produced by chance.

5.1.2 Using Actual Data Only

Make the following change in the Parameters dialog box: change to Actual Data Only.

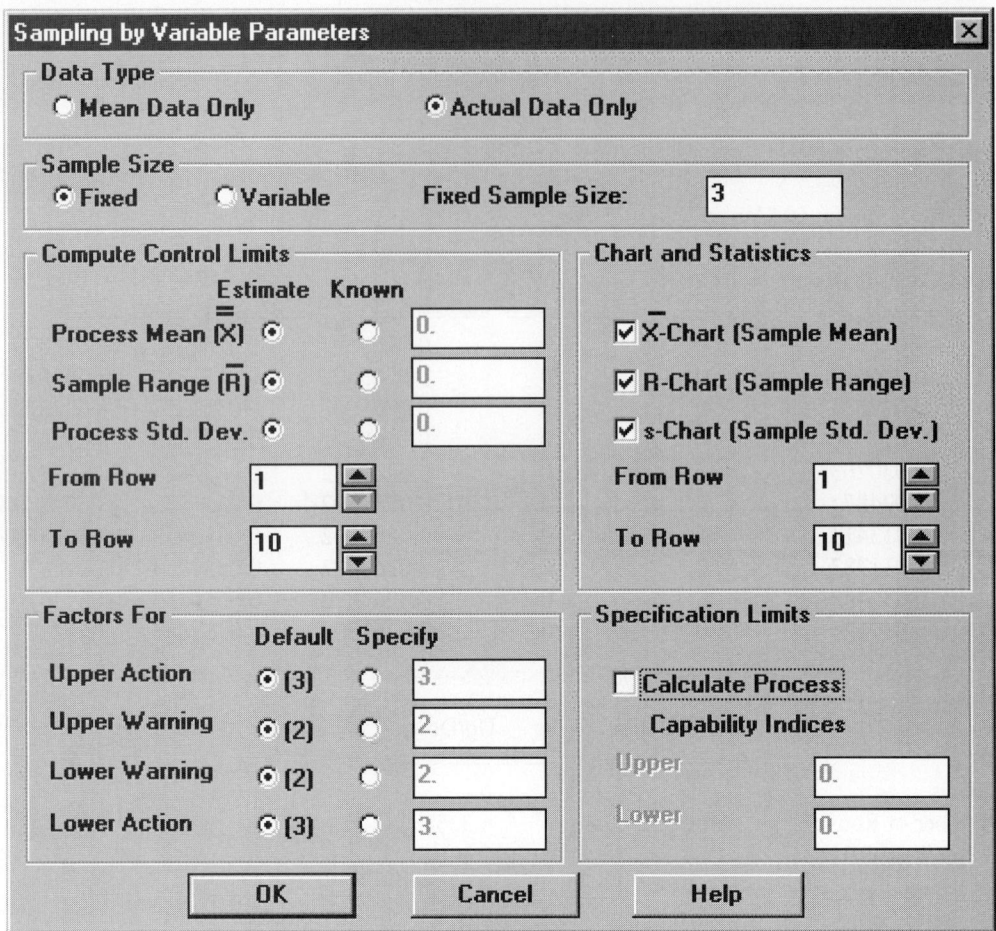

HOM will warn that the old data will be lost. If you have not saved your previous data, then choose No and save the data.

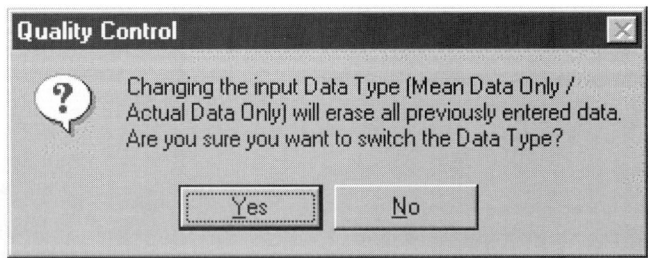

Close this dialog box and enter the data in the spreadsheet as shown below (this file is EXAMPLE2.VAR).

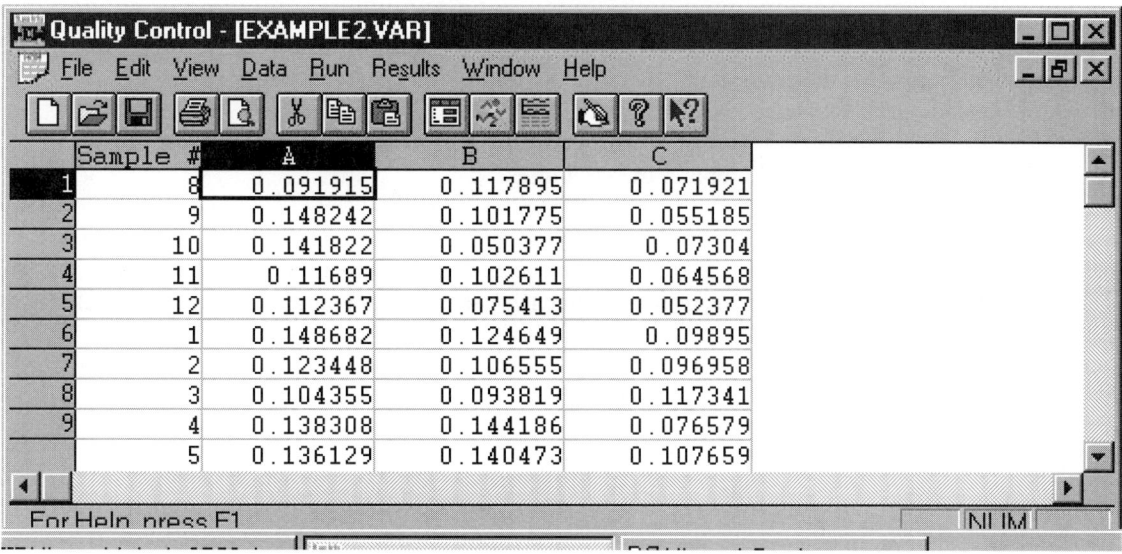

These data were generated in Excel. The data in each cell were generated using the formula 0.05 + 0.1*RAND(). Click on Run. The output will be identical to the one shown before.

5.1.3 Variable Sample Size

An example using all the data shown is included in EXAMPLE3.VAR. In this example, the sample size has been set as variable and the maximum sample size is set equal to 4. Upon running this example, notice that the control limits change with a change in the sample size.

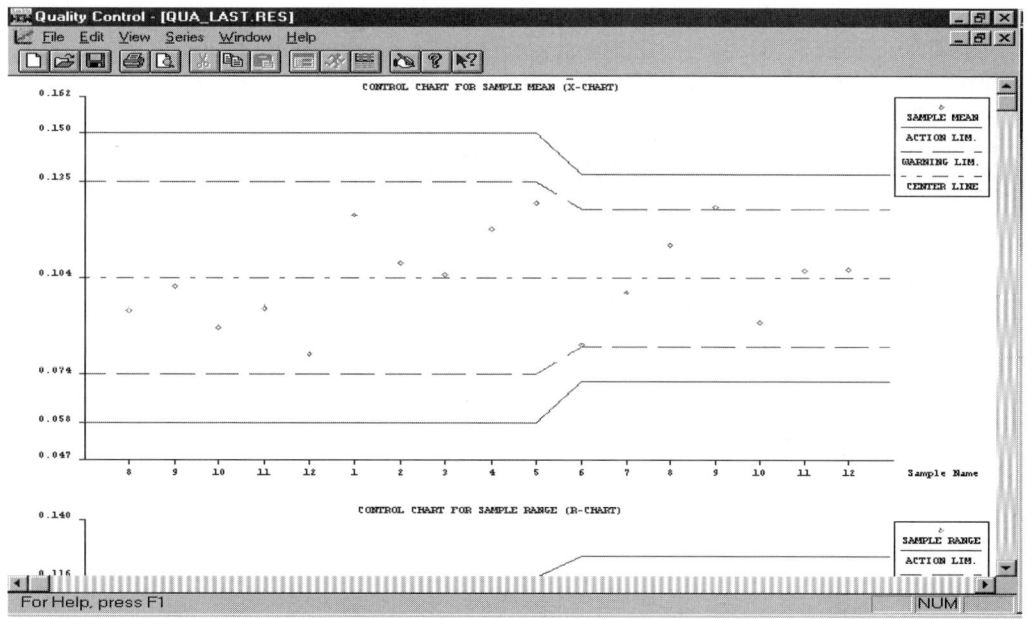

5.1.4 Known Process Parameters

The user can look at EXAMPLE4.VAR, in which the process mean has been specified as 0.10. In this case, HOM uses the given value rather than the estimate of the mean. Other examples are given in EXAMPLE5.VAR and EXAMPLE6.VAR.

5.2 Statistical Process Control: Sampling by Attributes

Consider the following data (adapted from Problem 8 in Chase, Aquilano, and Jacobs, 1998). During the period December 1 to December 10, 1000 diners were questioned each day as to whether their meal was satisfactory or not. The sample size was increased after 10 days as shown below. The data file is included as EXAMPLE1.ATT.

Date	Sample Size	No. of Unsatisfactory Meals
1-Dec	1000	74
2-Dec	1000	42
3-Dec	1000	64
4-Dec	1000	80
5-Dec	1000	40
6-Dec	1000	50
7-Dec	1000	65
8-Dec	1000	70
9-Dec	1000	40
10-Dec	1000	75
11-Dec	2000	82
12-Dec	2000	92
13-Dec	2000	123
14-Dec	2000	101
15-Dec	2000	97

These data can be analyzed either using a *p* chart or an *np* chart. Let us first analyze the first 10 day's data using a *p* chart. Start HOM, choose Sampling by Attributes, and click OK.

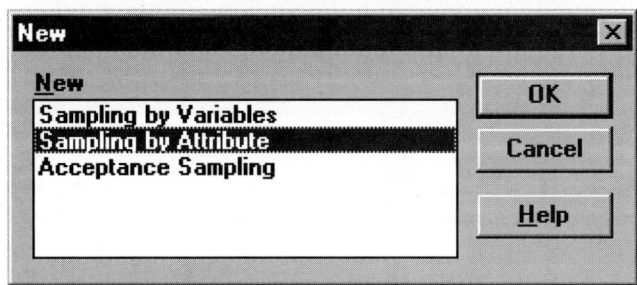

You will see the spreadsheet that is shown below.

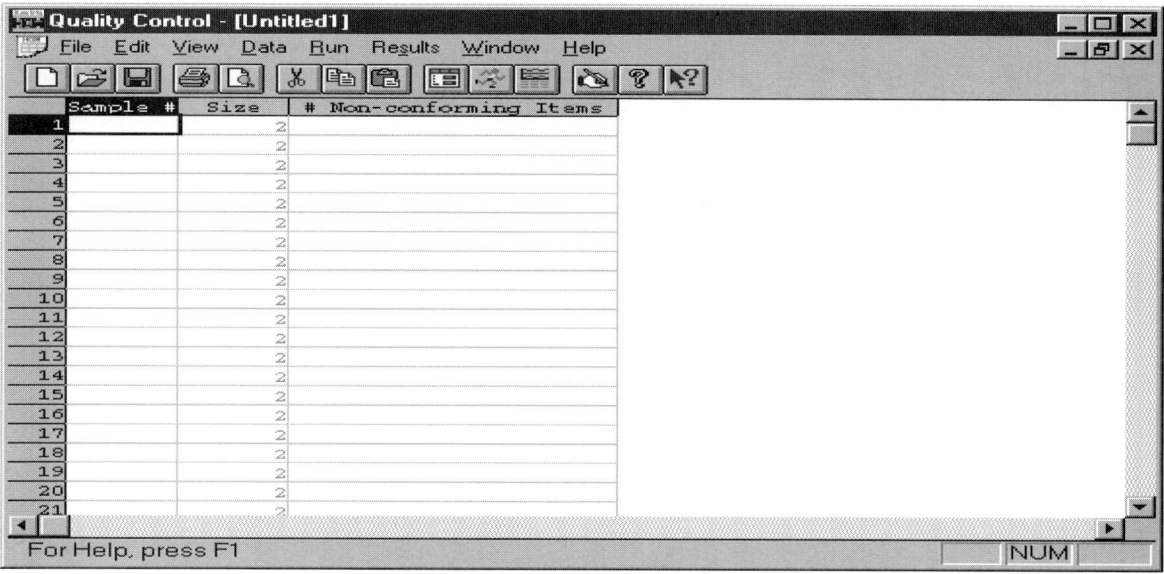

Open the Parameters dialog box and enter the choices as shown below. Click on OK.

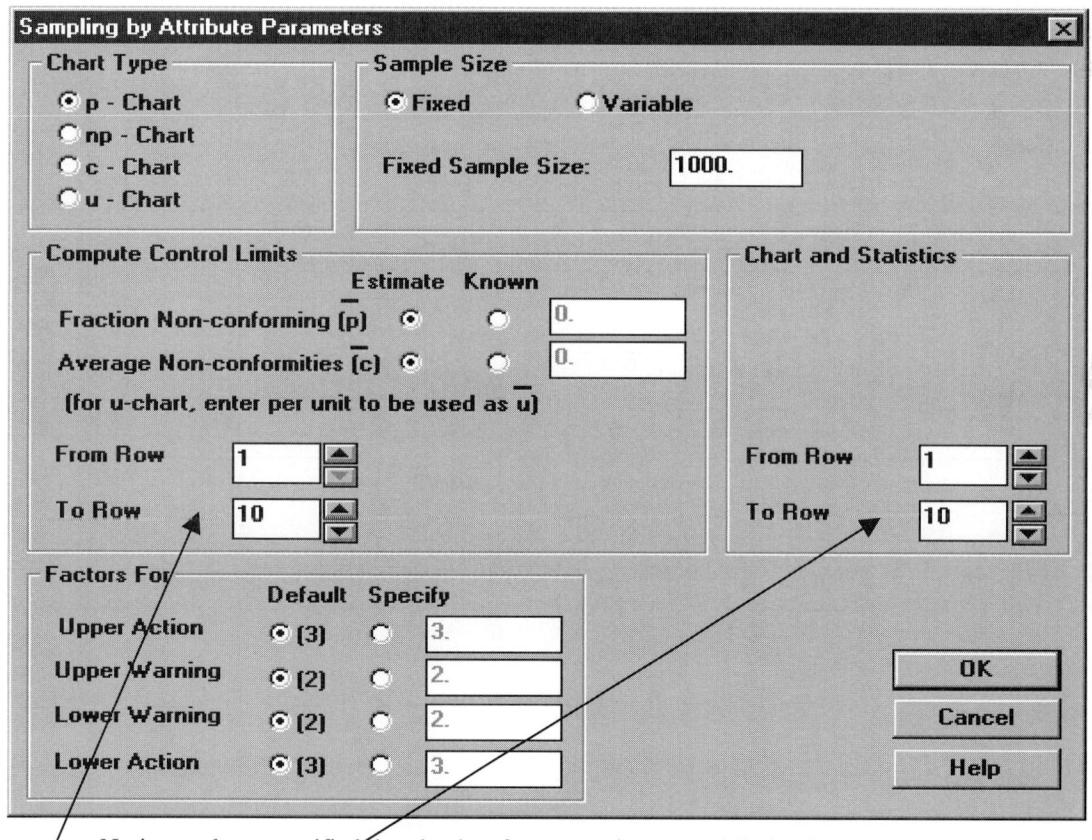

Notice we have specified that the data for computing control limits should be drawn from rows 1 to 10 and that the same rows of data should be plotted on the control chart.

Enter the data as shown below.

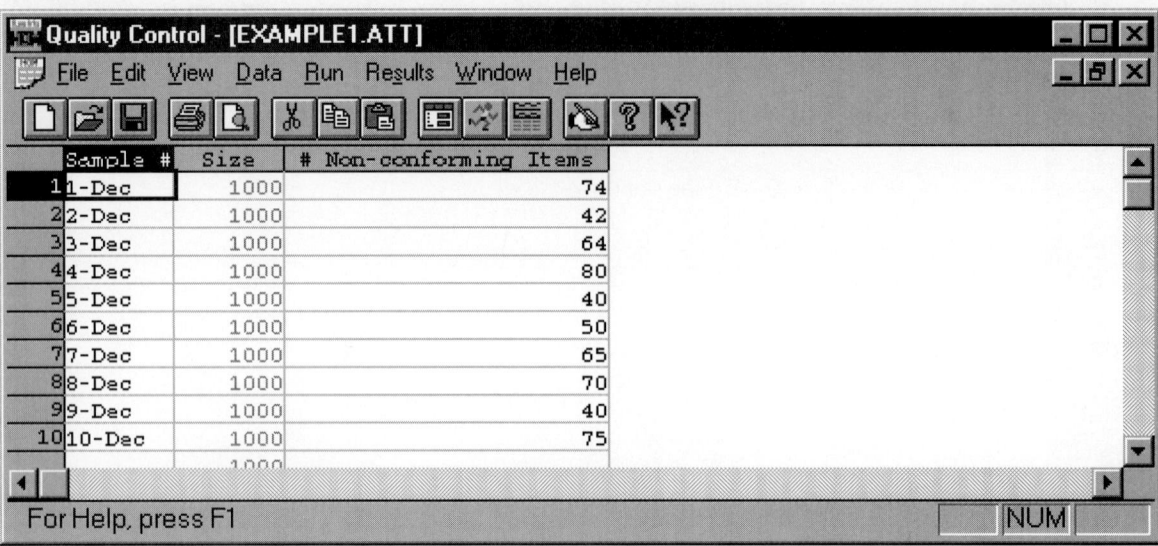

Clicking on Run produces the output shown below. The output was copied using EDIT --> Copy and pasted into this document. The chart was copied using Alt + Shift + PrtScr and pasted. The output has been annotated with notes.

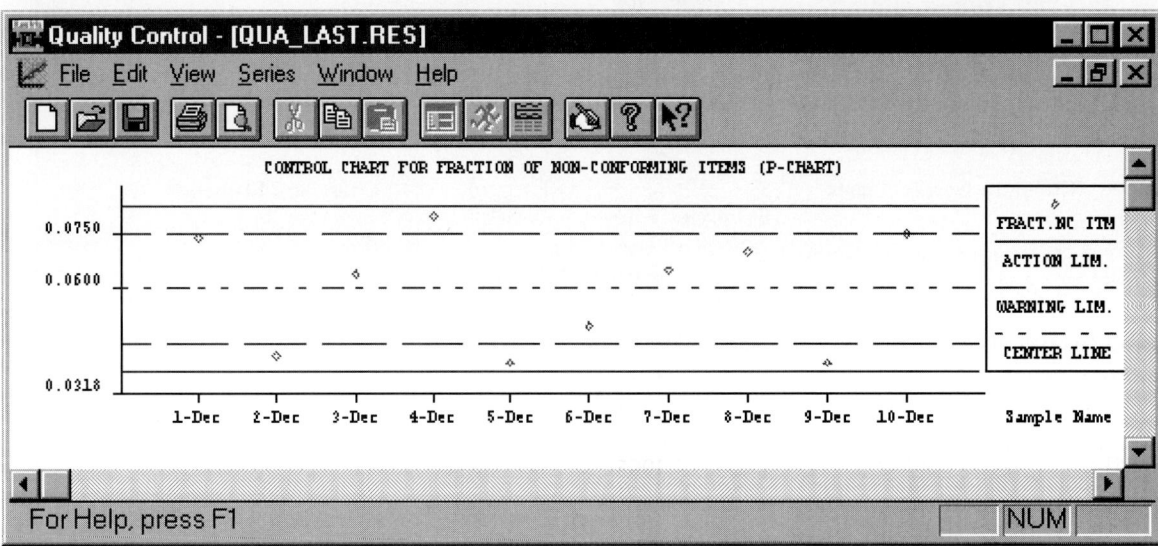

Sampling by Attribute
Control Chart for the Fraction of Non-Conforming Items (p-chart)
Estimated Fraction Non-Cnf :   0.06
Standard Deviation(p-chart):   0.00750999

Note: The standard deviation for the p - chart is computed using the following formula. Let pbar be the estimated fraction of nonconforming items. Then the standard deviation is given by $\rho_{pbar} = \sqrt{\dfrac{pbar(1-pbar)}{n}}$

No.	Sample Size	Fraction of Non-conf.Itm	LAL	LWL	Center	UWL	UAL
1-Dec	1000	0.074	0.03747	0.04498	0.06	0.07502	0.08253
2-Dec	1000	0.042	0.03747	0.04498	0.06	0.07502	0.08253
3-Dec	1000	0.064	0.03747	0.04498	0.06	0.07502	0.08253
4-Dec	1000	0.08	0.03747	0.04498	0.06	0.07502	0.08253
5-Dec	1000	0.04	0.03747	0.04498	0.06	0.07502	0.08253
6-Dec	1000	0.05	0.03747	0.04498	0.06	0.07502	0.08253
7-Dec	1000	0.065	0.03747	0.04498	0.06	0.07502	0.08253
8-Dec	1000	0.07	0.03747	0.04498	0.06	0.07502	0.08253
9-Dec	1000	0.04	0.03747	0.04498	0.06	0.07502	0.08253
10-Dec	1000	0.075	0.03747	0.04498	0.06	0.07502	0.08253

Run Test Results

	Above/Below	Up/Down
Number of Runs :	7	6
Expected Number of Runs :	6	6.33333
Std.Dev. of Number of Runs :	1.5	1.20646
Z-statistic :	0.666667	-0.276289
Number of Sample Points :	10	10

Note: These run tests are similar to the ones for Sampling by Variables.

Dispersion Test to Determine whether the Data could have been generated by a binomial distribution.
Observed Variance :   242.889
Theoretical Variance :   56.4
Chi-square Statistic :   38.7589
Degrees of Freedom :   9
Ratio Observed to Theor.Var: 4.30654

Note: The z-statistic of Run test could be used to determine whether the runs could have been produced by chance.
Note: Perform a two-sided Chi-square test using the provided statistic to determine whether there is reason to suspect that these observations could have been produced by a binomial distribution.
Warning: Ratio of Observed to Theoretical Variance does not fall into the range 0.8 to 1.25.

Note: Please see Section 7 for the formulae used.

Other examples are given in EXAMPLE2.ATT (variable sample size np - chart), EXAMPLE3.ATT (c - chart), and EXAMPLE4.ATT (u - chart). As an example, the entire data shown for 1-Dec to 15-Dec can be analyzed using an np chart (see EXAMPLE2.ATT). The chart alone is reproduced below.

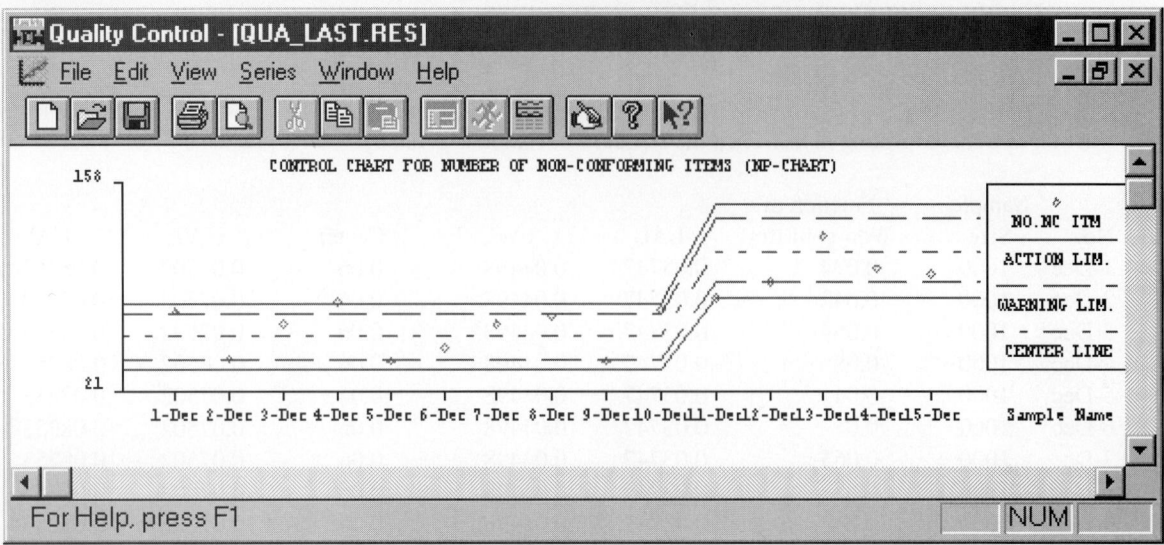

5. 3 Acceptance Sampling

Consider the problem of determining the probability of acceptance (OC curve) for different values of the fraction of defectives, when the sample size is 300 and the Acceptance Number is 3. Start HOM's Quality Management module, select Acceptance Sampling, and click on OK.

You will see the following screen. Click on the Parameters dialog box.

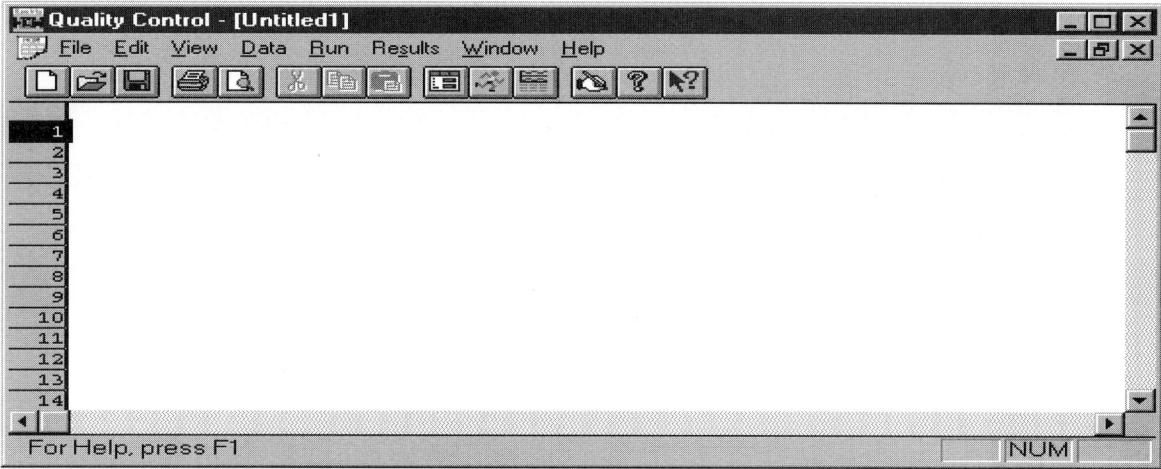

Make the entries shown below in the Parameters dialog box and click on OK.

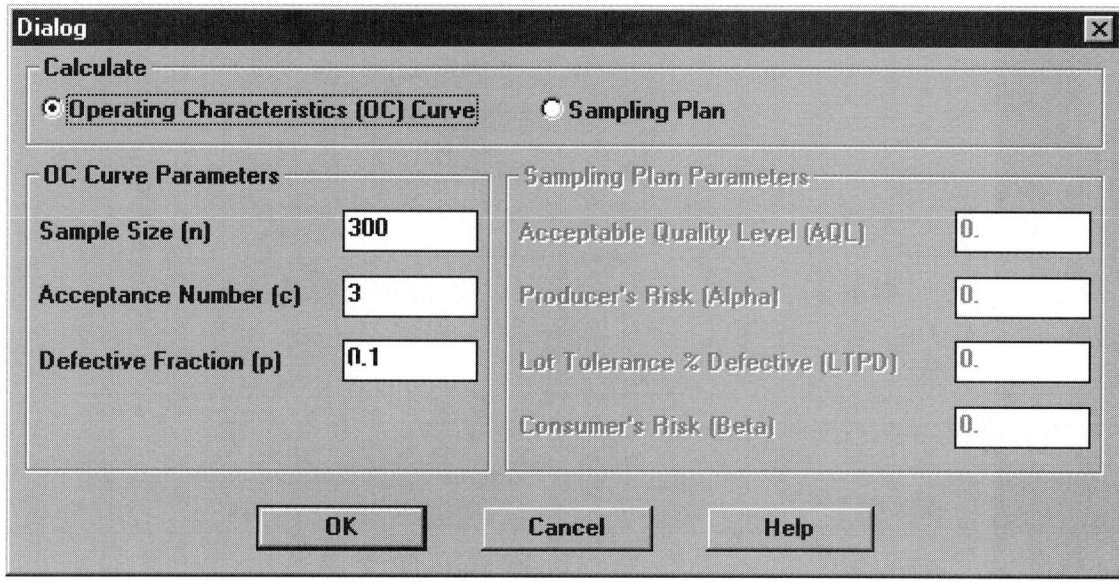

Run to obtain the output shown below. The graph has been copied to the clipboard and pasted. The text output was copied using EDIT --> Copy and pasted.

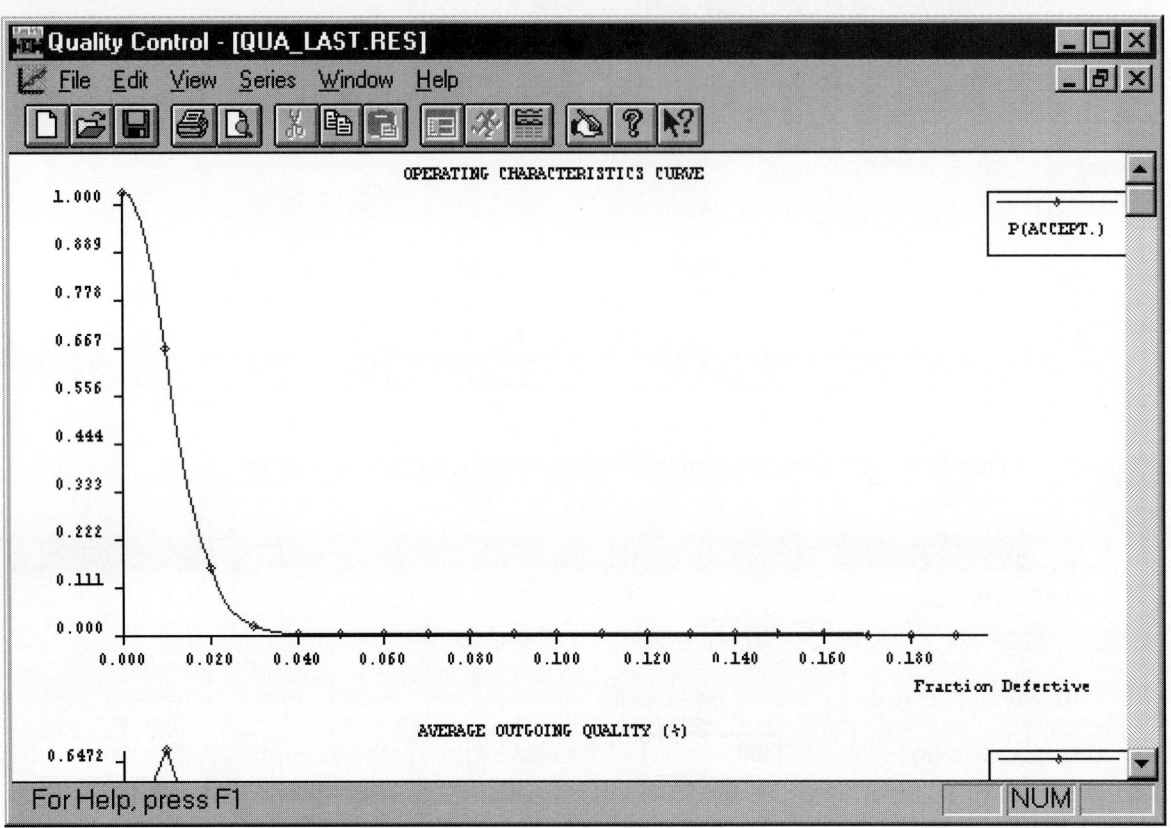

Acceptance Sampling

Operating Characteristics Curve and Average Outgoing Quality

Sample Size (n) :	300
Acceptance Number (c) :	3
Fraction Defective (p) :	0.1
Probability of Accepting :	1.2554e-010
Average Outgoing Quality :	1.2554e-009

Fraction Defect.(p)	Probabil. of Accept.Lot	AOQ (%)
===	===	===
0	1	0
0.0025	0.992801	0.2482
0.005	0.93483	0.467415
....	....	....
....	....	....
0.1925	8.74873e-024	1.68413e-022
0.195	3.61832e-024	7.05572e-023
0.1975	1.49148e-024	2.94567e-023

Note: Binomial distribution was used to calculate the Probability of Accepting the Lot.

Note: Please see section 7 for some of the assumptions and the formulae used to generate this output.

EXAMPLE1.ACP contains the data for the above example. The data file for determining a sampling plan is included in EXAMPLE2.ACP. The data in EXAMPLE2.ACP are as follows:

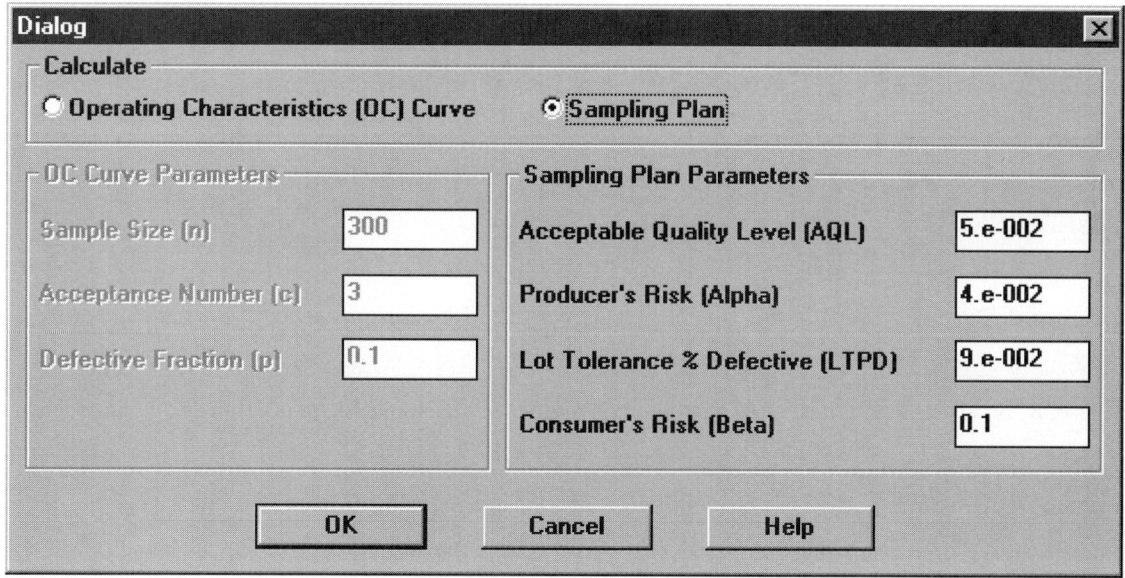

The OC curve of the sampling plan determined by HOM is shown below.

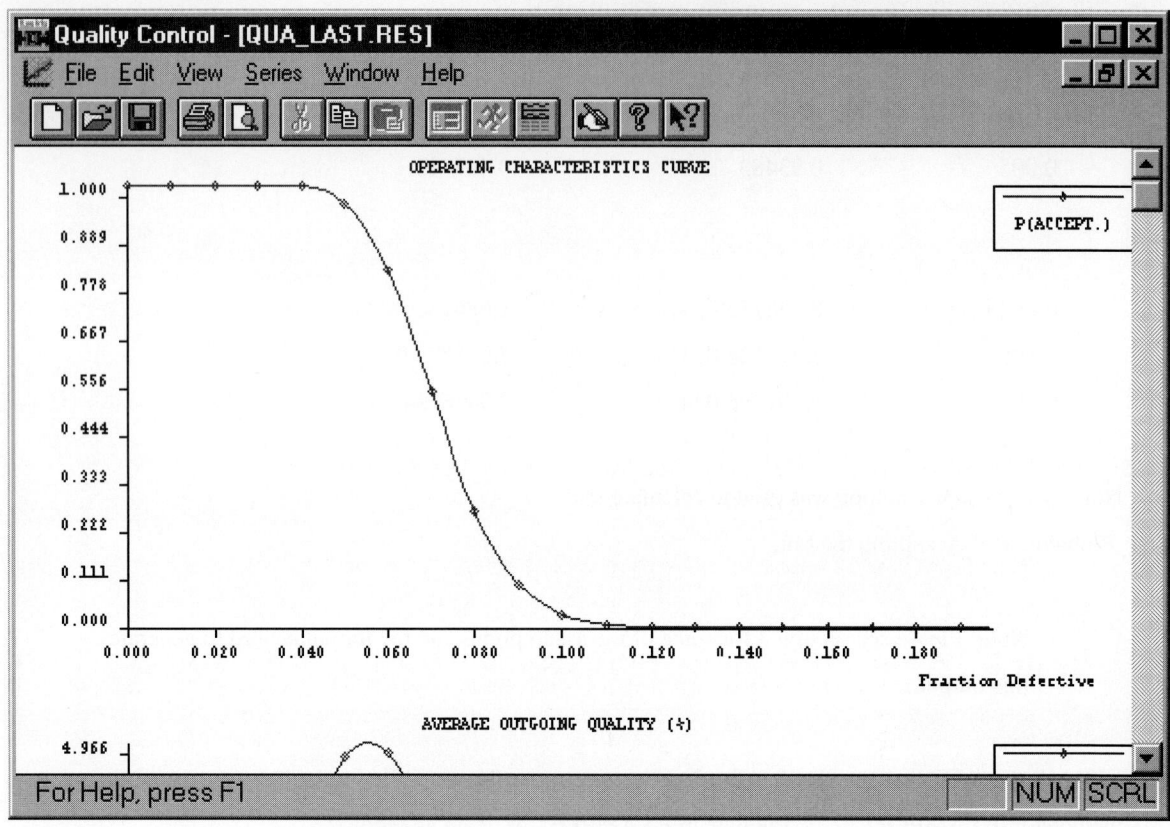

6. REFERENCES

Acheson, J. Duncan. *Quality Control and Industrial Statistics.* 5th ed. Homewood, Il: Ruchard D. Irwin., 1986.

Chase, R. B., and N. J. Aquilano. *Production and Operations Management.* 7th ed. Burr Ridge, IL: Richard D. Irwin, 1995.

Nahmias, S. *Production and Operations Analysis.* 3rd ed. Burr Ridge, IL: Richard D. Irwin, 1997.

Stevenson, W. J. *Production/Operations Management.* 5th ed. Burr Ridge, IL: Richard D. Irwin, 1996.

Grant, E. L., and R. S. Leavenworth. *Statistical Quality Control.* 7th ed., New York, NY: McGraw Hill, 1996.

Wetherill, G. B., and D. W. Brown. *Statistical Process Control: Theory and Practice.* London, Chapman and Hall: 1991.

7. TECHNICAL NOTES

7.1 Typical Calculations for Sampling by Variables

Let there be N1 rows of data. Row *i* had n_i data items, that is, the *i*th sample is of size n_i. Let the values entered in row *i* be $X_{i,1}, X_{i,2}, \ldots, X_{i,ni}$. Let Xbar$_i$ and R$_i$ be the mean and range of the *i*th sample. Let s$_i$ stand for the sample standard deviation. Xdoublebar and R bar stand for estimates of the process mean and average range.

For rows 1 to N1:
    If no actual data but mean data, let Xbar$_i$ be the mean value given by the user.
    If data, Xbar$_i = (X_{i,1} + X_{i,2} + \ldots + X_{i,ni})/n_i$
    If no actual data but mean data, R$_i$ = R given by user; else left blank.
    If data, always compute R$_i = \max_j\{X_{i,j}\} - \min_j\{X_{i,j}\}$
    If no actual data, s$_i$ equals the value given by the user; else left blank.
    If actual data, always compute:
    s$_i = [\,((X_{i,1} - \text{Xbar}_i)^2 + (X_{i,2} - \text{Xbar}_i)^2 + \ldots + (X_{i,n\_i} - \text{Xbar}_i)^2\,)/(n_i - 1)]^{0.5}$
    Xdoublebar = simple average of sample means = (Xbar$_1 + \ldots$ Xbar$_{N1})/(N1)$
    Rbar = simple average of the ranges *if sample sizes are equal or fixed in N1 and available*
    Process standard deviation (s_W)
    $= [\,((n_1 - 1)(s_1)^2 + (n_2 - 1)(s_2)^2 + \ldots + (n_{N1} - 1)(s_{N1})^2)/((n_1 - 1) + \ldots + (n_{N1} - 1))\,]^{0.5}$

The estimate of between group variation is given by
$s_B = [\,((\text{Xbar}_1 - \text{Xdoublebar})^2 + \ldots (\text{Xbar}_{N1} - \text{Xdoublebar})^2)/(N1-1)]^{0.5}$
If both s_W and s_B are available and there is a fixed sample size *n*, then compute the *F* statistic:
$F = (n\,(s_B)^2 / (s_W)^2]$ with degrees of freedom equal to (N1–1) and N1*(n–1)

7.2 Run Tests

Run tests apply only if the sample size is fixed. There are two types of runs, above and below the median runs and up/down runs. These tests apply to all types of charts.

7.2.1 Above/Below Median Runs

    Label data above the center line as A and below as B.
    Assume that there are N2 observations
    A run is a group of A's or B's. For example,

        AA   BBB   A   BB

is four runs.

    <u>Define</u>: Number of runs = r_{med}
              Expected number of runs $E(r_{med})$ = N2/2 + 1
              Standard deviation of number of runs, sigma$_{med}$ = sqrt((N2–1)/4)
              z statistic = $(r_{med} - E(r_{med}))$/sigma$_{med}$

7.2.2 Up/Down Runs

    Do not label the first point on the chart.
    Label a point as U if the value increased with respect to the previous one; else label as D
    Groups of U's and D's constitute the runs (as in the Above/Below runs).
    <u>Define</u>: Number of runs = $r_{(u/d)}$
              Expected number of runs $E(r_{(u/d)})$ = (2N2 – 1)/3
              Standard deviation of number of runs, sigma$_{(u/d)}$ = sqrt((16N2 – 29)/90)
              z statistic = $(r_{(u/d)} - E(r_{(u/d)}))$/sigma$_{(u/d)}$

The z statistic could be used to determine whether the runs could have been produced by chance.

7.3 Process Capability Indices Report

This report is generated only if the Upper and Lower Specification limits are given in the parameters dialog box. Let

> USL = Upper Specification Limit
> LSL = Lower Specification Limit
>
> Let the Process Standard Deviation = s_W
> (If fixed sample size, s_W = Rbar/ d_2;
> else if variable sample size, then use sigma given by the user or the estimate of s_W in that order of preference.)
>
> Process Capability Index, C_p = (USL − LSL)/6 s_W
>
> Process Performance Index, C_{PK} = Minimum of {|USL − Process Mean|, |Process Mean − LSL|}/3 s_W

7.4 Dispersion Test for the *p*, *np*, and *c* Charts

The *p* and *np* charts assume that the sampling distribution is the binomial. The *c* and *u* charts assume that the sampling distribution is the Poisson. The dispersion test is performed to check the validity of these claims.

7.4.1 Dispersion Test for the p and np Charts

Let x_i be the number of nonconforming items in row *i*. Let N2 be the number of samples and *n* the sample size.
pbar = $(x_1 + \ldots + x_{N2})/(N2*n)$
Average number of nonconforming items in a sample of size *n* = n*pbar
Observed variance*(Number of observations − 1) = $((x_1 - n*pbar)^2 + \ldots + (x_{N2} - n*pbar)^2)$
Theoretical variance = n*pbar*(1−pbar)

Chisquare = Observed variance*(Number of observations − 1)/Theoretical variance
with degrees of freedom, d.f. = N2 − 1

Perform a two-sided chi-square test to determine whether there is reason to suspect that these observations could not have been produced by a binomial distribution.

7.4.2 Dispersion Test for c chart

Let c_i be the number of nonconformities in sample *i* and N2 be the number of samples.
cbar = $(c_1 + \ldots + c_{N2})/N2$
Observed variance*(Number of observations − 1) = $((c_1 - cbar)^2 + \ldots + (c_{N2} - cbar)^2)$
Theoretical variance = cbar

Chisquare = Observed variance*(Number of observations − 1)/Theoretical variance
with degrees of freedom, d.f. = N2 − 1

Perform a two-sided chi-square test to determine whether there is reason to suspect that these observations could not have been produced by a Poisson distribution.

7.5 Acceptance Sampling

We assume

- The lot size is large when compared to the sample size. The lot size is constant.
- Nonconforming items conform to a binomial distribution.
- There is a single sampling plan.
- Average outgoing quality is computed assuming that nonconforming items in rejected lots are completely identified and replaced with good items before sending the lot to the customer.

There are two options, A and B.

A: Given a sampling plan and defective fraction, compute the operating characteristics (OC) curve and the average outgoing quality (AOQ). A sampling plan is specified by the sample size (n) and the acceptance number (c). Let p be the fraction of defective items in the population.

        n must be integral and greater than 1.
        c must be integral and nonnegative.
        p should be greater than and strictly less than 0.5.

B: Determine a sampling plan given
- The producer's risk point, which could also be considered to be the Acceptable Quality Level (see discussion in Grant and Leavenworth, 1996) (AQL).
- The producer's risk (alpha).
- The consumer's risk point, which could also be considered to be Lot Tolerance Percent Defective (LTPD).
- The consumer's risk (beta).

7.5.1 Procedure for A

Two different distributions could be used to approximate or exactly determine the probability of accepting a lot. Call this function $P(n,c,p)$.

    Exact: $P(n,c,p) = \text{sum for } i = 0 \text{ to } c \ \{n \text{ choose } i * p^i (1-p)^{(n-i)}\}$
                     Use this function for $n \leq 45$
    Poisson Approximation: Use for $n > 45$
                Let $m = n*p$
                $P(n,c,p) = e^{\{-m\}}\{\text{sum for } i = 0 \text{ to } c \ \{m^i/i!\}\}$

7.5.2 Procedure for B

A search technique is used to determine the optimal sampling plan. A sampling plan is considered to be optimal when it meets all the criteria above and has the smallest sample size.

FORECASTING METHODS

Eight different forecasting methods for forecasting demand and other variables are available in this application: Exponential Smoothing, FIT Smoothing, Exponential (Smoothing with) Regressed Trend, Simple Average, Moving Average, Weighted Average, Winter's Method, and Multiple Regression. The methods are described below.

In all methods:

> N = total number of periods when actual data are available
> A_i = actual demand in period i for i = 1, 2, ..., N
> F_i = forecast in period i for i = 1, 2, ..., N, N+1, N+2, ...
> T_i = Trend in period i for i = 1, 2, ..., N

where N+1 is the first forecast period.

1. EXPONENTIAL SMOOTHING

> $F_1 = A_1$
> $F_i = F_{i-1} + \alpha * (A_{i-1} - F_{i-1})$ for i = 2, 3, ..., N+1
> $F_i = F_{N+1}$ for i = N+2, N+3, ...

Sample Data File

FEXPSM.DAT

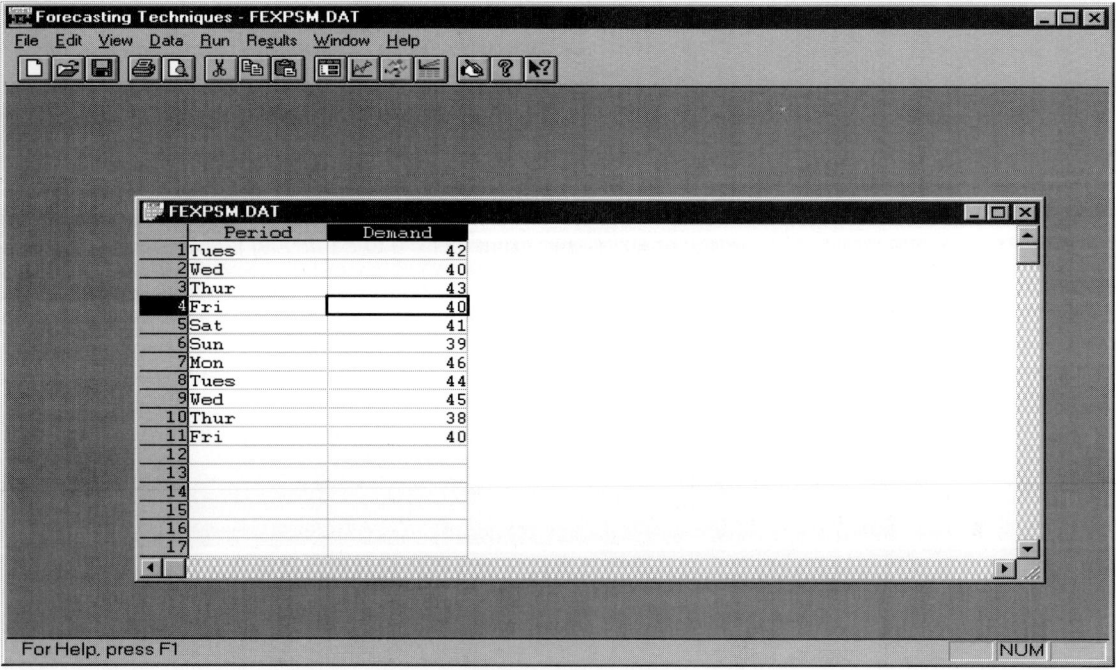

Exponential Smoothing Inputs

Method of Forecast	Exponential Smoothing
Variable to Forecast	Select from the drop-down list (corresponds to a column in the spreadsheet).
Seasonality	Choose a method for deseasonalizing the data before doing the forecast. Refer to "Seasonality" in section 9 for details.
Starting Period of Actual Data	Row number from which the Actual Data begin. [You can choose to omit *some* data when doing the forecast. For example, if there are data given in rows 11 through 100, you can choose to analyze any set of contiguous data (say from Row 14 to Row 64). However, all the data between the chosen starting and ending periods will be used to create the forecast.]
Ending Period of Actual Data	Row number at which Actual Data end.
How Many Periods to Forecast	Number of periods *beyond* the ending period for which to construct the forecast.
α	Smoothing constant between 0 and 1. The value of α is entered under "Data" in the Smoothing Constants section of the Parameters dialog box. You can choose to input α or leave it to the package to determine by selecting "Find Best Fit." The package finds the best α that minimizes the Root Mean Square Error (RMSE) using a bi-section search.
Find Best Fit	See above.
Initial Value of Forecast	The first period's forecast is by default set equal to the first period's actual demand. The user can override this by selecting "Define" and entering the value in the box provided.
MAD	See section 11 under MAD Updating.

Sample Parameters Dialog Box

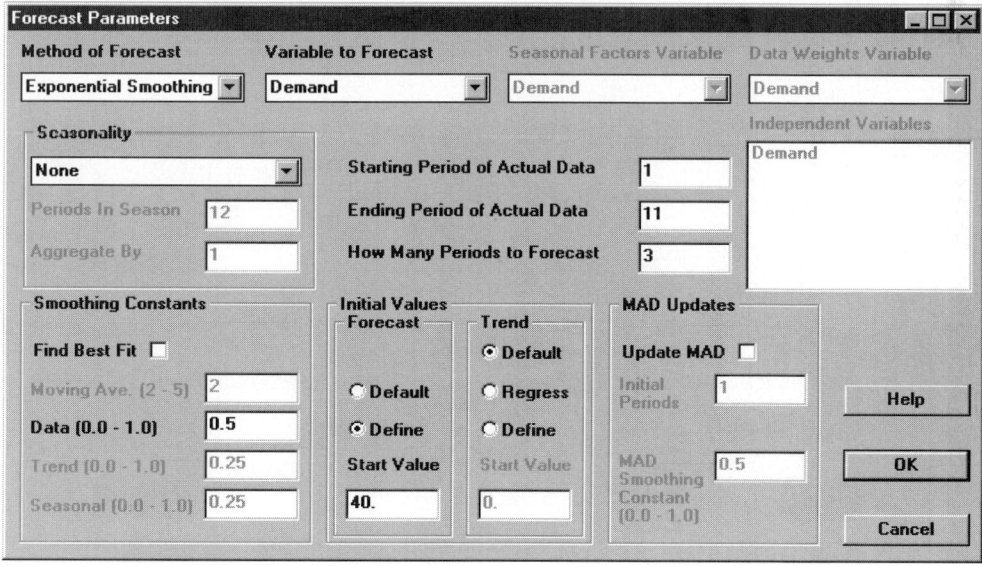

Output for Sample Data

FEXPSM.DAT   (Exponential Smoothing)

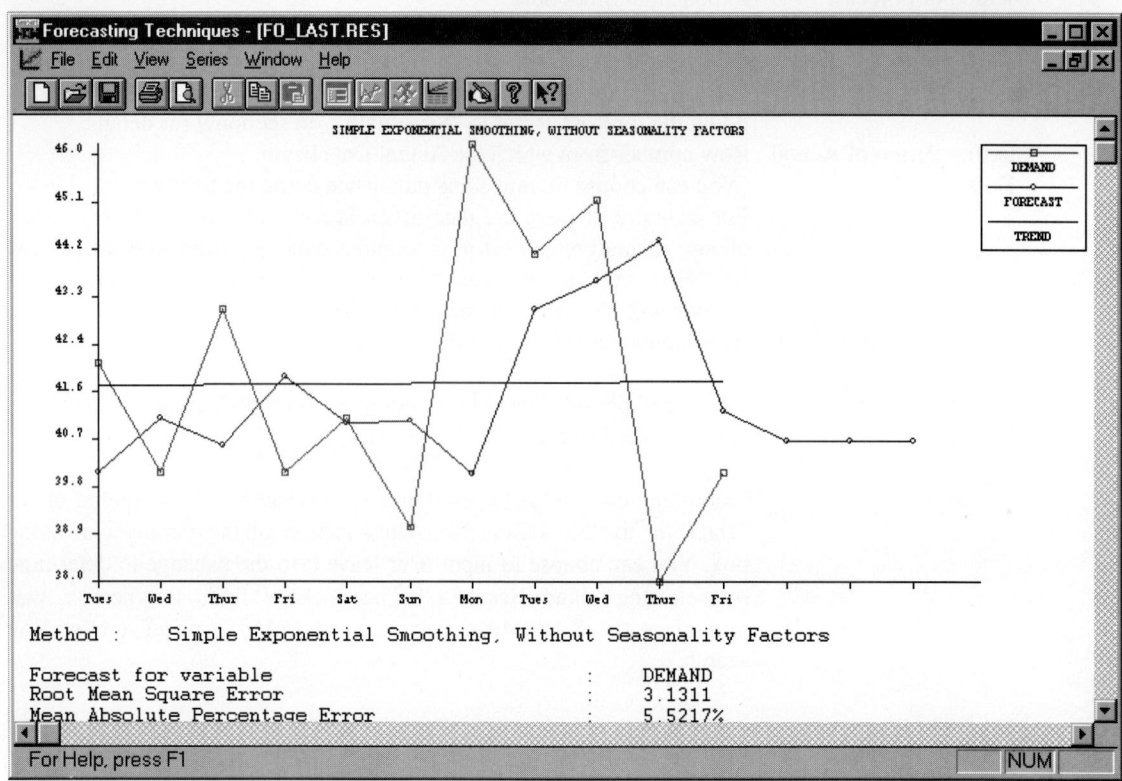

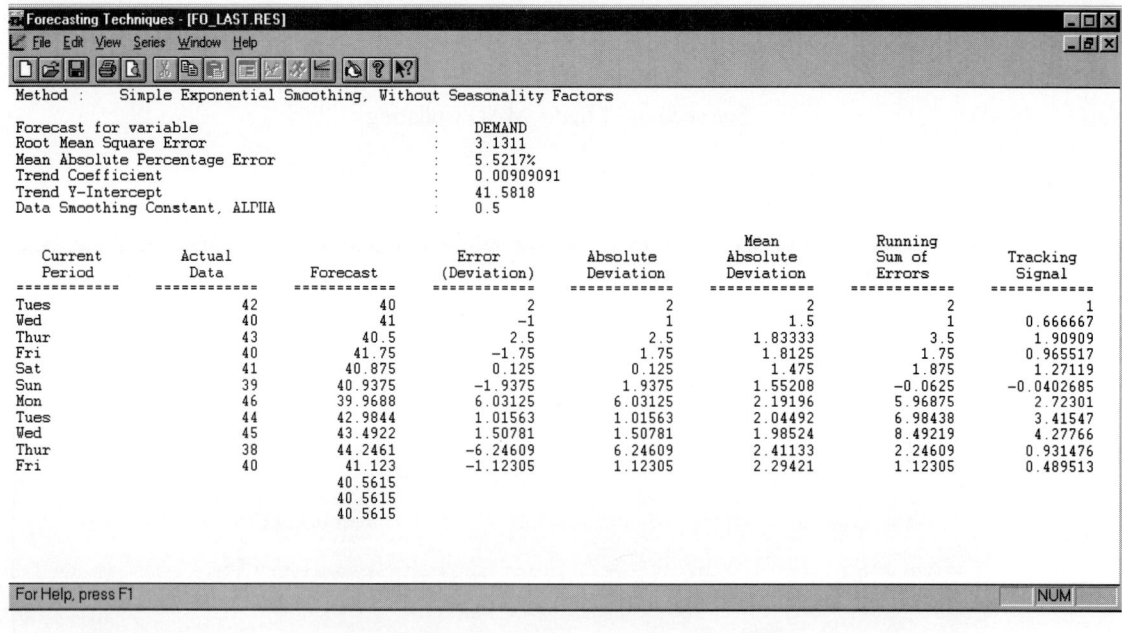

2. FIT SMOOTHING - EXPONENTIAL SMOOTHING INCLUDING TREND (FIT)

$$F_1 = A_1, T_1 = 0$$
$$F_i = F_{i-1} + \alpha * (A_{i-1} - F_{i-1})$$
$$T_i = T_{i-1} + \alpha * \delta * (A_{i-1} - FIT_{i-1}) \quad \text{for } i = 2, 3, ..., N+1$$
$$F_i = F_{N+1}, T_i = T_{N+1} * (i - N+1) \quad \text{for } i = N+2, N+3, ...$$
$$FIT_i = F_i + T_i \quad \text{for } i = 1, 2, ..., N, N+1, ...$$

Note: FIT Smoothing also called double exponential smoothing or Holt's method.

Sample Data File

FFIT.DAT

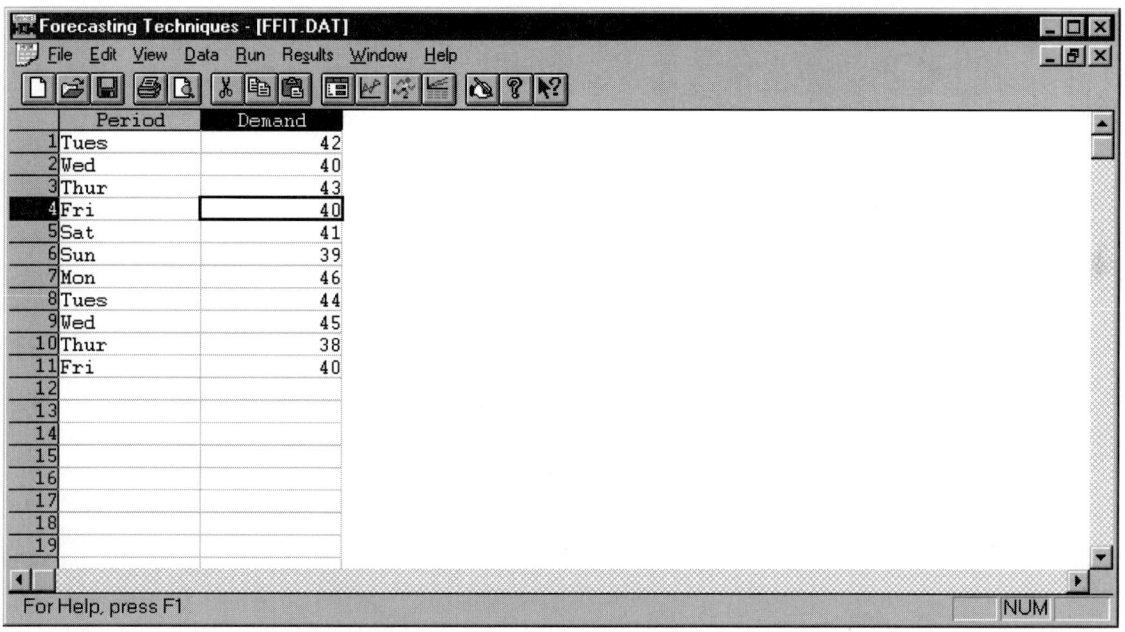

FIT Smoothing Inputs

Method of Forecast	FIT Smoothing
Variable to Forecast	Select from the drop-down list (corresponds to a column in the spreadsheet).
Seasonality	Choose a method for deseasonalizing the data before doing the forecast. Refer to "Seasonality" in section 9 for details.
Starting Period of Actual Data	Row number from which the Actual Data begin. [You can choose to omit *some* data when doing the forecast. For example, if there are data given in rows 11 through 100, you can choose to analyze any set of contiguous data (say from Row 14 to Row 64). However, all the data between the chosen starting and ending periods will be used to create the forecast.]
Ending Period of Actual Data	Row number at which Actual Data end.
How Many Periods to Forecast	Number of periods *beyond* the ending period for which to construct the forecast.
α	Smoothing constant between 0 and 1. The value of α is entered under "Data" in the Smoothing Constants section of the Parameters dialog box. You can choose to input α or leave it to the package to determine by selecting "Find Best Fit." The package finds the best α and δ that minimize the Root Mean Square Error (RMSE) using a bi-section search.
δ	Smoothing constant for trend between 0 and 1. The value of δ is entered under "Trend" in the Smoothing Constants section of the Parameters dialog box. You can choose to input δ or leave it to the package to determine by selecting "Find Best Fit." The package finds the best α and δ that minimize the Root Mean Square Error (RMSE) using a bi-section search.
Find Best Fit	See above.
Initial Value of Forecast	The first period's forecast is by default set equal to the first period's actual demand. The user can override this by selecting "Define" and entering the value in the box provided.
Initial Value of Trend	The default value for the first period trend is zero. This value can be set equal to the regressed value of the trend by choosing "Regress." The regression is carried out over the starting and ending periods of data. This value can be defined by the user by choosing "Define" and inputting a value in the box provided.
MAD	See section 11 under MAD Updating.

Sample Parameters Dialog Box

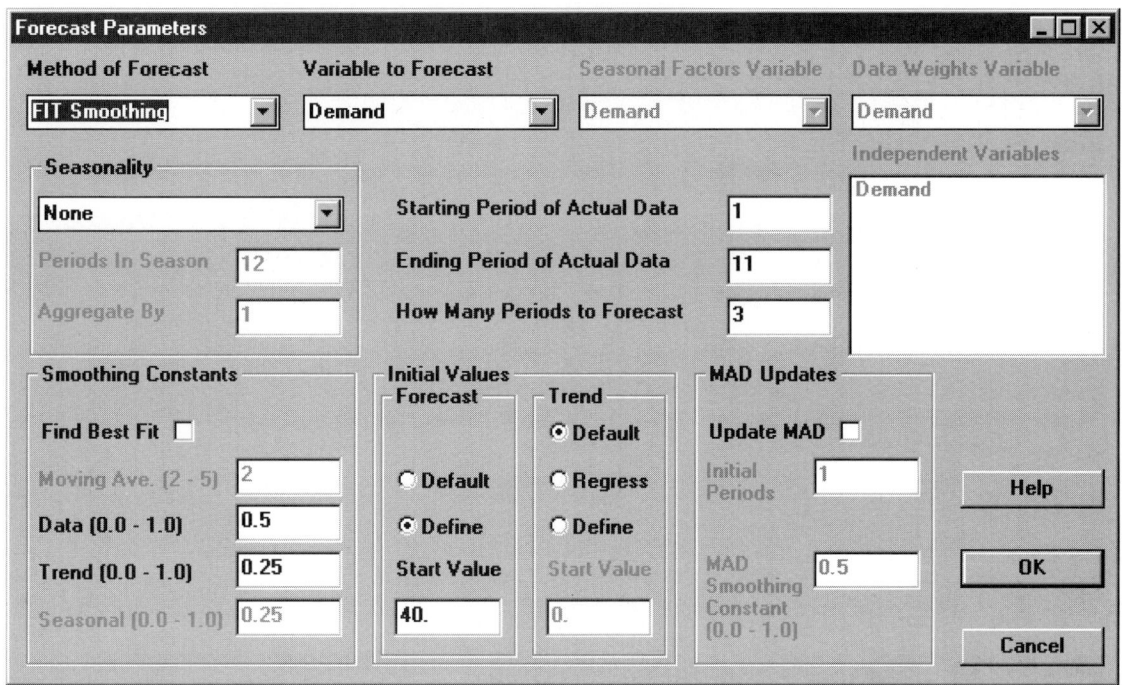

Output for Sample Data

FFIT.DAT   (FIT Smoothing)

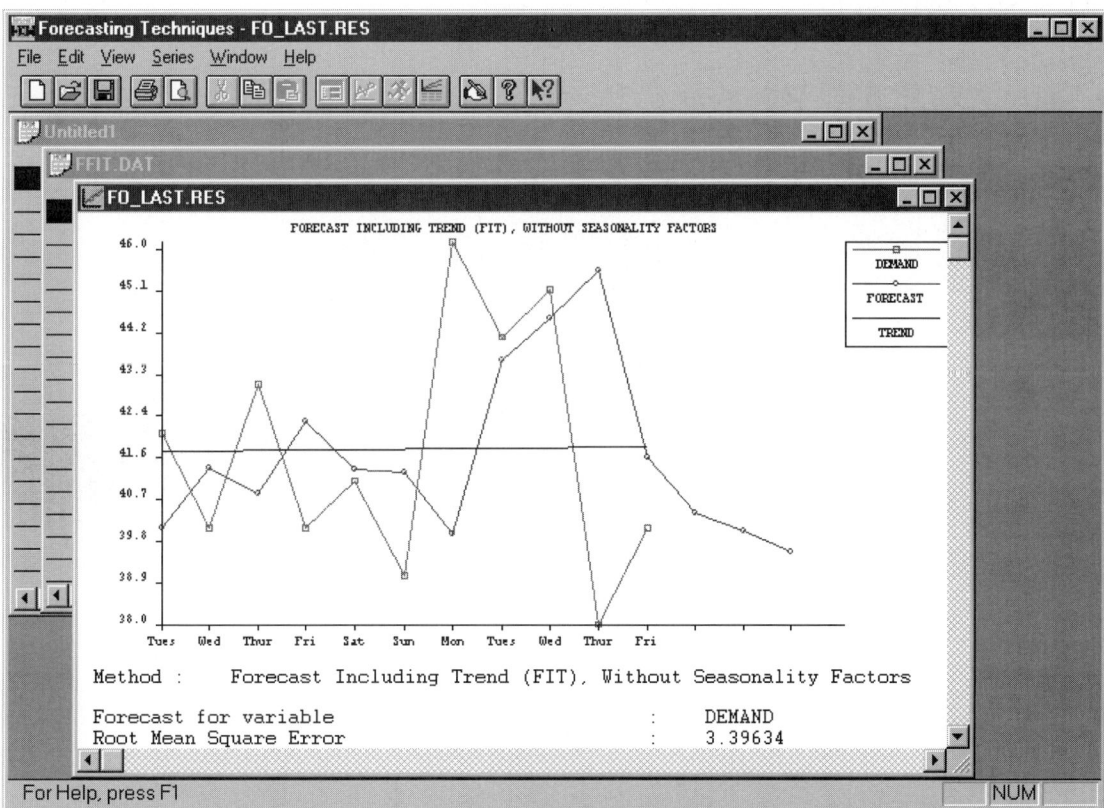

181

Output for FIT Smoothing Example (continued)

Text output exported to Microsoft Excel before copying to clipboard and pasting.

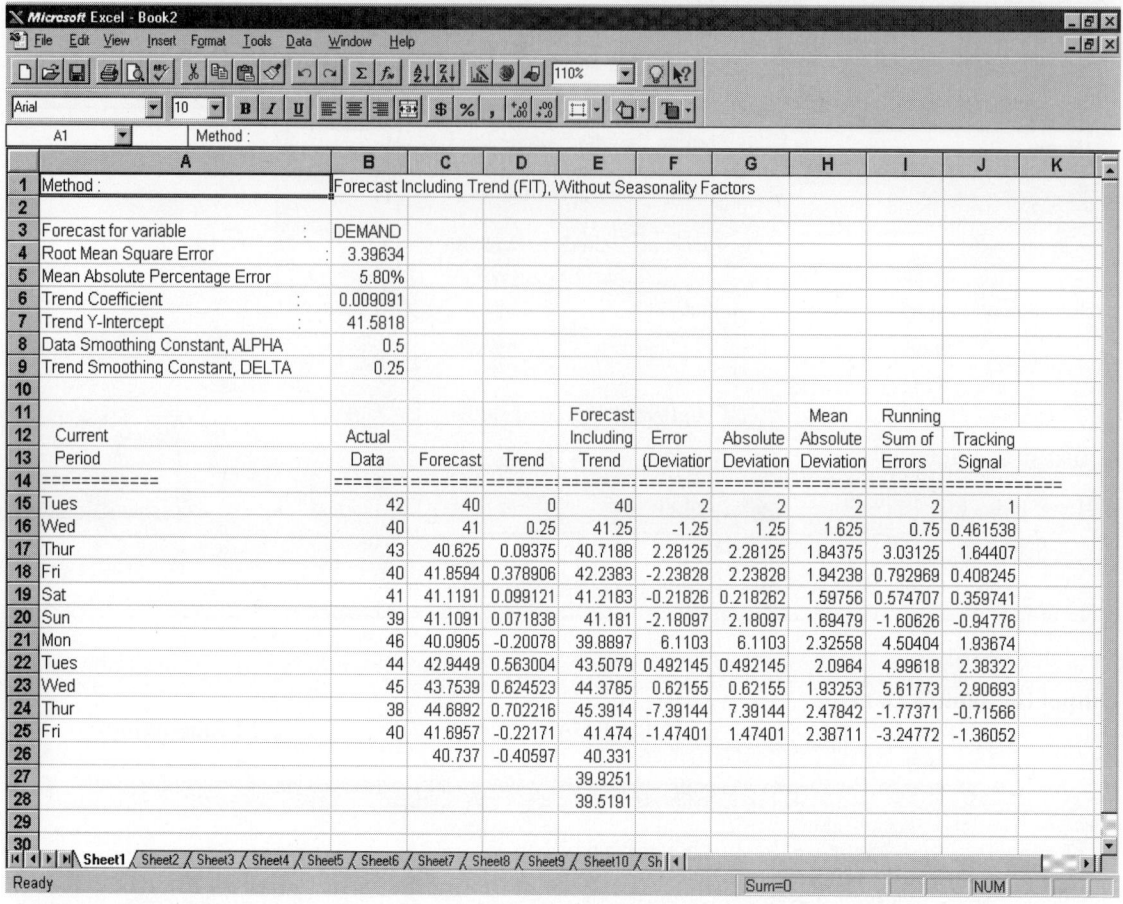

3. EXPONENTIAL SMOOTHING WITH REGRESSED TREND

In this method the "divide and conquer" approach is applied to eliminate the trend in the actual data at the first step. This method is advisable if the trend is relatively constant.

First, the regression equation is solved to fit:

$$A_i = \text{Constant} + A_x * i \qquad \text{where i is the time period}$$

The value of A_x is the trend. This trend is then subtracted from the actual data:

$$A'_i = A_i - [A_x * (i - 1)] \qquad \text{for } i = 1, 3, ..., N$$

The exponential smoothing is done next:

$$F_1 = A'_1 = A_1$$
$$F_i = F_{i-1} + \alpha * (A'_{i-1} - F_{i-1}) \qquad \text{for } i = 2, 3, ..., N+1$$
$$F_i = F_{N+1} \qquad \text{for } i = N+2, N+3, ...$$

The trend is added back to give forecast including trend (FIT):

$$FIT_i = F_i + [A_x * (i - 1)] \qquad \text{for } i = 1, 2, ..., N, N+1, ...$$

The inputs are similar to Exponential Smoothing. An example is given below.

Example:

    Input File   **TREND.DAT**

Period	Trend Data	Period	Trend Data
1	10	6	20
2	12	7	22
3	14	8	24
4	16	9	26
5	18	10	28

Method: Trend Regressed
       Seasonality = None
       Start Period = 1
       Ending Period = 10

Partial Text Output

<u>TREND.DAT</u>   (Regressed Trend)

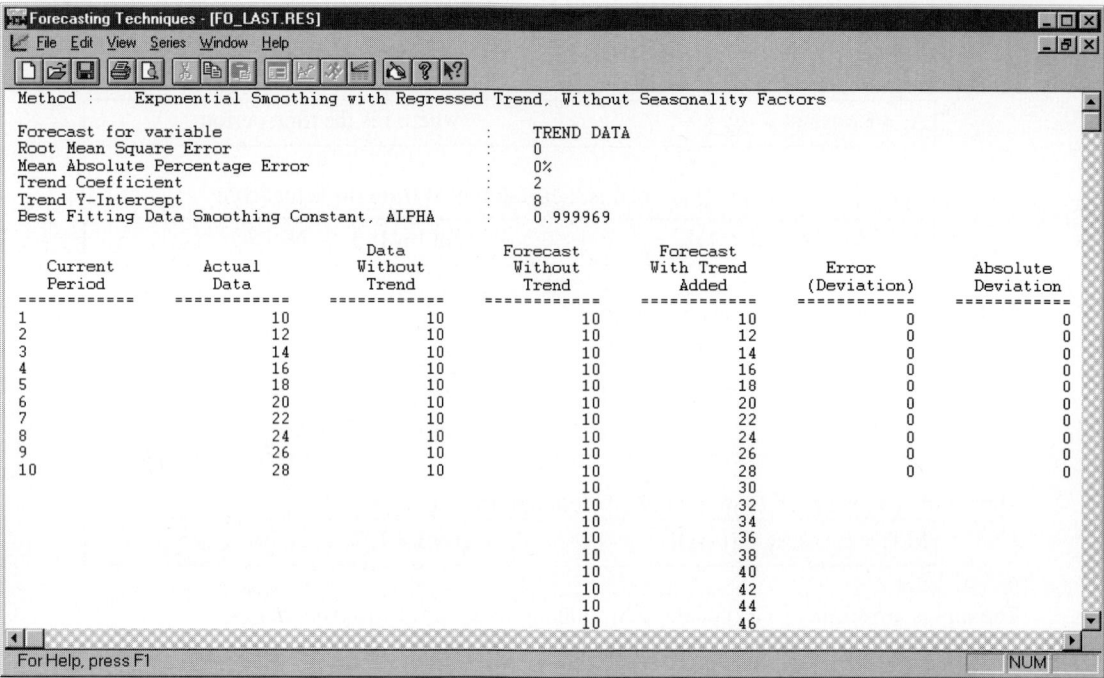

4. SIMPLE AVERAGE

$$F_i = (A_1 + A_2 + ... + A_N) / N \qquad \text{for } i = 1, 2, ..., N, N+1, N+2, ...$$

The inputs are similar to Exponential Smoothing *except* that no smoothing constants are necessary. See section 6, "Best of Above," for a sample output based on the data in FFIT.DAT.

5. MOVING AVERAGE (OVER M PERIODS)

$$F_i = 0 \qquad \text{for } i = 1, 2, ..., M$$
$$F_i = (A_{i-M} + A_{i-M+1} + ... + A_{i-1}) / M \qquad \text{for } i = M+1, M+2, ..., N+1$$
$$F_i = F_{N+1} \qquad \text{for } i = N+2, N+3, ...$$

The inputs are similar to Exponential Smoothing *except* that the user has to specify the number of periods, **M**, over which the Moving Average is computed. **M** can take values 2, 3, 4, 5. If the user chooses "Find Best Fit," then the program searches over these four values and determines the value that gives the smallest Root Mean Square Error (RMSE) (See Section 11).

6. BEST OF ABOVE

The user can ask HOM to determine the best of the first *five* methods, namely Exponential Smoothing, FIT, Regressed Trend, Simple Average, and Moving Average. The program then searches for the best method (*and* the best parameters for each method). The criterion used is minimization of the Root Mean Square Error (RMSE). For the data file FFIT.DAT, the "Best of Above" choice produces the following output.

Output for FFIT.DAT (Best of Above – Seasonality = None)

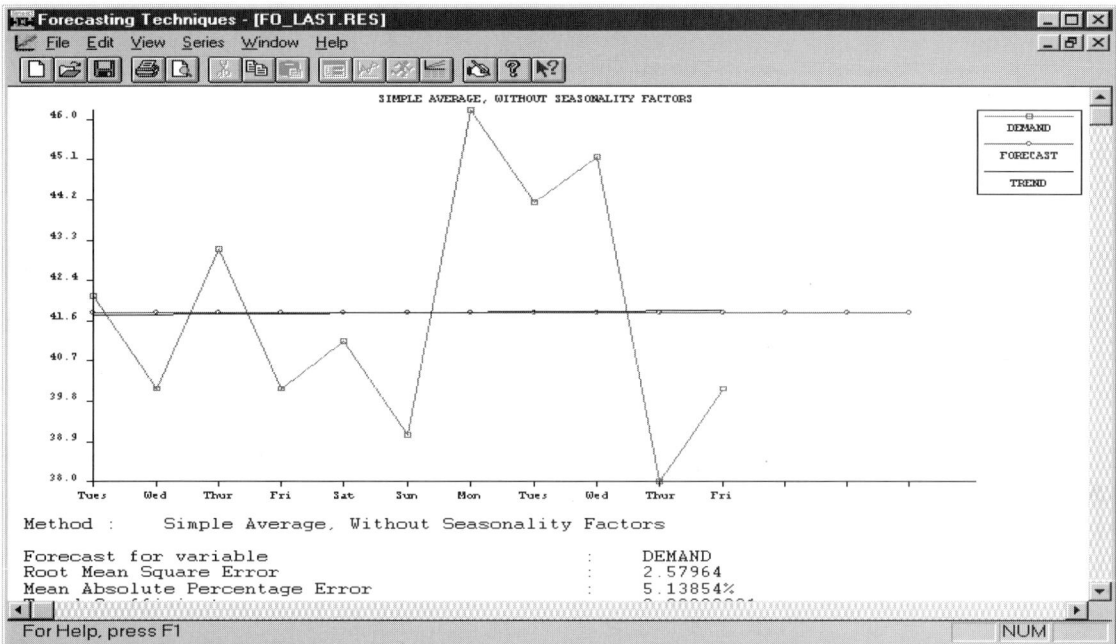

The best method is Simple Average with RMSE = 2.58. Note that HOM gives the name of the best method and the best fitting parameters.

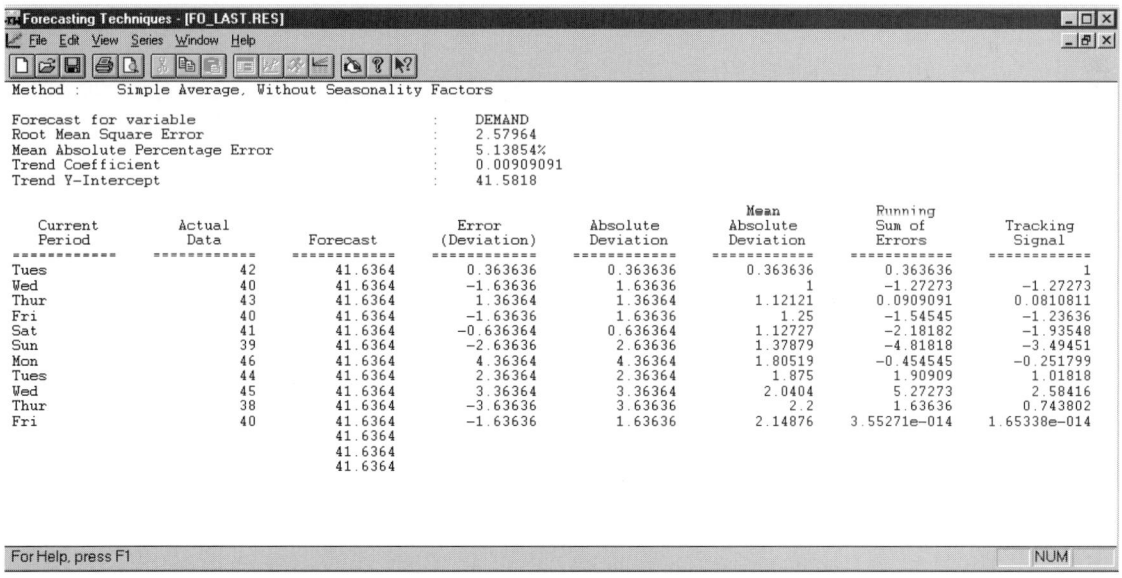

7. WEIGHTED AVERAGE (M WEIGHTS)

The weights are denoted as W_i, $i = 1, 2, ..., M$. The weights must be nonnegative and should add up to a strictly positive number. See below for input description.

$$F_i = A_i \qquad \text{for } i = 1, 2, ..., M$$
$$F_i = (A_{i-M} * W_1 + A_{i-M+1} * W_2 + ... + A_{i-1} * W_M) / (W_1 + W_2 + ... + W_M)$$
$$\text{for } i = M+1, M+2, ..., N+1$$
$$F_i = F_{N+1} \qquad \text{for } i = N+2, N+3, ...$$

Sample Data File

FWTDAVE.DAT

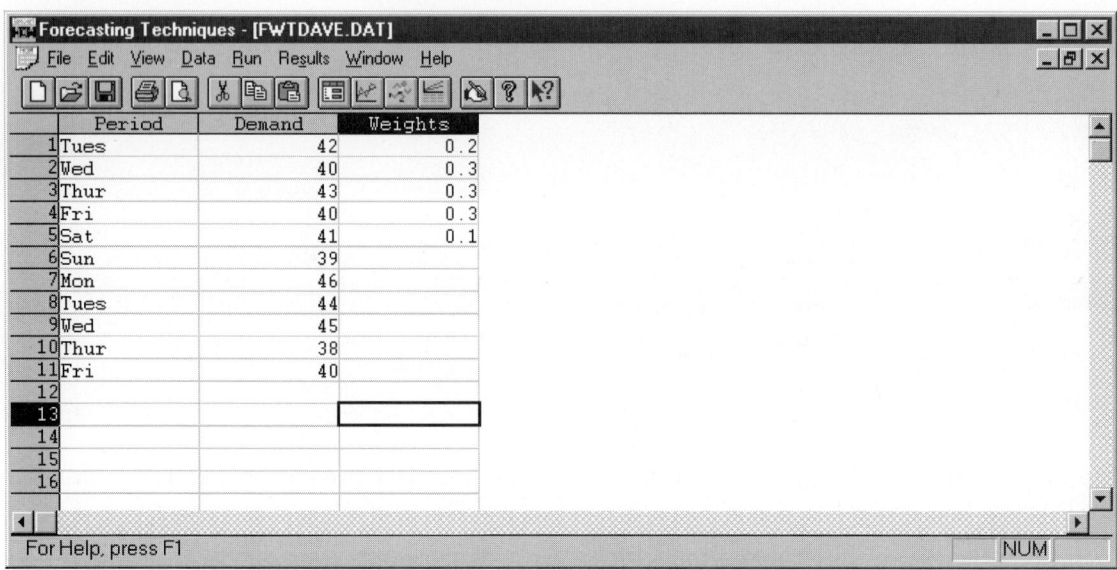

Weighted Average Inputs

Method of Forecast	Weighted Average
Variable to Forecast	Select from the drop-down list (corresponds to a column in the spreadsheet).
Seasonality	Choose a method for deseasonalizing the data before doing the forecast. Refer to "Seasonality" in section 9 for details.
Starting Period of Actual Data	Row number from which the Actual Data begin. (You can choose to omit *some* data when doing the forecast. For example, if there are data given in rows 11 through 100, you can choose to analyze data from Row 14 to Row 64. However, all the data between the starting and ending periods will be used to create the forecast.)
Ending Period of Actual Data	Row number at which Actual Data end.
How Many Periods to Forecast	Number of periods *beyond* the ending period for which to construct the forecast.

Data Weights Variable — Choose from the drop-down list. The weights *start* from the first row (Row 1). The package *automatically* scans down the Data Weights column starting from Row 1. It reads until it encounters a *blank*, *zero*, or *negative* entry in the column. Examples:

(a) 0.1, 0.2, blank, 0.4 - treated as if there are only two data weights: 0.1 and 0.2.

(b) 0.1, 0.2, 0.3, 0.0, 10.0 - treated as if there are three (3) data weights 0.1, 0.2, and 0.3.

(c) 0.1, -1, 2, 10 - treated as if there is only one weight, namely 0.1.

MAD — See section 11 under MAD Updating.

Sample Parameters Dialog Box

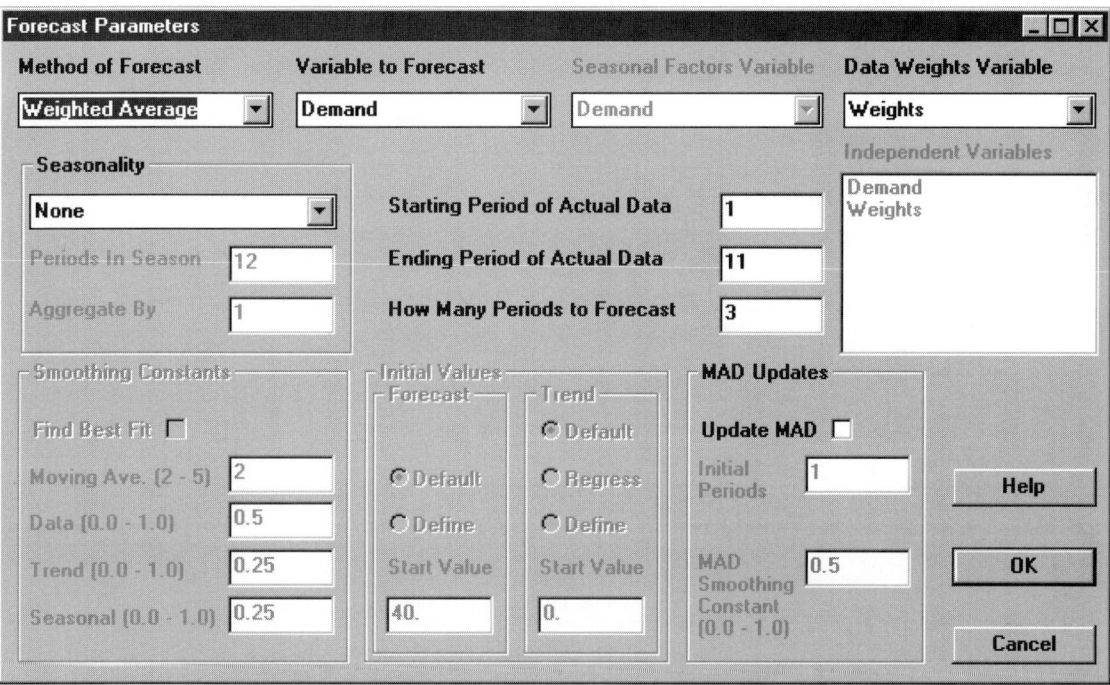

The data weights are in the variable Weights. See Sample Data File on previous page.

Output for Sample Data

<u>FWTDAVE.DAT</u>   (Weighted Average Method)

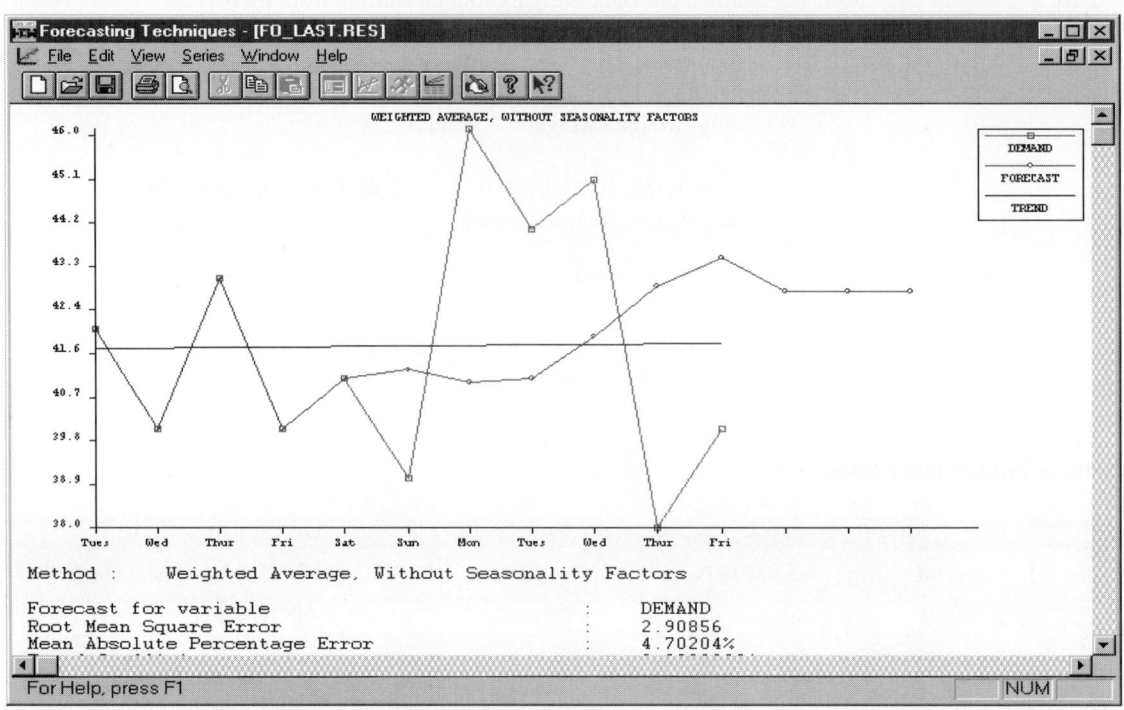

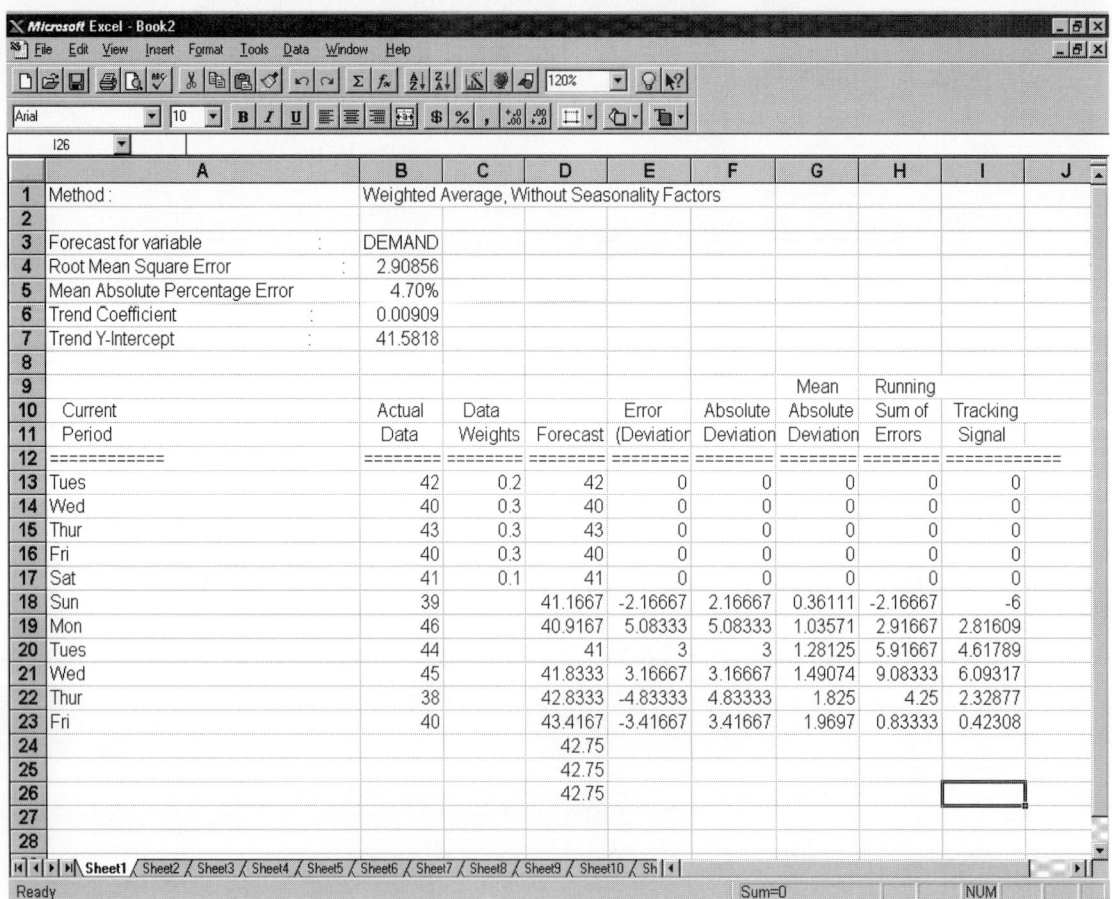

8. WINTER'S METHOD (SEE SECTION 9, "SEASONALITY.")

9. SEASONALITY

In HOM, the user has the options to (i) deseasonalize the data, (ii) incorporate seasonality using Winter's method, or (iii) ignore seasonality. The seasonal factors [for options (i) and (ii)] are displayed to the user in the text output after a successful RUN command

9.1 Deseasonalization of Data or the Divide and Conquer Approach (Seasonality Section of the Parameters Dialog Box)

The number of "Periods In Season" is defined as the number of periods after which the seasonal patterns repeat themselves. For example, if monthly sales depend on the month, then the number of periods in a season is equal to 12. If traffic patterns depend on the day of the week, then the number of periods in aseason is 7.

If the seasonal patterns apply over *blocks* of periods - such as the quarters of a year or January–February, March–April, and so forth - then the user can choose to define the size of such blocks using the variable "Aggregate By" (in the Seasonality section of the Parameters dialog box). For the two examples, "Aggregate By" will equal 3 and 2 respectively (and number of "Periods In Season" will equal 12).

The term *seasonal relative* is used to denote the weight assigned to each period in a season. It is defined as the demand in a period divided by the average demand over the season.

Deseasonalization of data involves (i) obtaining the seasonal relatives for each period and (ii) dividing the actual data for each period by its corresponding seasonal relative. See (d) below for an example of deseasonalization. Once the data have been deseasonalized, any of the forecasting methods (except Winter's method) can be used to develop a forecast employing the deseasonalized data. The forecast is then reseasonalized to produce the final forecast. All measures of error are based on the reseasonalized forecast.

Methods

There are four methods available for calculating the Seasonal Relatives in HOM: (a) Seasonal Factors Using Moving Averages; (b) Simple Seasonal Factors; (c) Quarterly Seasonal Factors; and (d) User Defined Seasonal Factors.

(a) Seasonal Factors Using Moving Averages

Inputs: Number of "Periods In Season," k, and actual data for at least two seasons.
Method: Please refer to Nahmias (1997) for the algorithms used. A pseudo-code is given below.
Output: The seasonal relatives are given by SA[i], i = 1, 2, ..., k.

Algorithm

Let a season consist of k periods. The procedure is different for even and odd values of k. We use the temporary arrays MA[], seasonal relatives SR[], and COUNT [].

```
If k is odd , let k' = (k-1)/2, number of data points = n
DO i = (k+1)/2, n
        Compute centered MA[i] = (A[i-k'] + A[i-k'+1] + ... + A[i+k'])/k for i > (k-1)/2
        MA[i] = A[i]/MA[i]           ! convert using centered average into a relative weight
        j = i (modulo) k
        COUNT[j] ++1                 ! counts how many seasonal factors we have
        SR[j] += MA[i]
ENDDO
sum = 0
DO i = 1,k {SR[i] /= float( COUNT[i] ), sum += SR[i] }
DO i = 1,k {SR[i] = SR[i]*k/sum}                       ! Normalize the SR[]'s to add up to k.
```

```
If k is even, let k' = k/2
DO  i = k/2 + 1, n
        compute centered MA[i] = (A[i-k'] + 2*A[i-k'+1] + 2*A[i-k'+2] + ... + 2*A[i+k'-1]
                                 + A[i+k'])/(2*k')
        j = i (modulo) k
        COUNT[j] ++1                 ! counts how many seasonal factors we have
        SR[j] += MA[i]
ENDDO
sum = 0
DO i = 1,k {SR[i] /= float( COUNT[i] ), sum += SR[i] }
DO i = 1,k {SR[i] = SR[i]*k/sum}                       ! Normalize the SR[]'s to add up to k.
```

(b) Simple Seasonal Factors

Inputs: Number of "Periods In Season" and "Aggregate By."
Method: The basic approach is to divide the actuals in a period by the average of all data and use the ratios to compute the seasonal relatives. Please refer to Nahmias (1997) for the algorithms used.

Let

Number of Periods in a Season	= k	
Aggregate By	= m	(default m = 1)
Number of Seasons of data	= n	

Note: k must be divisible by m

Algorithm

```
Step 1:  Aggregate the actual data every m periods - k must be divisible by m.
         That is, let
                 B[1] = (A[1]+A[2]+ ... + A[m])/m
                 B[2] = (A[m+1] + A[m+2] + ... + A[2m])/m
             and so on.
Step 2:  Find the sample mean for all the data. Denote the sample mean as A.
Step 3:  Normalize all the B's; that is, set  b[t] = B[t]/(m*A).
Step 4:  Find the seasonal factor:
             SR[i] = (b[1]+b[k/m+1]+...+b[nk/m+1])/n,       i = 1, 2, 3,..., k/m
Step 5:  Normalize the SR[i]'s to add up to k/m.
```

(c) Quarterly Seasonal Factors

Instead of finding the seasons period by period, sometimes it might be beneficial to find the seasonals using quarterly values (sum of 3 periods) of the data. The seasonal factor is then found not for a period, but for the first, second, third, and fourth quarters. The simple method described above in (b) is used to find the quarterly factors.

(d) User Defined Seasonal Factors

The user can choose to define the seasonal weights. When this option is chosen, the "Seasonal Factors" variable of the Parameters dialog box is highlighted.

Inputs: Seasonal Factors must be entered as a separate variable with a unique name using the Data --> Variable --> Add operation of HOM. The values are given in a separate column *starting from the first row*.

The name of the Seasonal Factors Variable *must be chosen* from the drop-down list. The "number of a Periods In Season" and "Aggregate By" values have to be specified.

The effect of "Aggregate By" is to first aggregate the data by the given number of periods and then apply the seasonal factors.

Example: To specify the seasonal factors 0.5, 1.5, 1.5, 0.5 for the four quarters in a year, define a new variable, say NEW. Enter the data starting from Row #1 of this variable. Select "User Defined" under Seasonality, "Periods In Season" = 12, and "Aggregate By" = 3. See below for the input screen and dialog box.
(The data file BLANCH.DAT is included. The variable NEW has to be added by the user.)

File:
BLANCH.DAT

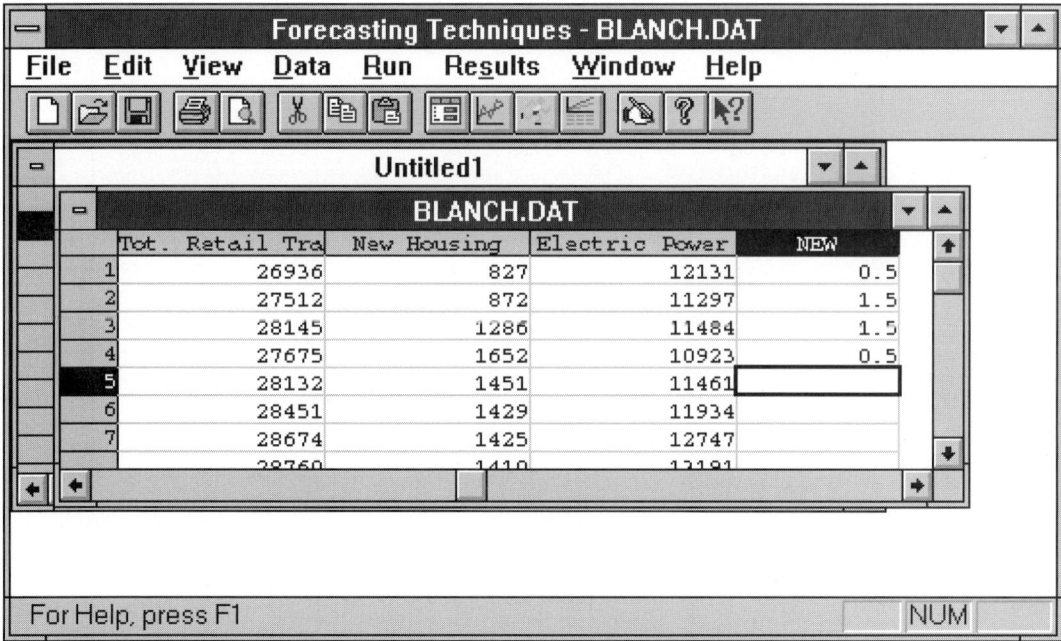

The effect of these choices can be seen from the output shown below.

Parameters Dialog Box

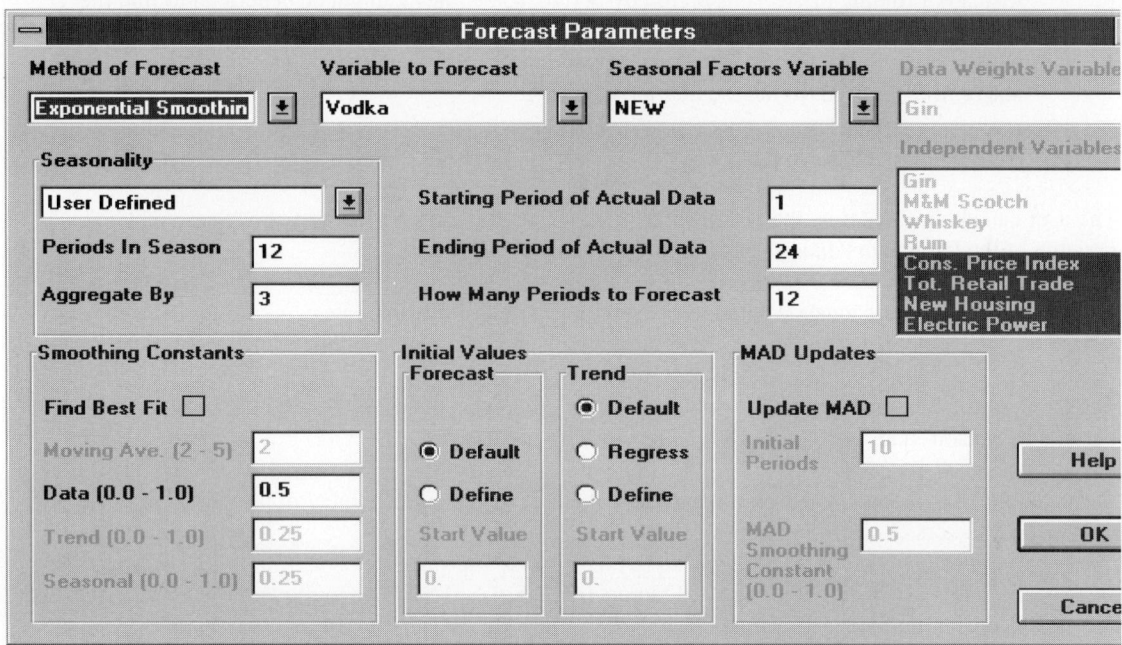

Partial Output for Sample Data

BLANCH.DAT   (User Defined Seasonal Factors)

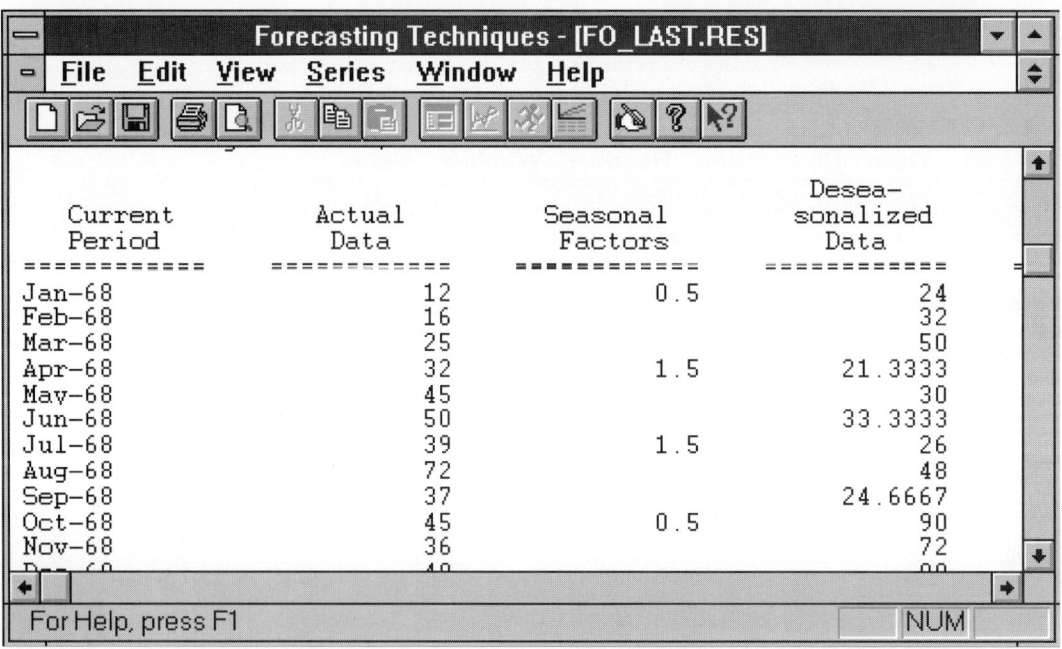

Note the effect of "Aggregate By" = 3.

9.2 Incorporating Seasonality Using Winter's Method

Inputs: Three smoothing constants: α, δ, and γ. α is used for the series, S; δ is used for the trend; and γ is used for the seasonal weights. The user has to define the "Periods In Season," k.

Note: The term "series" can be understood as being similar to deseasonalized data. The term "seasonal weights" is equivalent to "Seasonal Relatives." The terminology in this section has been kept consistent as far as possible with the terminology given in Nahmias (1997).

Method

Please consult Nahmias (1997) for a detailed explanation. A brief explanation is given below.

The forecast for period t, s periods in the future (i.e., forecast for the period (t+s) in period t) is written as

$$F_{t, t+s} = (S_t + s\, T_t)\, C_{(t+s\,(\text{mod})\,k\, + \,1)}$$

where S_t and T_t are the series and trend and $C_{(t+s\,(\text{mod})\,k\,+\,1)}$ stands for the seasonal weight for the period (t+s). [Technical note: t+s (mod) k stands for the remainder that is obtained by dividing t+s by k.].

Let tk = t (mod) k. Then, the triple smoothing procedure of Winter leads to

$$S_t = \alpha\,[A_t / C_{tk}] + (1-\alpha)\,(S_{t-1} + T_{t-1})$$

$$T_t = \delta\,[S_t - S_{t-1}] + (1-\delta)\,T_{t-1}$$

$$C_{tk} = \gamma\,(A_t/S_t) + (1-\gamma)\,C_{tk}$$

Note that after each step we need to renormalize the seasonal factors to add up to k ("Periods In Season").

Choice of Initial Values:

The user can choose to use the moving seasonal relatives [see (a) in section 9.1] *or* the simple method [see (b) in section 9.1] *or* user-defined values [see (d) in section 9.1] as the seasonal relatives for starting the forecasting procedure. The "Aggregate By" value is always equal to one (1). A regression line is fitted to the deseasonalized data to get the starting values of series, S, and trend, T.

Winter's Method Inputs

Method of Forecast	Winter's Method
Variable to Forecast	Select from the drop-down list (corresponds to a column in the spreadsheet).
Seasonality	Choose a method for deseasonalizing the data before doing the forecast. The methods allowed are Simple Seasonal Relatives, Moving Seasonal Relatives, or User Defined. "Aggregate By" always equals one.
Starting Period of Actual Data	Row number from which the Actual Data begin. (You can choose to omit *some* data when doing the forecast. For example, if there are data given in rows 11 through 100, you can choose to analyze data from Row 14 to Row 64. However, all the data between the starting and ending periods will be used to create the forecast.)
Ending Period of Actual Data	Row number at which Actual Data end.
How Many Periods to Forecast	Number of periods *beyond* the ending period for which to construct the forecast.
α	Smoothing constant between 0 and 1. The value of α is entered under "Data" in the Smoothing Constants section of the Parameters dialog box. You can choose to input α or leave it to the package to determine by selecting "Find Best Fit." The package finds the best α, δ, and γ that minimize the Root Mean Square Error (RMSE).
δ	Smoothing constant for trend between 0 and 1. The value of δ is entered under "Trend" in the Smoothing Constants section of the Parameters dialog box). You can choose to input δ or leave it to the package to determine by selecting "Find Best Fit." The package finds the best α, δ, and γ that minimize the Root Mean Square Error (RMSE).
γ	Smoothing constant for seasonality between 0 and 1. The value of γ is entered under "Seasonal" in the Smoothing Constants section of the Parameters dialog box). You can choose to input γ or leave it to the package to determine by selecting "Find Best Fit." The package finds the best α, δ, and γ that minimize the Root Mean Square Error (RMSE).
Find Best Fit	See above.
Initial Value of Forecast	The first period's forecast is by default set equal to the first period's actual demand. The user can override this by selecting "Define" and entering the value in the box provided.

Initial Value of Trend	The default value for the first period trend is zero. This value can be set equal to the regressed value of the trend by choosing "Regress." The regression is carried out over the starting and ending periods of data. This value can be defined by the user by choosing "Define" and inputting a value in the box provided.
MAD	See section 11 under MAD Updating.

Example File:

        BLANCH.DAT (please see section 9.1 for a sample of this data file)

Sample Parameters Dialog Box

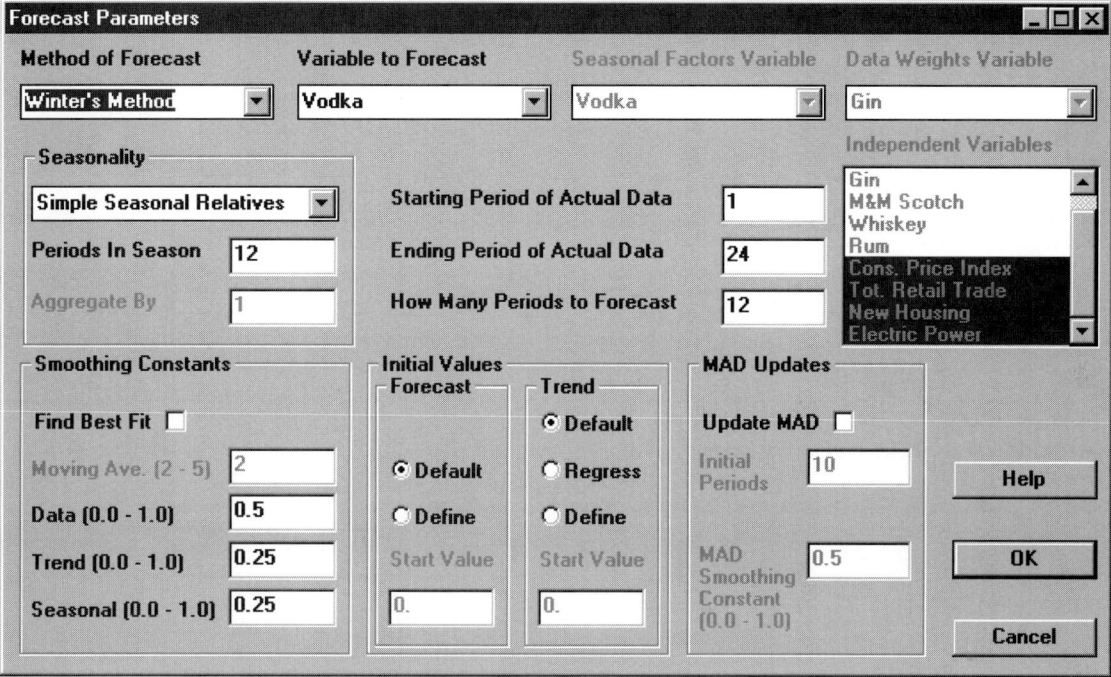

Output for Sample Data

BLANCH.DAT   (Winter's Method)

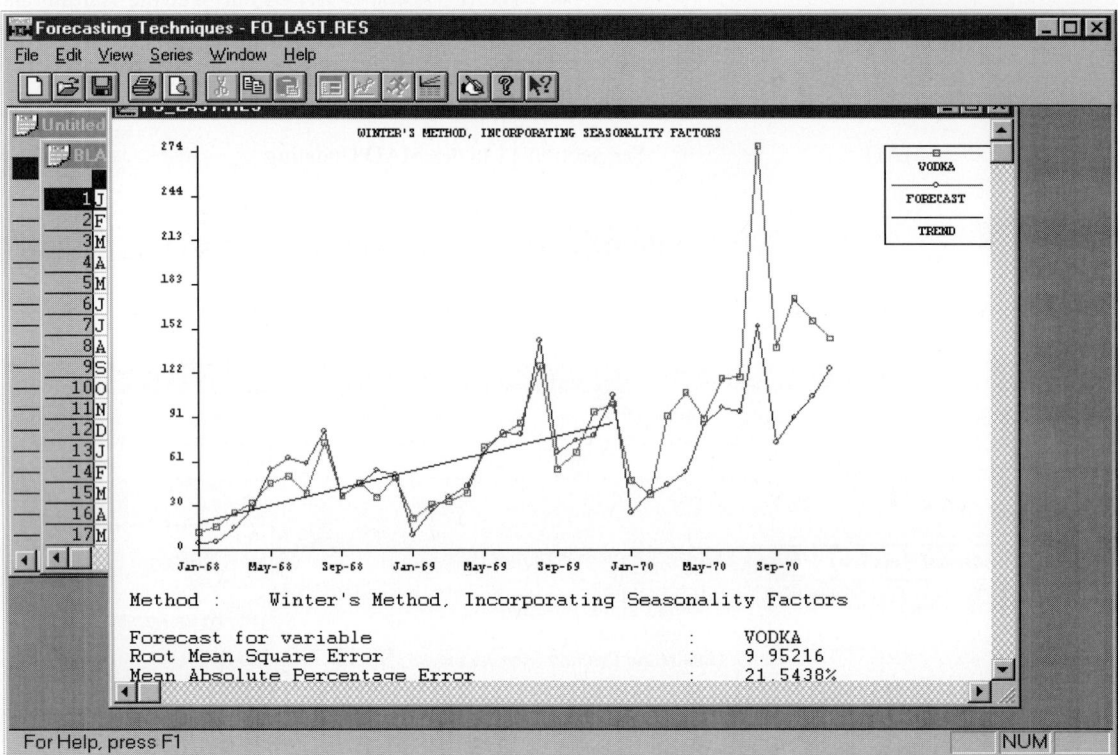

Output for Sample Data (continued)

BLANCH.DAT

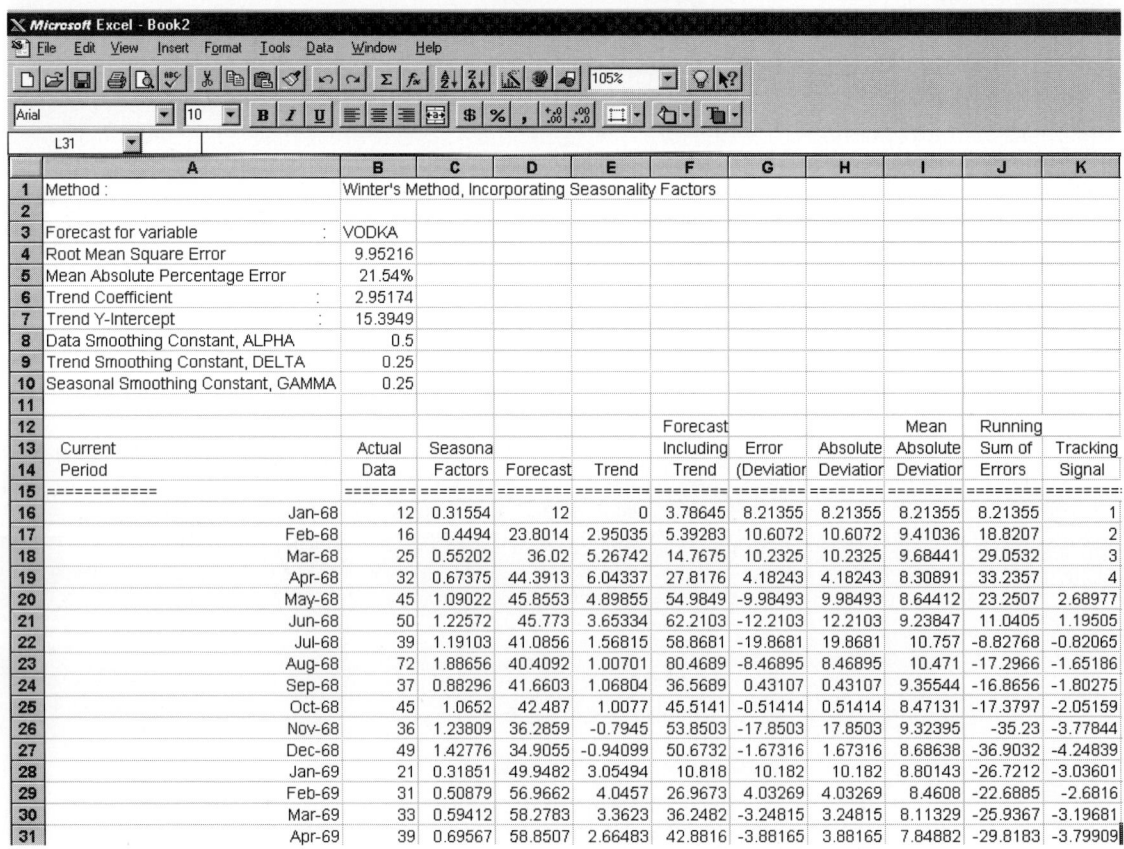

10. MULTIPLE REGRESSION

To calculate the forecast, HOM first carries out a regression of the chosen dependent variable (e.g., actual demand) against (up to six) independent variables (e.g., economic indicators). The forecast for period i is calculated as follows:

$$F_i = \text{Constant} + X_1 * VAR_{1i} + X_2 * VAR_{2i} + \ldots + X_K * VAR_{Ki}$$

where   K is a number of independent variables;
          $VAR_{1i}, VAR_{2i}, \ldots, VAR_{Ki}$ are the values for the independent variables for period i;
          Constant is a regression constant;
          $X_1, X_2, \ldots, X_K$ are regression coefficients for corresponding independent variables.

The names of the independent variables are selected from the drop-down list.

The dependent variable data can be deseasonalized (but not the independent variable data - at least within HOM) by selecting an appropriate method under Seasonality (see section 9). (The concept of deseasonalizing just the dependent variable might not be proper in applications. In that case, select a method such as Simple Average, select in turn each of the independent variables, deseasonalize the independent variables, store the deseasonalized data in an external or another input spreadsheet, import the deseasonalized data back into HOM, and then run the multiple regression.)

Please refer to a standard text for a discussion about the multiple regression technique.

Example Data File: BLANCH.DAT (see section 9.1 for input screen)

Sample Parameters Dialog Box

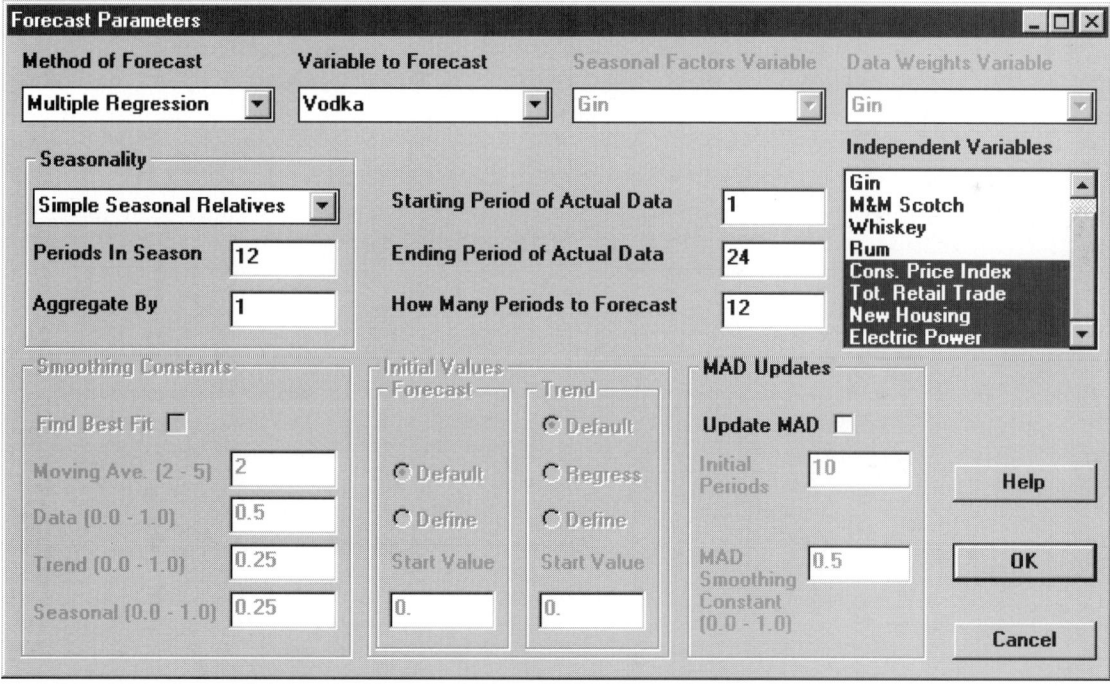

The dependent variable is Vodka. It will be deseasonalized using the simple method discussed in section 9.1(b). The dependent variables are the Consumer Price Index, Total Retail Trade, New Housing Starts, and Consumption of Electric Power (not deseasonalized).

Partial Output for Sample Data

<u>BLANCH.DAT</u> **(Multiple Regression)**

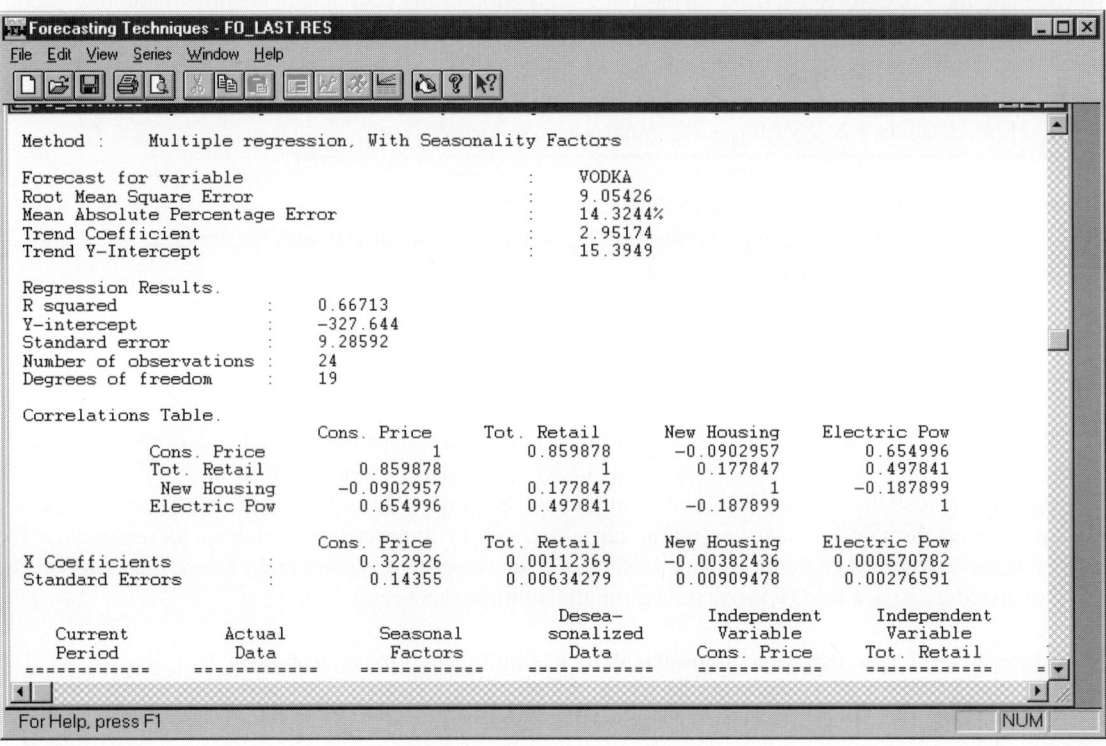

11. ERROR IN FORECAST

HOM reports the Root Mean Square Error (RMSE), the Mean Absolute Percentage Error (MAPE), the Mean Absolute Deviation (MAD), and the Tracking Signal. Please refer to any standard text for the explanation of these terms. The formulae used are as follows:

Measurements of error for the current period i, i = 1, ..., N.

(a) Absolute deviation in period i, $AD_i = abs(A_i - F_i)$; error, $e_i = (A_i - F_i)$.
$MAD_i = (AD_1 + AD_2 + ... + AD_i) / i$; (no update)
$= MAD(i - 1) + \alpha_{MAD} (|e_i| - MAD(i - 1))$

(c) Running sum of forecast errors in period i,
$RSFE_i = [(A_1 - F_1) + (A_2 - F_2) + ... + (A_i - F_i)]$

(d) Tracking signal in period i, $TS_i = RSFE_i / MAD_i$

(e) Root mean square error, $RMSE = \{(AD_1^2 + AD_2^2 + ... + AD_N^2) / N\}^{1/2}$.

MAD Updating: In HOM two ways are permitted for computing MAD.

1. Use all the data available to calculate the MAD, that is, $MAD_i = (AD_1 + AD_2 + ... + AD_i) / i$. This is the default.

2. Allow MAD to be updated each period. For this, we need the user to specify the initial number of periods (say INI) and a smoothing constant, αMAD. Then, HOM uses INI periods [i.e., start period to (start period + INI - 1] to compute the MAD (INI <= n). The tracking signal starts from start period + INI.

Thereafter, let the error in period *i* be $e_i = (A_i - F_i)$. Then
$$MAD(i) = MAD(I - 1) + \alpha_{MAD} (|e_i| - MAD(i - 1))$$

The smoothing constant, αMAD, is specified in the Update MAD section of the Parameters dialog box. The value of αMAD can range from 0 to 1.

REFERENCES

Chase, R. B., and N. J. Aquilano *Production and Operations Management* 7th ed. Burr Ridge, IL: Richard D. Irwin, 1995.

Nahmias, S. *Production and Operations Analysis* 3rd ed. Burr Ridge, IL: Richard D. Irwin, 1997.

Stevenson, W. J. *Production/Operations Management* 5th ed. Burr Ridge, IL: Richard D. Irwin, 1996.

INDEPENDENT DEMAND INVENTORY MANAGEMENT METHODS

The HOM Independent Demand Inventory Management calculation schema for Continuous and Periodic Review models are given below, followed by a summary of the models along with data requirements and calculations performed.

1. GETTING STARTED

A problem that has faced organizations throughout time is how much to have on hand (inventory) of the products it is selling (dresses at Bloomingdales, geraniums at local flower shops, syringes and bandages at hospital emergency rooms, newspapers at the local newsstand, etc.). Almost all sales are made from some amount of stock and not made to order, even though the latter is becoming the goal for many companies.

The key questions one would like to know about inventory are how much should be ordered; how often, or when, to order it; and how much is it costing the organization to order and hold it? HOM$^{\copyright}$ Inventory Management is designed to help answer these and other questions for a vast number of assumptions on the description of the business environment.

To solve these problems, we will first have to make assumptions on whether demand is constant, variable with certainty (known with certainty, but changeable each time period), or uncertain (describable by a probability distribution or its mean and standard distribution). Is the firm buying from a distributor (stock always available, but it takes a finite time to arrive after order—lead time), or producing what it sells? The latter case will also require a lead time, but each sale also has an effect on raw materials required for the manufacturing process (MRP—Materials Requirement Planning). What does it cost us to order the product, what is the cost of the item, and what is the cost of holding it in inventory for a period of time? Remember that inventory requires investment and thus, takes cash away from other productive opportunities; therefore, the opportunity cost of capital is the proper interest rate to use. Also remember that the cost data used in this module are such that they vary with the number of orders, the size of the order, or the average inventory—fixed costs are not relevant as inputs to inventory calculations.

2. SPECIFY DEMAND STRUCTURE

To initiate the Inventory Management module, you must first decide on the structure of demand. This manual describes Independent Demand inventory models that can be solved using HOM. Independent demand implies that the product is for "final" consumption. These could be products that you are selling or the ones that you acquire from a manufacturer or distributor (e.g., Wal-Mart, L.L. Bean).

3. SPECIFY PROBLEM STRUCTURE

If you have chosen Independent Demand, a spreadsheet will appear that has entries for numerous data items. However, before you enter any data, we recommend that you first use the Parameters dialog box (reached by its icon or by DATA, then choose the Parameters item on the command line) to specify your problem. We recommend this because, for this module, there are more numerous problem-alternative combinations than there are problem data. Once you specify the problem, the spreadsheet will again appear, and you will only be able to enter data in the "blue or gray" specified areas that are unique to that problem specification.

The Parameters dialog box is divided into six areas, each requiring a choice on the user's part:
      Type of Review
      Type of Demand
      Replenishment Rate
      Calculate Parameters
      Conversion Factor
      Quantity Discounts

A description of each of these items is given below.

3.1 Type of Review

This choice requires you to make an assessment of how you will know when to reorder your inventory. There are two choices:

1. Continuous Review assumes that you will continuously keep track of (count) your inventory position and place an order when it reaches a specific number/level [order more bandages when there are **3** (reorder point) boxes remaining].

2. Periodic Review assumes that you review inventory at specific time epochs (every 10 days, every Monday, etc.) independent of how much you have in stock.

3.1.1 Continuous Review

The decision variables in the Continuous Review inventory models in HOM are the quantity to order (Q) and the reorder level (R). The Continuous Review models can incorporate backlogs, Deterministic or Stochastic demand, and Finite or Infinite Replenishment Rate. The following calculations can be performed:

Determine the quantity to order and the reorder level (all Deterministic demand models). See models 1, 3, and 5.

Determine the best price range by performing Quantity Discount calculations (both with and without backlogging of demand)—only for Deterministic demand models. See models 2 and 4.

Determine Safety Stocks for Stochastic demand model given a desired service level. See model 6(a).

Do complete Cost Calculations and determine the optimal quantity to order and the reorder level for Stochastic demand models. See model 6(b).

Determine the Service Level given the values of the quantity to order and the reorder level—only for Stochastic demand models. See model 6(c).

3.1.2 Periodic Review

The Periodic Review model within HOM is also called an (S,S-1) model. Demand has to be Stochastic to be able to use HOM for the calculations. It is assumed that the inventory is reviewed periodically (once at the beginning of every review period—say, daily, weekly, or monthly). The user specifies a value of the review period. Uncertainties in lead time as well as demand can be modeled. An order is placed if at the time of review, the inventory on hand, I, is less than a predetermined (order up to) quantity, S. The quantity ordered will equal S minus I. The following calculations can be performed:

Determine the quantity to order given a desired service level.
Determine the service level given the quantity to be ordered.

3.2 Type of Demand

This choice requires you to decide on whether your demand is Deterministic (known with certainty) Stochastic (you may only know the mean and standard deviation of demand and/or its entire probability distribution). If you choose Deterministic Demand, you can also decide on whether you will allow back orders, that is, the filling of current demand some time after it has been requested. (Often my desire for Lands End and L.L. Bean products has been shared by others, and since I order many weeks after the catalog has arrived, they are usually out of stock and they ask me if I mind waiting a few weeks until they refill their stock. Offering this type of service implies back-ordering.)

If you choose Stochastic demand, back orders are not available, but you can choose to meet either fill-rate or lead-time service levels. Since demand is uncertain, and you may not be confident in your cost estimate for stockouts, you may want to carry extra inventory so that you can meet demand with some level of service (probability). Lead-time service level implies that you set a probability for not stocking out during the inventory cycle (the period between two orders or the time between two reviews). If this service level is 90%, it implies that (on the average) in nine out of every ten inventory cycles, we will not stock out during the lead time. Fill-rate service levels imply that we have enough in stock to meet the service-level fraction of demand. For example, if fill-rate service level equals 95%, then we plan to provide 95 percent of the items demanded each inventory cycle from off the shelf (existing) inventory.

3.3 Replenishment Rate

For Continuous Review and Deterministic demand situations, the user gets to choose the replenishment rate. Infinite and Finite Replenishment Rate options are available.

> Infinite Replenishment Rate implies that each order is delivered all at once—that is, order 100 items and obtain 100 items in one delivery.

> Finite Replenishment Rate is usually chosen to model a situation in which a part or product is being produced by the firm. The finite replenishment rate is then set equal to the capacity of the machine producing the item. It can be used to approximate uniformly staggered deliveries.

3.4 Calculate

For Continuous Review and Stochastic demand problems, the user has the choice (using either the fill-rate or lead-time scenarios) of calculating:
- Safety stock
- Costs
- Service level

A description of each type of calculation is given in section 6.

3.5 Conversion Factor

While product demand is usually assumed to be annual, measures for lead time, review period, and so on (data on lines 13–18 of the input data spreadsheet) are usually convenient to express in time units less than annually. The Conversion Factor subwindow has a drop-down list that allows the user to use shorter periods of time for these factors. Clicking on the down arrow in the subwindow box reveals the four alternatives (Daily, Weekly, Monthly, Yearly), and the user just needs to point and click on the desired option. At that time, HOM automatically produces the appropriate number of those time units in a year (e.g., 52 weeks in a year). The user can change this number by moving the cursor to the edit box, clicking, and then editing in a new number. Fifty weeks in a year might be appropriate if the firm is closed, say, for two weeks at New Year's time. The choice of Conversion Factor is also automatically shown in the data spreadsheet in the Supplemental Data section.

3.6 Quantity Discounts

Using the Continuous Review and Deterministic demand environment also allows for the possibility of quantity discounts if Infinite Replenishment Rate has also been used. It is allowable to have both back orders and quantity discounts.

Quantity Discounts (the more you order, the less you pay) can be broken into up to a maximum of 10 price points. Choice of the number of price points is up to the user and is specified after the quantity discount has been enabled by clicking on the appropriate box in the dialog box.

4. INPUT PROBLEM DATA

After using the Parameters dialog box to specify the problem environment, the data input spreadsheet now highlights all allowable data entry cells in "blue or gray" areas. The first two lines of the spreadsheet are highlighted and repeat the problem specification. If these key words do not match your selection, please return to the Parameters dialog box and check your entries. There are four sections in the spreadsheet:
- Basic Model Data
- Supplemental Data
- Sensitivity Analysis
- Quantity Discount Table

4.1 Basic Model Data

The first section for data entry is called Basic Model Data and requires inputs for some of the following variables: annual demand, cost per unit, annual holding cost rate, annual holding cost per unit, ordering cost, and annual cost per back order.

Remember, data are only necessary in the fields preceded by a word in blue or black. The third column indicates the units required. Thus, annual demand is in units per year. The cost per unit is in dollars; that is., 1.29 is equivalent to one dollar and 29 cents. The annual holding cost rate is that percent that you have chosen to calculate the cost of holding an item in inventory for one year. Remember to include pilferage, breakage, obsolescence, deterioration, theft, and so on. The annual holding cost per unit is the cost of the item times the holding cost rate. The ordering cost is incurred each time you order and is assumed to be independent of the quantity ordered. For production-based systems, this could be the cost of setting up production from one product to another. The annual back-order cost is per unit and requires an estimate by the user of the cost of meeting demand with a delay rather than on time. These costs could include, but not be limited to, special shipping and record-keeping charges, loss of future demand, and so forth

4.2 Supplemental Data

The second section for data entry is called Supplemental Data and may require inputs for the following variables (notice that most of the units have been adjusted to your choice of time periods):

- Usage rate refers to the daily, weekly, monthly, or annual demand.
- Production rate is the capacity of the machine producing the item and is used only in finite replenishment rate, continuous review models.
- Average lead time is the time it takes from order to delivery.
- When demand is stochastic, enter its standard deviation in units per time period.
- The standard deviation of the length of the lead time is required when both demand and lead time are stochastic.
- The length of the review period (time units between orders) is required when you are using periodic review with stochastic demand, as will be the inventory on hand at the start of the review period.
- A service level entry is also required under both fill-rate and lead-time scenarios.

4.3 Sensitivity Analysis

The third data section allows the user to do a Sensitivity Analysis to determine the effect of alternative order quantities and reorder levels in the Continuous Review setting. In the Periodic Review setting, service level can be determined for different values of the quantity ordered. Details are given in section 6.

4.4 Quantity Discount Table

The quantity discount modeled in HOM is an all-unit discount; that is, if the minimum quantity is purchased, then the discount will be applied to all the units. For example, if 99 or fewer units are purchased, then the cost will be $10.00 per unit; and if 100 or more units are purchased, then the unit price will be $9.90 for all units purchased. The table has two columns: the price per unit is given in the first column and the minimum quantity that has to be purchased to obtain that price is shown in the second column.

Be sure to specify the number of price ranges in the Parameters dialog box.

5. GLOSSARY OF TERMS AND NOTATION

Annual Cost per Backorder (C_B)
The Annual Cost per Backorder is the cost per year of an unfilled unit of the product, that is, the cost of filling an order for one unit one year late.

Annual Demand (D)
The Annual Demand is the anticipated annual demand for the product.

Annual Holding Cost Rate (i)
The Annual Holding Cost Rate is the cost of holding one *dollar* of inventory of the product for one year.

Annual Holding Cost Rate per Unit (C_H)
The Annual Holding Cost Rate per Unit is the cost of holding one unit of the product in inventory for one year. It also equals Annual Holding Cost Rate, i, times Cost per Unit, C.

Average Leadtime (LT)
The Average Leadtime is the average time it takes between the placement and the receipt of an order.

Backorder (maximum level B)
Unmet or unfulfilled demand (i.e., demand that cannot be met using off-the-shelf items) can be either lost or filled once replenishment orders are received. In HOM, only the latter case can be modeled. The quantity of demand that cannot be met and that is filled in the future is said to be a backorder.

Cost per Unit (C)
This is the purchase price of a unit. For the Finite Replenishment Rate model, the Cost per Unit is the value added per unit of a finished part or product by the machine.

Fill Rate Service Level (SL)
In HOM, two types of service levels can be modeled. Fill Rate Service Level equals the fraction of demand met from stock. Also see Leadtime Service Level.

Finite Replenishment Rate (p)
Choose the Finite Replenishment Rate option when the part or product is being produced at a machine or when deliveries are staggered at a constant rate (and Leadtime is zero).

Infinite Replenishment Rate
The replenishment rate is said to be infinite when each order is delivered all at once (i.e., if 100 widgets are ordered, 100 widgets are delivered together).

Inventory Cycle
The Inventory Cycle is the time between the placement of successive orders.

Inventory on Hand (I)
The Inventory on Hand is the quantity of the product in inventory at a given data.

Inventory Position
The Inventory Position is defined to be the sum of Inventory on Hand and the quantity on order.

Leadtime
The Leadtime is the time between the placement of an order and its receipt. It could be deterministic or stochastic.

Leadtime Service Level (LTSL)
The Leadtime Service Level is the fraction of time there is no inventory during an inventory cycle. Alternately, it is the probability of a stockout in an inventory cycle.

Length of Review Period (Review Period) (T)
The Length of Review Period is the time between reviews in a Periodic Review model (see below).

Ordering Cost (C_o)
The Ordering Cost is the cost incurred in placing an order. It is considered to be independent of the quantity ordered.

Production Rate (p)
The Production Rate is the rate at which the machine produces the item.

Quantity Discount Table: C(i), MINQ(i), i = 1,N
The quantity discount modeled in HOM is an all-unit discount. The quantity discount table has two columns: the price per unit [C(i)] is given in the first column and the minimum quantity [MINQ(i)] that has to be purchased to obtain this price is shown in the second column. The number of price ranges = N.

Reorder Level (R)
In a Continuous Review inventory model, an order is placed when the inventory position is at or below the Reorder Level.

Safety Stock (SS)
Safety Stock is used to guard against variations in demand and/or lead time.

Standard Deviation of Demand (SDD)
The Standard Deviation of Demand refers to the standard deviation of the daily, weekly, monthly, or annual demand—depending on the Conversion Factor chosen in the Parameters dialog box. If the demand is deterministic, then its standard deviation can be left blank (blanks are treated as zeros).

Standard Deviation of Leadtime (SDLT)
The Standard Deviation of Leadtime is the standard deviation of the time between placing and receipt of an order. If the lead time is deterministic, then this entry can be left blank (blanks are treated as zeros).

Usage Rate (u)
The Usage Rate applies to the Finite Replenishment Rate model. It refers to the rate of consumption of the product or part. The rate is expressed as a daily, weekly, monthly, or annual quantity depending on the Conversion Factor selected in the Parameters dialog box.

6. MODELING TECHNIQUES AND SAMPLE PROBLEMS

The nine models in HOM's Independent Demand system module are described below. Sample problems and outputs are also given.

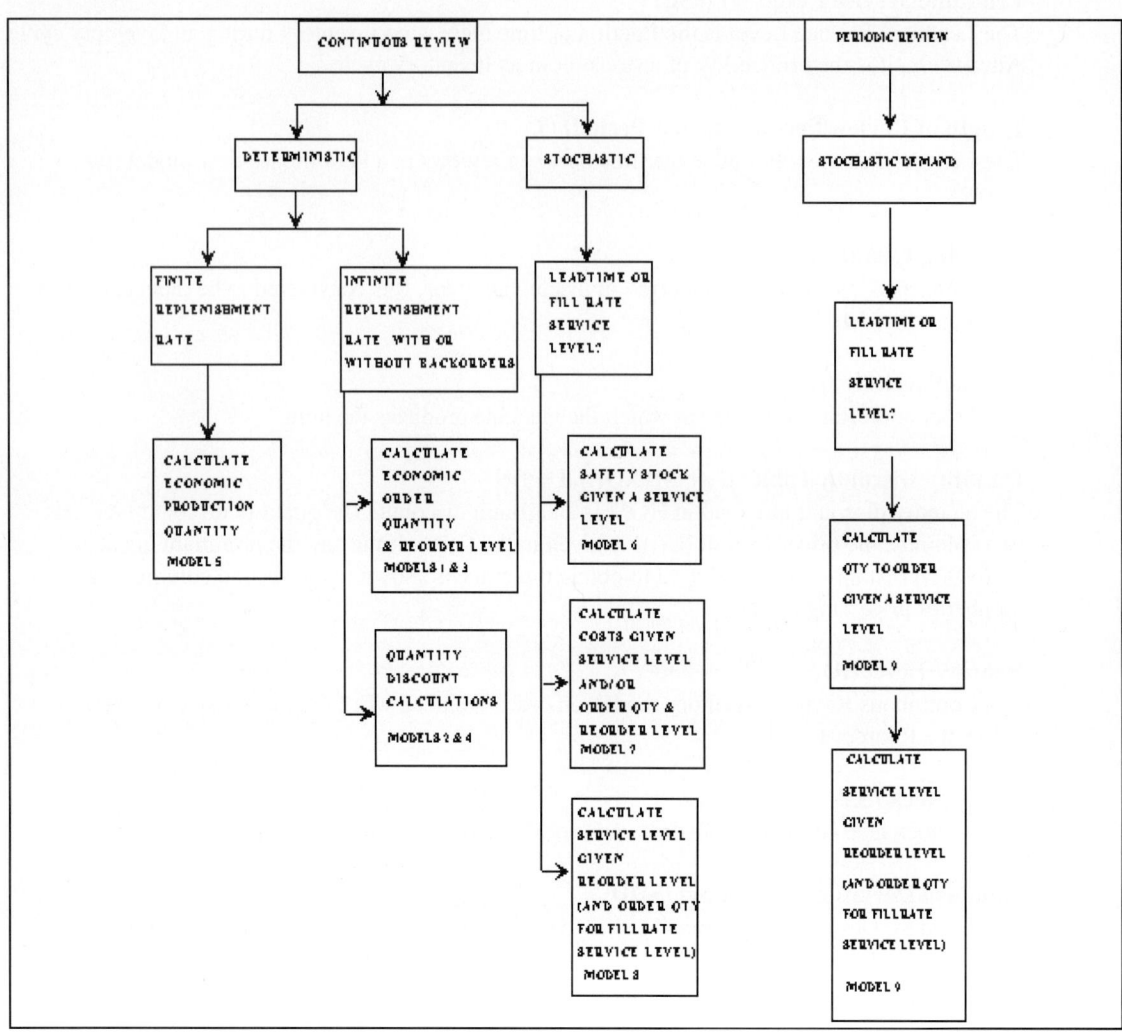

Summary of Deterministic Demand Models, Data Necessary, and Calculations Possible

Model No.	Type of Review	Repl. Rate	Backorders Allowed?	Qty. Disc.	Calculate	Data Necessary*
1	Continuous	Infinite	No	No	Order Quantity, Reorder Level, Costs	Annual Demand, Annual Holding Cost per Unit (or Cost per Unit and Annual Holding Cost rate), Ordering Cost, Average Leadtime
Sensitivity analysis automatically performed if given Alternate Order Quantities.						
2	Continuous	Infinite	No	Yes	Best Price Range, Order Quantity, Reorder Level, Costs	Annual Demand, Annual Holding Cost Rate, Ordering Cost, Average Leadtime, Quantity Discount Table
3	Continuous	Infinite	Yes	No	Order Quantity, Reorder Level, Costs	Annual Demand, Annual Holding Cost per Unit (or Cost per Unit and Annual Holding Cost Eate), Ordering Cost, Annual Cost per Backorder, Average Leadtime
Sensitivity analysis automatically performed if given Alternate Order Quantities. Note that the "optimal" reorder level is calculated corresponding to the Alternate Order Quantities (please see manual).						
4	Continuous	Infinite	Yes	Yes	Best Price Range, Order Quantity, Reorder Level, Costs	Annual Demand, Annual Holding Cost Rate, Ordering Cost, Annual Cost per Backorder, Average Leadtime, Quantity Discount Table
5	Continuous	Finite	No	No	Production Quantity, Costs	Annual Holding Cost per Unit (or Cost per Unit and Annual Holding Cost Rate), Setup Cost, Usage Rate (or Annual Demand), Production Rate
Sensitivity analysis automatically performed if given Alternate Order Quantities.						

*Note: The data items given below are necessary to perform calculations. For certain models additional data items can be entered. The entry of such data items is entirely optional. Please see below regarding how the additional data are used to perform calculations.

Summary of Stochastic Demand Models, Data Necessary, and Calculations Possible (concluded)

Model	Type of Review	Repl. Rate	Backorders Allowed?	Qty. Disc.	Calculate	Data Necessary*
6(a)	Continuous	Infinite	Implicit	No	Safety Stock given Leadtime Service Level	Usage Rate (Demand) (or Annual Demand), Average Leadtime, Std.Dev. of Demand, Std.Dev. of Leadtime, and Service Level
6(b)	Continuous	Infinite	Implicit	No	Safety Stock given Fill Rate Service Level Model first computes the Economic Order Quantity (EOQ)	Annual Demand (or Usage Rate), (Cost per Unit [and] Annual Holding Cost Rate) or Annual Holding Cost per Unit and Ordering Cost Usage Rate (Demand) (or Annual Demand), Average Leadtime, Std.Dev. of Demand, Std.Dev. of Leadtime, and Service Level
	*Alternate Safety Stock values* automatically computed if given Alternate Order Quantities.
7	Continuous	Infinite	Implicit	No	Calculate Costs Either Leadtime or Fill Rate Service Level	Annual Demand (or Usage Rate), (Cost per Unit [and] Annual Holding Cost Rate) or Annual Holding Cost per Unit and Ordering Cost Usage Rate (Demand) (or Annual Demand), Average Leadtime, Std.Dev. of Demand, Std.Dev. of Leadtime, and Service Level
	*Sensitivity Analysis* automatically performed if given Alternate Order Quantities.
8(a)	Continuous	Infinite	Implicit	No	Determine Leadtime Service Level	Usage Rate (Demand) (or Annual Demand), Average Leadtime, Std.Dev. of Demand, Std.Dev. of Leadtime, and Service Level Alternate Reorder Levels
8(b)	Continuous	Infinite	Implicit	No	Determine Fill Rate Service Level	Usage Rate (Demand) (or Annual Demand), Average Leadtime, Std.Dev. of Demand, Std.Dev. of Leadtime, and Service Level Alternate Order Quantities and Reorder Levels
9	Periodic	Infinite	Implicit	No	Determine Quantity to Order for either Leadtime or Fill Rate Service Level	Usage Rate (Demand) (or Annual Demand), Average Leadtime, Std.Dev. of Demand, Std.Dev. of Leadtime, and Service Level Length of Review Period and Inventory on Hand
	*Service Level* calculations are automatically performed if given Alternate Order Quantities.

[2] Note: The data items given below are necessary to perform calculations. For certain models additional data items can be entered. The entry of such data items is entirely optional. Please see below regarding how the additional data are used to perform calculations.

6.1 Model 1: Continuous Review, Deterministic Demand, Infinite Replenishment Rate, Backorders Not Allowed, No Quantity Discounts

Data Required
1. Annual Demand, D
2. Either   Cost per Unit, C [and]
                  Annual Holding Cost Rate, i
   Or   Annual Holding Cost per Unit, C_H
          <u>Note:</u> If all three values are given, then HOM checks if $C_H = C*i$. If this equality does not hold, then it prompts the user to change the data.
3. Ordering Cost, C_O
4. Average Leadtime, LT.
          <u>Note:</u> If the value of LT is not entered (left blank), then LT is set equal to zero.
5. Conversion Factor (in the Parameters dialog box).

Decision Variables
     Quantity to Order, Q, and Reorder Level, R

Formulae Used
     If C_H is not given, then $C_H = C*i$
     Total Inventory Cost per Year, $TIC(Q) = C_O*D/Q + C_H*Q/2$
     Total Cost per Year, $TC(Q) = D*C + TIC(Q)$
     Number of Orders per Year = D/Q
     Maximum Inventory = Q
     Average Inventory = Q/2
     Length of Inventory Cycle = Q/D years
     Reorder Level, R = LT*D/Conversion Factor

     (Optimal) Economic Order Quantity = $\sqrt{\dfrac{2DC_O}{C_H}}$

Sensitivity Analysis
Two types of sensitivity analysis are possible. (i) HOM by default creates a plot of various costs and relevant quantities using values of Q, ranging from 0.5*EOQ to 1.5*EOQ. (ii) In addition, the user can specify (up to 3) Alternate Order Quantities. The output (see below) contains the values corresponding to the EOQ as well as the Alternate Order Quantities.

Sample Problem
EOQ.DAT

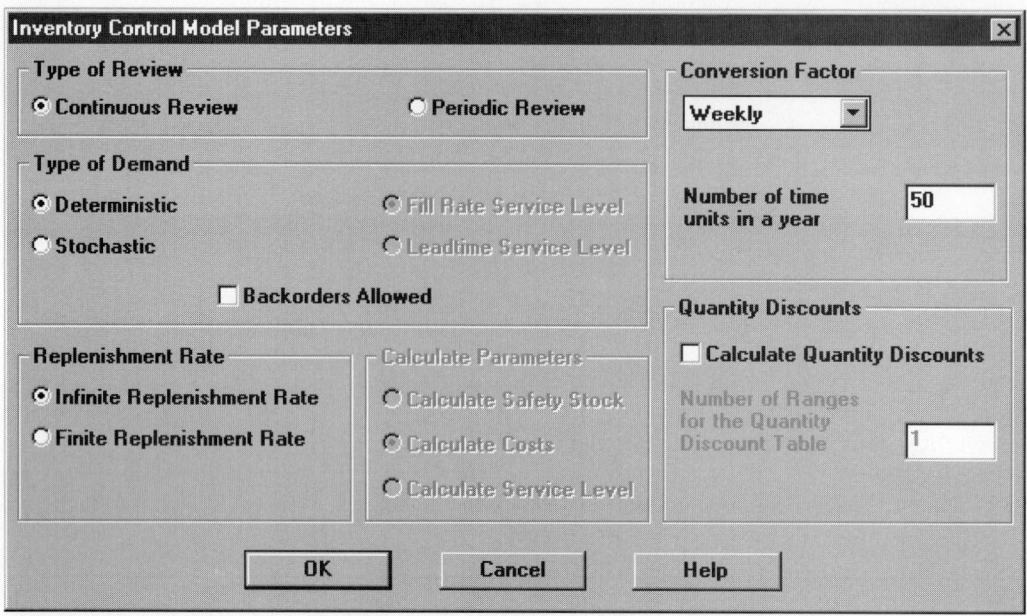

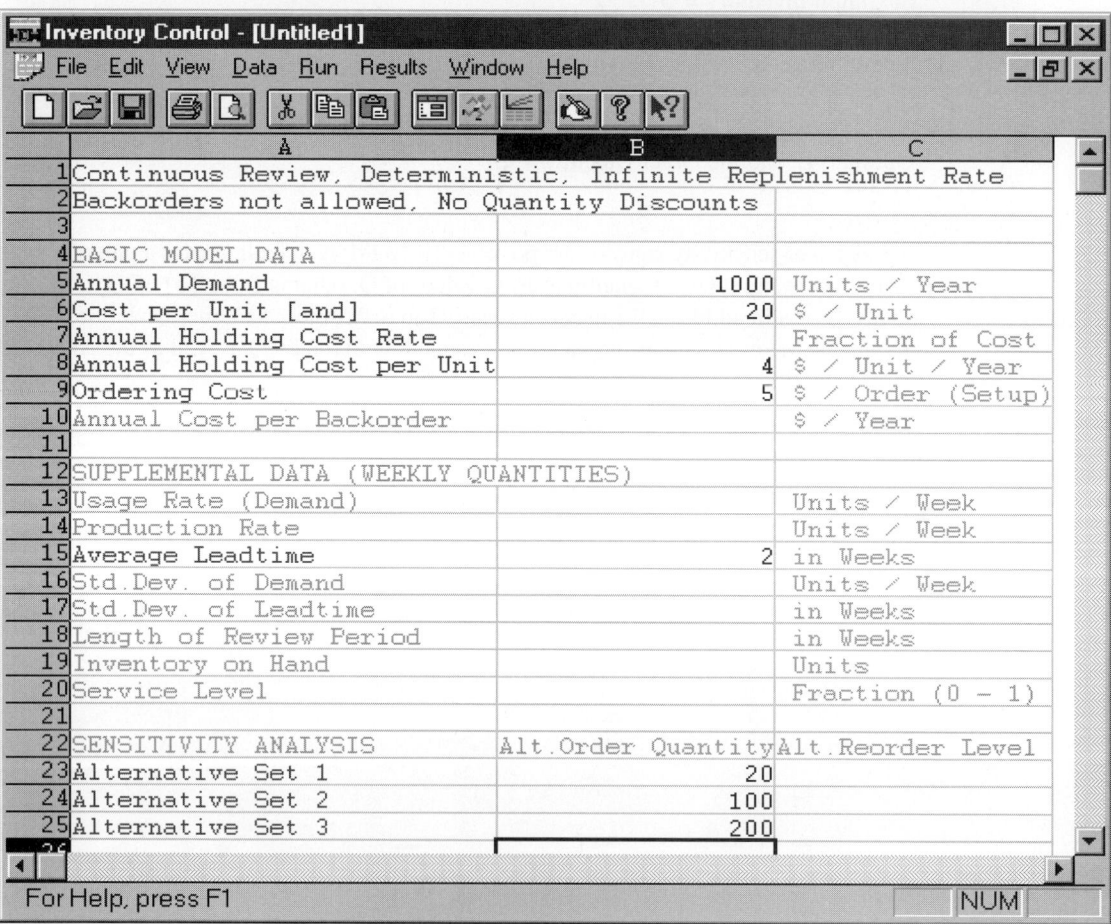

Sample Problem (continued)

EOQ.DAT

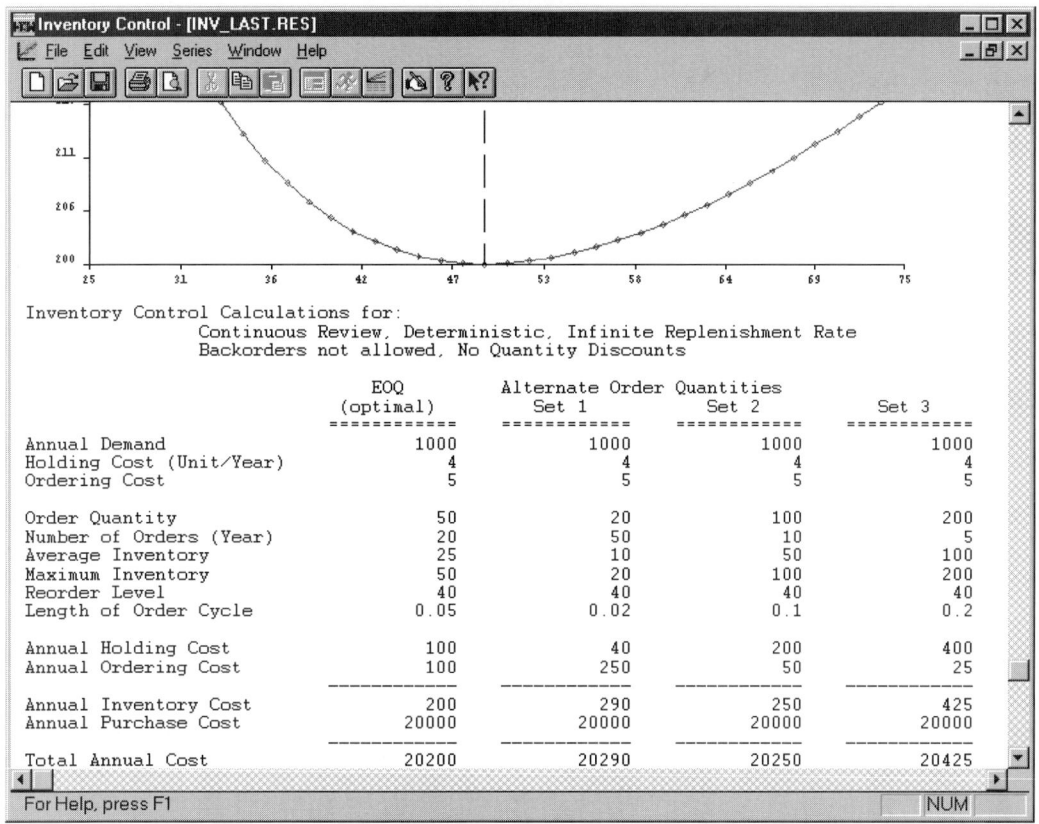

6.2 Model 2: Continuous Review, Deterministic Demand, Infinite Replenishment Rate, Backorders Not Allowed, Calculate Quantity Discounts

Data Required
1. Annual Demand, D
2. Annual Holding Cost Rate, i
3. Ordering Cost, C_o
4. Average Leadtime, LT.
   Note: If the value of LT is not entered (left blank), then LT is set equal to zero.
5. Conversion Factor (in the Parameters dialog box).

6. Quantity Discount Table, giving cost per unit C(j) and minimum quantity, MINQ(j) that has to be ordered to obtain the price, C(j), j = 1,..,N.
7. The number of price ranges, N (up to 10),has to be entered in the Parameters dalog box.

Decision Variables
   Best Price Range, Quantity to Order, Q, and Reorder Level, R

Formulae Used
   For each j = 1,N

   Calculate the Economic Order Quantity, $Q(j) = \sqrt{\dfrac{2DC_o}{C(j)*i}}$

   If Q(j) > MINQ(j+1) and j < N,then no results for this j.
   Elseif Q(j) < MINQ(j) then,Q(j) = MINQ(j).
   Compute TC(Q(j)) using Model 1 formula.

Sensitivity Analysis
   None.

Sample Problem   EOQQD.DAT

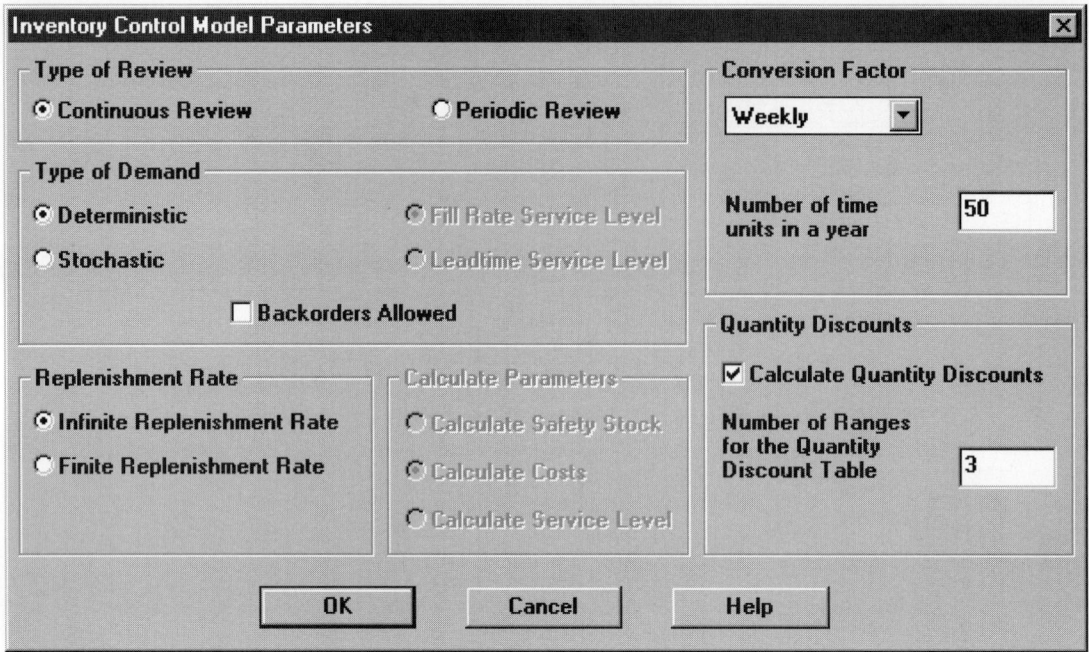

Sample Problem (continued)

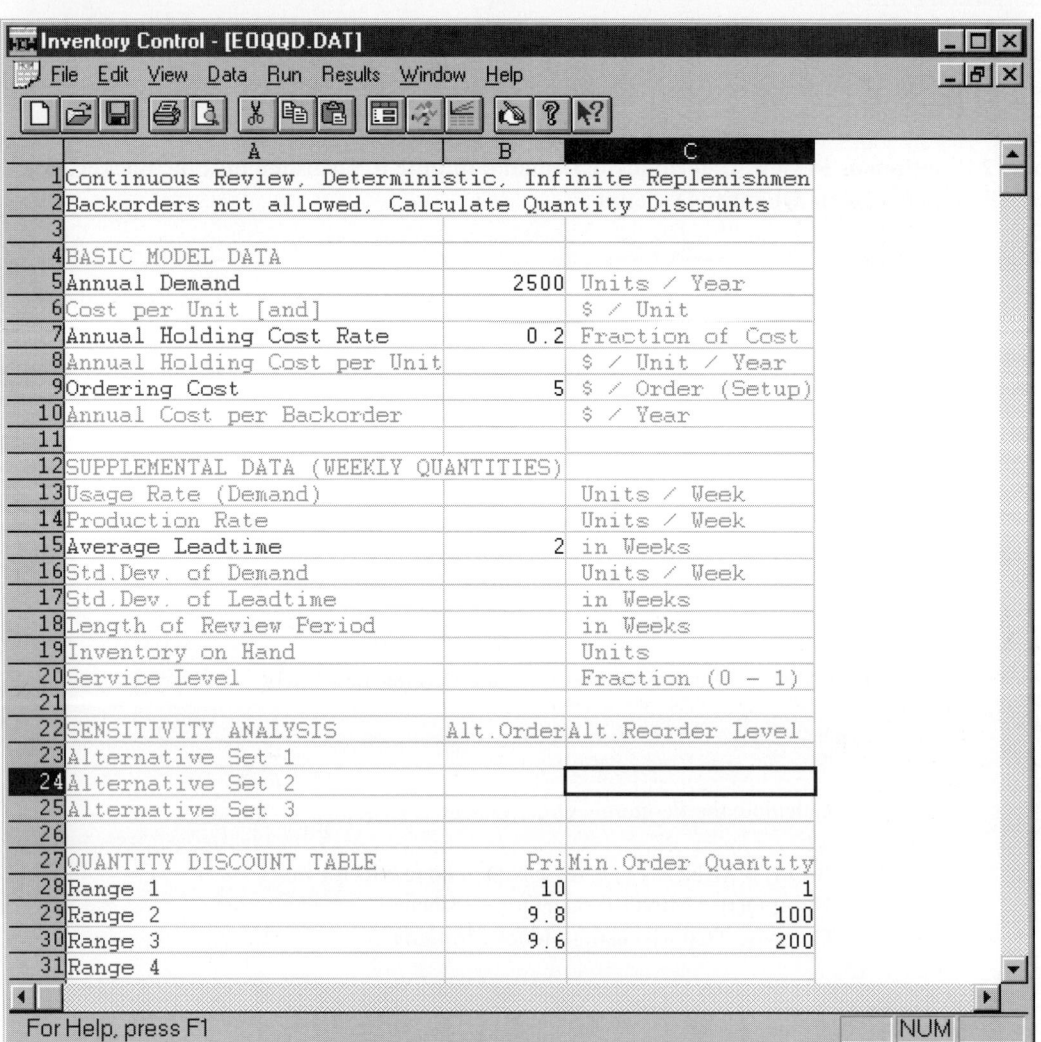

Sample Problem (continued)

EOQQD.DAT

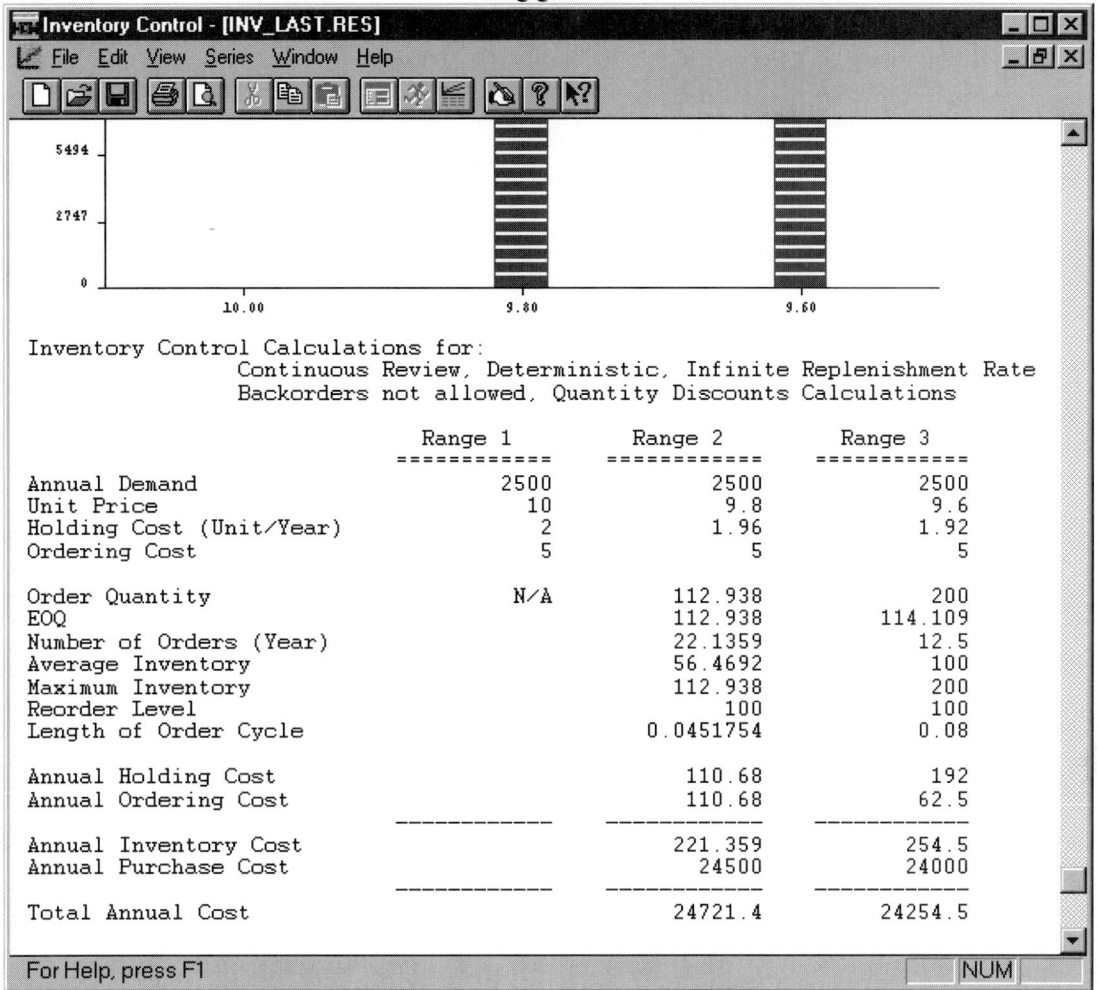

Inventory Control Calculations for:
    Continuous Review, Deterministic, Infinite Replenishment Rate
    Backorders not allowed, Quantity Discounts Calculations

	Range 1	Range 2	Range 3
Annual Demand	2500	2500	2500
Unit Price	10	9.8	9.6
Holding Cost (Unit/Year)	2	1.96	1.92
Ordering Cost	5	5	5
Order Quantity	N/A	112.938	200
EOQ		112.938	114.109
Number of Orders (Year)		22.1359	12.5
Average Inventory		56.4692	100
Maximum Inventory		112.938	200
Reorder Level		100	100
Length of Order Cycle		0.0451754	0.08
Annual Holding Cost		110.68	192
Annual Ordering Cost		110.68	62.5
		---------	--------
Annual Inventory Cost		221.359	254.5
Annual Purchase Cost		24500	24000
		---------	--------
Total Annual Cost		24721.4	24254.5

6.3 Model 3: Continuous Review, Deterministic Demand, Infinite Replenishment Rate, Backorders Allowed, No Quantity Discounts

Data Required
1. Data as per Model 1.
2. Annual Cost per Backorder, C_B

Decision Variables
Quantity to Order, Q; Maximum Level of Backorder in a Cycle, B; and Reorder Level, R

Formulae Used
If C_H is not given, then $C_H = C*i$
Total Inventory Cost per Year, $TIC(Q) = C_o*D/Q + C_H*(Q-B)^2/(2Q) + C_B*B^2/(2Q)$
Total Cost per Year, $TC(Q) = D*C + TIC(Q)$
Number of Orders per Year = D/Q
Maximum Inventory = $Q - B$
Average Inventory = $(Q - B)^2/(2Q)$
Maximum Backorders = B
Average Number of Backorders = $B^2/(2Q)$
Optimal value of B(Q) given a value of Q = $\text{argmin}_B \{ C_H*(Q-B)^2/(2Q) + C_B*B^2/(2Q)\}$
$\quad\quad \Rightarrow \quad B(Q) = Q* C_H/(C_H + C_B)$ $\quad\quad$ (differentiate w.r.t. B)
Length of Inventory Cycle = Q/D years
Reorder Level, $R = (LT*D)/(\text{Conversion Factor}) - B$.

(Optimal) Economic Order Quantity = $\sqrt{\dfrac{2DC_O}{C_H}\left(\dfrac{C_B}{C_B + C_H}\right)}$

Sensitivity Analysis

Two types of sensitivity analysis are possible. (i) HOM by default creates a plot of various costs and relevant quantities using values of Q, ranging from 0.5*EOQ to 1.5*EOQ. (ii) In addition, the user can specify (up to 3) Alternate Order Quantities. The output (see below) contains the values corresponding to the EOQ as well as the Alternate Order Quantities. Note that the value of B is computed using the alternate values of Q (see formulae above).

Sample Problem   EOQBO.DAT

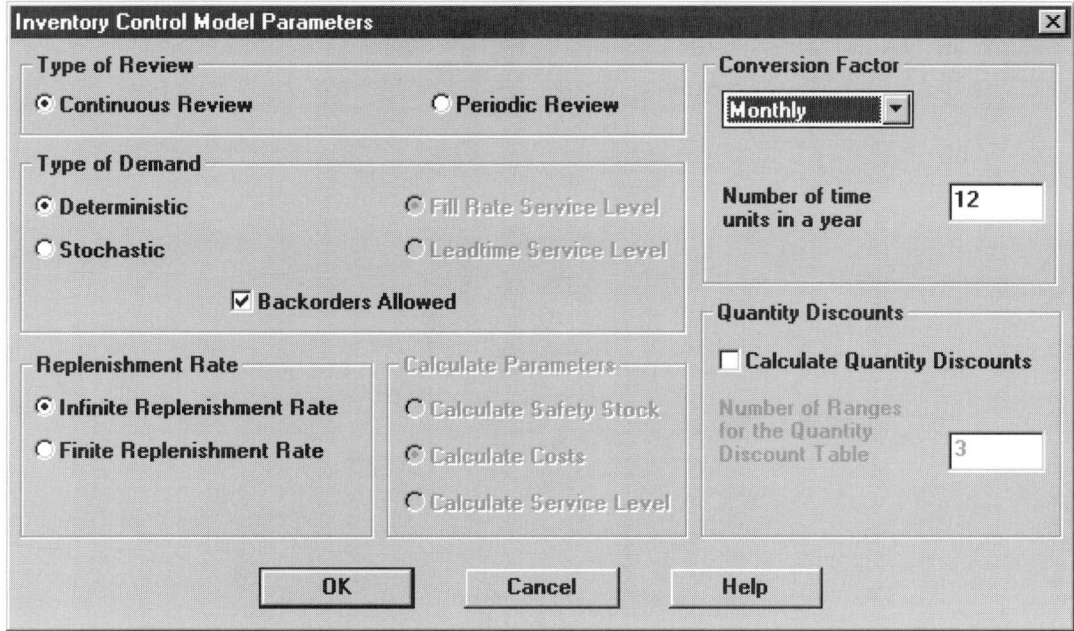

Sample Problem (continued)

EOQBO.DAT

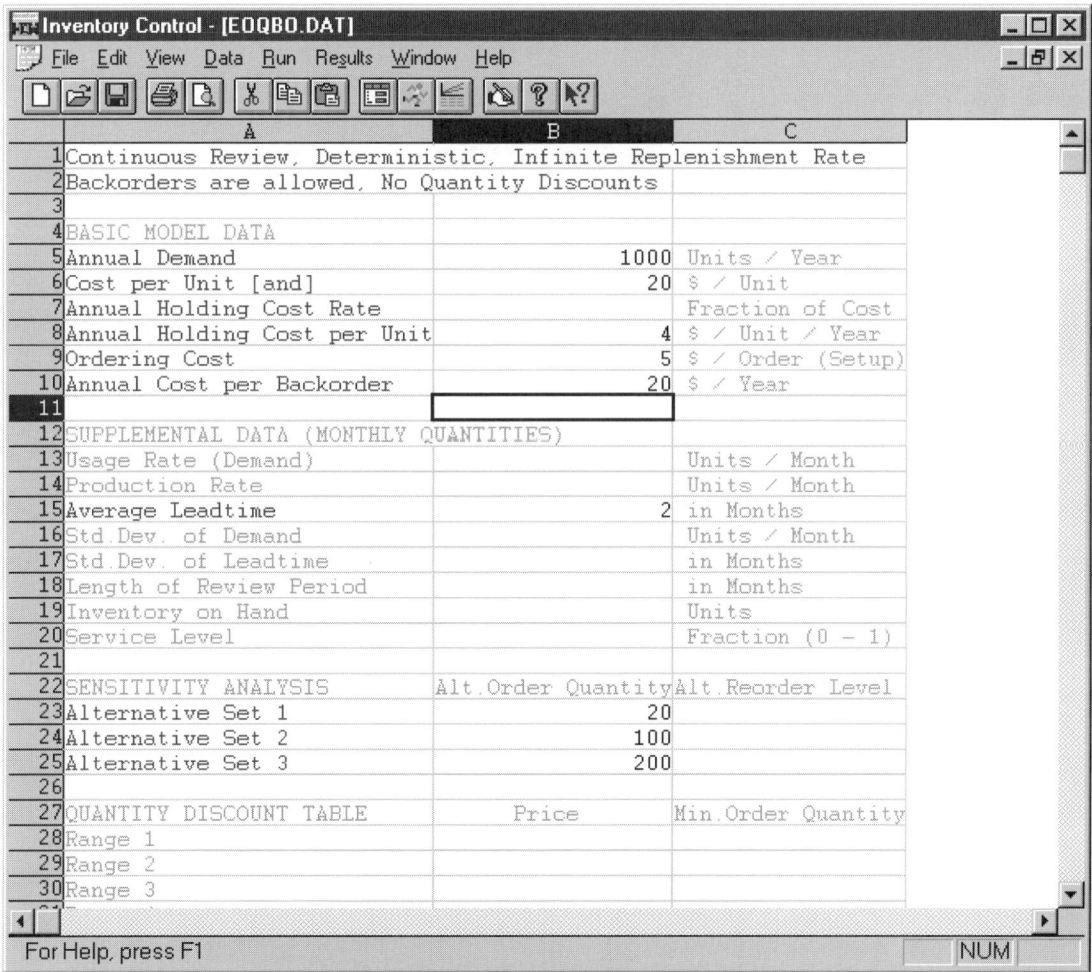

215

Sample Problem (continued)

<u>EOQBO.DAT</u>

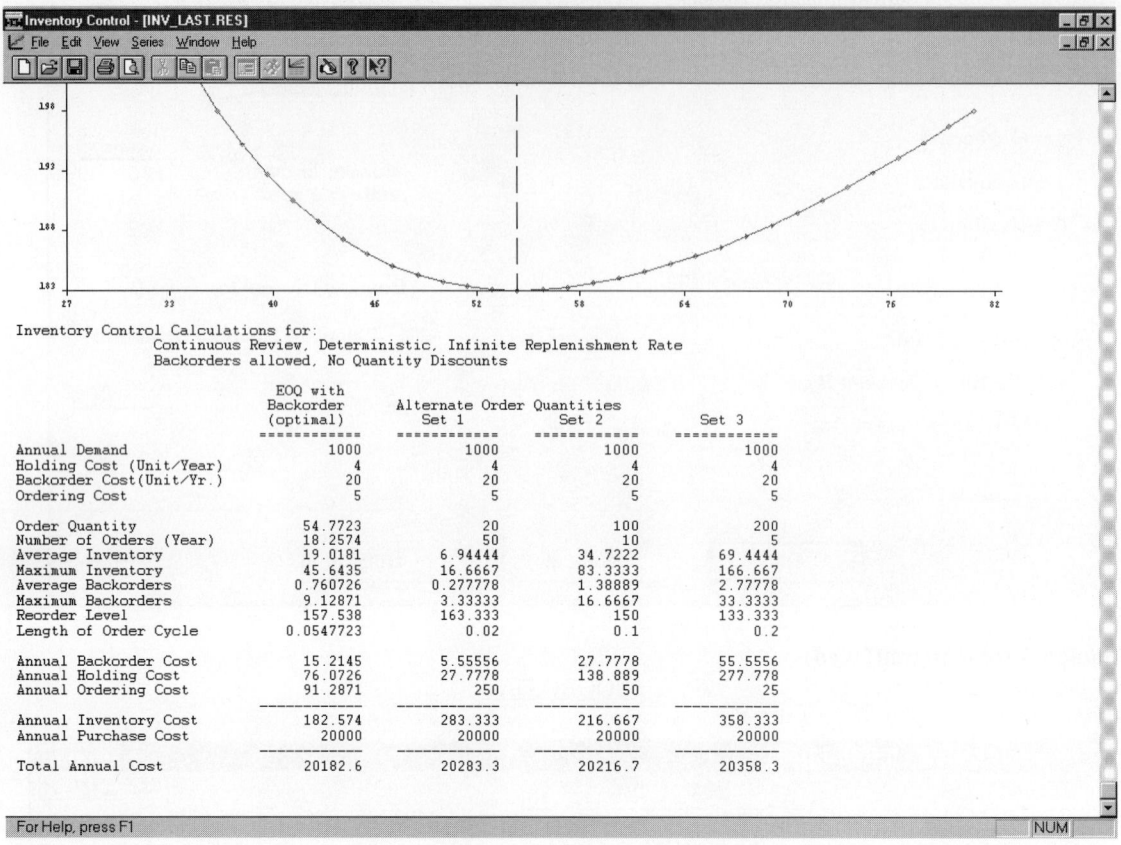

6.4 Model 4: Continuous Review, Deterministic Demand, Infinite Replenishment Rate, Backorders Allowed, Calculate Quantity Discounts

This model has been included mainly to illustrate the fact that if back orders are allowed, then the economic order quantities will be larger. The larger order quantities would make quantity discounts more attractive.

Data Required
1. Data as per Model 2.
2. Annual Cost per Backorder, C_B

Decision Variables
Best Price Range, j, Quantity to Order, Q, and Reorder Level, R

Formulae Used
Similar to Model 2.

Sensitivity Analysis
None.

Sample Problem   EOQBOQD.DAT

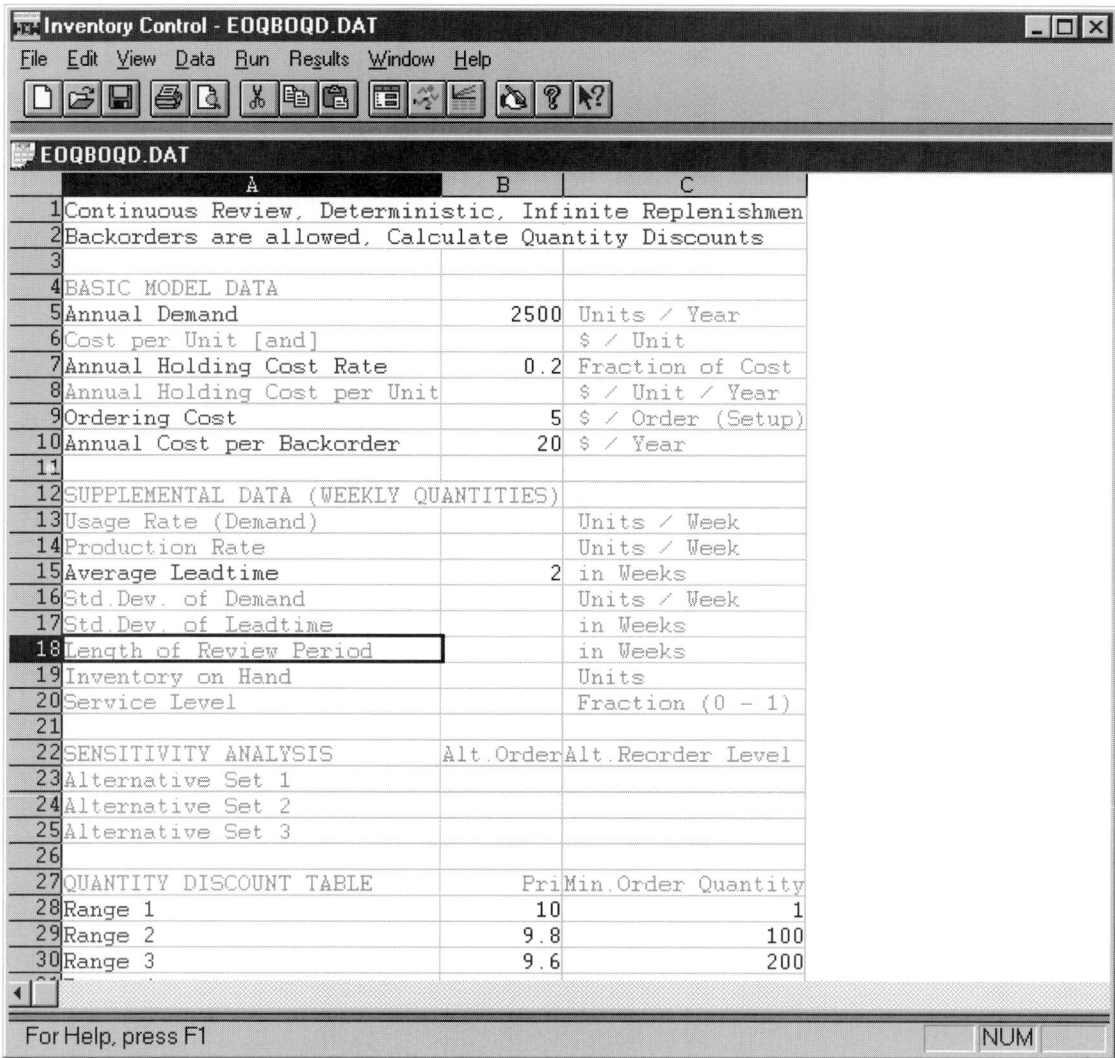

Note: Backorders Allowed box has to be checked in the Parameters dialog box.

Sample Problem (continued)

EOQBOQD.DAT

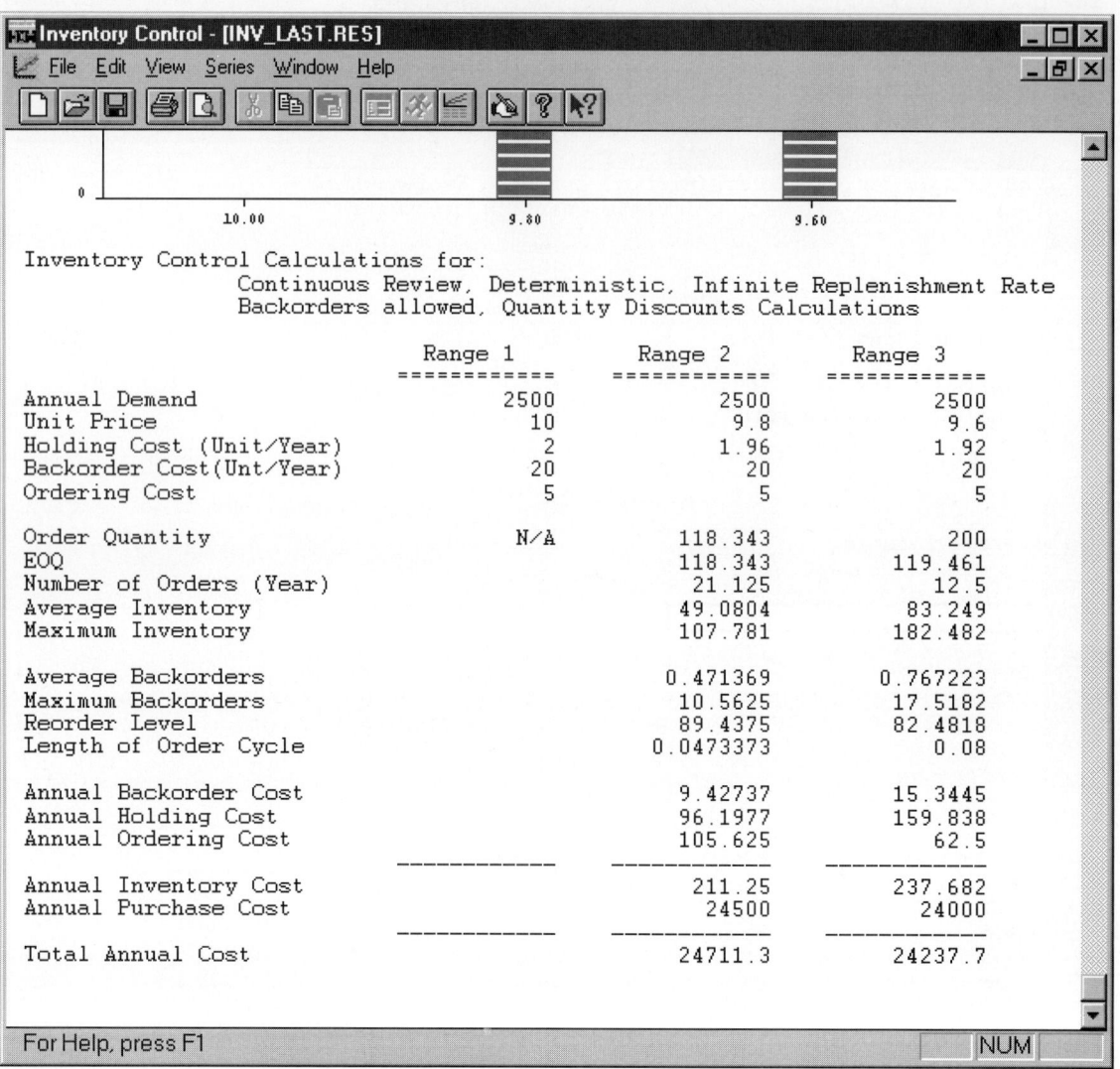

6.5 Model 5: Continuous Review, Deterministic, Finite Replenishment Rate, Backorders Not Allowed, No Quantity Discounts

Data Required
1. Either   Annual Demand, D
   Or   Usage Rate, u.
   <u>Note:</u> If both are given, then HOM checks whether D = Conversion Factor * u. If the equality does not hold, then HOM prompts the user to change these values.
2. Either   Cost per Unit, C [and]
   Annual Holding Cost Rate, i
   Annual Holding Cost per Unit, C_H
   <u>Note:</u> If all three values are given then HOM checks if $C_H = C*i$. If this equality does not hold, then it prompts the user to change the data.
3. Setup Cost, C_o
4. Leadtime is treated as equal to zero.
5. Conversion Factor (in the Parameters dialog box).
6. Production Rate, p.
   <u>Note:</u> The units of p and u are the same. The time unit is given by the Conversion Factor. HOM checks whether p is greater than u. If not, it prompts the user to change these values.

Decision Variables
     Quantity to Produce, Q.

Formulae Used
     If p is not given, set p = D/Conversion Factor
     If C_H is not given, set $C_H = C*i$
     Total Cost per Year = $C_o*D/Q + C_H*(Q*(p - u)/p)/2$
     Number of Setups per Year = D/Q
     Maximum Inventory = $Q*(p - u)/p$
     Average Inventory = $(Q*(p - u)/p)/2$
     Length of Order Cycle = (Q/D)*Conversion Factor

Sensitivity Analysis
     Similar to Models 1 and 3.

Sample Problem

FINITE.DAT

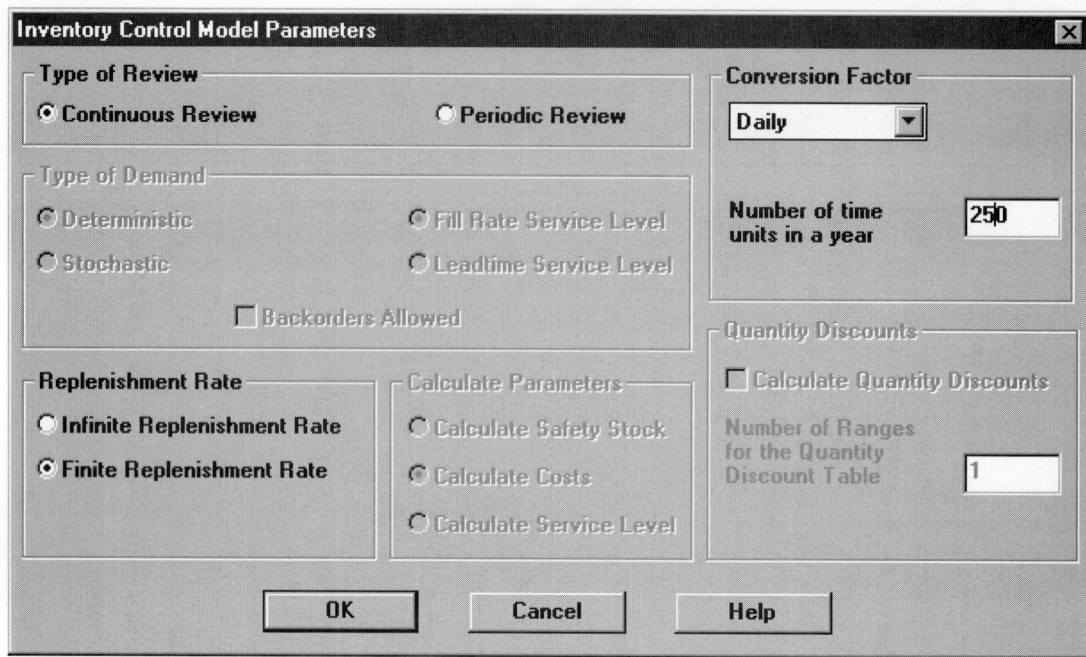

Sample Problem (continued)

FINITE.DAT

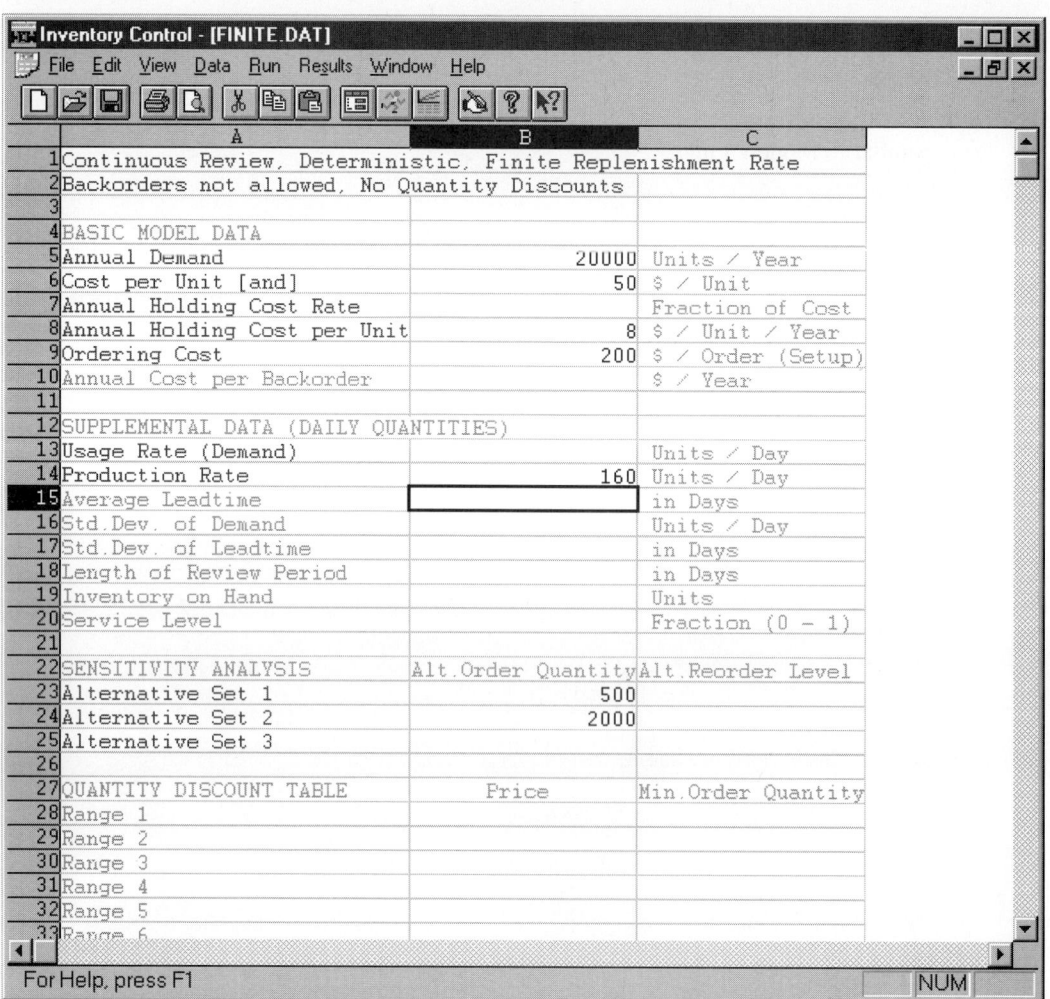

Sample Problem (continued)

FINITE.DAT

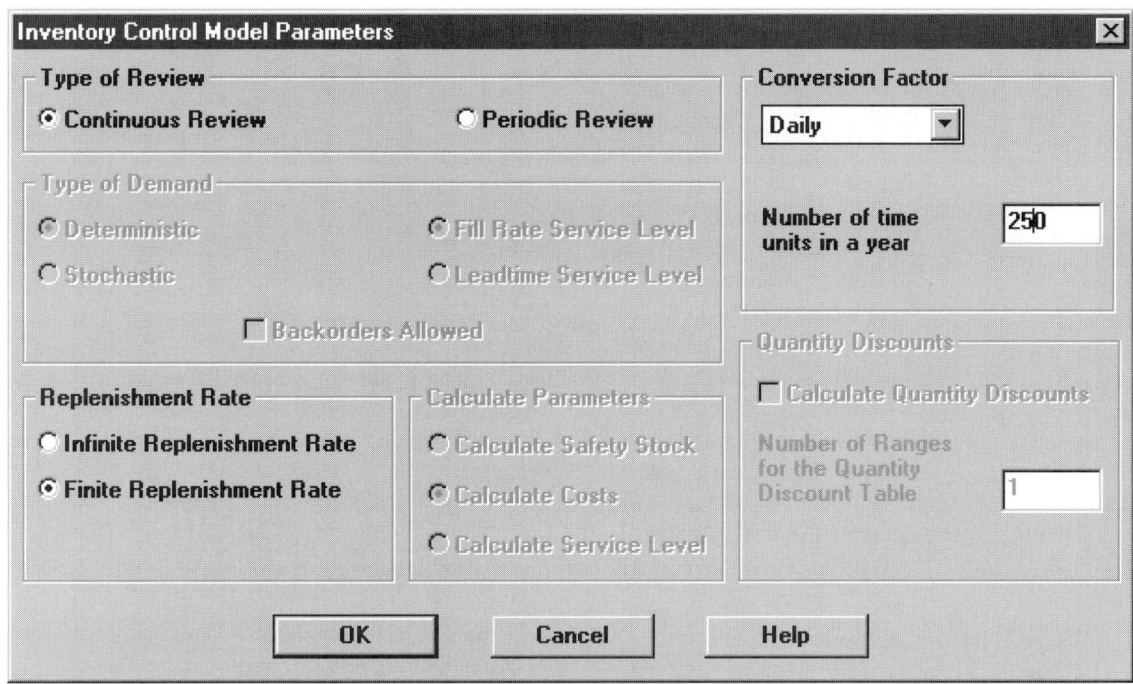

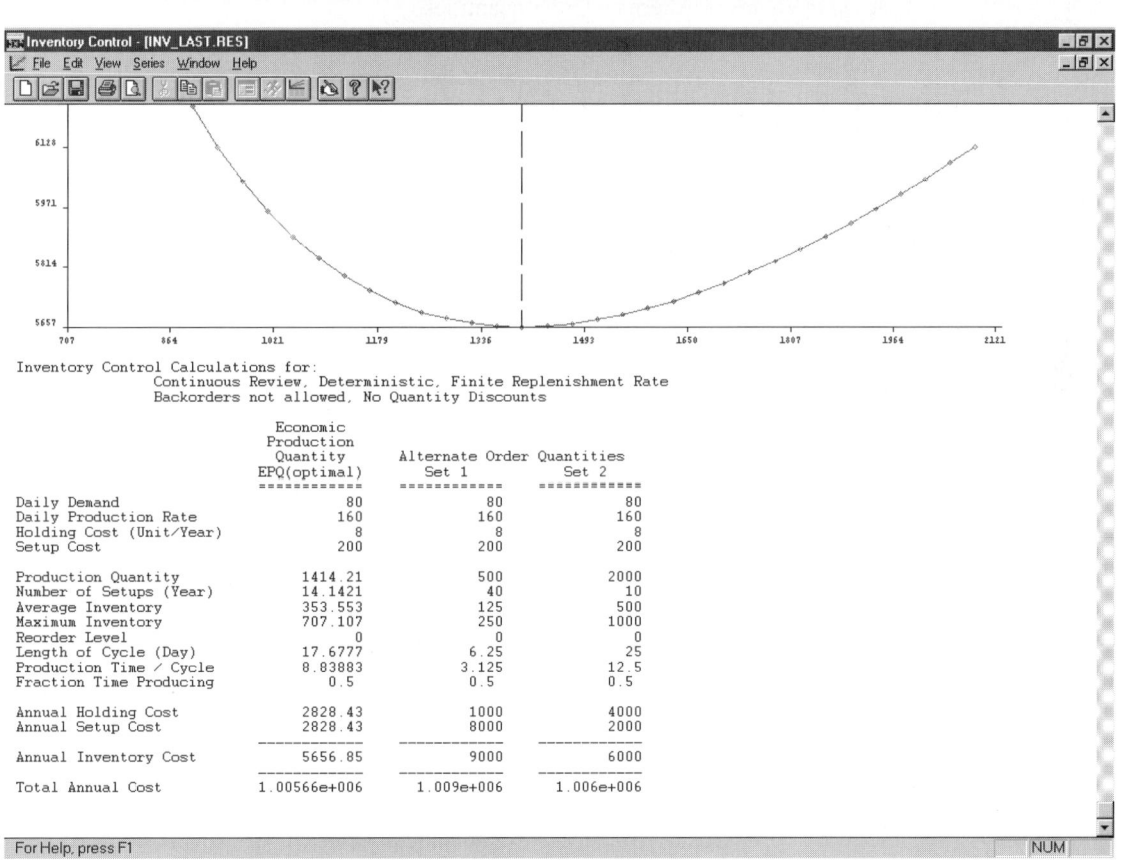

```
Inventory Control Calculations for:
    Continuous Review, Deterministic, Finite Replenishment Rate
    Backorders not allowed, No Quantity Discounts

                        Economic
                        Production
                        Quantity      Alternate Order Quantities
                        EPQ(optimal)  Set 1         Set 2
                        ============  ============  ============
Daily Demand                    80            80            80
Daily Production Rate          160           160           160
Holding Cost (Unit/Year)         8             8             8
Setup Cost                     200           200           200

Production Quantity        1414.21           500          2000
Number of Setups (Year)    14.1421            40            10
Average Inventory          353.553           125           500
Maximum Inventory          707.107           250          1000
Reorder Level                    0             0             0
Length of Cycle (Day)      17.6777          6.25            25
Production Time / Cycle    8.83883         3.125          12.5
Fraction Time Producing        0.5           0.5           0.5

Annual Holding Cost        2828.43          1000          4000
Annual Setup Cost          2828.43          8000          2000
                          --------      --------      --------
Annual Inventory Cost      5656.85          9000          6000
                          --------      --------      --------
Total Annual Cost      1.00566e+006   1.009e+006    1.006e+006
```

6.6 Model 6: Continuous Review, Stochastic, Infinite Replenishment Rate, Backorders Not Allowed, No Qty. Discounts, Calculate Safety Stock

Data Required

Model 6(a): Leadtime Service Level
1. Either   Annual Demand, D
   Or   Usage Rate, u
   Note: If both D and u are given, then HOM checks whether D=u*Conversion Factor. If not, it prompts the user to change the values.
2. Average Leadtime, LT   (zero if left blank).
3. Std.Dev. of Demand, SDD (zero if left blank).
4. Std.Dev. of Leadtime, SDLT (zero if left blank).
5. Service Level, LTSL
6. Conversion Factor (in Parameters dialog box).

Note: The time units for u, LT, SDLT, and SDD are given by the Conversion Factor. For example, if u is given in units per week, then the standard deviation of demand should be the standard deviation of the weekly demand, the average and standard deviation of the leadtime must be in weeks.

Model 6(b): Fill Rate Service Level
1. Data as per Model 6(a). (Except that the service level is the Fill Rate Service Level, SL.)
2. Either the data for Model 1 to enable HOM to compute the EOQ and thereby determine the fill rate service level corresponding to the EOQ
   And/Or Values of Alternate Order quantities.

Decision Variables

Safety Stock, SS, and Reorder Level, R.

Formulae Used

Let $\Phi(LTSL)$ be the CDF of the Normal Distribution.
Let $E(z)$ be the expected number of customers who are backlogged
in a cycle when the standard deviation of the demand during the leadtime equals one (1).

If u is not given, set u = D/Conversion Factor
Set Standard Deviation of Demand during Leadtime
$$SDD\&LT = (LT*SDD^2 + u^2*SDLT^2)^{0.5}$$
If Leadtime Service Level, then
  set $z = \Phi(LTSL)$
  If EOQ can be determined, then compute the Fill Rate Service Level (see Model 8).
  Else compute the Fill Rate Service Level for each positive Alternate Order Quantity.
Else If Fill Rate Service Level, then
  Attempt to compute the EOQ (if Data are adequate—see Model 1)
  If successful then search for a z such that $E(z) * SDD\&LT/EOQ \leq 1 - SL$.
  Repeat the calculations with EOQ substituted with each Alternate Order Quantity.
  Compute for each z the corresponding value of Leadtime Service Level (Model 8).
SS = z*SDD&LT
R = SS + u*LT

Sensitivity Analysis

As described above, sensitivity analysis is automatically carried out using Alterrnate Order Quantities.

Sample Problem

SAFETY.DAT

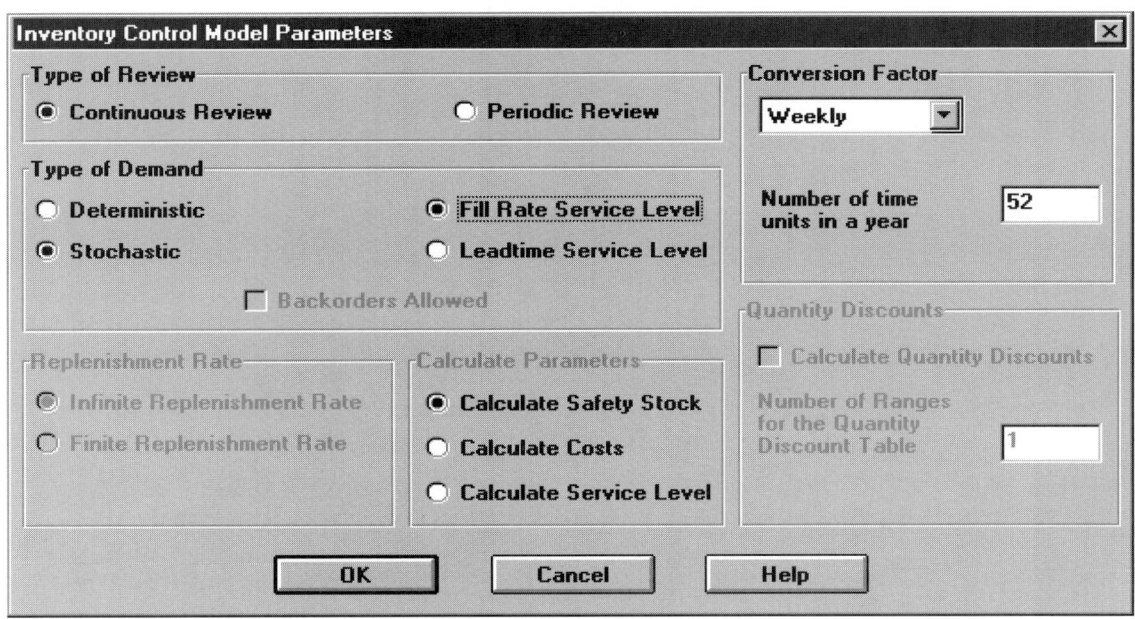

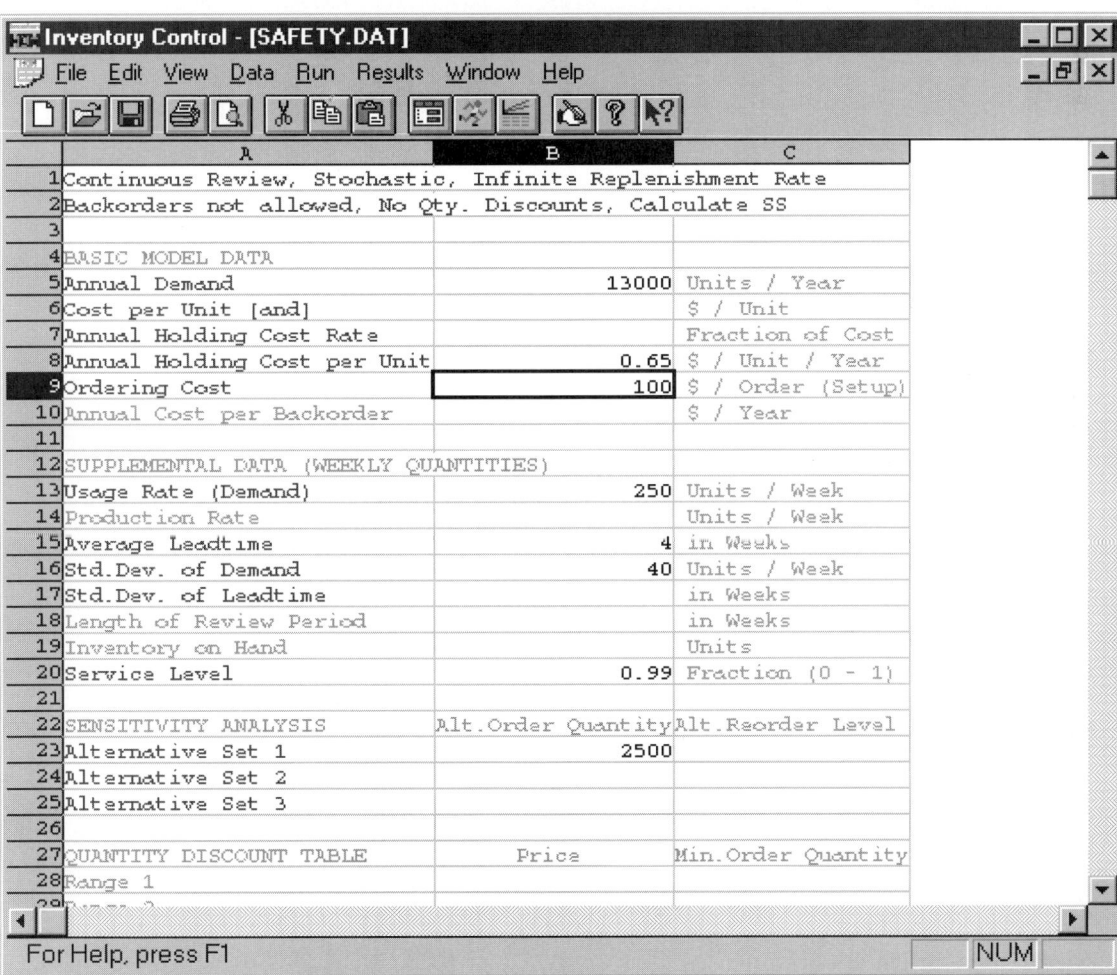

Inventory Control Calculations for:
 Continuous Review, Stochastic, Infinite Replenishment Rate
 Backorders Not Allowed, No Quantity Discounts
 Safety Stock Calculations Only

	Safety Stock EOQ(optimal)	Alternate Order Quantities Set 1
I. Demand, Ordering, and Cost		
Annual Demand	13000	13000
Holding Cost (Unit/Year)	0.65	0.65
Ordering Cost	100	100
Order Quantity	2000	2500
Number of Orders (Year)	6.5	5.2
Average Inventory	N/A	N/A
Maximum Inventory	N/A	N/A
Reorder Level	1027.2	1014.8
Length of Order Cycle	N/A	N/A
Annual Holding Cost	N/A	N/A
Annual Safety Stock Cost	N/A	N/A
Annual Ordering Cost	N/A	N/A
Annual Inventory Cost	N/A	N/A
Annual Purchase Cost	N/A	N/A
Total Annual Cost	N/A	N/A

Note: The outputs shown on this and the following pages in Helvetica Font (9 point) was copied to the clipboard using the EDIT --> COPY command and pasted into the Word document.

II. Safety Stock and Reorder Levels

Service Level Desired	0.99	0.99
Type of Service Level	Fill Rate	Fill Rate
Service Level Achieved		
Leadtime SL	0.633072	0.573385
Fill Rate SL	0.99	0.99
Avg. Leadtime (Weeks)	4	4
Std.Dev. of Leadtime (Week)	0	0
Avg. Demand (Units/Week)	250	250
Std.Dev. of Demand (Units/Week)	40	40
Std.Dev. of Demand during		
Leadtime (Units/Week)	80	80
Safety Stock	27.2	14.8
Reorder Level	1027.2	1014.8
Number of Std.Dev. of SS (z)	0.34	0.185
E(z)	0.25	0.3125
Expected Units Short/Cycle	20	25
Expected Units Short/Year	130	130

Note: Fill Rate Service Level and Expected Units Short per Year are reported as Not Available (N/A) if the EOQ cannot be computed. That is the case when the Holding or Ordering Cost is not given.

Same data file but solved for 99% Leadtime Service Level

Inventory Control Calculations for:
    Continuous Review, Stochastic, Infinite Replenishment Rate
    Backorders Not Allowed, No Quantity Discounts
    Safety Stock Calculations Only

	Safety Stock EOQ(optimal)	Alternate Order Quantities Set 1
I. Demand, Ordering, and Cost		
Annual Demand	13000	13000
Holding Cost (Unit/Year)	0	0
Ordering Cost	0	0
Order Quantity	0	2500
Number of Orders (Year)	0	0
Average Inventory	N/A	N/A
Maximum Inventory	N/A	N/A
Reorder Level	1186.4	1186.4
Length of Order Cycle	N/A	N/A
Annual Holding Cost	N/A	N/A
Annual Safety Stock Cost	N/A	N/A
Annual Ordering Cost	N/A	N/A
Annual Inventory Cost	N/A	N/A
Annual Purchase Cost	N/A	N/A
Total Annual Cost	N/A	N/A
II. Safety Stock and Reorder Levels		
Service Level Desired	0.99	0.99
Type of Service Level	Leadtime	Leadtime
Service Level Achieved		
Leadtime SL	0.99	0.99
Fill Rate SL	N/A	0.999893
Avg. Leadtime (Weeks)	4	4
Std.Dev. of Leadtime (Week)	0	0
Avg. Demand (Units/Week)	250	250
Std.Dev. of Demand (Units/Week) 40	40	
Std.Dev. of Demand during Leadtime (Units/Week)	80	80
Safety Stock	186.4	186.4
Reorder Level	1186.4	1186.4
Number of Std.Dev. of SS (z)	2.33	2.33
E(z)	0.00335237	0.00335237
Expected Units Short/Cycle	0.26819	0.26819
Expected Units Short/Year	N/A	1.39459

Note: Fill Rate Service Level and Expected Units Short per Year are reported as Not Available (N/A) if the EOQ cannot be computed. That is the case when the Holding or Ordering Cost is not given.

6.7 Model 7: Continuous Review, Stochastic, Infinite Replenishment Rate, Backorders Not Allowed, No Qty. Discounts, Calculate Costs

Data Required
    1. Data required for Model 6.
    2. Data required for Model 1.

Formulae Used
    Combines the formulae used in Models 1 and 6.
    Estimates the cost of holding Safety Stock as being equal to C_H*SS
    Note: This estimate could lead to a *negative* cost of holding safety stock if the value of SS is negative. SS can be negative if the value of $z < 0$ (see Model 6 formulae).

    Search for Optimality: As an indicator of the fact that the EOQ need not be optimal when the demand is stochastic, HOM reports the "optimal" value of the order quantity. This quantity is determined by searching in 20 equal steps between the values of 0.5*EOQ and 1.5*EOQ. The objective of the search is to determine the value of Q that gives the smallest cost while achieving the desired service level. See below for an example.

Sensitivity Analysis
    Two types of sensitivity analysis are possible. (i) HOM by default creates a plot of various costs and relevant quantities using values of Q, ranging from 0.5*EOQ to 1.5*EOQ. (ii) In addition, the user can specify (up to 3) Alternate Order Quantities. The output (see below) contains the values corresponding to the EOQ as well as the Alternate Order Quantities.

Sample Problem

SAFETY.DAT

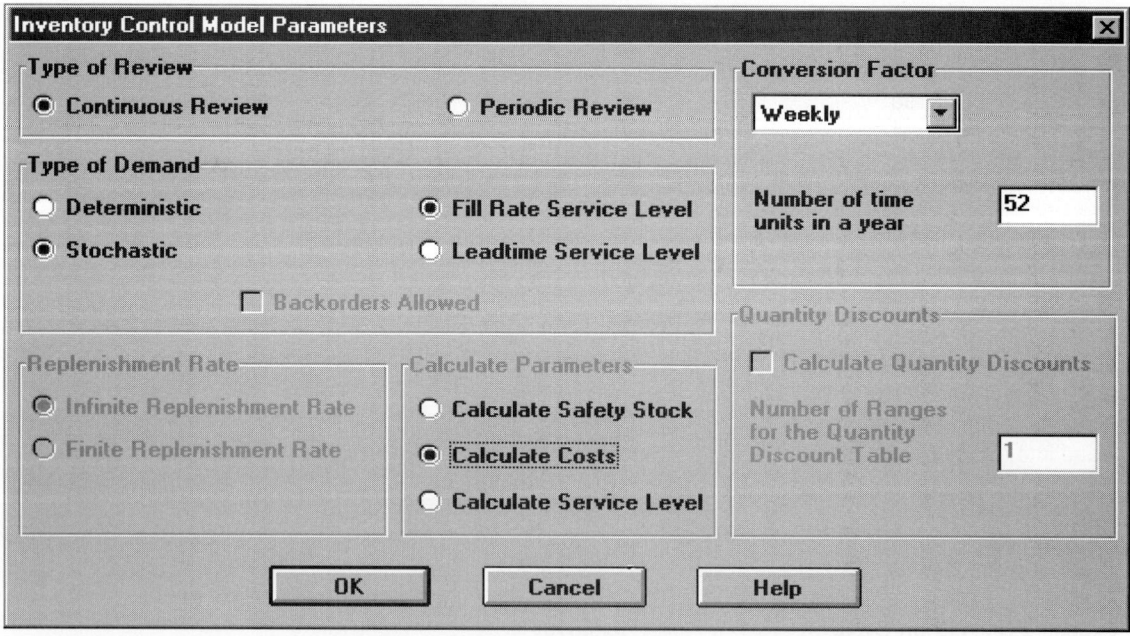

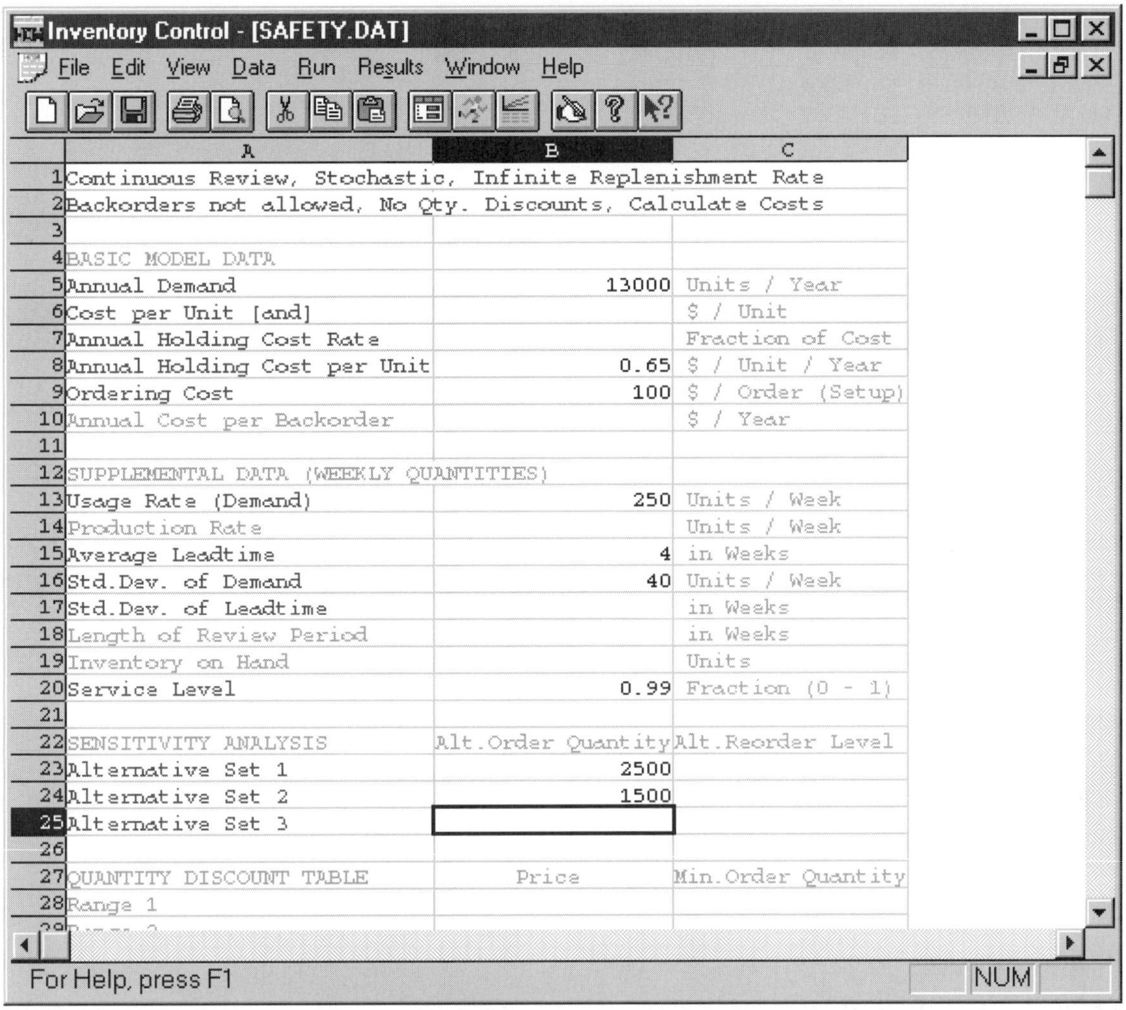

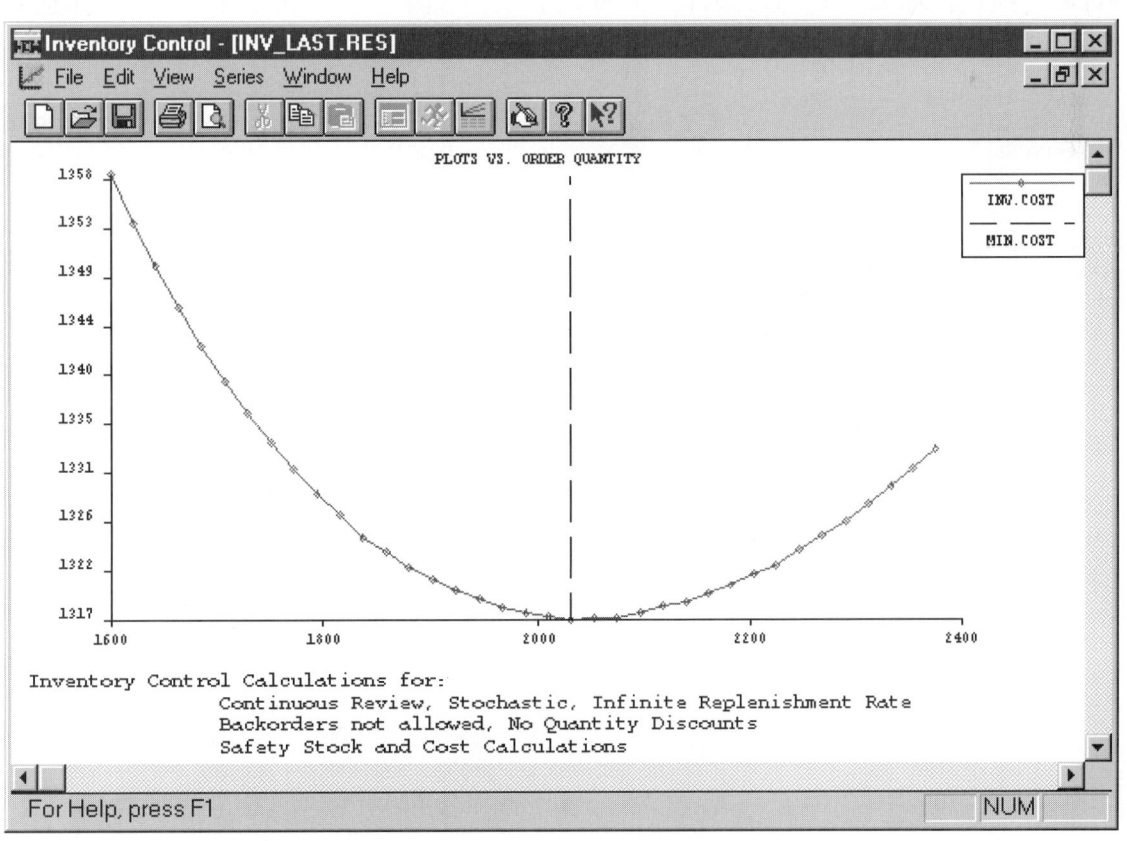

Inventory Control Calculations for:
 Continuous Review, Stochastic, Infinite Replenishment Rate
 Backorders Not Allowed, No Quantity Discounts
 Safety Stock and Cost Calculations

		Alternate Order Quantities		
	EOQ	Set 1	Set 2	Best Q
I. Demand, Ordering, and Cost				
Annual Demand	13000	13000	13000	13000
Holding Cost (Unit/Year)	0.65	0.65	0.65	0.65
Ordering Cost	100	100	100	100
Order Quantity	2000	2500	1500	2044.44
Number of Orders (Year)	6.5	5.2	8.66667	6.3587
Average Inventory	1027.2	1264.8	792.4	1048.22
Maximum Inventory	2027.2	2514.8	1542.4	2070.44
Reorder Level	1027.2	1014.8	1042.4	1026
Length of Order Cycle	0.153846	0.192308	0.115385	0.157265
Annual Holding Cost	650	812.5	487.5	664.444
Annual Safety Stock Cost	17.68	9.62	27.56	16.9
Annual Ordering Cost	650	520	866.667	635.87
Annual Inventory Cost	1317.68	1342.12	1381.73	1317.21
Annual Purchase Cost	0	0	0	0
Total Annual Cost	1317.68	1342.12	1381.73	1317.21
II. Safety Stock and Reorder Levels				
Service Level Desired	0.99	0.99	0.99	0.99
Type of Service Level	Fill Rate	Fill Rate	Fill Rate	Fill Rate
Service Level Achieved				
Leadtime SL	0.633072	0.573385	0.701944	0.627409
Fill Rate SL	0.99	0.99	0.99	0.99
Avg. Leadtime (Weeks)	4	4	4	4
Std.Dev. of Leadtime (Week) 0	0	0	0	
Avg. Demand (Units/Week)	250	250	250	250
Std.Dev. of Demand (Units/Week) 40	40	40	40	
Std.Dev. of Demand during Leadtime (Units/Week)	80	80	80	80
Safety Stock	27.2	14.8	42.4	26
Reorder Level	1027.2	1014.8	1042.4	1026
Number of Std.Dev. of SS (z)	0.34	0.185	0.53	0.325
E(z)	0.25	0.3125	0.1875	0.255556
Expected Units Short/Cycle	20	25	15	20.4444
Expected Units Short/Year	130	130	130	130

6.8 Model 8: Continuous Review, Stochastic, Infinite Replenishment Rate, Backorders Not Allowed, No Qty. Discounts, Calculate Service Level

Data Required
1. Data for Model 6 except
   The entry for service level is not required (but the type of service level must be specified).
2. For carrying out sensitivity analysis
   If Leadtime Service Level, then Alternate Reorder Levels must be entered.
   If Fill Rate Service Level, both Alternate Order Quantities as well as Alternate Reorder Levels must be entered.

Formulae Used
Similar to Model 6.

Sensitivity Analysis
Sensitivity analysis is automatically carried out by specifying Alternate Order Quantities and Alternate Reorder Levels (see Data Required above).

Sample Problem

SERVICE.DAT

Inventory Control Calculations for:
  Continuous Review, Stochastic, Infinite Replenishment Rate
  Backorders Not Allowed, No Quantity Discounts
  Service Level Calculations Only

	EOQ(optimal)	Alternate Order Quantities Set 1	Alternate Order Quantities Set 2
I. Demand, Ordering, and Cost			
Annual Demand	13000	13000	13000
Holding Cost (Unit/Year)	0.65	0.65	0.65
Ordering Cost	100	100	100
Order Quantity	0	2500	1500
Number of Orders (Year)	0	5.2	8.66667
Average Inventory	0	2450	3050
Maximum Inventory	0	3700	3800
Reorder Level	0	2200	3300
Length of Order Cycle	0	0.192308	0.115385
Annual Holding Cost	0	812.5	487.5
Annual Safety Stock Cost	0	780	1495
Annual Ordering Cost	0	520	866.667
Annual Inventory Cost	0	2112.5	2849.17
Annual Purchase Cost	0	0	0
Total Annual Cost	0	2112.5	2849.17
II. Safety Stock and Reorder Levels			
Type of Service Level	Fill Rate	Fill Rate	Fill Rate
Service Level Achieved			
Leadtime SL	0	0.787816	0.937135
Fill Rate SL	0	0.927628	0.972674
Avg. Leadtime (Weeks)	4	4	4
Std.Dev. of Leadtime (Week)	6	6	6
Order Quantity	0	2500	1500
Avg. Demand (Units/Week)	250	250	250
Std.Dev. of Demand (Units/Week)	40	40	40
Std.Dev. of Demand during Leadtime (Units/Week)	1502.13	1502.13	1502.13
Safety Stock	0	1200	2300
Reorder Level	0	2200	3300
Number of Std.Dev. of SS (z)	0	0.798865	1.53116
E(z)	0	0.120448	0.0272871
Expected Units Short/Cycle	0	180.929	40.9889
Expected Units Short/Year	0	940.83	355.237

6.9 Model 9: Periodic Review, Stochastic, Infinite Replenishment Rate, Backorders Not Allowed, No Quantity Discounts

Data Required
1. Data for Model 6(a).
2. Length of Review Period (in time units given by the Conversion Factor), T.
3. Inventory on Hand at the time of review, I.

Decision Variables
Quantity to Order, Q, given a service level; safety Stock, SS.

Formulae Used
Let F(LTSL) be the CDF of the Normal Distribution.
Let E(z) be the expected number of customers who are backlogged
in a cycle when the Standard Deviation of Demand during Leadtime equals one (1).
If u is not given, set u = D/Conversion Factor
Set Standard Deviation of Demand during Leadtime and review period (approximation)
$$SDD\&LT+T = ((T+LT)*SDD^2 + u^2*SDLT^2)^{0.5}$$
If Leadtime Service Level, then
set z = F(LTSL)
Compute the Fill Rate Service Level (see below)
For each Alternate Order Quantity, compute the Fill Rate and Leadtime Service Levels.

Else If Fill Rate Service Level , then
Set X = u*LT (average demand during a review period).
Search for a z such that E(z) * SDD&LT/EOQ <= 1 - SL.
SS = z*SDD&LT+T
R = SS + u*(LT+T)

Sensitivity Analysis
HOM computes the service levels for each Alternate Order Quantity.

Sample Problem

PERIODIC.DAT

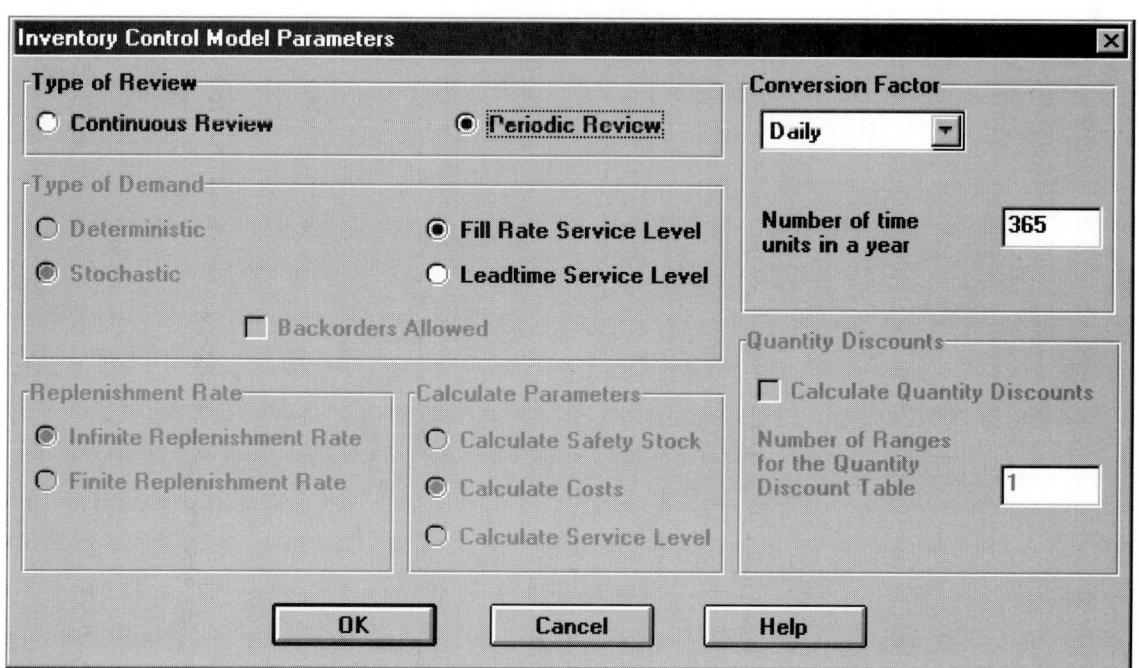

Sample Problem (continued)

PERIODIC.DAT

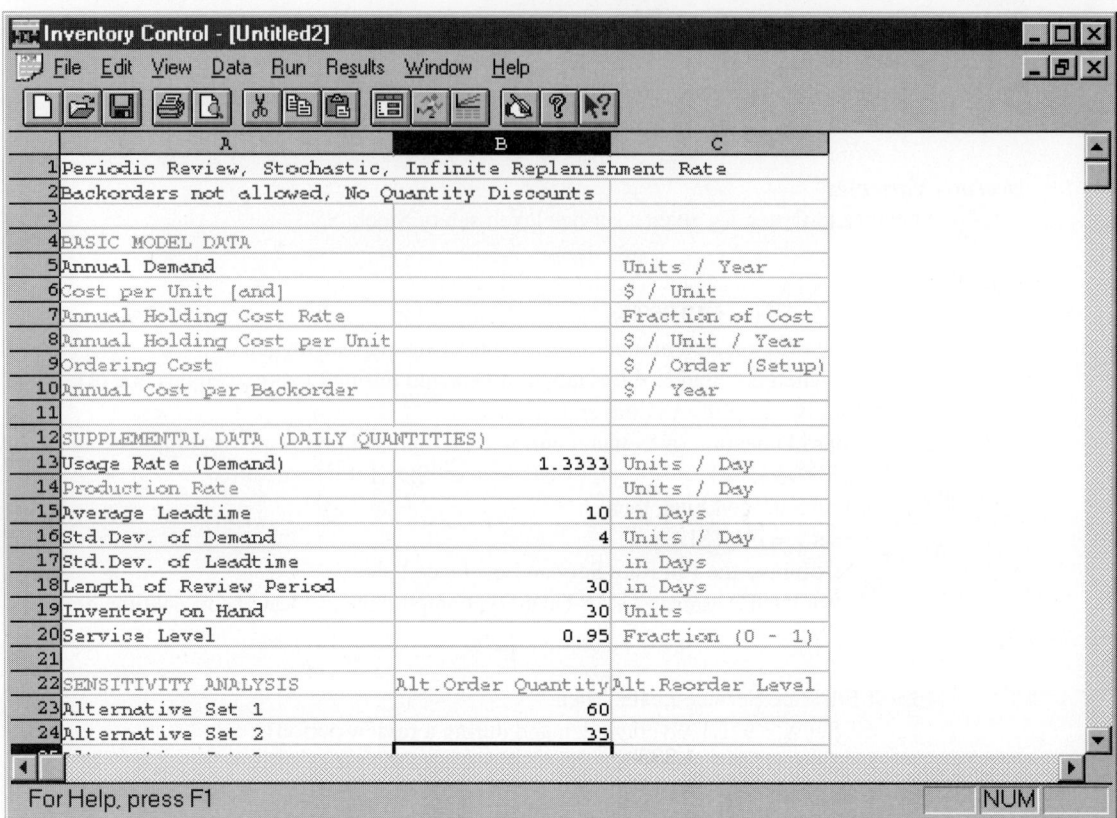

Inventory Control Calculations for:
- Periodic Review, Stochastic, Infinite Replenishment Rate
- Backorders Not Allowed, No Quantity Discounts
- Safety Stock and Service Level Calculations

	Base Case	Alternate Order Quantities Set 1	Alternate Order Quantities Set 2
I. Ordering			
Number of Orders (Year)	12.1667	12.1667	12.1667
Quantity to Order	49.2627	60	35
Length of Review Cycle	30	30	30
Inventory On Hand	30	30	30
II. Safety Stock and Reorder Levels			
Service Level Desired	0.95	0.95	0.95
Type of Service Level	Fill Rate	Fill Rate	Fill Rate
Service Level Achieved			
Leadtime SL	0.847318	0.926391	0.677679
Fill Rate SL	0.95	0.97922	0.867163
Avg. Leadtime (Days)	10	10	10
Std.Dev. of Leadtime (Day)	0	0	0
Avg. Demand (Units/Day)	1.3333	1.3333	1.3333
Std. Demand (Units/Day)	4	4	4
Std.Dev. of Demand during Leadtime (Units/Day)	25.2982	25.2982	25.2982
Safety Stock	25.9307	36.668	11.668
Number of Std.Dev. of SS (z) 1.025	1.44943	0.461218	
E(z)	0.079055	0.032855	0.210029
Expected Units Short/Cycle	1.99995	0.831174	5.31335
Expected Units Short/Year	24.3327	10.1126	64.6458

REFERENCES

Chase, R. B., and N. J. Aquilano *Production and Operations Management*, 7th ed., Burr Ridge, IL: Richard D. Irwin, 1995.

Nahmias, S. *Production and Operations Analysis*, 3rd ed., Burr Ridge, IL: Richard D. Irwin, 1997.

Stevenson, W. J. *Production/Operations Management*, 5th ed., Burr Ridge, IL: Richard D. Irwin, 1996.

The Nut Case[1]

David Nutt was worried. It appeared that he would soon have to close the family business that had run for three generations. The Nutt Company (TNC) was a supplier of special nuts to aircraft manufacturers. Its biggest customer was a large and very successful aircraft manufacturer headquartered in the Northwest USA. A forecasted decline in demand for aircraft had resulted in some downward pressure on earnings in the Big Aircraft Group (BAG). Due to this pressure, BAG was "asking" its suppliers to "share" some of the burden by lowering their prices at least 3 percent. For the over 200,000 parts that it purchased, BAG typically selected an exclusive vendor for its entire needs of each part. Of course, some vendors supplied more than one part to BAG. Recently, BAG was considering adopting a multi-vendor policy for some of its parts needs. David had heard that BAG was evaluating whether to find another vendor for the special nuts that TNC supplied.

TNC was the exclusive supplier of special nuts in various sizes and shapes that were used in extremely sensitive components installed on some of BAG's most successful aircraft. Typically, TNC supplied 400,000 cases of nuts each year at a price of $312 per case. TNC purchased these nuts from several manufacturers around the world for $240 per case. Since BAG had large backlogs of deliveries for the planes on which these nuts were installed, BAG built roughly the same number of aircraft each month although each aircraft was custom built according to BAG's customers' specifications. In fact, it seemed that BAG's needs for these special nuts was nearly constant from day–to–day.

TNC did not manufacture anything; it was simply a trading company. It cost TNC $1,200 to place each order with its suppliers. This was a very high cost because each order had to reflect the custom needs of all the planes for which nuts were being ordered. TNC incurred a cost of $60 per case per annum for handling and storing each case of nuts. Due to the high ordering cost, David was placing one order each month for the expected quantity of nuts needed. His suppliers had an extremely efficient operation that could deliver the entire order quantity essentially within 24 hours!!

David was wondering what he should do when his cousin, Peter (a recent graduate from the Stern School of Business currently employed at a very successful investment bank in New York; and rumored to be earning in excess of $5 million a year) called to say that he would be visiting David next weekend. He mentioned something about how his investment clients were earning upwards of 20 percent annum before tax and offered to do the same for David. David did not understand too much about what Peter did, but 20 percent sounded almost illegal to his ears. In any case, he soon forgot about it. David was simply delighted to hear that Peter was visiting. He and Peter had grown up together and were very close. In addition to their love for tennis and hiking, David and Peter would often discuss business issues through the night! This time David knew exactly what he was going to talk about. Since it was already Thursday, David set about preparing for the weekend.

David wanted to check whether there was any chance that his suppliers might be willing to also "share" in the burden being transferred by BAG. He called some of his main suppliers, and to his complete surprise he was able to get some discounts just by asking! Of course, there were some conditions. One possibility was that a 10 percent discount would be given in the form of a refund at the end of the year only if the quantity he ordered was at least 4,000 cases. Another possibility was a 5 percent discount if each order was at least 4,000 cases. A third possibility was that the suppliers could deliver a predetermined quantity of nuts daily (260 working days per year) to TNC for no extra charge. The daily quantity could only be set once each year. The last alternative discussed was a 15 percent discount if TNC accepted at least 400,000 cases in one delivery. Of course, these discounts could not be combined.

David was barely recovering from the shock of having obtained these concessions so easily when he got a call from the Executive Vice-President of Nut Purchasing at BAG. He had called to ask TNC to cut at least 5 percent off their prices immediately. Since David's firm only had a profit before tax of $6,240,000, David knew that this was the last nut in his coffin!

---

[1] By Praveen Nayyar, Operations Management Area, Stern School of Business. This case is for the use of students in a core course in Operations Management and is intended to have no actual relationship to any real person or organization. (11/98)

INPUT DATA

ANNUAL DEMAND	
ORDER COSTS PER ORDER	
UNIT COST PER CASE	
ANNUAL COST OF CAPITAL	
ANNUAL HOLDING COST PER CASE	
SELLING PRICE	

CURRENT PROFITABILITY

TOTAL ANNUAL SALES	
TOTAL ANNUAL COGS	
TOTAL ANNUAL MARGIN	
TOTAL OVERHEAD (INCL. INVENTORY COSTS	
TOTAL PROFIT BEFORE TAX	

ALTERNATIVE INVENTORY POLICIES

	CURRENT POLICY ONCE A MONTH	EOQ	5% PRICE DISCOUNT	ONE ORDER 15% DISCOUNT	ONE ORDER DELIVER DAILY
ORDER QUANTITY					
ANNUAL ORDER COSTS					
ANNUAL INVENTORY CARRYING COSTS					
ANNUAL TOTAL INVENTORY COSTS					
ANNUAL SAVINGS OVER CURRENT POLICY					
SAVINGS AS A % OF PROFIT BEFORE TAX					
YEAR-END DISCOUNTS					
ANNUAL SAVINGS AFTER DISCOUNTS					
MAXIMUM WORKING CAPITAL INVESTMENT					
TOTAL COSTS					
NOTES					

DEPENDENT DEMAND INVENTORY MANAGEMENT METHODS

1. INTRODUCTION

The HOM Dependent Demand Inventory module is a Materials Requirements Planning (MRP) system. MRP data files have the extension MRP. The MRP techniques can be used for the following categories of demand:

    a. When the demand for the item *depends* on the demand for *other* end or intermediate products, assemblies, and parts, the Dependent Demand model can be used to determine both the order quantities as well as the timing of the orders.

    b. The MRP module could be used for determining the lot sizes and timing of orders when the demand is independent and deterministic but varying over time.

Example

XYZ company manufactures two types of tables, ordinary and special, with part names ORD and SPE respectively. The only difference between the two types is the top portion of the table, and these are termed TOPO and TOPS for ORD and SPE respectively. The bill of materials for the two tables is given below. Quantities in parentheses indicate the quantity required to make the assembly. CASTERS are purchased items and the leadtime between the placement and the receipt of an order for CASTERS is one period. LEGS for the table require a leadtime of one period, and tops require a leadtime of two periods. The final assembly of the table requires one period.

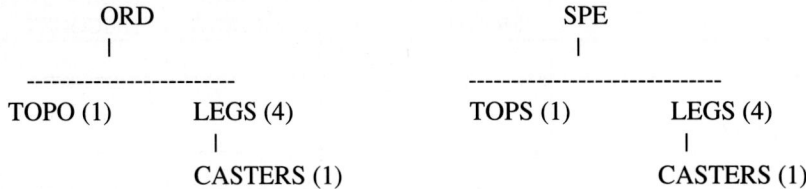

2. THE BILL OF MATERIALS INFORMATION

The bill of materials (BOM) is a list of the products (assemblies and subassemblies) and the name as well as the quantity of each of their assemblies, subassemblies, and components. Follow the steps given below to enter the data.

    a. Enter the name of a product (subassembly or assembly) in the first column of the spreadsheet in the column labeled as "Part." The entry could begin in any row.

    b. Enter the quantity required (assemblies, subassemblies and components required to make this part) for making this Part in the second column of the <u>same</u> row. This must be a nonnegative integer entry (0, 1, 2, 3,...). This second column is labeled "No. of Children."

    c. Beginning in the <u>same</u> row but in the third column, list the names of the components. Only *one* component name should be entered *per* row; <u>no</u> breaks are allowed between rows. The third column is labeled "Name of Child."

    d. Enter the quantity of the component required to make one unit of the Part, in the fourth column, labeled "Qty. Required."

    e. Repeat steps a, b, c, and d for each Part that requires components as well as for each part that is not a component but has independent demand. Blank rows may be left between parts.

Example:

Part	No. of Children	Name of Child	Qty. Required
ORD	2	TOPO	1
		LEGS	4
SPE	2	TOPS	1
		LEGS	4
LEGS	1	CASTERS	1

The filled spreadsheet is shown below (see <u>TABLES.MRP</u> data file).

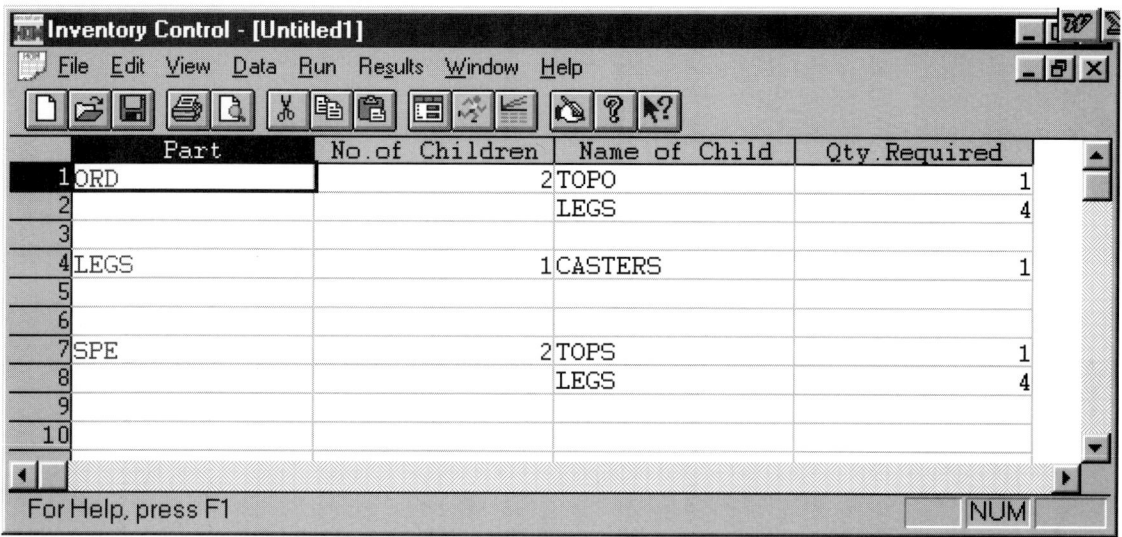

Note that the order of the entry of "Part" is not important; for example, the data for LEGS is followed by the data for the product SPE that uses LEGS. After entering the BOM data, save the data using the command SAVE.

3. ADD OR DELETE PARTS FROM THE BILL OF MATERIALS

You may wish to modify the BOM. New data for Parts can be inserted or appended anywhere in the spreadsheet (see Caution! below). Insertion of rows in the spreadsheet is accomplished via DATA --> Row --> Insert.

> **Caution!** HOM does not permit undo's. Therefore, either be very certain before deleting data or save your data before attempting to modify the BOM.

4. DEMAND AND SCHEDULED RECEIPTS (CREATE PART MASTER)

The Part Master should be created after entering the BOM data. To reach the Part Master data entry spreadsheet, click on the BOM spreadsheet using the right mouse button. The Part Master spreadsheet can also be reached via DATA --> Create/View Part Master. The BOM spreadsheet can be reached in a similar manner from the Part Master spreadsheet.

The names of all the parts (products, assemblies, subassemblies, and component parts) are shown in blue. Following the name of each part, there are 20 rows for data entry. Each row represents one period or time bucket. A total of 20 periods are allowed. You may have to scroll down to reach the data entry rows of some parts.

The data entry method given below should be followed for creating a new Part Master or editing an old one. See Section 5 for other options that are available for entering the Part Master data.

The Part Master has the following information for *each* part in the BOM:

The independent demand for the part in each period for up to 20 periods. If the part is a component or assembly or subassembly *and* has no independent demand, then this column can be left unfilled. For example, the independent demand for ORD and SPE would be the forecast demand during different time periods. The table tops (TOPO and TOPS) need not have independent demand unless they are sold separately as replacement parts. In our example, there is independent demand for replacement LEGS.

The scheduled receipts for the part in each period. If there are no scheduled receipts then this column can be left unfilled. For example, if orders have already been *released* to the department manufacturing the table tops, then scheduled receipts will be shown against the anticipated delivery dates.

(Optional) If the user wishes to see the effect of rescheduling the scheduled receipts, then enter the rescheduled receipts in the column labeled as "Resched. Receipts." See section 7.9 for a description of using this option in the Parameters dialog box for the Part Master.

(Optional) If the user wishes to see the effect of using his or her own planned receipts, then enter the planned receipts in the "Planned Receipts" column. See section 7.9 for a description of using this option in the Parameters dialog box for the Part Master. The computer will not calculate the planned receipts for this order and will instead use the given values of planned receipts.

After entering the Part Master data, save the data using the command SAVE.

Example

The forecast demand and scheduled receipts for ORD and SPE tables are as shown below.

Period	1	2	3	4	5	6	7	8
Forecast ORD	10	20	220	50	10	0	70	10
Sch. Recipts ORD	40	0	70	0	100	0	20	0
Forecast SPE	30	20	10	0	0	40	0	60
Sch. Receipts SPE	20	20	20	20	20	20	20	20
Sch. Receipts TOPO	40	40	0	0	0	0	0	0
Sch. Receipts TOPS	0	20	0	0	0	0	0	0
Forecast LEGS	3	3	3	3	3	3	3	3
Sch. Receipts LEGS	200	0	0	0	0	0	0	0
Sch. Receipts CASTERS	20	10	0	0	0	0	0	0

Part of the filled spreadsheet is shown below (see file <u>TABLES.MRP</u>). Please experiment with the feature that allows the user to toggle between the Part Master and the BOM by clicking the right mouse button.

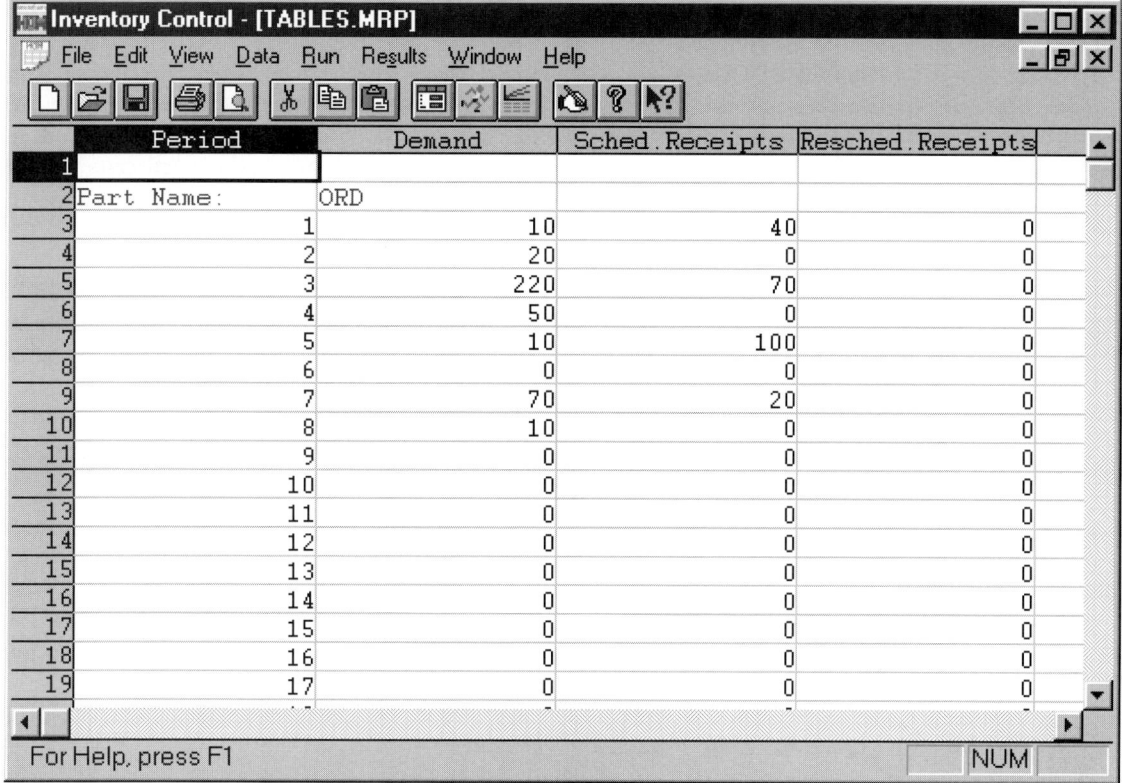

5. SAVING AND RETRIEVING THE PART MASTER

The BOM and Part Master are saved and retrieved together. Unlike the BOM, the Part Master containing data about Demand, Scheduled Receipts, and so forth, can be retrieved from different files. For a description of this feature see the next section.

6. CREATING A PART MASTER FROM SAVED DATA

Instead of entering all Part Master information you may wish to do either of the following:

> a. Read in all the Part Master data corresponding to the BOM parts from a previously saved file. This should be a HOM file with the extension MRP, created and saved in HOM.

> b. Selectively read in data for parts of your choice into the Part Master from a previously saved file. This should be a HOM file with the extension MRP, created and saved in HOM.

In both cases, the BOM should have been created first. These options are provided to permit the user to carry out a what–if analysis. For example, you may wish to add new products to the BOM and study the effect. You may wish to change the BOM (add parts or delete parts) and redo the calculations. In all such cases, save the original data as an MRP file. Create the modified BOM. Then use option (a) or (b).

To use option (a), create the BOM, go to DATA --> Part Master --> Create from File. HOM warns you that creating the Part Master in this fashion will erase previously entered data in the spreadsheet that you are *currently* editing. Choose "Yes." The File Open dialog box will be displayed. Select the name of the file from which you wish to copy the Part Master data and choose OK. HOM will copy the data (i.e., Demand, Scheduled Receipts, Rescheduled Receipts, and Planned Receipts) for all parts from that file. If there are parts in the current BOM that are not found in the file you have selected, then the Part Master data corresponding to those parts will be left unaffected.

To use option (b), you have to be in the Part Master data entry spreadsheet. This spreadsheet can be reached by clicking on the right mouse button. Once you are in the Part Master spreadsheet, go to DATA--> Part Master. Only one option will be displayed, namely that of Import Part Data. Select this item. HOM will warn you that all previously entered data for selected parts will be erased. Choose Yes. The File Open dialog box will be displayed. Select the name of the file from which you wish to *import* data selectively and click on OK. HOM will open a dialog box showing only the names of parts in the selected file that correspond to parts in the current BOM. In other words, if there are parts in the selected file that do not belong to the current BOM, then they will not be displayed. (Thus, if the selected file has *no* Part Master data that you can reuse, HOM will produce an appropriate error message.) The names of the selected parts will be in blue. Initially all the parts will be shown as selected. Unselect or select the parts using the mouse. Choose OK to execute the Import of Data. Only the data for the selected parts will be imported.

Example using Option (a)

Say you have already created and saved the TABLES.MRP file. We wish to delete the part SPE and create a new part VSPE (very special). We also wish to reuse as much as possible of the data in the part master of TABLES.MRP. The BOM of the new file is shown below (called TABLEVS.MRP):

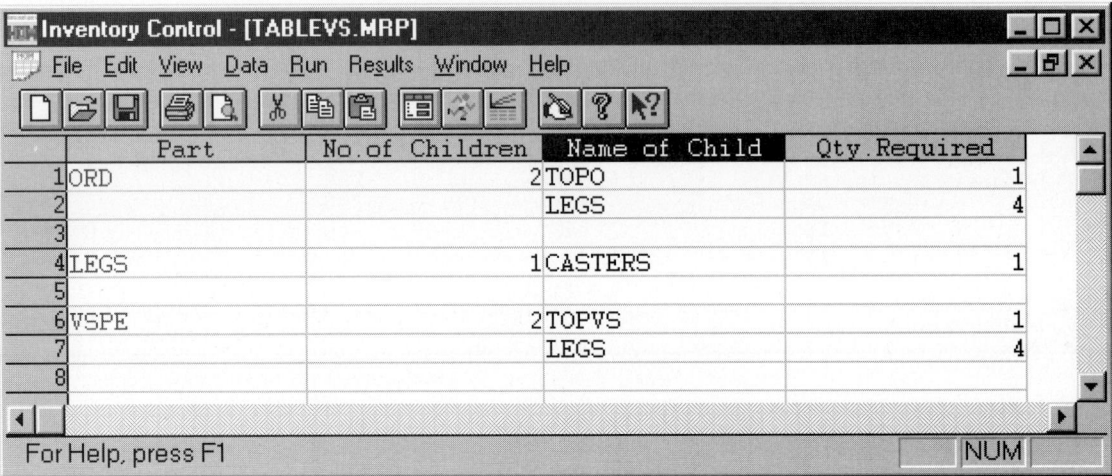

Notice that the new parts are VSPE and its corresponding top, TOPVS. Everything else is the same as before. In order to use option (a), go to DATA --> Part Master --> Create from File. HOM warns you that this step will erase data in the Part Master of the current file, TABLEVS.MRP. Choose Yes. The File Open dialog box is displayed as shown below:

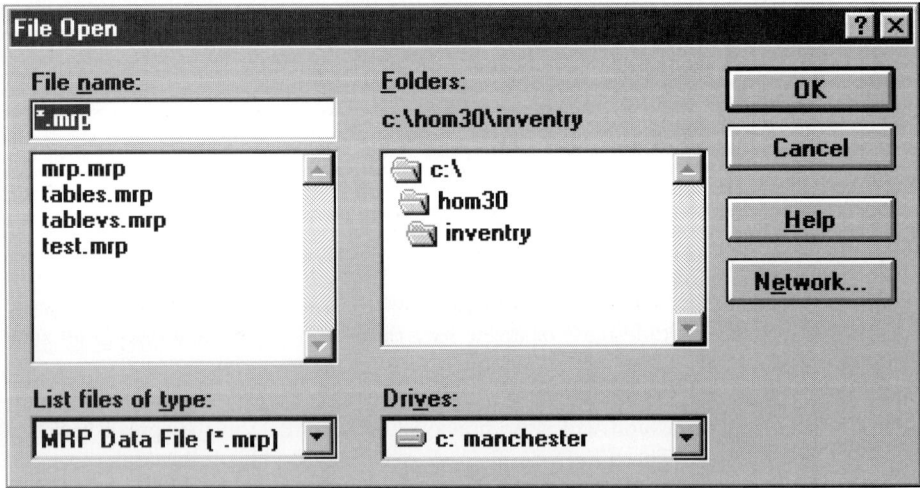

Select the file TABLES.MRP and choose OK. HOM will only read in the data corresponding to the *common* parts: ORD, LEGS, and TOPO.

Example using Option (b)

Now suppose you have file called TABLEVS1.MRP that has data only pertaining to the new product VSPE. You can selectively read in data into the Part Master of TABLEVS.MRP from that file by following the steps given below.

    Open the file TABLEVS.MRP

    Switch to its Part Master screen by right clicking on the mouse.

    Choose DATA --> Part Master --> Import Part Data.

HOM will warn you that entered data for the parts that you choose to import in the *current* file will be erased. (The current file is TABLEVS.MRP.) Select Yes. The File Open Dialog box is displayed as shown below:

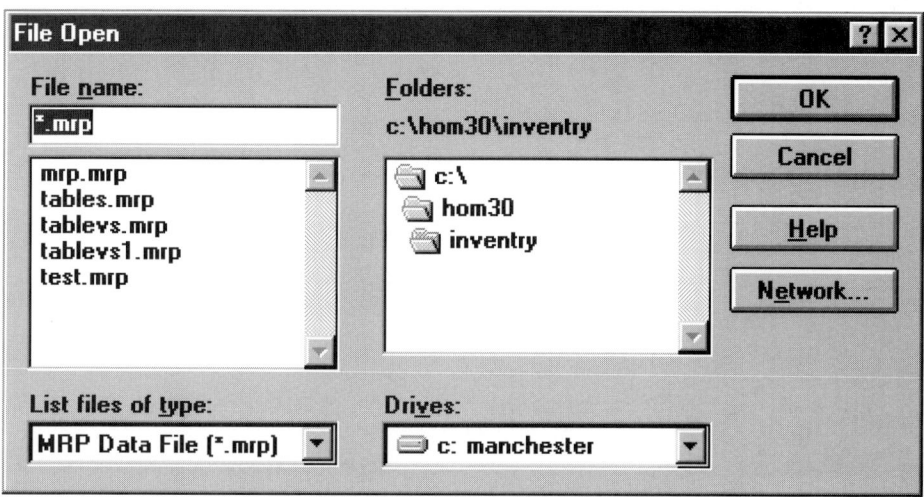

Choose the file TABLEVS1.MRP and click on OK. The following dialog box opens up:

241

This dialog box shows that there are four parts in the Part Master of TABLEVS1.MRP that are common to the Part Master of TABLEVS.MRP. You choose to import data only for the new product, so choose only VSPE and TOPVS. To do so, deselect LEGS and CASTERS (make them white in color by clicking on them):

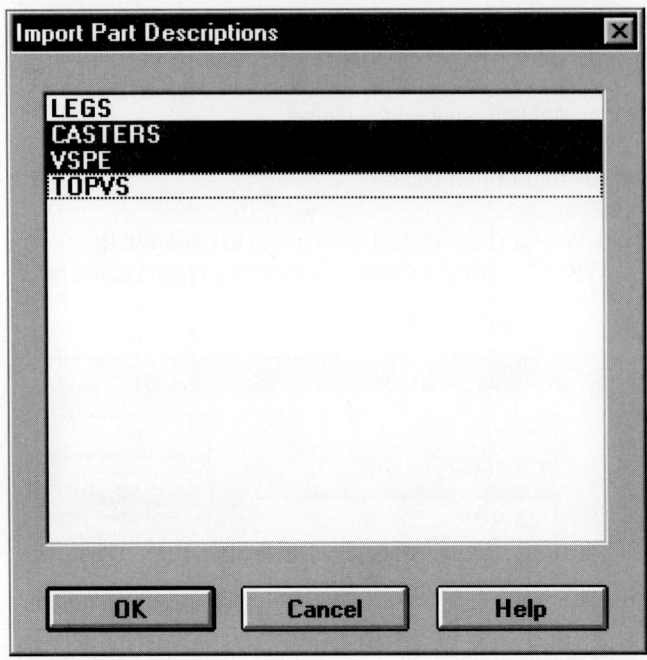

Choose OK. The data for the selected parts will be imported. The rest of the Part Master will be left unaffected.

7. SPECIFY THE LOT SIZING RULE, SAFETY STOCK, LEADTIME, AND OTHERS

The planning data for the parts in the BOM (and therefore in the Part Master) is entered via the Part Master Parameters dialog box. This dialog box can be activated in two ways: If the Part Master spreadsheet is open, then clicking on the Parameters Icon will open the dialog box. The user can also reach this box via DATA --> Parameters --> Part Master Parameters. The part number should be first selected from the drop-down list shown in the top center of the dialog box. (The drop-down list is context sensitive. If the cursor is currently located at LEGS in the Part Master spreadsheet, then LEGS will be shown in the drop-down list.) The user has the option of entering the following data:

    Safety Stock

    Order Policy (Lot Sizing Rule)

    Lead Time

    Lot Size (FOQ)

    Inventory on Hand

    No. of Periods (FPQ)

    Cost of One Setup

    Holding Cost

    Three check boxes called:

        Rescheduled Scheduled Receipts

        Allow Expedited Orders

        Enter Planned Receipts

Brief descriptions of these items are given below.

Example Data Entered in File TABLES.MRP:

	ORD	SPE	LEGS	TOPO	TOPS	CASTERS
Safety Stock	10	30	40	0	0	30
Order Policy	LTL	LTL	FOQ	FPQ	SILVER MEAL	LUC
Lead Time	1	1	1	2	3	1
Lot Size	0	0	100	0	0	0
Inventory on Hand	20	-5	50	25	10	35
No. of Periods	1	1	1	2	1	1
Cost of One Setup	50	50	20	100	150	10
Holding Cost	10	15	3	7	12	1

Hint: Once in the Parameters dialog box, the up or down arrow key can be used to scroll through the parameters for the different parts.

7.1 Safety Stock (Part Parameters Dialog Box)

The MRP calculations are carried out to ensure that the Projected Available Balance (i.e., the period ending inventory) does not fall below the value of the safety stock. However, if Expediting Orders is not allowed it might not always be possible to maintain the Projected Available Balance greater than or equal to the value of the safety stock.

Before carrying out the MRP calculations, the On Hand Inventory is reduced by the given amount of safety stock. The MRP calculations are carried out using the reduced On Hand Inventory. The safety stock is added back to the Projected Available Balance after carrying out the MRP calculations. See section 11 for the details of the algorithm.

The cost of holding safety stock is estimated as the total number of periods in the planning horizon times the safety stock times the Holding Cost. This value is added to the total cost of setup and the cost of holding inventory, and the total is reported in the output.

7.2 Order Policy (Lot Sizing Rule) (Part Parameters Dialog Box)

HOM allows the user to choose from one of six lot sizing rules. The lot sizing rules are aimed at reducing the total cost of setup and holding inventory. The rules can be set differently for different parts. Please consult a textbook or section 11 for the algorithms used. The rules are:

Rule	Brief Description
Lot for Lot (LTL)	No Lot Sizing, planned orders are equal to the Net Requirements
Fixed Order Quantity (FOQ)	Orders are released in multiples of the given lot size. The lot size has to be a positive integer and is specified in the same dialog box.
Fixed Period Quantity (FPQ)	Orders are combined for the given (fixed) number of periods. The number of periods has to be a positive integer and is specified in the same dialog box.
	The calculations for the FPQ rule are not straightforward when there are scheduled receipts. HOM searches for the first period in which the Net Requirements are positive. Starting from this period, it breaks up the rest of the periods into time buckets of length equal to the fixed number of periods. Thereafter, starting from the first such time bucket, HOM plans to release orders for the *largest cumulative* Net Requirements in each time bucket.
Silver Meal Heuristic	This heuristic rule attempts to greedily minimize the set up and holding cost.
Least Unit Cost (LUC)	This heuristic attempts to heuristically minimize the unit cost of setup and holding inventory.
Least Total Cost (LTC)	This heuristic rule attempts to balance the cost of holding inventory versus the cost of setup.

7.3 Lead Time (Part Parameters Dialog Box)

The lead time is expressed in number of periods.

The lead time should be a nonnegative integer. If the lead time is negligible, it can be entered as zero (0).

For MRP calculations, the lead time is the time required to assemble the part given that all its component parts are available. For purchased parts, the lead time retains the usual meaning; namely, it is the time between the placement and the receipt of an order.

7.4 Lot Size for Fixed Order Quantity (FOQ) Rule (Part Parameters Dialog Box)

When the Fixed Order Quantity (FOQ) rule has been selected, orders are released in multiples of the given lot size. The lot size has to be a positive integer and is specified in the corresponding edit box.

7.5 Inventory on Hand (Part Parameters Dialog Box)

The inventory on hand (On Hand Inventory) is the inventory at the beginning of the planning horizon.

The beginning of the planning horizon is the first period by default. The default value can be changed in the MRP Parameters dialog box; see Starting Period.

The value of the inventory can be set equal to any integer value.

7.6 Number of Periods for Fixed Period Quantity (FPQ) Rule (Part Parameters Dialog Box)

When the lot sizing rule is Fixed Period Quantity (FPQ), orders are combined for the given (fixed) number of periods. The number of periods has to be a positive integer and is specified in the same dialog box.

The calculations for the FPQ rule are not straightforward when there are scheduled receipts. HOM searches for the first period in which the Net Requirements are positive. Starting from this period, it breaks up the rest of the periods into time buckets equal to the fixed number of periods. Thereafter, starting from the first such time bucket, HOM plans to release orders for the *largest cumulative* Net Requirements in each time bucket. The algorithm is implemented in an iterative manner. For more details please consult section 11.

7.7 Cost of One Setup (Part Parameters Dialog Box)

The setup cost for the part is required data when using any of the three heuristic rules: Silver Meal, Least Unit Cost, or Least Total Cost. The set up cost should be a positive number. This cost reflects the cost of setting up for production or assembly, or the ordering cost for a purchased item.

7.8 Holding Cost (Part Parameters Dialog Box)

The holding cost is the cost of holding one unit of the part for one period.

The holding cost is assessed on period ending inventory, that is, the Projected Available Balance.

The cost of holding safety stock is estimated as the total number of periods in the planning horizon times the safety stock times the Holding Cost. This value is added to the total cost of setup and holding inventory, and the total cost is reported in the output.

7.9 Rescheduled Receipts, Expedited Orders, and Planned Receipts (Part Parameters Dialog Box)

> Rescheduled Receipts: The user can carry out sensitivity analysis by entering different values for the scheduled receipts for a part, see section 10. In order to force HOM to use these new values, select the Reschedule Scheduled Receipts check box for the part. This analysis is especially insightful, if the scheduled receipts do not match the gross requirements.

Expedited Orders: In order to meet the requirements, it might become necessary to expedite some orders. HOM normally assumes that Planned Orders will require an amount of time equal to the leadtime to become Planned Receipts. However, if the user selects the Allow Expedited Orders check box, then HOM will plan so that there are no shortages in any period. In addition, the output will indicate whether the Planned Order is an expedited one, and what part of the order will be delivered (in case of split orders) in which period.

Planned Receipts: The software allows the user to override HOM's calculations for the Planned Receipts using this device. The user could enter planned receipts and force HOM to use these values of Planned Receipts. This feature allows the user to mimic Firm Planned Orders to a degree. In order to activate this feature, the user should select the Enter Planned Receipts check box.

Please see section 10 for examples.

8. SET CALCULATION PARAMETERS AND RUN THE MODEL

The MRP calculation parameters are selected in the BOM Parameters dialog box. This box can be opened by clicking on the Parameters icon when the BOM spreadsheet is displayed or via DATA --> Parameters --> MRP Calculations Parameters.

HOM carries out low level coding once the data have been entered. Therefore, when the user opens this dialog box, the maximum level in the BOM has already been determined. The user can select the following items in the dialog box:

- From Level
- To Level
- Starting Period
- Ending Period

The controls have been designed to permit the user to explore step–by–step explosion of the material requirements, and see how the plan changes by rolling time forward.

Descriptions of the choices are given below. After having made your choices, click on OK. Click on the RUN icon.

Example: In the TABLES.MRP example, the number of levels is three; that is, level zero corresponds to ORD and SPE; level 1 corresponds to TOPO, TOPS, and LEGS; and the only level 2 part is CASTERS. The number of periods is eight as there are eight periods of data.

8.1 From Level and To Level (MRP Calculations Parameters Dialog Box)

Choose the low levels for which the MRP calculations have to be carried out. HOM automatically carries out low–level coding given the BOM data. The user however has to select the levels for which HOM carries out the MRP calculations. The default values for the From and To levels are zero. HOM will not permit the user to exceed the maximum level (depth) of the BOM. The dialog box is shown below for our example.

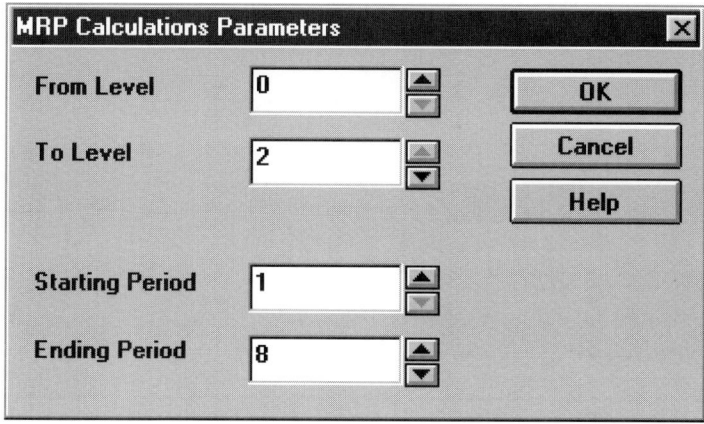

This feature allows the user to experiment with BOM explosion. For example, the User could carry out the calculations for just level zero (0), be satisfied with the results, and then complete the calculations for the remaining levels.

If the From Level is greater than zero, HOM assumes that the calculations have already been carried out for the levels smaller than the From Level.

8.2 Starting Period (MRP Calculations Parameters Dialog Box)

HOM permits the simulation of planning over time via the use of this feature. The Starting Period is one (1) by default. If the Starting Period is set equal to a value greater than one, then the following actions will ensue:

1. The Inventory on Hand will be assumed to be On Hand Inventory at the beginning of the Starting Period.

2. The MRP plan for Periods 1 through Starting Period minus 1 will be unaffected. If these values were computed earlier, then they will remain the same.

3. The MRP calculations will be carried out from the Starting Period.

Note that the Starting Period will be the same for all parts.

8.3 Ending Period (MRP Calculations Parameters Dialog Box)

Enter the Ending Period for the MRP calculations. MRP data beyond the ending period will be unaffected. The calculations will be carried out for the requirements between (and including) the Starting Period and the Ending Period.

9. VIEW THE RESULT

The results are displayed for the parts whose low–level codes fall within the From Level – To Level range. The format of the display is similar to the one found in most textbooks. The last four lines of the output for each part are unique to HOM. They depict whether the order is an expedited one, the Rescheduled Receipts, the Planned Order Receipts, the independent demand, and the dependent demand originating from the planned orders for higher level parts. See the next section for examples.

10. EXAMPLES

The data file is TABLES.MRP. The settings are as shown below. The output is attached, and it is followed by examples of what-if analysis carried out using the same data.

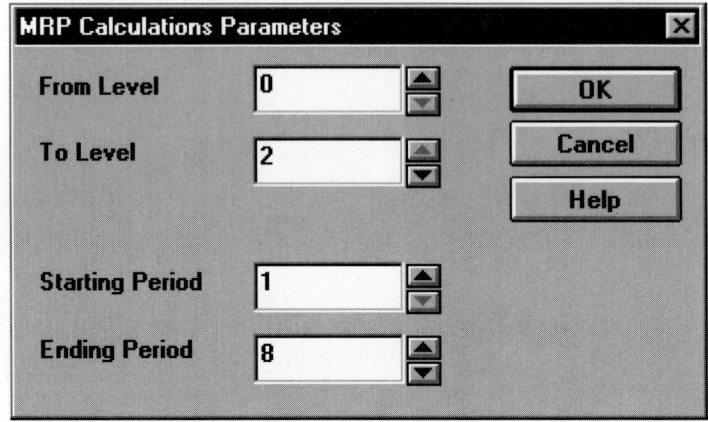

BILL OF MATERIAL
=====================================

Part Name	Number of Children	Child Name	Quantity Required
ORD	2	TOPO	1
		LEGS	4
LEGS	1	CASTERS	1
SPE	2	TOPS	1
		LEGS	4

MRP PARAMETERS
=====================================

From Level	0
To Level	2
Start Period	1
End Period	8

MRP PART RECORDS
====================================

PART NAME	ORD
Low Level	0
Ordering Policy	LTL
Safety Stock	10
Lead Time	1
On Hand Inventory	20
User Reschedules Receipts?	NO
Expediting allowed	NO
User Provides Planned Rcpts?	NO
Setup plus Holding Cost	4000

Period	1	2	3	4	5	6	7	8
Gross Requirements	10	20	220	50	10	0	70	10
Scheduled Receipts	40	0	70	0	100	0	20	0
Projected Available Balance	50	30	10	10	100	100	50	40
Planned Order Releases	0	130	50	0	0	0	0	0
Expedite Orders?	NO	NO	NO	NO	NO	NO	NO	NO
Rescheduled Scheduled Rcpts	0	0	0	0	0	0	0	0
Planned Order Receipts	0	0	130	50	0	0	0	0
Independent Demand	10	20	220	50	10	0	70	10
Dependent Demand	0	0	0	0	0	0	0	0

PART NAME	SPE
Low Level	0
Ordering Policy	LTL
Safety Stock	30
Lead Time	1
On Hand Inventory	-5
User Reschedules Receipts?	NO
Expediting allowed	NO
User Provides Planned Rcpts?	NO
Setup plus Holding Cost	6350

Period	1	2	3	4	5	6	7	8
Gross Requirements	30	20	10	0	0	40	0	60
Scheduled Receipts	20	20	20	20	20	20	20	20
Projected Available Balance	-15	30	40	60	80	60	80	40
Planned Order Releases	45	0	0	0	0	0	0	0
Expedite Orders?	NO	NO	NO	NO	NO	NO	NO	NO
Rescheduled Scheduled Rcpts	0	0	0	0	0	0	0	0
Planned Order Receipts	0	45	0	0	0	0	0	0
Independent Demand	30	20	10	0	0	40	0	60
Dependent Demand	0	0	0	0	0	0	0	0

PART NAME   **LEGS**

Low Level   1
Ordering Policy   FOQ
Safety Stock   40
Lead Time   1
On Hand Inventory   50
Lot Size (for FOQ)   100
User Reschedules Receipts?   NO
Expediting allowed   NO
User Provides Planned Rcpts?   NO
Setup plus Holding Cost   2496

Period	1	2	3	4	5	6	7	8
Gross Requirements	183	523	203	3	3	3	3	3
Scheduled Receipts	200	0	0	0	0	0	0	0
Projected Available Balance	67	44	41	138	135	132	129	126
Planned Order Releases	500	200	100	0	0	0	0	0
Expedite Orders?	NO	NO	NO	NO	NO	NO	NO	NO
Rescheduled Scheduled Rcpts	0	0	0	0	0	0	0	0
Planned Order Receipts	0	500	200	100	0	0	0	0
Independent Demand	3	3	3	3	3	3	3	3
Dependent Demand	180	520	200	0	0	0	0	0

PART NAME   **TOPO**

Low Level   1
Ordering Policy   FPQ
Safety Stock   0
Lead Time   2
On Hand Inventory   25
No. of Periods (for FPQ)   2
User Reschedules Receipts?   NO
Expediting allowed   NO
User Provides Planned Rcpts?   NO
Setup plus Holding Cost   555

Period	1	2	3	4	5	6	7	8
Gross Requirements	0	130	50	0	0	0	0	0
Scheduled Receipts	40	40	0	0	0	0	0	0
Projected Available Balance	65	-25	0	0	0	0	0	0
Planned Order Releases	75	0	0	0	0	0	0	0
Expedite Orders?	NO	NO	NO	NO	NO	NO	NO	NO
Rescheduled Scheduled Rcpts	0	0	0	0	0	0	0	0
Planned Order Receipts	0	0	75	0	0	0	0	0
Independent Demand	0	0	0	0	0	0	0	0
Dependent Demand	0	130	50	0	0	0	0	0

PART NAME TOPS

Low Level 1
Ordering Policy SILMEA
Safety Stock 0
Lead Time 3
On Hand Inventory 10
User Reschedules Receipts? NO
Expediting allowed NO
User Provides Planned Rcpts? NO
Setup plus Holding Cost 150

Period	1	2	3	4	5	6	7	8
Gross Requirements	45	0	0	0	0	0	0	0
Scheduled Receipts	0	20	0	0	0	0	0	0
Projected Available Balance	-35	-15	-15	0	0	0	0	0
Planned Order Releases	15	0	0	0	0	0	0	0
Expedite Orders?	NO	NO	NO	NO	NO	NO	NO	NO
Rescheduled Scheduled Rcpts	0	0	0	0	0	0	0	0
Planned Order Receipts	0	0	0	15	0	0	0	0
Independent Demand	0	0	0	0	0	0	0	0
Dependent Demand	45	0	0	0	0	0	0	0

PART NAME CASTERS

Low Level 2
Ordering Policy LUC
Safety Stock 30
Lead Time 1
On Hand Inventory 35
User Reschedules Receipts? NO
Expediting allowed NO
User Provides Planned Rcpts? NO
Setup plus Holding Cost 260

Period	1	2	3	4	5	6	7	8
Gross Requirements	500	200	100	0	0	0	0	0
Scheduled Receipts	20	10	0	0	0	0	0	0
Projected Available Balance	-445	30	30	30	30	30	30	30
Planned Order Releases	665	100	0	0	0	0	0	0
Expedite Orders?	NO	NO	NO	NO	NO	NO	NO	NO
Rescheduled Scheduled Rcpts	0	0	0	0	0	0	0	0
Planned Order Receipts	0	665	100	0	0	0	0	0
Independent Demand	0	0	0	0	0	0	0	0
Dependent Demand	500	200	100	0	0	0	0	0

The User could now begin experimenting with the planning parameters as follows.

Sensitivity Analysis (1): Permit Expedited Orders for SPE as a shortfall of 15 units is predicted at the end of the first period. Go to the Parameters dialog box when in the Part Master screen, select SPE from the drop down list, and check "Allow Expedited Orders." The user has to make these changes to the <u>TABLES.MRP</u> file.

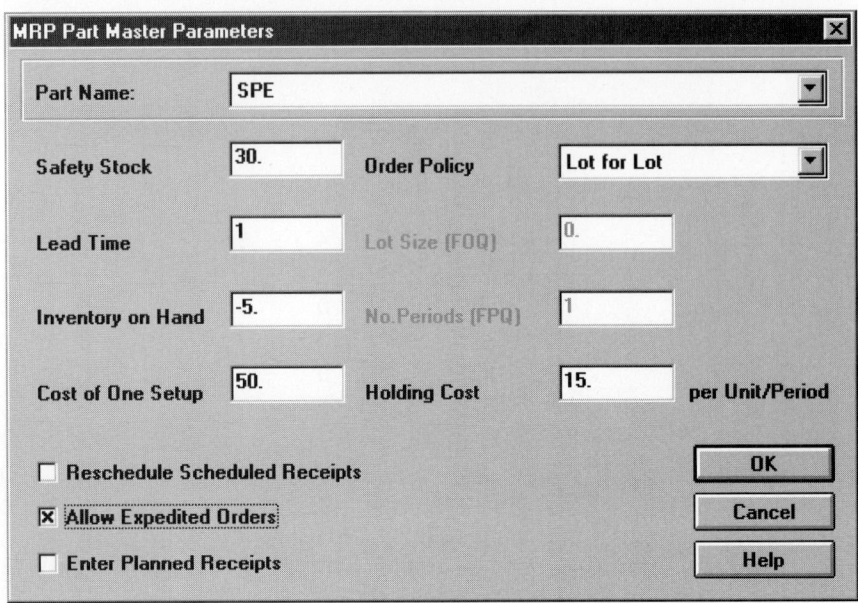

Run again. The output for SPE alone is shown below.

PART NAME	SPE							
Low Level	0							
Ordering Policy	LTL							
Safety Stock	30							
Lead Time	1							
On Hand Inventory	-5							
User Reschedules Receipts?	NO							
Expediting allowed	YES							
User Provides Planned Rcpts?	NO							
Setup plus Holding Cost	6350							
Period	1	2	3	4	5	6	7	8
Gross Requirements	30	20	10	0	0	40	0	60
Scheduled Receipts	20	20	20	20	20	20	20	20
Projected Available Balance	30	30	40	60	80	60	80	40
Planned Order Releases	45	0	0	0	0	0	0	0
Expedite Orders?	YES	NO	NO	NO	NO	NO	NO	NO
Rescheduled Scheduled Rcpts	0	0	0	0	0	0	0	0
Planned Order Receipts	45	0	0	0	0	0	0	0
Independent Demand	30	20	10	0	0	40	0	60
Dependent Demand	0	0	0	0	0	0	0	0

Sensitivity Analysis (2): Let us *continue* with the above example. Notice that if the scheduled receipts for TOPS are adjusted, then some of the shortfall for TOPS can be mitigated. We could attempt to reschedule the scheduled receipts of 20 units of TOPS in the second period to the first period. To do so, copy the scheduled receipts to the Resched. Receipts column and make the change as shown below. The user has to make these changes.

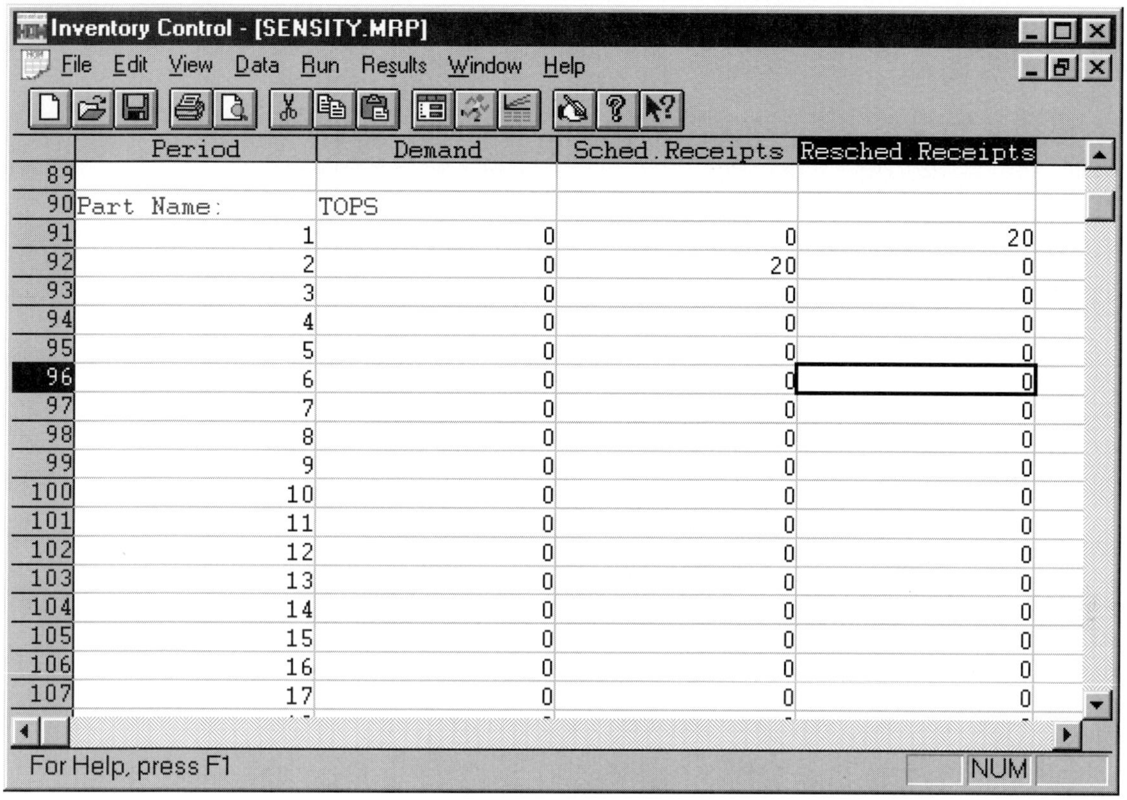

	Period	Demand	Sched. Receipts	Resched. Receipts
89				
90	Part Name:	TOPS		
91	1	0	0	20
92	2	0	20	0
93	3	0	0	0
94	4	0	0	0
95	5	0	0	0
96	6	0	0	0
97	7	0	0	0
98	8	0	0	0
99	9	0	0	0
100	10	0	0	0
101	11	0	0	0
102	12	0	0	0
103	13	0	0	0
104	14	0	0	0
105	15	0	0	0
106	16	0	0	0
107	17	0	0	0

<u>Sensitivity Analysis (2) continued</u>: Go to the dialog box and check the Reschedule Scheduled Receipts box for TOPS. The user has to make this change.

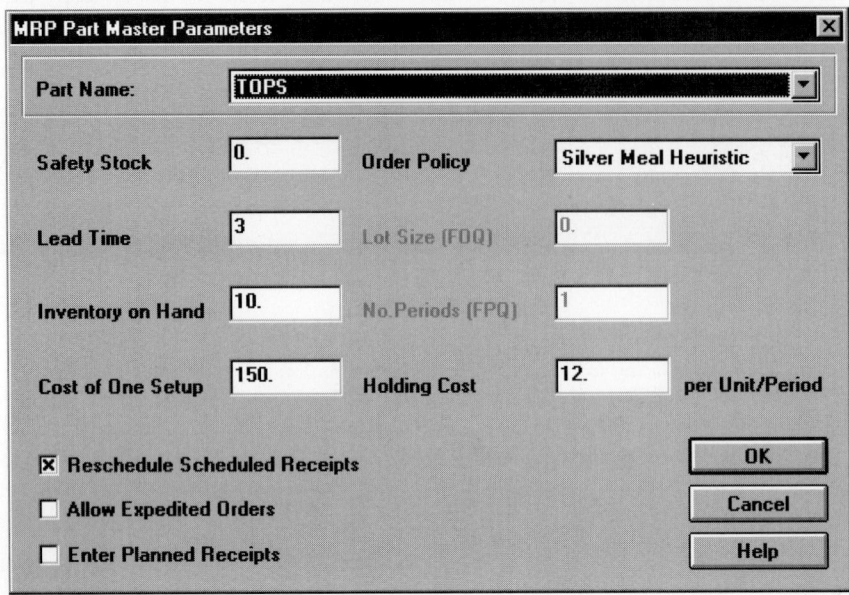

Run again. The output for TOPS will be as shown below.

PART NAME	TOPS							
Low Level	1							
Ordering Policy	SILMEA							
Safety Stock	0							
Lead Time	3							
On Hand Inventory	10							
User Reschedules Receipts?	YES							
Expediting allowed	NO							
User Provides Planned Rcpts?	NO							
Setup plus Holding Cost	150							
Period	1	2	3	4	5	6	7	8
Gross Requirements	45	0	0	0	0	0	0	0
Scheduled Receipts	0	20	0	0	0	0	0	0
Projected Available Balance	-15	-15	-15	0	0	0	0	0
Planned Order Releases	15	0	0	0	0	0	0	0
Expedite Orders?	NO	NO	NO	NO	NO	NO	NO	NO
Rescheduled Scheduled Rcpts	20	0	0	0	0	0	0	0
Planned Order Receipts	0	0	0	15	0	0	0	0
Independent Demand	0	0	0	0	0	0	0	0
Dependent Demand	45	0	0	0	0	0	0	0

Sensitivity Analysis (3): Finally, the user might wish to change the Planned Order Releases for ORD. Notice that after the two steps given above, there are still some shortages showing for TOPS and TOPO. (CASTERS should be expedited, and the planner makes a note of that -- but does not worry as much. because it is a bought out part, and the supplier is known to be reliable!) One method of reducing the shortages would be to reduce the planned order quantity of 130 units of ORD in period 2 to an order quantity of 120, and to increase the order quantity to 60 (from 50) in period 3. The user should verify that all that this change does with regard to the requirements for ORD is to drive the period ending balance for period 2 to zero, i.e., below the safety stock level established for this part. A method for accomplishing the postponement of planned orders of ORD would be to change the planned *receipts* corresponding to these two orders (currently the planned receipts are shown as 130 and 50 in periods 3 and 4 respectively). To do this, enter the planned receipts of 120 and 60 in periods 3 and 4 in the fourth column labeled "Planned Receipts," as shown below. The user has to make these changes.

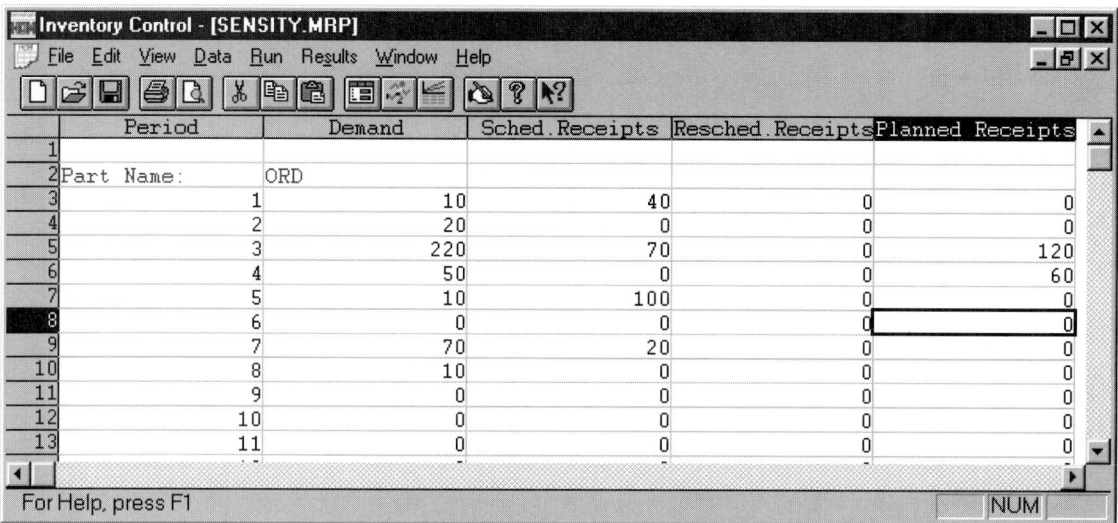

Check the "Enter Planned Receipts" check box for ORD.

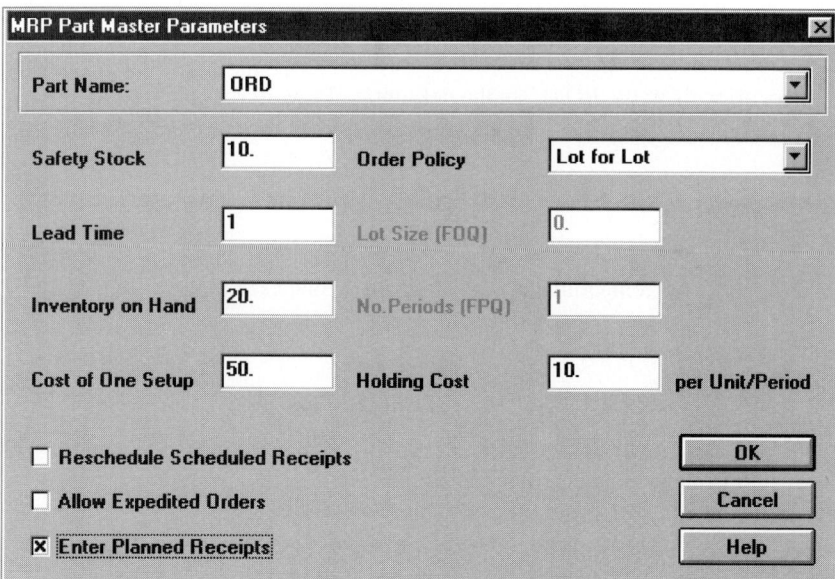

Sensitivity Analysis (3) continued: Run once again. The output for ORD alone is shown below. The shortage for TOPO in period 2 would have reduced by 10 units. The data file with all the above changes (1 through 3) is called SENSITY.MRP.

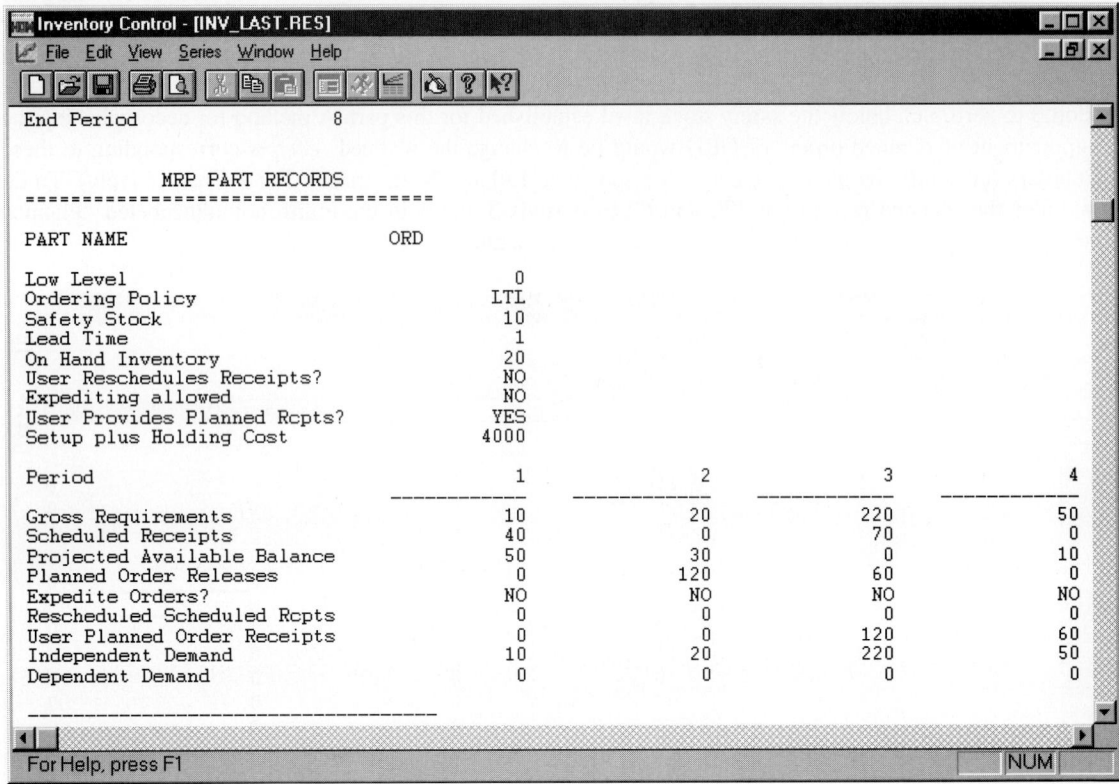

11. OUTLINE OF ALGORITHM

begin

1. Compute the low–level code for all parts in the BOM. By the definition of low–level coding, parts with low–level code i, can only have components with low–level code $j > i$. We shall refer to the low–level code as "Level."

2. MRP Calculations:

For code = lowest Level to highest Level, incrementing the value of code by one each time

Set startpd = Either 1 or the value entered by the user.

    2.1 Determine dependent demand
        For each parent — look at each child
        If the child's level = code, then add the parent's demand to the
        dependent demand for the child after multiplication by qtychild — because say
        parent has a demand in period 1 of 20, and 3 of the child are used to
        make one of the parent, then need 3*20 = 60 of the child.

    2.2 Find gross requirement
        Gross requirement is defined as the dependent demand
        plus the part's (independent) demand. The demand is a user input.
        For example demand could be for spare parts,
        whereas dependent demand could be what is required to make a complete product
        using this child.

2.3 Compute net requirements
   This is the Cumulative net requirement (repeat, cumulative).
   The projected on hand of the starting period is set equal to On Hand Inventory minus the safety stock.

There are 2 cases — has user rescheduled receipts?
If yes, use the rescheduled receipts, else use the scheduled receipts

Cumulative Net Requirements of period (j+1)
   = Gross Requirements of period (j) - Projected Available Balance at the
      end of period (j) - Scheduled (or Rescheduled Receipts) for period (j+1)

Projected Available Balance of period (j+1) = (-1)*Cumulative Net Requirements of period (j+1)

2.4 Carry out lot sizing calculations
   If expediting is not allowed, start the calculations in period (startpd + leadtime)
   else start from startpd.

   Case 1: Lot for Lot (LTL) or User Enters Planned Receipts
   This is the case when order code is LTL or user does not want
   the computer to calculate the planned orders.
   The logic is called lot for lot (LTL). This means that
   if 101 parts are needed in period 4 and lead time is 2 periods,
   simply plan an order in period, 4 - 2 = 2 for a quantity of 101.
   Recompute the cumulative net requirements for the remaining periods after determining each planned order.

   Case 2: The Fixed Order Quantity Rule (FOQ)
   Here the planned order must be in a multiple of the lot size.
   An example is 100 of the part are needed in period 4, lead time = 2 periods,
   and lot size = 75. Release order in period, 4 - 2 = 2, for 150 units (round up)
   Note that lot size must be > 0.
   Recompute the cumulative net requirements for the remaining periods after determining each planned order.

   Case 3: The Fixed Period Quantity (FPQ) Rule
   Here the user must plan for a fixed number of periods, say "PD."
   This is a fairly complex rule.
      Find the first period with positive net requirements.
      If no such period, go to next part.
      Starting from the first such period, call it first,

         Do in steps of PD, set j = first, first + PD + 1, first+ 2*PD+1 ....

            Find the cumulative maximum net requirement over the time
            bucket which starts with j, that is, max over the periods
            j, j+1, ..., j+PD.
            The max is needed because the cumulative net requirement
               need not be an increasing function of the period, this would be
               the case when there is a shipment expected in between in
               period j+1.
               Plan a receipt for period j equal to the maximum net
               requirement. Recompute the cumulative net requirements for
               the remaining periods.

         End do

<u>Cases 4, 5, 6 deal with the Silver Meal, Least Total Cost and Least Unit Cost Heuristics</u>
The heuristics attempt to tradeoff setup cost versus the inventory holding cost. A setup cost for a part is assumed to be incurred in each period in which there is a planned order for the part. Inventory holding cost is assessed based on the Projected Available Balance.

Please consult a textbook for a description of these heuristics.

    2.6 Determine the setup and holding costs, add back the safety stock to the Projected Available Balance. Write results to the Part Master.

end

12. GLOSSARY OF TERMS USED IN MATERIAL REQUIREMENTS PLANNING[*]

Bill of Material (BOM)	A listing of all subassemblies, intermediates, parts, and raw materials that go into a parent assembly showing the quantity required to make an assembly.
Dependent Demand	Demand that is directly related o or derived from the bill of materials structure for other items and end products. A given inventory item may have both dependent and independent demand at any given time. For example, a part may simultaneously be the component of an assembly and sold as a service part.
Expedited Orders	Planned orders that are required to be completed sooner than the lead time.
Fixed Order Quantity	A lot sizing technique in MRP that will always cause planned or actual orders to be generated for a predetermined fixed quantity, or multiples thereof, if net requirements for a period exceed the fixed order quantity.
Firm Planned Orders	A planned order that can be frozen in quantity and time. The computer is not allowed to change it automatically.
Fixed Period Quantity	A lot sizing technique that sets the order quantity equal to the net requirements for a given number of periods.
Gross Requirements	The total of dependent demand and independent demand for a component before the netting of on hand inventory and scheduled receipts. By convention the requirements are at the beginning of the period.
Independent Demand	Demand for an item that is unrelated to the demand for other items. For example, demand for finished goods, parts required for destructive testing, and service parts requirements.
Lead Time	A span of time required to perform a process (or series or operations). In MRP, the number of periods required to assemble (or manufacture) the item given all its subassemblies and components.
Least Total Cost	A dynamic lot sizing technique that calculates the order quantity by comparing the setup (or ordering) costs and the carrying cost for various lot sizes and selects the lot size where these costs are most nearly equal.
Least Unit Cost	A dynamic lot sizing technique that adds ordering cost and inventory holding cost for each trial lot size, picking the lot size with the lowest unit cost.
Lot For Lot	A lot sizing technique that generates planned orders in quantities exactly equal to the net requirements in a period.
Lot Size	The amount of a particular item that is ordered from the plant or a supplier or issued as a standard quantity to the production system.

---

[*] Source: *APICS Dictionary*, 8th ed.

Lot Sizing	The process or techniques used in determining lot sizes.
Low Level Code	A number that identifies the lowest level in any bill of material at which a particular component appears. Net requirements of a given component are not calculated until all the gross requirements have been calculated down to that level.
Net Requirements	In MRP, the net requirements for a part or an assembly are derived as a result of applying gross requirements and allocations against inventory on hand, scheduled receipts, and safety stock. Net requirements, when lot sized and offset for lead time become planned orders.
On Hand Inventory	On hand inventory or on hand balance is the quantity shown in the inventory as being physically in stock. By convention the quantity is available at the beginning of the first period in the planning horizon.
Planned Orders	A suggested order quantity, release date, and due date created by the planning system's logic when it encounters net requirements in processing MRP. Planned orders are created by the computer, exist only within the computer, and may be changed by the computer during subsequent processing if conditions change. Planned orders at one level will be exploded into gross requirements for components at the next level.
Planned Orders Receipts	That quantity planned to be received at a future date as a result of a planned order.
Projected Available Balance	An inventory balance projected into the future. It is the running sum of on hand inventory minus gross requirements plus scheduled receipts and planned orders. It is the projected period ending inventory.
Safety Stock	In general a quantity of stock planned in inventory to protect against fluctuations in demand or supply.
Scheduled Receipts	An open order that has been assigned a due date. An open order is a released manufacturing order or purchase order. By convention scheduled receipts should become available if production proceeds as per plan at the beginning of the period.
Silver Meal Heuristic	A dynamic lot sizing heuristic.

REFERENCES

Chase, R. B. and N. J. Aquilano. *Production and Operations Management*, 7th ed. Burr Ridge, IL: Richard D. Irwin, 1995.

Cox, J.F., III; J.H. Blackstone, Jr.; and M.S. Spencer, eds. *APICS, Dictionary, 8th ed.* VA: American Production and Inventory Control Society, 1995.

Nahmias, S. *Production and Operations Analysis*, 3rd ed. Burr Ridge, IL: Richard D. Irwin, 1997.

Stevenson, W. J. *Production/Operations Management*, 5th ed. Burr Ridge, IL: Richard D. Irwin, 1996.

Vollman, T. E.; W. L. Berry; and D. C. Whybark. *Manufacturing Planning and Control Systems,* 4th ed. Burr Ridge, IL: Richard D. Irwin, 1997.

AGGREGATE PLANNING

HOM's Capacity Management module uses a combination of linear, mixed integer, and dynamic programming as well as heuristics to solve problems. The methods used vary depending on the inputs given by the user. There are two parts to the solution procedure. In the first part, the problem is defined through user inputs (i.e., the objective function and constraints are generated). In the second part, the appropriate solution technique is invoked. The following are described below:

- The class of problems that can be solved using this module.
- The parameters and input data required.
- Methods used to solve the problems.
- The outputs generated by HOM.

1. PROBLEMS THAT CAN BE SOLVED USING THIS MODULE

The HOM Capacity Management module is designed for solving problems dealing with the determination of production activity levels and work force levels necessary to meet demand for various products over an intermediate range planning horizon. This type of planning, also called *aggregate planning,* is usually done over a 12- to 24-month horizon. The modeling capability of this HOM module is shown below.

Number of products	1 to 3
Planning horizon	2 to 24 periods
Types of strategy (plan types)	Optimal, Chase (zero inventory), Level Workforce, and Level Production
Number of constraining resources	1
Number of labor types	1
Process specification	Both run time as well as setup time for each product can be modeled
Option of subcontracting	Can be modeled
Option of operating second shift	Can be modeled
Shift premium for second shift	Can be modeled
Variable number of days in a period	Can be specified
Safety stock	Can be specified for each period and each product
Opening and desired ending inventory levels	Can be specified
Costs that can be modeled	Wages, overtime, undertime, hiring, firing, inventory holding cost, setup cost, cost of lost sales, and cost of backlogging sales
Other	Upper bounds on hiring, firing, inventory, and subcontracting; lower bounds on work force for operating a shift.

2. PARAMETERS AND DATA REQUIRED

2.1 Enter Period, Days in Period, Overtime

2.1.1 Period Names
When the opening DATA input spreadsheet of this module appears, you will notice that by default the periods have been named from 1 through 24. If you want to use your own period names, simply edit them into the appropriate cell.

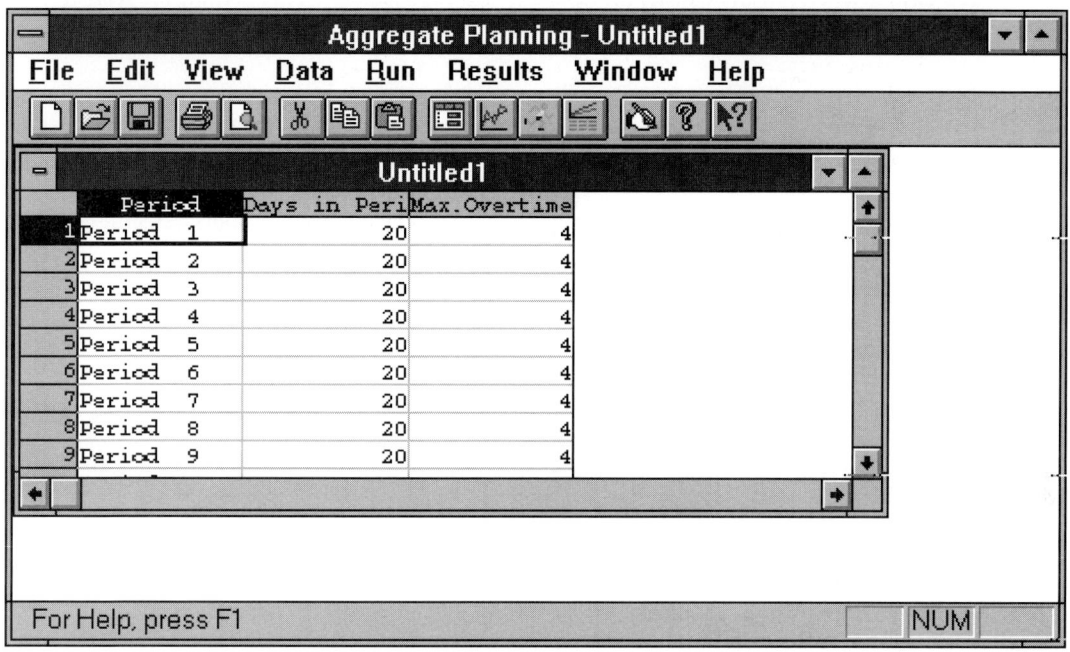

If you are using less than 24 periods, use the first n *periods and ignore the remaining ones.* If this bothers your artistic sensibility, simply edit out the unused rows using the Edit or DATA functions. Before doing a complete analysis, HOM will always prompt you as to the contiguous range of time periods you intend to use.

2.1.2 Days in a Period and Maximum Overtime
The default setting assumes that a period is a month with 20 days and that the maximum overtime allowable in a day is four hours. If you want to vary the number of working days in a month or the maximum hours of overtime that can be worked in a day of that month, edit the appropriate cells of the spreadsheet.

2.1.3 Modeling Permutations
HOM is very adaptable. Thus, if you want to plan for up to 24 weeks with varying numbers of days and varying maximum allowable overtime in each week, or you want to split each month into two 10–14-day periods and plan accordingly, simply enter the desired data. Caution, however, must be exercised by the user to ensure that Time Units— that is year, month, day, or hour— are consistent for any one problem analysis (see box below).

2.1.4 Column Too Small?
If your data is too big for a column, and/or there are words in a column you cannot completely read, you can expand the column width by clicking on the right side of the column heading and dragging it, or using the DATA, Product, Add, Column Width functions on the HOM command line.

After specifying your inputs, it is strongly recommended that you save your work using the FILE, Save As function on the HOM command line.

> **Time Units and Related Decisions in the Capacity Management Module**
>
> The unit of planning is a period.
>
> The planning horizon is made up of n periods, with $1 <= n <= 24$.
>
> Each period has a given number of days. The default is 20 days per period.
>
> The days in a period can be different from one period to another. This permits the realistic modeling of a working calendar.
>
> There can be up to two shifts in a day. The second shift option is modeled as a 0 or 1 decision variable for each period. In words, the decision each period is whether there should be a second shift for the entire period or no second shift at all during that period.
>
> Each shift has a fixed and equal number of hours in it. The default is 8 hours per shift (see Parameters dialog box).
>
> Wages are paid either on a per hour basis or on a per period basis (choose in Parameters dialog box).
>
> The run time and setup time are specified in hours (and fractions thereof). For example, 1.2 hours = 1 hour 12 minutes. The user can choose time units suitable for the problem at hand—while conforming to this framework.

2.2. Enter Product Name, Demand and Desired Safety Stock (SS)

Provide the demand data for up to three products you are going to produce.

2.2.1 Adding a product
Use the DATA, Product, Add functions from the HOM command line to add a product. Each time you do so, HOM will give the new product an incremental name (by default set to Product 1, Product 2, etc.). You can edit in your own product names if you desire.

2.2.2 Demand and Safety Stock
Each time you Add a variable, HOM will generate two incremental columns on your DATA input spreadsheet. The columns will be labeled, **D**:<name of product> and **SS**: <name of product>, where **D** stands for Demand and **SS** for Safety Stock. The columns for entering Demand are grouped together and so are the columns for entering the Safety Stock. (You may have to scroll to the right to see the newly created Safety Stock column.) The two extra columns so generated should be filled in.

> The first of the new columns corresponds to the demand for the product that you have just added. Enter the demand for the product in each period. If in your problem the planning horizon is only six periods, you should enter the demand in the first six rows.
>
> In the second new column, enter a safety stock level for the product (you have added) for each period. The safety stock can be different for different periods. It should be a number greater than or equal to zero, and of a magnitude such that its availability at the end of the specified period will give you some assurance of meeting demand if it is viewed as being uncertain.
>
> Once you have completed enumerating all the products, their demand, and safety stocks, we recommend saving the data using the Save As capability of the FILE function on the HOM command line.

A sample spreadsheet with data for 3 products and 24 periods (labeled January through December) is shown below.

Sample Data File

CHASE.DAT

Period		Days	Max.O	D: Product 1	D: Product 2	D: Product 3	SS: Product 1	SS: Product 2	SS: Product 3
1	Jan	20	4	87	0	0	200	20	20
2	Feb	20	4	2740	520	326	20	20	20
3	Mar	20	4	3210	2466	653	20	20	20
4	Apr	20	4	3210	2466	653	200	20	20
5	May	20	4	2675	477	294	20	20	20
6	Jun	20	4	4012	637	418	20	20	20
7	Jul	20	4	2675	1814	1310	20	20	20
8	Aug	20	4	4012	3183	1633	2000	20	20
9	Sep	20	4	6220	2390	2613	200	20	20
10	Oct	20	4	9362	2390	2613	20	20	20
11	Nov	20	4	9710	143	196	20	20	20
12	Dec	20	4	2740	520	326	20	20	20
13	Jan	20	4	3210	2466	653	20	20	20
14	Feb	20	4	3210	2466	653	2000	20	20
15	Mar	20	4	2675	477	294	20	20	20
16	Apr	20	4	4012	637	418	200	20	20
17	May	20	4	2675	1814	1310	20	20	20
18	Jun	20	4	4012	3183	1633	20	20	20
19	Jul	20	4	6220	2390	2613	20	20	20
20	Aug	20	4	9362	2390	2613	20	20	20
21	Sep	20	4	9710	143	196	20	20	20
22	Oct	20	4	2740	520	326	20	20	20
23	Nov	20	4	3210	2466	653	20	20	20
24	Dec	20	4	3210	2466	653	20	20	20

Product Cost/Time Data

2.3 Enter Other Product Data

Capacity management requires product-specific data other than demand and safety stock. For simplicity's sake, these items are input on the bottom half of the DATA spreadsheet rather than in an entirely new spreadsheet or window. As this data is product specific, it is incorporated below the product demand data. To reach this area, scroll down the DATA spreadsheet until you reach the section entitled Product Cost/Time Data. The data items and their default values and units are listed below in a table. Sample data is shown, followed by brief descriptions of the data items.

Product Cost/Time Data	Default Value	Units
Inventory Holding Cost		$/Unit/Period
Backorder Cost	1,000,000,000	$/Unit/Period
Lost Sales Cost	1,000,000,000	$/Unit/Period
Setup Time		Hours/Setup
Setup Cost		$/Setup
Run Time		Hours/Unit
Subcontracting Cost	1,000,000,000	$/Unit
Max. Subcontracting Qty. / Period	1,000,000,000	Units
Starting Inventory		Units
Desired Ending Inventory		Units
Maximum Inventory	1,000,000,000	Units

When you have completed this section remember to save your data using <u>FILE</u> and <u>Save As</u>.

Sample Data

CHASE.DAT

Period	Days in Period	Max. Overtime	D:Product 1	D:Product 2	D:Product 3	SS:Product 1
Jan	20	4	3210	2466	653	20
Feb	20	4	3210	2466	653	2000
Mar	20	4	2675	477	294	20
Apr	20	4	4012	637	418	200
May	20	4	2675	1814	1310	20
Jun	20	4	4012	3183	1633	20
Jul	20	4	6220	2390	2613	20
Aug	20	4	9362	2390	2613	20
Sep	20	4	9710	143	196	20
Oct	20	4	2740	520	326	20
Nov	20	4	3210	2466	653	20
Dec	20	4	3210	2466	653	20

Product Cost/Time Data

Inventory Holding Cost	2.12	3.47	3.72	$/Unit/Period
Backorder Cost	1000	1000	1000	$/Unit/Period
Lost Sales Cost	105	172	184	$/Unit/Period
Setup Time	80	80	80	Hours/Setup
Setup Cost	1000	1000	1000	$/Setup
Run Time	0.3458	0.379	0.4013	Hours/Unit
Subcontracting Cost	50000	50000	50000	$/Unit
Max. Subcontracting Qty. / Period	1000000	1000000	1000000	Units
Starting Inventory	780	0	426	Units
Desired Ending Inventory	5000	3000	3000	Units
Maximum Inventory	1000000	1000000	1000000	Units

2.3.1 Inventory Holding Cost

The inventory holding cost of a product is the dollar cost of holding one unit of the product in inventory for one period. The default value is zero (blanks are treated as zero).

2.3.2 Backorder Cost
The cost of backorder is the cost of satisfying current demand in the future, in dollars per unit per period. Setting this cost at a high level ($1,000,000,000—by default) will be tantamount to excluding backordering as a feasible way of satisfying current demand. Please note that the model assumes backorders will be filled in the future and also that there should be no backorders at the end of the planning horizon.

2.3.3 Lost Sales Cost
This is the penalty a firm might incur by not having a unit to sell when it is demanded. The minimum this cost should be is the lost profit margin and contributions to overhead of that product, and it could be much greater if future lost sales may be engendered by the current lost sale. The cost is in dollars per unit of lost sales. Setting this cost at a high level ($1,000,000,000—by default) will be tantamount to excluding lost sales as an option for matching demand and supply.

2.3.4 Setup Time
The setup time for a product is the total regular-shift labor hours necessary to set up the chosen product (i.e., 20 people each working four hours to set up would be 80 hours of setup time). This can vary from product to product. The default value is zero (blanks are treated as zero).

2.3.5 Setup Cost
The setup cost is any extra costs, other than the cost of labor, incurred by changing from one product to another, such as special equipment, cleansers, part-time labor, special talent labor, and so on. The default value is zero (blanks are treated as zero).

> Repeat: the setup cost should *NOT include* the cost of the labor hours required to carry out the setup (HOM accounts for this automatically).

2.3.6 Run Time
The run time is the amount of time required to produce a unit of a specific product. It is given as a decimal equivalent to a fraction of an hour. The model assumption is that labor time and run time are equivalent—that is, if 1.8 hours is the run time for Product 1, then in order to produce 100 units of Product 1, 100×1.8 hours = 180 hours of labor are necessary. The default value is zero (blanks are treated as zero).

2.3.7 Subcontracting Cost and Maximum Subcontracting Quantity
One way of meeting demand is outsourcing production to another vendor. HOM allows for this, and the user must enter the subcontracting cost for a unit for each product.

The user can also specify the maximum amount of demand that can be satisfied in this manner. The default has been set as a very large number, namely 1,000,000,000.

If no subcontracting is desired, set a very high cost of subcontracting ($1,000,000,000—by default) and set the maximum quantity at zero.

2.3.8 Starting, Ending, and Maximum Inventory Levels
Starting and ending inventory levels by product, as well as the maximum amount of inventory that can be carried, are input in the last three rows of the spreadsheet.

(a) Starting Inventory
The starting inventory level is the quantity of product available at the *beginning* of the first period.

(b) Desired Inventory Level
The desired ending inventory level is the desired quantity of product at the *end* of the planning horizon. Note that it may not always be possible to attain the desired ending inventory level. For example, if the starting inventory is 1000 and demand during the planning horizon is zero, then the ending inventory level cannot be different from 1000. HOM will try to achieve an ending inventory level that is the closest possible to the one desired by the user—please see formulation below.

(c) Maximum Inventory Level

The maximum amount of inventory could also be unachievable. For example, with a level production policy, very high inventories might be unavoidable. HOM makes suitable adjustments to the maximum inventory level when the level production policy is specified or when the opening inventory is itself too high. Details of the adjustments can be found in the section on formulation.

2.4 Plot Demand

Before you start the specification of your problem, you might like to plot the demand data that you have entered to get a better feel for it. To do this, use the Parameters dialog box and specify which of the products you would like to inspect by clicking on it in the Select Products section of the box, then click on OK. Next click on the DATA menu item on the command line and click on Plot Demand. Plots of the demand for all the products you choose will appear. To make the graph bigger, simply click on the maximize arrow (up arrow, right-hand corner of the box). To return to the Parameters dialog box, use the command line or appropriate icon. The plot of demand for the three products in the sample data file is shown below.

Sample Data

CHASE.DAT   **Plot of Demand**

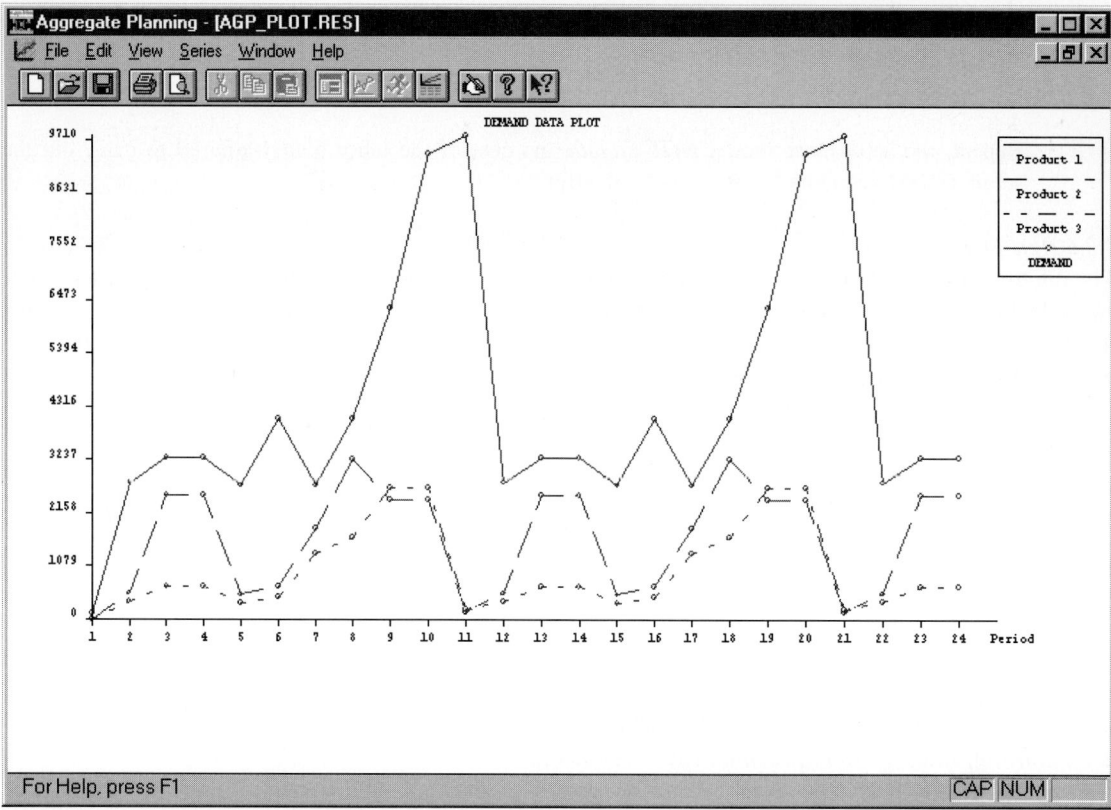

2.5 Input Data Necessary For Specifying A Model

To complete specification of your capacity management problem, information is needed on,
(i) the planning horizon, product selection, plan type, and solution technique
(ii) the wage rates
(iii) the work force composition
(iv) the cost of changes to the work force.

This data has to be input in the Parameters dialog box. The Parameters dialog box as shown below has been divided into four subareas to address each of these issues.

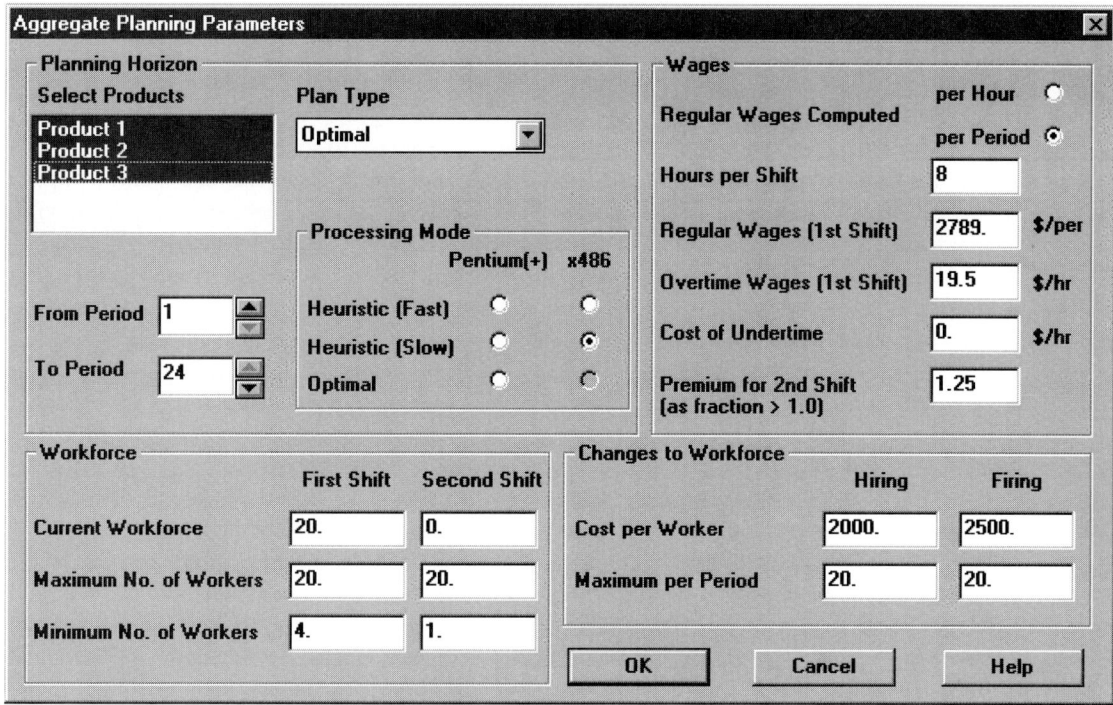

Once you have completed the PARAMETERS dialog box, you should click on the OK element and move onto the RUN command line function.

2.5.1 Planning Horizon, Product Selection, Plan Type, and Solution Technique.

(a) Planning Horizon

        The number of time periods to plan for.

        The user can manipulate the up/down buttons to choose the time periods to be planned. Make sure your ending period is at least one greater than your starting period, or else the computer gives you a warning to which you must respond several times to advance to the ending period.

(b) Select Products

        Choose the products to include in the aggregate plan.

        The upper-left-hand side subbox of the Parameters dialog box gives you the opportunity to select any subset of the products previously specified in the spreadsheet by clicking on each one on the list that you want to include. (Active products will have a blue background.)

(c) Plan Type

        Select from one of four types of planning strategies.

        HOM gives you the opportunity to select one of four plans. If you click on the down arrow by Plan Type, you will see the possibilities: Optimal, Chase (zero inventory), Level Workforce, and Level Production. The first will search for the "optimal" allocation of all the variables that minimizes the cost of meeting the demand subject to the restrictions of the problem. The solution methodology uses a mixed integer programming technique to find the true optimal solution. Historically, several other potentially nonoptimal approaches were used due to their often shorter solution times. We have emulated these historical approaches, but still use optimum seeking methodologies, by further constraining the problem to have zero inventory (chase), a level work force, or level production. There may be many practical reasons to use one of the latter strategies, and thus, it is good to investigate the cost tradeoffs among the alternatives. Also see the description of the Plan Types given below and Section 3 on problem formulation.

(d) Processing Mode

Customize the amount of computing resources to devote to solving the problem.
The solution of these types of capacity management problems are very computer intensive. Thus, we have given the user the opportunity to use methodologies that employ cutoff strategies for stopping a solution run. These run quicker. The results gained by these heuristics are often close enough to optimal that it might be beneficial doing extensive sensitivity analysis investigations using a heuristic rather than waiting several hours for a slow processor to find a true optimal solution. To choose which processing mode you want to use, simply click on the appropriate button. Please see the formulation for more details about the cutoff strategies. Also see Processing Mode as described below.

Plan Type (Parameters Dialog Box)

There are four options to choose from the drop down list. The options are briefly described below. More details can be found in a standard text book.

Optimal: The problem to solved to optimality or using heuristic procedures. Briefly, if there are no setups, setup cost, or second shift options, then the problem is solved using Linear Programming. The workforce levels are made integral using a dynamic programming algorithm. Else if the number of products times the number of periods in the planning horizon is less than or equal to 24, then too the above procedures are invoked. In all other cases, the planning horizon is partitioned and the problem solved using a rolling planning horizon heuristic, see section 3.

Chase (0 inventory): The period ending inventories are constrained to be equal to the safety stock specified for the products for that period. This could result in infeasibility if the initial inventory is too high (free disposal of extra inventory is not permitted). The HOM module eliminates this possibility by preprocessing the data to ensure feasibility. The problem is solved either to optimality or using heuristic procedures, see section 3.

Level Workforce: The workforce is constrained to be the same every period. However production levels and subcontract quantities are allowed to vary period to period. The problem will be solved either to optimality or based on a heuristic (please see manual) subject to this constraint on the workforce. *Due to the nature of the heuristics employed – please experiment with different values of the minimum number of workers in the first and second shift to obtain the "best" possible solution.*

Level Production: The production is constrained to be equal every period. However subcontract quantities can vary from one period to another. The problem is solved to optimality. The number of workers is made integral using a dynamic programming algorithm, see section 3.

Processing Mode (Parameters Dialog Box)

The Aggregate Planning module uses Linear or Mixed Integer Programming techniques to solve problems. The Mixed Integer Programming techniques are time consuming. This technique will be used when there are setups, and/or second shift options and/or setup costs.

In the absense of these three, the problem will be solved as a Linear Program, fairly rapidly. The processing mode *does not play a role* in this case.

The module provides the user some flexibility in determining how much computing resources to devote to solving a particular problem. The user can select from one of five options: two for x486 machines and three for Pentium machines.

The heuristic procedures limit the number of iterations performed. Please section 3.

Selecting Optimal (for Pentium machines) *does not* guarantee an optimal solution if the number of products times the length of the planning horizon exceeds 24. Please consult section 3 for details.

2.5.2 Wages.

Regular Wage Computed The first choice is to decide on whether labor will be paid by the hour or by the period. If you specify "per Hour" then labor is somewhat variable within a period, while paying labor "per Period" assumes that labor is somewhat fixed. Labor with any level of skill is usually considered to be fixed for a period. You would not hire skilled workers for a day, fire them the next, and then rehire them the following day. The effect of these two alternatives is important to investigate in a sensitivity analysis. Make your choice and click on the appropriate button.

Hours per Shift You next need to specify the hours in a shift. The default value is set at eight.

Regular Wages (1st Shift) If you have chosen the per Period wage, then the value to be entered is obtained by multiplying the hours worked in a period (the number of days in a period times the number of hours in a day) by the wage rate, including benefits. If you have previously chosen the per Hour option, simply enter the per hour wage rate.

Overtime wages (1st Shift) The overtime rates are given on a dollar per hour basis.

Cost of Undertime Some professionals feel that the lack of work can be as costly as overtime work, and thus, a cost of undertime possibility is also provided. It should also be entered on a dollar per hour basis. No distinction can be made between cost of undertime in the first versus cost of undertime in the second shift.

Premium for 2nd Shift Most organizations give non–prime time labor a shift differential. This premium is entered in the last box in the wages section. A shift premium of 10 percent would be entered as 1.1. The default value for the premium has been set equal to one.

2.5.3 Work Force Composition.

Current Workforce
First specify the number of workers that are currently working on the first and seconds shift (if active) by filling in the appropriate boxes.

Maximum/Minimum No. of Workers
Most operating facilities cannot expand and contract the number of workers continuously without eventually affecting productivity or, equivalently, the run time needed to produce a specific unit of product. HOM thus gives the user the

opportunity to enter a maximum and minimum number of workers that can be used for each shift to maintain the run time numbers previously given in the spreadsheet.

(Envision Charlie Chaplin having the run of an entire factory in the film Modern Times to produce just one unit of output. The user can specify a minimum number of workers on both shifts, which makes using a shift reasonable. Similar arguments can be made for shift maximums.)

2.5.4 Cost of Changes to the Work Force.

Hiring costs would normally incorporate the time required for training and lost productivity due to lack of familiarity with job tasks. The cost of firing workers is dependent on labor contracts.

Most labor markets are constrained, and thus, you might be limited with regard to the maximum number of people you could hire in any period. Likewise, firing too many workers in a period might give the organization a bad reputation, which it would like to avoid. The cost numbers should be entered as a one-time cost, not a per hour value (i.e., $2,500). The default values are set extremely high.

3. METHODS AND TECHNIQUES EMPLOYED

3.1 Notation

Number of periods = m
Number of products = n
Demand for product i in period j = $d(i,j)$
Holding cost for product i = $h(i)$ per unit per period
Backlog cost for product i = $b(i)$ per unit per period
Lost sales cost for product i = $l(i)$ per unit
Opening inventory of product i = $I(i,1)$
Desired ending inventory for product i = $I(i,m+1)$
Safety stock for product i in period j = $ss(i,j)$
Runtime for product i = $r(i)$
Setup time for product i = $s(i)$
Setup cost for product i = $setupcost(i)$ per setup
Cost of subcontracting out production for product i = $subconcost(i)$ per unit
Number of workers at beginning of planning period in shift k = $Men(k,0)$, $k=1, 2$
Normal wages per person per period = $wages$
Normal hours per person in a shift = $hours$
Normal cost of overtime per hour = $otcost$
Undertime cost per hour = $utcost$
Number of days in period j = $days(j)$
Maximum overtime permitted per person in period j = $otmax(j)$
Second shift premium = $secshift$
    Wages for second shift = $wages * secshift$
    Otcost in second shift = $otcost * secshift$
Maximum number of workers in the first shift = $maxmen1$
Minimum number of workers in the first shift = $minmen1$
Maximum number of workers in the second shift = $maxmen2$
Minimum number of workers in the second shift = $minmen2$
Maximum inventory level for product i = $maxinv(i)$
Maximum subcontract quantity per period for product i = $maxsub(i)$
Maximum number of workers that can be hired in a period = $maxhire$
Maximum number of workers that can be fired in a perioood = $maxfire$
Cost of hiring one worker = $hire$
Cost of firing one worker = $fire$

3.2 Decision Variables

Production of product i in period j = $P(i,j)$
Opening inventory of product i in period j = $I(i,j)$
Opening backlog of product i in period j = $B(i,j)$
Lost sales of product i in period j = $L(i,j)$
Subcontracted quantity of product i in period j = $SC(i,j)$
Setup variable for product i in period j = $SET(i,j)$
    { = 0 if no production and = 1 if there is any production of product i in period j}
Workers in period j in shift k = $Men(k,j)$
Secondshift variable for period j = $SEC(j)$
    { = 0 if there is no second shift and = 1 if there is a second shift in period j }
Overtime given in period j in shift k = $OT(k,j)$
Undertime in period j = $UT(j)$
Number of workers hired in period j = $H(j)$
Number of workers fired in period j = $F(j)$

3.3 Constraints

(a) <u>People Balance Constraints</u>

$$Men(1,j) + Men(2,j) = Men(1,j-1) + Men(2,j-1) + H(j) - F(j), \quad \text{for } j = 1, 2, \ldots, m$$

(b) <u>Setup Constraints</u>

$$P(i,j) <= M * SET(i,j) \quad \text{for } j = 1, 2, \ldots, m, \; i = 1, 2, \ldots, n$$

where <u>M</u> is a large number (set equal to total demand for periods j to m <u>plus</u> desired ending inventory for product i)

c) <u>Inventory Balance Constraints</u>

$$I(i,j) + P(i,j) - B(i,j) + SC(i,j) = d(i,j) + I(i,j+1) - L(i,j+1) - B(i,j)$$
$$\text{for } j = 1, 2, \ldots, m, \; i = 1, 2, \ldots, n$$

d) <u>Production (Resource Availability)</u>

$$r(1) * P(1,j) + s(1) * SET(1,j) + \ldots + r(m) * P(m,j) + s(m) * SET(m,j) + UT(j) =$$

$$days(j)*hours*Men(1,j) + OT(1,j) + days(j)*hours*Men(2,j) + OT(2,j) \,;$$

$$\text{for } j = 1, 2, \ldots, m$$

e) <u>Bounds on Inventory</u>

$$I(i,j) >= ss(i,j) \quad \text{for } i = 1, 2, \ldots, n, \; j = 2, 3, \ldots, m$$

$$I(i,j) <= \max\{ I(i,1) - (d(i,1)+d(i,2)+\ldots+d(i,j)), maxinv(i)\}$$

$I(i,1)$ and $I(i,m+1)$ are given as data items. The value of $I(i,m+1)$, that is, the desired ending inventory, is checked for feasibility. If the program turns out to be infeasible or the lost sales excessive, then the value of maximum inventory is relaxed completely and run again.

When the strategy is zero inventory, that is, Chase, it may be impossible to achieve the zero inventory criterion, namely, $I(i,j) = ss(i,j)$. Instead we employ the following procedure:

z = min of safety stock for periods 1 to m for product i.
$x = 0$
if(x.lt.I(i,1)-z-d(i,1)+1) then
$x = I(i,1)-z-d(i,1)+1$
endif
maxinv(i,1) = x + ss(i,1)
endif
for period $m > j > 1$
   $x = I(i,1)$ - (sum of demand from periods 1 to j) - z
   maxinv(i,j) = max(x,0) + ss(i,j)
for period m
   $x = I(i,1)$ - (sum of demand from periods 1 to m) - z
   maxinv(i,m) = max(x,0) + I(i,m+1)

(f)   <u>Maximum and Minimum Work Force and Adjustments Possible</u>

$H(j) <= maxhire$	
$F(j) <= maxfire$	
$minmen1 <= Men(i,1) <= maxmen1$	
$Men(i,2) <= maxmen2$	
$minmen2*SEC(j) <= Men(2,j)$	for $j = 1, 2, ... , m$

(g)   <u>Maximum Overtime and Subcontracting Possible</u>

$OT(1,J) <= Men(1,j)*maxot(j)$	
$OT(2,j) <= Men(2,j)*maxot(j)$	for $k = 1, 2, \ j=1, 2, ... , m$
$SC(i,j) <= maxsub(i)$	for $i = 1,2,..,n, \ j = 1,2,...,m$

3.4 Objective Function

$$
\begin{aligned}
\text{MIN} \quad & h(1) * (I(1,1) + I(1,2) + \ldots + I(1,m)) + \ldots + h(n) * (I(n,1) + I(n,2) + \ldots I(n,m)) + \\
& b(1) * (B(1,1) + B(1,2) + \ldots + B(1,m)) + \ldots + b(n) * (B(n,1) + B(n,2) + \ldots B(n,m)) + \\
& l(1) * (L(1,1) + L(1,2) + \ldots + L(1,m)) + \ldots + l(n) * (L(n,1) + L(n,2) + \ldots L(n,m)) + \\
& subconcost(1) * (SC(1,1) + SC(1,2) + \ldots + SC(1,m)) + \ldots + subconcost(n) * (SC(n,1) + \\
& SC(n,2) + \ldots SC(n,m)) + setupcost(1) * (SET(1,1) + \ldots + SET(1,m)) + \ldots + \\
& setupcost(n) * (SET(n,1) + \ldots + SET(n,m)) + wages * (Men(1,1) + \ldots + Men(1,m)) + secshift * wages * \\
& (Men(2,1) + \ldots + Men(2,m)) + otcost * (OT(1,1) + \ldots + OT(1,m)) + secshift * otcost * (OT(2,1) + \ldots \\
& + OT(2,m)) + utcost * (UT(1) + UT(2) + \ldots + UT(m)) + hire * (H(1) + H(2) + \ldots + H(m)) + fire * \\
& (F(1) + F(2) + \ldots + F(m))
\end{aligned}
$$

<u>Note</u>: If wages are paid on a hourly basis, then the wages are suitably modified [i.e., to $wages*days(j)*hours*(Men(j,1) + secshft*Men(j,2))$].

3.5 Other Conventions

IF	THEN
maxmen1 < 0	maxmen1 = 1.0e09
maxmen2 < 0	maxmen2 = 1.0e09
maxhire < 0	maxhire = maxmen1 + maxmen2
maxfire < 0	maxfire = maxmen1 + maxmen2
utcost < 0	utcost = 0
maxot(j) < 0	maxot(j) = 0

3.6 Solution Technique

The problem is solved in two passes. The LP and MILP solvers are based on codes developed by the authors. These codes are being revised to improve the speed as well as the accuracy of the solution.

Pass I Initially, the number of workers is *not* constrained to be integer.
If the setup time as well as setup costs are zero, then the program is solved to optimality as a linear program using the dual simplex method.
Else If the strategy is chosen as Level Production, then the problem is solved to optimality using a mixed integer programming (MILP) technique that incorporates a branch-and-bound procedure to solve for integer values of the zero-one variables (setup, *SET(i,j)*, and second-shift option, *SEC(j)*).
Else If the (number of products+1) times the number of periods is less than 24, then the problem is once again solved to optimality using a MILP.
Else a heuristic procedure is used. In this procedure, a rolling planning horizon, *RPH,* is first selected. The value of this horizon is equal to 12 when there is one product, 8 when there are two products, and 6 when there are three products. The problem is solved initially for *RPH* periods—and the solution is used to set up a problem for another *RPH* period, and so forth. The psuedo code for the procedure is as follows:

```
        do nplan = 1, ceiling(2n/NPH) - 1        !ceiling rounds up a number to its nearest
                                                 ! integer value
    {       start_period = NPH/2*(nplan-1) + 1;
            end_period = min(start_period + NPH - 1, m);

            if(start_period != 1)
            {set initial inventory and workforce = initial workforce of start_period
                    obtained during the last solution}
            else
            {set initial inventory and workforce = given data}

            if(end_period != m)
            {set ending inventory = safety stock of end_period}
            else
            {set ending inventory = desired ending inventory}
                            !feasibility of this setting is checked before
                            !calling the MILP procedure.

            solve the subproblem to optimality using the MILP procedure;
    }
        enddo
```

Pass II The LP or MILP solution will usually contain fractional values for the number of workers. A dynamic programming procedure is then used to round up and down the values of workers so as to select the final combination of workers. This process may lead to violation of the maximum overtime hours that can be worked in a shift. Experience with this procedure suggests that such violations are usually small. The dynamic program is based on the assumption that the number of workers can only be either rounded down or rounded up. A backward induction procedure is used.

Note of Caution: The heuristic procedure described above could produce very poor solutions when the strategy chosen is "Level Workforce." Please see section 3.7, "Variations" for a fix to the problem.

3.7 Variations

If the user does not want a particular decision variable in the final solution, then the corresponding cost for that variable could be set to a large value. This can be done to prevent second-shift operation (set second shift premium to be 100,000, say), subcontracting, lost sales, backlogged sales, or even hiring and firing of workers.

The Optimal and Chase (zero inventory) strategies are produced using the procedure described above.

The Level Production strategy is obtained by constraining the production of each product (as well as the work force) to be the same in each period. As no heuristic is employed, a true optimal solution is obtained for this case.

The Level Workforce strategy poses the most serious problem when using the above procedure. However, the fix is quite simple. Experiment with different levels of minimum number of workers in the first and second shift until a reasonable solution has been obtained.

4. RUN MODEL

To run a previously specified model, simply click on the RUN icon or the RUN menu item on the command line. Once a RUN has commenced, a message appears on the screen informing you that the RUN will take some time. The run time can be up to 30 minutes if setup times are greater than zero and the second-shift option has been specified. The computer will be unavailable to the user during this time.

The only way to stop a RUN is to hit the Ctrl, Alt, and Delete keys simultaneously. A message will appear, giving you the option of returning to Windows or starting the machine over again. Choose the Enter option and return to HOM to start your analysis over again. When you exit in this manner your data will be lost, so we advise you to save your data as often as possible.

5. RESULTS

At the end of a RUN, the output results will appear on the screen automatically. These results can be recalled at any time by clicking on the RESULTS icon or the RESULTS_toolbar menu item and then clicking on Last Results. Results can be saved using the FILE --> Save As function. Similarly, the Open command of the RESULTS function may be used to recall previous results that have been named and saved using the FILE --> Save As toolbar function.

The default RESULTS graph plots the production in each period (remember that these results can be enlarged by using the maximize arrow in the top right corner of this window). Below the graph is a textual output depicting the optimal production cost numbers for the problem specified in the Parameters dialog box. Period costs for Setup, Subcontracting, Inventory, Backlog, and Lost Sales are listed.

Scrolling down the document, you encounter these costs totaled for all periods. The work force costs, namely, period costs for wages, overtime, undertime, hiring, and firing, are given next. Continuing to scroll down the output file, one encounters the total cost of these items, plus the total cost of production.

Then, for each product in turn, data is given for the actual amounts demanded, produced, and subcontracted; opening period inventories and backlog; and, scrolling to the right, lost sales. Continuing down the file, the data on the work force is shown, such as the number of workers on each shift and their overtime hours, as well as the amount of undertime. The number of workers hired and fired in each period completes the RESULTS file. Remember that the non-graphical results can be exported to a spreadsheet or word processing program.

5.1 Customizing Output

To portray more information in a graphical manner, the Series function can be used on the HOM toolbar. For each product, demand, production, and inventory levels can be plotted simultaneously. Total work force can also be plotted, but is often very small in comparison to production and thus often conforms to the x axis. It should thus be plotted separately. The graphical output cannot be exported easily. The text below the graph can be easily exported to a spreadsheet by using EDIT. It can also be eliminated by clicking on the appropriate box in the Series window. To view multiple outputs at the same time, the Window function can be used. The use of this function is described more fully in the forecasting module. A snapshot of the Series dialog box is shown below.

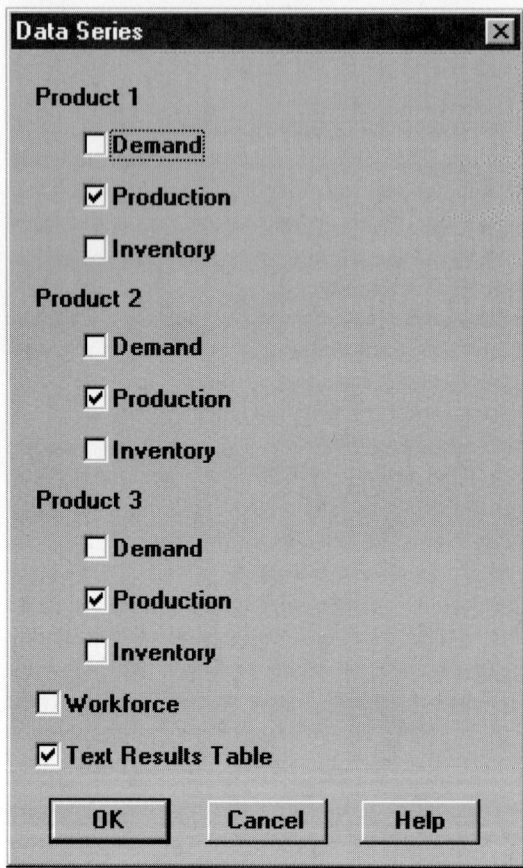

5.2 Sample Outputs (Run Times for Pentium Pro 200 Machine)

Sample Data File

<u>CHASE.DAT</u>   **Optimal**   **(8 minutes)**

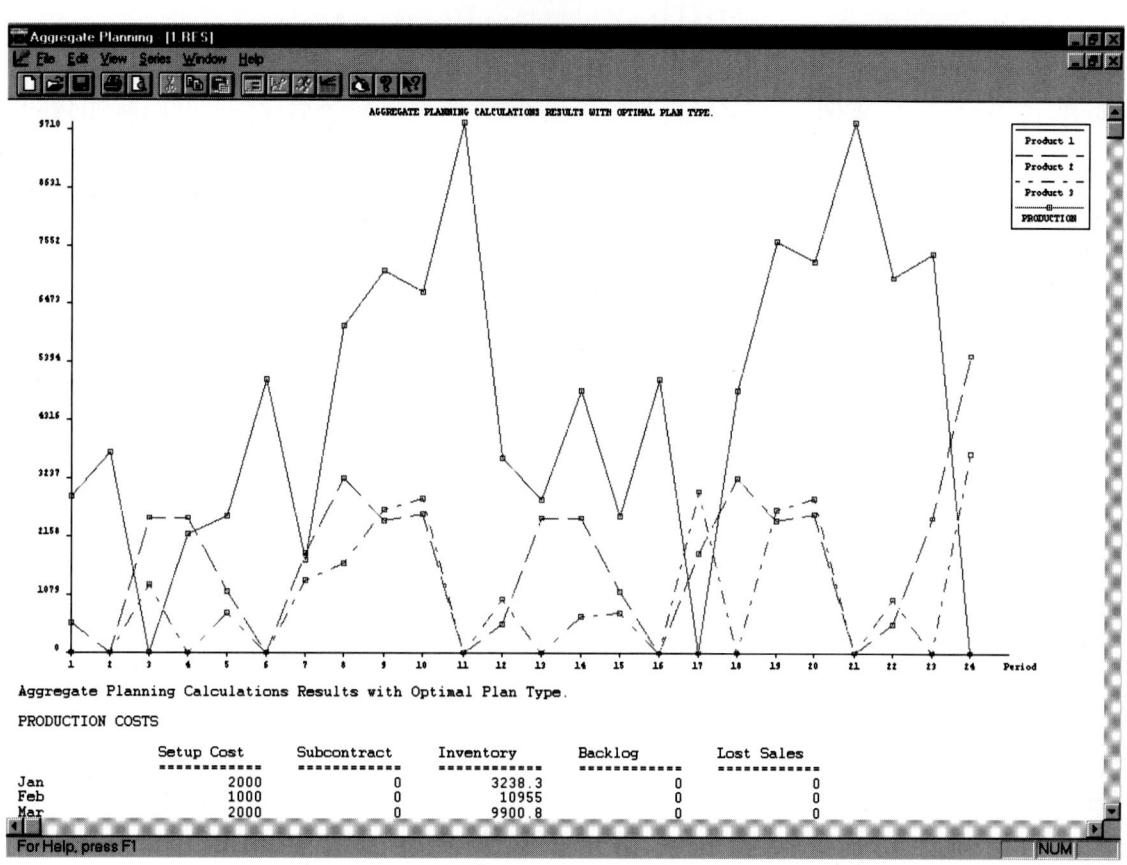

Aggregate Planning Calculations Results with Optimal Plan Type.

PRODUCTION COSTS

	Setup Cost	Subcontract	Inventory	Backlog	Lost Sales
Jan	2000	0	3238.3	0	0
Feb	1000	0	10955	0	0
Mar	2000	0	9900.8	0	0
Apr	2000	0	5227.2	0	0
May	3000	0	567.8	0	0
Jun	1000	0	3951.6	0	0
Jul	3000	0	2291.1	0	0
Aug	3000	0	186.2	0	0
Sep	3000	0	4383.8	0	0
Oct	3000	0	6022.8	0	0
Nov	1000	0	1411.5	0	0
Dec	3000	0	186.2	0	0
Jan	2000	0	4353.7	0	0
Feb	3000	0	1044	0	0
Mar	3000	0	4383.8	0	0
Apr	1000	0	7762	0	0
May	2000	0	6095.9	0	0
Jun	2000	0	6499.7	0	0
Jul	3000	0	2086.2	0	0
Aug	3000	0	4873.9	0	4.6276
Sep	1000	0	1411.5	0	0
Oct	3000	0	186.2	0	0
Nov	2000	0	11337	0	0
Dec	2000	0	17549	0	0
Total:	54000	0	115905	0	4.6276

WORKFORCE COSTS

	Wages	Overtime	Undertime	Hiring Cost	Firing Cost
Jan	25101	0	0	0	27500
Feb	25101	0	0	0	0
Mar	25101	2858.8	0	0	0
Apr	30679	1576.9	0	4000	0
May	30679	989.04	0	0	0
Jun	30679	989.04	0	0	0
Jul	33468	2240.2	0	2000	0
Aug	55780	18986	0	16000	0
Sep	55780	27545	0	0	0
Oct	55780	27545	0	0	0
Nov	55780	4634.8	0	0	0
Dec	36257	0	0	0	17500
Jan	36257	0	0	0	0
Feb	36257	19723	0	0	0
Mar	33468	0	0	0	2500
Apr	33468	0	0	0	0
May	33468	2115.4	0	0	0
Jun	52991	0	0	14000	0
Jul	55780	31200	0	2000	0
Aug	55780	31200	0	0	0
Sep	55780	4635.5	0	0	0
Oct	55780	0	0	0	0
Nov	55780	8076.5	0	0	0
Dec	55780	9398.2	0	0	0
Total:	1.02E+06	193713	0	38000	47500

TOTAL COST: 1.47E+06

PRODUCTION (FOR EACH PRODUCT)

Product 1

Period	Demand	Production	Sucontract	Opening Inventory	Opening Backlog	Lost Sales
Jan	87	2842.9	0	780	0	0
Feb	2740	3666.1	0	3535.9	0	0
Mar	3210	0	0	4462	0	0
Apr	3210	2158	0	1252	0	0
May	2675	2495	0	200	0	0
Jun	4012	5004.9	0	20	0	0
Jul	2675	1682.1	0	1012.9	0	0
Aug	4012	5992	0	20	0	0
Sep	6220	6993.1	0	2000	0	0
Oct	9362	6608.9	0	2773.1	0	0
Nov	9710	9710	0	20	0	0
Dec	2740	3560	0	20	0	0
Jan	3210	2794.7	0	839.95	0	0
Feb	3210	4785.4	0	424.64	0	0
Mar	2675	2492.4	0	2000	0	0
Apr	4012	5002.2	0	1817.4	0	0
May	2675	0	0	2807.6	0	0
Jun	4012	4795.6	0	132.6	0	0
Jul	6220	7535	0	916.24	0	0
Aug	9362	7150.8	0	2231.2	0	0.044072
Sep	9710	9710	0	20	0	0
Oct	2740	6853.8	0	20	0	0
Nov	3210	7286.2	0	4133.8	0	0
Dec	3210	0	0	8210	0	0

Product 2

Period	Demand	Production	Sucontract	Opening Inventory	Opening Backlog	Lost Sales
Jan	0	540	0	0	0	0
Feb	520	0	0	540	0	0
Mar	2466	2466	0	20	0	0
Apr	2466	2466	0	20	0	0
May	477	1114	0	20	0	0
Jun	637	0	0	657	0	0
Jul	1814	1814	0	20	0	0
Aug	3183	3183	0	20	0	0
Sep	2390	2390	0	20	0	0
Oct	2390	2533	0	20	0	0
Nov	143	0	0	163	0	0
Dec	520	520	0	20	0	0
Jan	2466	2466	0	20	0	0
Feb	2466	2466	0	20	0	0
Mar	477	1114	0	20	0	0
Apr	637	0	0	657	0	0
May	1814	1814	0	20	0	0
Jun	3183	3183	0	20	0	0
Jul	2390	2390	0	20	0	0
Aug	2390	2533	0	20	0	0
Sep	143	0	0	163	0	0
Oct	520	520	0	20	0	0
Nov	2466	2466	0	20	0	0
Dec	2466	5446	0	20	0	0

Product 3

Period	Demand	Production	Sucontract	Opening Inventory	Opening Backlog	Lost Sales
Jan	0	0	0	426	0	0
Feb	326	0	0	426	0	0
Mar	653	1226	0	100	0	0
Apr	653	0	0	673	0	0
May	294	712	0	20	0	0
Jun	418	0	0	438	0	0
Jul	1310	1310	0	20	0	0
Aug	1633	1633	0	20	0	0
Sep	2613	2613	0	20	0	0
Oct	2613	2809	0	20	0	0
Nov	196	0	0	216	0	0
Dec	326	979	0	20	0	0
Jan	653	0	0	673	0	0
Feb	653	653	0	20	0	0
Mar	294	712	0	20	0	0
Apr	418	0	0	438	0	0
May	1310	2943	0	20	0	0
Jun	1633	0	0	1653	0	0
Jul	2613	2613	0	20	0	0
Aug	2613	2809	0	20	0	0
Sep	196	0	0	216	0	0
Oct	326	979	0	20	0	0
Nov	653	0	0	673	0	0
Dec	653	3633	0	20	0	0

WORKFORCE

Period	No. Workers in 1st Shift	Overtime in 1st Shif	No. Workers in 2nd Shift	Overtime in 2nd Shi	Undertime	No. Workers to Hire	No. Workers to Fire
Jan	9	0	0	0	92.265	0	11
Feb	9	0	0	0	92.263	0	0
Mar	9	146.6	0	0	0	0	0
Apr	11	80.868	0	0	0	2	0
May	11	50.72	0	0	0	0	0
Jun	11	50.72	0	0	0	0	0
Jul	12	114.88	0	0	0	1	0
Aug	20	973.64	0	0	0	8	0
Sep	20	1412.5	0	0	0	0	0
Oct	20	1412.5	0	0	0	0	0
Nov	20	237.68	0	0	0	0	0
Dec	13	0	0	0	18.999	0	7
Jan	13	0	0	0	18.979	0	0
Feb	13	1011.5	0	0	0	0	0
Mar	12	0	0	0	110.2	0	1
Apr	12	0	0	0	110.24	0	0
May	12	108.48	0	0	0	0	0
Jun	19	0	0	0	15.325	7	0
Jul	20	1600	0	0	0	1	0
Aug	20	1600	0	0	0	0	0
Sep	20	237.72	0	0	0	0	0
Oct	20	0	0	0	0.00326	0	0
Nov	20	414.18	0	0	0	0	0
Dec	20	481.96	0	0	0	0	0

Sample Data

<u>**CHASE.DAT**</u>   **Chase or Zero Inventory Strategy (5 minutes)**

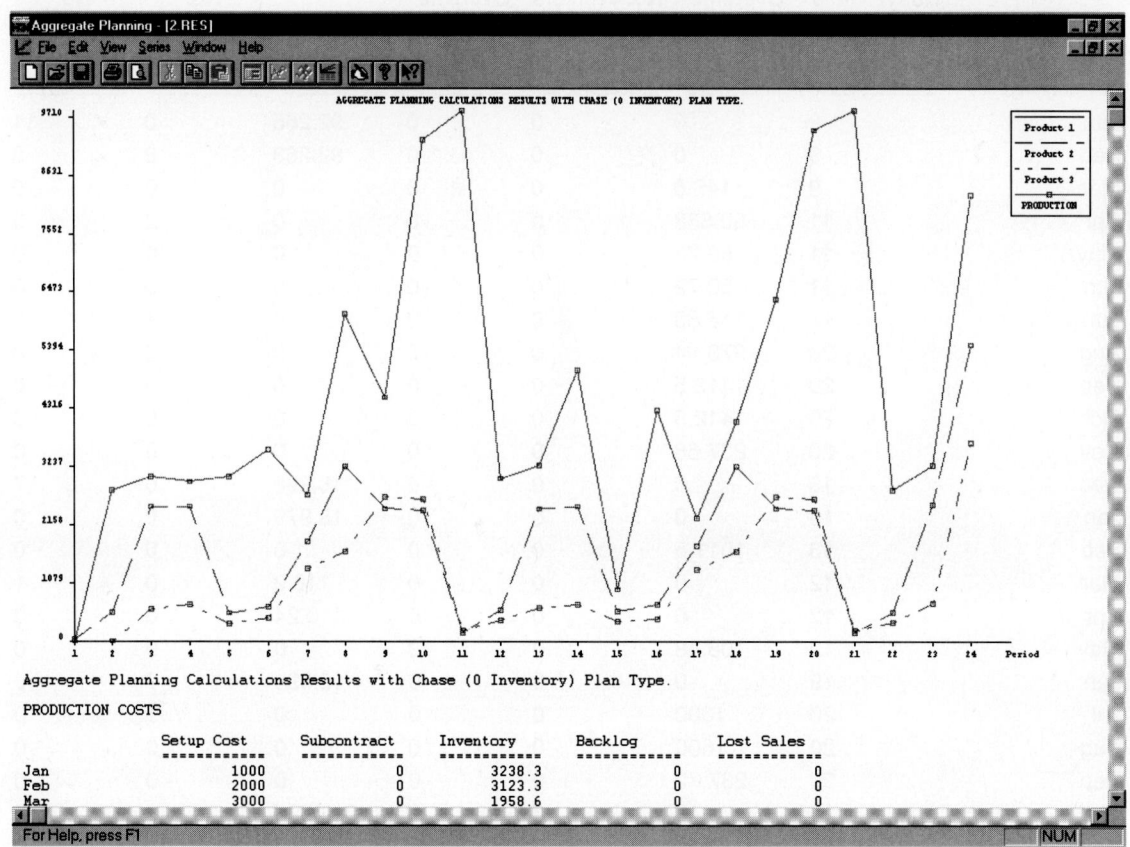

Aggregate Planning Calculations Results with Chase (0 Inventory) Plan Type.

PRODUCTION COSTS

	Setup Cost	Subcontract	Inventory	Backlog	Lost Sales
Jan	1000	0	3238.3	0	0
Feb	2000	0	3123.3	0	0
Mar	3000	0	1958.6	0	0

Aggregate Planning Calculations Results with Chase (0 Inventory) Plan Type.

PRODUCTION COSTS

	Setup Cost	Subcontract	Inventory	Backlog	Lost Sales
Jan	1000	0	3238.3	0	0
Feb	2000	0	3123.3	0	0
Mar	3000	0	1958.6	0	0
Apr	3000	0	1212.2	0	0
May	3000	0	567.8	0	0
Jun	3000	0	1407.7	0	0
Jul	3000	0	186.2	0	0
Aug	3000	0	186.2	0	0
Sep	3000	0	4383.8	0	0
Oct	3000	0	763.31	0	0
Nov	3000	0	186.2	0	0
Dec	3000	0	186.2	0	0
Jan	3000	0	958.82	0	0
Feb	3000	0	657.07	0	0
Mar	3000	0	4383.8	0	0
Apr	3000	0	1085.2	0	0
May	3000	0	1482.7	0	0
Jun	3000	0	186.2	0	0
Jul	3000	0	186.2	0	0
Aug	3000	0	381.71	0	0
Sep	3000	0	186.2	0	0
Oct	3000	0	186.2	0	0
Nov	3000	0	230.72	0	0
Dec	3000	0	381.71	0	0
Total:	69000	0	27706.3	0	0

WORKFORCE COSTS

	Wages	Overtime	Undertime	Hiring Cost	Firing Cost
Jan	25101	0	0	0	27500
Feb	25101	0	0	0	0
Mar	30679	13290	0	4000	0
Apr	30679	13290	0	0	0
May	30679	0	0	0	0
Jun	30679	1666.1	0	0	0
Jul	39046	2695.7	0	6000	0
Aug	55780	18987	0	12000	0
Sep	55780	10657	0	0	0
Oct	66239	32806	0	6000	0
Nov	55780	10346	0	0	7500
Dec	39046	0	0	0	15000
Jan	39046	5342	0	0	0
Feb	39046	17834	0	0	0
Mar	39046	0	0	0	0
Apr	39046	0	0	0	0
May	39046	0	0	0	0
Jun	55780	5636.1	0	12000	0
Jul	55780	22794	0	0	0
Aug	66239	34323	0	6000	0
Sep	55780	10346	0	0	7500
Oct	47413	0	0	0	7500
Nov	47413	0	0	0	0
Dec	83670	43154	0	22000	0
Total:	1.09E+06	243167	0	68000	65000

TOTAL COST: 1.56E+06

PRODUCTION (FOR EACH PRODUCT)

Product 1

Period	Demand	Production	Sucontract	Opening Inventory	Opening Backlog	Lost Sales
Jan	87	0	0	780	0	0
Feb	2740	2761	0	693	0	0
Mar	3210	3000	0	714	0	0
Apr	3210	2906	0	503.97	0	0
May	2675	3000	0	200	0	0
Jun	4012	3507	0	524.97	0	0
Jul	2675	2675	0	20	0	0
Aug	4012	5992	0	20	0	0
Sep	6220	4441	0	2000	0	0
Oct	9362	9161	0	221	0	0
Nov	9710	9710	0	20	0	0
Dec	2740	2962	0	20	0	0
Jan	3210	3210.1	0	242	0	0
Feb	3210	4967.9	0	242.11	0	0
Mar	2675	938	0	2000	0	0
Apr	4012	4213	0	263	0	0
May	2675	2231	0	464	0	0
Jun	4012	4012	0	20	0	0
Jul	6220	6241	0	20	0	0
Aug	9362	9341	0	41	0	0
Sep	9710	9710	0	20	0	0
Oct	2740	2761	0	20	0	0
Nov	3210	3210	0	41	0	0
Dec	3210	8169	0	41	0	0

Product 2

Period	Demand	Production	Sucontract	Opening Inventory	Opening Backlog	Lost Sales
Jan	0	20	0	0	0	0
Feb	520	521	0	20	0	0
Mar	2466	2465	0	21	0	0
Apr	2466	2466	0	20	0	0
May	477	498	0	20	0	0
Jun	637	616	0	41	0	0
Jul	1814	1814	0	20	0	0
Aug	3183	3183	0	20	0	0
Sep	2390	2411	0	20	0	0
Oct	2390	2369	0	41	0	0
Nov	143	143	0	20	0	0
Dec	520	562	0	20	0	0
Jan	2466	2424	0	62	0	0
Feb	2466	2466	0	20	0	0
Mar	477	540	0	20	0	0
Apr	637	658	0	83	0	0
May	1814	1730	0	104	0	0
Jun	3183	3183	0	20	0	0
Jul	2390	2411	0	20	0	0
Aug	2390	2369	0	41	0	0
Sep	143	143	0	20	0	0
Oct	520	520	0	20	0	0
Nov	2466	2487	0	20	0	0
Dec	2466	5425	0	41	0	0

WORKFORCE COSTS

	Wages	Overtime	Undertime	Hiring Cost	Firing Cost
Jan	55780	0	0	0	0
Feb	55780	0	0	0	0
Mar	55780	0	0	0	0
Apr	55780	0	0	0	0
May	55780	0	0	0	0
Jun	55780	0	0	0	0
Jul	55780	0	0	0	0
Aug	55780	0	0	0	0
Sep	55780	12136	0	0	0
Oct	55780	31200	0	0	0
Nov	55780	4635.5	0	0	0
Dec	55780	0	0	0	0
Jan	55780	0	0	0	0
Feb	55780	0	0	0	0
Mar	55780	0	0	0	0
Apr	55780	0	0	0	0
May	55780	0	0	0	0
Jun	55780	0	0	0	0
Jul	55780	1046.5	0	0	0
Aug	55780	31200	0	0	0
Sep	55780	4635.5	0	0	0
Oct	55780	0	0	0	0
Nov	55780	8076.5	0	0	0
Dec	55780	9398.2	0	0	0
Total:	1.34E+06	102328	0	0	0

TOTAL COST: 1.61E+06

PRODUCTION (FOR EACH PRODUCT)

Product 1

Period	Demand	Production	Sucontract	Opening Inventory	Opening Backlog	Lost Sales
Jan	87	0	0	780	0	0
Feb	2740	2067	0	693	0	0
Mar	3210	3210	0	20	0	0
Apr	3210	3390	0	20	0	0
May	2675	2495	0	200	0	0
Jun	4012	5963.4	0	20	0	0
Jul	2675	3156.4	0	1971.4	0	0
Aug	4012	5302.6	0	2452.8	0	0
Sep	6220	4707.8	0	3743.4	0	0
Oct	9362	7150.8	0	2231.2	0	0.015442
Nov	9710	9710	0	20	0	0
Dec	2740	2740	0	20	0	0
Jan	3210	3300.7	0	20	0	0
Feb	3210	5099.3	0	110.7	0	0
Mar	2675	695	0	2000	0	0
Apr	4012	7376.6	0	20	0	0
May	2675	5051.4	0	3384.6	0	0
Jun	4012	0	0	5761.1	0	0
Jul	6220	6702.1	0	1749.1	0	0
Aug	9362	7150.8	0	2231.2	0	0
Sep	9710	9710	0	20	0	0
Oct	2740	6853.8	0	20	0	0
Nov	3210	7286.2	0	4133.8	0	0
Dec	3210	0	0	8210	0	0

Product 2

Period	Demand	Production	Sucontract	Opening Inventory	Opening Backlog	Lost Sales
Jan	0	20	0	0	0	0
Feb	520	520	0	20	0	0
Mar	2466	2466	0	20	0	0
Apr	2466	2466	0	20	0	0
May	477	477	0	20	0	0
Jun	637	637	0	20	0	0
Jul	1814	1814	0	20	0	0
Aug	3183	3183	0	20	0	0
Sep	2390	2390	0	20	0	0
Oct	2390	2533	0	20	0	0
Nov	143	0	0	163	0	0
Dec	520	520	0	20	0	0
Jan	2466	2466	0	20	0	0
Feb	2466	2466	0	20	0	0
Mar	477	477	0	20	0	0
Apr	637	637	0	20	0	0
May	1814	1814	0	20	0	0
Jun	3183	5573	0	20	0	0
Jul	2390	0	0	2410	0	0
Aug	2390	2533	0	20	0	0
Sep	143	0	0	163	0	0
Oct	520	520	0	20	0	0
Nov	2466	2466	0	20	0	0
Dec	2466	5446	0	20	0	0

Product 3

Period	Demand	Production	Sucontract	Opening Inventory	Opening Backlog	Lost Sales
Jan	0	0	0	426	0	0
Feb	326	0	0	426	0	0
Mar	653	573	0	100	0	0
Apr	653	653	0	20	0	0
May	294	294	0	20	0	0
Jun	418	418	0	20	0	0
Jul	1310	2943	0	20	0	0
Aug	1633	0	0	1653	0	0
Sep	2613	2613	0	20	0	0
Oct	2613	2809	0	20	0	0
Nov	196	0	0	216	0	0
Dec	326	326	0	20	0	0
Jan	653	653	0	20	0	0
Feb	653	653	0	20	0	0
Mar	294	294	0	20	0	0
Apr	418	418	0	20	0	0
May	1310	1310	0	20	0	0
Jun	1633	2312.1	0	20	0	0
Jul	2613	1933.9	0	699.07	0	0
Aug	2613	2809	0	20	0	0
Sep	196	0	0	216	0	0
Oct	326	979	0	20	0	0
Nov	653	0	0	673	0	0
Dec	653	3633	0	20	0	0

WORKFORCE

Period	No. Workers in 1st Shift	Overtime in 1st Shift	No. Workers in 2nd Shift	Overtime in 2nd Shift	Undertime	No. Workers to Hire	No. Workers to Fire
Jan	20	0	0	0	3112.4	0	0
Feb	20	0	0	0	2128.2	0	0
Mar	20	0	0	0	685.42	0	0
Apr	20	0	0	0	591.08	0	0
May	20	0	0	0	1798.5	0	0
Jun	20	0	0	0	488.69	0	0
Jul	20	0	0	0	0	0	0
Aug	20	0	0	0	0.00392	0	0
Sep	20	622.38	0	0	0	0	0
Oct	20	1600	0	0	0	0	0
Nov	20	237.72	0	0	0	0	0
Dec	20	0	0	0	1684.6	0	0
Jan	20	0	0	0	621.96	0	0
Feb	20	0	0	0	0	0	0
Mar	20	0	0	0	2420.9	0	0
Apr	20	0	0	0	0.00532	0	0
May	20	0	0	0	0.01688	0	0
Jun	20	0	0	0	0	0	0
Jul	20	53.666	0	0	0	0	0
Aug	20	1600	0	0	0	0	0
Sep	20	237.72	0	0	0	0	0
Oct	20	0	0	0	0.00326	0	0
Nov	20	414.18	0	0	0	0	0
Dec	20	481.96	0	0	0	0	0

Sample Dat

<u>CHASE.DAT</u>   **Level Production Strategy**   **(2-3 seconds)**

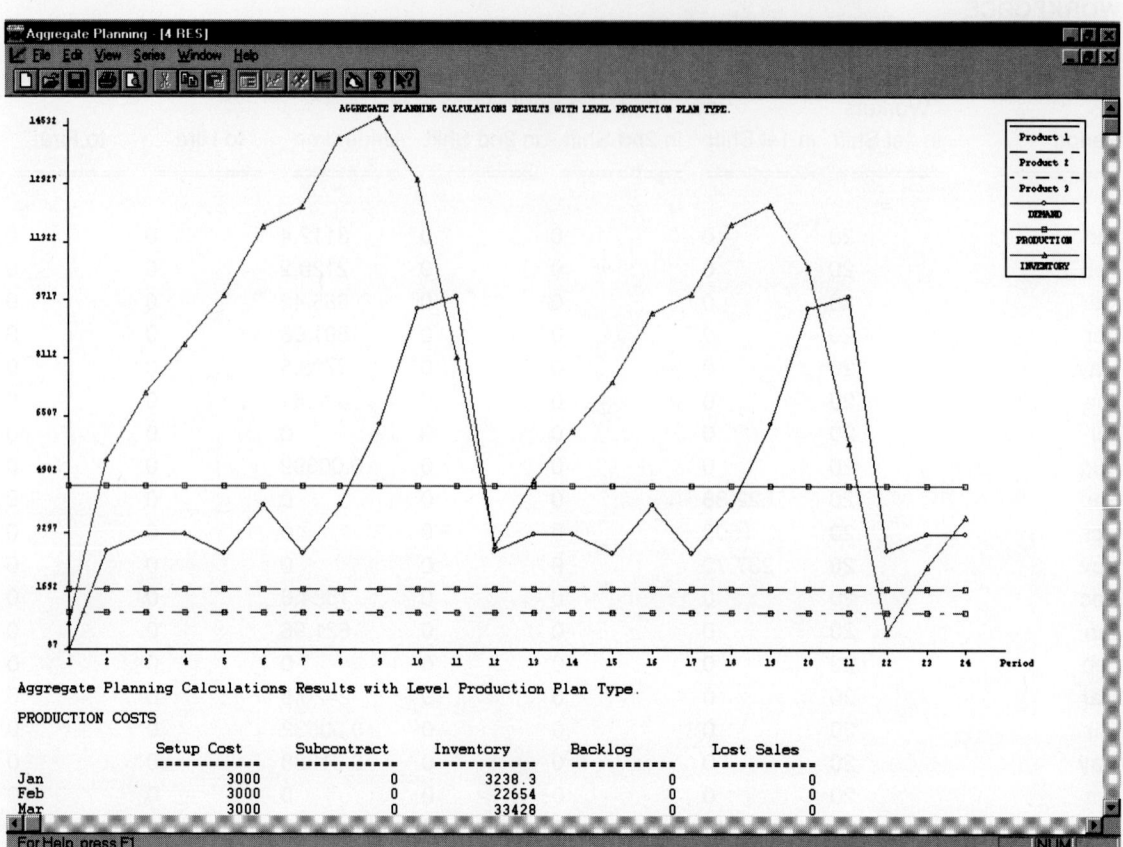

Aggregate Planning Calculations Results with Level Production Plan Type.

PRODUCTION COSTS

	Setup Cost	Subcontract	Inventory	Backlog	Lost Sales
Jan	3000	0	3238.3	0	0
Feb	3000	0	22654	0	0
Mar	3000	0	33428	0	0
Apr	3000	0	35236	0	0
May	3000	0	37044	0	0
Jun	3000	0	48224	0	0
Jul	3000	0	55554	0	0
Aug	3000	0	58314	0	0
Sep	3000	0	52289	0	0
Oct	3000	0	40689	0	0
Nov	3000	0	22427	0	0
Dec	3000	0	20216	0	0
Jan	3000	0	30990	0	0
Feb	3000	0	32799	0	0
Mar	3000	0	34607	0	0
Apr	3000	0	45787	0	0
May	3000	0	53116	0	0
Jun	3000	0	55878	0	0
Jul	3000	0	49851	0	0
Aug	3000	0	38252	0	0
Sep	3000	0	19990	0	0
Oct	3000	0	17779	0	0
Nov	3000	0	28553	0	0
Dec	3000	0	30362	0	0
Total:	72000	0	867277	0	0

WORKFORCE COSTS

	Wages	Overtime	Undertime	Hiring Cost	Firing Cost
Jan	52991	0	0	0	2500
Feb	52991	0	0	0	0
Mar	52991	0	0	0	0
Apr	52991	0	0	0	0
May	52991	0	0	0	0
Jun	52991	0	0	0	0
Jul	52991	0	0	0	0
Aug	52991	0	0	0	0
Sep	52991	0	0	0	0
Oct	52991	0	0	0	0
Nov	52991	0	0	0	0
Dec	52991	0	0	0	0
Jan	52991	0	0	0	0
Feb	52991	0	0	0	0
Mar	52991	0	0	0	0
Apr	52991	0	0	0	0
May	52991	0	0	0	0
Jun	52991	0	0	0	0
Jul	52991	0	0	0	0
Aug	52991	0	0	0	0
Sep	52991	0	0	0	0
Oct	52991	0	0	0	0
Nov	52991	0	0	0	0
Dec	52991	0	0	0	0
Total:	1.27E+06	0	0	0	2500

TOTAL COST: 2.21E+06

PRODUCTION (FOR EACH PRODUCT)

Product 1

Period	Demand	Production	Sucontract	Opening Inventory	Opening Backlog	Lost Sales
Jan	87	4546.6	0	780	0	0
Feb	2740	4546.6	0	5239.6	0	0
Mar	3210	4546.6	0	7046.3	0	0
Apr	3210	4546.6	0	8382.9	0	0
May	2675	4546.6	0	9719.5	0	0
Jun	4012	4546.6	0	11591	0	0
Jul	2675	4546.6	0	12126	0	0
Aug	4012	4546.6	0	13997	0	0
Sep	6220	4546.6	0	14532	0	0
Oct	9362	4546.6	0	12859	0	0
Nov	9710	4546.6	0	8043.3	0	0
Dec	2740	4546.6	0	2879.9	0	0
Jan	3210	4546.6	0	4686.5	0	0
Feb	3210	4546.6	0	6023.1	0	0
Mar	2675	4546.6	0	7359.8	0	0
Apr	4012	4546.6	0	9231.4	0	0
May	2675	4546.6	0	9766	0	0
Jun	4012	4546.6	0	11638	0	0
Jul	6220	4546.6	0	12172	0	0
Aug	9362	4546.6	0	10499	0	0
Sep	9710	4546.6	0	5683.5	0	0
Oct	2740	4546.6	0	520.13	0	0
Nov	3210	4546.6	0	2326.8	0	0
Dec	3210	4546.6	0	3663.4	0	0

Product 2

Period	Demand	Production	Sucontract	Opening Inventory	Opening Backlog	Lost Sales
Jan	0	1726	0	0	0	0
Feb	520	1726	0	1726	0	0
Mar	2466	1726	0	2932	0	0
Apr	2466	1726	0	2192	0	0
May	477	1726	0	1452	0	0
Jun	637	1726	0	2701	0	0
Jul	1814	1726	0	3790	0	0
Aug	3183	1726	0	3702	0	0
Sep	2390	1726	0	2245	0	0
Oct	2390	1726	0	1581	0	0
Nov	143	1726	0	917	0	0
Dec	520	1726	0	2500	0	0
Jan	2466	1726	0	3706	0	0
Feb	2466	1726	0	2966	0	0
Mar	477	1726	0	2226	0	0
Apr	637	1726	0	3475	0	0
May	1814	1726	0	4564	0	0
Jun	3183	1726	0	4476	0	0
Jul	2390	1726	0	3019	0	0
Aug	2390	1726	0	2355	0	0
Sep	143	1726	0	1691	0	0
Oct	520	1726	0	3274	0	0
Nov	2466	1726	0	4480	0	0
Dec	2466	1726	0	3740	0	0

Product 3

Period	Demand	Production	Sucontract	Opening Inventory	Opening Backlog	Lost Sales
Jan	0	1067.7	0	426	0	0
Feb	326	1067.7	0	1493.7	0	0
Mar	653	1067.7	0	2235.3	0	0
Apr	653	1067.7	0	2650	0	0
May	294	1067.7	0	3064.7	0	0
Jun	418	1067.7	0	3838.3	0	0
Jul	1310	1067.7	0	4488	0	0
Aug	1633	1067.7	0	4245.7	0	0
Sep	2613	1067.7	0	3680.3	0	0
Oct	2613	1067.7	0	2135	0	0
Nov	196	1067.7	0	589.67	0	0
Dec	326	1067.7	0	1461.3	0	0
Jan	653	1067.7	0	2203	0	0
Feb	653	1067.7	0	2617.7	0	0
Mar	294	1067.7	0	3032.3	0	0
Apr	418	1067.7	0	3806	0	0
May	1310	1067.7	0	4455.7	0	0
Jun	1633	1067.7	0	4213.3	0	0
Jul	2613	1067.7	0	3648	0	0
Aug	2613	1067.7	0	2102.7	0	0
Sep	196	1067.7	0	557.33	0	0
Oct	326	1067.7	0	1429	0	0
Nov	653	1067.7	0	2170.7	0	0
Dec	653	1067.7	0	2585.3	0	0

WORKFORCE

Period	No. Workers in 1st Shift	Overtime in 1st Shift	No. Workers in 2nd Shift	Overtime in 2nd Shift	Undertime	No.Workers to Hire	No.Workers to Fire
Jan	19	0	0	0	145.16	0	1
Feb	19	0	0	0	145.16	0	0
Mar	19	0	0	0	145.16	0	0
Apr	19	0	0	0	145.16	0	0
May	19	0	0	0	145.16	0	0
Jun	19	0	0	0	145.16	0	0
Jul	19	0	0	0	145.16	0	0
Aug	19	0	0	0	145.16	0	0
Sep	19	0	0	0	145.16	0	0
Oct	19	0	0	0	145.16	0	0
Nov	19	0	0	0	145.16	0	0
Dec	19	0	0	0	145.16	0	0
Jan	19	0	0	0	145.16	0	0
Feb	19	0	0	0	145.16	0	0
Mar	19	0	0	0	145.16	0	0
Apr	19	0	0	0	145.16	0	0
May	19	0	0	0	145.16	0	0
Jun	19	0	0	0	145.16	0	0
Jul	19	0	0	0	145.16	0	0
Aug	19	0	0	0	145.16	0	0
Sep	19	0	0	0	145.16	0	0
Oct	19	0	0	0	145.16	0	0
Nov	19	0	0	0	145.16	0	0
Dec	19	0	0	0	145.16	0	0

REFERENCES

Chase, R. B., and N. J. Aquilano *Production and Operations Management* 7th ed. Burr Ridge, IL: Richard D. Irwin, 1995.

Nahmias, S. *Production and Operations Analysis* 3rd ed. Burr Ridge, IL: Richard D. Irwin, 1997.

Stevenson, W. J. *Production/Operations Management* 5th ed., Burr Ridge, IL: Richard D. Irwin, 1996.

Hax, A. C., and D. Candea *Production and Inventory Management*, Englewood Cliffs, NJ: Prentice Hall, 1984.

Padberg, M. W. *Linear optimization and extensions* Berlin and New York: Springer-Verlag, 1995.

TC Bank Corp.[1]

Check Processing Unit

To cover market share gains, TC Bank Corp (TCBC) has augmented its own check clearing operation by outsourcing its overflow to a small vendor. This subcontracting cost is $14.50 per thousand checks (monthly contract accepted); and under the leadership of Myron Goodcheck, the vendor's quality is equivalent to that of the bank's. Myron's firms' processing capacity available to TCBC is 1.5 million checks per week. Within that limit, Myron can process any combination of retail and commercial checks. Unfortunately, Myron was getting older and wanted to retire and enjoy his remaining years. His son, Myron Jr., had just received his MBA, and ran the business this year. Not satisfied with the returns his father had garnered, but unwilling to raise prices in the competitive check processing market, he reengineered the company by firing older experienced workers and replaced them with younger and cheaper, but inexperienced employees. As a result, the firm suffered a substantive decrease in quality. This caused TCBC to reevaluate its current contract, assuming the bank would have to process a maximum of 14 million checks per month during its peak periods next year.

TCBC has capacity to process 8 million checks per month in one–shift operations using forty employees and forty clearing machines. Each operator/machine can process 1,250 checks per hour. The holiday season leads to December, January and February being the heaviest months, with peak demand exceeding base demand by 4 million checks per month. Due to an aggressive marketing campaign for new customers, TCBC's monthly check processing volume has grown by 2 million checks each month for the past two years (Table 1).

Twenty percent of monthly demand is for commercial checks. These are of bigger size than normal checks and, thus, require the machines to be reset. This takes each operator three hours to accomplish. An additional three hours are required when switching back to personal checks. A special piece of software must also be run to recalibrate the machine after each change over. The lease with the vendor of the software requires a $10 fee per machine for each time it is used. To avoid confusion, all machines run the same size check at the same time. The bank's customer guarantee requires checks to be processed at least twice a month. All check processing demand is such that sixty percent of monthly demand occurs during the first two weeks of the month.

Overtime work, according to the union contract, requires a premium of 50% and no more than two hours per day. The second shift wage premium is 10%. TCBC Management is leery about the loss of control and quality that may occur during a second shift. They require an additional assistant manager at a cost of $3,500 per month if a second shift is used. To justify this overhead, the firm feels that a 2nd shift should have a minimum of 10 employees. For these reasons, they have used firms like Myron's in the past instead of a second shift.

Trained operators and managers are in scarce supply in TCBC's area. A search firm would be required to find part or full–time candidates. The fee for this service is 10% of their annual wage each time they are hired independent of the number of months they work. In addition, one month's TCBC specific training is needed before new employees are allowed to work on an independent basis. The Human Resources department feels that it can not handle any more than 20 new hires and 20 dismissals in any one period. The cost of dismissing an employee (unemployment compensation, etc.) is $4,000.

TCBC can add two additional processing machines rated at 1,250 checks per hour each in their existing check processing center (CPC). Machines cost $25,000 each, and have a ten– year life, with no salvage value. Each machine requires an operator whom is paid the same as the current operators, $2,500 per month, including benefits. Any additional machines over this level would require an additional $100,000 in fixed investment to open a new CPC and $50,000 annually for a new manager. The firm uses straight line depreciation, has a cost of capital of 10 percent, and an opportunity cost of capital of 20 percent.

- A. Discuss the building of inventory before demand, peak load pricing, and back ordering as possible aggregate planning strategies in the TCBC business environment.
- B. Excluding the buying of new equipment, which aggregate plan strategies are feasible for TCBC?

---

[1] By Michael Moses, Operations Management Area, Stern School of Business. This case is for the use of students in a core course in Operations Management and is intended to have no actual relationship to any real person or organization. (11/98)

C. Which of the strategies discussed in (B) should be used; and is Myron Jr. included? Explain why the specific strategy was chosen and why (cost, quality, etc.) it was better than the alternative strategies.

D. Myron Jr.'s reduced quality has cost the bank an increased loss of customers. Additional advertising is needed to make up for these losses. This is tantamount to increasing Myron's subcontracting cost by 30%. Does this change your decision? Why? What would happen if the true cost of lost business increased Myron's cost by 40%?

E. Without new equipment, is it feasible (and for how many years) for TCBC to continue their market share gain campaign into the future, assuming it adds 2 million checks per month as it has in the past?

F. How would the ability to purchase new equipment affect your responses to A through E?

TABLE 1
TOTAL CHECKS SUBMITTED TO TCBC FOR PROCESSING

	ACTUAL Two Years Ago	ACTUAL Previous Year	ACTUAL Current Year	FORECAST Next Year
DEC	10,000,000	12,000,000	14,000,000	14,000,000
JAN	10,000,000	12,000,000	14,000,000	14,000,000
FEB	10,000,000	12,000,000	14,000,000	14,000,000
MAR	6,000,000	8,000,000	10,000,000	10,000,000
APR	6,000,000	8,000,000	10,000,000	10,000,000
MAY	6,000,000	8,000,000	10,000,000	10,000,000
JUN	6,000,000	8,000,000	10,000,000	10,000,000
JUL	6,000,000	8,000,000	10,000,000	10,000,000
AUG	6,000,000	8,000,000	10,000,000	10,000,000
SEP	6,000,000	8,000,000	10,000,000	10,000,000
OCT	6,000,000	8,000,000	10,000,000	10,000,000
NOV	6,000,000	8,000,000	10,000,000	10,000,000

INTEGRATIVE CASES

United Bank Branches[1]
A Comprehensive Service Operations Case

On March 31, 1996, The Chase Manhattan Corporation merged with Chemical Banking Corporation to form a huge behemoth of a bank. The new Chase will eclipse New York neighbor Citicorp as the largest U.S. banking company, with nearly $300 billion in assets and $15 billion in annual revenues. The merger is expected to pare annual expenses by $1.7 billion by combining branch and office operations (at a one–time cost of $1.9 billion), resulting in the closing of over 100 of its 626 branches. This case is written as a hypothetical example of the problems encountered in one such unification.

CUSTOMER SERVICE IMPROVEMENT VIA WAITING LINE DESIGN

To evaluate the opportunities for combining branch operations, management would like you to analyze the feasibility of combining the two branches in the vicinity of 86th Street and Lexington Avenue in New York City. The branch on 86th Street is the larger of the two. It has a ground floor with 10 ATMs in the front and select customer services such as new account origination, loans, brokerage, and other services in the back. The Select Services personnel could be moved, should the need arise, to add up to a maximum of four more ATMs. The mezzanine floor has 12 human teller locations divided into four commercial customer teller positions and eight retail customer positions as well as the back-office operations and branch management space. The back office-operations could also be moved, by adding a third floor, and thus make room for up to six additional human teller positions.

    Most branch customers (both commercial and retail) become impatient if they are forced to wait for more than a few minutes at any one time. Both retail and commercial customers are serviced by dedicated tellers (commercial customers cannot be handled by retail tellers and vice versa) and waiting occurs in two independent "s" lines (first–come, first–served), which, for all intents and purposes, have no physical capacity. Tables 1–3 give the peak interarrival rates for retail customers at the 86th Street branch and the Lexington Ave. branch, and the pro forma rate for the combined branches. Tables 4–6 give the corresponding interarrival rates for commercial customers. Tables 7 and 8 give service time information for the typical teller at each branch. Arrivals peak between 11:00 AM and 1:00 PM at both branches when local offices let workers out for their lunch hour.

    Management would like to know whether the existing 86th Street branch can handle the combined volume of the two branches while maintaining the same level of service prior to the merger. To benchmark the current 86th Street Branch operation, you want to determine the customer's service parameters of the current service facility as well as the utilization of its tellers and ATMs if it had continued operations as an independent entity. Does the existing 86th Street branch have enough teller capacity in the mezzanine area to handle the joint workload? What is the optimal arrangement of tellers to ensure that no customer (retail or commercial) has to wait in line for more than two or three minutes, and that tellers are busy at least 80 percent of the time. Do commercial customers get a benefit from having their own separate line, or would they be better off if they were mixed in with the general population? (Hint: See Table 9 for combined arrival rate data, and think about what to do with the service time data.) Both retail and commercial customers have some very long service–time activities that they share in common. In particular, money orders have a mean service rate of four minutes and a mean arrival rate of 12 per hour during peak periods. Removing these customers from the combined data yields a combined mean arrival rate of 8.5 customers per minute and a mean service time of 70 seconds. Does this class of service warrant a special line? Arrival data for the rest of the day is contained in Table 10 and should be used to develop an appropriate staffing plan for all periods of the day. The bank is also considering a more personalized approach to

---

[1] By Michael Moses and Don Weinstein, Operations Management Area, Stern School of Business. This case is for the use of students in a core course in Operations Management and is intended to have no actual relationship to any real person or organization. (11/98)

banking by restoring an old system of letting customers queue up behind an individual (favorite) teller if they like. Would this be feasible for either the retail or commercial customer classes? How would this type of service discipline affect waiting time and teller efficiency?

The 10 ATMs on the ground floor are accessible 10 hours a day. The remainder of the branch is open 9–5. The peak arrival rates and service times for the combined ATM traffic are given in Tables 11 and 12, respectively. The ATM area can hold a maximum of 20 people before customers start spilling out into the street, and an "s" service line is impractical due to the shape of the lobby. Does the ATM area have enough capacity to combine operations? If not, how many ATMs are needed to ensure that customers do not have to wait for more than one minute on average. If the entire first–floor back–office area is converted, there will be sufficient space for an "s" line of 30 people. Is this helpful? Due to the mechanical nature of the ATM machines (they may overheat if they are actively processing transactions all the time without a break to cool down), utilization rates in excess of 90-95 percent during peak periods is undesirable.

RAPID TIME–TO–MARKET VIA PROJECT AND TIME MANAGEMENT

Management is concerned that the 86th Street branch may need to be expanded in order to service the increased customer load from the Lexington Ave. branch. However, experience from a prior merger was not encouraging. At that time, the 86th Street branch was expanded to absorb customers from another branch in the area. That project lasted six months and resulted in the branch losing approximately 10 percent of its customers. Management wants to know how long it would take to expand the ATM area on the first floor and add a third floor for non-teller and back–office operations to make more room on the second floor for additional human teller locations.

The construction project manager has sketched out the following plan. First, she must reconfigure once more the offices on the first floor to make room for more ATMs. Then, the kiosk frames for the additional ATMs must be built and the ATM kiosks must be wired. Once that is complete, installation of the additional ATMs can be completed. They are coming from the Lexington Ave. branch and can be moved at any time. When the ATMs are installed, they must be circuit–tested before being connected to the network, followed by a circuit test of the network connection. After the ATMs are up and running, the construction manager and his crew do a final walk–through of the ATM area to look for any structural or cosmetic defects and then touch up those defects before the project is complete and ready for live operation.

While all that is happening on the first floor, another construction team must lay out and install the new third floor and then put up the framing around the new floor. Once the framing is up, they can simultaneously put the siding on the exterior walls and shingle the roof. Afterwards, separate contractors simultaneously install the plumbing, wiring, and HVAC systems inside the new floor. Then the interior can be filled with insulation and the interior walls put up. Next, the area can be painted. When the paint dries, the construction team installs all the necessary office fixtures and furniture and then lay the carpeting down. The construction manager and his crew then do a final walk– through to look for defects and must touch up those defects before the project is complete and ready for live, on-line operation. The design for additional human teller stations on the second floor can start any time, but demolition of this space must await the completion of the new first and third floors. After demolition, the sequential steps of framing, spackling, installing partitions, painting, installing electronics, and final testing can be accomplished. Table 13 gives a summary of the described activities along with their normal (most likely) duration times.

In order to stem the tide of lost customers during the disruptive construction project, management considers it worthwhile to spend up to $10,000 a week for every week that the project schedule can be compressed. Referring to the data in Table 13, by how many weeks can you reduce the completion time (crash the project) and up to what point will it remain financially advisable?

Management is also concerned that unforeseen circumstances may hinder the crashing efforts. What is the probability that the project will be completed within the crashing timetable assuming that all the "most likely crash duration" estimates in Table 13 are used as the most likely time estimates? Table 13 also gives information on optimistic and pessimistic duration times. If you had to give a 90 percent confidence level for the completion of the crashed project, when would you commit to it being complete? How would you allocate your managerial time to the separate project tasks?

COST IMPROVEMENT VIA INVENTORY MANAGEMENT AND DEMAND FORECASTING

One of the concerns of expanding the ATM and teller areas at the branch is increasing the amount of cash being held at the branch rather than invested in more productive opportunities. As a result, management would like to review the current cash inventory policy based on the number of tellers and ATMs you've recommended.

The branch borrows money from its depositors in various forms of savings and checking accounts, certificates of deposits (CDs), and so on, and pays depositors a weighted average interest rate of 5.2 percent on these accounts, which is its cost of funds. The branch uses these funds to make loans to customers and currently has a weighted interest rate of 9.1 percent on all loans outstanding, including first home mortgages, home equity loans, car loans, personal loans, and small business loans and credit lines. The bank uses the proceeds from its gross spread between deposits and loans to pay for its operating costs, write off bad loan losses, and earn a 19 percent return on invested capital for its shareholders. This mainly takes the form of investing the bank's capital in acquisitions of competitors to accumulate market power.

The forecasted demand for cash at each ATM is $150,000 each month, and $90,000 per month at each teller station. Currently, the branches have an armored car deliver cash once each week. The cost of this delivery is $300 per trip, which is constant for any size delivery. To save money, the local branch signed a contract with the armored car company for the upcoming year worth $10,400 (to be paid at the start of the year in one lump sum) to provide these deliveries (52 total for the year) for an average cost of $200 per delivery. The contract stipulates that additional deliveries outside of the normal schedule can be made at an additional cost of $250 per delivery and that 24 hours' advance notice must be provided for any delivery.

The assistant branch manager is responsible for monitoring the cash reserves in the branch and ensuring they do not fall below the minimum threshold. Her salary is a straight $45,000 per year, plus 30 percent for benefits with unpaid overtime, all of which is attributed to overhead. Part-time tellers earn $15 per hour plus 20 percent for benefits. When the armored car arrives, the assistant manager, with the help of one of the part-time tellers, immediately fills the ATM trays and puts the remaining cash for the teller trays in the vault. Each ATM tray can hold up to $40,000. Each tray takes five minutes to fill due to the care required in the stacking of bills so that misfeeds can be prevented. Individual teller trays are filled by each teller from the vault at the beginning of each shift, and then counted and returned to the vault at the end of each shift, which takes about ten minutes for each transaction. ATMs typically experience two types of problems leading to an economic loss: (1) theft from stolen ATM cards which amounts to 0.5 percent of the total cash used in the ATM for each 12–hour shift of operation, and (2) transaction errors from bills loaded incorrectly. Both types of losses come out of the branch profits and currently add up to 2.0 percent of the total cash used in the ATMs.

Since the introduction of high capability ATMs some 10 years ago, demand for their use has been growing steadily. After the initial burst of excitement when minimal function ATMs were introduced 15 years ago, basic growth has increased whenever new functionality has been introduced. For the 86th Street branch, significant improvements in functionality occurred in 1987 when account balance data was introduced, in 1990 when transferring money between accounts was introduced, and in 1994 when multilingual machines as well as the issuance of traveler's checks were introduced. The next major functionality improvement is planned for 1998, when stock sale and purchases will be allowed, as well as the issuance of money orders. All new introductions have been made during the first quarter of each year and have normally caused an increase in the average time customers spend at the ATMs, as well as the amount of cash withdrawn.

Before you develop your cash inventory level for the branch, the manager wants you to check on the forecast being used for the demand for cash at the ATMs over the next few years. Ten years of historical quarterly data have been made available to you by the branch (see Table 14). Forecasts on the independent macroeconomic and company controlled variable are also available in Table 14. In addition, the manager would like your advice on how frequently the branch should order cash deliveries and how much cash it should order each time. What is the average amount of cash on hand in the ATMs and how much does it cost the bank to hold that cash on an annual basis?

TOTAL QUALITY MANAGEMENT

Management is concerned about possible side effects from the merger announcements, like an increase in the error rates at branches and a general decrease in service times leading to long lines and irritated customers. As a key advisor to the bank's top management and merger team, you've had the chance to visit numerous branches and assess the situation. You've noted that most of the lower level employees in the back office and teller operations are highly anxious about the merger and feel like they may be fodder for the inevitable downsizing which they believe to be the management's chief strategy.

This is especially distressing since these employees interact most frequently with the customers and often vent their concerns openly in front of them. In addition, the stress and discontent are prime distractions that could lead to errors. Management fears the problems will get worse as the pace of merger activity increases and new complexities are undertaken such as combining the back offices, accounting, and information systems of the two banks; combining branches and management teams; and moving new tellers with seniority into unfamiliar branches and displacing lower seniority workers. There is the perception that the period following the previous merger was marked by lower quality and reduced customer service levels at some branches, as the combined bank struggled with its new identity.

Since all of the cost justifications for the merger depend on maintaining and improving quality and service levels, management has requested a proactive plan from you to ensure that the new 86th Street branch meets its service goals. Develop a brief quality statement that addresses all of a typical branch bank's operations. How do you maintain consistently high levels of fast, friendly service in an environment of fear and culture clash? How can you avoid costly errors and smoothly integrate the operations, management, personnel practices, and systems of the two different banks without degenerating into competitiveness and territorial behavior over whose methods will prevail?

To get started, the corporate vice chairman responsible for quality has asked you to look into a particular incident at a location where the bank was pilot testing a branch combination. It started with a complaint that a deposit transaction made a few weeks prior did not appear on the customer's monthly statement. Having endured a long wait at the bank the day the deposit was made, the customer was particularly irate. The vice chairman gives you a copy of the customer's letter which contains both the receipt from the missed transaction and the monthly statement.

A quick check of the branch's records from that day via the bank's on-line operations system confirms that the transaction was never entered. However, as you scroll through the records from that day, you notice something else a little unusual: a pair of offsetting transactions after the branch closed for the day.

The assistant manager at the branch explains the after hours transactions. On that day, one of the first of pilot operations, a senior teller reported that his drawer count was too low following the end of his shift. The teller was visibly upset, as he had never had a problem like this before and was especially nervous about keeping his job in light of the upcoming staff reductions. The assistant manager was very understanding about the incident, as the pilot branch had been off to a rough start during its first week. There were long lines throughout the day, at times spilling through the doors onto the sidewalk outside, and tellers worked furiously to keep pace with the seemingly endless onslaught of customers.

Fortunately, the manager explains, the imbalance was soon reconciled. Another teller came back at the end of her shift who had an incorrect drawer count that was too high by the same amount that the first teller's was too low. It then became immediately obvious to everyone involved what the problem was: the drawers must have been filled incorrectly at the start of the shifts with some cash being incorrectly placed into the second teller's drawer from the first teller's. This was especially understandable since both of the tellers came from the other bank, which used different shaped drawers and different procedures for filling the drawers.

In order not to upset the tellers any more than they already were, the assistant manager agreed to simply process a pair of phantom transactions to net out the count in the two tellers' drawers. Everyone was quite relieved at the speedy resolution to this incident. The manager continued to explain that he decided not to report it any further in order to calm some of the jittery feelings that were sweeping through the pilot branch's personnel during its stressful first week.

As you report back to the vice-chairman of quality, will you describe this incident? What issues for quality can be gleaned from the incident? What actions can the bank take to fix any problems you believe exist in the pilot branch and prevent them from infecting the rest of the bank as more operations are merged? Having just come from an American Management Association short course on total quality management, you are wondering whether to use a fishbone diagram to help explain the overage and underage in the cash drawers and other branch quality issues.

COST IMPROVEMENT VIA PROCESS ANALYSIS AND DESIGN

One of the major purposes of a branch bank is to facilitate the opening of new "line of credit" accounts by private and commercial customers. The 86th and Lexington location is a major crossroads on the Upper East Side, being strategically located near major bus and subway express stops, as well as local hospitals and many large apartment buildings. Demand for new accounts is relatively constant throughout the year, except for September, when college students return to start school. The location, with its good transportation and walking distance to many of the 2nd Avenue clubs serving college age students, has made the location increasingly popular with students sharing apartments in local buildings. The management of the to-be-consolidated branches wants to make a big effort to try and win over the business for new local accounts. They are trying to decide on an advertising program based on the branch's ability to handle a September peak of opening new line–of–credit accounts over and above the normal base business. Not having much familiarity with this part of branch operations, the manager has requested your assistance in determining the capabilities of the current system, and whether substantial new business could be handled by the current staff or if it would require the assistance of a corporate level team or the hiring of independent contractors.

The assistant manager with the responsibility for new accounts has described the current system as follows: The initial contact with a potential new account customer occurs at the branch or by a phone call to the branch. The breakdown between these two approaches is often determined by advertising. Normally they are divided 50/50, but a small amount of local radio advertisements can shift the mix to 75 percent phone. The initial phone contact is handled by a secretary, but an initial branch contact is handled by a customer account manager (CAM). The purpose of the initial contact is to answer some basic questions and to give the customer an application form to be filled out (phone contacts gets these forms by mail). Phone contacts usually take three minutes and branch contacts take five minutes, and do not vary if the customer is retail or commercial.

After receipt of the completed application, the CAM is required to obtain historical and employment information for a line of credit checking account. This can be obtained by a branch interview taking 10 minutes or a phone interview taking five minutes. Seventy five percent of retail customers avail themselves of an in-branch interview. The remainder use the phone. Commercial customers can only be interviewed at the branch due to the requirement that pertinent corporate documents must be inspected by the CAM, thus doubling the process time.

No matter how the information is obtained, the conservative nature of the branch requires the CAM to verify certain of the data in the application and approve the continuation of the process to the next phase, credit check. This verification takes 10 minutes for retail customers and 20 minutes for commercial customers. The credit check requires the use of an on-line computer to contact certain commercial entities for credit verification. The branch currently has only one of these machines. To process a credit check, the user must sign on to a network and do other tasks that usually take five minutes. After the system has been set up it will accept up to five different names to analyze. The average run time per name is 10 minutes. The CAM must remain at the terminal for this period since intermittent requests for additional information are often made by the computer. Once a printout has been obtained for a prospective applicant, an additional 45 minutes of CAM work are required for completion of the credit check and approval of the account. Other than the on–line service setup time, all run time estimates should be doubled for commercial customers. For new accounts with a line of credit exceeding $10,000, a division credit office (DCO) approval is required. This approval usually takes three days to obtain and requires about 30 minutes of CAM time for preparation and phone conversations with the DCO. Eighty percent of this three-day interval is spent in the in-box of the DCO and twenty percent is spent getting the paper application to and from the DCO's office in Long Island City. The DCO usually takes no more than 15 minutes on any one file. Approximately 10 percent of all new accounts request this expanded service.

After completing the credit check, the CAM must then inform the customer of the reasons for denial (this usually only happens with about 10 percent of the retail customers and 25 percent of the commercial customers). Either explanation takes 15 minutes. An approval moves the process to the next step, which is the ordering of the previously requested check styles and the ATM card and the establishment of a computer banking account, which is a new service of the bank. The check printing is done by an outside vendor and only requires an application completed by the CAM, which takes two minutes. It takes five business days to produce the checks, which are then mailed to the customer. The ATM card is created at a corporate headquarters facility, where it takes three business days, and it takes the CAM two minutes to order. The establishment of a computer banking account requires the CAM to spend 15 minutes on his or her desktop PC interacting with the corporate host computer. There is no setup time required for this operation. The checks, ATM card, and computer account can all be processed simultaneously and independently.

The ATM card is delivered to the branch and the customer is called so that he or she can pick it up and establish a PIN security code. This takes five minutes of CAM time. At this time, the CAM can also explain the operation of the computer banking system. Half of the customers avail themselves of this service, which requires 30 minutes for retail customers and 60 minutes for commercial customers. The remaining 50 percent are computer literate enough to establish their accounts on their own using only the printed material supplied by the bank. The delivery of the ATM card completes the opening of a new account.

Most CAMs spend only 20 percent of their time on new checking account activities. The remainder is split between mortgage and other loan applications, doing "due diligence" on existing loans, selling investment vehicles, and other activities. Assume that the demand for new accounts occurs uniformly throughout the hours of the day and days of the week and month. To stay competitive the bank feels it must be able to open an account and deliver an ATM card in five business days. Is this feasible? Given that the combined branch will have eight CAMs, how many new accounts could the branch process a month? Typically, 20 percent of the branch customers are commercial. New student accounts are considered to be 100 percent retail. The combined branches are forecast to open 50 new accounts per month. Is this feasible? The new student accounts will be incremental to this base. How many customer accounts could they open in September if CAMs worked two hours of overtime per day dedicated to the opening of these accounts?

The branch manager is considering using an outside agency to help with credit checks. This would involve the CAM filling out a form, requiring two minutes. The forms would be sent to the branch manager for approval and communication with the outside agency at the end of each day. It would take the branch manager 10 minutes to connect with the outside vendor's computer system and two minutes for each entry thereafter for a given day. The credit checks would be complete by the start of the third business day after the order at a cost of $10 per credit check (retail and commercial). A CAM receives $800 per week in salary and benefits. The branch manager receives $1,200 per week in salary and benefits. How much additional capacity would using the outside service create for the branch? Is it cost effective? The manager also wants to know whether any new advertising should be done to swing the mix of customers to those with a phone orientation and the maximum he should pay for the service.

Corporate marketing management has launched an advertising campaign, without seeking your advice or approval, that quoted a service guarantee to customers of a three day turnaround on new loan requests exceeding $10,000, but less than $500,000. The credit check for a new loan for an existing customer is identical to that described here for credit checks for new line–of– credit accounts with above $10,000 approval. Does your branch process need to be redesigned so that it can meet this service guarantee? What suggestions would you make to improve the process? Prepare a memo to the marketing department explaining your reactions to their campaign.

CAPACITY MANAGEMENT

Success in bringing in new "line of credit" accounts to the branch, as well as other positive market share forecasts by corporate as the result of the merger, is causing concern about the capacity of the branch to meet its growing demand. Unlike some operating systems that can store previously created products for future consumption (inventory), a service organization can only store capacity to serve, but not the service itself (i.e., extra ATMs). Both types of organizations maintain the ability to shift the time pattern of demand (if the branch was open more hours, then peak hour demand might be reduced), but not completely.

A small store next to the branch has just been vacated, and the branch has been given the opportunity to lease the space before it goes on the open market by a local real estate company, which is also a branch commercial customer. This space could be added to the existing first floor space so that the ATM area could be increased by 10 machines with a second or third "s" line service structure established. Multiple "s" lines might allow for some ATMs to be dedicated to long cycle transactions such as stock and insurance purchases.

For planning purposes, demand for service at the branch can be divided into two product categories; those requiring teller/ATM assistance (i.e., check cashing, account balance verification, etc.) and those requiring a Customer Account Manager (CAM) (loan applications, investment advice, etc.). Typically, demand for CAM services occurs somewhat uniformly over the day and within the week, with only a slight peak between 11:00 a.m. and 1:00 p.m. On average, a CAM can service the demand generated by six branch retail customers or three commercial customer per hour. History has shown that a branch with 10,000 retail customers and 2,500 commercial accounts would generate the hourly demand for CAM services shown in Table 15. Every 1% growth in accounts would increase these numbers by 1%. CAMs can only work four or eight hour shifts. The eight-hour shift workers are branch employees costing $800 per week, including benefits. The four-hour shift CAMs are part-timers hired from a temp agency and cost $500 per week, without benefits. Eight- and four-hour workers must work contiguous hours (i.e., 9-5, 9-1, 1-5, etc.). The branch's contract with the part-time employment agency states that a worker hired requires an up-front finder's fee of $1,000 and has no firing cost. Any break in service of more than one week requires the finder's fee to be paid again. Thus, the branch uses a rule of thumb that any part-time CAM will be on the payroll for at least six months. The demand patterns for both teller/ATM and CAM services are assumed to be stable for six months. New corporate forecasts for account growth assume that the commercial accounts should be growing by 5% every six months, and that a successful student account promotional campaign should add an additional 5% increase in retail accounts every year.

Currently, the branch is open for full service operation for eight hours a day (9:00AM – 5:00 PM)and the customer demand for teller/ATM services is given in Tables 1-12 previously discussed. The peak demand for teller services is forecasted to continue to grow in direct proportion to customer growth. A 20% increase in new accounts will increase peak demand by 20%. It is felt that expanding the branch hours might ameliorate this pattern even if it created incremental demand. The arrival data in Tables 1 to 12 is for the existing shift. Two additional increases in shift hours requiring complete branch services are being contemplated. The first would have the bank open two hours earlier (7:00 – 9:00 AM.) and stay open two hours later (5:00-7:00 PM). The second, only feasible if the first expansion is completed, would include these new hours and expand the evening hours to 11 PM. If both changes were made, the branch would be open 16 hours a day for full operations. It is felt that a minimum staff of five employees is required whenever the branch is in full operation (an assistant branch manager, two tellers able to perform both commercial and consumer transactions, a receptionist, and one CAM). Each four-hour shift addition is forecasted to cut peak day checking/ATM demand by 10%. Each four-hour shift increase is assumed to add 5% to the number of new accounts at the branch. The weekly wages plus benefits for the assistant manager is $900, for tellers - $600, and for secretaries - $450. A shift premium of 20% would be required to induce these people to work the 3 PM – 11 PM shift, as well as a 7 PM – 11 PM four-hour shift. Consistent overtime is not feasible over and above two hours per day. Overtime requires a 50% incentive. It costs $5,000 to hire and train a new full-time employee and $2,500 to fire one.

The neighboring store would require a one time refurbishment fee of $50,000 and an all-in weekly cost per ATM of $1,000 assuming a machine life of 3 years with no residual value. Each human teller requires processing equipment with a monthly fee of $200. The peak demand for services determines the maximum amount of equipment required.

Corporate management would like to know what the staffing plan of the branch would look like one to two years in the future if the promotion plan is successful. Management would also like to know the desired breakdown between tellers and ATMs, whether to rent the additional space, and what hours the branch should operate. The branch is considered a cost center where long term cost is expected to be minimized subject to specific service targets on customer waiting and transaction times (i.e., average teller/ATM waits of less than two minutes, standard deviation of teller/ATM waits of less than one minute, and new loan approval throughput time of less than five days, etc.).

Table 1
Chi-Square Goodness-of-Fit Test for Retail Customer Inter-arrival Times at 86th Street Branch

Inter-Arrival Times (seconds)	Number of Observ.-s	Cumulative Observ.-s	Fraction Of Total	Interval Mean	Squared Mean	Expected Exponential	Deviation From Exponential
2	29	29	0.1686	29	29.00	20.7613	3.2693
4	19	48	0.2791	57	171.00	18.3135	0.0257
6	9	57	0.3314	45	225.00	16.1542	3.1684
8	17	74	0.4302	119	833.00	14.2495	0.5309
10	11	85	0.4942	99	891.00	12.5694	0.1960
12	8	93	0.5407	88	968.00	11.0874	0.8597
14	8	101	0.5872	104	1,352.00	9.7802	0.3240
16	4	105	0.6105	60	900.00	8.6270	2.4817
18	5	110	0.6395	85	1,445.00	7.6099	0.8951
20	9	119	0.6919	171	3,249.00	6.7126	0.7794
22	5	124	0.7209	105	2,205.00	5.9212	0.1433
24	7	131	0.7616	161	3,703.00	5.2230	0.6046
26	4	135	0.7849	100	2,500.00	4.6072	0.0800
28	2	137	0.7965	54	1,458.00	4.0640	1.0482
30	4	141	0.8198	116	3,364.00	3.5848	0.0481
32	6	147	0.8547	186	5,766.00	3.1622	2.5468
34	2	149	0.8663	66	2,178.00	2.7893	0.2234
36	1	150	0.8721	35	1,225.00	2.4604	0.8669
38	2	152	0.8837	74	2,738.00	2.1703	0.0134
40	1	153	0.8895	39	1,521.00	1.9145	0.4368
42	1	154	0.8953	41	1,681.00	1.6887	0.2809
44	2	156	0.9070	86	3,698.00	1.4896	0.1749
46	3	159	0.9244	135	6,075.00	1.3140	2.1634
48	2	161	0.9360	94	4,418.00	1.1591	0.6101
50	2	163	0.9477	98	4,802.00	1.0224	0.9348
52	1	164	0.9535	51	2,601.00	0.9019	0.0107
54	3	167	0.9709	159	8,427.00	0.7955	6.1089
56	2	169	0.9826	110	6,050.00	0.7017	2.4020
58	1	170	0.9884	57	3,249.00	0.6190	0.2345
60	2	172	1.0000	118	6,962.00	0.5460	3.8719

Sample mean: 15.94
Variance: 238.21
35.3337

Table 2
Chi-Square Goodness-of-Fit Test for Retail Customer Inter-arrival Times at Lexington Ave. Branch

Inter-Arrival Times (seconds)	Num. of Observ.-s	Cum. Observ.-s	Fraction of Total	Interval Mean	Squared Mean	Expected Exponential	Deviation From Exponential
2	21	21	0.1221	21	21.00	19.0312	0.2037
4	15	36	0.2093	45	135.00	16.9827	0.2315
6	18	54	0.3140	90	450.00	15.1547	0.5342
8	14	68	0.3953	98	686.00	13.5234	0.0168
10	10	78	0.4535	90	810.00	12.0677	0.3543
12	5	83	0.4826	55	605.00	10.7688	3.0903
14	8	91	0.5291	104	1,352.00	9.6096	0.2696
16	6	97	0.5640	90	1,350.00	8.5752	0.7734
18	5	102	0.5930	85	1,445.00	7.6522	0.9192
20	9	111	0.6453	171	3,249.00	6.8285	0.6906
22	7	118	0.6860	147	3,087.00	6.0935	0.1349
24	7	125	0.7267	161	3,703.00	5.4376	0.4489
26	6	131	0.7616	150	3,750.00	4.8523	0.2715
28	3	134	0.7791	81	2,187.00	4.3300	0.4085
30	4	138	0.8023	116	3,364.00	3.8639	0.0048
32	2	140	0.8140	62	1,922.00	3.4480	0.6081
34	2	142	0.8256	66	2,178.00	3.0768	0.3769
36	3	145	0.8430	105	3,675.00	2.7456	0.0236
38	2	147	0.8547	74	2,738.00	2.4501	0.0827
40	2	149	0.8663	78	3,042.00	2.1864	0.0159
42	1	150	0.8721	41	1,681.00	1.9510	0.4636
44	2	152	0.8837	86	3,698.00	1.7410	0.0385
46	2	154	0.8953	90	4,050.00	1.5536	0.1283
48	2	156	0.9070	94	4,418.00	1.3864	0.2716
50	4	160	0.9302	196	9,604.00	1.2372	6.1701
52	2	162	0.9419	102	5,202.00	1.1040	0.7272
54	2	164	0.9535	106	5,618.00	0.9852	1.0454
56	2	166	0.9651	110	6,050.00	0.8791	1.4292
58	3	169	0.9826	171	9,747.00	0.7845	6.2570
60	2	171	0.9942	118	6,962.00	0.7000	2.4140
		Sample mean:		17.56		Chi-square Statistic:	28.4040
		Variance			257.56		

Table 3
Chi-Square Goodness-of-Fit Test for Retail Customer Inter-arrival Times at the Combined Branches

Inter-Arrival Times (seconds)	Number of Observ.-s	Cum. Observ.-s	Fraction of Total	Interval Mean	Squared Mean	Expected Exponential	Deviation From Exponential
1	50	50	0.1458	25	12.50	39.7107	2.6660
2	34	84	0.2449	51	76.50	35.2411	0.0437
3	27	111	0.3236	67.5	168.75	31.2745	0.5842
4	31	142	0.4140	108.5	379.75	27.7544	0.3795
5	21	163	0.4752	94.5	425.25	24.6305	0.5351
6	13	176	0.5131	71.5	393.25	21.8583	3.5899
7	16	192	0.5598	104	676.00	19.3980	0.5952
8	10	202	0.5889	75	562.50	17.2147	3.0237
9	10	212	0.6181	85	722.50	15.2771	1.8228
10	18	230	0.6706	171	1,624.50	13.5576	1.4556
11	12	242	0.7055	126	1,323.00	12.0316	0.0001
12	14	256	0.7464	161	1,851.50	10.6774	1.0339
13	10	266	0.7755	125	1,562.50	9.4756	0.0290
14	5	271	0.7901	67.5	911.25	8.4091	1.3821
15	8	279	0.8134	116	1,682.00	7.4626	0.0387
16	8	287	0.8367	124	1,922.00	6.6227	0.2864
17	4	291	0.8484	66	1,089.00	5.8773	0.5996
18	4	295	0.8601	70	1,225.00	5.2157	0.2834
19	4	299	0.8717	74	1,369.00	4.6287	0.0854
20	3	302	0.8805	58.5	1,140.75	4.1077	0.2987
21	2	304	0.8863	41	840.50	3.6454	0.7426
22	4	308	0.8980	86	1,849.00	3.2351	0.1809
23	5	313	0.9125	112.5	2,531.25	2.8709	1.5789
24	4	317	0.9242	94	2,209.00	2.5478	0.8277
25	6	323	0.9417	147	3,601.50	2.2610	6.1829
26	3	326	0.9504	76.5	1,950.75	2.0065	0.4919
27	5	331	0.9650	132.5	3,511.25	1.7807	5.8201
28	4	335	0.9767	110	3,025.00	1.5803	3.7051
29	4	339	0.9883	114	3,249.00	1.4024	4.8114
30	4	343	1.0000	118	3,481.00	1.2446	6.1005
		Sample mean:		8.37		Chi-square Statistic:	49.1753
		Variance			62.13		

Table 4
Chi-Square Goodness of Fit Test for Commercial Inter-arrival Times at 86th Street Branch

Inter-Arrival Times (seconds)	Number of Observ.-s	Cum. Observ.-s	Fraction of Total	INterval Mean	Squared Mean	Expected Exponential	Deviation From Exponential
4	6	6	0.0674	12	24	8.0606	0.5268
8	5	11	0.1236	30	180	7.3829	0.7691
12	6	17	0.1910	60	600	6.7623	0.0859
16	8	25	0.2809	112	1,568	6.1938	0.5267
20	5	30	0.3371	90	1,620	5.6731	0.0799
24	3	33	0.3708	66	1,452	5.1961	0.9282
28	4	37	0.4157	104	2,704	4.7593	0.1211
32	4	41	0.4607	120	3,600	4.3592	0.0296
36	2	43	0.4831	68	2,312	3.9927	0.9945
40	3	46	0.5169	114	4,332	3.6570	0.1180
44	2	48	0.5393	84	3,528	3.3496	0.5438
48	2	50	0.5618	92	4,232	3.0680	0.3718
52	2	52	0.5843	100	5,000	2.8101	0.2335
56	3	55	0.6180	162	8,748	2.5738	0.0706
60	3	58	0.6517	174	10,092	2.3575	0.1751
64	3	61	0.6854	186	11,532	2.1593	0.3273
68	2	63	0.7079	132	8,712	1.9777	0.0003
72	3	66	0.7416	210	14,700	1.8115	0.7798
76	3	69	0.7753	222	16,428	1.6592	1.0835
80	2	71	0.7978	156	12,168	1.5197	0.1518
84	2	73	0.8202	164	13,448	1.3919	0.2656
88	3	76	0.8539	258	22,188	1.2749	2.3342
92	2	78	0.8764	180	16,200	1.1677	0.5932
96	2	80	0.8989	188	17,672	1.0696	0.8094
100	1	81	0.9101	98	9,604	0.9796	0.0004
104	3	84	0.9438	306	31,212	0.8973	4.9275
108	1	85	0.9551	106	11,236	0.8219	0.0386
112	0	85	0.9551	0	0	0.7528	0.7528
116	3	88	0.9888	342	38,988	0.6895	7.7428
120	1	89	1.0000	118	13,924	0.6315	0.2150

Sample mean: 45.55

Variance: 1,161

Chi-square Statistic: 25.5970

Table 5
Chi-Square Goodness of Fit Test for Commercial Inter-arrival Times at Lexington Ave. Branch

Inter-Arrival Times (seconds)	Number of Observ.-s	Cum. Observ.-s	Fraction of Total	Interval Mean	Squared Mean	Expected Exponential	Deviation From Exponential
4	4	4	0.0449	8	16	6.0131	0.6740
8	3	7	0.0787	18	108	5.6209	1.2221
12	3	10	0.1124	30	300	5.2542	0.9671
16	3	13	0.1461	42	588	4.9115	0.7439
20	1	14	0.1573	18	324	4.5911	2.8089
24	2	16	0.1798	44	968	4.2917	1.2237
28	2	18	0.2022	52	1,352	4.0117	1.0088
32	1	19	0.2135	30	900	3.7500	2.0167
36	3	22	0.2472	102	3,468	3.5054	0.0729
40	3	25	0.2809	114	4,332	3.2768	0.0234
44	3	28	0.3146	126	5,292	3.0630	0.0013
48	3	31	0.3483	138	6,348	2.8632	0.0065
52	2	33	0.3708	100	5,000	2.6765	0.1710
56	3	36	0.4045	162	8,748	2.5019	0.0992
60	2	38	0.4270	116	6,728	2.3387	0.0490
64	3	41	0.4607	186	11,532	2.1861	0.3030
68	3	44	0.4944	198	13,068	2.0435	0.4477
72	3	47	0.5281	210	14,700	1.9102	0.6217
76	4	51	0.5730	296	21,904	1.7856	2.7460
80	4	55	0.6180	312	24,336	1.6692	3.2548
84	4	59	0.6629	328	26,896	1.5603	3.8148
88	3	62	0.6966	258	22,188	1.4585	1.6292
92	3	65	0.7303	270	24,300	1.3634	1.9646
96	2	67	0.7528	188	17,672	1.2744	0.4131
100	2	69	0.7753	196	19,208	1.1913	0.5490
104	2	71	0.7978	204	20,808	1.1136	0.7055
108	3	74	0.8315	318	33,708	1.0410	3.6868
112	3	77	0.8652	330	36,300	0.9731	4.2222
116	1	78	0.8764	114	12,996	0.9096	0.0090
120	2	80	0.8989	236	27,848	0.8503	1.5547
	Sample mean:			59.30		Chi Square Statistic:	37.0106
	Variance				1,133		

Table 6
Chi-Square Goodness-of-Fit Test for Commercial Inter-arrival Times at the Combined Branches

Inter-Arrival Times (seconds)	Number of Observ.-s	Cum. Observ.-s	Fraction of Total	Interval Mean	Squared Mean	Expected Exponential	Deviation From Exponential
2	10	10	0.0592	10	10	13.8838	1.0865
4	8	18	0.1065	24	72	12.8570	1.8348
6	9	27	0.1598	45	225	11.9061	0.7094
8	11	38	0.2249	77	539	11.0256	0.0001
10	6	44	0.2604	54	486	10.2102	1.7361
12	5	49	0.2899	55	605	9.4550	2.0991
14	6	55	0.3254	78	1,014	8.7558	0.8673
16	5	60	0.3550	75	1,125	8.1082	1.1915
18	5	65	0.3846	85	1,445	7.5085	0.8381
20	6	71	0.4201	114	2,166	6.9532	0.1307
22	5	76	0.4497	105	2,205	6.4390	0.3216
24	5	81	0.4793	115	2,645	5.9628	0.1554
26	4	85	0.5030	100	2,500	5.5218	0.4194
28	6	91	0.5385	162	4,374	5.1134	0.1537
30	5	96	0.5680	145	4,205	4.7352	0.0148
32	6	102	0.6036	186	5,766	4.3850	0.5948
34	5	107	0.6331	165	5,445	4.0607	0.2173
36	6	113	0.6686	210	7,350	3.7604	1.3339
38	7	120	0.7101	259	9,583	3.4823	3.5536
40	6	126	0.7456	234	9,126	3.2247	2.3885
42	6	132	0.7811	246	10,086	2.9862	3.0416
44	6	138	0.8166	258	11,094	2.7654	3.7835
46	5	143	0.8462	225	10,125	2.5609	2.3232
48	4	147	0.8698	188	8,836	2.3715	1.1184
50	3	150	0.8876	147	7,203	2.1961	0.2943
52	5	155	0.9172	255	13,005	2.0337	4.3268
54	4	159	0.9408	212	11,236	1.8832	2.3792
56	3	162	0.9586	165	9,075	1.7440	0.9046
58	4	166	0.9822	228	12,996	1.6150	3.5222
60	3	169	1.0000	177	10,443	1.4955	1.5134
Sample mean:					26.03	Chi-square Statistic:	42.8536
Variance					299		

Table 7
Chi-Square Goodness of Fit Test for Retail Customer Service Times

Service Times (sec)	Number of Observ.-s	Cum. Observ.-s	Fraction of Total	Interval Mean	Squared Mean	Erlang-2 Deviation	Erlang-3 Deviation	Erlang-4 Deviation
10	0	0	0.0000	0	0.00	0.1900	0.5915	1.3012
20	4	4	0.0597	60	900.00	5.8596	0.1018	0.9419
30	7	11	0.1642	175	4,375.00	7.2984	0.1424	0.8617
40	9	20	0.2985	315	11,025.00	7.0144	0.2488	0.2831
50	11	31	0.4627	495	22,275.00	8.4638	1.0608	0.1444
60	9	40	0.5970	495	27,225.00	2.7505	0.2096	0.1013
70	6	46	0.6866	390	25,350.00	0.0640	0.1210	0.0096
80	5	51	0.7612	375	28,125.00	0.0235	0.1369	0.0362
90	2	53	0.7910	170	14,450.00	1.8940	1.6782	0.4857
100	1	54	0.8060	95	9,025.00	2.9560	2.1423	0.6927
110	2	56	0.8358	210	22,050.00	1.2367	0.3562	0.1540
120	1	57	0.8507	115	13,225.00	2.1011	0.7649	0.0000
130	2	59	0.8806	250	31,250.00	0.5586	0.0302	2.7553
140	1	60	0.8955	135	18,225.00	1.2656	0.0784	0.7894
150	2	62	0.9254	290	42,050.00	0.1024	1.0706	11.1269
160	1	63	0.9403	155	24,025.00	0.5985	0.1132	4.0550
170	0	63	0.9403	0	0.00	1.7928	0.5194	0.1064
180	1	64	0.9552	175	30,625.00	0.1660	1.0456	13.1987
190	1	65	0.9701	185	34,225.00	0.0482	1.9987	22.5559
200	1	66	0.9851	195	38,025.00	0.0008	3.4316	37.9730
210	0	66	0.9851	0	0.00	0.8443	0.1351	0.0153
220	0	66	0.9851	0	0.00	0.6902	0.0952	0.0093
230	0	66	0.9851	0	0.00	0.5618	0.0668	0.0056
240	1	67	1.0000	235	55,225.00	0.6511	19.4605	293.5165
250	0	67	1.0000	0	0.00	0.3679	0.0325	0.0020
260	0	67	1.0000	0	0.00	0.2962	0.0226	0.0012
270	0	67	1.0000	0	0.00	0.2377	0.0156	0.0007
280	0	67	1.0000	0	0.00	0.1903	0.0108	0.0004
290	0	67	1.0000	0	0.00	0.1519	0.0074	0.0003
300	0	67	1.0000	0	0.00	0.1209	0.0051	0.0002
Sample mean:				67.39		48.4969	35.6939	391.1235
Variance					2,200.27			

Table 8
Chi-Square Goodness-of-Fit Test for Commercial Customer Service Times

Service Times (sec)	Number of Observ.-s	Cum. Observ.-s	Fraction of Total	Interval Mean	Squared Mean	Erlang-2 Deviation	Erlang-3 Deviation	Erlang-4 Deviation
10	0	0	0.0000	0	0.00	0.0843	0.2485	0.5565
20	3	3	0.0448	45	675.00	8.8137	0.9680	0.0739
30	5	8	0.1194	125	3,125.00	8.4147	0.5054	0.4904
40	7	15	0.2239	245	8,575.00	8.6572	0.4289	0.6039
50	9	24	0.3582	405	18,225.00	9.5250	0.6230	0.3201
60	6	30	0.4478	330	18,150.00	0.7821	0.4657	2.5379
70	7	37	0.5522	455	29,575.00	0.9016	0.2558	1.5322
80	9	46	0.6866	675	50,625.00	2.2968	0.0151	0.1841
90	9	55	0.8209	765	65,025.00	1.6698	0.0297	0.0127
100	9	64	0.9552	855	81,225.00	1.3355	0.0933	0.0825
110	7	71	1.0597	735	77,175.00	0.0836	0.0482	0.0000
120	6	77	1.1493	690	79,350.00	0.0144	0.1394	0.0023
130	3	80	1.1940	375	46,875.00	1.6762	1.7456	0.7187
140	3	83	1.2388	405	54,675.00	1.5638	1.2411	0.2418
150	3	86	1.2836	435	63,075.00	1.4075	0.7933	0.0148
160	3	89	1.3284	465	72,075.00	1.2217	0.4277	0.0696
170	3	92	1.3731	495	81,675.00	1.0194	0.1645	0.4450
180	2	94	1.4030	350	61,250.00	1.8168	0.4899	0.0931
190	3	97	1.4478	555	102,675.00	0.6125	0.0152	2.3902
200	3	100	1.4925	585	114,075.00	0.4281	0.1630	4.1386
210	3	103	1.5373	615	126,075.00	0.2679	0.4847	6.5841
220	3	106	1.5821	645	138,675.00	0.1394	1.0044	9.9267
230	2	108	1.6119	450	101,250.00	0.5833	0.2351	5.3347
240	2	110	1.6418	470	110,450.00	0.3986	0.5553	7.9675
250	2	112	1.6716	490	120,050.00	0.2451	1.0341	11.5241
260	2	114	1.7015	510	130,050.00	0.1261	1.6963	16.3054
270	2	116	1.7313	530	140,450.00	0.0448	2.5738	22.7210
280	1	117	1.7463	275	75,625.00	0.5713	0.3466	6.9168
290	0	117	1.7463	0	0.00	1.8824	0.4603	0.0855
300	1	118	1.7612	295	87,025.00	0.2805	1.0254	13.6457
		Sample mean:		112.46		56.8640	18.2772	115.5195
		Variance			4,791.84			

Table 9
Chi-Square Goodness of Fit Test for Total Customer Population Interarrival Times

Inter-Arrival Time (seconds)	Number of Observ.(s)	Cum. Observations	Fraction of Total	Interval Mean	Squared Mean	Expected Exponential	Exponential Deviation
1	29	29	0.1790	14.50	7.25	23.9121	1.0826
2	24	53	0.3272	36.00	54.00	20.4132	0.6302
3	16	69	0.4259	40.00	100.00	17.4263	0.1167
4	17	86	0.5309	59.50	208.25	14.8764	0.3031
5	14	100	0.6173	63.00	283.50	12.6996	0.1332
6	8	108	0.6667	44.00	242.00	10.8414	0.7447
7	8	116	0.7160	52.00	338.00	9.2550	0.1702
8	4	120	0.7407	30.00	225.00	7.9008	1.9259
9	5	125	0.7716	42.50	361.25	6.7447	0.4513
10	3	128	0.7901	28.50	270.75	5.7578	1.3209
11	5	133	0.8210	52.50	551.25	4.9153	0.0015
12	2	135	0.8333	23.00	264.50	4.1961	1.1494
13	4	139	0.8580	50.00	625.00	3.5821	0.0488
14	2	141	0.8704	27.00	364.50	3.0580	0.3660
15	1	142	0.8765	14.50	210.25	2.6105	0.9936
16	1	143	0.8827	15.50	240.25	2.2285	0.6772
17	2	145	0.8951	33.00	544.50	1.9024	0.0050
18	1	146	0.9012	17.50	306.25	1.6241	0.2398
19	2	148	0.9136	37.00	684.50	1.3864	0.2715
20	1	149	0.9198	19.50	380.25	1.1836	0.0285
21	1	150	0.9259	20.50	420.25	1.0104	0.0001
22	2	152	0.9383	43.00	924.50	0.8625	1.5000
23	0	152	0.9383	0.00	0.00	0.7363	0.7363
24	2	154	0.9506	47.00	1,104.50	0.6286	2.9921
25	2	156	0.9630	49.00	1,200.50	0.5366	3.9909
26	1	157	0.9691	25.50	650.25	0.4581	0.6411
27	1	158	0.9753	26.50	702.25	0.3911	0.9482
28	2	160	0.9877	55.00	1,512.50	0.3338	8.3157
29	1	161	0.9938	28.50	812.25	0.2850	1.7939
30	1	162	1.0000	29.50	870.25	0.2433	2.3536
		Sample mean		6.32		Chi-square statistic:	33.9320
		Variance			49.30		

Table 10
Chart of Daily Average Customer Arrival Rates

Time of Day	Average Customer Arrivals					
	Peak Day (Monday and Friday)			Normal Day		
	Retail	Commercial	Total	Retail	Commercial	Total
9:00-9:59	257	121	378	224	94	318
10:00-10:59	212	103	315	168	80	248
11:00-11:59	419	128	547	353	107	460
12:00-12:59	432	139	571	366	112	478
1:00-1:59	238	116	354	217	72	289
2:00-2:59	97	82	179	72	31	103
3:00-3:59	198	107	305	151	88	239
4:00-4:59	284	129	413	238	74	312

Table 11
Chi-Square Goodness-of-Fit Test for ATM Customer Inter Arrival Times at the Combined Branches

Inter-Arrival Times (seconds)	Number of Observ.-s	Cum. Observations	Fraction of Total	Interval Mean	Squared Mean	Expected Expon.	Expon. Deviation
1	65	65	0.3250	32.5	16.25	56.7760	1.1912
2	44	109	0.5450	66	99.00	40.6591	0.2745
3	28	137	0.6850	70	175.00	29.1173	0.0429
4	14	151	0.7550	49	171.50	20.8519	2.2515
5	12	163	0.8150	54	243.00	14.9327	0.5760
6	11	174	0.8700	60.5	332.75	10.6938	0.0088
7	5	179	0.8950	32.5	211.25	7.6582	0.9227
8	3	182	0.9100	22.5	168.75	5.4843	1.1253
9	4	186	0.9300	34	289.00	3.9275	0.0013
10	3	189	0.9450	28.5	270.75	2.8126	0.0125
11	2	191	0.9550	21	220.50	2.0142	0.0001
12	2	193	0.9650	23	264.50	1.4424	0.2155
13	2	195	0.9750	25	312.50	1.0330	0.9053
14	1	196	0.9800	13.5	182.25	0.7397	0.0916
15	1	197	0.9850	14.5	210.25	0.5298	0.4174
16	1	198	0.9900	15.5	240.25	0.3794	1.0153
17	0	198	0.9900	0	0.00	0.2717	0.2717
18	1	199	0.9950	17.5	306.25	0.1946	3.3344
19	0	199	0.9950	0	0.00	0.1393	0.1393
20	1	200	1.0000	19.5	380.25	0.0998	8.1219
21	0	200	1.0000	0	0.00	0.0715	0.0715
22	0	200	1.0000	0	0.00	0.0512	0.0512
23	0	200	1.0000	0	0.00	0.0366	0.0366
24	0	200	1.0000	0	0.00	0.0262	0.0262
25	0	200	1.0000	0	0.00	0.0188	0.0188
26	0	200	1.0000	0	0.00	0.0135	0.0135
27	0	200	1.0000	0	0.00	0.0096	0.0096
28	0	200	1.0000	0	0.00	0.0069	0.0069
29	0	200	1.0000	0	0.00	0.0049	0.0049
30	0	200	1.0000	0	0.00	0.0035	0.0035

Sample mean 3.00

Variance 11.50

Chi-Square Statistic: 21.1620

Table 12
Chi-Square Goodness of Fit Test for ATM Customer Service Times

Service Times (sec)	Num. of Observ.-s	Cum. Observ.-s	Fraction of Total	Interval Mean	Squared Mean	Erlang-2 Deviation	Erlang-3 Deviation	Erlang-4 Deviation
5	2	2	0.0286	5	12.01	10.3449	1.4249	0.0036
10	7	9	0.1286	52.5	175.00	14.6437	1.0360	0.3627
15	10	19	0.2714	125	1,000.00	11.2292	0.5013	0.4745
20	11	30	0.4286	192.5	2,475.00	6.9479	0.2540	0.1595
25	8	38	0.5429	180	3,200.00	0.6844	0.2137	0.5725
30	9	47	0.6714	247.5	5,625.00	1.0835	0.0316	0.1395
35	4	51	0.7286	130	3,600.00	0.8707	1.3827	0.4834
40	5	56	0.8000	187.5	6,125.00	0.1775	0.0937	0.3551
45	2	58	0.8286	85	3,200.00	2.2551	1.3406	0.1028
50	1	59	0.8429	47.5	2,025.00	3.1344	1.6425	0.2222
55	2	61	0.8714	105	5,000.00	1.2298	0.0868	1.0224
60	1	62	0.8857	57.5	3,025.00	1.9523	0.3423	0.2554
65	1	63	0.9000	62.5	3,600.00	1.4256	0.0568	1.1054
70	1	64	0.9143	67.5	4,225.00	0.9704	0.0131	2.8299
75	1	65	0.9286	72.5	4,900.00	0.5970	0.2323	5.9787
80	1	66	0.9429	77.5	5,625.00	0.3110	0.7672	11.5648
85	1	67	0.9571	82.5	6,400.00	0.1156	1.7168	21.4175
90	1	68	0.9714	87.5	7,225.00	0.0141	3.2480	38.8241
95	1	69	0.9857	92.5	8,100.00	0.0116	5.6287	69.6953
100	0	69	0.9857	0	0.00	0.7121	0.0894	0.0079
105	0	69	0.9857	0	0.00	0.5616	0.0595	0.0044
110	0	69	0.9857	0	0.00	0.4409	0.0395	0.0025
115	0	69	0.9857	0	0.00	0.3446	0.0261	0.0014
120	1	70	1.0000	117.5	13,225.00	1.9960	56.3363	1,294.2951
125	0	70	1.0000	0	0.00	0.2081	0.0112	0.0004
130	0	70	1.0000	0	0.00	0.1609	0.0073	0.0002
135	0	70	1.0000	0	0.00	0.1240	0.0048	0.0001
140	0	70	1.0000	0	0.00	0.0953	0.0031	0.0001
145	0	70	1.0000	0	0.00	0.0730	0.0020	0.0000
150	0	70	1.0000	0	0.00	0.0558	0.0013	0.0000
		Sample Mean:		29.64		62.7710	76.5935	1,449.8813
		Variance			389.33			

Table 13: Project Schedule

Activity Name	Predecessor	Normal Duration (days)	Normal Cost	Most Likely Crash Duration (days)	Crash Cost	Cost/ Time	Crash Duration (days) Optimistic	Pessimistic
Reconfigure Back Offices	none	15	$25,000	10	31,000	$1,200	7	12
Move ATMs	none	6	$5,000	3	6,000	$333	2	4
Frame Addt'l ATM Space	RBO	10	$10,000	5	15,000	$1,000	3	8
Install ATM Wiring	Frame-1	20	$30,000	12	50,000	$2,500	8	15
Install ATMs	Wire-1, Move	2	$4,000	1	6,000	$2,000	1	2
Circuit Test ATMs	ATM	6	$7,500	3	15,000	$2,500	2	4
Connect to Network	Ckt-a	2	$4,000	1	6,000	$2,000	1	2
Circuit Test Connection	Conn	6	$7,500	3	10,500	$1,000	2	4
Final Walk Through	Ckt-b	2	$2,500	1	4,000	$1,500	1	2
Touch Up Operations	Walk-1	4	$3,000	2	5,000	$1,000	1	4
Layout 3rd Floor	none	10	$25,000	6	31,000	$1,500	4	8
Put Up Framing	Floor	15	$14,000	8	21,000	$1,000	5	12
Shingle the Roof	Frame-3	10	$12,000	6	18,000	$1,500	4	8
Close Exterior Walls	Frame-3	8	$10,000	5	12,000	$667	3	7
Install Plumbing	Ext, Roof	12	$16,000	6	20,000	$667	3	10
Install Wiring	Ext, Roof	15	$20,000	8	34,000	$2,000	5	12
Install HVAC System	Ext, Roof	10	$12,000	5	15,000	$600	3	7
Install Insulation	Plumb, Wire-3, HVAC	6	$8,000	3	12,000	$1,333	2	4
Close Interior Walls	Insul	4	$6,000	2	9,000	$1,500	1	3
Paint Interior	Int	3	$3,000	2	5,000	$2,000	1	3
Install Fixtures	Paint	3	$4,000	2	6,000	$2,000	1	4
Lay Carpeting	Fixt	2	$3,000	1	5,000	$2,000	1	2
Final Walk Through	Carpet	2	$2,500	1	5,000	$2,500	1	2
Touch Up Operations	Walk-3	4	$3,000	2	5,000	$1,000	1	3
Design New 2nd Floor	none	20	$20,000	10	35,000	$1,500	6	15
Demolish Office Space	T/U-1, T/U-3	5	$10,000	3	15,000	$2,500	2	4
Frame Teller Stations	Demolish	10	$12,000	5	24,000	$2,400	3	7
Spackle	Frame-2	5	$6,000	3	10,000	$2,000	2	4
Install Partitions	Spackle	6	$8,000	3	15,000	$2,333	2	4
Paint	Part	3	$3,000	2	5,000	$2,000	1	3
Install Electronics	Paint	10	$15,000	5	25,000	$2,000	3	7
Final Test	Elec	4	$5,000	2	10,000	$2,500	1	3

Table 14

Year/ Quarter	# Branch Customers	Cash With-drawals ($000s)	ATM Cash With-drawals ($000s)	# ATM's	Gross U.S. Income	NY Employment (000's)	City NY Unemployment Rate (%)	NY Inflation 84=100	Corp. Adv. Expenditures ($000s)	Branch Promotions ($000s)	Local Population	Inflation Adjusted Inc*	Adv*	Promo*
87/1	9862	2652.115	262.115	2	1609	3543.2	6.5	115.3	19091	10900	49922	1609	19091	10900
87/2	9987	2720.688	270.608	2	1639	3592.4	5.6	117.2	19088	11200	49865	1612	18779	11018
87/3	9908	2671.15	276.511	2	1659	3585.1	5.5	118.9	18966	11500	49605	1609	18392	11152
87/4	10201	1816.9	199.61	2	1678	3639.4	5.3	120.4	19089	12000	49481	1607	18280	11492
88/1	10295	2901.027	292.701	2	1707	3581.0	4.9	121.3	19408	12250	49212	1623	18448	11644
88/2	10380	2894.13	309.814	2	1706	3611.5	4.5	122.8	19076	12500	49183	1602	17911	11737
88/3	10433	2988.517	427.558	3	1761	3586.5	5.2	124.6	19211	12500	49402	1630	17777	11567
88/4	10402	2939.69	449.535	3	1766	3644.0	5.4	126.0	19480	12750	49577	1616	17826	11667
89/1	10566	3066.54	489.195	3	1812	3587.6	6.0	127.8	19951	13000	49673	1635	18000	11728
89/2	10574	3043.6	628.72	4	1832	3627.1	7.4	130.1	20176	13200	49887	1624	17881	11698
89/3	10691	3076.16	635.221	4	1835	3590.6	7.2	131.2	20843	13500	49904	1613	18317	11864
89/4	10619	3082.562	656.346	4	1883	3627.7	6.9	133.1	21673	13600	49892	1631	18775	11781
90/1	10312	2892.664	605.832	4	1901	3569.3	7.0	135.7	21752	13500	49961	1615	18482	11471
90/2	10467	2973.939	674.857	4	1925	3595.3	6.4	137.2	22304	13800	49857	1618	18744	11597
90/3	10448	2972.034	694.802	4	1964	3553.2	7.1	139.7	23021	14000	50034	1621	19000	11555
90/4	10640	3090.943	688.166	4	2000	3547.2	7.2	141.6	23300	14500	50006	1629	18972	11807
91/1	10249	2909.024	711.432	4	2033	3394.8	8.0	143.3	23741	14000	49918	1636	19102	11264
91/2	10523	3084.33	867.205	6	2062	3399.1	8.4	144.1	23912	14500	49890	1650	19133	11602
91/3	10736	3197.189	909.259	6	2086	3338.9	8.9	145.5	24188	15000	50046	1653	19168	11887
91/4	10264	3000.669	956.187	6	2117	3366.2	9.5	146.3	24403	14750	50024	1668	19232	11625
92/1	10055	2948.129	907.282	6	2170	3266.2	10.7	148.1	24806	14500	49899	1689	19312	11289
92/2	10210	3039.494	944.781	6	2192	3292.6	10.7	149.2	23203	15000	49985	1694	17931	11592
92/3	10594	3237.073	981.284	6	2218	3269.0	11.5	150.7	21988	15500	50097	1697	16823	11859
92/4	10815	3472.901	997.622	6	2305	3297.6	11.2	152.1	22089	16500	50192	1747	16745	12508
93/1	10775	3301.397	1044.378	6	2247	3239.2	11.3	153.6	21896	16500	50108	1687	16436	12386
93/2	10619	3339.595	1041.919	6	2316	3282.2	10.1	154.0	21788	16250	50056	1734	16313	12166
93/3	10523	3275.926	1058.614	6	2321	3281.0	10.0	155.0	21987	16250	50222	1727	16355	12088
93/4	10837	3685.834	1072.815	6	2466	3331.0	10.1	155.5	22473	16500	50173	1828	16663	12234
94/1	10692	3505.059	1107.572	6	2431	3265.9	10.1	157.1	22389	17100	50160	1784	16432	12550
94/2	10861	3735.031	1179.622	6	2518	3313.7	8.8	157.6	22206	17500	50121	1842	16246	12803
94/3	11090	3998.562	1229.305	6	2619	3307.0	8.3	158.8	22198	18000	50298	1902	16117	13069
94/4	11176	4059.83	1359.868	6	2639	3356.1	7.6	159.3	23077	18000	50287	1910	16703	13028
95/1	11568	4333.501	1966.75	10	2701	3286.9	8.2	160.4	23481	18500	50176	1942	16879	13298
95/2	11580	4317.535	1958.765	10	2710	3324.9	8.0	161.8	23102	19000	50213	1931	16463	13540
95/3	11475	4199.239	2009.619	10	2691	3308.6	8.2	162.8	22482	19000	50368	1906	15922	13456
95/4	11812	4503.28	2051.642	10	2782	3371.0	8.2	163.7	23404	19500	50323	1959	16484	13735
96/1	11279	4322.018	2061.009	10	2867	3304.8	9.0	165.7	23677	18500	50312	1995	16475	12873
96/2	10921	4151.981	2075.9905	10	2886	3359.4	8.6	166.3	23708	19000	50356	2001	16437	13173
96/3	11035	4166.867	2083.4335	10	2876	3354.2	8.7	167.4	23911	19250	50518	1981	16469	13259
96/4	11143	4264.351	2127.553	10	2918	3411.6	8.8	168.4	24021	19500	50457	1998	16447	13351
97/1	11499	4412.688	2162.421	10	2930	3355.8	9.9	170.0	23989	19800	50488	1987	16270	13429
97/2	11446	4500.973	2181.584	10	2998	3400.8	9.6	170.1	24166	20000	50432	2032	16381	13557
97/3				10	2982	3450.2	9	170.3	24197	20500	50632	2019	16382	13879
97/4				10	3002	3470.6	8.8	170.9	24288	20000	50548	2025	16386	13493
98/1				12	3012	3468.2	8.6	172.1	24315	19700	50591	2018	16290	13198
98/2				12	3080	3490.8	8.5	172.6	24508	20000	50577	2057	16372	13360
98/3				12	3065	3510.2	8.4	173.1	24429	20800	50668	2042	16272	13855
98/4				12	3080	3550.4	8.4	175.2	24781	20500	50689	2027	16309	13491
99/1				12	3000	3500.3	9	175.6	24562	20600	50592	1970	16128	13526
99/2				12	2950	3460.7	8.8	174.9	24881	20200	50627	1945	16402	13317

Table 15: Customer Arrivals Requiring CAM Service

Time of Day	Retail Customers	Commercial Customers
9:00-10:00	21	9
10:00-11:00	14	6
11:00-12:00	31	8
12:00-1:00	34	5
1:00-2:00	17	6
2:00-3:00	11	5
3:00-4:00	12	7
4:00-5:00	19	9

Ice Queen Snow Blowers Inc.[1]

A Comprehensive Manufacturing Operations Case

BACKGROUND AND COMPANY HISTORY

Ice Queen Snow Blowers has been in existence for the last 15 years and has successfully developed a market niche in the northern tier of the United States and Canada for high-quality snow blowers. The company started initially with just one model, the 18-inch push (P) type blower. Ten years ago the 22-inch self-propelled (SP) model was added to the line, and five years ago a 28-inch self-propelled blower with an electric starter (SPES) was introduced.

The origins of Ice Queen's operating expertise were the metal bending and casting industries. The company previously made architect-designed air-conditioning ducts for homes and offices, as well as cast shovels and rakes for gardening supply stores. In the late 1970s, the president, Ms. Bowe, decided to enter a more value-added line of business and chose snow blowers, due to their high cast metal content. The snow blower business had grown significantly so that it was now the firm's only product line. Aside from casting the metal parts and blades, Ice Queen principally assembled their machines from parts and subassemblies supplied by other manufacturers in the northeast. These parts included the engine, transmission, starter mechanism, and wheels.

Ice Queen's financial position was quite good. An abbreviated profit and loss statement for the last two years is given in Table 1. The current debt cost to Ice Queen was 15 percent and it felt that every extra dollar it had available to spend on advertising would result in an after-tax return of 20 percent. Management wants to take on more debt at this time only as a last resort.

A total of 235 employees are involved in the manufacturing process at Ice Queen's Massachusetts plant. These employees include on average 20 assembly-line workers; 140 in the smelting, casting, and milling operation (2 shifts); 40 in shipping, receiving, and materials movement; 10 in maintenance, and 25 in quality assurance, engineering, and other supervisory functions. An experienced assembly-line/shipping type worker receives $10/hour, and the remaining high-skill workers average about $14/hour. Benefits cost about 30 percent of base salary for all employees and are incremental. The plant runs from 7:00 a.m. to 4:00 p.m. with a half-hour lunch and two 15-minute breaks, one in the morning and one in the afternoon. The plant is unionized, and while labor strife is not a current problem, there have been periods of unrest that culminated in a four-week walkout in 1987. The company feels that to hire and train a new employee costs about $4,000, including productivity losses during training. To lay off an employee costs the company about $4,500 in severance pay and incremental unemployment insurance charges.

Ice Queen's strategy was to continue to grow in the snow blower business by supplying a high-quality product at a fair price and servicing its dealers with quick response to market demand variation. Some consideration was currently being given to substantially expanding the firm's product offerings.

RAPID TIME TO MARKET USING PROJECT MANAGEMENT METHODS

In the spring (March) of 1995, the management of Ice Queen got together to consider the possibility of expanding the product line to include lawn mowers and snowmobiles. The advantage of lawn mowers is that they would be sold through the same 10,000 small lawn and garden equipment retailers that currently handle the snow blowers. Unfortunately, the market for lawn mowers is dominated by several large national and international competitors and price competition is fierce and almost every market niche seems to be filled. Snowmobiles, however, offer a retail distribution channel somewhat different than Ice Queen's and a market without a large group of dominant competitors, and thus favorable pricing opportunities. Snowmobiles were of particular interest to Ice Queen's growing customer base of large discount store chains.

To enter either of these markets would require an intense product development cycle on Ice Queen's part. Due to the fact that the current date (March) would require Ice Queen to miss this summer's season for lawn mowers, a development cycle of 12 months was first proposed. However, for snowmobiles a seven-month development cycle would make possible their introduction for the upcoming winter season. Ice Queen management wanted to make a decision on which new venture to initiate by next month. The major concern

---

[1] By Michael Moses, Operations Management Area, Stern School of Business and Donald Weinstein, Associate, Price Waterhouse Coopers. This case is intended to be used with the core course—Competitive Advantage from Operations. (11/98)

was how long each development task would require, and whether or not they could be managed in a way that would allow the meeting of each of their individual deadlines. Several months had been spent prior to the impending meeting preparing a detailed development plan for each alternative (Appendix 1). As an assistant to Ray Leon, Operations Analysis Manager, your job is to recommend which alternative to undertake at the upcoming meeting.

The product development cycles for both new products were originally forecasted to take approximately 12 months. Both products required the same set of development tasks except that it had been previously decided that snowmobiles would require a totally new production line, while lawn mowers would be integrated into the existing snow blower assembly line. Thus, the task of designing the new line (DNL) for snowmobiles would be replaced by the task of design integration with the snow blower line (DTSBL) for lawn mowers. The task of building the new line (BNL) for snowmobiles would be replaced by the task of making changes to the snow blower line (MCSBL) for lawn mowers. The product development cycle for snowmobiles is described below. Appendix 1 contains time estimates for each task for both products.

The product development cycle begins with a thorough analysis of the market (AM) that must be completed before the design of the product concept (DPC) can begin. Once the product concept has been determined, the marketing group can begin the development of a marketing plan (DMP). Simultaneously (with DMP), the engineering team can begin the specification, ordering, and receiving process of the internally produced and outsourced components to be used in the product (SC).

Once the marketing plan has been developed, it can be analyzed and approved (AMP). The preparation of the sales force training material can begin (PST) once the marketing plan has been approved. While the sales force training material is being developed, the advertising material can also be developed (DAM) and then prepared (PAM). The preparation of the advertising material must await the completed building of a product mock up (BMU) by the engineering team. Before the sales force is trained (TSF) they must be moved to the corporate headquarters site (MSF). This training also cannot commence until the sales training material (PST) and advertising material preparations (PAM) have been completed. Once the sales force completes its training, they are returned to the field (MSF2) where they can start the task of convincing current customers to carry the line and take initial orders (CCTIO). In addition, this stage, (CCTIO), cannot be initiated until the product design has been finalized (FPD). After the initial product orders (CCTIO) have been fed to the production center, the manufacturing cycle can begin (SM).

Once the product concept has been designed (DPC), and the engineering team has specified and obtained the product's component parts (SC) from both inside and outside sources, the building of the mock-up can commence (BMU). Once the mock-up has been created, it can be tested (TMU), and simultaneously with the testing, the manufacturing team can begin the development of the manufacturing plan (DMP2). After testing changes are made to the mock-up (CMU) it is tested again (TMU2). These tests allow for the next task, the finalization of the product design (FPD), which is then communicated to the marketing team in the field, which has been awaiting it to start its contact of store owners. After the product design has been finalized (FPD), purchase orders can be placed with suppliers for the outsourced components (PPO). These components must be received (RSC) before manufacturing can begin.

After the general manufacturing plan has been developed (DMP2), a more detailed allocation of tasks to work stations can be made (AWS). These tasks are then used to design the new manufacturing line (DNL). Before the line can be built (BNL), new special equipment must be ordered and received (OSE). These orders cannot take place until the line design task (DNL) has been completed. The specialized equipment also cannot be safely ordered until the first mock-up has been tested, changed, and tested again (TMU2). Once the special equipment has arrived the line can be built and then initially tested (TL). Using data from the initial test run and the finalized product design (FPD), the line is changed (MCL), then tested again (TL2), and then finalized (FLD). Once the line is finalized, initial manufacturing can begin (SM).

Given the time estimates indicated for each task for each product in Appendix 1, Ray Leon wants to know the earliest (in weeks) each product could be started in manufacturing if the current project development plan was approved April 1.

The current schedule for the snowmobile development did not envision a current-year introduction. In order to accelerate the process Mr. Leon has gone back to each task manager and asked how much it would cost to cut the time on each task. Those managers who felt they had this flexibility have submitted the cost data illustrated in Appendix 2. These data are given in units that indicate the total costs for accelerating the activity and the maximum time reduction allowable at these costs. Mr. Leon wants to know if there is now a way to accomplish the snowmobile project in 35 weeks (compared to the time computed from Appendix 1), and what is its incremental cost? Is there more than one path that has this minimum cost?

The Marketing Department feels that every week's improvement beyond 35 weeks would gain the company $40,000 in profits. Is it cost effective to improve beyond the 35-week target? If so, by how many weeks if our goal is to maximize profits?

While the task managers were somewhat confident in their original time estimates, the push to 35 weeks has left most of them with a degree of increased anxiety over their new time estimates. Data were also gathered on the optimistic, most likely, and pessimistic times for completing the accelerated tasks (Appendix 3). Management requires a likelihood of 80 percent or better on project completion in 35 weeks. As part of your overall evaluation of the project, you need to tell them how confident you are that this will occur, (use the data in Appendix 3 for your analysis). What is the likelihood that the development cycle will be completed in 30 weeks? Rank order the tasks that you would recommend require the most managerial attention if a push to project completion in 35, and then 30, weeks is decided upon.

LOW COST AND CAPACITY SUFFICIENCY BY PROCESS ANALYSIS AND DESIGN

Currently, the snow blowers are assembled on a U-shaped assembly line (Figure 1). The first operation is the assembly of the frame from parts produced in the casting and milling part of the plant. Each employee working at a separate station at this point in the line can assemble a frame in 2½ minutes each. There is no setup time and only one snow blower can be worked on at a time at each station. There are two stations available at this point in the line.

Frame parts are cast in a separate part of the plant in large molds. The casting machines have a cycle time of 15 minutes. Each mold makes enough parts for six snow blowers of the same type. Each mold weighs five tons and requires the four-person operating crew[2] 90 minutes to change to another mold for a different blower size. All cast parts have to be cooled overnight before they can be used on the assembly line. Molds typically last two years and have just been replaced for an investment of $150,000 ($50,000 each). There is **more than enough** **casting and milling capacity** in the plant, and thus, it should not be considered a constraint on the plant's output.

The next step, bolting the engine to the assembled frame, occurs as the partially assembled blower moves down an elevated and paced assembly line. This elevated line is also used for the preceding step. Each body size requires a different engine size. Each of up to four workers at this stage can attach an engine to a frame in five minutes. The engine supplier, C.A. Inc., is located in northern Maine, about one day's drive from the Ice Queen factory, weather permitting, and has the capacity to deliver 400 engines of the same size per day (five days/week).

Wheels, and transmission if the blower is self-propelled, are added at the six identical work centers of the next stage. This operation has no setup time and requires 1¾ minutes for one person if the blower is a push type (P), four minutes if it is self-propelled (SP), and seven minutes if it is self-propelled with an electric starter (SPES). Currently, when push blowers are being produced only one work center (out of the six) with one employee is used. When self-propelled blowers are being produced, the line has been designed so that two of the six work centers can be used, each with one employee. If SPES blowers are being produced, three of the six work centers can be used, each with one employee. Transmissions and wheels are readily available, and Ice Queen has contracts with several suppliers who guarantee delivery of parts for up to 500 snow blowers on one day's notice. Transmissions cost $25.00 and represent 12 percent of the materials cost of goods sold for the SP model. For the SPES model, the transmission and starter package costs $31.24 and represents 14 percent of its materials cost. In addition to these parts, the SP and SPES are made of more costly basic components than the P model.

---

[2] Each Caster has a four-person operating crew.

FIGURE 1

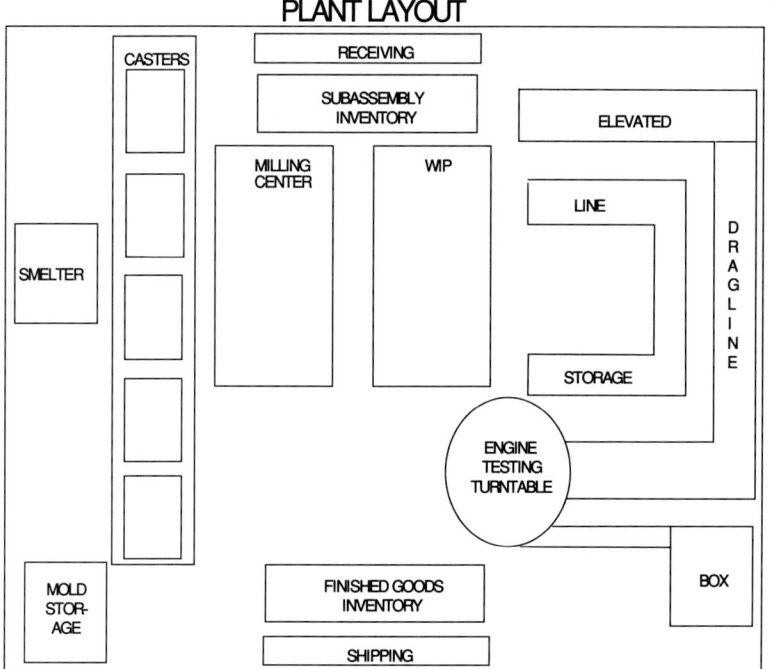

After this step, the blower is capable of moving on its own wheels and a much less expensive dragline conveyor system is used to move the blower along. The only problem with this system is that the blowers tend to move randomly in either direction perpendicular to the dragline. Thus, restraining rails have to be put in place to guide the blower. These rails have to be changed for each different blower size, which takes all the assembly line workers a half day to complete. All the rails must be unscrewed from their current locations and re-screwed to other fixed locations depending on the size of the blower being produced. Attaching the blower to the dragline takes no time.

The next operation is to attach the housing that covers the engine to the frame. This operation takes one employee 1¾ minutes. The housing is also cast and milled in-house. The molds for the housing can make three of the same size in each mold. The cycle time, setup time, and cost for this operation are the same as for the frame operation, except that there are two casters dedicated to this operation.

After the housing has been attached, the reel and blower assembly is attached. This requires one employee and can be accomplished in a total time of 3½ minutes. There is enough equipment for up to two employees to work at this station. Again, these parts are made in-house in molds capable of producing six pieces of the same blower size. Two casters, one for reels and one for blowers, are dedicated to this operation. Again the cycle and setup time and cost of this operation are the same as for the previous one.

The next step in the process is to attach the push handle lever and link it to the starter and transmission. This task requires two minutes of labor, and there is enough equipment for two employees. The blower is then gassed up and started by an employee (½ minute). It is then rolled onto a round circulating platter, that can handle up to 10 blowers, and attached to monitoring equipment for testing (½ min). This is a continuous-process piece of equipment and is kept rotating during all assembly shifts. An additional employee is required to continuously monitor progress and roll the blowers off the platter. Each blower stays on the platter until it reaches the exit, which takes a total elapsed time of 10 minutes. The transmission is tested by driving the blower from the platter exit to the boxing area, which takes 30 seconds and needs one employee. The blowers are packed in special-strength boxes that allow vertical stacking and are moved by forklift trucks to the finished goods storage area. Packing takes five minutes per blower per worker, and there are four packing stations as well as a holding area for 100 blowers awaiting packing.

Table 2 gives last year's actual production for all models and sales for each model for each month. Daily production rates by model type, assumed for planning purposes, are also given on the last line of the table.

Currently, the assembly line is run only one shift a day, with overtime and inventory being used to buffer unexpected increase in demand or decreases in production capability. The workers in the casting and milling operation are high-skill workers and are not easy to find in the labor market. The assembly-line workers are of moderate skill and are in ample supply in the local labor market. A new assembly-line worker takes four to six weeks before he or she can achieve the production output and quality equal to a seasoned employee. The production planning rates given in Table 2 assume experienced employees. Normally 20 percent of the production workers do not return from plant shutdowns of more than two weeks. Assembly-line maintenance is done during the second shift, and casting and milling maintenance is done in the third shift.

As a recent hire you have been asked to verify the single product production capacities indicated in Table 2. Can Ice Queen produce the 82,800 blowers forecast for 1995 (Table 3) using only a one-shift operation production strategy? If not, how much overtime or extra capacity would be required? Would there be any change in five-week capacity if products are produced on a daily schedule and the product mix is produced in a ratio of 3:1:1 for P:SP:SPES (i.e., three days P, one day SP, and one day SPES) compared to a weekly cycle of three weeks P, one week SP, and one week SPES. How would the average time an order stays in the system change under these two operating environments? Should product shift changes be done during regular shift or on an overtime basis? How much would capacity increase if the wheel and transmission workcenter were re-engineered so that any machine could work on any type of snow blower?

CUSTOMER SERVICE ANALYSIS THROUGH WAITING LINE MODELS

Ice Queen receives orders for its products throughout the year, but the most intensive ordering period is from mid-October to mid-December. Traditionally, orders have been accepted by two full-time employees and two temporary employees (hired for the peak period). Each store owner would call in and could request to speak to a preferred order taker. Full-time order takers are long-term Ice Queen employees and have developed a high degree of camaraderie over the years with particular storeowners. Storeowners do not mind having to wait several minutes so that they could exchange pleasantries and family status with their preferred order takers. The old telecommunications technology used by Ice Queen randomly allocated incoming calls to one of the four lines, each of which allowed for a queue of up to 10 waiting calls. Once a call was allocated to a line it was impossible for the call to be switched to a different line. If a particular storeowner wanted to speak to a particular order taker, the order takers simply switched positions to accommodate the request. Ice Queen was considering changing over to a more modern hands-free system that would allow waiting calls to be automatically routed to the next available operator in order of their arrival. A pre-recorded message feature was also available so customers could be informed of special sales and promotions while they waited. The new system had the ability to hold an unlimited number of calls and allowed for shorter service time for wrong numbers. Ice Queen had approximately 10,000 customers who ordered, on average, 6 to 10 blowers over a season, requiring approximately three phone orders. The service times for these calls varied considerably and were based on the amount of pleasantries exchanged and the complexity of the orders. The shortest calls could take 15 seconds (wrong numbers, approximately 5 percent of total calls), or up to 10 minutes for an annual call for a well-acquainted pair of owner and order taker. Some data had been collected last year on call inter-arrival and service time distributions and is given in Appendix 4. Data for busy and normal months was collected.

Ice Queen management has been getting complaints, especially from the new high-volume mass market store accounts, that waiting time to place their orders was too long. Most of these customers felt that a wait of any more than 90 seconds was unreasonable. Could the current system handle this performance guarantee? Would adopting the new telephone system meet these requirements? As part of a cost-improvement program, Ice Queen wanted to ensure that each of the order takers was busy at least 80 percent of the time. How many order takers and which system should they adopt to guarantee these results? Can the service guarantee of no more than 90 seconds of waiting and operating efficiency goal of approximately 80 percent utilization be achieved simultaneously? Ice Queen feels that new product introduction could increase call volume by 30 percent, but leave service time uneffected. Could this scenario be handled with the old or new system, and with what results?

QUALITY ENHANCEMENT THROUGH TESTING AND PROCESS CONTROL

A new dashboard console had been created for the SPES model. It was a major product innovation with oil and gas level indicators at handle level rather than the industry standard that forced the user to reach down and inspect a dipstick at the engine level. In addition, an electronic engine temperature gauge and snow throwing direction setting were also included on this new control panel. This panel was assembled on a separate assembly line in the Ice Queen facility. It utilized electronic and mechanical parts functionally specified by Ice Queen but produced by several local manufacturers. Some of these parts were quite expensive, and thus added substantial value to the overall product. Unfortunately, Ice Queen was having substantial quality assurance problems with this line and was trying to decide on how to handle them. The in-process testing currently being done occurred at the end of the process and ensured that no bad product would be delivered to the final mower assembly line. This final test had a yield of 80 percent (i.e., one out of five assemblies was bad and it found all of them) and cost $3 in labor, $2.50 in variable overhead, and $5 in allocated fixed costs for the testing machine. Labor, overhead, and materials costs per stage of the manufacturing process are given in Appendix 5. The dashboards that failed the final function test were discarded and had no scrap or salvage value.

A new in-process test was being considered. It would be done immediately after the engine temperature gauge was attached and would have a yield of 90 percent and would also improve the final function test yield to 89 percent. The labor cost for this test was $3 and had an allocated variable overhead cost of $2 per test. Again, there was no salvage value for the rejected material. Does this test reduce the total cost of a good dashboard?

As an alternative, Ice Queen was considering a new piece of test equipment that would detect a greater percentage of defects in process and pinpoint the source of the failure for rework. The new test will have an 80 percent yield, and Ice Queen will be able to rework 75 percent of the defective units. This will raise the final test yield to 95 percent. The new test adds $2 in direct labor and $1 in variable overhead costs, and the rework adds $2 in material, $2 in labor, and $1.00 in variable overhead costs. Does this test reduce the total cost of a good dashboard? Should Ice Queen purchase the test equipment if it costs $60,000 and has a four-year life (assume straight-line depreciation and zero salvage value)?

COST IMPROVEMENT VIA LEAN PRODUCTION AND TAILORED DISTRIBUTION SYSTEMS

Ray Leon worked for the vice president of manufacturing and was also responsible for managing the parts inventory for the mechanized mower line. The principal parts that required ordering were the motors and transmissions and dashboard gauges.

The firm had been trying to follow a level production strategy in the past and ordered motors once a week. Ray, in addition to his other duties, had just taken over the inventory responsibility from a recently departed employee and was reviewing the inventory plan for the coming year. He assumed the departure might have had something to do with the piles of outmoded engines stacked all over the inventory cage. Last year's orders for motors were 60,000 and this year's planned production was 82,800. Lead time from CA, the engine provider, was one week for orders placed during the week. The transportation cost amounted to about $2 per engine for these orders. CA allowed for fast response ordering and responded to urgent need orders on a 2nd-day air express basis, which added $5 to the cost of each engine and a special expedite fee of $100 per order. The previous employee used one fifth of his annual salary of $30,000 as part of the order cost, as well as the cost of the long-distance phone call and express mail confirmation ($7.50) required to place an order. Due to the popularity of the engines, a pilferage rate of 5 percent was forecast. The projected average cost of the engines for this year was $30 per engine. In addition to inventory, Ray was in charge of purchasing non-mechanical parts and raw materials. Ray's assessment of his job was that even if he wanted to order three times as often as was currently planned, it would not affect his job performance. However, if ordering more often than that was required, he would have to hire a part-time worker, which would end up costing approximately $50 per order for all orders.

Along with a level production strategy, a modified chase strategy was being considered that would divide the year into quarters with a constant production rate forecast for all of the 13 weeks in each quarter (quarterly production: 10, 20, 33, 20 thousand). An almost just-in-time monthly chase production strategy with constant weekly production within the month (monthly production: 2, 5, 3, 5, 6, 9, 11, 11, 11, 10, 5, 5 thousand) was also being considered.

You have been asked to help Ray by evaluating the inventory cost of these alternative strategies, as well as any other you can devise. You should first assume that demand is known with certainty. Secondly, you may want to develop an inventory policy that allows management to see the effects of varying service levels if weekly demand is uncertain, with mean equal to average weekly demand and standard deviation equal to one tenth of average weekly demand. Stocking out of motors any more than 2% of the time is unacceptable to Ice Queen Management. CA has also offered a quantity discount of 20 percent for all engines if each order is for more than 250 units. Should Ice Queen take advantage of this offer if it is following the annual level production strategy?

CAPACITY SUFFICIENCY VIA DEMAND FORECASTING AND AGGREGATE PLANNING

Total sales have been growing almost every year, except during 1987. Due to last year's harsh winter, total sales increased the most since the year the company opened for business. Key factors that influence total demand, in units, seem to be the farmer's almanac forecast for winter weather, total degree days in December, new and existing home sales, and disposable personal income. (Historical data and future forecasts of these variables are given in Appendix 6.)

Liza Michaels, the vice president for marketing, had just recently finished her sales forecast for the coming year for total demand and demand for each model. She was on her way to see the vice president for manufacturing, Andrew Daniels, to discuss the marketing plan that she had sent him the previous day. It was March 15, and everyone had recently returned from the annual mandatory plant closing of two weeks. Michaels had only been with the company for 12 months and was a little nervous since this was the first annual forecast that was entirely her responsibility. Michaels' condition was not improved by her finding that the president of the company, Jennifer Bowe, was also in Andrew Daniels' office. (Michaels' forecast is given in Table 3, along with previous forecasts and their concomitant actuals.)

At the start of the meeting, Daniels expressed his concern that the forecast was for an aggressive increase in demand of 15 percent and that the individual model forecasts were substantially different than what had been predicted in previous years. Michaels' response to this was that she was quite confident in her forecast for total demand. For the last 10 years her predecessors had also been quite good at predicting total demand, but had no luck in predicting demand by product. She was trying a new technique for forecasting mix that she hoped would be more successful, but she could not guarantee it. She commented to Daniels that it would be nice if the company's operating system could be made flexible enough to accommodate these last-minute mix variations. At this, Daniels, attempting to hold his anger in check, explained that the manufacture of quality snow blowers required careful workmanship and special equipment that had high setup times. Thus to keep costs in line, long product runs were required. Also, since there was not enough one-shift capacity to meet peak demand during the November-through-February period, and to keep production somewhat level over the year, seasonal sales had to be made from inventory.

The bickering between the two vice presidents went on for some time until the president stepped into the fray. Ms. Bowe instructed her two vice presidents to work together and come up with an aggregate plan for the coming production year by the following Friday. The plan could include investments in setup time reduction, as well as cycle time enhancement and other classic aggregate planning alternatives. But since the current model year was fast approaching, all changes had to be implemented by next month and could not interfere with production.

The next day Michaels and Daniels met to try to sort out their differences and come up with an aggregate plan for the following year. Daniels explained to Michaels that, since last year's marketing forecast was for a product mix in the proportion of 3:1:1 (P, SP, SPES respectively), he had planned for 50 weeks of production assuming the following rotation: Three weeks of P blowers followed by one week of SP blowers and then one week of SPES blowers. All changeovers were to be made during normal shift hours on the Friday afternoon before the next model was to be run. If demand had been as predicted, this would have resulted in the loss of a manageable number of production days due to product mix changeovers. But due to the poor mix forecasts and an irregular flow of total orders, more than twice the planned number of setups were required. An unexpected quality problem with C.A. Inc.'s engines during the late fall also caused the loss of over 10 days of production time. Substantial overtime was required to make up for the lost production time caused by both these events.

You were hired by Ice Queen in September to assist both the marketing and operations vice presidents. They have now turned to you for a draft proposal for an aggregate plan. What do you recommend? They suggested that answering some of the following questions might help frame your response:

1. Verify the current demand and mix forecast utilizing all forecasting techniques at your disposal.
2. Does Ice Queen have enough one–shift capacity to meet next year's demand assuming they want to start any new year with 2,000 units on hand? Any more starting inventory is considered useless due to annual design changes.
3. Should Ice Queen still build inventory off-season (level production strategy), or should they follow a chase production strategy for increasing output by using more overtime (overtime pay is time and a half)? Should Ice Queen initiate a second shift (full-or part-time) to help increase capacity (the second-shift wage premium is 10 percent)? To technically operate the line on a second shift, each station must be operated by at least one individual.
4. What other classical aggregate planning strategies might you recommend (peak load pricing, outsourcing, etc.)?
5. Given all these alternatives, is there an optimal (minimum cost) solution that you would recommend, and why? How sensitive is it to any of the assumptions you have made in order to solve the problem?

How much would it be worth to Ice Queen if the model change setup time could be reduced to one-half hour? How might you reengineer this task to accomplish this goal?

Table 1 Profit and Loss Statement (000)

	Current Year (just ended March 1)	Previous Year
Sales	$26,450	$20,160
Cost-of-goods sold materials	10,800	9,450
Direct labor[3]	7,295	5,560
Depreciation	2,166	1,650
Overhead	1,083	825
General and administrative	722	550
Advertising expenses	542	413
Sales expenses	361	275
Pre-tax profit	3,481	1,437

[3] Includes benefits

Table 2
Actual Production and Sales for the Year Just Ended

Production 1994 Total/Monthly			Actual Sales for 1994 Total/Monthly	P	SP	SPES
Production and inventory	72,000	**Sales**	71375	43,440	14,355	13,580
March	2,480		65	65		
April	5,200		2,625	2,050	325	250
*May	5,450		4,450	2,400	1,550	500
June	5,200		4,450	2,400	1,550	500
July	4,950		2,525	2,000	300	225
*August	5,450		3,720	3,000	400	320
September	4,950		5,140	2,000	1,140	2,000
*October	5,400		7,250	3,000	2,000	2,250
November	4,950		13,150	6,650	3,500	3,000
*December	4,700		11,500	7,000	2,500	2,000
*January	6,000		11,500	8,260	1,090	2,150
*February	5,270		5,000	4,615		385
Starting Inventory	12,000		12,000**	3,000**	4,000**	5,000**
Ending Inventory			625	400	125	100
Planned Production rate/shift				272	232	208

*   Overtime required for assembly operation

**   This initial inventory has been allocated to the Sales in the months above, and thus, should not be added to the monthly numbers in trying to arrive at the total Sales numbers by product.

Table 3

Year	Total Sales History Forecast	Actual	Sales Mix History Push Actual	Forecast	SP Actual	Forecast	SPES Actual	Forecast
1985	37,000	37,740	18,870		18,870			
1986	41,250	41,514	24,908		16,605			
1987	42,500	37,363	26,154		11,208			
1988	41,500	41,847	20,923		20,923			
1989	43,000	42,684	25,610		17,073			
1990	47,000	47,380	28,428	23,500	14,214	14,100	4,738	9,400
1991	52,500	53,066	29,186	31,500	10,613	10,500	13,266	10,500
1992	57,750	57,311	28,655	34,650	17,193	11,550	11,462	11,550
1993	62,500	63,043	37,825	31,250	15,760	15,625	9,456	15,625
1994	72,000	71,375	43,440	36,000	14,355	18,000	13,580	18,000
1995 forecast	82,800			51,820		16,560		14,420

Appendix 1 Normal Project Durations

Activity	Normal Duration (weeks) Snow	Lawn	Normal Cost Snow	Lawn
Analyze market (AM)	4	4	$16,000	$16,000
Develop marketing plan (DMP)	4	4	$22,000	$22,000
Approve marketing plan (AMP)	2	2	$4,000	$4,000
Develop advertising materials (DAM)	4	4	$9,000	$9,000
Prepare advertising materials (PAM)	4	4	$32,000	$32,000
Prepare sales force training materials (PST)	4	4	$25,000	$25,000
Move sales force (MSF)	2	2	$5,000	$5,000
Train sales force (TSF)	4	4	$32,000	$32,000
Move sales force (MSF2)	2	2	$5,000	$5,000
Convince customers to carry line and take initial orders (CCTIO)	12	12	$48,000	$48,000
Develop product concept (DPC)	4	4	$16,000	$16,000
Specify components (SC)	2	2	$9,000	$9,000
Build mock-up (BMU)	2	2	$6,000	$6,000
Test mock-up (TMU)	1	1	$4,000	$4,000
Change mock-up (CMU)	2	2	$6,000	$6,000
Test mock-up (TMU2)	1	1	$4,000	$4,000
Finalize product design (FPD)	5	5	$20,000	$20,000
Place purchase orders (PPO)	5	5	$12,000	$12,000
Receive special components (RSC)	12	12	$400,000	$400,000
Develop manufacturing plan (DMP2)	3	2	$14,000	$10,000
Allocate tasks to work stations (AWS)	1	1	$4,000	$4,000
Design line/integrate with blower line (DNL)/(DTSBL)	4	2	$16,000	$8,000
Order special equipment (OSE)	12	8	$180,000	$120,000
Build line/make changes to line (BNL)/(MCSBL)	6	4	$45,000	$30,000
Test line (TL)	2	2	$16,000	$16,000
Make changes to line (MCL)	4	3	$32,000	$24,000
Test line (TL2)	2	2	$16,000	$16,000
Finalize line design (FLD)	2	2	$8,000	$8,000
Start manufacturing (SM)				
			$1,006,000	$911,000

Appendix 2 Accelerated Project Durations

Activity	Minimum Time (weeks)		Crash Cost	
	Snow	Lawn	Snow	Lawn
Analyze market (AM)	3	3	$20,000	$20,000
Develop marketing plan (DMP)	3	3	$36,000	$36,000
Approve marketing plan (AMP)	1.5	1.5	$6,000	$6,000
Develop advertising materials (DAM)	3	3	$15,000	$15,000
Prepare advertising materials (PAM)	3	3	$40,000	$40,000
Prepare sales force training materials (PST)	3	3	$40,000	$40,000
Move sales force (MSF)	1.5	1.5	$10,000	$10,000
Train sales force (TSF)	3	3	$40,000	$40,000
Move sales force (MSF2)	1.5	1.5	$10,000	$10,000
Convince customers to carry line and take initial orders (CCTIO)	8	8	$80,000	$80,000
Develop product concept (DPC)	3	3	$28,000	$28,000
Specify components (SC)	1.5	1.5	$12,000	$12,000
Build mock-up (BMU)	1	1	$10,000	$10,000
Test mock-up (TMU)	1	1	$4,000	$4,000
Change mock-up (CMU)	1	1	$10,000	$10,000
Test mock-up (TMU2)	1	1	$4,000	$4,000
Finalize product design (FPD)	3	3	$42,000	$42,000
Place purchase orders (PPO)	3	3	$36,000	$36,000
Receive special components (RSC)	7	7	$580,000	$580,000
Develop manufacturing plan (DMP2)	2	1	$21,000	$15,000
Allocate tasks to work stations (AWS)	1	1	$4,000	$4,000
Design line/integrate with blower line (DNL)/(DTSBL)	2	1	$20,000	$10,000
Order special equipment (OSE)	7	6	$300,000	$200,000
Build line/make changes to line (BNL)/(MCSBL)	4	3	$75,000	$50,000
Test line (TL)	1.5	1.5	$20,000	$20,000
Make changes to line (MCL)	2	2	$40,000	$30,000
Test line (TL2)	1.5	1.5	$20,000	$20,000
Finalize line design (FLD)	1.5	1.5	$12,000	$12,000
Start manufacturing (SM)				
			$1,535,000	$1,384,000

Appendix 3 Accelerated Project Probabilities for Snowmobiles

Activity	Crash Time Probability (weeks)		
	Optimistic	**Most Likely**	**Pessimistic**
Analyze market (AM)	2	3	4
Develop marketing plan (DMP)	2	3	4
Approve marketing plan (AMP)	1	1.5	2
Develop advertising materials (DAM)	2	3	4
Prepare advertising materials (PAM)	2	3	4
Prepare sales force training materials (PST)	2	3	4
Move sales force (MSF)	1	1.5	2
Train sales force (TSF)	2	3	4
Move sales force (MSF2)	1	1.5	2
Convince customers to carry line and take initial orders (CCTIO)	6	8	10
Develop product concept (DPC)	2	3	4
Specify components (SC)	1	1.5	2
Build mock-up (BMU)	0.5	1	2
Test mock-up (TMU)	1	1	1
Change mock-up (CMU)	0.5	1	2
Test mock-up (TMU2)	1	1	1
Finalize product design (FPD)	2	3	4
Place purchase orders (PPO)	2	3	4
Receive special components (RSC)	4	7	10
Develop manufacturing plan (DMP2)	1	2	3
Allocate tasks to work stations (AWS)	1	1	1
Design line (DNL)	1	2	3
Order special equipment (OSE)	4	7	10
Build line (BNL)	3	4	5
Test line (TL)	1	1.5	2
Make changes to line (MCL)	1	2	3
Test line (TL2)	1	1.5	3
Finalize line design (FLD)	1	1.5	2
Start manufacturing (SM)			

Appendix 4 Service and Arrival Time Data

Table 1 – Time In Seconds
Chi-Square Goodness-of-Fit Test for Existing Phone Service System

Service Times	Number of Observations	Cumulative	Fraction of Total	Interval Mean	Squared Mean	Expected Erlang-3	Expected Exponent	Erlang-3 Deviation	Exponent Deviation
30	11	11	0.050	165	2475	1.0639	27.0333	92.7995	9.5092
60	15	26	0.118	675	30375	6.7056	24.0068	10.2596	3.3791
90	16	42	0.191	1200	90000	13.0450	21.3192	0.6694	1.3271
120	15	57	0.260	1575	165375	17.9063	18.9324	0.4717	0.8168
150	16	73	0.333	2160	291600	20.7301	16.8128	1.0793	0.0393
180	15	88	0.401	2475	408375	21.6875	14.9306	2.0621	0.0003
210	14	102	0.465	2730	532350	21.2137	13.2591	2.4530	0.0414
240	12	114	0.520	2700	607500	19.7797	11.7747	3.0599	0.0043
270	11	125	0.570	2805	715275	17.7927	10.4564	2.5932	0.0283
300	12	137	0.625	3420	974700	15.5653	9.2858	0.8167	0.7933
330	11	148	0.675	3465	1091475	13.3167	8.2462	0.4030	0.9196
360	10	158	0.721	3450	1190250	11.1872	7.3230	0.1260	0.9786
390	10	168	0.767	3750	1406250	9.2566	6.5032	0.0597	1.8803
420	9	177	0.808	3645	1476225	7.5615	5.7751	0.2737	1.8008
450	9	186	0.849	3915	1703025	6.1092	5.1286	1.3679	2.9224
480	7	193	0.881	3255	1513575	4.8889	4.5544	0.9116	1.3132
510	7	200	0.913	3465	1715175	3.8800	4.0445	2.5090	2.1596
540	7	207	0.945	3675	1929375	3.0566	3.5917	5.0874	3.2342
570	7	214	0.977	3885	2156175	2.3923	3.1896	8.8747	4.5519
600	5	219	1.000	2925	1711125	1.8614	2.8325	5.2919	1.6585

Sample Mean 252.67 Chi-square statistic 141.1693 37.3584

Variance 26280.33

Table 2 – Time in Seconds
Chi-Square Goodness-of-Fit Test for Proposed Phone Service System

Service Times	Number of Observations	Cumulative	Fraction of Total	Interval Mean	Squared Mean	Expected Erlang-3	Expected Exponent	Erlang-3 Deviation	Exponent Deviation
30	5	5	0.022	75	1125	1.0639	27.0333	14.5630	17.9581
60	8	13	0.059	360	16200	6.7056	24.0068	0.2499	10.6727
90	16	29	0.132	1200	90000	13.0450	21.3192	0.6694	1.3271
120	15	44	0.200	1575	165375	17.9063	18.9324	0.4717	0.8168
150	16	60	0.274	2160	291600	20.7301	16.8128	1.0793	0.0393
180	15	75	0.342	2475	408375	21.6875	14.9306	2.0621	0.0003
210	14	89	0.406	2730	532350	21.2137	13.2591	2.4530	0.0414
240	12	101	0.461	2700	607500	19.7797	11.7747	3.0599	0.0043
270	11	112	0.511	2805	715275	17.7927	10.4564	2.5932	0.0283
300	12	124	0.566	3420	974700	15.5653	9.2858	0.8176	0.7933
330	11	135	0.616	3465	1091475	13.3167	8.2462	0.4030	0.9196
360	10	145	0.622	3450	1190250	11.1872	7.3230	0.1260	0.9786
390	10	155	0.707	3750	1406250	9.2566	6.5032	0.0597	1.8803
420	9	164	0.748	3645	1476225	7.5615	5.7751	0.2737	1.8008
450	9	173	0.790	3915	1703025	6.1092	5.1286	1.3679	2.9224
480	7	180	0.821	3255	1513575	4.8889	4.5544	0.9116	1.3132
510	6	286	0.849	2970	1470150	3.8800	4.0445	1.1584	0.9454
540	5	291	0.872	2625	1378125	3.0566	3.5917	1.2356	0.5522
570	3	194	0.885	1665	924075	2.3923	3.1896	0.1544	0.0113
600	2	196	0.895	1170	684450	1.8614	2.8325	0.0103	0.2447

Sample Mean 252.09 Chi-square statistic 33.7187 43.2501

Variance 21348.18

Table 3 – Interarrival Times Are In Seconds
Chi-Square Goodness-of-Fit Test for Peak Month Interarrival Times

Arrival Times	Number of Observations	Cumulative	Fraction of Total	Interval Mean	Squared Mean	Expected Exponent	Exponent Deviation
20	76	76	0.182	760	7600	92.2679	2.8682
40	65	141	0.338	1950	58500	71.9443	0.6703
60	57	198	0.476	2850	142500	56.0973	0.0145
80	48	246	0.591	3360	235200	43.7409	0.4147
100	43	289	0.694	3870	348300	34.1062	2.3192
120	27	316	0.759	2970	326300	26.5983	0.0062
140	28	344	0.826	3640	473200	20.7360	2.5446
160	26	370	0.889	3900	585000	16.1686	5.9781
180	19	389	0.935	3230	549100	12.6072	3.2417
200	4	393	0.944	760	144400	9.8302	3.4579
220	3	396	0.951	630	132300	7.6649	2.8391
240	6	402	0.966	1380	317400	5.9766	0.0001
260	4	406	0.976	1000	250000	4.6602	0.0935
280	2	408	0.980	540	145800	3.6337	0.7345
300	3	411	0.988	870	252300	2.8333	0.0098
320	0	411	0.988	0	0	2.2092	2.2092
340	3	414	0.995	990	326700	1.7226	0.9473
360	1	415	0.997	350	122500	1.3432	0.0877
380	0	415	0.997	0	0	1.0473	1.0473
400	1	416	1.000	390	152100	0.0412	0.0412

Sample Mean 80.38 Chi-square statistic 29.5250

Variance 4522.93

Table 4 – Interarrival Times Are In Seconds
Chi-Square Goodness-of-Fit Test for Normal Month Interarrival Times

Arrival Times	Number of Observations	Cumulative	Fraction of Total	Interval Mean	Squared Mean	Expected Exponent	Exponent Deviation
30	8	8	0.102	120	1800	8.0184	0.0000
60	6	14	0.179	270	12150	7.2735	0.2230
90	3	17	0.217	225	16875	6.5978	1.9619
120	2	19	0.243	210	22050	5.9849	2.6533
150	3	22	0.282	405	54675	5.4289	1.0867
180	4	26	0.333	660	108900	4.9246	0.1736
210	3	29	0.371	585	114075	4.4671	0.4818
240	4	33	0.423	900	202500	4.0521	0.0007
270	4	37	0.474	1020	260100	3.6757	0.0286
300	3	40	0.512	855	243675	3.3342	0.0335
330	4	44	0.564	1260	396900	3.0245	0.3146
360	2	46	0.589	690	283050	2.7435	0.2015
390	4	50	0.641	1500	562500	2.4887	0.9178
420	3	53	0.679	1215	492075	2.2575	0.2442
450	2	55	0.705	870	378450	2.0477	0.0011
480	1	56	0.717	465	216225	1.8575	0.3959
510	4	60	0.769	1980	980100	1.6850	3.1807
540	3	63	0.807	1575	826875	1.5284	1.4168
570	4	67	0.858	2220	1232100	1.3864	4.9268
600	5	72	0.923	2925	1711125	1.2576	11.1361
630	1	73	0.935	615	378225	1.1408	0.0174
660	0	73	0.935	0	0	1.0348	1.0348
690	3	76	0.974	2025	1366875	0.9387	4.5264
720	2	78	1	1410	994050	0.8515	1.5491

Sample Mean 307.6923077 Chi-square statistic 36.5065

Variance 43919.67

Appendix 5 Dash Board Process

	Yield (%)	Material	Labor	Variable overhead	Fixed overhead
Attach fuel sensor gauge		$2	$1	$0.5	
Attach oil level gauge		2	1	0.5	
Attach engine temperature gauge		3	2	1	
Attach snow direction lever		4	3	2	
Bundle wiring harness		0.5	5	1.5	
Complete functional test	80		3	2.5	$5

Appendix 6

Year	Farmer's Almanac Forecast	December Degree Days	New Home Sales	Existing Home Sales	Disposable Personal Income
1995	64	-150	$16,994	$35,277	$52,120
1994	54	-160	14,333	28,119	52,150
1993	46	0	15,168	24,924	40,175
1992	50	-40	17,052	21,191	44,180
1991	41	-120	12,148	22,747	48,100
1990	45	0	13,984	21,934	40,900
1989	39	80	16,808	11,461	42,175
1988	44	-20	21,551	19,236	45,160
1987	32	160	12,065	16,484	32,150
1986	45	20	18,122	19,297	41,750
1985	37	90	21,437	15,131	45,100